Microsoft® Help Desk for

Microsoft® Windows™ 98

PUBLISHED BY
Microsoft Press
A Division of Microsoft Corporation
One Microsoft Way
Redmond, Washington 98052-6399

Library of Congress Cataloging-in-Publication Data
Nelson, Stephen L., 1959–
    Microsoft Help Desk for Microsoft Windows 98 / Stephen L. Nelson.
        p.   cm.
    ISBN 0-7356-0632-3
    1. Microsoft Windows (Computer file)   2. Operating systems
(Computers)   3. Computer industry--Customer services.   I. Title.
QA76.76.063N4453   1999
005.4'469--dc21   99-10771
                                                            CIP

Printed and bound in the United States of America.

1 2 3 4 5 6 7 8 9   WCWC   4 3 2 1 0 9

Distributed in Canada by ITP Nelson, a division of Thomson Canada Limited.

A CIP catalogue record for this book is available from the British Library.

Microsoft Press books are available through booksellers and distributors worldwide. For further
information about international editions, contact your local Microsoft Corporation office. Or
contact Microsoft Press International directlyat fax (425) 936-7329. Visit our Web site at
mspress.microsoft.com.

Macintosh, QuickTime, and TrueType fonts are registered trademarks of Apple Computer, Inc.
Kodak is a registered trademark of Eastman Kodak Company. MechWarrior is a registered
trademark of FASA Corporation. Intel is a registered trademark of Intel Corporation.
Active Desktop, ActiveMovie, ActiveX, DirectX, DoubleSpace, DriveSpace, FrontPage,
IntelliMouse, Microsoft, Microsoft Press, MS-DOS, MSN, NetMeeting, Outlook, Picture It!,
SideWinder, Visual Basic, Visual C++, Visual Studio, WebTV, Win32, Windows, the Windows
logo, and Windows NT are either registered trademarks or trademarks of Microsoft Corporation
in the United States and/or other countries. Scholastic and The Magic School Bus are trademarks
of Scholastic Inc. Nickelodeon is a registered trademark of Viacom New Media. Other product
and company names mentioned herein may be the trademarks of their respective owners.

The example companies, organizations, products, people and events depicted herein
are fictitious. No association with any real company, organization, product, person or
event is intended or should be inferred.

Acquisitions Editor: Christey Bahn
Project Editor: Kim Fryer

Microsoft Help Desk for

Microsoft Windows 98

Compiled by Stephen L. Nelson

*Dedicated to all the hardworking people in
Microsoft Product Support Services*

Contents

Hot Topic

Chapter 5   Internet   269

Hot Topic

Acknowledgments

Special thanks to Christey Bahn, Ed Belleba, Casey Doyle, Barb Ellsworth, and Kim Fryer of Microsoft Press.

Thanks to Jeff Adell, Amy Calkins, Pat Coleman, Kaarin Dolliver, Peter Dyson, Michael Furdyk, Jason Gerend, Michael Jang, Julie Kawabata, Stefan Knorr, Brian Milbrath, Kevin Murray, Paula Thurman, Rebecca Whitney, and Todd Young of Stephen L. Nelson, Inc. Your contributions and hard work made this book possible.

Introduction

Few people want to spend much time reading an Introduction, and you're probably no exception. Nevertheless, by getting a quick overview of what the *Microsoft Help Desk for Microsoft Windows 98* does and how it's organized, you'll more easily use and benefit from this book.

What the Help Desk Does

The *Microsoft Help Desk for Microsoft Windows 98* summarizes the problem-solving information available from Microsoft's Product Support Services Knowledge Base. Developed from responses to requests, the Help Desk gives experienced users concise overviews of known problems and step-by-step instructions of available solutions.

How to Use the Help Desk

The *Microsoft Help Desk for Microsoft Windows 98* supplies nearly 1,200 problem-and-solution descriptions. Each problem-and-solution description starts by describing a problem and its symptoms and ends by providing one or more solutions you can use to solve, work-around, or avoid the problem. The book organizes these problem-and-solution descriptions into chapters of related topics, which are further categorized into smaller sections.

You can locate problem-and-solution descriptions by using either the index or one of the tables of contents. The Help Desk index, predictably, works like any book's index. You look up a keyword or phrase in the index, and then use the page numbers to begin searching the pages where the word or phrase is used.

For ease of use, the Help Desk supplies two types of tables of contents: One all-inclusive table of contents appears at the beginning of the book. Chapter-specific tables of contents also appear at the beginning of each chapter. You use both tables in the same way: Find the chapter and then the section that lists problems similar to the one you're experiencing, scan the list for your specific problem, and then turn to the page and read the problem-and-solution description to help you get on your way and back to work. (To make them stand out, problems that people most frequently encounter are marked with a "hot topic" icon in the tables of contents.)

If You Can't Find a Problem or Solution

If you can't find a problem-and-solution description that matches your own problem, your first tactic should be to scan other chapters and chapter sections. Some problem-and-solution descriptions can fit into more than one chapter or section. For example, network printer problems might reasonably be included in either the Networks chapter or the Printing chapter. The Help Desk includes network printer problems in the Printing chapter, however; so if you looked in the Networks chapter, you wouldn't find the information.

Your second tactic, assuming you have a working Internet connection, is to search the actual Product Support Services Knowledge Base at *http://support.microsoft.com.* Product Support Services continues to add to and enhance the Microsoft Windows 98 Knowledge Base. So although this book was based on a rich and very complete Knowledge Base, what's available in the future will be even richer and deeper. And if you locate the appropriate problem-and-solution description, but you find that you would like more information, note that each problem-and-solution description identifies its source article in the Knowledge Base. You may sometimes be able to get additional or updated information from the original article.

A final tactic, of course, is to contact Product Support Services directly. You can find the direct support telephone number for any Microsoft product at the *http://support.microsoft.com* web site. Note that the Windows 98 support telephone number for the United States is (425) 635-7222 and for Canada it is (905) 568-4494.

A Final Important Note

A handful of the problem-and-solution descriptions explain how to edit the Windows Registry. Before you make any change in the Registry, heed this important warning: If you make a mistake while editing the Registry, you can cause serious problems that may require you to reinstall Windows. Please be extremely careful. In particular, before you start, first make a backup copy of your Registry files. These files are called SYSTEM.DAT and USER.DAT and are hidden files located in your WINDOWS folder. (Refer to KB article Q132332, "How to Back Up the Registry," for information on how to back up these two files.) Note, too, that if you need more information on how to use the Regedit tool, you can get this information from the Regedit tool's online help. To access this information, follow these steps:

1. Click the Start button, click Run, enter *Regedit* in the Open text box, and click OK.

2. Choose Help Topics from the Help menu.

3. Review the "Changing Keys And Values" topic for information on adding a key or value, changing a value, or deleting or renaming a key or value in the Registry.

CHAPTER 1

Accessories

Backup

Destination Folder Changes to Default Folder

You specify a destination folder under Where To Back Up in Microsoft Backup and then change your backup options by clicking Options under How To Back Up, but the destination folder is changed to the default folder instead of the folder you specified.

This can happen if both of the following conditions exist:

- You click Browse to locate the destination folder
- You change the Microsoft Backup options after you specify the destination folder

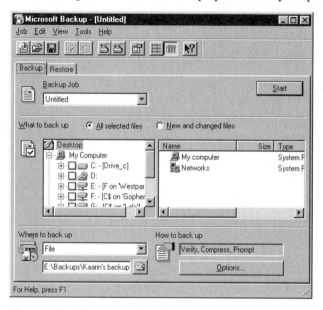

Figure 1-1. *The Microsoft Backup window.*

Solution

Manually type the path to the destination folder, or change the Microsoft Backup options before you specify the destination folder.

Related KB article Q182011

Driver or Device Error Occurs Using Microsoft Backup

You start Microsoft Backup in Windows 98 and receive the following error message:

Driver already installed Ref 00-02-00-00-0000

After Microsoft Backup starts, you might also receive this error message:

No device found

Also, backup devices in your computer might not work correctly and running the Add New Hardware Wizard might not correctly detect your backup device or devices.

This problem can occur if Seagate Direct Tape Access version 2.0 or 3.0 is installed on your computer.

Solution

Work around this issue by uninstalling Seagate Direct Tape Access version 2.0 or 3.0 or uninstalling Microsoft Backup in Windows 98. For information about how to uninstall Seagate Direct Tape Access version 2.0 or 3.0, see the documentation included with Direct Tape Access, or contact Seagate. To uninstall Microsoft Backup in Windows 98, follow these steps:

1. Click the Start button, choose Settings, and click Control Panel.

2. Double-click the Add/Remove Programs icon.

3. Click the Windows Setup tab, select System Tools (the words, not the check box), and click Details.

4. Clear the Backup check box, and click OK.

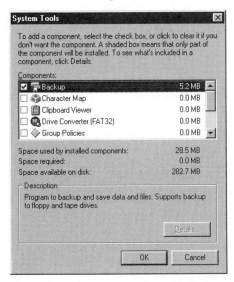

Figure 1-2. *The System Tools dialog box.*

5. Follow the instructions on the screen to finish uninstalling Backup.

Related KB article Q187398

Error Message Occurs Backing Up to Removable Media

You use Microsoft Backup to back up files to removable media and receive the following error message:

An error occurred while writing the backup data. The end of the media was approached unexpectedly. (08-22-07-01-0000)

After this message is displayed, you cannot insert the next media. This problem can occur if you back up to a removable device that has been compressed with DriveSpace and Backup needs to span multiple media to finish.

Solution

Do not compress your removable media with DriveSpace if you need to create a backup that spans multiple media.

Related KB articles Q188158, Q183810

Error or Warning Message Occurs During Backup

You use Microsoft Backup to create a full system backup or a backup that includes the Windows folder and the status box indicates that errors occurred during the backup. When you click Report to view the backup report, you might receive one of the following error messages:

Error: C:\WINDOWS\Cookies\index.dat - busy

Error: C:\WINDOWS\History\index.dat - busy

Error: C:\WINDOWS\Temporary Internet Files\index.dat - busy

Warning: C:\WINDOWS\Cookies\index.dat was busy during backup. It cannot be restored or compared.

Warning: C:\WINDOWS\History\index.dat was busy during backup. It cannot be restored or compared.

Warning: C:\WINDOWS\Temporary Internet Files\index.dat was busy during backup. It cannot be restored or compared.

This problem can occur because the INDEX.DAT files in these locations are open when Internet Explorer is running. Because Internet Explorer is part of the Windows 98 graphical user interface (GUI), these files are always open and therefore cannot be backed up.

Solution

These INDEX.DAT files are actually re-created each time Internet Explorer starts, so you don't need to back them up. All the other files you selected are backed up successfully.

Related KB article 185713

File Doesn't Restore

When you try to use Microsoft Backup to restore a backup set created in Windows 95 that spans multiple disks, Backup creates a new folder but does not restore the file in the backup set.

This problem occurs when your backup set contains a file that spans multiple disks. Windows 98 cannot restore a Windows 95 backup set that consists of a single file that spans two or more disks.

Solution One

Use Backup in Windows 95 to restore your file.

Solution Two

To prevent this problem from occurring in the future, do not use Backup in Windows 95 to back up a single file that spans multiple disks.

Solution Three

Back up more than one file from your Windows 95–based computer and verify that the additional file is on the first disk in its entirety.

Related KB article Q189602

File Doesn't Restore from Windows 95 Backup

You try to use Microsoft Backup to restore an individual file from a Windows 95 backup set, but the restored file might be damaged and the resulting file is 0 bytes.

This problem can occur when you try to restore an individual file from a multiple-file backup set that spans more than one disk or tape. Design variations between Windows 98 and Windows 95 in the implementation of the QIC format cause this problem.

Solution

Work around this problem by restoring the entire Windows 95 backup set and then deleting any of the other restored files you do not want.

Related KB article Q190897

Media Is Damaged Error Message

You try to use Microsoft Backup to restore files from a backup that spans multiple tapes, but you receive an error message that says the backup media is damaged. If you then click OK or Cancel, the restore process stops, and you are not prompted to insert the next tape. This problem can occur if one of your backup tapes is damaged.

Solution

To work around this issue, you must manually restore the files on each tape. To do so, follow these steps:

1. Click the Start button, choose Programs, choose Accessories, choose System Tools, and click Backup.

2. Insert one of the tapes from your backup set into the tape drive, and then click Refresh on the Restore tab.

Note You will not be able to restore files from the damaged tape.

3. When you see a message that says your backup spans multiple tapes, click No.

4. On the list of files on the tape, click the files you want to restore, and then click Start. Repeat steps 2–4 with another tape until you restore all the files you want, and then quit Backup.

Related KB article Q186946

Media Not Supported

You use Microsoft Backup to read a backup tape and receive the following error message:

The media is not supported by this product. Please insert another media.

Using a different tape generates the same error message. The error message occurs with any operation that attempts to read the tape.

This error message occurs if the tape drive does not support the Quick File Access format (QFA), which is also known as media partitioning. Backup requires that the tape drive support QFA. QFA allows tapes to be divided into a large data partition and a small directory partition. The directory partition holds information about each of the backup sets on the tape and can also be used to store the exact block address of each file on the tape. This allows for the fastest file retrieval possible with the tape drive.

Solution

Determine whether your tape drive supports QFA by contacting your tape drive manufacturer. Some earlier tape drives do not support QFA. Many newer drives do support QFA.

If possible, get updated firmware to add QFA support. Note, however, that this is typically an option for only a few high-end tape drives.

Related KB article Q191796

Network Share Files Don't Back Up

You try to back up files or folders on a password-protected network share and receive the following error message:

Backup complete - error reported

If you view the log for this backup, you might receive one of the following error messages (in which <share> is the name of the network share):

Error: \\<share> - accessed denied

Error: \\<share> - could not be accessed

This problem can occur because Microsoft Backup does not prompt you for a password to access a password-protected network share.

Solution

Connect to the network share, and enter your password before you try to back up files or folders from this share.

Related KB article Q181628

Registry Doesn't Back Up

You configure Microsoft Backup to back up your Registry, but the Registry does not back up. This problem can occur if either or both of the following conditions exist:

- You are not backing up the WINDOWS folder.
- All the files that you are backing up are on a drive other than the boot drive.

The Registry contains several references that are dependent on device drivers and dynamic-link library (.DLL) files located in the Windows folder. The Registry cannot be restored properly without the corresponding Windows folder.

Solution

Back up the WINDOWS folder when you back up the Registry, or back up at least one file on the boot drive when you back up the Registry.

Related KB article Q187585

Removable Media Doesn't Appear on Backup List

You click the Where To Back Up box in Microsoft Backup to view your backup devices and removable media does not appear on the list. Note that removable media include devices such as floppy drives, Zip drives, and Jazz drives. This behavior is by design. Removable media are not recognized as a backup device (such as a tape drive) but instead are recognized as a regular drive with a drive letter (such as a hard disk).

Solution

If you want to back up to removable media, select File from the Where To Back Up box when you make a backup. For more information about making a backup to removable media, start Backup, choose Help Topics from the Help menu, click the Index tab, enter *files* in the text box, select Backups To from the list, and then click Display.

If your computer has a removable media drive for backup purposes only, when you start Backup for the first time, you will see a message stating there are no backup devices. When you are prompted to use the Add New Hardware Wizard to find a backup device, or to continue without looking for a backup device, click No.

Related KB article Q186168

Shared Network Drive Backup Causes Error Messages

You attempt to use Microsoft Backup to back up files or folders to a Windows 95 shared network drive and receive one of the following error messages:

This media is not formatted with this product's backup software format.

Formatting will require one to 30 minutes. All existing data on the media will be lost.

Do you want to format the media?

When you attempt to back up to a Windows NT shared network drive, you might receive the following message:

This media is write-protected. Remove the write protection or insert another media to continue.

The shared network drive to which you are attempting to back up files or folders is password protected.

Microsoft Backup does not prompt you for a password when you attempt to back up files or folders to a password-protected shared network drive.

When you connect to and specify a password for the shared network drive, the password is added to the WINDOWS\<USERNAME>.PWL file. (<USERNAME> is the name you use to log on to Windows 98.) When you attempt to back up files or folders to the shared network drive, the appropriate password in the WINDOWS\<USERNAME>.PWL file is used.

Solution

Connect to and specify a password for the shared network drive before you attempt to back up files or folders to it. To do so, follow these steps:

1. Click the Start button, and choose Run.

2. Enter \\<*COMPUTER NAME*>\<*SHARE NAME*> in the Run box (in which <COMPUTER NAME> is the name of the network computer and <SHARE NAME> is the name of the shared drive on that computer).

Figure 1-3. *The Run dialog box.*

3. Click OK.

4. In the Enter Network Password dialog box, enter the password in the Password box, and verify that the Save This Password In Your Password List check box is selected.

5. Click OK, and then attempt to back up files or folders to the shared network drive again.

Related KB article Q182344

Unattended Backup Job Doesn't Complete

You use Task Scheduler to start an unattended backup job in Microsoft Backup, but the backup job does not complete if it is left unattended. This problem occurs even if you configured Backup to perform an unattended backup and then added this task to Task Scheduler. Task Scheduler only starts Microsoft Backup, not the backup job. The version of Backup that is included with Windows 98 does not support a backup job being started automatically.

Solution One

Be present when beginning a backup job.

Solution Two

Upgrade to a backup program that supports completely unattended backup jobs.

Related KB article Q184756

Communications

HyperTerminal Doesn't Answer Incoming Calls

You try to use HyperTerminal to answer an incoming call, but it is not configured to do so.

Solution

Configure HyperTerminal to answer an incoming call. To do this, follow these steps:

1. Click the Start button, choose Programs, choose Accessories, choose Communications, and click HyperTerminal.

2. Double-click the Hypertrm.exe icon.

3. Enter a name for the connection, and click OK. (You might want to name the connection something like "Answer Mode.")

4. Enter the connection information, including a phone number in the Phone Number box, and click OK.

Figure 1-4. *The Connect To dialog box.*

Note The phone number you enter is not important because you will use this connection to answer only incoming calls. You must enter a phone number however.

5. Click Cancel to bypass the connect process.

6. Choose Properties from the File menu.

7. Click the Settings tab, and click ASCII Setup.

8. Optionally, select the following check boxes to properly display characters in the Terminal window:

   - Send Line Ends With Line Feeds

   - Echo Typed Characters Locally

   - Append Line Feeds To Incoming Line Ends

   - Wrap Lines That Exceed Terminal Width

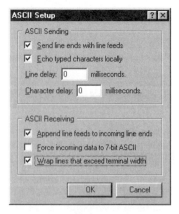

Figure 1-5. *The ASCII Setup dialog box.*

9. Click OK, and click OK again to return to HyperTerminal.

10. When you hear the phone ring or see the "ring" command, enter the answer command for your modem. The answer command for many modems is ATA. If your modem supports automatic answering mode, type *ATS0=1* for it to answer incoming calls automatically.

Related KB article Q142899

HyperTerminal Doesn't Connect to French Minitel

Your modem doesn't connect to French Minitel when using HyperTerminal.

Solution

To connect to the French Minitel, follow these steps:

1. Check your modem manual for a command that enables your modem to connect in V.23 modulation to Minitel.

2. Click the Start button, choose Settings, and click Control Panel.

3. Double-click the Modems icon, select your modem, and then click Properties.

4. Click the Connection tab, and then click Advanced.

5. Enter the V.23 command you looked up in the Extra Settings text box, and then click OK.

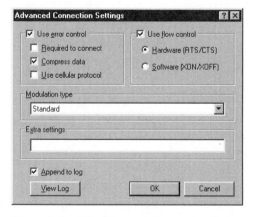

Figure 1-6.   *The Advanced Connection Settings dialog box.*

Related KB article Q191480 or HARDWARE.TXT in your WINDOWS folder

HyperTerminal Doesn't Display Characters

You attempt to type characters in HyperTerminal, but the characters do not display on the screen. This behavior can occur even if the Echo Typed Characters Locally check box is selected in the connection's properties. This behavior occurs because the Echo Typed Characters Locally check box does not work properly in the version of HyperTerminal included with Windows 98.

Solution

Download and install HyperTerminal Private Edition, version 4.0, from Hilgraeve's web site at *http://www.hilgraeve.com,* or obtain it from Hilgraeve Technical Support.

Related KB article Q192456

HyperTerminal Doesn't Install

After you choose Typical Install and perform a clean install of Windows to a new folder or hard disk, you notice that the HyperTerminal program is not installed.

When you upgrade to Windows 98 with HyperTerminal already installed, HyperTerminal is installed and functional.

Solution

To resolve this problem, manually install HyperTerminal. To do this, follow these steps:

1. Click the Start button, choose Settings, and click Control Panel.

2. Double-click the Add/Remove Programs icon.

3. Click the Windows Setup tab, select Communications (the word, not the check box) from the list, and then click Details.

4. Select the HyperTerminal check box, and then click OK.

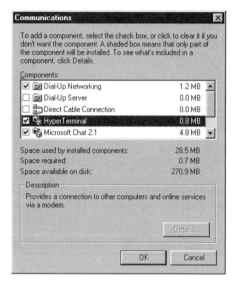

Figure 1-7. *The Communications dialog box.*

5. Click OK, and then follow the instructions on the screen to complete the installation.

Related KB article Q186939

HyperTerminal Reports Invalid Page Fault Error Message

You attempt to create a new connection in HyperTerminal and receive the following error message:

HyperTerminal caused an invalid page fault in module MSVCRT.DLL at <xxxx>:<xxxxxxxx>

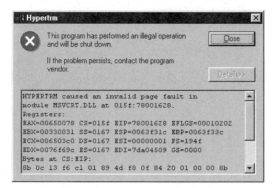

Figure 1-8. *HyperTerminal displays an error message.*

This behavior can occur if you have version 6.0 of the MSVCRT.DLL file installed. This version of the file is included with Microsoft Visual Studio 6.0.

Solution

HyperTerminal is developed by Hilgraeve. To resolve this issue, download and install HyperTerminal Private Edition, version 4.0, from the following Hilgraeve web site:

http://www.hilgraeve.com

Note This behavior might also occur in other programs. For more information, see KB article Q190536.

Related KB article Q192123

Phone Dialer Doesn't Complete Call

You attempt to place a call using Phone Dialer, but Phone Dialer stops before the complete phone number is dialed or the Call Status and Dialing dialog boxes close before you hang up the phone. This behavior can occur when the phone number you are dialing includes letters (A–Z). Phone Dialer supports dialing only numerals.

Solution

Type the phone number as numerals (0–9), not letters (A–Z).

Related KB article Q177254

Phone Dialer Doesn't Disable Call Waiting

Phone Dialer does not dial the code to disable call waiting even though the To Disable Call Waiting, Dial <code> check box is selected in the Dialing Properties dialog box.

This problem occurs because Phone Dialer does not use this setting. This behavior is by design. The disable call waiting setting is used for modem and fax calls only.

Solution One

Insert the code to disable call waiting as part of the number you are dialing in Phone Dialer. For example:

70,555-1212

Figure 1-9. *The Phone Dialer program window.*

Note Depending on your area or phone type, the code used to disable call waiting could be *70, 70#, or 1170. Contact your local phone company to find out what your code is.

Solution Two

Insert the code to disable call waiting as part of the outside line access number in the Dialing Properties dialog box.

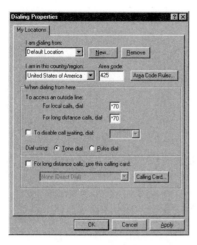

Figure 1-10. *The Dialing Properties dialog box.*

Note If you do this, make sure to clear the To Disable Call Waiting, Dial <code> check box in the Dialing Properties dialog box to avoid the code being dialed twice in other programs (such as Dial-Up Networking).

Related KB article Q139516

Telnet Most-Recently-Used List Should Be Cleared

The Telnet program included with Windows maintains a most-recently-used (MRU) list of host names entered in the Remote System/Host Name box. You can use the MRU list to easily select commonly accessed Telnet locations. To clear the Telnet MRU list, display the Registry key:

```
HKEY_USERS\.Default\Software\Microsoft\Telnet
```

and delete the following values:

```
Machine<X>
```

```
LastMachine
```

```
LastTermType
```

```
LastService
```

```
Service<X>
```

```
TermType<X>
```

where <X> is any number from 1 to 8.

Solution

To clear the MRU values, follow these steps:

Warning Please read the Introduction for information on how to safely edit the Registry.

1. Click the Start button, and choose Run.

2. Enter *Regedit* in the Run box, and click OK.

3. Navigate your way down through the folders in the left pane.

4. Right-click the appropriate values, and choose Delete from the shortcut menu.

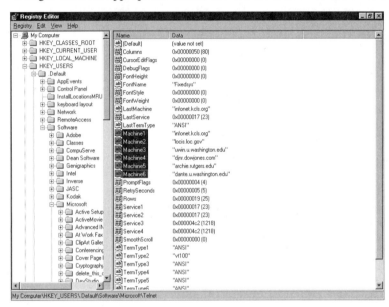

Figure 1-11.   *The Registry Editor window.*

5. Close the Registry Editor window.

6. Restart Windows.

Related KB article Q148820

Entertainment and Multimedia

ActiveMovie Displays Blank Select The Movie Size Box

You attempt to resize a video file you are viewing using ActiveMovie by right-clicking the video, choosing Properties from the shortcut menu, and then clicking the Movie Size tab, but the Select The Movie Size box appears to be blank when the ActiveMovie window is currently maximized. If the ActiveMovie window is not maximized when you right-click the video, choose Properties from the shortcut menu, and then click the Movie Size tab. The current movie size appears in the Select The Movie Size box.

Solution One

Click the Restore button, and then resize the window.

Solution Two

1. Right-click the video, and then choose Properties from the shortcut menu to open the Properties dialog box.

2. On the Movie Size tab, click the Select The Movie Size box, and then click a size other than Maximized.

3. Click OK.

Related KB article Q178562

CD Player Doesn't Play Audio CDs Automatically

You start CD Player, but it does not automatically play the CD in the CD-ROM drive. You must first click Play.

This problem occurs when the Auto Insert Notification option is disabled or unavailable.

Solution

To cause audio CDs to play automatically when you start CD Player, follow these steps:

1. Right-click the Start button, and choose Explore from the shortcut menu.

2. Double-click the WINDOWS folder, double-click the Start Menu folder, double-click the Accessories folder, and double-click the Entertainment folder.

3. Right-click CD Player, and choose Properties from the shortcut menu.

4. Click the Shortcut tab, and change the entry in the Target box to C:\WINDOWS\CDPLAYER.EXE /PLAY.

Figure 1-12.   *The CD Player Properties dialog box.*

5. Click OK.

Related KB article Q142361

CD Player Doesn't Start Automatically

You insert an audio CD in your CD-ROM drive, but CD Player does not start automatically. If you attempt to start CD Player, you receive one of the following error messages:

Please insert an audio compact disc

Data or no disc loaded

This problem occurs when the CD audio device driver is missing or damaged.

Solution

Remove and then reinstall the CD audio device driver. To do so, follow these steps:

1. Click the Start button, choose Settings, click Control Panel, and then double-click the Multimedia icon.

2. On the Devices tab, double-click the Media Control Devices branch to expand it.

3. Click CD Audio Device (Media Control), and then click Properties.

Figure 1-13. *The Devices tab of the Multimedia Properties dialog box.*

4. Click Remove, and then click Yes when you are prompted to remove the device.

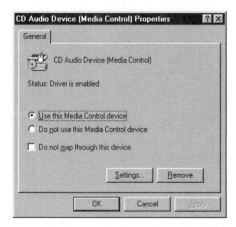

Figure 1-14. *The CD Audio Device (Media Control) Properties dialog box.*

5. Click OK, click OK again, and then restart your computer.

6. Click the Start button, choose Settings, click Control Panel, and then double-click the Add New Hardware icon.

7. Click Next, click Next again, click No, I Want To Select The Hardware From A List, and then click Next.

8. Click Sound, Video, And Game Controllers, and then click Next.

9. In the Manufacturers box, click Microsoft MCI, and then click CD Audio Device (Media Control) in the Models box.

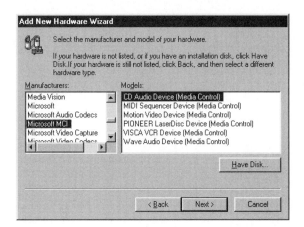

Figure 1-15. *The Add New Hardware Wizard dialog box.*

10. Click Next, click Finish, and then click Yes when you are prompted to restart your computer.

Note A missing or damaged CD audio device driver affects only audio CDs, not CD-ROMs.

Related KB article Q192988

CD Player Settings Don't Transfer

You move from one computer to another and your user-defined Artist, Track, and Title CD settings are not installed on the new computer. The Artist, Track, and Title settings are stored in the CDPLAYER.INI file in the WINDOWS folder.

Solution One

Copy the CDPLAYER.INI file from the WINDOWS folder to a floppy disk, and then copy the file from the floppy disk to the WINDOWS folder on the other computer.

If there is already a CDPLAYER.INI file in the WINDOWS folder on the second computer, you must rename it before you copy the file from the first computer or you will overwrite the existing file. You can merge the contents of two CDPLAYER.INI files using the Copy and Paste commands in a text editor (such as Notepad).

Solution Two

If the computers are connected over a network, you can copy the CDPLAYER.INI file from the first computer's WINDOWS folder to the second computer's WINDOWS folder directly using Windows Explorer.

Related KB article Q147802

CD Player Shortcut Remains in Multimedia Folder

You click the Start button, choose Programs, choose Accessories, choose Multimedia, and then click CD Player, and you receive the following error message:

The item "Cdplayer.exe" that this shortcut refers to has been changed or moved.

This problem can occur if a shortcut to CD Player (CDPLAYER.EXE) is located in both the EN-TERTAINMENT and MULTIMEDIA folders on the Start menu, and you remove CD Player using the Add/Remove Programs tool in Control Panel: only the shortcut in the ENTERTAINMENT folder is removed. Microsoft has confirmed this to be a problem in Windows 98.

Solution

To work around this problem, manually remove the shortcut to CD Player in the MULTIMEDIA folder. To do so, follow these steps:

1. Click the Start button, choose Programs, choose Accessories, and then choose Multimedia.

2. Right-click CD Player, and then choose Delete from the shortcut menu.

Figure 1-16. *Deleting the CD Player shortcut.*

Related KB article Q187657

DirectX 6.0 Won't Remove

After you install the Microsoft DirectX 6.0 upgrade, you cannot remove DirectX 6.0 and revert to the earlier version of DirectX included with Windows 98. This problem occurs because DirectX 6.0 is an update to the operating system itself, it is not an add-on component.

Uninstalling DirectX Drivers on the Install/Uninstall tab in the Add/Remove Programs tool in Control Panel does not uninstall DirectX 6.0.

Solution

To revert to the earlier version of DirectX included with Windows 98, you must reinstall Windows 98 from MS-DOS.

Related KB article Q193719

Media Player Doesn't Play Compressed .AVI File Correctly

You try to play an audio-video interleaved (.AVI) file compressed with the Intel Indeo 4.x codec, but the file is displayed incorrectly or not at all in the Media Player tool included with Windows 98.

Note that ActiveMovie 2.0 can play the .AVI file properly.

When you install Windows 98 on a blank hard disk or in an empty folder, a necessary driver entry may not be created in the SYSTEM.INI file.

The Indeo codec included with Windows 98 is both a Video for Windows codec and a DirectShow filter. As a filter, the file registers itself in the Registry so that DirectShow can use it. Media Player is based on the older model in which an entry is required in the SYSTEM.INI file in order for Video for Windows to recognize the installed codec.

Solution

To resolve this issue, follow these steps:

1. Click the Start button, and then choose Run.

2. In the Open box, enter *sysedit*, and then click OK.

3. Choose C:\WINDOWS\SYSTEM.INI from the Window menu.

4. In the [drivers32] section of the SYSTEM.INI file, add the following line:

```
VIDC.IV41=ir41_32.ax
```

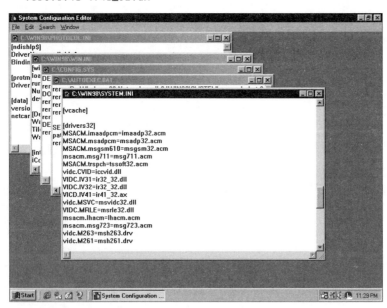

Figure 1-17. *The window for the SYSTEM.INI file in the System Configuration Editor.*

5. Choose Save from the File menu.

6. Choose Exit from the File menu.

7. Restart your computer.

Related KB article Q191533

File Management Tools

Briefcase Doesn't Prompt to Delete Original File

You delete a file in Briefcase and click Update All, but you are not prompted to delete the original file if you modify the original file before you delete the copy in Briefcase.

Solution

Delete the original file before you delete the copy of the file in Briefcase.

Related KB article Q179174

Briefcase Doesn't Receive Files Sent to It

You right-click a file or folder, choose Send To from the shortcut menu, and then choose My Briefcase from the submenu, but the file or folder is not sent to Briefcase if user profiles are enabled on the computer.

The Send To command assumes My Briefcase is in the <DRIVE>:\<WINDOWS>\ desktop folder (in which <DRIVE> is the drive letter of the hard disk on which Windows is installed and <WINDOWS> is the folder in which Windows is installed). With user profiles enabled, My Briefcase is in the <DRIVE>:\<WINDOWS>\PROFILES\<USERNAME> \DESKTOP folder (where <USERNAME> is the name you use to log on to Windows). For more information about how to use Briefcase, see KB article Q142574, "How to Install and Use Briefcase."

Solution

Copy the file or folder to Briefcase instead of using the Send To command.

Related KB article Q193764

Briefcase Doesn't Uninstall in Add/Remove Programs

You attempt to use the Add/Remove Programs tool to remove a Briefcase from the computer but find that Briefcase is not listed on the Windows Setup tab, so it seems that you cannot completely remove a Briefcase from the computer as you can other Windows components.

This problem occurs because Windows excludes Briefcase from the list of components that you can uninstall to prevent data loss. If Windows enabled you to uninstall a Briefcase, any existing Briefcase on your computer would become inaccessible.

Solution

Delete any specific Briefcase on your computer by right-clicking it and choosing Delete from the shortcut menu.

Related KB article Q132653

Copy Disk Command Causes Fatal Exception

You use the Copy Disk command in My Computer or Windows Explorer, and you receive the following error message after you insert the destination disk and click OK:

Fatal Exception 0D has occurred at <address> in VxD V86MMGR (01)+

In addition, the Performance tab in the System tool in Control Panel might indicate that your floppy drives are using MS-DOS Compatibility mode. This problem occurs when the HSFLOP.PDR file is missing or damaged.

Solution

To solve this problem, follow these steps:

1. Click the Start button, choose Find, and then click Files Or Folders.

2. Enter *hsflop.pdr* in the Named box, and click Find Now.

3. If the HSFLOP.PDR file is found, right-click it, choose Rename from the shortcut menu, and then enter a new name for the HSFLOP.PDR file (such as HSFLOP.XXX). If the HSFLOP.PDR file is not found, proceed to step 4.

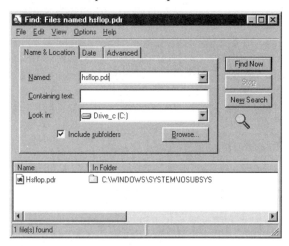

Figure 1-18. *The Find window.*

4. Click the Close button.

5. Use the System File Checker tool to extract a new copy of the HSFLOP.PDR file from your original Windows 98 disks or CD-ROM to the C:\WINDOWS\SYSTEM\IOSUBSYS folder (assuming C is the drive on which you installed Windows 98 and WINDOWS is the folder in which you installed Windows 98.)

Note For more information about how to use the System File Checker to extract files, see KB article Q129605.

Solution Two

To work around this behavior, type *diskcopy<source drive>: <destination drive>* at a command prompt (in which <source drive> is the drive from which you are copying files and <destination drive> is the drive to which you are copying files) and then press the Enter key.

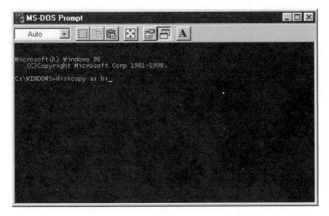

Figure 1-19. *The MS-DOS Prompt window.*

Related KB article Q192835

Copying Files Displays Error Message

You attempt to copy files to a drive that is low on free disk space and receive the following error message:

Cannot create or replace <file>: There is not enough free disk space.

Solution

If you do not want to receive this error message, and do not want to use the Disk Cleanup tool to free disk space, create a DWORD value named DisableLowDiskSpaceBroadcast in the following Registry key:

`HKEY_LOCAL_MACHINE\System\CurrentControlSet\Control\FileSystem`

To do so, follow these steps:

Warning Please read the Introduction for information on how to safely edit the Registry.

1. Click the Start button, choose Run, and enter *Regedit* in the Open box. Click OK.

2. Navigate your way down through the folders in the left pane until you locate the key named above.

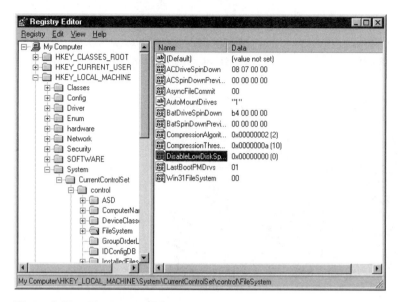

Figure 1-20. *The Registry Editor window.*

3. Double-click the DisableLowDiskSpaceBroadcast value, and set the data value to the appropriate value from the following table:

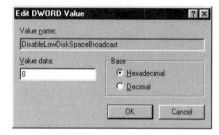

Figure 1-21. *The Edit DWORD Value dialog box.*

Table 1-1.   Data Values for DisableLowDiskSpaceBroadcast

Drive letter	Data value
A	1
B	2
C	4
D	8
E	16
F	32
G	64
H	128
I	256

Drive letter	Data value
J	512
K	1024
L	2048
M	4096
N	8192
O	16384
P	32768
Q	65536
R	131072
S	262144
T	524288
U	1048576
V	2097152
W	4194304
X	8388608
Y	16777216
Z	33554432

4. Close Regedit.

5. Restart Windows.

If you want to disable the error message for more than one drive, you can add the data values of the drives located in the table and then set the data value of the DisableLowDiskSpaceBroadcast value using the sum of these data values. For example, drive E has a value of 16 and drive G has a value of 64. These two data values added together equal 80. To disable the low disk space notification for drive E and drive G, set the data value of the DisableLowDiskSpaceBroadcast value to 80.

Note For more information about using the Disk Cleanup tool, see KB article Q186099.

Related KB article Q188074

Deleting Files Prompts Confirmation

You attempt to delete a file and are prompted to confirm the deletion.

Solution

To disable the Delete Confirmation dialog box, follow these steps:

1. Right-click the Recycle Bin icon on the desktop, and choose Properties from the shortcut menu.

2. Clear the Display Delete Confirmation Dialog Box check box, and then click OK.

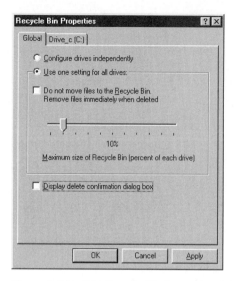

Figure 1-22.   *The Recycle Bin Properties dialog box.*

Related KB article Q185257

Deleting or Renaming Folder Causes Error Message

You try to delete a folder and receive one of the following error messages:

Cannot remove folder <folder name>: Access is denied. Make sure the disk is not full or write protected and that the file is not currently in use.

Cannot delete *.*. Cannot find the specified file. Make sure you specify the correct path and filename.

Or you rename a folder and receive the following message:

This operation may affect some registered applications.

This message occurs for the same reason as the message you receive when you try to delete a folder. You can ignore this message and continue.

These messages occur because the directory structure for the folder you want to remove is longer than the maximum allowable length.

Solution One

Rename some of the parent folders that are closer to the root directory with shorter names, and then try to delete the folder.

Solution Two

Run ScanDisk, and then try to delete the folder.

Related KB article Q132650

Disk Drives Don't Appear in My Computer or Windows Explorer

You view My Computer or Windows Explorer and some or all of your drives are missing. When you view Device Manager, the missing drives are not displayed, and you are not able to gain access to the drives by clicking the Start button, choosing Run, entering the drive letter in the Open box, and then clicking OK.

This behavior can occur if the PowerToys TweakUI tool is installed and configured to hide one or more of your drives.

Note For information about the TweakUI tool, see KB articles Q190643 and Q188920.

Solution

To solve this problem, follow these steps:

1. Click the Start button, choose Settings, and then click Control Panel.

2. Double-click the TweakUI icon.

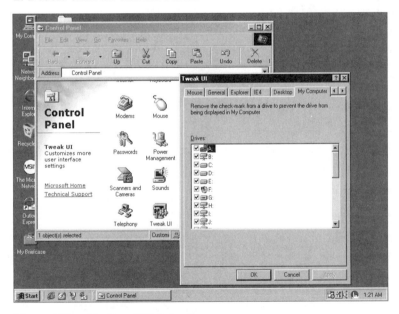

Figure 1-23. *The TweakUI dialog box.*

3. On the My Computer tab, select the check boxes of the drives that are currently hidden.

4. Click Close, and then restart your computer.

Related KB article Q191579

.DLL Files Do Not Move

You try to move (or cut and paste) multiple read-only dynamic-link library (.DLL) files to another disk or network drive and receive an error message similar to one of the following:

Error Moving File Cannot move <Filename>.dll: The file exists.

Error Copying File Cannot copy <Filename>.dll: There has been a sharing violation. The source or destination file may be in use.

Note that the <FILENAME>.DLL file on the destination drive has a size of 0 bytes. You try to delete this file and receive the following error message:

Cannot delete <Filename>.dll: Access is denied. Make sure the disk is not full or write-protected and that the file is not currently in use.

Solution One

Delete the <FILENAME>.DLL 0-byte file. To do so, restart the computer and then delete the file.

Solution Two

Move the read-only .DLL files by copying the .DLL files to the destination disk and then deleting the .DLL files on the source disk.

Related KB article Q192848

Explorer Causes Page Fault

You attempt to open MY COMPUTER, CONTROL PANEL, or the PRINTERS folder and receive one of the following error messages:

Explorer caused a page fault in module Shell32.dll.

Explorer caused a divide error in module Shell32.dll.

This problem occurs when you are running an old version of Plug-In for Windows (PLUGIN.EXE) which is not compatible with Windows. Versions older than version 2.5 cause these errors.

Solution One

Obtain an updated version of Plug-In for Windows from Plannet Crafters.

Solution Two

To work around this problem, disable Plug-In for Windows. To do so, remove PLUGIN.EXE from the STARTUP folder or from the "load=" line in the WIN.INI file in the WINDOWS folder. Restart your computer.

Note For more information about other possible causes for the error message "Explorer caused a divide error in module Shell32.dll," see KB article Q136475.

Related KB article Q148322

File Type Won't Register

You try to add a file type to the Registered File Types list and receive the following error message, even if you cannot find the file extension in the list:

The extension '.<EXT>' is already in use by file type '<Name>'.Choose another extension.

This problem occurs because multiple file types can be registered to one program. In this case, the file type does not appear in the Registered File Types list, but instead it appears in the details for another registered file type.

For example, the registered file type Microsoft Word 6.0 Document can contain .RTF, .DOC, and .DOT extensions. Even though these file types do not appear in the Registered File Types list, they are registered to Microsoft Word 6.0.

Solution

Change the association of a file type that does not appear in the Registered File Types list. To do this, follow these steps:

1. In My Computer or Windows Explorer, select a file of the type you want to register, and then hold down the Shift key while you right-click the file.

2. Choose Open With from the shortcut menu.

3. If you are prompted to, enter a description for the file type. Select the program you want to use for this file type in the Choose The Program You Want To Use box.

4. Select the Always Use This Program To Open This Type Of File check box, and click OK.

Figure 1-24. *The Open With dialog box.*

Related KB article Q129050

Find Target Command Causes Explorer Errors

You right-click an icon on the desktop, choose Properties from the shortcut menu, click Find Target, and then receive the following error message:

Explorer: This program has performed an illegal operation and will be shut down. If the problem persists, contact the program vendor.

If you click Details, you might see the following information:

EXPLORER caused an invalid page fault in module SHDOCVW.DLL at <memory address>.

If you click Close, you might receive the following error message:

There was an internal error and one of the windows you were using will be closed. It is recommended that you save your work and close all programs, and then restart your computer.

Solution

Restart your computer.

Related KB article Q188604

Hard Disk Icon Appears As CD-ROM Icon

You open My Computer, and your hard disk icon appears as a CD-ROM icon. If you double-click (or right-click and then choose Open from the shortcut menu) the CD-ROM icon in My Computer, you might receive the following error message:

Cannot find autorun.exe.

This problem occurs when the AUTORUN.INF file is in the root folder of your hard disk.

Solution

Rename the AUTORUN.INF file to AUTORUN.XXX. To do so, follow these steps:

1. Click the Start button, choose Find, and then click Files Or Folders.

2. Enter *autorun.inf* in the Named box, and click Find Now.

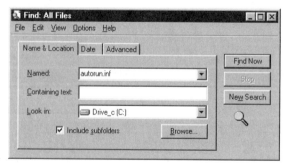

Figure 1-25. *The Find: All Files dialog box.*

3. Right-click AUTORUN.INF in the list of found files, and choose Properties from the shortcut menu.

4. Click the Read-Only check box to clear it, and then click OK.

5. Right-click AUTORUN.INF in the list of found files, and choose Rename from the shortcut menu.

6. Enter *autorun.xxx,* and then press the Enter key.

7. Restart your computer.

Related KB article Q185552

Install Command Unavailable for .INF File

You right-click an .INF file, and the Install command does not appear on the shortcut menu. The Install command can be unavailable if the association for .INF files is changed from the default value. This is often done by right-clicking an .INF file while holding down the Shift key, selecting a different program to open the .INF file, and then selecting the Always Use This Program To Open This Type Of File check box.

Solution One

Use Registry Editor to change the (Default) value in the following Registry key:

`HKEY_CLASSES_ROOT\.inf`

To do so, follow these steps:

Warning Please read the Introduction for information on how to safely edit the Registry.

1. Click the Start button, and choose Run.

2. Enter *Regedit* in the Open box, and click OK.

3. Navigate your way down through the folders in the left pane.

4. Double-click the (Default) value, and enter *inffile* in the Value Data box.

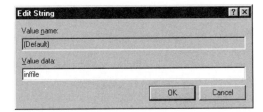

Figure 1-26. *The Edit String dialog box.*

5. Close Regedit.

6. Restart Windows.

Solution Two

Restore the standard Windows shell commands. To do so, follow these steps:

1. Click the Start button, and choose Run.

2. Enter the following line in the Open box:

```
rundll setupx.dll,InstallHinfSection DefaultInstall 132
c:\windows\inf\shell.inf
```

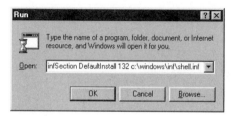

Figure 1-27. *The Run dialog box.*

Note If you installed Windows in a folder other than the WINDOWS folder, adjust this command accordingly.

3. Click OK.

4. When hard disk activity stops, restart Windows.

Solution Three

Create a new file association action for .INF files by following these steps:

1. Right-click the Start button, and choose Explore from the shortcut menu.

2. Choose Folder Options from the View menu, and then click the File Types tab.

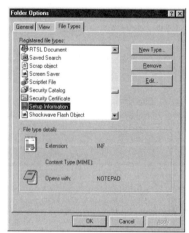

Figure 1-28. *The Folder Options dialog box.*

3. In the Registered File Types box, select Setup Information, and then click Edit.

4. Click New, enter *Install* in the Action box, and then enter the following line in the Application Used To Perform Action box:

```
c:\windows\rundll.exe setupx.dll,InstallHinfSectionDefaultInstall 132
```

Note If you installed Windows in a folder other than the WINDOWS folder, adjust this command accordingly.

5. Click OK until you return to Windows Explorer.

6. Restart Windows.

Related KB article Q145810

JPEG and GIF Files Open by Default in Internet Explorer

You double-click a JPEG (.JPG) or GIF (.GIF) file, and the image opens in Internet Explorer. Internet Explorer automatically changes the file associations for these files when it is installed.

Solution

To change the file association for these files, follow these steps:

1. Double-click the My Computer icon on the desktop.

2. Choose Folder Options from the View menu.

3. Click the File Types tab, select the file type you want to change from the Registered File Types box, and then click Remove. Click Yes when you are prompted to confirm the change.

Figure 1-29.   *The File Types tab of the Folder Options dialog box.*

4. Click OK.

5. Double-click a .JPG or .GIF file in My Computer or Windows Explorer. When you are asked which program to open the file with, select the program you want to use.

Related KB article Q135955

Multimedia Files Don't Preview in Windows Explorer

You view a folder as a web page and click a multimedia file, but a preview of the file does not display on the left side of the right pane. This behavior occurs because the preview feature is disabled by default.

Solution

To enable the multimedia preview feature, follow these steps:

1. In Windows Explorer, click the WINDOWS folder, and then double-click the Web folder.

2. Choose Customize This Folder from the View menu, click Next, and click Next again.

3. Choose Find from the Search menu, enter *wantmedia*, click Find Next, and then click Cancel.

4. Change the "false" entry in the following line to *true*:

   var wantMedia   = false; // cool, but may hinder media file manipulation

   After you make this change, the line should look like this:

   var wantMedia   = true; // cool, but may hinder media file manipulation

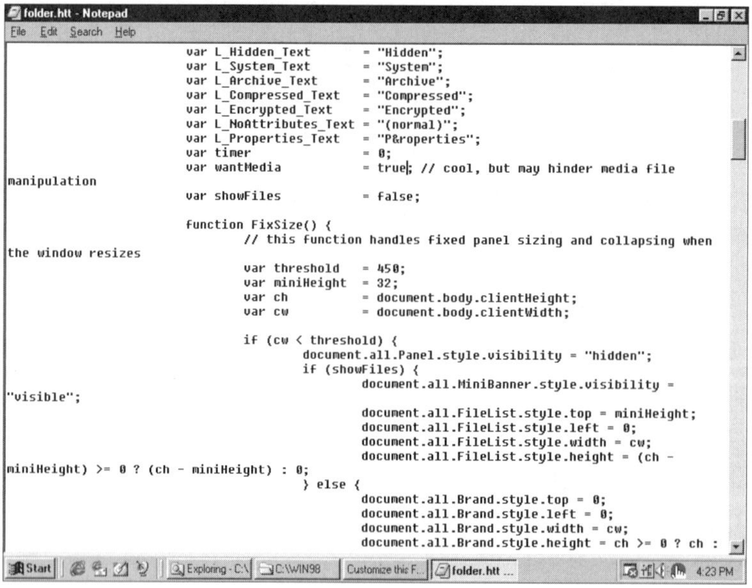

Figure 1-30.   *The Notepad program window.*

5. Choose Save from the File menu.

6. Close Notepad, click Finish, and then close Windows Explorer.

Note For more information about the FOLDER.HTT file and customizing folders, see KB articles Q181689 and Q182000.

Related KB article Q191242

My Documents Displays Error Message

You double-click or right-click the My Documents shortcut on the desktop and receive the following error message:

Explorer

This program has performed an illegal operation and will be shut down.

If you then click Details, you might see either of the following informational messages:

Explorer caused a stack fault in module KERNEL32.DLL at <address>

Explorer caused a stack fault in module SHDOCVW.DLL at <address>

This problem can occur if a value in the Registry points to the wrong path or is blank.

Solution

Restart your computer, and then use Registry Editor to edit the Personal value in the following Registry key:

```
HKEY_CURRENT_USER\Software\Microsoft\Windows\CurrentVersion\Explorer\User  Shell
Folders
```

Warning Please read the Introduction for information on how to safely edit the Registry.

1. Click the Start button, and choose Run.

2. Enter *Regedit* in the Open box, and click OK.

3. Navigate your way down through the folders in the left pane until you locate the key described above.

4. Double-click the Personal value, and modify the Value Data box so that it describes the path to the MY DOCUMENTS folder. (By default, this is C:\MY DOCUMENTS.)

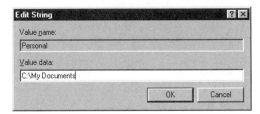

Figure 1-31. *The Edit String dialog box.*

5. Close Regedit.

6. Restart Windows.

Note For information about a similar issue, see KB article Q188604.

Related KB article Q189952

Read-Only File Doesn't Copy to Core SMB Server

You use Windows Explorer or XCOPY to copy a read-only file to a core SMB server (such as a LAN Manager for UNIX server) and receive the following error message:

Error 5 - Access Denied

Solution

To work around this issue, use File Manager (WINFILE.EXE) to transfer the files. To do so, follow these steps:

1. Click the Start button, choose Find, and click Files Or Folders.

2. Enter WINFILE.EXE in the Named box, select the C: drive from the Look In drop-down list box, and click Find Now.

3. Double-click WINFILE in the list of found files, and use the program to transfer your files.

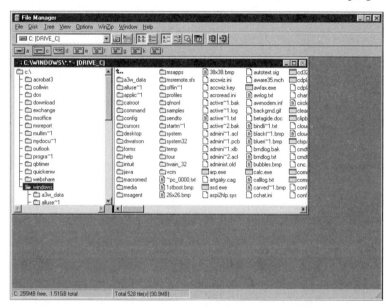

Figure 1-32. *The File Manager program window.*

Note If this is not a viable solution, Microsoft has created a fix for this problem, which can be obtained by contacting Microsoft Technical Support.

Related KB article Q136834

Recycle Bin Emptying Displays Error Message

You attempt to empty the Recycle Bin and receive the following error message:

Can not delete Thumbs: Access is denied.

Make sure the disk is not full or write protected and that the file is not currently in use.

This problem can occur when the following conditions exist:

- You delete a folder for which you have enabled Thumbnail view

- You are viewing the contents of the folder in Windows Explorer when you delete it

When this behavior occurs, the folder is not deleted from the Recycle Bin, but the contents of the folder are deleted. Microsoft has confirmed this to be a problem in Windows 98.

Solution One

Close Windows Explorer, and then empty the Recycle Bin.

Solution Two

In Windows Explorer, click another folder to view its contents, and then empty the Recycle Bin.

Related KB article Q185698

Recycle Bin Properties Reports Incorrect Disk Size

You view Recycle Bin Properties to view the size of a partition on a hard disk in your computer and see a partition larger than 1.99 gigabytes (GB) incorrectly reported to be 1.99 GB. Microsoft has confirmed this to be a problem in Windows 98.

Solution

To work around this problem, use Windows Explorer to view the size of a partition on a hard disk in your computer. To do so, follow these steps:

1. Click the Start button, choose Programs, and click Windows Explorer.

2. Right-click the drive you want to view, and choose Properties from the shortcut menu.

Related KB article Q187188

Renaming File, Folder, or Shortcut Causes Error Message

You rename a file, folder, or shortcut and receive the following error message:

A filename cannot contain any of the following characters: \ / : * ? " < > |

These characters cannot be used in file, folder, or shortcut names.

Solution

Use a valid character that is not listed in the error message.

You can rename the system desktop icons (such as My Computer, My Documents, Internet Explorer, and Network Neighborhood) using the invalid characters. The icons are system objects and do not follow the same naming convention as files, folders, and shortcuts.

The Tab key and inserted characters are also accepted after you press the Enter key or click the icon when the renaming process is complete. Tab characters used in the names of the system icons are displayed as spaces.

Characters that are valid for naming files, folders, or shortcuts include any combination of letters (A–Z) and numbers (0–9), plus the following special characters:

- $ (dollar sign)
- % (percent)
- ' (apostrophe)
- ' (opening single quotation mark)
- - (hyphen)
- @ (at sign)
- { (left brace)
- } (right brace)
- ~ (tilde)
- ! (exclamation point
- # (number sign)
- ((opening parenthesis)
-) (closing parenthesis)
- & (ampersand)
- _ (underscore)
- ^ (caret)

Note For more information about invalid characters, see KB article Q132660, "Invalid Characters Allowed When Creating File Association."

Related KB article Q177506

Send To Command Missing

You search for files using the Find tool and when you right-click a file in the list of found files, the Send To command is missing.

This problem can occur if you select multiple files at once and you have the Windows Desktop Update component installed.

Solution

Right-click each file, and then choose Send To from the shortcut menu.

Related KB article Q184962

Send To Menu Missing Desktop As Shortcut Command

You choose Send To from the File menu, or you right-click a file and then choose Send To from the shortcut menu, and the Desktop As Shortcut command is missing.

This behavior can occur if the DESKTOP AS SHORTCUT.DESKLINK file is missing from the SENDTO folder.

Solution

Create a DESKTOP AS SHORTCUT.DESKLINK file in the SENDTO folder. To do so, follow these steps:

1. Click the Start button, choose Programs, and then click Windows Explorer.

2. Navigate to the WINDOWS\SENDTO folder.

3. Choose New from the File menu, and choose Text Document from the submenu. Enter *Desktop as Shortcut.DESKLINK*, and then press the Enter key.

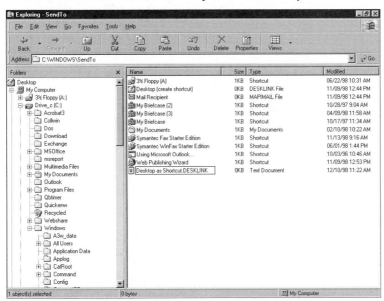

Figure 1-33. *The WINDOWS\SENDTO folder in Windows Explorer.*

4. Click Yes, and then close Windows Explorer.

Related KB article Q191882

Thumbnail Folder Missing Columns

The contents of a folder are displayed in one column when you enable Thumbnail view for the folder.

This behavior can occur if you are running Internet Explorer 4.01 Service Pack 1.

Solution

Choose Refresh from the View menu to display the contents of the folder in multiple columns.

Related KB article Q185350

Thumbnail View Causes Explorer Errors

You attempt to view the contents of a folder using Thumbnail view and receive one of the following error messages:

> *EXPLORER caused an invalid page fault in module THUMBVW.DLL at 015f:799eaee4*

> *EXPLORER caused an invalid page fault in module KERNEL32.DLL at 015f:bff9d709*

This problem occurs when the THUMBS.DB file, which contains the thumbnails for a particular folder, is corrupt.

Solution

To solve this problem, follow these steps:

1. Delete the THUMBS.DB file in the folder for which Thumbnail view is enabled.

Note You need to be able to view hidden files to see the THUMBS.DB file. To view hidden files, choose Folder Options from the View menu in Windows Explorer, click the View tab, click the Show All Files option button under Hidden Files, and then click OK.

2. Re-create the THUMBS.DB file by selecting the folder in Windows Explorer and then choosing Thumbnails from the View menu.

Note If you receive an error message indication that access is denied when you attempt to delete the THUMBS.DB file, see KB article Q185698.

Related KB article Q188540

Two CD-ROM Drives Display When Only One Exists

You view My Computer or Windows Explorer and two CD-ROM drives are displayed even though you have only one CD-ROM drive in your computer. You try to access both CD-ROM drives, and your computer stops responding.

This problem occurs when you have both the real-mode CD-ROM device drivers and the Windows 98 CD-ROM device drivers installed.

Solution

Use the System Configuration Editor tool (MSCONFIG.EXE) to disable the real-mode CD-ROM device drivers. To do so, follow these steps:

1. Click the Start button, choose Run, enter *sysedit* in the Open box, and then click OK.

2. Click the CONFIG.SYS window, locate the line that loads the real-mode CD-ROM device drivers, and then type *rem* in front of the line. For example, the line in your CONFIG.SYS file may be similar to the following line:

    Device=C:\Cdrom\Cdrom.sys /d:mscd001

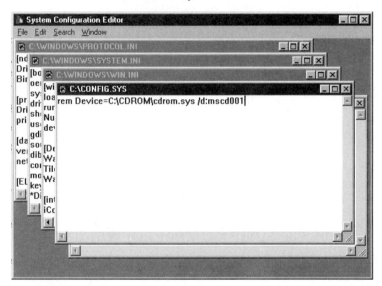

Figure 1-34. *The Config.sys window of the System Configuration Editor.*

3. Click the Autoexec.bat window, locate the line that loads the real-mode CD ROM device drivers, and then type *rem* in front of the line. For example, the line in your AUTOEXEC.BAT file may be similar to the following line:

    C:\Windows\Command\Mscdex.exe /d:mscd001

4. Close System Configuration Editor, click Yes to save AUTOEXEC.BAT and CONFIG.SYS, and then restart your computer.

Related KB article Q192802

Windows Explorer Can't See Local Hard Disk

You look in My Computer or Windows Explorer, and you are not able to view or gain access to a local hard disk. This problem can occur if all of the following conditions are true:

- You have installed the Microsoft Client for NetWare Networks.

- The First Network Drive in Microsoft Client for NetWare Networks is set to drive F (the default setting).

- You have four or more logical hard disks on your computer.

Under these conditions, the network drive maps over the local drive. However, you do not lose data on the disks that are no longer available. You can have problems processing a NetWare login script if drive F is assumed to be the first network drive letter. If you have problems gaining access to network resources, contact your network administrator. Microsoft has confirmed this to be a problem in Windows 98.

Solution

To work around this problem, change the First Drive Letter setting in Microsoft Client For NetWare Network Properties. To do so, follow these steps:

1. Determine the next available drive letter after you take into account all of your logical disk drives. For example, if your last disk drive is drive G, then the next available drive letter is drive H.

2. Click the Start button, choose Settings, and click Control Panel.

3. Double-click the Network icon, select Client For NetWare Networks from the list box, and then click Properties.

4. Click the letter corresponding to the next available drive driver, click OK, and then click OK in the Network box.

Related KB article Q187279

Windows Explorer Doesn't Display Contents of Window

You enable the View As Web Page feature in Windows Explorer, but you are unable to view the contents of the window. This can occur if style sheets in Internet Explorer are disabled.

Solution

To work around this issue, use Registry Editor to enable style sheets. To do this, change the data value of the Use Stylesheets value to Yes in the following Registry key:

```
HKEY_CURRENT_USER\Software\Microsoft\Internet Explorer\Main
```

Create this key if it does not exist.

To do so, follow these steps:

Warning Please read the Introduction for information on how to safely edit the Registry.

1. Click the Start button, and choose Run.

2. Enter *Regedit* in the Open box, and click OK.

3. Navigate your way down through the folders in the left pane until you locate the key described above.

4. Double-click the Use Stylesheets value, and enter *yes* in the Value Data box.

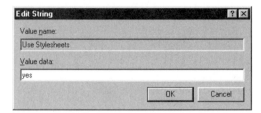

Figure 1-35. *The Edit String dialog box.*

5. Close Regedit.

6. Restart Windows.

Related KB article Q192337

Windows Explorer Doesn't Display Picture Preview

You click an image icon in Windows Explorer, but the picture preview does not display on the left side of the pane. This problem can occur if a third-party program has changed the file association for the type of file you are trying to preview. Note that previews are available only if you have the View As Web Page option enabled for the folder containing the image file.

Solution

Verify that the following entries exist in the

`HKEY_CLASSES_ROOT\<file type>`

Registry key for the type of file you are trying to preview:

`HKEY_CLASSES_ROOT\<file type>\ShellEx`

`HKEY_CLASSES_ROOT\<file type>\ShellEx\{BB2E617C-0920-11d1-9A0B-00C04FC2D6C1}`

with the value:

`(Default)="{7376D660-C583-11d0-A3A5-00C04FD70GEC}"`

The following file types use the Registry values listed above:

.ART

.BMP

.DIB

.GIF

.JFIF

.JPE

.JPEG

.JPG

.PNG

.WMF

Follow these steps:

Warning Please read the Introduction for information on how to safely edit the Registry.

1. Click the Start button, and choose Run.

2. Enter *Regedit* in the Run box, and click OK.

3. Navigate your way down through the folders in the left pane until you locate the key described above.

4. Confirm or modify the value.

5. Close Regedit.

6. Restart Windows.

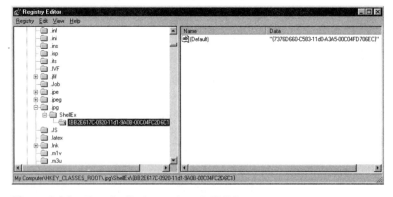

Figure 1-36. *Regedit displays value of .JPG key.*

Related KB article Q192573

Windows Explorer Doesn't Display Shortcut Menu

You right-click the root object in Windows Explorer, but a shortcut menu does not display. However, a shortcut menu is available for all other objects in Windows Explorer. This behavior is by design.

Note Desktop is the default root object in Windows Explorer. To view a shortcut menu for Desktop, right-click the DESKTOP folder in the folder where Windows is installed.

Solution

To work around this behavior, change the root object for Windows Explorer by adding the /root, <object> parameter to the Windows Explorer command line. Set the root object so that the object for which you want a shortcut menu is no longer the root object.

Note For more information about Windows Explorer command line switches, see KB article Q130510, "Command-Line Switches for Windows Explorer."

Related KB article Q150256

Windows Explorer Is Empty

You start Windows Explorer and the All Folders pane is missing or the entire Windows Explorer window is empty. This can occur if the ExplorerBar value in the Registry is damaged. The ExplorerBar value contains positioning information for the All Folders pane in Windows Explorer. The value is created only if the window has been resized. Removing the value returns the window to the default position.

Solution

Use Registry Editor to delete the ExplorerBar value in the following Registry key:

```
HKEY_CURRENT_USER\Software\Microsoft\Internet  Explorer\Main
```

Restart your computer, and then follow these steps:

Warning Please read the Introduction for information on how to safely edit the Registry.

1. Click the Start button, and choose Run.

2. Enter *Regedit* in the Open box, and click OK.

3. Navigate your way down through the folders in the left pane until you locate the key described above.

4. Delete the ExplorerBar value.

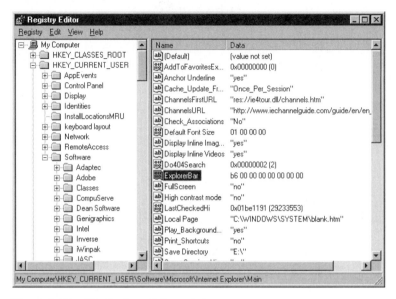

Figure 1-37.   *The Registry Editor window.*

5. Close Regedit.

6. Restart Windows.

Related KB article Q192315

Windows Explorer Missing Summary Information

You view files or folders in My Computer or Windows Explorer, but the summary information on the left side of the window is missing. This can occur for either of the following reasons:

- The View as Web Page feature is not enabled.

- The window size is too small to correctly display the summary information on the left side of the window.

Solution One

To enable the View As Web Page feature in My Computer or Windows Explorer, start Windows Explorer or open My Computer, and then choose As Web Page from the View menu.

Solution Two

To resize the window to a larger size, click the Maximize button, or choose Size from the System menu, press the arrow keys until you size the window appropriately, and then press the Enter key.

Related KB article Q186704

Windows Explorer Truncates Folder Names

When you install Windows 98 from MS-DOS, various folders are created in the PROGRAM FILES folder (such as the ACCESSORIES, ONLINE SERVICES, and OUTLOOK EXPRESS folders). If you choose not to install some optional Windows 98 components, some of these folders might be empty. If you manually delete any of these empty folders in Windows and then install the accessory that belongs in that folder, the folder is re-created with a short folder name instead of a long folder name. For example, the PROGRAM FILES\ACCESSORIES\HYPERTERMINAL folder might be re-created as the PROGRAM FILES\ACCESSORIES\HYPERT~1 folder. The accessories installed in these re-created folders work correctly, even though the folder has a short folder name.

This situation occurs because of architectural limitations inherent in the 16-bit, MS-DOS Setup program. No functionality is lost—and no problems occur—when this happens.

Solution

If you want to change the short folder names to long folder names, follow these steps:

1. Using Windows, rename the folder to an arbitrary intermediate name. For example, rename the HYPERT~1 folder to TEST.

Warning Do not rename the folder to the correct long folder name in one step. Doing so may cause shortcuts to programs in the folder not to work.

2. Rename the intermediate folder name to the correct long folder name. For example, rename the TEST folder to HYPERTERMINAL.

3. Repeat these steps for all folders you want to rename.

Related KB article Q188162

Image Programs and Other Accessories

Calculator Button Labels Disappear

You start Calculator, but you are unable to see any text on any of the buttons. This can occur if you configure the appearance of your computer's 3D Objects to be the same color as the text on the buttons in Calculator. Windows cannot change the colors used for the text on the buttons in Calculator, so the color of the buttons and the text on the buttons remain the same.

Solution

To work around this problem, change the color of 3D Objects to a different color. To do so, follow these steps:

1. Click the Start button, choose Settings, click Control Panel, and double-click the Display icon.

2. Click the Appearance tab, click 3D Objects in the Item box, click a different color in the Color box, and then click OK.

Figure 1-38. *The Appearance tab of the Display Properties dialog box.*

Related KB article Q187190

Calculator Decimal/Hexadecimal Converter Gives Unexpected Results

You use Calculator to convert a decimal number to a hexadecimal number, but some digits in the hexadecimal number are missing. As a result, if you convert back to a decimal number, the number is different from what you originally typed.

This problem can occur if you attempt to convert a very large decimal number to hexadecimal. If the hexadecimal equivalent of a decimal number is more than eight digits, only the eight rightmost digits are displayed. Microsoft has confirmed this to be a problem in Windows 98.

Solution One

To prevent this problem from occurring, do not use Calculator to convert large decimal numbers to hexadecimal.

Solution Two

To work around this problem so that you receive an error message if the hexadecimal number is too large, use the version of Calculator included with Windows 95. To do so, follow these steps:

1. Click the Start button, choose Find, and then click Files Or Folders.

2. Enter *calc.exe* in the Named box, and click Find Now.

3. In the list of found files, right-click the CALC.EXE file, and then enter a new name for the CALC.EXE file (such as CALC.XXX).

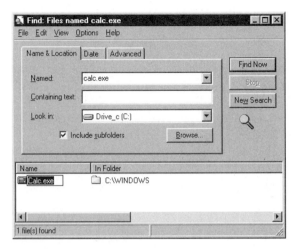

Figure 1-39. *The Find window.*

4. Extract a new copy of the CALC.EXE file from your original Windows 95 disks or CD-ROM into the WINDOWS folder. The CALC.EXE file is located in the following locations:

- The WIN95_02.CAB cabinet file on the Windows 95 CD-ROM.

- The WIN95_03.CAB cabinet file on the Windows 95 OEM Service Release 2 (OSR2) CD-ROM.

- The WIN95_03.CAB cabinet file on disk 3 of the original Windows 95 DMF floppy disks.

- The WIN95_03.CAB cabinet file on disk 3 of the original Windows 95 non-DMF floppy disks.

Related KB article Q187514

Imaging Causes Errors

You attempt to start Imaging, it does not start, and you receive one of the following error messages:

> *Error starting program, the IMGCMN.DLL file is linked to missing export MFC42.DLL:6453.*

> *Error starting program, the ANNCLIST.EXE file is linked to missing export MFC42.DLL:6453.*

This problem occurs when you run the installation program for the Kodak DC120 digital camera from the CD-ROM included with the camera. The installation program overwrites the MFC42.DLL file with an earlier version that is not compatible with Imaging.

Solution

Remove and then reinstall Imaging. To do so, follow these steps:

1. Click the Start button, choose Settings, and then click Control Panel.

2. Double-click the Add/Remove Programs icon, and then click the Windows Setup tab.

3. Select Accessories from the list box, and click Details.

4. Clear the Imaging check box, click OK, and then click Apply.

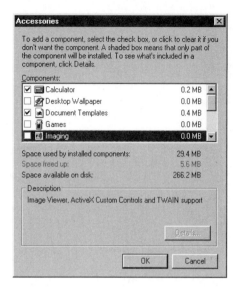

Figure 1-40. *The Accessories dialog box.*

5. Select Accessories from the list box and click Details.

6. Select the Imaging check box, click OK, and then click OK again.

Note This behavior does not occur if you use the drivers for the Kodak DC120 digital camera included with Windows 98.

Related KB article Q188392

Imaging Displays Wang Image Control Error Message

You attempt to open an editable fax using Imaging and receive one of the following error messages:

Wang Image Control Cannot Be Found.

A problem occurred with (or connecting to) a linked or embedded object or its source application.

This behavior can occur if you are using Imaging for Windows 95.

Solution

Remove Imaging for Windows 95, and install the version of Imaging included with Windows 98. To do so, follow these steps:

1. Click the Start button, choose Settings, and then click Control Panel.

2. Double-click the Add/Remove Programs icon, and then click the Windows Setup tab.

3. Select Accessories from the list box, and then click Details.

4. Clear the Imaging check box, click OK, and then click Apply.

Figure 1-41. *The Accessories dialog box.*

5. Click Accessories, and then click Details.

6. Select the Imaging check box, click OK, and then click OK again. When you are prompted to do so, insert your Windows 98 CD-ROM or floppy disks into your CD-ROM or floppy disk drive.

Related KB article Q190232

Imaging's Show Annotations Command Unavailable

You attempt to hide annotations on an image file using Imaging, but the Show Annotations command on the Annotation menu is unavailable. This can happen if you are attempting to hide annotations on a Windows bitmap (BMP) or Microsoft Fax (AWD) image file. In Imaging, you can hide annotations only on a tagged image file format (TIFF) image file.

Solution

Save the BMP or AWD image file as a TIFF image file, and then hide the annotations. To do this, follow these steps:

1. Click the Start button, choose Programs, choose Accessories, and click Imaging.

2. Choose Open from the File menu, locate and click the BMP or AWD image file, and then click Open.

3. Choose Save As from the File menu.

4. Enter a new name for the image file in the File Name box.

5. Select TIFF Document (*.TIF) from the Save As Type drop-down list box, and then click Save.

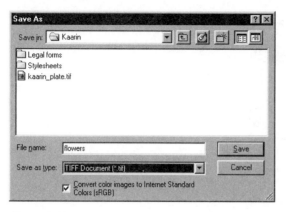

Figure 1-42. *The Save As dialog box in Imaging.*

6. Choose Show Annotations from the Annotation menu to clear the check mark.

You can add annotations to a BMP, AWD, or TIFF image file by clicking the command associated with the annotation you want on the Annotation menu.

Note For more information about how to use annotation in Imaging, choose Imaging Help from the Help menu in Imaging, click the Index tab, enter *annotating* in the text box, and then select the topic you want.

Related KB article Q180029

JPEG File Doesn't Save

You use Microsoft Picture It! Express or Microsoft Paint to save an image as a Joint Photographic Experts Group (JPEG) file, but the file is not saved. The program might appear to save the file, but it is not listed in the folder in which you chose to save it. Also, when you attempt to open a JPEG file in Paint, you receive the following error message:

> *Paint*
>
> *<path><filename>.jpg*
>
> *Paint cannot read this file.*
>
> *This is not a valid bitmap file, or its format is not currently supported.*

This problem can occur if the JPEG graphics filter is missing or damaged or if the Registry entries for the JPEG graphics filter are missing or damaged.

Solution

Remove Picture It! Express, rename the JPEG graphics filter, remove the JPEG graphics filter Registry entries, and then reinstall Picture It! Express. To do so, follow these steps:

1. Click the Start button, choose Settings, and then click Control Panel.

2. Double-click the Add/Remove Programs icon.

3. On the Install/Uninstall tab, select Microsoft Plus! 98, click Add/Remove, click Add/Remove again, and then click Next.

4. Clear the Picture It! Express check box, click Next, click Next again, click Finish, and then click OK.

5. Click the Start button, choose Find, and then click Files Or Folders.

6. Enter *jpegim32.flt* in the Named box, and then click Find Now.

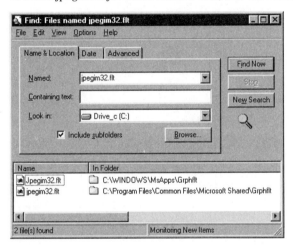

Figure 1-43. *The Find window.*

7. Rename all of the JPEGIM32.FLT files to JPEGIM32.OLD.

8. Use Registry Editor to remove the JPEG value from the following Registry keys:

    HKEY_LOCAL_MACHINE/Software/Microsoft/Shared Tools/Graphic Filters/Export

    HKEY_LOCAL_MACHINE/Software/Microsoft/Shared Tools/Graphic Filters/Import

Warning Please read the Introduction for information on how to safely edit the Registry.

9. Click the Start button, and choose Run.

10. Enter *Regedit* in the Run box, and click OK.

11. Navigate your way down through the folders in the left pane until you locate the key described above.

12. Delete the JPEG values.

13. Close Regedit.

14. Restart Windows.

15. Click the Start button, choose Settings, and then click Control Panel.

16. Double-click the Add/Remove Programs icon.

17. On the Install/Uninstall tab, click Microsoft Plus! 98, click Add/Remove, click Add/Remove again, and then click Next.

18. Select the Picture It! Express check box, click Next, click Next again, click Finish, and then click OK.

Related KB article Q193354

Notepad Causes Memory Error Message

You open a file in Notepad and receive the following error message:

Not enough memory available to complete this operation. Quit one or more applications to increase available memory, and then try again.

This behavior can occur because the Notepad program in Windows 98 is slightly larger and the space to edit data slightly smaller than the Notepad program in Windows 3.x. Therefore, some files that you can open in Notepad in Windows 3.x might be too large for Notepad in Windows 98.

Solution

Reduce the size of the file, or open it in a different text editor, such as WordPad.

Related KB article Q132841

Notepad Undo Command Is Unavailable

You attempt to remove a date and time stamp in Notepad, but the Undo command on the Edit menu is unavailable.

Solution

Manually delete the date and time stamp text.

Related KB article Q177495

Paint's Brush Tool Leaves Trail of Black Dots

You create a new image using Paint, but black dots trail the Brush tool as you move it across the canvas. This problem can occur if you selected the Black And White option button in the Attributes dialog box.

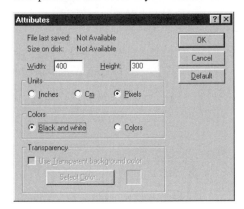

Figure 1-44. *The Attributes dialog box.*

Solution One

To work around this problem, open and modify an existing black and white image instead of creating a new one.

Solution Two

Create a new color image using only black and white. When you create a new image using Paint, the image is in color by default.

Related KB article Q191800

Paint Causes Page Fault Error

You type text in Paint, select a font size from the Font Size toolbar button on the Text toolbar, press the Esc key to close the Text toolbar, and then receive the following error message:

MSPAINT caused an invalid page fault in module MSPAINT.EXE at 015f:010259e2.

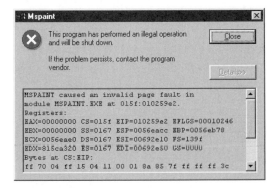

Figure 1-45. *Paint displays an error message.*

You click Close, and receive the following error message:

MSPAINT caused an invalid page fault in module MFC42.DLL at 015f:5f4012b3.

Solution

Close the Text toolbar by choosing Text Toolbar from the View menu to remove the check mark.

Related KB article Q185501

Paint Starts Slow or Doesn't Start

You try to start Paint or view a bitmap (.BMP) file in Paint and the program takes a long time to start or you receive the following error message:

Not enough memory or resources. Close some programs and try again.

This problem could occur for one of the following reasons:

- The bitmap file is in a compressed format that Paint cannot read. For example, Paint does not support CVID compressed bitmap files. If you try to open such a file in Paint, the error message stated above occurs.

- The default image attributes for Paint are set too large. This setting is dependent upon memory and disk space.

- You convert a tagged image file format (.TIF) file to a bitmap file using Imaging, and you try to open the bitmap using Paint included with Windows 95.

Solution One

If you receive the above error message while opening a bitmap in Paint, open the bitmap file in another program.

Solution Two

If you receive the above error message while opening Paint, your computer might not be able to open Paint. To solve this problem, follow these steps:

1. Open an existing bitmap.

2. Choose Attributes from the Image menu.

3. Click Default, and then click OK.

4. Choose Save As from the File menu, and save the bitmap under a new name.

5. Close and restart Paint.

Related KB article Q129545

Paint Tools Cause Unexpected Results

You use the Fill With Color tool or Brush tool in Paint, and you experience unexpected behavior. For example, if you attempt to fill only part of the canvas using the Fill With Color tool, the entire canvas might be filled. Alternately, if you attempt to fill the entire canvas using the Fill With Color tool, only part of the canvas might be filled. If you select the Brush tool, a trail of dots might appear when you move the cursor across the canvas. This problem can occur if you set the image attributes to 1024 x 768 pixels and enable the Black And White option. Microsoft has confirmed this to be a problem in Windows 98.

Solution

To work around this problem, set the image width to something other than 1024 pixels, set the image height to something other than 768 pixels, and enable the Colors option. To do so, follow these steps:

1. Choose Attributes from the Image menu.

2. Enter a number other than 1024 in the Width box.

3. Enter a number other than 768 in the Height box.

4. Click the Colors option button.

5. Click OK.

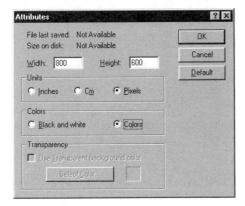

Figure 1-46. *The Attributes dialog box.*

Related KB article Q185972

Paint Won't Open PCX Files

You try to open a ZSoft Image file (.PCX) in Paint, but you are unable to do so. This is because the version of Paint included in Windows 98 does not include support for .PCX files.

Solution

Use a different program, such as Imaging, to open or view .PCX files. To start Imaging, click the Start button, choose Programs, choose Accessories, and then click Imaging.

Related KB article Q186967

Quick View Displays Additional Boxes

You use Quick View to view a document, but one or more boxes are displayed in addition to the document's text. This problem can occur if the document contains embedded objects, such as images or files. This behavior is by design. Quick View is not designed to display embedded objects.

Solution

To work around this behavior, view the document using a program that can open the document's file type and display embedded objects. For example, if you are trying to view a Microsoft Word (.DOC) document, use Word or Microsoft WordPad to view the document.

Related KB article Q187322

WordPad Doesn't Change Font

You change the font type or size in WordPad and then press the Delete key, but the font reverts to its previous type or size. Microsoft has confirmed this to be a problem in Windows 98.

Solution

Type at least one character in the new font type or size before pressing the Delete key.

Related KB article Q178477

WordPad Doesn't Correctly Handle Unicode Text Documents

You attempt to use WordPad to save a Unicode text document as a text document or an MS-DOS-format text document, but the document remains in Unicode format. Also, every other character in the document might be unintelligible.

Solution

To work around this problem, copy and paste the Unicode text document into a new WordPad document, and then save it as a text document. To do so, follow these steps:

1. Open the Unicode text document in WordPad.

2. Choose Select All from the Edit menu, and then choose Copy from the Edit menu.

3. Choose Exit from the File menu.

4. Click the Start button, choose Programs, choose Accessories, and then click WordPad.

5. Choose Paste from the Edit menu, and then choose Save As from the File menu.

6. Select Text Document or Text Document – MS-DOS Format from the Save As Type box.

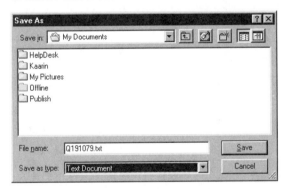

Figure 1-47.   *The Save As dialog box in WordPad.*

7. Enter a new name for the file in the File Name box.

8. Click Save, and then choose Exit from the File menu.

Related KB article Q191079

Pre-Windows 95 Accessories

BOOTDISK.BAT File Displays Error Message

You try to run the BOOTDISK.BAT batch file and receive the following error message:

The EBD directory does not exist.

Change to the WINDOWS\COMMAND directory and try again.

This problem can occur if you run Windows 98 Setup using the /IE switch or run Setup by using a BATCH.INF file with an EBD=0 entry. These Setup methods do not create Startup disks or a WINDOWS\COMMAND\EBD folder, so the files and folders that are referenced in the BOOTDISK.BAT batch file do not exist. This problem can also occur if Windows 98 Setup does not detect a floppy drive controller. Microsoft has confirmed this to be a problem in Windows 98.

Solution One

Create a Windows 98 Startup Disk manually. To do so, follow these steps:

1. Click the Start button, choose Settings, click Control Panel, and then double-click the Add/Remove Programs icon.

2. Click the Startup Disk tab, and then click Create Disk. Follow the instructions on the screen to finish creating the Windows 98 Startup disk.

Figure 1-48.   *The Startup Disk tab of the Add/Remove Programs Properties dialog box.*

Solution Two

Redetect your floppy drive controller. To do so, follow these steps:

1. Click the Start button, choose Settings, click Control Panel, and then double-click the Add New Hardware icon.

2. Follow the instructions on the screen to finish detecting your floppy drive controller.

Related KB article Q187691

COPY Command Loses Attributes of Files Copied from a NetWare Volume

You use the COPY command at an MS-DOS prompt in Windows 98 to copy read-only files from a NetWare volume, but the read-only attribute is not applied to the files. This problem occurs because the MS-DOS COPY command does not have the ability to copy NetWare file attributes.

Solution

Use the Novell NCOPY command to copy the files instead of the MS-DOS COPY command.

Note For more information about the NetWare NCOPY command, consult your NetWare product documentation.

Related KB article Q189191

EMM386.EXE No Longer Loads

After you install Windows 98, EMM386.EXE no longer loads when you start your computer. This problem can occur if you load EMM386.EXE with the /HIGHSCAN switch. The /HIGHSCAN switch interferes with hardware detection during Setup, so it is disabled by Windows 98 Setup.

Solution

To reenable EMM386.EXE, follow these steps:

1. Using any text editor (such as Notepad), open the CONFIG.SYS file.

2. Locate the line that loads EMM386.EXE, and then remove the following text from the beginning of the line:

```
rem -- by Windows 98 setup -
```

3. Save and then close the CONFIG.SYS file.

4. Restart Windows.

Related KB article Q187694

File Does Not Open When You Drag the File to a Shortcut

You drag a file from File Manager to an application shortcut on the desktop, and you receive no error message, but the file does not open and the mouse pointer does not change to indicate that the action is invalid.

File Manager is a Windows 3.1–based program and does not support the enhanced features of OLE and drag and drop.

Solution

Make sure the program on the desktop is open before you drag a file from File Manager to the shortcut or from Windows Explorer to the shortcut.

Related KB article Q132574

File Overwritten When XCOPY32 Command Used

You use the XCOPY32 command to copy files, and you are not prompted before it overwrites files that are already present.

The XCOPY32 command is not designed to prompt you before overwriting existing files.

XCOPY32.EXE is an internal helper program that is not designed to run directly from the command line. It is designed to run only as a helper by the main XCOPY.EXE program.

Solution One

Use the XCOPY command. The XCOPY command prompts you before files are overwritten, provided the COPYCMD environment variable has not been set to the value "/Y." If you set this environment variable, you can force overwrite protection by changing the command to SET COPYCMD=/-Y

Solution Two

Use Windows Explorer to copy files.

Related KB article Q134772

MEM Command Reports Multiple Copies of COMMAND.COM

You restart your computer in MS-DOS mode, and the MEM command reports two or more copies of COMMAND.COM in memory. This situation occurs for two reasons.

- COMMAND.COM loads itself in multiple pieces, which might be reported separately.

- When you restart your computer in MS-DOS mode, Windows checks the EXIT TO DOS.PIF file. Or, when you run a program shortcut that specifies MS-DOS mode, Windows checks the program information file (PIF) for the shortcut. In either case, Windows uses that information to build the following batch file that describes how MS-DOS mode should be configured:

```
rem This is the batch file for MS-DOS mode

<custom Autoexec.bat information><n><n>

<custom batch file information>

command.com

<restart the Windows graphical user interface (GUI)>
```

After the Windows graphical user interface (GUI) is shut down, COMMAND.COM runs the batch file. Therefore, two copies of COMMAND.COM are resident in memory. The outer copy runs the batch file, and the inner copy processes your commands. When you type *exit* in the inner copy of COMMAND.COM, control returns to the outer copy of COMMAND.COM, which restarts the Windows GUI.

Note Two copies of COMMAND.COM require less than twice the amount of memory as one copy because the second and any subsequent copies share information with the first copy.

Solution

Instead of exiting to MS-DOS mode and then running the program manually, create a shortcut for the program, and configure the shortcut to use MS-DOS mode. When you want to run the program, double-click the shortcut instead of exiting to MS-DOS mode manually.

Note For more information about MS-DOS mode settings, see KB article Q134400, "General Tips for Using MS-DOS Mode."

Related KB article Q149548

MS-DOS Utility Doesn't Work in Windows 98

If you need to use an MS-DOS utility, a number of MS-DOS utilities are enhanced for use with Windows 98 and are located in the \WINDOWS\COMMAND directory. Most other MS-DOS utilities that worked with earlier versions of Windows should continue to work with Windows 98, but some may not.

Note See PROGRAMS.TXT in your WINDOWS folder for a list of deleted MS-DOS utility files and upgraded MS-DOS utility files.

Solution

Use the MS-DOS SETVER command to enable MS-DOS utilities specific to older versions of MS-DOS. For more information on using the SETVER command, see KB article Q96767.

Warning Do not use the disk repair utilities that shipped with older versions of MS-DOS.

Related KB article Q188978

Program Manager Doesn't Display Groups

You click the Start button, choose Run, enter *PROGMAN.EXE* in the Open box, and then click OK, but no program groups or icons are visible in Program Manager. Also, if you choose New from the File menu, the Program Groups dialog box might open automatically instead of prompting you to choose to create a new program group or a new program item.

This behavior can occur if you install Windows 98 on a computer that does not already have an operating system (such as Windows 3.x or Windows 95) installed or if you install Windows 98 into a folder that does not contain an earlier version of Windows. Because of this, the PROGMAN.INI file does not contain a Groups section with corresponding information about program groups.

Solution

To work around this behavior, manually create program groups and items within the program groups. To do so, follow these steps:

1. Click the Start button, choose Run, enter *PROGMAN.EXE* in the Open box, and then click OK.

2. Choose New from the File menu.

3. In the Description box, enter the name of the program group you want to create, and then click OK.

Note The name that you type in the Description box appears on the title bar of the program group window.

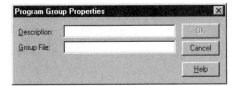

Figure 1-49. *The Program Group Properties dialog box.*

Note You now have the option to create a program group or a program item.

To create program items, follow these steps:

1. Choose the program group name from the Window menu to open the program group to which you want to add an item.

2. Choose New from the File Menu.

3. Click the Program Item option button, and then click OK.

4. In the Description box, enter the name of the program item you are creating, click Browse, open the folder that contains the program item you want, click the appropriate file, and then click OK.

Note The name that you type in the Description box is the name that appears below the item's icon in the program group.

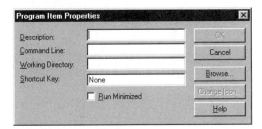

Figure 1-50. *The Program Item Properties dialog box.*

Related KB articles Q185146, Q178367

Program Manager Doesn't Function

You upgrade from Windows 95 and Program Manager doesn't work, possibly resulting in one of the following problems:

- When you drag a link from the desktop to a Program Manager group, the item description is truncated to eight characters.

- When you copy a link or item from the desktop to Program Manager, the item's icon is lost.

- You cannot drag an item from a Program Manager group to the desktop.

- You cannot copy the MY COMPUTER, NETWORK NEIGHBORHOOD, CONTROL PANEL, or PRINTERS folders to a Program Manager group. The Info Center folder can be copied to the group, but it does not work properly because of an "Invalid Path" error.

- You make changes to the Start menu, but the changes are not reflected in Program Manager group files.

Although Program Manager ships with Windows 95 and therefore is available to Windows 98 users who upgrade from Windows 95, Program Manager has not been updated from the previous version of Microsoft Windows. It is provided to ease the transition from Program Manager to the Windows desktop.

Program Manager uses the filename minus the extension when you take advantage of the drag-and-drop capability to create an icon. For example, if you drag the MS-DOS Prompt link from the desktop to a Program Manager group, the MS-DOS Prompt description is shortened to "MS-DOSPR." This occurs because the MS-DOS Prompt link uses the MS-DOS name "MS-DOSPR.LNK."

Solution One

To work around the truncated description problem, manually edit the description of an item in Program Manager by selecting the item and choosing Properties from the File menu.

Solution Two

To work around the lost icon problem, follow these steps:

1. Select the item in Program Manager.

2. Choose Properties from the File menu.

3. Click Change Icon.

3. Click OK when you receive the following error message:

> *The path "%1" is invalid.*

5. Type the path to the icon you want to use, or select an icon from the choices given, and then click OK.

Figure 1-51.   *The Change Icon dialog box.*

Solution Three

If you want changes to the Start menu to be reflected in Program Manager group files, perform the changes manually by adding new program items to the appropriate program groups. Although Windows automatically updates the Start menu with changes to Program Manager group files, the reverse does not occur.

Related KB article Q116245

Write Program Not Available

Windows 95/98 does not include Write, a word processing tool included with earlier versions of Windows. Write has been replaced with WordPad, a word processing tool with more features. For backward compatibility, Windows 98 includes a file called WRITE.EXE located in the WINDOWS folder.

The WRITE.EXE file included with Windows 98 is a small program that accepts the same parameters as the version of Write included with earlier versions of Windows. The WRITE.EXE file included with Windows 98 starts WordPad and then passes the command-line parameters to WordPad. This behavior allows 16-bit programs that use WRITE.EXE to run without modification in Windows 98. For future portability, 32-bit programs should use WordPad instead of Write.

Solution

If you want to use the version of Write included with earlier versions of Windows, expand the WRITE.EXE file from your original Windows or Windows for Workgroups version 3.x disks. To do so, follow these steps:

1. Rename the WRITE.EXE file in the WINDOWS folder to a different name.

2. Locate the WRITE.EXE file using the table below. Insert the appropriate disk in a floppy disk drive.

3. At a command prompt, type the following command:

```
expand -r a:\write.ex_ c:\windows
```

4. Press the Enter key.

Note These steps assume you have inserted the floppy disk in drive A and that Windows is installed in the WINDOWS folder on drive C. If you are using a different drive or folder, modify the line accordingly.

Table 1-2.   Location of the WRITE.EXE Files

Windows version	1.44 MB disks	1.2 MB disks
Windows 3.1	Disk 3	Disk 3
Windows 3.11	Disk 4	Disk 5
WFWG 3.1	Disk 6	Disk 8
WFWG 3.11	Disk 6	Disk 6

Related KB article Q140360

XCOPY Causes Invalid Path Error

You receive an *Invalid Path, 0 Files Copied* error message when you type either of the following commands at a command prompt:

```
XCOPY \\<server>\<share>\<file(s)> <destination>

XCOPY32 \\<server>\<share>\<file(s)> <destination>
```

This problem occurs when the Prevent MS-DOS-Based Programs From Detecting Windows check box is selected in the Advanced Program Settings dialog box in the properties for the .PIF file for the command prompt you are using.

This problem occurs because XCOPY.EXE and XCOPY32.EXE are MS-DOS-based programs, but the network redirector needed to broadcast the UNC request is a Windows-based program. The network redirector cannot be accessed by the command prompt if the Prevent MS-DOS-Based Programs From Detecting Windows setting is enabled. The COPY command does work in this case because the COPY command is an internal COMMAND.COM command instead of a program running on top of COMMAND.COM. Therefore, the COPY command can use the network redirector.

Solution One

To solve this problem, follow these steps:

1. Right-click the shortcut (.PIF file) you use to start the command prompt, and choose Properties from the shortcut menu.

2. Click the Program tab, and click Advanced.

3. Clear the Prevent MS-DOS-Based Programs From Detecting Windows check box, and then click OK.

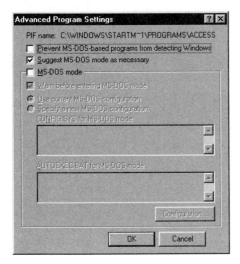

Figure 1-52. *The Advanced Program Settings dialog box.*

4. Click OK.

If you do not want to clear the Prevent MS-DOS-Based Programs From Detecting Windows check box because you need this setting enabled, use one of the following solutions.

Solution Two

Map a network drive pointing to the share you want to use by using one of the following methods:

Method One

1. Browse to the share from which you want to copy files in Network Neighborhood.

2. Right-click the share, and choose Map Network Drive from the shortcut menu.

3. Select the drive letter you want to map to that share, and then click OK.

Figure 1-53. *The Map Network Drive dialog box.*

Method Two

1. Click the Start button, and choose Run. Enter \\<*server*> (in which <server> is the name of the server containing the share you want to use), and then click OK.

2. In the window that opens, right-click the share you want to use, and then choose Map Network Drive from the shortcut menu.

Figure 1-54. *The shared resources on the server Westpark.*

3. Select the drive letter you want to use, and then click OK.

Use the XCOPY or XCOPY32 command with the drive letter of the mapped network drive.

Solution Three

Use the COPY command instead of the XCOPY or XCOPY32 command. If you use the COPY command, you can use Universal Naming Convention (UNC) paths to define the server you want to use. Note that the COPY command cannot copy folders within the selected folder.

Related KB article   Q192808

XCOPY Doesn't Copy Folder Attributes

You use XCOPY to copy a folder and the source folder's attributes are not copied to the new folder.

XCOPY does not have the ability to copy attributes for folders.

Solution One

Manually set the attributes for the new folder using ATTRIBE.EXE at an MS-DOS prompt. For example, the following command sets a folder's read-only attribute:

```
Attrib +r <foldername>
```

Solution Two

Manually set the attributes for the folder. To do so, follow these steps:

1. Right-click the Start button, and choose Explore from the shortcut menu.

2. Right-click the new folder's icon, and choose Properties from the shortcut menu.

3. Click the attributes you would like to ascribe to that folder.

4. Click OK.

Related KB article Q133351

WebTV

All-In-Wonder Display Driver Displays Blank Screen

After you install the ATI All-In-Wonder DirectX 5.0 display adapter driver or the ATI All-In-Wonder Pro DirectX 5.0 display adapter driver, Microsoft WebTV for Windows displays a blank screen. This can occur because the ATI All-In-Wonder DirectX 5.0 display adapter driver and the ATI All-In-Wonder Pro DirectX 5.0 display adapter driver provided by ATI may be incompatible with WebTV for Windows.

Solution

To solve this problem, install the DirectX 5.0 display adapter driver from the Windows 98 CD-ROM. To do so, follow these steps:

1. Click the Start button, choose Settings, click Control Panel, and then double-click the Display icon.

2. On the Settings tab, click Advanced.

3. On the Adapter tab, click Change, click Next, click Display A List Of All The Drivers In A Specific Location, So You Can Select The Driver You Want, click Next, and then click Have Disk.

4. Insert the Windows 98 CD-ROM in the CD-ROM drive. If the Windows 98 screen appears, click Cancel, and then click Browse. If the Windows 98 screen does not appear, click Browse.

5. On the Windows 98 CD-ROM, double-click the DRIVERS folder, double-click the DISPLAY folder, double-click the ATI folder, click OK, and then click OK.

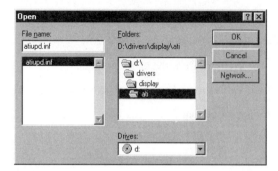

Figure 1-55. *The Open dialog box.*

6. Click the appropriate display adapter driver, click Next, click Next, click Finish, and then click Yes to restart your computer.

If you want to use the programs that are included with the ATI All-In-Wonder or the ATI All-In-Wonder Pro display adapter, you must use the DirectX 5.0 display adapter drivers provided by ATI.

Related KB article Q185658

Channel Cannot Display Error Message

You run Microsoft WebTV for Windows and see a black screen with the following error message:

> *Cannot display this channel. Check your TV tuner card and make sure the other video applications (e.g. DVD player) are not running.*

This problem occurs when the Hardware Acceleration setting in the Display Properties dialog box is set to No Accelerator Functions or Basic Accelerator Functions.

Solution

Change to a higher setting before running WebTV for Windows if you are using a lower setting for another program. To change the setting, follow these steps:

1. Click the Start button, choose Settings, and then click Control Panel.

2. Double-click the Display icon, and then click the Settings tab.

3. Click Advanced, and then click the Performance tab.

4. Move the Hardware Acceleration slider to the setting you want.

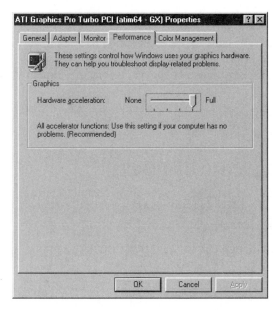

Figure 1-56. *The Performance tab of the display adapter's Properties dialog box.*

5. Click OK, and then click OK.

6. If you are prompted to restart your computer, click Yes.

Related KB article Q190227

Content Is Missing

You have WebTV for Windows, but the following content is not displayed on your screen:

- Active content with a television program

- Closed Captioning

- Electronic Programming Guide (EPG)

- Software subscriptions

This situation can occur if the Closed Captioning feature on your ATI All-In-Wonder or ATI All-In-Wonder Pro display adapter is disabled.

WebTV for Windows uses the information contained in the vertical blanking intervals (VBI) broadcast on the television (TV) channel you are viewing to display Closed Captioning and other content. When the jumper for the Closed Captioning feature on your ATI All-In-Wonder or ATI All-In-Wonder Pro display adapter is disabled, all information broadcast through the VBI cannot be used.

Solution

To work around this issue, set the jumper to enable the Closed Captioning feature on your ATI All-In-Wonder or ATI All-In-Wonder Pro display adapter. For information about how to do so, consult the documentation included with your display adapter, or contact the manufacturer of your display adapter.

Related KB article Q185771

Folders Don't Delete When Program Is Uninstalled

You uninstall WebTV for Windows using the Add/Remove Programs tool in Control Panel and the PROGRAM FILES\TV VIEWER and PROGRAM FILES\WEBCAST folders remain on your hard disk. Microsoft has confirmed this to be a problem in Windows 98.

The PROGRAM FILES\TV VIEWER and PROGRAM FILES\WEBCAST folders are re-created if you reinstall WebTV for Windows.

Solution

Manually delete the PROGRAM FILES\TV VIEWER and PROGRAM FILES\WEBCAST folders from your hard disk. To do so, follow these steps:

1. Click the Start button, choose Find, and then click Files Or Folders.

2. Enter *tv viewer* in the Named box, press the Spacebar, enter *webcast*, and then click Find Now.

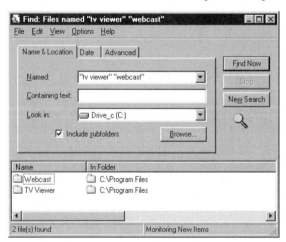

Figure 1-57. *The Find window.*

3. In the list of found folders, right-click each folder, and then click Delete.

4. Close the Find window.

Related KB article Q179486

Graphics Not Visible on Desktop or in WebTV

Graphics are not visible on the desktop or in WebTV for Windows if your computer is not configured to display graphics.

Solution

To configure your computer to display graphics, follow these steps:

1. Click the Start button, choose Settings, click Control Panel, and then double-click the Internet icon.

2. Click the Advanced tab, scroll to the Multimedia branch, and then select the Show Pictures check box.

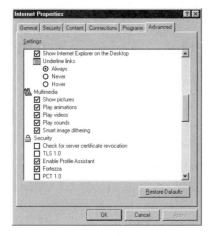

Figure 1-58. *The Advanced tab of the Internet Properties dialog box.*

3. Click OK.

Related KB article Q181510

Network Protocol Is Incorrect

If you install Windows 98 on a computer that has only MS-DOS and a Novell network client (such as Netx or VLM) installed, and you then choose to install the Microsoft WebTV for Windows optional component, the correct network protocol is not bound to the TV Data adapter that is installed in Network properties.

Setup does not install Transport Control Protocol/Internet Protocol (TCP/IP) for the TV Data adapter when you install Windows 98 over a network using Internetworking Packet Exchange/Session Packet Exchange protocol (IPX/SPX), which is used by the Novell network clients listed above.

Solution

To solve this problem, install TCP/IP and bind it to the TV Data adapter. To do this, follow these steps:

1. Click the Start button, choose Settings, and click Control Panel.

2. Double-click the Network icon, and then click the Configuration tab.

3. Click Add, select Protocol from the list, and then click Add.

4. In the Manufacturers box, select Microsoft. In the Network Protocols box, select TCP/IP, and then click OK.

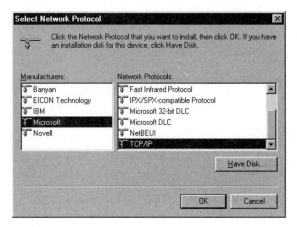

Figure 1-59. *The Select Network Protocol dialog box.*

5. Click OK. Restart your computer when you are prompted to do so.

6. Click the Start button, choose Settings, and click Control Panel.

7. Double-click the Network icon, and then click the Configuration tab.

8. Select TV Data Adapter, and then click Properties.

9. On the Bindings tab, clear the IPX/SPX check box, and then click OK.

10. Click OK. Restart your computer when you are prompted to do so.

Related KB article Q187587

Program Guide Is Incomplete

If you change channels in Microsoft WebTV for Windows while the program guide is being downloaded, the download is not completed. This happens because program guide data is available on only one channel, and changing channels interrupts the download process.

Solution

Do not change channels while the program guide is being downloaded. Wait until the download is finished before you change channels. You can also change the scheduled program guide download time to a later time. When the program guide is being downloaded, a Guide Loader icon appears on the right side of the taskbar. Do not run WebTV for Windows or attempt to change the channel until the icon disappears.

Related KB article Q187660

WebTV Doesn't Start

You are unable to start Microsoft WebTV for Windows. This can occur if the Vidsvr string value has a value of something other than null (" ") in the Registry.

Solution

To fix this problem, follow these steps:

Warning Please read the Introduction for information on how to safely edit the Registry.

1. Click the Start button, choose Run, enter *Regedit* in the Open box, and click OK.

2. Navigate your way down through the folders in the left pane until you locate the following key:

   HKEY_LOCAL_MACHINE\Software\Microsoft\Windows\CurrentVersion\RunServices

3. Delete the value data for the Vidsvr string value.

4. Close Regedit.

5. Click the Start button, choose Settings, click Control Panel, and then double-click the Add/Remove Programs icon.

6. Click the Windows Setup tab.

7. Clear the WebTV For Windows check box, and click OK.

8. Click Yes when you are prompted to restart your computer.

9. Click the Start button, choose Settings, click Control Panel, and then double-click the Add/Remove Programs icon.

10. Click the Windows Setup tab.

11. Select the WebTV For Windows check box, and click OK.

12. Click No when you are prompted to restart your computer.

13. Click the Start button, choose Shut Down, click the Shut Down option button, and then click OK.

14. Turn your computer off and then back on.

Note If you do not turn your computer off and then back on before you start Microsoft WebTV for Windows, the sound in WebTV will not work.

Related KB article Q191066

C H A P T E R   2

Application Software

Antivirus Software

Cheyenne AntiVirus 4.0 Causes Windows to Hang

You install Cheyenne AntiVirus 4.0 and restart your computer, and Windows 98 stops responding. Microsoft has confirmed that this behavior is not caused by a problem in Windows 98, but may be caused by design changes in Windows 98.

Solution One

Remove Cheyenne AntiVirus by following these steps:

1. Restart your computer. After your computer completes the Power On Self Test (POST), press and hold down the Ctrl key until you see the Windows 98 Startup menu, and then choose Safe Mode.

2. Click the Start button, choose Settings, and then click Control Panel.

3. Select Cheyenne AntiVirus For Windows 95 from the list of installed programs, and then click Add/Remove.

4. Click Uninstall, click OK, and then click Yes when you are prompted to restart your computer.

Solution Two

Obtain a patch from Cheyenne and apply it immediately after you install Cheyenne AntiVirus. Do not restart your computer before you apply the patch. To obtain this patch, contact Cheyenne Technical Support or download it from the following Cheyenne web site:

`http://www.cheyenne.com/CheyTech/Download/patches/techptch.html`

Related KB article Q186835

Dr. Solomon's WinGuard Anti-Virus Won't Start Automatically

You upgrade Microsoft Windows 95 to Windows 98, and Dr. Solomon's WinGuard Anti-Virus no longer starts automatically when you start Windows 98.

This occurs because a virtual device driver (.VXD), included with versions of WinGuard Anti-Virus earlier than version 7.81, can cause your computer to perform slowly and stop responding when you attempt to gain access to your floppy disk drive. For this reason, Windows 98 Setup disables WinGuard Anti-Virus. Microsoft has confirmed that this behavior is not caused by a problem in Windows 98, but may be caused by design changes in Windows 98.

Start WinGuard Anti-Virus automatically when you start Windows 98 by using either of the following solutions:

Solution One

Obtain WinGuard Anti-Virus version 7.81 or later from Dr. Solomon's Software Ltd.

Solution Two

If you are using WinGuard Anti-Virus version 7.81 or later, manually start it. You have an option to reenable WinGuard Anti-Virus, which results in it being run every time you start Windows 98. If you are using a version of WinGuard Anti-Virus earlier than version 7.81, Microsoft recommends that you obtain a later version of WinGuard Anti-Virus instead of reenabling it.

Related KB article Q187538

IBM Anti-Virus Produces Error Messages on FAT32 Drives

When you are installing IBM Anti-Virus, the Setup program offers to scan for viruses. You choose to scan and receive an error message stating that the master boot record could not be read.

When you are scanning for viruses on a drive using the FAT32 file system, IBM Anti-Virus may report that errors occurred while it was checking for viruses. The error log may contain the following information:

Errors during virus checking: unexpected error code 18

IBM Anti-Virus is not written to work with the new FAT32 file system included with Windows 98.

Solution

Contact IBM for an updated copy of IBM Anti-Virus.

The third-party product discussed in this article is manufactured by a vendor independent of Microsoft; Microsoft makes no warranty, implied or otherwise, regarding this product's performance or reliability.

Related KB article Q158853

McAfee's VirusScan Causes Fatal Error

You receive the following error message during Windows 98 Setup:

A fatal exception 06 has occurred at <XXXX>:<XXXXXXXX>.

This problem occurs when an older version of McAfee's VirusScan (antivirus software) loads from the AUTOEXEC.BAT file.

Solution

Disable McAfee VirusScan by following these steps:

1. Restart your computer. After your computer completes the Power On Self Test (POST), press and hold down the Ctrl key until you see the Windows 98 Startup menu, and then choose Command Prompt Only.

2. At the command prompt, type the following line, and then press Enter:

```
edit c:\AUTOEXEC.BAT
```

3. Type *rem* and then a space at the beginning of the line that contains VSHIELD.EXE.

4. Save and then close the AUTOEXEC.BAT file.

5. Restart your computer. Setup should continue normally.

Related KB article Q190123

McAfee WebScanX Does Not Block Access

If you are running Windows 98, McAfee WebScanX may not be able to block access to servers or Internet Protocol (IP) addresses. You may notice this if you are watching the Status window's Internet filter. Although programs are detected, scanned, and counted (if this option is enabled), no Internet sites may be counted or displayed in the Last Item window. This may occur with all web browsers in Windows 98 if you are using WebScanX 3.1.2, which is not compatible with changes made to the WINSOCK.DLL file in Windows 98.

Solution

Upgrade WebScanX to version 3.1.6 or later using either of the following methods:

Contact McAfee to receive an update disk. North American customers can contact McAfee Customer Care at 408-988-3832. International customers can contact McAfee Customer Care Amsterdam at +31 (0) 20 586 6100.

Download the upgrade from the following McAfee web site:

```
http://www.nai.com/regs/oemreg.asp
```

Use your Internet Explorer Plus 4.0 product ID for the password. No login ID is necessary.

Customers who install WebScanX from the Internet Explorer Plus 4.0 CD-ROM will be required by McAfee to provide a validation code to receive the update. The validation code is the product ID located in the Help About section of Internet Explorer Plus 4.0.

Related KB article Q191633

MSDOS.SYS File Size Triggers Virus Warning

Some programs expect the MSDOS.SYS file to be at least 1024 bytes in length. If it's not, these programs may not work correctly. For example, if an antivirus program detects that the MSDOS.SYS file is less than 1024 bytes in length, the program may assume that the MSDOS.SYS file is infected with a virus.

If you use the SYS command to transfer system files from your Windows Startup disk to the hard disk, the MSDOS.SYS file that is copied to the hard disk is less than 1024 bytes in length,

Solution

Modify your MSDOS.SYS file to make it more than 1024 bytes long by taking the following steps:

1. At the command prompt, type the following lines, pressing Enter after each line:

```
attrib -s -h -r c:\msdos.sys

edit c:\msdos.sys
```

2. Add the following lines in the MSDOS.SYS file (if required):

```
[Paths]

WinDir=<Windows>

WinBootDir=<Windows>

HostWinBootDrv=C

[Options]

BootGUI=1
```

In these lines, <Windows> is the folder containing Windows (for example, C:\Windows). If you are using disk compression software (such as DriveSpace), change the letter in the HostWinBootDrv= line to the letter of the host drive.

3. Add these lines as well to the MSDOS.SYS file:

```
;Some programs on this system expect the Msdos.sys file to be at least 1024 bytes in
;length; therefore, add the following lines to create an Msdos.sys file that is
;greater than 1024 bytes in length. These lines are not needed for Windows to boot or
;run.

;xxxxxxxxxxxxxxxxxxxxxxxxxxxxxxxxxxxxxxxxxxxxxxxxxxxxxxxxxxxxxxxxxa

;xxxxxxxxxxxxxxxxxxxxxxxxxxxxxxxxxxxxxxxxxxxxxxxxxxxxxxxxxxxxxxxxxb

;xxxxxxxxxxxxxxxxxxxxxxxxxxxxxxxxxxxxxxxxxxxxxxxxxxxxxxxxxxxxxxxxxc

;xxxxxxxxxxxxxxxxxxxxxxxxxxxxxxxxxxxxxxxxxxxxxxxxxxxxxxxxxxxxxxxxxd

;xxxxxxxxxxxxxxxxxxxxxxxxxxxxxxxxxxxxxxxxxxxxxxxxxxxxxxxxxxxxxxxxxe

;xxxxxxxxxxxxxxxxxxxxxxxxxxxxxxxxxxxxxxxxxxxxxxxxxxxxxxxxxxxxxxxxxf

;xxxxxxxxxxxxxxxxxxxxxxxxxxxxxxxxxxxxxxxxxxxxxxxxxxxxxxxxxxxxxxxxxg

;xxxxxxxxxxxxxxxxxxxxxxxxxxxxxxxxxxxxxxxxxxxxxxxxxxxxxxxxxxxxxxxxxh

;xxxxxxxxxxxxxxxxxxxxxxxxxxxxxxxxxxxxxxxxxxxxxxxxxxxxxxxxxxxxxxxxxi

;xxxxxxxxxxxxxxxxxxxxxxxxxxxxxxxxxxxxxxxxxxxxxxxxxxxxxxxxxxxxxxxxxj

;xxxxxxxxxxxxxxxxxxxxxxxxxxxxxxxxxxxxxxxxxxxxxxxxxxxxxxxxxxxxxxxxxk

;xxxxxxxxxxxxxxxxxxxxxxxxxxxxxxxxxxxxxxxxxxxxxxxxxxxxxxxxxxxxxxxxxl

;xxxxxxxxxxxxxxxxxxxxxxxxxxxxxxxxxxxxxxxxxxxxxxxxxxxxxxxxxxxxxxxxxm
```

```
;xxxxxxxxxxxxxxxxxxxxxxxxxxxxxxxxxxxxxxxxxxxxxxxxxxxxxxxxxxxxxxxxn

;xxxxxxxxxxxxxxxxxxxxxxxxxxxxxxxxxxxxxxxxxxxxxxxxxxxxxxxxxxxxxxxxo

;xxxxxxxxxxxxxxxxxxxxxxxxxxxxxxxxxxxxxxxxxxxxxxxxxxxxxxxxxxxxxxxxp

;xxxxxxxxxxxxxxxxxxxxxxxxxxxxxxxxxxxxxxxxxxxxxxxxxxxxxxxxxxxxxxxxq

;xxxxxxxxxxxxxxxxxxxxxxxxxxxxxxxxxxxxxxxxxxxxxxxxxxxxxxxxxxxxxxxxr

;xxxxxxxxxxxxxxxxxxxxxxxxxxxxxxxxxxxxxxxxxxxxxxxxxxxxxxxxxxxxxxxxs
```

4. Save the file, and exit EDIT.COM.

5. Type the following line, and then press Enter:

   `attrib +s +h +r c:\msdos.sys`

6. Restart your computer.

Related KB article Q129998

Norton Antivirus 4.0 Displays Error Message

You enable the Check Floppies On Reboot option in Norton Antivirus 4.0, restart your computer, and see the following error message:

Windows Protection Error.

You need to restart your computer.

This behavior occurs if you are using a computer with a Matrox Millennium or Matrox Mystique video adapter.

Solution

Obtain and install the latest drivers for your video adapter from Matrox.

Related KB article Q186351

Norton Desktop's Antivirus Program Disabled in Windows Startup

You install Windows, and Setup removes the antivirus program installed by Norton Desktop for Windows 2.0 from the CONFIG.SYS file, and the antivirus program no longer runs. This antivirus program is a terminate-and-stay-resident program (TSR) that requires exclusive disk access, which is prohibited in Windows.

Solution

Upgrade to the latest version of Norton Desktop for Windows

Related KB article Q135178

Virus Protection Software Causes Errors When You Install Windows

You attempt to install Windows with virus protection software, and one of the following problems occurs:

- Windows stops responding during Setup, either when it attempts to load or at the End User License Agreement screen.

- You are asked whether you want to overwrite the boot sector. Choosing Yes may allow you to complete the Setup procedure, but Windows hangs when it attempts to load.

- The images on the screen become distorted.

After you restart the computer, you receive the following message:

Windows Setup was unable to update your system files.

This problem occurs for one of two reasons:

- Some computers include a feature that prevents applications from writing to the boot sector. Such features are normally in the form of antivirus protection set in your computer's CMOS settings.

- Some computers have virus-detection software installed.

If antivirus protection is enabled, Windows either can't complete its installation or it doesn't load properly.

Solution

Check your computer's CMOS settings for antivirus features. If present, you will need to run the configuration program for the CMOS that came with your machine to disable these features. If this is not clear in your CMOS settings, you may need to contact your machine manufacturer.

Next, disable any virus-detection software you have on your system by removing the lines that start the program from your AUTOEXEC.BAT and/or CONFIG.SYS files.

After you have disabled virus protection in your CMOS and software, restart your machine and rerun Windows Setup. Once you have successfully installed Windows, you can reenable the virus detection features in your CMOS and software.

Related KB article Q125480

DOS Programs

Helix Hurricane Causes Errors in Windows

You encounter one of the following error messages running Helix Hurricane with Windows:

- You use the RAM Doubler feature and receive the following error message when Windows starts:

  While initializing device ARPL:

  Windows protection error. You must restart your computer.

- You run the Hurricane Control Center (HCC.EXE) and receive an error message on a blue screen similar to the following message:

  An exception xx has occurred at 0028:0000xxxx in VxD ---

Note If you press Enter, the Hurricane Control Center runs successfully.

- You enable the Hurricane Screen Accelerator, and the Windows desktop becomes inactive, or, when Windows starts, you see a black screen with an active mouse pointer.

- You enable Hurricane WinGuard and receive a Windows protection error.

These problems occur because Hurricane and its utilities are not compatible with Windows.

Solution One

Remove the program by using the Hurricane unistall tool:

1. Restart your computer. After your computer completes the Power On Self Test (POST), press and hold down the Ctrl key until you see the Windows 98 Startup menu, and then choose Safe Mode.

2. Consult the program's documentation to find the location of the Hurricane Folder on your hard drive.

3. Open the Hurricane folder and double-click the uninstall tool.

Solution Two

Disable the program by taking the following steps:

1. Click the Start button, click Run, enter *Sysedit* in the text box, and then click OK.

2. Select the C:\WINDOWS\SYSTEM.INI window.

3. Disable the following lines in the [386Enh] section of the file by placing a semicolon (;) at the beginning of each line:

```
device=<path>arpl.386

device=<path>Winsa.386

device=<path>Winguard.386

device=<path>vxmsems.386
```

```
device=<path>windrv.386

device=<path>vcache16.386

device=<path>vsectd.386

device=<path>heapx.386
```

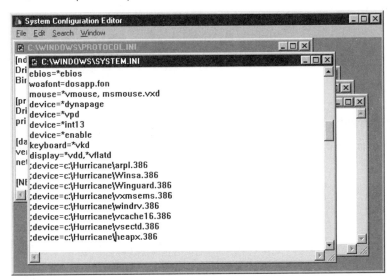

Figure 2-1. *The [386Enh] section of the SYSTEM.INI file in the System Configuration Editor.*

4. Change the following lines in the [Boot] section of the file:

From	To
system.drv=<path>sysdrv.drv	system.drv=System.drv
display.drv=<path>winsa256.drv	display.drv=Pnpdrvr.drv

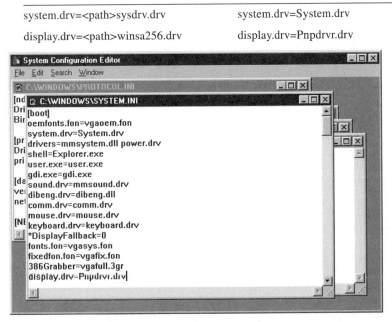

Figure 2-2. *The [Boot] section of the SYSTEM.INI file in the System Configuration Editor.*

Note If your original display driver was not PNPDRVR.DRV, start Windows in Safe mode and change the video driver.

5. Reboot your computer.

Solution Three

Upgrade to Helix Hurricane Version 2.0 or later. For information on upgrading Helix Hurricane, please contact Helix.

Related KB article Q136776

Netroom 3.04 Incompatible with Windows 98 Setup

Netroom 3.04's CACHECLK.EXE, STACKS.EXE and SETCFG.EXE interfere with Windows 98 setup.

Solution

Disable CACHECLK.EXE, NETROOM\STACKS.EXE and NETROOM\SETCFG.EXE before setting up Windows 98.

Related KB article Q188978 or PROGRAMS.TXT in your WINDOWS folder

No Sound from MS-DOS Programs

You change the preferred playback audio device on a computer with multiple sound cards, and MS-DOS-based programs no longer play sound. This occurs if either of the following conditions exists:

Your computer contains a sound card using a Windows Driver Model (WDM) driver and another sound card using a virtual device driver (VxD). In this configuration, the sound card using a VxD may prevent Sound Blaster emulation from starting even if it is specified in the AUTOEXEC.BAT file. This causes MS-DOS-based programs to use the VxD sound card.

Your computer contains two sounds cards that use WDM drivers. In this configuration, some MS-DOS-based programs bypass Sound Blaster emulation and attempt to communicate directly with the hardware on the sound card.

Solution

Use the following steps to work around this issue:

1. Disable the sound card using the VxD in Device Manager.

2. Disable the SET BLASTER= line in the AUTOEXEC.BAT file. Click Start, and then click Run. In the Open box, type *sysedit,* and then click OK. Click the Autoexec.bat window. Locate the line that starts with SET BLASTER=, and then type *rem* in front of the line. Click OK.

3. Close System Configuration Editor, click Yes, and then restart your computer.

4. Create a forced hardware configuration based on Sound Blaster emulation for the sound card. Set the resources of the audio device to I/O=220, IRQ=5, and DMA=1.

Related KB article Q188136

Program Causes Windows to Hang

You attempt to view an MS-DOS-based program in full-screen mode or restart your computer in MS-DOS mode on a computer with a Rendition Verite 2x00–based video adapter, and your computer stops responding. This occurs when you are using older drivers for your Rendition Verite 2x00–based video adapter. Several video adapter manufacturers may use the Rendition chip set.

Solution

To resolve this issue, contact the manufacturer of your video adapter to inquire about updated drivers.

Related KB article Q187217

Program Does Not Run

You have problems running an MS-DOS program which worked correctly in an earlier version of Windows.

This problem occurs when the MS-DOS-based program is using a Windows 3.x program information file (PIF) instead of a newer PIF optimized for Windows.

Solution One

Rename the PIF that is located in the same folder as the MS-DOS-based program. Then, run the MS-DOS-based program by double-clicking the program's executable file in Windows Explorer or My Computer.

Solution Two

If that doesn't work, or you don't have a PIF file for this program, refer to the program's documentation to determine the optimal settings for the program and activate those settings as follows:

1. Right-click the program's executable file, and then choose Properties from the shortcut menu.

2. In the program's properties box, enter any specific PIF configuration information suggested in the program's documentation, then click OK.

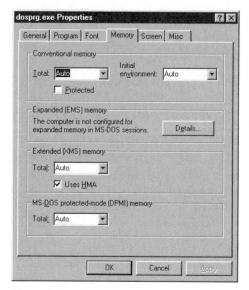

Figure 2-3. *The Memory tab of a MS-DOS program's Properties dialog box.*

Solution Three

If the program still does not run correctly, you can try running the program in MS-DOS mode, or you can contact the program's manufacturer for additional information.

Related KB article Q138410

Program Does Not Run Properly

Most MS-DOS based programs run correctly in Windows 98, however some will refuse to launch, run slowly, or crash.

Solution

Run the program in an MS-DOS environment by restarting your computer in MS-DOS mode or by setting up your program to launch in MS-DOS mode automatically, as described below.

Note When you run a program in MS-DOS mode, Windows 98 shuts down and loads the program in an MS-DOS environment. You do not have access to devices that require Windows 98 drivers while you are in the MS-DOS environment; only MS-DOS drivers loaded in your AUTOEXEC.BAT and CONFIG.SYS files are available to your program.

1. Right-click the MS-DOS based program, and choose Create Shortcut from the shortcut menu.

2. Right-click the shortcut you previously created, and then choose Properties from the shortcut menu.

3. Click the Program tab, and then click Advanced.

4. Select the MS-DOS mode check box.

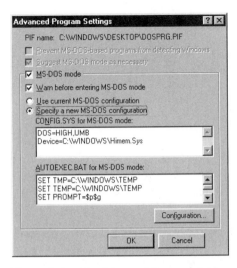

Figure 2-4. *The Advanced Program Settings dialog box.*

5. Optionally, click the Specify A New MS-DOS Configuration option button, and enter the text you want to appear in the CONFIG.SYS and AUTOEXEC.BAT files for this program.

6. Click OK

Related KB article Q188978 or PROGRAMS.TXT in your WINDOWS folder

Program Does Not Switch from Full Screen

You run an MS-DOS-based program in full screen mode and are unable to switch to another program using the Alt+Tab or Ctrl+Esc key combinations. When you try, the computer may beep.

This occurs with the following types of programs:

- Programs that use high-resolution graphics mode (such as SVGA or VESA modes) or text modes
- Hard disk tools such as disk defragmenter or undelete tools

Solution One

If you are using a program that uses a high-resolution graphics or text mode, configure the program to use a lower resolution. Consult the program's documentation or manufacturer to learn how to do this.

Solution Two

If you are running a hard disk tool, you cannot switch programs until you close the tool program. Windows does not switch away from an MS-DOS-based-program that has locked a drive.

Related KB article Q139473

Program Returns Error Message on Startup

When you attempt to run an MS-DOS-based program, including:

- AutoCAD for DOS version 12 by AutoDesk

- DOS GIS by Surpac

- FIFA Soccer by Electronic Arts

Windows returns the error message:

Phar Lap err 74: Can't use - REALBREAK under this version of DPMI

This occurs because the program you're trying to run requires services from the DPMI server that are not available in Windows.

When you run a program in Windows, the program invokes the currently loaded DPMI server that Windows launched at startup. Microsoft Windows supports the DPMI specification version 0.9 with the math coprocessor functions 1.0. If the program makes a call to a service that is supported by DPMI 1.0, you receive an error message, and the program halts. Phar Lap is a DOS extender that has its own set of libraries of services for the DPMI specification level 1.0. If your MS-DOS-based program needs services from level 1.0 of this specification, it cannot run in Windows.

Solution

Run the program in MS-DOS mode. To restart your computer in MS-DOS mode, click the Start button and choose Shut Down. Then click the Restart In MS-DOS Mode option button, and click OK.

Related KB article Q121962

Program Runs Slowly While in the Background

You run an MS-DOS program, and it runs very slowly while in the background (when you're using another program). This occurs because Windows 98 considers the DOS application in the background unimportant and reduces processor allocation to it.

Solution

Modify the properties of the MS-DOS program by following these steps:

1. Right-click your MS-DOS program on the taskbar, and then choose Properties from the short-cut menu.

2. Click the Misc tab.

3. Drag the Idle Sensitivity slider toward Low.

4. In the Background section of the dialog box, make sure the Always Suspend check box is cleared.

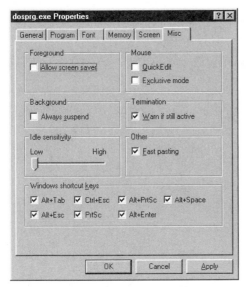

Figure 2-5. *The Misc tab of a MS-DOS program's Properties dialog box.*

5. Click OK.

Related KB article Q188978 or PROGRAMS.TXT in your WINDOWS folder

SoftRam Version 1.03 Is Not Compatible with Windows

You install Windows, and your computer displays a blue screen and the following error message:

> *Invalid VxD dynamic link call from IOS(03) +00000B5D to device "Pagefile", service 7. Your Windows configuration is invalid, run the windows Setup program again to correct this problem.*

> *To continue to run Windows, press Y or ENTER. To quit the current program, press N. If you continue running Windows, your system may become unstable. Do you want to continue?*

This problem occurs because Softram, version 1.03, is not compatible with the Windows operating system.

Solution One

Remove Softram by taking the following steps:

1. Click the Start button, choose Settings, and then click Control Panel.

2. Double-click the Add/Remove Programs icon.

3. In the list of programs, click Softram 1.03, and then click Add/Remove.

4. Click OK.

Solution Two

Disable Softram by taking the following steps:

1. Click the Start button, click Run, and then enter *Sysedit* in the text box.

2. Select the SYSTEM.INI file.

3. Disable the following lines in the [386Enh] section of the SYSTEM.INI file by placing a semi-colon (;) at the beginning of each line:

```
Device=C:\Softram\softram1.386

Device=C:\Softram\softram2.386

SoftRam=1

SoftRamOnTop=0

SoftRamSize=12000 (value varies)

SoftRamMaxPhys=100

SoftRamMinoper=2500

SoftRamSpeed=10

SoftRamExtended=12288 (value varies)

SoftRamLowmemExt=1

SoftRamResourceExt=1

PageOverCommit=10
```

4. Choose Save from the File menu, and then close Sysedit.

5. Right-click an empty area on the Windows taskbar, and then choose Properties from the short-cut menu.

6. Select the Start Menu Programs tab, and click Remove.

7. Double-click the Startup folder, click the SoftRam icon, and then click Remove.

Note Do not remove the SoftRam folder which is listed above the Startup folder. Make sure to remove the SoftRam icon in the Startup folder.

8. Click Close, and then click OK.

9. Reboot your computer.

Related KB article Q135737

Games and Entertainment

Alt+Tab Causes Windows to Stop Responding

You run a game program, and then press Alt+Tab to switch to another program, and Windows stops responding.

This problem occurs when you are running one of the following programs:

- Sierra Space Quest 6

- Sierra Police Quest 4

- Sierra Gabriel Knight

Solution

Don't press Alt+Tab to switch to another program while you are running one of these programs.

Related KB article Q190604

Chessmaster 4000 Causes Display Problems

When you run the Book Editor in Chessmaster 4000 and drag a window, video problems occur.

Solution

Turn off the Show Window Contents While Dragging option in the Display Properties control panel by following these steps:

1. Right-click a blank spot on your desktop, and choose Properties from the shortcut menu.

2. Click the Effects tab.

3. Clear the Show Window Contents While Dragging text box.

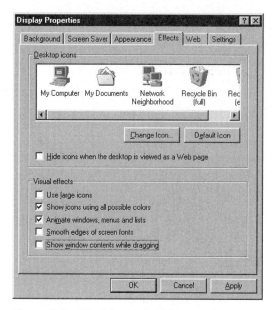

Figure 2-6. *The Effects tab of the Display Properties dialog box.*

4. Click OK.

Related KB article Q188978 or PROGRAMS.TXT in your WINDOWS folder

---

Delphine Software's MotoRacer Program Displays Error Message

You try to run Delphine Softw1are's MotoRacer program after you upgrade to Windows 98 and see the following error message displayed:

Program Incorrectly Installed. Please Reinstall it.

Microsoft has confirmed that this behavior is not caused by a problem in Windows 98, but may be caused by design changes in Windows 98.

Solution

Reinstall MotoRacer. For information about reinstalling MotoRacer, consult the program's documentation or contact Delphine.

Related KB article Q186922

Hardball III Stops Windows from Responding

You attempt to install Hardball III, and the computer stops responding. This occurs when the Active Desktop is enabled, because some older games do not support the Active Desktop.

Solution

Disable the Active Desktop by taking these steps:

1. Right-click the desktop, click Properties, and then click the Web tab.

2. Clear the View My Active Desktop As A Web Page check box, and then click OK.

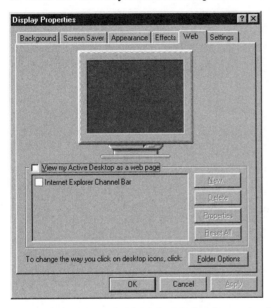

Figure 2-7. *The Web tab of the Display Properties dialog box.*

Related KB article Q186095

Heroes of Might and Magic Causes Display Problems

You run Heroes of Might and Magic by New World Computing in Windows 98, and clicking an object with the mouse leaves a residual rectangle on the screen.

This occurs when you run the game in full-screen mode and use a Trident Super VGA display adapter.

Solution One

Do not run Heroes of Might and Magic in full-screen mode. To switch from full-screen mode, press the F4 key.

Solution Two

Reduce your Hardware Acceleration setting in Windows 98 by taking the following steps:

1. Click the Start button, choose Settings, click Control Panel, and then double-click the Display icon.

2. Choose the Settings tab, and then click Advanced.

3. Click the Performance tab.

4. Move the Hardware Acceleration slider one notch to the left of the Full setting (to the Most Acceleration Functions setting).

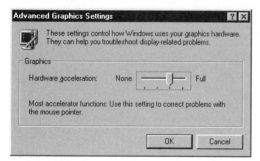

Figure 2-8. *The Advanced Graphics Settings dialog box.*

5. Click OK, and then click OK. If prompted, restart your computer.

Related KB article Q189154

Interplay MAX2 Won't Install

You have DirectX 6.0 installed on your computer and are unable to install Interplay MAX2 from the screen that opens automatically when you insert the MAX2 CD-ROM.

Solution

Install the MAX2 CD-ROM. Use Windows Explorer to navigate to the root folder of the MAX2 CD-ROM, and then double-click the SETUP.EXE file. Click No when you are prompted *Newer version of DX is on CD. Install it?* Select your installation type and then follow the instructions on the screen.

Related KB article Q190912

Jane's US Navy Fighter or Advanced Tactical Fighter Quits Unexpectedly

You play Jane's US Navy Fighter or Advanced Tactical Fighter, and the game quits unexpectedly. Microsoft has confirmed that this behavior is not caused by a problem in Windows 98, but may be caused by design changes in Windows 98.

Solution

Contact Electronic Arts Technical Support to inquire about obtaining a patch to resolve this issue.

Related KB article Q187512

Joystick Stops Responding in Jane's AH-64D Longbow

You use the Microsoft SideWinder Pro joystick in Jane's AH-64D Longbow program and, when you switch resolutions from 640 x 480 to 320 x 240, the joystick stops responding.

Solution

Press one of the arrow keys to restore joystick input, or download a patch that fixes this problem from the vendor at *http://www.janes.ea.com.*

Related KB article Q188978 or PROGRAMS.TXT in your WINDOWS folder

Kyrandia 3 Causes EMS Memory Error

You run Kyrandia 3 Malcolm's Revenge in Windows 98 and see an EMS memory error.

Solution

Right-click the MALCOM.PIF file, and choose Properties from the shortcut menu. Click the Memory tab, and choose 4096 from the Expanded (EMS) Memory and Extended (XMS) Memory drop-down list boxes. Click the Apply button, change the settings back to Auto, and click OK.

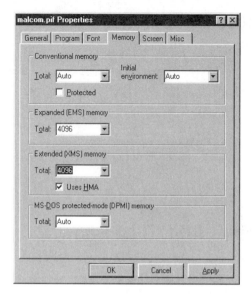

Figure 2-9. *The Memory tab of the MALCOM.PIF Properties dialog box.*

Related KB article Q188978 or PROGRAMS.TXT in your WINDOWS folder

Links LS 97 Installer Locks Up

You install Links LS 97, choose the Disable Task Scheduler option, and the Setup program minimizes the taskbar and locks up.

Solution

Do not choose to disable the Task Scheduler when running the Setup program.

Related KB article Q188978 or PROGRAMS.TXT in your WINDOWS folder

Links LS Legends in Sport 1997 Edition Displays Error Message

You install Links LS Legends in Sport 1997 Edition and see the following message:

Warning: The System Agent is currently running on your system.

This program can interrupt Links LS without notice. It is strongly

recommended that this program is closed before running Links LS.

If you choose to close it, it will automatically be restarted.

If you then click Continue, Links may stop responding.

Solution

Disable Task Scheduler by taking the following steps:

1. Restart your computer.

2. On the taskbar, double-click Task Scheduler, and then choose Stop Using Task Scheduler from the Advanced menu.

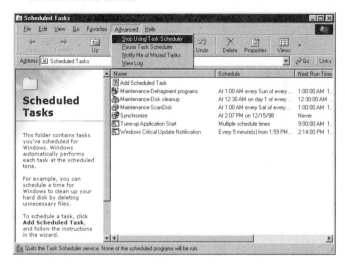

Figure 2-10.   *The Scheduled Tasks window.*

3. Restart your computer.

Related KB article   Q186924

Logical Journey Of The Zoombinis Displays Startup Error Message

You attempt to start Logical Journey Of The Zoombinis, your screen becomes distorted, and you see the following error message:

Unable to initialize graphics.

This occurs if you're using more than 256 colors. Logical Journey Of The Zoombinis cannot be run using a color depth greater than 256 colors.

Solution

Set the color depth to 256 colors by following these steps:

1. Click the Start button, choose Settings, and then click Control Panel.

2. Double-click the Display icon.

3. Click the Settings tab.

4. In the Colors box, select 256 Colors, and then click OK.

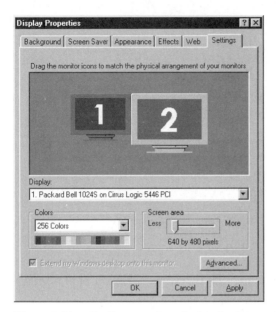

Figure 2-11. *The Settings tab in the Display Properties dialog box.*

5. If you are prompted to restart your computer or wish to apply the new settings without restarting your computer, click Apply The New Color Settings Without Restarting, and then click OK.

Related KB article Q186089

Magic School Bus Demo Doesn't Run

You try to run Scholastic's The Magic School Bus: Explores the Rainforest demonstration by double-clicking the MSBRAIN.EXE file in the CDSAMPLE\DEMOS\MSB\RAIN folder on the Windows 98 CD-ROM and receive the following error message:

Failed to retrieve initialization data

Solution One

Run the game from the Microsoft Interactive CD Sampler tool:

1. Insert the Windows 98 CD-ROM into the CD-ROM drive.

2. Navigate to the CDSAMPLE folder on your Windows 98 CD-ROM and then double-click the SAMPLER.EXE file.

Solution Two

Start Interactive CD Sampler manually by double-clicking the SAMPLER.EXE file in the CDSAMPLE folder on the Windows 98 CD-ROM.

Related KB article Q185133

Maxis SimGolf Doesn't Minimize, Maximize, or Close

You click the Minimize, Maximize, or Close buttons in the Maxis SimGolf program, and nothing happens.

This problem occurs when you run Maxis SimGolf on a monitor other than your primary monitor.

Solution

Don't run Maxis SimGolf on a monitor other than your primary.

Related KB article Q188221

MCS Stereo 1.05 Mixer Controls Are Disabled

You switch between standard and enhanced environments in MCS Stereo version 1.05, and the mixer controls are disabled.

Solution One

Close the program and reopen it.

Solution Two

Upgrade MCS Stereo to a version designed for Windows 98 by contacting Animotion Development. Their US number is (205) 591-5715. Alternately, call the product support number that came with your copy of MCS Stereo.

Related KB article Q188978 or PROGRAMS.TXT in your WINDOWS folder

MechWarrior 2 Doesn't Run Correctly

Activision's MechWarior 2 for MS-DOS does not work properly.

Solution

Download the MECH2V11.EXE patch from Activision's web site at *http://www.Activision.com.*

Related KB article Q188978 or PROGRAMS.TXT in your WINDOWS folder

MS-DOS Game Doesn't Play Sounds

You try to play an MS-DOS-based game with sounds after you upgrade to Windows 98, and you don't hear the sounds.

This problem occurs when your sound card uses a Windows Driver Model (WDM) driver, the MS-DOS-based game uses Sound Blaster Emulation, and this game uses Sound Blaster FM Synthesis for music playback. Sound Blaster Emulation does not support FM synthesis.

Solution

Configure your game to use General MIDI (0x330) for music instead of FM Synthesis. For information about how to do this, please refer to the documentation included with the game, or contact the program's manufacturer.

Related KB article Q192231

MS-DOS Game Doesn't Play Sounds Properly

You upgrade your computer to Windows 98, and the sounds in MS-DOS-based games do not work properly.

This problem occurs when you use any of the following sound cards:

- Aztech
- ESS Technology
- Yamaha (OPL3-SA)

If the driver for your sound card is upgraded from a virtual device driver (VxD) to a Windows Driver Model (WDM) driver, the Sound Blaster compatibility components may not be loaded.

Solution

Disable the BLASTER= line in the AUTOEXEC.BAT file by taking the following steps:

1. Click the Start button, click Run, enter *sysedit* in the Open box, and then click OK.

2. Click the Autoexec.bat window, type *rem* in front of the BLASTER= line, close the program, click Yes, and then restart your computer.

Note You may need a BLASTER= line in the AUTOEXEC.BAT file when you start in MS-DOS mode to play games. If so, add a BLASTER= line to the DOSSTART.BAT file.

Related KB article Q192232

NBA Jam Extreme Displays Error Message

You attempt to install Acclaim Entertainment's NBA Jam Extreme onto a Windows 98-based computer and receive the following error message:

Cannot install this program on Windows NT

This error message displays because the NBA Jam Extreme Setup program looks for a specific Windows version number that has changed in Windows 98. Microsoft has confirmed that this behavior is not caused by a problem in Windows 98, but may be caused by design changes in Windows 98. For more information about resolving this issue, contact the program's manufacturer.

Solution

Change the data value of the Version value to Windows 95 in the Registry, install the NBA Jam Extreme program, and then change the value back to its original setting.

Warning Please read the Introduction for information on how to safely edit the Registry.

1. Click Start, click Run, enter *Regedit* in the Run box, and then click OK.

2. Navigate your way down through the folders in the left pane to the following Registry key:

   HKEY_LOCAL_MACHINE\Software\Microsoft\Windows\Current_Version

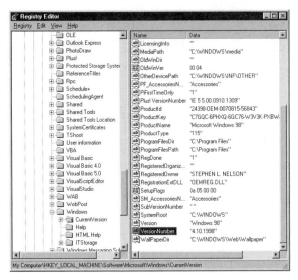

Figure 2-12. *The Registry Editor.*

3. Double-click the Version value, enter *Windows 95* in the Value Data box, and click OK.

4. Double-click the VersionNumber value, record the current value data, and then change the value data to *4.00.1111*.

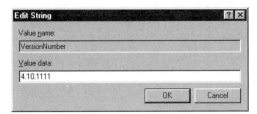

Figure 2-13. *The Edit String dialog box.*

5. Install the NBA Jam Extreme program.

6. Go to the following Registry key and change the value data of the Version value to *Windows 98*:

   `HKEY_LOCAL_MACHINE\Software\Microsoft\Windows\Current_Version`

7. Change the data value of the VersionNumber value in the following Registry key to the data value you recorded earlier:

   `HKEY_LOCAL_MACHINE\Software\Microsoft\Windows\Current_Version`

Related KB article   Q187748

Nickelodeon Director's Lab Installation Program Crashes

You install Nickelodeon Director's Lab, and the following error message appears:

Setup Message: Script or DLL has been corrupted.

Unable to load dialog template: 'mscuistf.dll: 2'.

Solution

Manually close the installation program by pressing Ctrl+Alt+Delete, select the Director's Lab Setup program,and then click End Task. This does no harm, as the program is finished installing at this point.

Related KB article Q188978 or PROGRAMS.TXT in your WINDOWS folder

PF Magic DOGZ and CATZ Don't Work As Expected

You click a toy from the toy box in the PF Magic DOGZ and CATZ version 1.08p, 1.08q, or 1.09 program, and the toy's icon is replaced with a different icon, and the toy doesn't work correctly.

Microsoft has confirmed that this behavior is not caused by a problem in Windows 98, but may be caused by design changes in Windows 98.

Solution

Upgrade to the most current version of DOGZ and CATZ or contact PF Magic to inquire about the availability of a fix for this problem.

Related KB article Q187703

Puzzle Collection Reports Error Message

You install Puzzle Collection from the Interactive CD Sampler link on the page that opens when you install the Windows 98 CD-ROM and receive an error message that consists of only an "X"in a red circle.

Solution

This occurs if Windows is set to use only 16 colors. Choose a color palette of more than 16 colors by taking the following steps

1. Click the Start button, choose Settings, and then click Control Panel.

2. Double-click the Display icon.

3. Click the Settings tab.

4. In the Colors box, select 256 Colors (or a higher setting).

Figure 2-14.   *The Settings tab of the Display Properties dialog box.*

5. Click OK. If you are prompted to restart your computer, do so.

Related KB article Q191948

Savage: The Ultimate Quest for Survival Exhibits Problems

Viridis's Savage: The Ultimate Quest for Survival stops responding during Setup, displays a double-cursor, or malfunctions with a S3 Trio64+ based display card.

Solution

Restart your computer. If the problems persists, install the 16-bit version of the game.

Related KB article Q188978 or PROGRAMS.TXT in your WINDOWS folder

Sierra Power Chess Causes Windows to Hang

If you install Sierra's Power Chess 1.0 and Power Chess 98 on a Windows 98–based computer, Power Chess may stop responding (hang) while you play. When this occurs, you must reboot the computer. Pressing Ctrl+Alt+Delete has no effect. Microsoft has confirmed that this behavior is not caused by a problem in Windows 98, but may be caused by design changes in Windows 98.

Solution

For more information or possible updates, please contact the game's manufacturer.

Related KB article Q187320

SimTown Changes Taskbar Icons

You install SimTown version 1.0 and restart your computer, and the Show Desktop and View Channels icons on the taskbar appear as small houses. If you click one of these icons, you may receive an Open With dialog box that prompts you to choose a program to use to open the View CHANNELS.SCF file or the Show DESKTOP.SCF file. This behavior occurs because SimTown alters the .SCF file association.

Microsoft has confirmed that this behavior is not caused by a problem in Windows 98, but may be caused by design changes in Windows 98. For more information about resolving this issue, contact the program's manufacturer.

Solution

Manually edit the .SCF file association as follows:

1. Double-click My Computer, choose Folder Options from the View menu, and then click the File Types tab.

2. In the Registered File Types box, select SimTown Sounds, and then click Edit.

3. In the Description Of Type box, type *Windows Explorer Command*, and then click New.

4. In the Action box, type *Open*, and then in the Application Used To Perform Action box, type *c:\progra~1\intern~1\iexplore.exe*.

Figure 2-15. *The New Action dialog box.*

5. Click the Use DDE check box to select it, and then type *[ShellFile("%1","%1",%S)],* in the DDE Message box.

6. In the Application box, type *Folders*, and then type *AppProperties* in the Topics box.

7. Click OK, click Change Icon, click Browse, choose an icon to replace the missing icon, click OK, click OK again, and then restart your computer.

Related KB article Q186228

SoftDVD Program Has Playback Problems

You view a DVD movie using the SoftDVD program included with some computers and experience various playback problems.

Solution

To solve this problem, follow these steps:

1. Click the Start button, choose Find, and then click Files Or Folders.

2. In the Named box, enter *SOFTDVD.INI* and click Find Now.

3. In the list of found files, double-click the SOFTDVD.INI file.

4. Type the following lines in the SOFTDVD.INI file:

```
[dvdfs]

AlignedAccess=0
```

Be sure to type a blank line above and below these two lines.

5. Choose Save from the File menu, and then choose Exit from the File menu.

6. Restart Windows.

If these steps do not resolve your problem, please contact your computer manufacturer for additional assistance.

Related KB article Q187329

Splice 2.0 Crashes

You create an optimal palette for a video file in Asymetrix Splice 2.0 and find the program has a General Protection Fault.

Solution

Upgrade to a more recent version of the program (now called Digital Video Producer). This upgrade is free to registered users. For more information, contact Asymetrix Technical Support at (425) 637-1600.

Related KB article Q188978 or PROGRAMS.TXT in your WINDOWS folder

The 7ᵗʰ Guest Audio Doesn't Work Properly

You play The 7ᵗʰ Guest on a computer with a Pro Audio Spectrum 16 sound card and your audio doesn't play properly.

Solution One

Enable and use Sound Blaster compatibility mode.

Solution Two

Configure your Pro Audio Spectrum card to use IRQ 5 and DMA 3. See your hardware documentation for more information.

Related KB article Q188978 or PROGRAMS.TXT in your WINDOWS folder

---

Tornado Game Causes Insufficient Memory Error

You run the game Tornado and receive an error message that says there is insufficient memory to run the program. This problem occurs because Tornado requires at least 606K of free conventional memory. Depending on the fragmentation in your system, Tornado may require up to 693K of free memory (based on your 1 MB total of conventional and upper memory).

Solution One

Create additional free conventional memory on your computer by editing the CONFIG.SYS file. To do so, follow these steps:

1. Click the Start button, and then click Run. Enter *Sysedit* in the text box, and then click OK.

2. Select the CONFIG.SYS window and enter the following lines in the file:

```
device=c:\windows\himem.sys

device=c:\windows\emm386.exe noems

dos=high,umb
```

3. Save the file, close the System Configuration Editor, and then restart Windows.

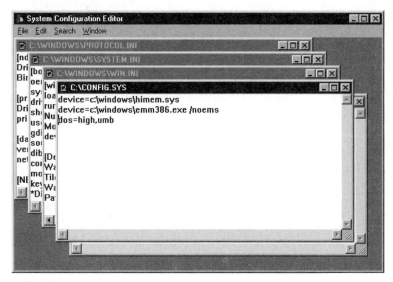

Figure 2-16. *The CONFIG.SYS file in the System Configuration Editor.*

Solution Two

Disable nonessential drivers and programs in the CONFIG.SYS and AUTOEXEC.BAT files by
following these steps:

1. If Sysedit is already open, skip to step 2. Otherwise, click the Start button, and then click Run.
   Enter *Sysedit* in the text box, and then click OK.

2. Select the CONFIG.SYS window and type *Rem* and a space at the beginning of the lines that have
   nonessential drivers or programs. This includes any real-mode drivers that have protected-mode
   equivalents.

3. Select the AUTOEXEC.BAT window and type *Rem* and a space at the beginning of the lines that
   have nonessential drivers or programs. This includes any real-mode drivers that have protected-
   mode equivalents.

5. Choose Save from the File menu. Then close the Sysedit windows and reboot the computer.

Solution Three

Edit the TORNADO.BAT file by following these steps

1. Click the Start button, choose Find, and then click Files Or Folders.

2. Enter *Tornado.bat* in the text box, enter your boot drive (usually C:) in the Look In box, then click
   Find Now.

3. When found, right-click the TORNADO.BAT file icon. In the shortcut menu, click Edit.

4. Change the line that reads apm to 1h apm.

5. Save your changes to the TORNADO.BAT file.

6. Double click the TORNADO.BAT file to verify that the problem has been resolved.

Related KB article Q132801

Triple Play 98's Autorun Crashes

You insert the Triple Play 98 CD-ROM to install the program, and the autorun feature causes a general protection fault.

Solution

Use the SETUP.EXE file on the CD-ROM. For more information, visit the Electronic Arts web site at *http://www.easports.com.*

Related KB article Q188978 or PROGRAMS.TXT in your WINDOWS folder

Ultima VI/Wing Commander Doesn't Work Properly

Ultima VI/Wind Commander does not run properly when run from the CD-ROM.

Solution

Copy the programs from the CD-ROM to your hard drive by following the instructions provided with the game.

Related KB article Q188978 or PROGRAMS.TXT in your WINDOWS folder

Virtual Pool 2 and Where in the USA Is Carmen San Diego? Don't Run with More than 256 Colors

Virtual Pool 2 and Where in the USA is Carmen San Diego? don't run when the color depth is set higher than 8 bits (256 colors).

Solution One

Change your color depth to 8 bits (256 colors). To do so, right-click an empty spot of the Desktop and choose Properties from the shortcut menu. Click the Settings tab, then choose 256 colors from the Colors drop-down listbox.

Figure 2-17. *The Settings tab of the Display Properties dialog box.*

Solution Two

Look for an upgrade to Virtual Pool 2 at the VRSports web site at *http://www.vrsports.com*.

Related KB article Q188978 or PROGRAMS.TXT in your WINDOWS folder

Westwood's Lands of Lore Displays Black Screen

You quit Westwood's Lands of Lore: Guardians of Destiny, and your computer stops responding and displays a black screen. Microsoft has confirmed that this behavior is not caused by a problem in Windows 98, but may be caused by design changes in Windows 98.

Solution

Reboot the computer. Contact the program's manufacturer for information about a fix for this problem.

Related KB article Q186940

Where in the World Is Carmen San Diego? Displays Error Message

You try to start Where in the World is Carmen San Diego? version 1.01 and receive the following error message:

Carmen caused a general protection fault in module CARMEN.EXE at 000c:0000446d.

Solution

Disable your Active Desktop. To do this, right-click on an empty part of your Desktop, choose Properties from the shortcut menu, click the Web tab and then clear the View My Active Desktop As A Web Page check box.

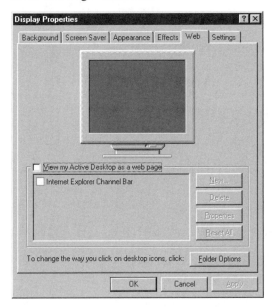

Figure 2-18. *The Web tab of the Display Properties dialog box.*

Related KB article Q186187

Where in the World Is Carmen San Diego? Game Doesn't Play MIDI Music Files

You run the Where in the World Is Carmen San Diego? version 1.0 game, and the MIDI music does not play, even when the Wave (.WAV) audio files play correctly. This occurs because the program sends the sound to the external MIDI output even if you selected internal playback during program installation.

Solution

Upgrade Where in the World Is Carmen San Diego? to version 1.01 or later.

Note The Version 1.0 CD-ROM has the words MPC (Windows) printed on it, while version 1.01 does not.

Related KB article Q136256

Yukon Trail Graphics Unclear

You run the Yukon Trail program, and the graphics displayed on the screen are unclear. This occurs because the Yukon Trail program is not totally compatible with the Active Desktop.

Solution

Disable the Active Desktop by taking the following steps:

1. Right-click the desktop, click Properties, and then click the Web tab.

2. Clear the View My Active Desktop As A Web Page check box, and then click Apply.

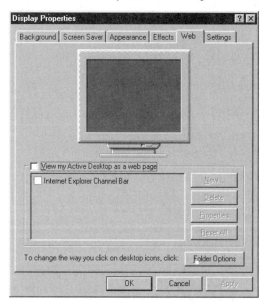

Figure 2-19. *The Web tab of the Display Properties dialog box.*

3. Click OK, and then restart your computer.

Related KB article Q186363

General

ADI Mathe Klasse 3+4 Version 2.5 Doesn't Work with Multiple Monitors

You try to start the ADI Mathe Klasse 3+4 version 2.5 program using multiple monitors, and you receive the following general protection (GP) fault error message:

ADI2 caused a General Protection Fault in module ADIWIN.EXE at 0011:000000a0

Solution

Disable all your non-primary monitors by taking the following steps:

1. Right-click the Windows desktop and choose Properties from the shortcut menu

2. Click the Settings tab.

3. Click the nonprimary monitor, and clear the Extend My Windows Desktop Onto This Monitor check box, and then click OK. If prompted, restart your computer.

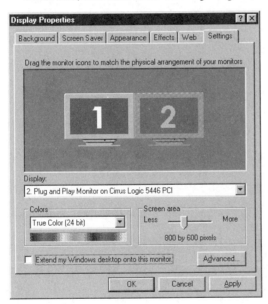

Figure 2-20. *The Settings tab of the Display Properties dialog box.*

Related KB article Q189311

Avantos ManagePro 3.1 Has Window Problems

If you have the Show Window Contents While Dragging option enabled, you may experience problems with Avantos ManagePro 3.1. For example, you may be unable to resize the ManagePro window. This behavior occurs if the program you're using isn't fully compatible with the Show Window Contents While Dragging feature.

Solution

Disable the Show Window Contents While Dragging option by taking the following steps:

1. Click the Start button, choose Settings, click Folder Options, and then click the View tab.

2. In the Advanced Settings box, click the Show Window Contents While Dragging check box to clear it, and then click OK.

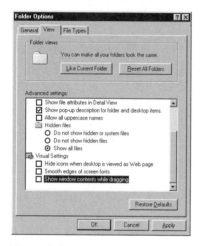

Figure 2-21. *The View tab in the Folder Options dialog box.*

Related KB article Q186299

Corel and MicroStar Programs Cause Problems

You run Corel and MicroStar programs and experience any of the following symptoms:

- You receive fatal exception error messages while Windows 98 Setup is copying files to your computer.

- One or more drives use MS-DOS Compatibility mode.

- You are unable to run ScanDisk for Windows.

- Your CD-ROM drive cannot be found after Windows 98 Setup is complete.

Some programs, such as Corel Graphics, Microsoft Word, and other Microsoft Office programs do not run properly, and you experience unexpected behavior when running these programs.

These problems occur if you are running a program that installs the UPDAT_CD.COM file, which is not compatible with Windows 98. This file prevents Windows operations that require direct disk access from functioning properly by incorrectly hooking interrupt 21. The UPDAT_CD.COM file is installed by earlier Corel programs and by the following programs distributed by MicroStar:

- 200 Great Games for Windows

- 300 Great Games for Windows

- Casino Games Gold Edition

- Unearthed Arsenal (a Diablo add-on package)

Solution

1. Restart your computer. After your computer completes the Power On Self Test (POST), press and hold down the Ctrl key until you see the Windows 98 Startup menu, and then choose Command Prompt Only.

2. After the command prompt type the following commands, pressing Enter after each:

   ```
   cd\Windows
   ```

   ```
   edit WINSTART.BAT
   ```

3. Type *rem* and a space in front of the following line:

   ```
   C:\Windows\updat_cd.com c:\cd.sav.
   ```

4. Press Alt+F, and press S (to save). Then press Alt+F, and then press X (to exit the Edit utility).

5. Restart your computer.

Related KB article Q186670

DirectX Settings Changes Result in Unexpected Behavior

You change settings in the DirectX tool included with the DirectX Software Developer Kit (DIRECTX.CPL) in Control Panel and experience unexpected behavior. This occurs if you change any of the original settings in the DirectX tool.

Note The DirectX settings vary by system and software. It is impossible to determine what the original DirectX settings were unless you have noted them.

Solution One

Restore the original settings in the DirectX tool, and then restart your computer.

Solution Two

If you don't know the original settings, Microsoft suggests that you restore your system from a known good backup. If you don't have a backup copy of your system, you may need to install Windows into a new folder, and then install your programs again to re-create affected Registry entries. For more information about how to troubleshoot DirectX issues, see KB article Q178098, "How to Troubleshoot DirectX Video Problems."

Related KB article Q184892

General Protection (GP) Fault Error Message When Restarting a Program

You close a 16-bit program that is listed as not responding in the Close Program dialog box by pressing Ctrl+Alt+Delete. When you restart the program, you receive a general protection (GP) fault error message.

When you use the Close Program dialog box to close a program that is not responding, the program's DLLs are not unloaded and reinitialized properly when you restart the program

Solution

Reboot the computer.

Related KB article Q135163

Grolier Multimedia Encyclopedia Displays Error Messages

You install the 1995 Grolier Multimedia Encyclopedia version 7.01, your computer restarts, and you receive one or more of the following general protection (GP) fault error messages:

IS20DEL caused a segment not present fault in module USER.EXE at 004:00002ca4

MMTASK caused a general protection fault in module MMSYSTEM.DLL at 0004:00001837

MMTASK caused a segment not present fault in module KRNL386.EXE at 0002:00000d82

This occurs because the MSCAM.DLL file is loaded into memory by Windows 98 when it starts. The Grolier Multimedia Encyclopedia Setup program overwrites and then restores this file while it is resident in memory, and this causes the copy of the file that is memory-resident to become unstable.

Solution

Use the Microsoft System File Checker tool to restore the following original Windows 98 files:

- Msacm.drv
- Msacm.dll

Related KB article Q186126

Installation Fails When .INF File Is on Hard Disk

You install a program by right-clicking the program's .INF file and then clicking Install, then you see a dialog box asking you to insert a disk even if the program is already on the hard disk:

The disk labeled <name> is now required. This disk is provided by your computer manufacturer. Click OK to continue.

This behavior occurs if the .INF file is located in a folder with a long file name.

Solution

Rename the folder containing the .INF file so that its name conforms to the MS-DOS 8.3 naming convention. You may also need to rename parent folders of the folder containing the .INF file.

Note For information about a similar problem, see KB article Q141350, ".INF File Install Fails with Error."

Related KB article Q151674

Kurzweil Voice 2 Displays Error Messages

You close the Kurzweil Voice 2 program and receive the following error messages:

KVTRCKER: Could not Free the DLL 'KVTRCK95'

KVSNDKEY: Could not Free the DLL 'KVSNDKEY'

Microsoft has confirmed that this behavior is not caused by a problem in Windows 98, but may be caused by design changes in Windows 98.

Solution

Contact Kurzweil Applied Intelligence for information about this problem and a possible solution.

Related KB article Q186838

Learn To Speak French 4.02 Doesn't Display Correctly

You use Hyperglot Learn to Speak French 4.02 with 256 colors and find the dialog boxes are discolored.

Solution

Disable the Active Desktop. To do so, follow these steps:

1. Right-click the desktop, and choose Properties from the shortcut menu.

2. Click the Web tab, then clear the View My Active Desktop As A Web Page check box, and then click Apply.

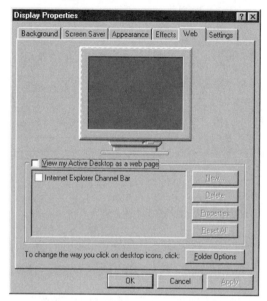

Figure 2-22. *The Web tab of the Display Properties dialog box.*

3. Click OK, and then restart your computer.

Related KB article Q188978 or PROGRAMS.TXT in your WINDOWS folder

Macromedia Director Doesn't Start

You install Macromedia Director version 4.x and attempt to run the program. The screen flashes briefly, but the program won't start. This occurs if you try to run Director 4.x on a hard disk with more than 2 gigabytes (GB) of free space. Microsoft has confirmed this to be a problem in Windows 98.

Solution

Work around this behavior by installing Director on a hard disk with less than 2 GB of free space.

Related KB article Q186824

Microsoft Batch 98 MSBATCH.INF File Installs AT&T WorldNet

You create an MSBATCH.INF file using the Microsoft Batch98 tool, click the AT&T WorldNet Service check box to clear it, save the MSBATCH.INF file, and then open it again using the Batch98 tool, and the AT&T WorldNet Service check box is still selected.

Solution

Prevent the MSBATCH.INF file from automatically installing the AT&T WorldNet service by taking the following steps:

1. Click the Start button, choose Programs, and then click Microsoft Batch 98.

2. Choose the file, click Open, and then double-click the MSBATCH.INF file.

3. Click Optional Components, and then click Online Services.

4. Click the AT&T WorldNet Service check box to clear it, click OK, and then click Save Settings to INF.

Note If you open the MSBATCH.INF file again using the Batch98 tool, the AT&T WorldNet Service check box will be selected.

Related KB article Q189112

Microsoft Fortran 5.1 Doesn't Properly Create QuickWin Applications

Microsoft Fortran 5.1 doesn't correctly compile QuickWin applications.

Solution

Delete or comment out the following line in the FL.DEF:

APPLOADER '___MSLANGLOAD'

After removing this line, recompile any QuickWin programs built with Fortran version 5.1.

Related KB article Q188978 or PROGRAMS.TXT in your WINDOWS folder

MS-DOS-Based Setup Program Doesn't Work Properly

Some Windows-based programs also include an MS-DOS version of Setup. If you set up such a program in MS-DOS mode, the program may not work correctly in Windows. Windows uses different AUTOEXEC.BAT and CONFIG.SYS files in MS-DOS mode. Changes to these files during the program's installation are not made in the files that Windows uses.

Solution One

Run the Windows-based version of the program's Setup program.

Solution Two

Restart the computer to a command prompt, and run the program in MS-DOS mode.

Related KB article Q148800

Out Of Memory Error When Starting a Program

You start a program on a computer using disk compression, and you receive one of the following error messages:

Out of memory

There is not enough memory to perform this operation. Close unneeded applications and then try the operation again.

If Windows 98 is installed on a compressed drive, the Setup program places the swap file on the host drive of the compressed drive. If the host drive doesn't have enough free space, the swap file isn't able to grow enough to accommodate large programs.

Solution One

If you are using a Microsoft compression program (DrvSpace or DblSpace), the swap file can be safely placed on the compressed drive (assuming there is enough free space on the compressed drive).

Solution Two

If you are using a non-Microsoft compression program, you must enlarge the host drive or move the swap file to another uncompressed drive.

Related KB article Q132810

Program Causes Errors

You install or run a program in Windows 98 and receive one of the following error messages:

Windows cannot run this program because it is in invalid format. The <drive>:\windows\system\imm32.dll file cannot load at the desired address, and is not relocatable. Contact your vender to get a version that is compatible with this version of Windows.

Error starting program the <drive>:\windows\system\imm32.dll file cannot load in the desired address and is not locatable. Contact your vender to get a version that is compatible with this version of Windows.

This occurs when the MFC42.DLL and IMM32.DLL files are damaged or replaced by another program, and if you install the RichWin 97 program either before or after installing Windows 98.

Solution

Extract a new copy of the MFC42.DLL and IMM32.DLL files from your original Windows 98 CD-ROM into the WINDOWS\SYSTEM folder using the System File Checker tool.

Related KB article Q189495

Program Causes Windows to Run Slowly

You use a Windows-based application, and Windows operates slowly.

This occurs when Windows uses a dynamic virtual memory manager to handle file swap functions. In order to provide more memory to applications than is physically present in RAM, Windows uses hard disk space to simulate RAM. If you have limited hard disk space, other applications may use virtual memory needed by Windows to run its applications.

Solution

Take the following steps to solve this problem:

1. Click the Start button, choose Settings, and then click Control Panel.

2. Double-click the System icon, and then click the Performance tab.

3. Click Virtual Memory and select the Let Me Specify My Own Virtual Memory Settings option button.

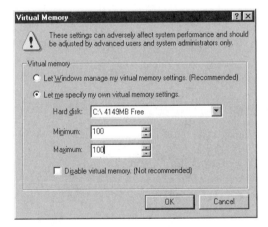

Figure 2-23. *The Virtual Memory dialog box.*

4. Enter an amount in the Minimum or Maximum text box.

Note If your computer has enough RAM to meet the needs of Windows and all its applications, you may select the Disable Virtual Memory (Not Recommended) check box.

Related KB article Q128327

QuickBooks 2.0 Causes General Protection (GP) Fault Errors

You use Intuit QuickBooks version 2.0 or 3.0, and it causes various general protection (GP) fault error messages when performing different functions

Solution One

Upgrade to Quick Books 3.1 or higher.

Solution Two

Edit the WIN.INI file by following these steps:

1. Click the Start button, and then click Run.

2. Enter *sysedit* in the Open text box and click OK.

3. Click the WIN.INI window.

4. Enter *QBW=0X08000000* in the [Compatibility] section of the file.

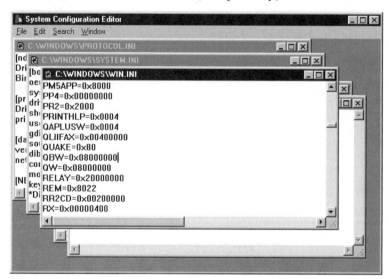

Figure 2-24.   *The WIN.INI file in the System Configuration Editor.*

5. Choose Save from the File menu.

6. Close the program.

7. Restart Windows

Note If you insert the QBW=0x08000000 line in the WIN.INI file, you must remove the line if you later upgrade to QuickBooks 3.1 or higher. If you upgrade QuickBooks and do not remove this line, you may have printing errors.

Related KB article Q130147

QuickBooks 2.0 Runs Poorly

QuickBooks 2.0 crashes or exhibits other errant behavior under Windows 98.

Solution

1. Click the Start button, and then click Run.

2. Enter *sysedit* in the Open text box, and click OK.

3. Click the WIN.INI window.

4. Enter *QBW=0x08000000* in the [Compatibility] section of the file.

5. Choose Save from the File menu.

6. Close the program and restart Windows.

Related KB article Q188978 or PROGRAMS.TXT in your WINDOWS folder

QuickBooks 3.0 Runs Incorrectly

You minimize QuickBooks before registering the product, and QuickBooks 3.0 doesn't operate correctly.

Solution

Register QuickBooks before minimizing the program. If you have already minimized it and are experiencing problems running QuickBooks, delete the QBW.INI file in the QuickBooks directory on your hard disk.

Related KB article Q188978 or PROGRAMS.TXT in your WINDOWS folder

Starting a Program Produces Error Message

You attempt to start a program and see the following error messages:

A device attached to the system is not functioning

The <filename> file is linked to missing export MFC42.DLL:6453

This occurs when you install the trial version of PC-Cillin v2.0, which replaces the Windows 98 version of the MFC42.DLL file, or if the MFC42.DLL file is damaged.

Solution

Extract a new copy of the MFC42.DLL file from your original Windows 98 CD-ROM into the WINDOWS\SYSTEM folder using the System File Checker tool by taking the following steps:

1. Click the Start button, click Run, enter *sfc.exe* in the Open box, and then click OK.

2. Select Extract One File From Installation Disk, enter *MFC42.DLL* in the text box, insert your Windows 98 installation CD-ROM, and then click the Start button.

Related KB article Q184799

System Resources Are Low with No Open Programs

You monitor your computer's free system resources (memory in particular) and note that the resources have decreased even though no programs are currently running. This occurs if you start a program and then quit it before it has completely started. When you do so, memory is leaked, and your free system resources decrease. Leaking memory can lead to memory becoming so low that your computer becomes unstable. If you restart your computer, all of your system resources should be available.

Solution One

Do not quit a program before it has completely started.

Solution Two

Restart your computer to free your system resources.

Related KB article Q185832

System Resources Do Not Return to Previous Value

You start a program and then close it, and the Free System Resources value doesn't return to the same value it had before you started the program.

This occurs because Windows waits until the first time a program asks for a particular service to initalize the system. For example, each font is initialized when a program first asks for it. If a program uses a service that uses this deferred initialization, the service remains initialized so that the next program that requests the service doesn't have to wait. Because of this, the system resources associated with that service are not freed. This behavior is by design.

This problem occurs because Windows does not free system resources abandoned by Windows 3.1-programs until all those programs have been closed. Windows only releases abandoned system resources when there are no Windows 3.1-based programs running.

Solution

Close all Windows 3.x-based programs to allow Windows to perform maximum system resource reclamation.

Related KB article Q146418

Visual Basic 16-Bit Programs Stay on Task List and Cause System Instability

When multiple instances of a 16-bit Microsoft Visual Basic program are run at the same time and then shut down, they all appear to close; however, the program may still appear in the task list. Once a computer has experienced this problem, the operating system can become unpredictable. This is because the Windows 98 COMPOBJ.DLL file sometimes does not fully unload the Visual Basic program.

Solution

Restart Windows. Fix the problem permanently by installing a Windows 98 Service Pack that contains an updated COMPOBJ.DLL file or contact Microsoft Technical Support.

Related KB article Q192515

Windows 3.1 Program Can't Access Network Resources

You use a program designed for Windows 3.1 and can't access network resources such as hard drives or printers.

Solution One

For disks and tape drives, assign a drive letter to the network resource.

1. Click the Start button, choose Programs, and then click Windows Explorer.

2. Choose Map Network Drive from the Tools menu.

3. Select a drive letter for the network drive from the Drive drop-down list box.

4. Choose a network resource or enter the path in the Path drop-down list box.

5. Click OK.

Figure 2-25. *The Map Network Drive dialog box.*

Solution Two

For printers, assign a network printer to a local printer port.

1. Click the Start button, choose Settings, and then click Printers.

2. Right-click the network printer you want to use and choose Properties from the shortcut menu.

3. Click the Details tab, and then click the Capture Printer Port button.

4. Choose the printer port you want to use from the Device drop-down list box.

5. Choose a network printer or enter the path to the printer you want to use in the Path drop-down list box.

Figure 2-26. *The Capture Printer Port dialog box.*

6. Click OK.

Related KB article Q188978 or PROGRAMS.TXT in your WINDOWS folder

Window-Eyes Version 2.1 Stops Working

You upgrade from Microsoft Windows 95 to Windows 98 and find that GW Micro Window-Eyes version 2.1 does not work.

To function properly, Window-Eyes (and possibly other screen readers) attempt to hook the operating system to obtain information about the programs that are currently running. When Window-Eyes 2.1 is unable to hook Windows 98, it displays one or more *Cannot Create Hook* error messages followed by the particular Windows function that cannot be hooked.

Solution

According to GW Micro, Window-Eyes 3.0 will support Windows 98 and is scheduled to be released in the summer of 1998. For more information, contact GW Micro at *support@gwmicro.com* or (219) 489-3671.

Related KB article Q191703

Windows Programs Cannot Launch from a DOS Prompt on a LANtastic Network

You cannot start Windows-based programs from an MS-DOS prompt when you use Windows with a LANtastic network. LANtastic keeps individual drive mappings for each virtual machine (VM). When the current working directory is on a remote drive on the LANtastic network, you cannot start Windows-based programs from an MS-DOS prompt unless the current VM is the system VM.

Solution

Change the drive mappings to the exact settings you use in the MS-DOS session.

Related KB article Q135130

World Watch 4.3 Displays Error Message

You click World Watch Help Topics on the Help menu in World Watch 4.3 and see the following error message:

Cannot find the Watch32.hlp file. Do you want to try to find this file yourself?

Microsoft has confirmed that this behavior is not caused by a problem in Windows 98, but may be caused by design changes in Windows 98. For more information about resolving this issue, contact the program's manufacturer.

Solution

To resolve this issue, click Yes when you are prompted to locate the file, locate and click the WATCH32.HLP file in the C:\PROGRAM\FILES\EXPRESS TECHNOLOGIES\WORLD WATCH folder, and then click Open.

Related KB article Q186883

Graphics, Fonts, and Desktop

Adobe Type Manager Causes Fatal Exception

You start Windows and see a blue screen with the following error message:

WINDOWS This program has caused a Fatal Exception 0D at

00457:000040B1 and will be terminated.

Pressing any key turns the screen black and causes the computer to stop responding.

This occurs when you use Adobe Type Manager and the Hardware Acceleration setting is not set to Full.

Solution

Take the following steps to solve this problem:

1. Restart your computer. After your computer completes the Power On Self Test (POST), press and hold down the Ctrl key until you see the Windows 98 Startup menu, and then choose Safe Mode.

2. Click the Start button, choose Settings, and then click Control Panel.

3. Double-click the System icon.

4. Choose the Performance tab, and then click Graphics.

5. Move the Hardware Acceleration slider all the way to the right, and then click OK.

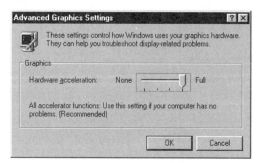

Figure 2-27. *The Advanced Graphics Settings dialog box.*

6. Click OK, and, when you are prompted to restart your computer, click Yes.

Related KB article Q133440

Adobe PhotoShop 3.0.4 or Macromedia Director 4 Does Not Run

Adobe PhotoShop 3.0.4 may not launch if your startup hard drive has more than 2 GB of free space. Macromedia Director 4 will not start on a hard disk with more than 2 GB of free space. To check how much free space you have, right-click on your startup drive in Windows Explorer and choose Properties from the shortcut menu.

Solution

Set a large minimum size for your swap file by following these steps:

1. Click the Start button, choose Settings, and then click Control Panel.

2. Double-click the System icon, and then click the Performance tab.

3. Click the Virtual Memory button.

4. Click the Let Me Specify My Own Virtual Memory Settings option button.

5. Select your startup drive from the Hard Disk drop-down list box.

6. Enter the amount of free space you have, minus 2 GB, in the Minimum text box.

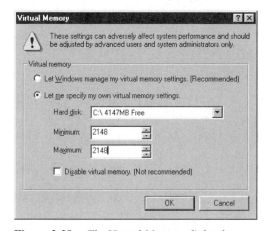

Figure 2-28. *The Virtual Memory dialog box.*

7. Click OK. If you see a **Warning**, click Yes. Click Close back in the System Properties dialog box.

8. When prompted, click Yes to restart your computer.

Note Macromedia Director can also be run by installing it on a hard disk with less than 2 GB of free space.

Related KB article Q188978 or PROGRAMS.TXT in your WINDOWS folder

Adobe PhotoShop 4.0 Crashes

You choose the Color Range command from the Select menu in Adobe, and a page fault occurs.

Solution

Download the patch to PhotoShop 4.0.1 from Adobe's web site at *http://www.adobe.com.*

Related KB article Q188978 or PROGRAMS.TXT in your WINDOWS folder

Allaire HomeSite Displays Error Message

You open a Hypertext Markup Language (HTML) document using the Allaire HomeSite 2.5a program and see the following error messages:

> *Invalid floating point operation*
>
> *Access violation at address 00D87OD4. Read of address 10004798*

This occurs if you are using HomeSite 2.5a and the Active Desktop is enabled.

Solution One

Disable the Active Desktop by following these steps:

1. Right-click the desktop, click Properties, and then click the Web tab.

2. Clear the View My Active Desktop As A Web Page check box, and then click Apply.

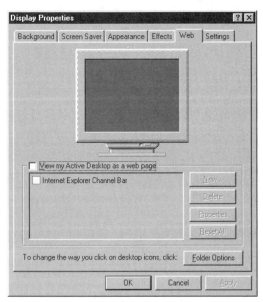

Figure 2-29. *The Web tab in the Display Properties dialog box.*

3. Click OK, and then restart Windows.

Solution Two

To resolve this issue, upgrade to HomeSite version 3.0, or contact Allaire for information about a possible update that resolves this issue with HomeSite 2.5a.

Related KB article Q187578

Digital Video 1.0 (DVCAP.EXE) Causes Error Message

You start the Digital Video 1.0 (DVCAP.EXE) program included with your Sony DVBK-2000 digital still image capture card, and you receive the following error message:

PDCLIB.DLL caused an invalid page fault in module KERNEL32.DLL

Solution

Contact Sony Corporation to obtain an updated DVBK-2000 driver.

Related KB article Q189222

FORTRAN PowerStation Compiles Bad Graphics Programs

Graphics programs that were compiled in Microsoft FORTRAN PowerStation version 1.0 can fail when executed under Windows 98, presenting a run time error instead of the usual graphic output. This error does not occur in version 1.0a. To determine which version you are running, run LINK.EXE from the BIN directory. If you are running version 1.0a, the text Version 1.0F appears.

Solution

Upgrade to version 1.0a. To obtain the patch to upgrade PowerStation, contact Microsoft Product Support Services at the number listed in your documentation, or, if you live in the U.S. or Canada, call (425) 635-7015. You can also download the file FPSFIX.EXE from the Microsoft Software Library (MSL) on CompuServe or on Anonymous FTP.

Related KB article Q188978 or PROGRAMS.TXT in your WINDOWS folder.

HiJaak Graphic Suite Causes a Loss of System Resources

You run SMUGGLER.EXE and lose system resources or have other problems.

Solution One

Use the screen capture utility for only short periods and periodically restart your computer to regain system resources.

Solution Two

Obtain a Windows 98 version of this program. If you are in the U.S., call Inset Systems, Inc., at (800) DR-INSET. Otherwise, call (203) 740-2400.

Related KB article Q188978 or PROGRAMS.TXT in your WINDOWS folder

HP Picture Link Software Causes Errors

You run Windows 98 and receive one of the following error messages:

> *DTOLE caused an invalid page fault in module KERNEL32.DLL*

> *PROCDB caused a General Protection Fault in module Kernel32.dll*

This occurs when you have installed the Hewlett-Packard PictureLink software included with the Hewlett-Packard Office Jet drivers.

Solution

Contact Hewlett-Packard for an update for this software.

Related KB article Q192969

Picture It! Trial Version Does Not Install

You try to install the trial version of Microsoft Picture It! 2.0 included in the CDSAMPLE\DEMOS\PITRIAL.CD folder on your Windows 98 CD-ROM and receive the following error message:

> *Setup Error 544: Setup is unable to open the data file "<CD-ROM drive letter>:\cdsample\demos\pitrial.cd\acmsetup.stf"; run Setup again from where you originally ran it.*

If you then click OK, you receive the following error message:

> *Setup Error 723: Setup was unable to read configuration information from the first section of the setup file <CD-ROM drive letter>:\cdsample\demos\pitrial.cd\acmsetup.stf.*

This occurs if you try to install the trial version of Microsoft Picture It! 2.0 by double-clicking the ACMSETUP.EXE file instead of SETUP.EXE.

Solution

Double-click the SETUP.EXE file instead of the ACMSETUP.EXE file.

Related KB article Q193500

QuarkXPress 3.3 or PageMaker 5.0 Network Error Message

You run QuarkXPress 3.3 or Pagemaker 5.0 on a computer using Microsoft Client for Netware and Dial-Up Networking and get the following error message:

> *Unable to access network [116]*

This happens when only the Dial-Up Networking/IPX components are loaded and the computer is not logged onto a valid network.

Solution One

Connect your computer to a valid network.

Solution Two

Remove the Dial-Up Networking/IPX components as described in the following steps:

1. Click the Start button, choose Settings, and then click Control Panel.

2. Double-click the Network icon.

3. Select Dial-Up Adapter from the list box, and then click Properties.

4. Click the Bindings tab, and clear the check box next to IPX/SPX-Compatible Protocol.

Figure 2-30.   *The Dial-Up Adapter Properties dialog box.*

5. Click OK, and then restart your system when prompted.

Solution Three

Upgrade to QuarkXPress 3.32 or higher.

Related KB article   Q188978 or PROGRAMS.TXT in your WINDOWS folder

---

QuarkXPress 3.3 Out-of-Memory Error

When you run QuarkXPress 3.3, you encounter an out-of-memory error.

Solution

Upgrade to QuarkXPress version 3.32 or higher.

Related KB article   Q188978 or PROGRAMS.TXT in your WINDOWS folder

---

Internet and Communications

Ascend 97 Franklin Day Planner Does Not Install Properly

Ascend Franklin Day Planner does not install properly in Windows 98.

Solution

Rename the MFC42.DLL in the WINDOWS\SYSTEM folder before installing the program.

1. Close all open programs.

2. Click the Start button, choose Find, and then click Files Or Folders.

3. Enter *mfc42.dll* in the Named text box.

4. Click Browse, locate your WINDOWS\SYSTEM directory, and then click OK.

5. Click Find Now.

6. Right-click the MFC42.DLL file, and choose Rename from the shortcut menu.

7. Rename the file, and then install Ascend Franklin Day Planner.

Related KB article Q188978 or PROGRAMS.TXT in your WINDOWS folder

Compaq Phone Center Jetfighter Upgrade Causes Windows to Hang

You restart your computer during the installation of Compaq Phone Center Jetfighter Upgrade and see a blank screen, or Windows 98 stops responding. This is because Compaq Phone Center Jetfighter Upgrade installs a version of the VRTWD.386 file that is incompatible with Windows 98. Microsoft has confirmed that this behavior is not caused by a problem in Windows 98, but may be caused by design changes in Windows 98.

Solution One

1. Restart your computer using your Windows 98 Startup disk, and enable support for your CD-ROM drive when you are prompted to do so.

2. Extract a new copy of the VRTWD.386 file from your original Windows 98 CD-ROM to the C:\REALTIME\SYSTEM folder. The VRTWD.386 file is located in the WIN98_22.CAB cabinet file. For information about how to use the Extract tool, type *extract* at a command prompt.

3. Remove your Windows 98 Startup disk, and then restart your computer.

Solution Two

Contact Compaq Technical Support for information about this issue and a possible solution.

Related KB article Q186843

Crescendo! Internet Explorer Plug-In May Not Work Correctly

You try to use the Crescendo! plug-in for Internet Explorer, and it doesn't work correctly. This can occur under any of the following conditions:

- If you upgrade Internet Explorer version 4.0 to 4.01.
- If you upgrade Microsoft Windows 95 to Windows 98.
- If you reinstall Internet Explorer version 4.0 or 4.01.

Solution

To resolve this issue, reinstall the Crescendo! plug-in. For information about how to do so, contact Crescendo!

Related KB article Q187693

DirectPC 1.6D Causes Windows to Hang

You quit the ISA version of DirectPC 1.6D, and your computer stops responding. This happens if you are using a Sound III 336SP modem. Windows 98 installs drivers for this modem provided by ZyXEL which are incompatible with DirectPC 1.6D.

Microsoft has confirmed that this behavior is not caused by a problem in Windows 98, but may be caused by design changes in Windows 98.

Solution

Install the Sound III 336SP modem drivers from the disk included with your modem by following these steps:

1. Click the Start button, choose Settings, and then click Control Panel.
2. Double-click the System icon, and then click the Device Manager tab.
3. Double-click the Modems branch to expand it, and then click Sound III 336SP.
4. Click Properties, click the Driver tab, and then click Update Driver.
5. Click Next.
6. Click Display A List Of All Drivers In A Specific Location, So You Can Select The Driver You Want, and then click Next.
7. Click Have Disk, specify the drive or folder containing the manufacturer's disk in the Copy Manufacturer's Files From box, and then click OK.

If you do not have the original driver disk included with your modem, contact the modem manufacturer to obtain the appropriate drivers.

Related KB article Q188105

Exchange and Schedule+ Advanced Tools Menus Don't Work

The advanced Tools menus in Exchange and Schedule+ don't work properly.

Solution

After installing or reinstalling Windows 98, reinstall Microsoft Exchange and Microsoft Schedule+.

Related KB article Q188978 or PROGRAMS.TXT in your WINDOWS folder

FaxWorks 3.0 Call Center Does Not Appear

When your default printer has a very long name, FaxWorks 3.0 may not display the Call Center dialog box.

Solution One

If your default printer is local, shorten your default printer's name by following these steps:

1. Click the Start button, choose Settings, and then click Printers.

2. Click the printer's name, and then click it again after a second or two.

3. Enter a shorter name in the text box.

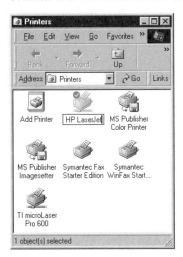

Figure 2-31. *The Printers folder.*

Solution Two

If your printer is a network printer, capture the printer port by following these steps:

1. Click the Start button, choose Settings, and then click Printers.

2. Right-click the network printer you want to use, and choose Properties from the shortcut menu.

3. Click the Details tab, and then click Capture Printer Port.

4. Choose the printer port you want to use from the Device drop-down list box.

5. Choose a network printer or enter the path to the printer you want to use in the Path drop-down list box.

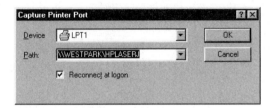

Figure 2-32. *The Capture Printer Port dialog box.*

6. Click OK.

Related KB article Q188978 or PROGRAMS.TXT in your WINDOWS folder

FaxWorks 3 Causes Lost Hard Disk Space or System Lockup

You use the Advanced AGC option (Audio Gain Control) designed to adjust incoming call voice volume on FaxWorks 3.00f.041, and your hard drive gradually fills up and eventually locks up Windows 98.

Solution

Do not use the Advanced AGC control. To regain lost hard disk space, delete any large .TMP files in your WINDOWS\TEMP directory.

Related KB article Q188978 or PROGRAMS.TXT in your WINDOWS folder

Hilgraeve HyperACCESS Script Won't Run

You attempt to use a script with Hilgraeve HyperACCESS version 8.1, but the script won't run. This occurs because the VBSCRIPT.DLL file included with Internet Explorer is incompatible with HyperACCESS 8.1.

Solution

For more information about this issue, please contact Hilgraeve Technical Support for an upgrade compatible with Internet Explorer.

Related KB article Q187250

Lotus cc:Mail Doesn't See New Calling Card Rules

You upgrade Microsoft Windows 95 to Windows 98, and the new calling card rules you create using the Modems tool in Control Panel do not appear in Lotus cc:Mail versions 6.1, 7.0, or 8.01. These versions of cc:Mail obtain dialing properties directly from the TELEPHON.INI file. Windows 98 stores dialing properties in the following Registry key instead of in the TELEPHON.INI file:

`HKEY_CURRENT_USER\Software\Microsoft\Windows\CurrentVersion\Telephony\Cards`

Microsoft has confirmed that this behavior is not caused by a problem in Windows 98, but may be caused by design changes in Windows 98.

Solution One

Create new calling card rules in cc:Mail by following these steps:

1. In cc:Mail, choose Locations from the Actions menu.

2. Click Edit Office, and then click Edit Dialing Rule to create your calling card rule.

Solution Two

Contact Lotus Technical Support for information on retaining the calling card rules created using the Modems tool in Windows 95.

Related KB article Q186745

Lotus Notes Displays Error Messages

You try to install Lotus Notes and receive a general protection fault (GPF) error message. Also, you may experience the following symptoms in Internet Explorer after you install Lotus Notes:

- If you configure Internet Explorer to use a proxy, this proxy server setting is disabled whenever you start Lotus Notes.

- If you enable the Every Visit To The Page or Every Time You Start Internet Explorer option in the Internet Options dialog box, the option is changed to Never whenever you start Lotus Notes.

This occurs because Lotus Notes changes a Registry setting that is associated with the proxy server.

Solution One

Upgrade to Lotus Notes version 4.61.

Solution Two

Contact Lotus to inquire about the availability of a fix for this issue.

Solution Three

Modify the WINDOWS\NOTES.INI file to keep Lotus Notes from writing to any of Internet Explorer's Registry settings by following these steps:

1. Click the Start button, choose Find, and then click Files Or Folders.

2. In the Named box, enter *Notes.ini*, and click Find Now.

3. Double-click the NOTES.INI file in the Windows folder, and then add the following line:

```
NOSYNCINTERNETSETTINGS=1
```

4. Choose Save from the File menu.

5. Restart your computer.

Related KB article Q186202

Lotus Notes Doesn't Install from a Network

The Lotus Notes installation program refuses to work properly when launched from a computer on a network.

Solution

Map a drive letter to the network computer with the Lotus Notes setup files by following these steps:

1. Click the Start button, choose Programs, and then click Windows Explorer.

2. Choose Map Network Drive from the Tools menu.

3. Select a drive letter for the network drive from the Drive drop-down list box.

4. Choose a network resource or enter the path in the Path drop-down list box.

Figure 2-33. *The Map Network Drive dialog box.*

5. Click OK.

6. Choose the drive that you just mapped. Find the Lotus Notes Setup Program.

7. Install Lotus Notes on your computer.

Related KB article Q188978 or PROGRAMS.TXT in your WINDOWS folder

Lotus Notes Windows Client 3.2 Doesn't Work Properly

You use Lotus Notes Windows Client 3.2 on a computer using the NetBIOS interface over IPX and NetBEUI protocol stacks and encounter problems. This occurs if the port for NetBIOS is not configured to use the correct unit number for each protocol.

Solution

Configure the port for NetBIOS using the correct unit number for each protocol. In the Lotus Notes Windows client, choose Setup from the Tools menu, and then click Ports. The default number for the first NetBIOS protocol is initially set to 0; then any additional NetBIOS interface starts at port 7 through 1. NetBIOS will probably use 7 or 6 if NetBEUI is using 0.

Related KB article Q188978 or PROGRAMS.TXT in your WINDOWS folder

Microsoft Mail Is Corrupted

You upgrade from Windows for Workgroups 3.x, and Microsoft Mail is corrupted.

Solution

Install Windows Messaging Update and update your Microsoft Message files by following these steps:

1. Insert your Windows 98 CD-ROM.

2. In Windows Explorer, double-click the EXUPDUSA.EXE file in the \TOOLS\OLDWIN95\ EXCHANGE folder on your Windows 98 CD.

3. After installing and configuring Windows Messaging, launch Windows Messaging.

4. To connect to your post office, choose Import Folder from the File menu.

5. Locate and import your Microsoft Mail message file (*.MMF) into Windows Messaging.

Note Installation of the Windows Messaging Update disables the group scheduling functionality of Schedule+ 1.0.

Related KB article Q188978 or PROGRAMS.TXT in your WINDOWS folder

Netmeter Causes an Invalid Page Fault

You try to use Dial-Up Networking to connect to another computer (such as your Internet service provider), or you try to connect to your Handheld PC (H/PC) using Microsoft Windows CE Services, and you receive one or more of the following error messages:

NETMETER caused an invalid page fault in module <unknown> at 0000:88595f1e

RNAAPP caused an invalid page fault in module <unknown> at 0000:88595f1e

RUNDLL32 caused an invalid page fault in module KERNEL32.DLL at 0157:bff79fcf.

The memory address in any of these error messages may vary.

This occurs if you are running the Starfish Internet Utilities 97 program called Netmeter, which is not compatible with Windows 98.

Solution

Uninstall Netmeter. For information about how to do so, consult the documentation included with Netmeter.

Related KB article Q186399

Outlook 98 Reports You Have an Earlier Version of MSN

You start Microsoft Outlook 98 by using the Inbox icon on the desktop, and you receive a message stating that you have an earlier version of MSN, The Microsoft Network, installed, and that a newer version is available.

Note When you install Outlook 98, the Inbox icon is normally changed to an Outlook icon, but in some cases the Inbox icon may not be changed.

Solution One

Install a newer version of The Microsoft Network.

Solution Two

Continue to start your mail program.

Solution Three

Create a new Outlook shortcut by following these steps:

1. Click the Start button, choose Programs, and then right-click Microsoft Outlook.

2. Click Copy.

3. Right-click the desktop, and then click Paste.

Related KB article Q189077

Packard Bell Comm Central Program Has Incoming Fax Problem

You upgrade to Windows 98, and the Packard Bell Comm Central program doesn't correctly receive incoming faxes.

Solution One

Quit Comm Central before you try to receive a fax.

Solution Two

Contact Packard Bell for more information about resolving this issue.

Related KB article Q186233

ProComm Plus 4.0 for Windows Stops Responding

You try to view Browser properties in the web browser included with ProComm Plus 4.0 for Windows, and the Properties window doesn't appear, and ProComm Plus stops responding.

Solution

Upgrade to ProComm Plus for Windows version 4.51 or later, or contact Quarterdeck to inquire about the availability of a fix for this issue.

Related KB article Q186280

ProComm Plus Web Browser Displays Error Message

You attempt to view a web page using the web browser included with ProComm Plus version 4.0 and receive a general protection (GP) fault in the KERNEL32.DLL file.

Solution One

Use Internet Explorer instead of the web browser included with ProComm Plus version 4.0 by following these steps:

1. Click the Start button, choose Programs, choose Accessories, and then click Dial-Up Networking.

2. Double-click the Dial-Up Networking connection for your Internet service provider (ISP).

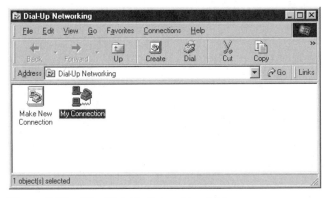

Figure 2-34. *The Dial-Up Networking folder.*

3. When you are connected to your ISP, click the Start button, choose Programs, choose Internet Explorer, and then click Internet Explorer.

Solution Two

For information about a possible resolution to this issue, contact Quarterdeck.

Related KB article Q187360

Symantec pcANYWHERE Displays Modem Error Message

You use Symantec pcANYWHERE to dial out by modem to establish a connection and receive an *Error initializing modem* error message. When this occurs, the modem continues to dial out and the connection is established. This behavior is caused by pcANYWHERE 7.0 trying to make two calls at once. The functionality of pcANYWHERE is not affected, but the error message may appear every time you dial out with a modem to establish a pcANYWHERE connection.

Solution One

Click OK when you receive the *Error initializing modem* error message.

Solution Two

Contact Symantec to upgrade to pcANYWHERE 7.5 or later.

Related KB article Q190840

Windows Messaging Reports Error Receiving Fax

You view message headers using Microsoft Windows Messaging and see the following fax header: *Error receiving fax from <xxx-xxx-xxxx>* This header may be present even if no errors occurred during transmission. When this occurs, you may be unable to open the fax because no program is associated with the Microsoft Fax (.AWD) file type.

This behavior occurs for noneditable faxes if Imaging for Windows is not installed. Imaging for Windows is used to render noneditable faxes in Windows 98.

Solution

Install Imaging for Windows by following these steps:

1. Insert your Windows 98 CD-ROM.

2. Click the Start button, choose Settings, click Control Panel, and then double-click the Add/Remove Programs icon.

3. Click the Windows Setup tab, select Accessories, and then click Details.

4. Click the Imaging check box to select it, and then click OK.

5. Click OK.

Related KB article Q192465

Utilities

Adaptec EZ-SCSI 4.0 and Adaptec Easy-CD Pro 95 Display Error Messages

You install the Adaptec EZ-SCSI 4.0 and the Adaptec Easy-CD Pro 95 programs and see the following error message:

Windows Protection Error: You need to restart your computer.

You may be able to use Windows, but you may not be able to use the EZ-SCSI 4.0 and Easy-CD Pro 95 programs. Microsoft has confirmed that this behavior is not caused by a problem in Windows 98, but may be caused by design changes in Windows 98.

Solution

Uninstall these programs by following these steps:

1. Restart your computer. After your computer completes the Power On Self Test (POST), press and hold down the Ctrl key until the Windows 98 Startup menu appears, and then choose Safe Mode.

2. Uninstall the EZ-SCSI 4.0 and Easy-CD Pro 95 programs.

3. Restart your computer normally.

Related KB article Q186844

Chameleon 4.0 Utilities Cause System Errors

You use the Chameleon 4.0 utilities and receive general protection (GP) faults and system errors. Chameleon 4.0 is incompatible with Microsoft Transmission Control Protocol/Internet Protocol (TCP/IP); Chameleon requires its own (user-mode) TCP/IP. Chameleon utilities run only with NetManage TCP/IP.

Solution One

Remove Microsoft TCP/IP from the list of installed network components by following these steps:

1. Click the Start button, choose Settings, and then click Control Panel.

2. Double-click the Network icon.

3. Select TCP/IP from the Components box, and then click Remove.

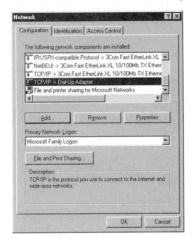

Figure 2-35. *The Configuration tab of the Network dialog box.*

4. Click OK.

5. When prompted, click Yes to restart your computer.

Solution Two

If you want to keep Microsoft TCP/IP installed on your computer, install NetManage TCP/IP included with Chameleon and unbind Microsoft TCP/IP from all installed network clients and services.

To unbind Microsoft TCP/IP, follow these steps:

1. Click the Start button, choose Settings, and then click Control Panel.

2. Double-click the Network icon.

3. Select Microsoft TCP/IP from the Components box, and then click Properties.

4. Click the Bindings tab.

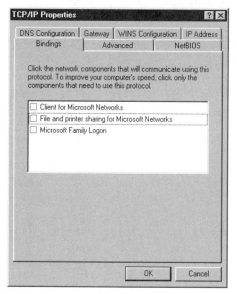

Figure 2-36.   *The Bindings tab of theTCP/IP Properties dialog box.*

5. Make sure all check boxes are cleared (not selected), and then click OK.

6. Click OK.

7. When prompted, click Yes to restart your computer.

Microsoft TCP/IP should now be unbound. When you need to use Microsoft TCP/IP again, it must be rebound to the network clients and services.

Solution Three

Contact NetManage to inquire about a possible updated version of Chameleon that is compatible with Microsoft TCP/IP.

Related KB article Q124047

CleanSweep 3.0 Renders Windows 98 Inoperable

You install Quarterdeck CleanSweep 3.04 or earlier and find key Windows files are overwritten, making Windows 98 unusable.

Solution One

If you have already installed CleanSweep 3.04 or earlier, you may need to reinstall Windows. If you must install CleanSweep 3.04 or earlier, consult the Quarterdeck support web site's Windows 98 issues pages for the procedure. Read and follow the instructions for installing this software carefully.

Solution Two

Install CleanSweep version 3.05 or later.

Related KB article Q188978 or PROGRAMS.TXT in your WINDOWS folder

Colorado Backup Does Not Detect Tape Drive

You try to use Hewlett-Packard's Colorado Backup for Windows 95 program in Windows 98, but it doesn't detect your tape drive. This happens even though your tape drive is listed in Device Manager. This behavior occurs if Microsoft Backup is currently installed or has been installed in the past.

Solution

Substitute Colorado Backup for Microsoft Backup:

1. Click the Start button, choose Settings, and then click Control Panel.

2. Double-click the Add/Remove Programs icon, and then click the Windows Setup tab.

3. Click System Tools (click the phrase, not the check box), and then click Details.

4. Clear the Backup check box, click OK, click OK again, and then click Yes to restart your computer.

Figure 2-37. *The System Tools dialog box in the Add/Remove Programs tool.*

5. Delete the following files, if they exist:

File Name	Location
PNPWPROP.DLL	WINDOWS\SYSTEM
PNPWRENU.DLL	WINDOWS\SYSTEM
PNPWFDC.INF	WINDOWS\INF
PNPWIDE.INF	WINDOWS\INF
PNPWPPT.INF	WINDOWS\INF
PNPWTAPE.INF	WINDOWS\INF
PNPWTAPE.CAT	WINDOWS\CATROOT\{F750E6C3-38EE-11D1-85E5-00C04FC295EE}

6. Click the Start button, click Run, and enter *Regedit* in the Run box. Click OK.

7. Navigate your way down through the folders in the left pane until you locate the following Registry keys, if they exist:

```
HKEY_LOCAL_MACHINE\System\CurrentControlSet\Services\Class\Tape
```

```
HKEY_LOCAL_MACHINE\System\CurrentControlSet\Services\Class\TapeController
```

```
HKEY_LOCAL_MACHINE\System\CurrentControlSet\Services\Class\TapeDetection
```

Warning Please read the Introduction for information on how to safely edit the Registry.

8. Delete the keys.

9. Close Regedit.

10. Restart your computer.

11. Check Device Manager to verify that the Windows 98 tape icons and drivers no longer exist, and remove them if they are present.

For information about removing a device in Device Manager, click Start, click Help, click the Index tab, enter *device manager*, and then double-click the Removing Hardware topic.

Note There are two different tape drive icons: a gray icon from Microsoft, and a blue icon from Colorado Backup. After you uninstall Microsoft Backup, the gray icon may remain in Device Manager, and you may need to remove it manually.

12. Reinstall Colorado Backup and test to determine if the issue is resolved by verifying that your tape drive is detected. For more information about how to do so, contact the program's manufacturer or review the documentation included with your tape drive.

13. If the tape drive is still not detected by the tape software, contact Hewlett-Packard or view the documentation included with your tape drive.

Note Microsoft Backup is not installed by default in Windows 98. If Backup was installed in Microsoft Windows 95 before you installed Windows 98, Backup is upgraded to the Windows 98 version.

Related KB article Q189870

CyberMedia First Aid 97 Causes Illegal Operation Error Message

The following error messages can occur the first time you reboot after installing Windows 98 or when you access a web site that runs a Java program if you have installed a version of CyberMedia First Aid 97 earlier than version 4.02.

This program has performed an illegal operation and will be shut down. If the problem persists, contact the program vendor.

If you click Details, you receive an error message similar to one of the following:

<Program> caused an access violation fault in module Gdi32.dll.

<Program> caused an invalid page fault in module Gdi32.dll.

<Program> caused an invalid page fault in module Kernel32.dll.

Solution

To prevent this problem, contact CyberMedia or visit its Web site to obtain and install a First Aid 97 update.

Related KB article Q166209

CyberMedia First Aid 97 Displays Error Message

You run an inventory report in CyberMedia First Aid 97 Deluxe in Windows 98 and receive the following error message:

```
FAP32.EXE caused an "Access Violation" fault in module FAINV32.DLL at
015F:00BB66D6
```

Note that the memory address in this error message may vary.

This problem can occur because First Aid 97 is looking for system information that exists in Microsoft Windows 95 but is not in Windows 98.

Solution One

Upgrade to CyberMedia First Aid 98.

Solution Two

Contact CyberMedia Technical Support to inquire about obtaining an update for First Aid 97.

Related KB article Q186019

CyberMedia First Aid 97 Displays Invalid Page Fault Error

You try to log on to your computer after you log off and see an invalid page fault error message. Also, you may receive the same invalid page fault error message when you try to start or a program. This occurs if you are running CyberMedia First Aid 97.

Solution One

Instead of logging off, restart your computer.

Solution Two

Upgrade to CyberMedia First Aid98.

Related KB article Q186693

CyberMedia Guard Dog Slows Windows 98 Startup

Windows 98 may start and run slowly when you run a version of CyberMedia Guard Dog earlier than version 1.09. When you start your computer, the Windows 98 startup process may take up to 10 times longer than normal, and, after startup, Windows 98 may run very slowly.

Solution One

Upgrade to Guard Dog version 1.09 or later from CyberMedia.

Solution Two

Uninstall Guard Dog. If required, contact CyberMedia Technical Support for instructions.

Related KB article Q191845

Icon Disappear or Icon Ripper Causes Computer to Hang

You install Icon Disappear 2.0 or Icon Ripper and restart your computer, and it stops responding (hangs), and you receive the following error message:

> *Error Starting Program. The SHELL32.DLL file is linked to missing export COMCTL32:386.*

This behavior occurs because Icon Disappear 2.0 overwrites the COMCTL32.DLL file. To solve this problem, you will need to extract and replace the COMCTL32.DLL file from your Windows 98 CD-ROM. The method you choose depends on your hardware. Solutions One and Two require a Windows 98 Startup Disk. If you do not already have one, create one by following these steps:

1. Click the Start button, choose Settings, click Control Panel, and then double-click the Add/Remove Programs icon.

2. Click the Startup Disk tab, click Create Disk, and then follow the instructions on the screen.

Solution One

If your computer has an IDE CD-ROM drive, follow these steps.

Note To determine what type of CD-ROM drive you have, see the documentation included with your computer or CD-ROM drive.

1. Insert the Windows 98 Startup disk in the floppy disk drive, and then restart your computer.

2. Choose Load IDE CDROM Driver from the Startup menu, and then press Enter.

3. At the command prompt, type the following commands, pressing Enter after each one:

```
c:

cd \windows\system

ren comctl32.dll comctl32.xxx

a:
```

4. Insert the Windows 98 CD-ROM in the CD-ROM drive, type the following line, and then press Enter:

```
extract /a <drv>:\win98\base3.cab comctl32.dll /l c:\windows\system
```

   (<drv> is one letter after the drive letter normally assigned to your CD-ROM drive. For example, if the drive letter normally assigned to your CD-ROM drive is D, type E in the command.)

5. Remove the Windows 98 Startup disk from the floppy disk drive, and then restart your computer.

Solution Two

If your computer has a Small Computer System Interface (SCSI) CD-ROM drive and an Adaptec, Mylex, or BusLogic SCSI adapter, follow these steps:

Note To determine what type of CD-ROM drive and SCSI adapter you have, see the documentation included with your computer, SCSI adapter, or CD-ROM drive.

1. Insert the Windows 98 Startup disk in the floppy disk drive, and then restart your computer.

2. Choose Load SCSI CDROM Driver (Adaptec) or Load SCSI CDROM Driver (Mylex\BusLogic) from the Startup menu, and then press Enter.

3. At the command prompt, type the following commands, pressing Enter after each one:

```
c:

cd \windows\system

ren comctl32.dll comctl32.xxx

a:
```

4. Insert the Windows 98 CD-ROM in the CD-ROM drive, type the following line, and then press Enter:

```
extract /a <drv>:\win98\base3.cab comctl32.dll /l c:\windows\system
```

(<drv> is one letter after the drive letter normally assigned to your CD-ROM drive. For example, if the drive letter normally assigned to your CD-ROM drive is D, you should type E in the command.)

5. Remove the Windows 98 Startup disk from the floppy disk drive, and then restart your computer.

Solution Three

If your computer can boot from your CD-ROM, follow these steps:

Note To determine if your computer can boot from your CD-ROM, see the documentation included with your computer. For information about how to configure your computer to use the CD-ROM drive as the bootable device, see the documentation included with your computer

1. Configure your computer to use the CD-ROM drive to boot your computer.

2. Insert the Windows 98 CD-ROM in the CD-ROM drive, restart your computer, and then choose Boot From CD-ROM when you are prompted.

3. Choose Command Prompt With CD-ROM Support (IDE) or Command Prompt With CD-ROM Support (SCSI) when you are prompted.

4. At the command prompt, type the following commands, pressing Enter after each one:

```
c:

cd \windows\system

ren comctl32.dll comctl32.xxx

<drv>:

cd \win98

extract /a <drv>:\win98\base3.cab comctl32.dll /l c:\windows\system
```

(<drv> is the drive letter assigned to your CD-ROM drive.)

5. Restart your computer, configure your computer to use the hard disk as the bootable device, and then restart your computer again.

Related KB article Q179302

Iomega Ditto Tools 3.0 Displays Error Message

You try to start the The Works program included with Iomega Ditto Tools version 3.0 and see the following error message:

DT Caused an Invalid Page Fault in Module TFSWNTFY.DLL at 015f:00d713d8

Also, the Ditto Tools and File!Flash programs included with Iomega Ditto Tools version 3.0 may not work correctly, or at all, as these programs in combination are not fully compatible with Windows 98. Microsoft has confirmed that this behavior is not caused by a problem in Windows 98, but may be caused by design changes in Windows 98.

Solution One

Uninstall either Ditto Tools or File!Flash.

Solution Two

Contact Iomega to inquire about the availability of a fix for this issue.

Related KB article Q186737

Iomega Ditto Tools Folder and Icons Missing

After you install Iomega Ditto Max Tools version 3.0 in Windows 98, restart your computer, click the Start button, and then choose Programs, you may notice that the Ditto Tools folder and icons are missing. This occurs because when you install Iomega Ditto Max Tools version 3.0 in Windows 98, Ditto Max Tools does not install the Ditto Max Tools folder and icons into the WINDOWS\START MENU\PROGRAMS folder correctly. Microsoft has confirmed that this behavior is not caused by a problem in Windows 98, but may be caused by design changes in Windows 98.

Solution

Copy the appropriate folder to the WINDOWS\START MENU\PROGRAMS folder by following these steps:

1. Click the Start button, choose Programs, and then click Windows Explorer.

2. Right-click the WINDOWS\PROFILES\SOFTWARE\START MENU\PROGRAMS\IOMEGA BACKUP folder, and then click Copy.

3. Right-click the WINDOWS\START MENU\PROGRAMS folder, and then click Paste.

   If you are using User Profiles, right-click the WINDOWS\PROFILES\<USERNAME>\START MENU\PROGRAMS folder, and then click Paste.

Related KB article Q187545

Matrox Diagnostic Utility Displays Error Message

You start your computer after you upgrade to Windows 98and receive a Matrox diagnostic utility error message that says you are using an older version of DirectX. This occurs even if you have the current version of DirectX installed on your computer, or because the Matrox diagnostic utility incorrectly reports that versions of DirectX newer than version 3.0 are out of date.

Solution One

Ignore the Matrox diagnostic utility error message.

Solution Two

Contact Matrox to inquire about the availability of a fix.

Related KB article   Q187270

MicroHelp Compression Plus 4.0 Doesn't Install Properly

MicroHelp Compression Plus 4.0 doesn't install correctly.

Solution

Add the word *progman* to the end of the *SHELL= line* in your SYSTEM.INI file, then reinstall MicroHelp Compression Plus by following these steps:

1. Click the Start button, and then click Run.

2. Enter *msconfig* in the Open text box, and click OK.

3. Click the SYSTEM.INI tab in the System Configuration Utility.

4. Click the plus sign next to the [boot] folder, and then select the shell=Explorer.exe entry.

5. Click Edit, and then enter a space followed by *progman* at the end of the entry.

Figure 2-38. *The SYSTEM.INI file in the System Configuration Utility.*

6. Click OK, restart your computer, and then reinstall MicroHelp Compression Plus.

7. Follow steps 1–4 after you're finished installing your program and delete *progman* from the shell=Explorer.exe line.

Related KB article Q188978 or PROGRAMS.TXT in your WINDOWS folder

Norton Backup Doesn't Run Properly

Norton Backup doesn't run correctly. Windows 98 requires new settings for this program.

Solution

Before you run Norton Backup, delete the *NBACKUP.PIF* file located in the Norton Backup directory.

Related KB article Q188978 or PROGRAMS.TXT in your WINDOWS folder

Norton Disk Doctor Does Not Run Automatically

You upgrade Microsoft Windows 95 to Windows 98 or reinstall Windows 98, and the Norton Disk Doctor utility included with Symantec Norton Utilities 2.0s or 3.0x does not automatically run after an improper shutdown of Windows. ScanDisk for MS-DOS runs instead.

This occurs because Norton Utilities updates the WIN.COM file to run the Norton Disk Doctor (NDD.EXE) utility when Windows is shut down improperly. When you upgrade Windows 95 to Windows 98 or reinstall Windows 98, the WIN.COM file is replaced, and ScanDisk is used as the default disk diagnostic utility. This is a known issue with Symantec Norton Utilities versions 2.0s and 3.0x. For additional information about this issue, please contact Symantec Technical Support.

Solution One

Install Norton Utilities again.

Solution Two

At a command prompt from within Windows 98, type the following commands, pressing Enter after each one:

```
cd c:\

cd \windows\command

copy ndd.exe scandisk.alt
```

This creates a copy of the Norton Disk Doctor utility named SCANDISK.ALT. When Windows is shut down improperly, the SCANDISK.ALT file (which is now the Norton Disk Doctor utility) automatically runs.

Related KB article Q186885

Norton Disk Doctor 2.0 Doesn't Run After an Improper Shutdown

You shut down Windows improperly, and Norton Disk Doctor 2.0 doesn't run if you installed Norton Utilities 2.0 prior to upgrading to Windows 98.

Solution One

Reinstall Norton Disk Doctor

Solution Two

Modify the Norton Disk Doctor files as follows:

1. Click the Start button, choose Programs, and then click MS-DOS Prompt.

2. Use the CD command to change to a \WINDOWS prompt, then type `CD Command` and press Enter to change to the COMMAND directory.

3. Type *copy ndd.exe scandisk.alt*, and then press Enter.

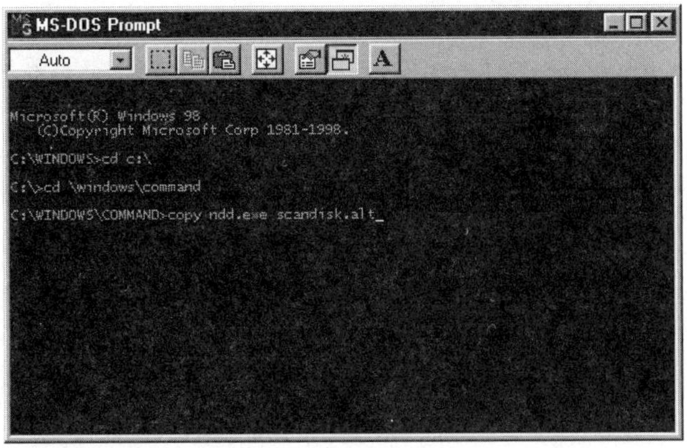

Figure 2-39. *The MS-DOS Prompt.*

4. Type *exit* to return to Windows. Norton Disk Doctor will now run correctly after improper shutdowns.

Related KB article Q188978 or PROGRAMS.TXT in your WINDOWS folder

Norton Navigator's Icons Do Not Launch Any Applets

You install Norton Navigator on a clean install of Window 98, and the shortcut icons placed on the Start menu do not work.

Solution

Manually edit these shortcuts to point to the correct *.CPL files in your \WINDOWS\SYSTEM directory.

Related KB article Q188978 or PROGRAMS.TXT in your WINDOWS folder

Nuts & Bolts Version 1.03 or 1.04 Causes General Protection Fault Error

You try to view the System Resources category in the Discover section of the NAI Nuts & Bolts version 1.03 or 1.04 program, and you receive a general-protection (GP) fault error message in either the DISCPRO.EXE or KRNL386.EXE module. This problem may not have occurred when you have previously used this feature on a Microsoft Windows 95–based computer. It occurs because some of the NAI Nuts & Bolts version 1.03 or 1.04 program files are not totally compatible with Windows 98.

Solution

Contact NAI to inquire about the availability of a fix for this problem.

Related KB article Q192801

Nuts & Bolts DiskMinder Displays Error Message

You start your computer after improperly shutting it down and receive an NAI Nuts & Bolts DiskMinder error message that says an invalid command line argument was used. This occurs if you are using the NAI Nuts & Bolts DiskMinder program instead of ScanDisk as your disk repair program. NAI Nuts & Bolts DiskMinder is unable to correctly interpret the /simpleui switch used with ScanDisk in the WIN.COM file.

Solution

Ignore the error message, and DiskMinder can then continue normally.

Related KB article Q187290

Nuts & Bolts Registry Wizard Displays Error Message

You attempt to use the Registry Wizard tool included with Network Associates Nuts & Bolts version 1.04 or earlier and receive an error message stating that the module cannot be run in this version of Windows. The Registry Wizard tool included with these versions of Nuts & Bolts does not work in Windows 98. Microsoft has confirmed that this behavior is not caused by a problem in Windows 98, but may be caused by design changes in Windows 98.

Solution

Contact Network Associates Technical Support for information about a possible solution.

Related KB article Q186853

PCTools Shortcuts Are Missing

You install PCTools versions 7 through 9, and no shortcuts are created in Windows 98.

Solution

Create shortcuts for PCTools by following these steps:

1. Click the Start button, and then click Run.

2. Enter *cpsdos.grp* in the text box, and click OK.

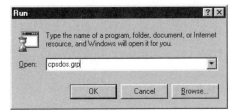

Figure 2-40. *The Run dialog box.*

3. Click the Start button, and then click Run.

4. Enter *notepad c:\autoexec.bat* in the text box, and then click OK.

5. Enter *PATH C:\PCTOOLS* or the path to wherever you installed PCTools on a new line.

6. Choose Save from the File menu, close Notepad, and then restart your computer.

Note Because of changes to the Windows 98 file system, these disk utilities do not work correctly with long filenames. For information about purchasing disk utilities that are designed for Windows 98, contact Symantec, or view their website at *http://www.symantec.com*.

Related KB article Q188978 or PROGRAMS.TXT in your WINDOWS folder

Quarterdeck CleanSweep Displays Error Messages

You restart your computer after you install Quarterdeck CleanSweep 95 version 3.04 or earlier and experience either of the following symptoms:

You receive the following error message:

> *Explorer*
>
> *This program has performed an illegal operation and will be shut down.*

If you then click Details, you may see the following information:

> *Explorer caused an exception 6d007fH in module Webcheck.dll at <memory address>.*

If you do not receive this error message, your computer may start, but it may display a gray-colored desktop. Note that when you start to install Quarterdeck CleanSweep 95 version 3.04 or earlier, you may receive the following message:

> *This program may not run correctly on Windows 98 because of enhanced operating system features.*

If you then click Details, you may receive a message stating that the installation will replace some vital system files and cause Windows 98 and other programs to work improperly. It then lists the files that will be overwritten and recommends you backup these files and restore them once the installation is finished.

This occurs because when you install CleanSweep 95 version 3.04 or earlier, the following system files are overwritten with older versions:

- ADVAPI32.DLL
- MFC40.DLL
- MFC42.DLL
- MSVCRT.DLL
- MSVCRT40.DLL
- OLEPRO32.DLL
- URLMON.DLL
- WININET.DLL

Solution One

Upgrade to CleanSweep version 4.02 or later.

Solution Two

Use System File Checker to extract the files listed above.

Related KB article Q185854

Quarterdeck SpeedyROM Version 1.0 Displays Error Message

You restart your computer after you upgrade to Windows 98 and see the following Quarterdeck SpeedyROM version 1.0 error message:

CD-ROM cache acceleration file is invalid. It will be reconstructed.

Also, even though SpeedyROM offers to reconstruct this file, you may continue to see this same error message whenever you restart your computer. This occurs if the your computer's Basic Input/ Output System (BIOS) is configured to use the Fast Reboot feature. Microsoft has confirmed that this behavior is not caused by a problem in Windows 98, but may be caused by design changes in Windows 98.

Solution

Disable the Fast Reboot feature in your computer's BIOS. For information on how to do so, see the documentation included with your computer or motherboard, or consult the manufacturer of your computer.

Related KB article Q187189

Quarterdeck QEMM 97 Displays Error Messages

If you are running Quarterdeck QEMM 97 and you choose Details from the File menu in QEMM Control Panel and then click Help, you may receive either of the following error messages:

QEMMDETA caused a general protection fault in module DETAILS.EXE at 0003:000070ce.

Program Error. Integer Divide by 0.

Microsoft has confirmed that this behavior is not caused by a problem in Windows 98, but may be caused by design changes in Windows 98.

Solution

Contact Quarterdeck for more information about resolving this issue.

Related KB article Q186712

Quarterdeck's QEMM Causes Computer to Stop Responding

You boot your computer in MS-DOS mode (either from the Shut Down Windows dialog box or from the properties for an MS-DOS-based application) with Quarterdeck's QEMM, the computer may stop responding (hang). This problem occurs because the QEMM QuickBoot feature does not operate correctly in Windows.

Solution One

Turn off your computer, wait several seconds, then turn your computer back on.

Solution Two

Disable the QuickBoot feature by adding the parameter *BOOTENABLE:N* to the QEMM386.SYS line in the CONFIG.SYS file. For example, after you add this parameter the line might look like

```
device=<path>\qemm386.sys bootenable:n
```

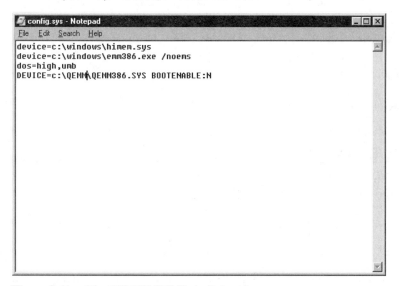

Figure 2-41. *The CONFIG.SYS file in Notepad.*

Related KB article Q127915

Seagate Backup Exec Displays Error Message After Uninstalling

You uninstall the Seagate Backup Exec program and the network protocol it used and you receive a general-protection (GP) fault in BKUPAGNT, or, when you restart your computer, you receive the following error message:

Backup Exec Agent:

Communication transport failure:

The Backup Exec Agent is unable to run because a required network component (DLL) was not found. Please check your network configuration.

This occurs because the Seagate Backup Exec program does not remove all of its registry entries when you uninstall it.

Solution

Use Registry Editor to delete the BackupExecAgent (BKUPAGNT.EXE) value.

Warning Please read the Introduction for information on how to safely edit the Registry.

---

1. Click the Start button, click Run, and enter *Regedit* into the Run box. Click OK.

2. Navigate your way down through the folders in the left pane until you locate the following Registry key:

   `HKEY_LOCAL_MACHINE\Software\Microsoft\Windows\Current\Version\RunServices`

3. Delete the BKUPAGNT.EXE value from this Registry key.

4. Close Regedit.

5. Restart your computer.

Related KB article Q188882

WIN32 SDK Debug Components Don't Work Properly

WIN32 SDK and DDK Debug components from the MSDN CD-ROM might not work properly with some Windows 98 components.

Solution

Reinstall Windows 98.

Related KB article Q188978 or PROGRAMS.TXT in your WINDOWS folder

---

Windrenalin Displays Error Message

You run Windrenalin in Windows 98 and see the following error message:

An error prevented Windrenalin from functioning.

The error code is 3441.

Windrenalin is incompatible with the updated memory management architecture of Windows 98.

Solution

Contact Syncronys Softcorp to inquire about a possible update.

Related KB article Q186295

WinShield 1.0.1 Deletes All Devices in Device Manager

You upgrade to Windows 98 without uninstalling WinShield 1.0.1, and all devices in Device Manager are deleted, or other system problems occur.

Solution One

Before upgrading to Windows 98, follow these steps to properly uninstall WinShield:

1. Remove WinShield by using the Setup program on the installation disks for the program.

2. When the program is finished uninstalling, immediately upgrade to Windows 98.

Warning To avoid deletion of all devices in Device Manager, install Windows 98 immediately after WinShield is removed. Do not restart, use the Add New Hardware Wizard, or attempt to use Device Manager before the Windows 98 installation is complete.

Solution Two

Install WinShield version 1.5 or higher.

Related KB article Q188978 or PROGRAMS.TXT in your WINDOWS folder

---

XtraDrive Does Not Load Properly

XtraDrive does not load properly when starting your system.

Solution

Insert the SETVER command in your AUTOEXEC.BAT file before XTRADRV.SYS.

Related KB article Q188978 or PROGRAMS.TXT in your WINDOWS folder

Word Processors, Spreadsheets, and Presentation Programs

Adobe Persuasion 3.0 Does Not Install

Adobe Persuasion 3.0 will not install on a computer running Windows 98 with an empty or nonexistent CONFIG.SYS file.

Solution

Create a CONFIG.SYS file or add to your existing CONFIG.SYS file by following these steps:

1. Click the Start button, choose Programs, choose Accessories, and then click Notepad.

2. Choose the File menu's Open command, enter *c:\CONFIG.SYS* in the File Name text box, and then click OK.

3. If you get an error message saying that the file was not found, click OK and then click Cancel. Choose Save As from the File menu, enter *C:\CONFIG.SYS* in the File Name text box, and then click OK.

4. Type *rem This is a temporary CONFIG.SYS file.*

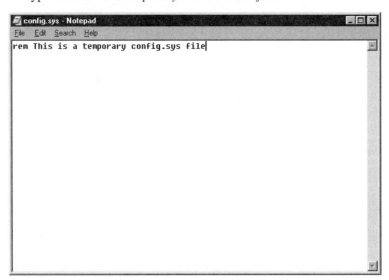

Figure 2-42. *The CONFIG.SYS file in Notepad.*

5. Choose Save As from the File menu, and then continue with your Adobe Persuasion 3.0 installation.

Related KB article Q188978 or PROGRAMS.TXT in your WINDOWS folder

Ami Pro 3.01 Tutorial Doesn't Work Right

You run the AmiPro 3.01 tutorial, and the Windows 98 taskbar interferes.

Solution

Set your taskbar to Auto Hide. To do this, click the Start button, choose Settings, and then click Taskbar And Start Menu. Select the Auto Hide check box, and then click OK.

Figure 2-43. *The Taskbar Properties dialog box.*

Related KB article Q188978 or PROGRAMS.TXT in your WINDOWS folder

ClarisWorks for Windows 3.0 Doesn't Install Properly

You install ClarisWorks for Windows 3.0 v1 from the Setup program on disk 1, and Setup will not work properly.

Solution

Run the SETUPCW program on disk 2.

Related KB article Q188978 or PROGRAMS.TXT in your WINDOWS folder

Media Blitz 3.0 Doesn't Work Properly

Media Blitz 3.0 does not run correctly when you launch the program immediately after installing it.

Solution

Restart Windows 98 after installing the program. This allows Windows to detect changes made by the Setup program.

Related KB article Q188978 or PROGRAMS.TXT in your WINDOWS folder

Microsoft Office Standard Version 7.0 Error in Data Access

You install Microsoft Office Standard for Windows version 7.0 on a computer running Windows 98, and a *Failure to load expression service* error message appears when you use the Access ODBC driver from Office programs such as Excel or Word.

Solution

Obtain the free update of Microsoft Office for Windows version 7.0b from Microsoft Product Support. If you are in the U.S., call the Microsoft Order Desk at (800) 360-7561 to obtain a copy. If you are outside the U.S., contact the Microsoft subsidiary in your area. To locate your subsidiary, call the Microsoft International Sales Information Center at (425) 936-8661.

Related KB article Q188978 or PROGRAMS.TXT in your WINDOWS folder

C H A P T E R   3

Desktop and Start Menu

Active Desktop

Channel Bar Causes Problems

You remove the Channel bar from the desktop, but the Internet Explorer Channel Bar option is unavailable in the Display tool in Control Panel.

Solution

To work around this problem, use Registry Editor to change the data value of the SHOW_CHANNELBAND value to No in the following Registry key:

HKEY_CURRENT_USER\Software\Microsoft\Internet Explorer\Main

To do so, follow these steps:

Warning Please read the Introduction for information on how to safely edit the Registry.

1. Click the Start button, click Run, enter *Regedit* in the Run box, and click OK.

2. Navigate your way down through the folders in the left pane until you locate the key described above.

3. Choose Modify from the Edit menu.

4. Modify the data value of SHOW_CHANNELBAND to No.

Figure 3-1. *The Edit String dialog box.*

5. Close Regedit.

6. Restart Windows.

Related KB article Q194173

Channel Bar Does Not Display Active Channels

You install Windows 98, and the Channel bar does not display any active channels.

This problem occurs when you copy the WIN98 folder from the Windows 98 CD-ROM to your hard disk and then install Windows 98 from the folder on your hard disk. The Channel bar files are located in the WIN98\CHANNELS folder on the Windows 98 CD-ROM. If you do not copy the folders in the WIN98 folder from the Windows 98 CD-ROM to your hard disk, this problem occurs.

Solution

To solve this problem, follow these steps:

1. Create a temporary folder on your hard disk.

2. Click the Start button, choose Programs, and then click Windows Explorer.

3. Locate the WIN98\CHANNELS folder on the Windows 98 CD-ROM.

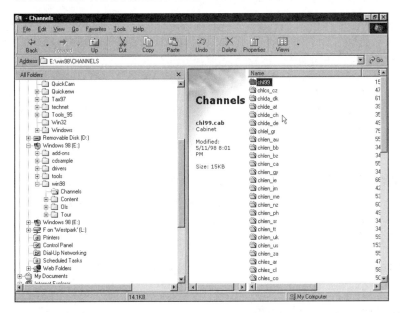

Figure 3-2. *The WIN98\CHANNELS folder holds the CHL99.CAB file.*

4. Double-click the CHL99.CAB cabinet file.

5. Choose Select All from the Edit menu.

6. Choose Extract from the File menu.

7. In the Browse For Folder dialog box, click the folder you created in step 1, and then click OK.

8. Repeat steps 3–7 to extract the CHLEN_US.CAB cabinet file.

9. Locate the folder you created in step 1.

10. Right-click the CHL99.INF file, and choose Install from the shortcut menu.

11. Right-click the CHLEN-US.INF file, and choose Install from the shortcut menu.

12. Click the Start button, choose Shut Down, click Restart, and then click OK.

13. Delete the folder you created in step 1.

Related KB article Q189466

Channel Bar Stuck Off Screen

You position the Channel bar off the screen and then try to move it back to the visible portion of the screen, but you are unable to do so.

Solution One

To resolve this problem, follow these steps:

1. Click the Start button, choose Settings, click Control Panel, and then double-click the Display icon.

2. Click the Web tab, and then clear the Internet Explorer Channel Bar check box.

3. Click OK.

4. Double-click Display, click the Web tab, and then select the Internet Explorer Channel Bar check box.

5. Click OK, and then close Control Panel.

Solution Two

If you are using multiple monitors and the Channel bar is positioned off the screen of a secondary monitor, you can clear the Extend My Windows Desktop Onto This Monitor check box to attempt to reposition the Channel bar.

Related KB article Q193151

Folder Contents Are Unavailable

You try to connect to a Windows 98 network share of the WINDOWS, WINDOWS\SYSTEM, or PROGRAM FILES folder from a Windows 95 or Windows NT computer with Active Desktop enabled, and you see one of the following messages:

Warning. Modifying the contents of this folder may cause your programs to stop working correctly. To view the contents of this folder, click Show Files.

Warning. To add or remove programs, click Start, point to Settings, click Control Panel, and then click Add/Remove programs.

Solution

To work around this problem, click Show Files.

Related KB article Q182590

HTML File Missing

You enable the Active Desktop and because of a missing or damaged MSHTML.DLL file or Registry entries, you encounter one of the following problems.

■ You receive the following error message when you attempt to enable Active Desktop:

Internet Explorer cannot find the Active Desktop HTML file. This file is needed for your Active Desktop. Click OK to turn off Active Desktop.

■ When you select As Web Page from the View menu in Windows Explorer or My Computer, nothing happens.

■ When you attempt to view a web page, Internet Explorer prompts you to open or save the file to a disk instead of displaying the web page.

Solution One

Extract a new Active Desktop HTML file. To do so, follow these steps:

1. Click the Start button, choose Find, and click Files Or Folders.

2. Enter *mshtml.dll* in the Named text box, and then click Find Now.

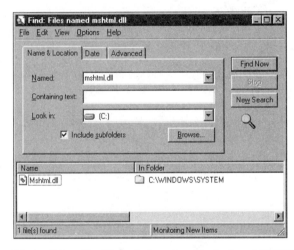

Figure 3-3. *The Find window showing the found MSHTML.DLL file.*

3. If the MSHTML.DLL file is found, right-click it, click Rename, and then type a new name for the MSHTML.DLL file (such as MSHTML.XXX).

4. Close the Find tool.

5. Use the System File Checker to extract a new copy of the MSHTML.DLL file to the WINDOWS\SYSTEM folder from your original Internet Explorer CD-ROM, the folder to which you downloaded the Internet Explorer Setup files, or your original Windows 98 disks or CD-ROM.

Note If you previously applied an update to the MSHTML.DLL file provided by Microsoft, reinstall the updated version of the MSHTML.DLL file instead of the version included with Internet Explorer or Windows 98.

Solution Two

Fix the Registry entries for the MSHTML.DLL file. To do so, follow these steps:

1. Click the Start button, and then click Run.

2. Type *regsvr32 /i mshtml.dll* in the Open text box, click OK, and then click OK again.

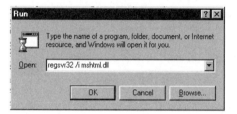

Figure 3-4. *The Run dialog box.*

3. Restart your computer.

Related KB articles Q193110, Q129605

HTML Wallpaper Causes Problems

After you select a Hypertext Markup Language (HTML) file for your desktop wallpaper, you experience one or more of the following symptoms:

- The background of your desktop appears blank.

- No icons are visible on the desktop.

- When you right-click the desktop, you do not see a context menu.

- You see your HTML wallpaper displayed in a browser window, and a bitmap file appears as the background of your desktop.

These problems can happen if any of the following conditions exist:

- Active Desktop is not enabled.

- System Policy Editor is configured to prevent the use of HTML files for wallpaper.

- System Policy Editor is configured to hide all desktop items.

Solution One

To enable the Active Desktop, follow these steps:

1. Right-click an empty area on the desktop.

2. Choose Active Desktop from the shortcut menu, and then click View As Web Page.

Solution Two

To use HTML files for wallpaper, use System Policy Editor to disable the No HTML Wallpaper policy. To do so, follow these steps:

1. Click the Start button, and click Run.

2. Type *poledit* in the Open box, and click OK.

3. Choose either Open Policy or Open Registry, as appropriate, from the File menu.

4. Double-click the user's policy file or Local User, as appropriate.

5. Double-click the Desktop category to expand it, and then click Desktop Wallpaper Settings. (Click the words, not the check box.)

6. Clear the No HTML Wallpaper check box, and then click OK.

7. Choose Save from the File menu, and then close Policy Editor.

8. Restart your computer.

Solution Three

Use System Policy Editor to disable the Hide All Items on Desktop policy. To do this, follow these steps:

1. Click Start, and click Run.

2. Type *poledit* in the Open box, and click OK.

3. Choose either Open Policy or Open Registry, as appropriate, from the File menu.

4. Double-click the user's policy file or Local User, as appropriate.

5. Double-click the Windows 98 System category to expand it, double-click the Shell category to expand it, and then click the Restrictions. (Click the words, not the check box.)

6. Clear the Hide All Items On Desktop check box, and then click OK.

7. Choose Save from the File menu, and then close Policy Editor.

8. Restart your computer.

Related KB article Q190693

IBM Aptiva Desktop Customization Doesn't Work Correctly

IBM Aptiva Desktop Customization does not work properly when the Windows 98 Active Desktop is enabled.

Solution

Disable the Active Desktop. To do so, follow these steps:

1. Click the Start button, choose Settings, and choose Active Desktop.

2. Clear the check box next to View As Web Page.

3. Click OK

Related KB article Q188978 or PROGRAMS.TXT in your WINDOWS folder

Java Programs Don't Work Offline

Active Desktop items that host Java programs stop working when Internet Explorer is offline. This can occur if the Java program has been removed from the TEMPORARY INTERNET FILES folder. Active Desktop items are retrieved from the cache when Internet Explorer is offline. If the cache reaches its maximum size, Java programs may be automatically removed from the cache to make room for current downloads. If an Active Desktop item hosts a Java program that has been removed from the cache and Internet Explorer is offline, the Active Desktop item stops working.

Solution One

Empty the TEMPORARY INTERNET FILES folder. To empty the TEMPORARY INTERNET FILES folder, follow these steps:

1. In Internet Explorer, choose Internet Options from the View menu.

2. Click the General tab, and in the Temporary Internet Files section, click Delete Files.

3. Click OK when you are prompted to delete the files, and then click OK again.

Solution Two

Increase the amount of hard disk space the Temporary Internet Files folder uses. To do so, follow these steps:

1. In Internet Explorer, choose Internet Options from the View menu.

2. Click the General tab, and in the Temporary Internet Files section, click Settings.

Figure 3-5. *The Settings dialog box.*

3. Move the Amount Of Disk Space To Use slider to the right.

4. Click OK, and then click OK again.

5. Connect to the Internet.

6. Right-click an empty area on the desktop, choose Active Desktop from the shortcut menu, and then click Update Now to update the Active Desktop items.

Related KB article Q172922

Offline Web Pages and ActiveX Content Slow to Display

You configure your desktop to display as a web page, and you add one or more web pages to your desktop, but the web pages are not displayed for several minutes after you log on, even though you're offline.

Or similarly, if you have ActiveX content on your Active Desktop, the ActiveX content does not display for several minutes after you log on but are offline. For example, if you have added the Microsoft Investor stock ticker to your Active Desktop, you might see the message *Downloading quotes* for several minutes before the quotes are loaded from the cache.

Solution

This problem can occur if your Internet Explorer connection type is set to Connect To The Internet Using A Local Area Network. When you use this setting, Internet Explorer waits several minutes for a local area network (LAN) connection before using the content from the cache.

To work around this problem, set Internet Explorer to connect to the Internet using a modem when you are not connected to the LAN. To do this, follow these steps:

1. Right-click the Internet Explorer icon on the desktop, and then choose Properties from the shortcut menu.

2. On the Connection tab, click Connect To The Internet Using A Modem, and then click Settings.

3. Select the appropriate Dial-Up Networking connection for your Internet service provider (ISP) from the Use The Following Dial-Up Networking Connection box.

4. Type the appropriate user name and password in the User and Password boxes, click OK, and then click OK.

5. Restart your computer

Related KB article Q192122

Screen Flashes and Wallpaper Changes Colors

You click an icon on the desktop, and your screen flashes and your desktop wallpaper changes colors if you are using the CLOUDS.BMP file as your desktop wallpaper or you are using a color depth of 256 colors or lower.

Solution One

Set the color depth to high or true color. To do so, follow these steps:

1. Click the Start button, choose Settings, and then click Control Panel.

2. Double-click the Display icon.

3. Click the Settings tab.

4. Select High Color (16 Bit) or a higher color in the Colors list box, and then click OK.

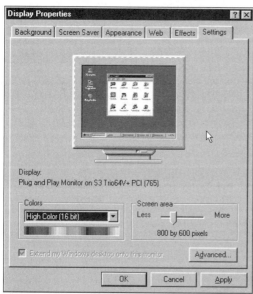

Figure 3-6. *The Settings tab of the Display Properties dialog box.*

5. If you are prompted to restart your computer or apply the new settings without restarting your computer, click Apply The New Color Settings Without Restarting, and then click OK.

Solution Two

Use different desktop wallpaper. To change your desktop wallpaper, follow these steps:

1. Click the Start button, choose Settings, and then click Control Panel.

2. Double-click the Display icon.

3. On the Background tab, select the desktop wallpaper you want from the list box, and then click OK.

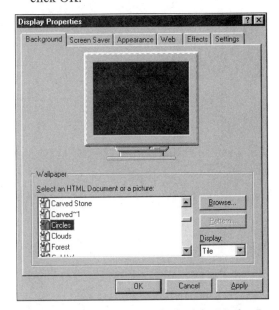

Figure 3-7. *The Background tab of the Display Properties dialog box.*

Related KB article Q191002

Visual C++ 4.2 Installation Disables Desktop

You install Microsoft Visual C++ version 4.2 and allow the setup program to copy older versions of existing files, but the Windows 98 Active Desktop is disabled.

Solution

When installing Visual C++, do not copy older versions of files over the newer versions.

Related KB article Q188978 or PROGRAMS.TXT in your WINDOWS folder

Web Tab and Active Desktop Command Are Missing

You open the Display Properties dialog box, and the Web tab is missing. Also, when you right-click the desktop, the Active Desktop command is missing. This problem can occur if you are using the TweakUI program and the Active Desktop Enabled feature is not enabled.

Solution

To resolve this problem, enable the Active Desktop Enabled feature. To do so, follow these steps:

1. Click the Start button, choose Settings, click Control Panel, and then double-click the TweakUI icon.

2. Click the Internet Explorer 4 tab, select the Active Desktop Enabled check box, and then click OK.

Related KB articles Q192400, Q192351, Q188920

Help

Book Icon Displays Incorrectly in Help

In Windows 98 Help, if you click a book icon in the left pane on the Contents tab to open the Help topic and then press the Plus sign key on the numeric keypad, the book icon is displayed incorrectly. The icon is displayed with a red mark, and then cycles through various icons ending as a folder icon as you press the Plus sign key.

Solution

This is a cosmetic problem only; it does not affect the functionality of Help. To work around this issue, press the Minus sign key on the numeric keypad to cycle the icon back to the book icon. Or, you can close and restart Help.

Related KB article Q186085

Invalid Page Fault Error Message When Quitting Help

If you quit Windows Help while a Windows 98 Troubleshooter is starting, you might see the following error message:

Winhlp32 caused an Invalid Page Fault in Module Winhlp32.exe

Solution

To work around this problem, do not quit Windows Help while a Windows 98 Troubleshooter is starting.

Related KB article Q179746

Jump To URL Command Causes Windows to Not Respond

You right-click Windows Help on the taskbar while Windows Help is minimized and then click Jump To URL, but Windows Help no longer seems to respond. The Jump To URL dialog box opens inside the minimized Windows Help tool, where you cannot see it.

Solution

To work around this problem, follow these steps:

1. Press Ctrl+Alt+Delete to open the Close Program dialog box.

2. Click Windows Help, click End Task, and then click End Task.

Related KB article Q182462

Unreadable Text in Windows Help

You can't read the text in Windows Help because of an incompatible background contrast color.

Solution

To change the background contrast color in Windows Help, follow these steps:

1. Click the Start button, choose Settings, and click Control Panel.

2. Double-click the Internet icon.

3. Click the General tab, and click Accessibility.

4. Select the Ignore Colors Specified On Web Pages check box, and then click OK.

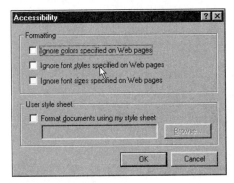

Figure 3-8. *The Accessibility dialog box.*

5. Click OK.

Related KB article Q185643

Windows Report Tool Starts Minimized

You start the Windows Report tool from Windows Help, but it is minimized (in other words, it appears as a button on the taskbar) because Windows Help calls the tool to start minimized.

Solution

Click the Winrep button on the taskbar to restore the program.

Related KB article Q194511

Screen Savers

Old Screen Saver Activates Instead of New

After you change your screen saver, your previous screen saver still starts when your computer is idle for the appropriate amount of time. If you then view the Screen Saver tab in the Display tool in Control Panel, your previous screen saver selection is visible instead of your new screen saver selection.

Solution

Remove the Read-Only attribute from the SYSTEM.INI file. To do so, follow these steps:

1. Click the Start button, choose Find, and then click Files Or Folders.

2. Enter *system.ini* in the Named box, and then click Find Now.

3. Right-click the SYSTEM.INI file, and choose Properties from the shortcut menu.

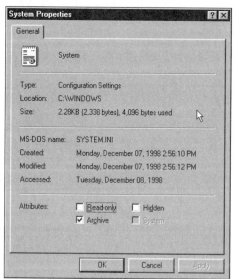

Figure 3-9. *The System Properties dialog box.*

4. Clear the Read Only check box, click OK, and then close the Find window.

Related KB article Q193794

Password Protection Does Not Work

You run a screen saver, and it does not prompt you for a password when you reengage Windows, even though password protection is enabled.

This problem occurs when you enable password protection, but do not assign a password.

Solution

To solve this problem, assign a password. To do this, follow these steps:

1. Click the Start button, choose Settings, and click Control Panel.

2. Double-click the Display icon.

3. Select the Screen Saver tab, and click Change.

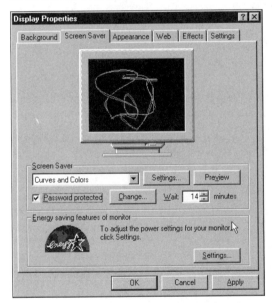

Figure 3-10. *The Screen Saver tab of the Display Properties dialog box.*

4. Type the password you want to use in both boxes, and click OK.

Related KB article Q141942

Preview Displays When None Is Selected

You click (None) in the Screen Saver box in Display Properties and a screen saver is displayed in the preview box.

This problem occurs when there is a screen saver (.SCR) file whose name begins with one of the following characters:

- %

- #

- &

- $

- !

- (

Solution

To solve this problem, follow these steps:

1. Click the Start button, choose Find, and click Files Or Folders.

2. Type *.scr in the Named box.

3. In the Look In box, click the drive on which Windows is installed, and then click Find Now.

4. In the list of found files, locate any .SCR file whose name begins with any of the characters listed above. Right-click the file, click Rename, press the Right arrow key, press the Home key, press the Delete key, and then press the Enter key.

5. Repeat step 4 for any other .SCR files whose name begins with any of the characters listed earlier in this article.

Related KB article Q192264

Screen Saver Does Not Start

Your screen saver does not start when your computer has been inactive for the specified wait time.

Solution One

This problem can occur because a key or mouse button is held down. To solve this problem, release the key or mouse button.

Solution Two

This problem can occur because the active program is an MS-DOS program for which the Allow Screen Saver function is disabled. To solve this problem, click the Misc tab in the program's properties, and then select the Allow Screen Saver check box.

Solution Three

This problem can occur because the active program is an MS-DOS-based program that uses a high-resolution graphics or text mode, or it is a disk utility. To solve this problem, close the program.

Related KB article Q146440

Wrong Screen Saver Displays

Your computer displays a screen saver, but it is not the screen saver you selected.

This problem occurs when your computer has two or more user profiles. If the screen saver is changed during a session in one user profile, that user profile overwrites the previous screen saver selection in another user profile.

Solution

Select the screen saver you prefer using the Display Properties Screen Saver tab.

Related KB article Q188227

Shortcuts

Briefcase Icon Appears As a Folder

You enable user profiles and log on to Windows as a different user and the Briefcase icon appears as a folder.

Solution

Windows does not copy the Briefcase to new user profiles because of its unique properties. To change the Briefcase icon from a folder to a briefcase, follow these steps:

1. Right-click an empty area on the desktop, choose New from the shortcut menu, and click Briefcase.

2. Right-click the old Briefcase icon, and choose Delete from the shortcut menu.

Related KB article Q132382

Connect To The Internet Icon Doesn't Delete

You get an error message when you try to delete the Connect To The Internet icon from your desktop.

Solution

To work around this problem, right-click the Connect To The Internet icon, and then choose Delete from the shortcut menu.

Related KB article Q185199

Desktop Contains Too Many Icons

After upgrading to Windows 98 from an earlier version of Windows or Windows for Workgroups, each file in the DESKTOP subfolder of the WINDOWS folder has a corresponding icon on the desktop. This problem occurs when you have a Windows-based (or Windows for Workgroups) program, such as Desktop Set by OKNA Corporation, that places files in the WINDOWS\DESKTOP folder.

Solution One

Move the unnecessary files to another folder or delete the files if the program is no longer needed. To move the files to another folder using Windows Explorer, follow these steps:

1. Click the Start button, choose Programs, and click Windows Explorer.

2. Display the contents of the Desktop by clicking the DESKTOP folder in the folder pane.

3. Drag the unnecessary files from the file pane to another folder in the folder pane.

Warning Moving the files could affect the performance or the ability to run the program.

Solution Two

Delete the unnecessary files. To delete a file using Windows Explorer, follow these steps:

1. Click the Start button, choose Programs, and click Windows Explorer.

2. Display the contents of the desktop by clicking the DESKTOP folder in the folder pane.

3. Right-click the file you want to remove, and choose Delete from the shortcut menu. Be sure not to delete any Windows shortcuts you want to maintain on the desktop.

4. When Windows asks you to confirm moving the file to the Recycle Bin, click Yes.

Related KB article Q124855

Desktop Icons Disappear or Will Not Move

You add a new icon to the desktop and it disappears when the desktop already has a large number of icons. Or, you move an icon from one location on the desktop to another and the icon returns to the original position.

These problems occur when the Auto Arrange function is activated on the Windows Desktop.

Solution One

To allow more icons to fit on the desktop, turn off the Auto Arrange function on the desktop and place the icons where you want them. To do this, follow these steps:

1. Right-click an empty space on the desktop.

2. Choose Arrange Icons from the shortcut menu, and click Auto Arrange to clear it.

Solution Two

To allow more icons to fit on the desktop, create folders on the desktop and drag and drop the icons into the folders to allow more room on the desktop. To do this, follow these steps:

1. Right-click an empty space on the desktop.

2. Choose New from the shortcut menu, and click Folder.

Solution Three

Adjust the icon spacing on the desktop. To do so, adjust the Icon Spacing (Vertical) and Icon Spacing (Horizontal) items on the Appearance tab in the Display Properties dialog box. To do so, follow these steps:

1. Right-click an empty space on the desktop.

2. Choose Properties from the shortcut menu.

3. Click the Appearance tab.

4. Select the Icon Spacing (Horizontal) entry from the Item list box. Then reduce the value shown in the Size box. (The value sets the number of pixels used for spacing.)

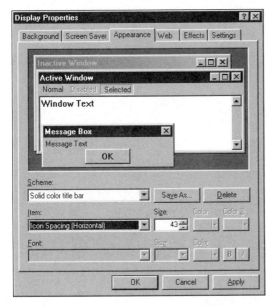

Figure 3-11. *The Appearance tab of the Display Properties dialog box.*

5. Select the Icon Spacing (Vertical) entry from the Item list box. Then reduce the value shown in the Size box.

6. Click OK.

Solution Four

Use a higher screen resolution, so you can see more of the desktop. (Your monitor must be capable of handling this.)

Solution Five

To allow the icons to move from one place on the desktop to another, turn off the Auto Arrange function. To do so, follow these steps:

1. Right-click an empty space on the desktop.

2. Choose Arrange Icons from the shortcut menu, and click Auto Arrange to clear it.

Related KB article Q137069

Desktop Icons or Shortcut Menu Are Missing

You start your computer with Policy Editor's Hide All Items On Desktop policy enabled, but your desktop icons disappear and a menu is missing when you right-click the desktop. Also, when you click Show Desktop, you might receive the following error message:

This operation has been cancelled due to restrictions in effect on this computer. Please contact your system administrator.

Solution

To resolve this issue, disable the Hide All Items On Desktop policy. To do so, follow these steps:

Note If your computer is on a network, you might be unable to perform the following steps because of policies your system administrator has enabled. Microsoft recommends you contact your system administrator before you try this procedure.

1. Click the Start button, click Run, enter *poledit* in the Open text box, and then click OK.

2. In System Policy Editor, choose Open Registry from the File menu.

3. Double-click the Local User branch to expand it, and then double-click the Windows 98 System branch to expand it.

4. Double-click Shell, and then double-click Restrictions.

5. Clear the Hide All Items On Desktop check box.

6. Click OK, choose Exit from the File menu, click Yes, and then restart your computer.

Related KB article Q192393

Icon Text Disappears

On a computer running Internet Explorer 4.0, you point to an icon on the desktop and the text under the icon disappears. This happens when selected items and desktop items use the same color.

Solution One

Configure Windows so that selected items and desktop items are not the same color. To do so, follow these steps:

1. Click the Start button, choose Settings, and then click Control Panel.

2. Double-click the Display icon.

3. Click the Appearance tab.

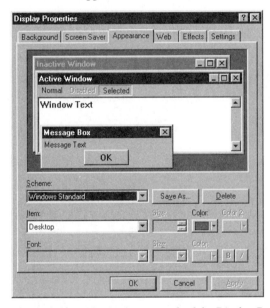

Figure 3-12. *The Appearance tab of the Display Properties dialog box.*

4. Select Desktop or Selected Items in the Item list box.

5. Select a different color in the Color drop-down list box.

6. Click OK.

Solution Two

Configure Windows so that you must double-click to open an object. To do so, follow these steps:

1. Double-click My Computer.

2. Choose Folder Options from the View menu.

3. Click the General tab.

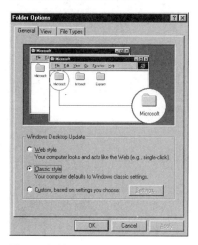

Figure 3-13. *The Folder Options dialog box.*

4. Select the Classic Style option button.

5. Click OK.

Related KB article Q165837

Icons Appear Fuzzy

You use Windows and the icons on the desktop or in Windows Explorer appear fuzzy and distorted.

This problem occurs when the icon size is set above or below 32 or 48. The icons appear clearly when set to 32 or 48.

Solution

To solve this problem, follow these steps:

1. Click the Start button, choose Settings, and click Control Panel.

2. Double-click the Display icon.

3. Click the Appearance tab, and click Icon.

4. Select 32 or 48 from the Size box to the right of the Item list box.

5. Click OK.

Related KB article Q146213

Icons Change Randomly

Icons in My Computer, Windows Explorer, on the Quick Launch toolbar or on the desktop change randomly.

Solution

To solve this problem, reboot the computer. If this does not work, delete the SHELLICONCACHE folder from the Windows file. This is a hidden file. To delete it, follow these steps:

1. Right-click the Start button, and choose Explore.

2. Click the Windows file icon, and choose Folder Options from the View menu.

3. Click the View tab, and click the Show All Files option button under the Hidden Files heading.

4. Click OK.

5. Choose Find from the Tools menu, and click Files Or Folders.

6. Enter *ShellIconCache* in the text box, and click Find Now.

7. Right-click the SHELLICONCACHE folder, and choose Delete from the shortcut menu.

8. Click Yes when you are asked to confirm that you want to send it to the Recycle Bin.

9. Right-click the Recycle Bin icon on the desktop, choose Empty Recycle Bin from the shortcut menu, and click Yes when asked to confirm.

10. Reboot the computer.

Related KB article Q132668

Shortcut Icons Display Arrow in Lower Left Corner

You create a shortcut or program information file (.PIF), and the icon displays an arrow in the lower left corner. The Windows Registry setting called IsShortcut causes this arrow to appear.

Solution

If you do not want your new shortcut icons to display an arrow, use Registry Editor to search for and remove the IsShortcut value from:

```
HKEY_CLASSES_ROOT\lnkfile
```

```
HKEY_CLASSES_ROOT\piffile
```

Warning Please read the Introduction for information on how to safely edit the Registry.

To remove the IsShortcut value, follow these steps:

1. Click the Start button, click Run, enter *Regedit* in the Run box, and click OK.

2. Navigate your way down through the folders in the left pane until you locate the LNKFILE folder.

3. Open the LNKFILE folder, and then right-click IsShortcut in the right pane.

4. Choose Delete from the shortcut menu.

5. Continue to navigate your way down the folders in the left pane until you locate the PIFFILE folder.

6. Open the PIFFILE folder, and then right-click IsShortcut in the right pane.

7. Choose Delete from the shortcut menu.

8. Close Regedit.

9. Restart Windows.

You can also use Windows PowerToys to change the appearance of shortcut icons. For more information about PowerToys, see KB article Q145688.

Related KB article Q126631

Shortcut Key Does Not Function

You try to assign a shortcut key combination used by another desktop shortcut in Windows with Internet Explorer 4.0 or 4.01 installed, and you are unable to do so. This occurs even when the other desktop shortcut is deleted.

Solution One

Clear the shortcut key combination you want to reuse. To do this, follow these steps:

1. Right-click the desktop shortcut that is assigned the key combination you want to reuse, and then choose Properties from the shortcut menu. If necessary, click the Shortcut tab.

2. Click the Shortcut Key box, and press the Delete key. Note that the value of the Shortcut Key is changed to None.

3. Click OK. You can now reassign the key combination to another desktop shortcut.

Solution Two

If you have already deleted the desktop shortcut that was assigned the key combination you want to reuse, restart your computer. You can now reassign the key combination to another desktop shortcut.

Related KB article Q192804

Shortcut Key Does Not Open Program

You press a shortcut key for an assigned program and the program does not open.

Solution

Shortcut keys work differently depending on the location of the shortcut. If the shortcut is on the desktop or in the Start menu hierarchy, you can use its shortcut key to start the assigned program, or switch to the program if it is already running.

If the shortcut is not on the desktop or in the Start menu hierarchy, however, you cannot use its shortcut key to start the assigned program, but you can use its shortcut key to switch to the assigned program if it is already running.

Related KB article Q134552

User Profile Settings Are Lost

You disable the user profiles option and icons are missing from the desktop or the Start menu.

This problem occurs because Windows returns to the default user profile when the User Profiles option is disabled.

Solution

You can access these profiles in the user-specific folders to regain the user's settings. To do this, follow these steps:

1. Click the Start button, choose Programs, and click Windows Explorer.

2. Navigate your way down through the folders in the left pane until you locate the WINDOWS folder and then the PROFILES subfolder.

3. Click the folder corresponding to the user whose settings you want to retrieve.

4. To regain the user's desktop shortcuts, drag the shortcuts from the DESKTOP folder to the Windows desktop.

5. To regain the user's Start Menu settings, drag the START MENU folder to the WINDOWS START MENU folder.

Related KB article Q130330

Start Menu

ActiveMovie and Media Player Not Present on Start Menu

Installing Microsoft Windows Media Player version 5.2 removes the shortcuts for Media Player and ActiveMovie Control from the Start menu. Windows Media Player version 5.2 replaces ActiveMovie and Media Player as the default media file player. This behavior is by design.

Solution One

Add the ActiveMovie Control shortcut back to the Entertainment menu in Windows 98. To do this, follow these steps:

1. Click the Start button, choose Settings, and then click Taskbar & Start Menu.

2 Click the Start Menu Programs tab, and then click Advanced.

3. In the left list, click the plus sign (+) next to the PROGRAMS folder, and then click the plus sign next to the ACCESSORIES folder to open it.

4. Click the ENTERTAINMENT folder.

5. Choose New from the File menu, and then click Shortcut.

6. Type *c:\<windows>\rundll32.exe amovie.ocx,RunDll* in the Command Line box, replacing <windows> with the name of your WINDOWS folder. (Note that the word *RunDll* must be capitalized exactly as shown.)

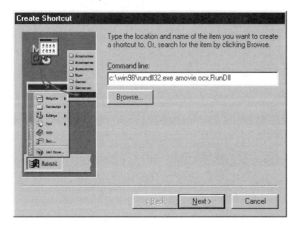

Figure 3-14. *The Create Shortcut dialog box.*

7. Click Next.

8. Type *ActiveMovie* in the Select A Name For The Shortcut box, and then click Finish.

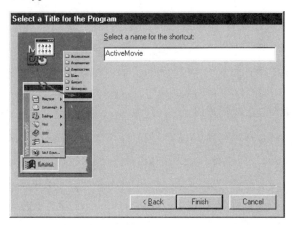

Figure 3-15.   *The Select A Title For The Program dialog box.*

9. Right-click the new ActiveMovie shortcut, choose Properties from the shortcut menu, and then click Change Icon.

10. Type *c:\<windows>\system\amovie.ocx* in the File Name box replacing <windows> with the name of your WINDOWS folder, and then click OK.

Figure 3-16.   *The Change Icon dialog box.*

11. Click OK, and then click OK.

Solution Two

To add the Media Player shortcut back to the Entertainment menu, follow these steps:

1. Follow steps 1–5 above.

2. Type *c:\<windows>\mplayer.exe* in the Command Line box, replacing <windows> with the name of your WINDOWS folder.

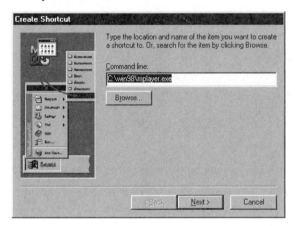

Figure 3-17.   *The Create Shortcut dialog box.*

3. Click Next.

4. Type *Media Player* in the Select A Name For The Shortcut box, and then click Finish.

Related KB article Q191531

Documents Command Shouldn't Appear on Start Menu

You use Windows and do not want the Documents command on the Start menu.

Solution

Remove the Documents command from the Start menu by using Registry Editor to add a DWORD entry named NoRecentDocsMenu with a hexadecimal value of 1 to the following Registry key:

`HKEY_CURRENT_USER\Software\Microsoft\Windows\CurrentVersion\Policies\Explorer`

Follow these steps:

Warning Please read the Introduction for information on how to safely edit the Registry.

1. Click the Start button, click Run, enter *Regedit* in the Run box, and then click OK.

2. Navigate your way down through the folders in the left pane until you find the key.

3. Right-click in a blank part of the right pane, and choose New from the shortcut menu.

4. Create the new entry.

5. Close Regedit.

6. Restart Windows.

Related KB article Q181342

Log Off <Username> Command Shouldn't Appear on Start Menu

You use Windows and do not want the Log Off <Username> command on the Start menu.

Solution

Remove the Log Off <Username> command from the Start menu by using Registry Editor to locate the following key:

```
HKEY_CURRENT_USER\Software\Microsoft\Windows\CurrentVersion\Policies\Explorer
```

Add a new binary value named NoLogOff to this key with the following value:

```
01 00 00 00
```

Follow these steps:

Warning Please read the Introduction for information on how to safely edit the Registry.

1. Click the Start button, click Run, enter *Regedit* in the Run box, and click OK.

2. Navigate your way down through the folders in the left pane.

3. Right-click in a blank area of the right pane, and choose New Binary Value from the shortcut menu.

4. Enter the name of the new value, right-click the name, and choose Modify from the shortcut menu to enter the new data.

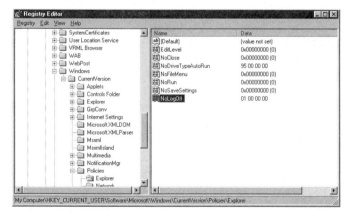

Figure 3-18. *The Registry Editor window.*

5. Close Regedit.

6. Restart Windows.

Related KB article Q177903

Naleco RADFind 96 Version 1.0a Causes EXPLORER Errors

You start Windows, and click the Start button while the startup sound is playing, and receive the following error message:

Explorer An error has occurred in your program. To keep working anyway, click Ignore and save your work to a new file. To quit this program, click Close. You will lose information you entered since your last save.

Clicking Ignore causes the error message to be repeated. Clicking Close causes the following error message to be displayed:

Explorer This program has performed an illegal operation and will be shut down. If the problem persists, contact the program vendor.

Clicking Details displays the following information:

EXPLORER caused a general protection fault in module mmsystem.dll at 0004:xxxxxxxx

---

Note If you are using the Active Desktop, the Active Desktop Recovery screen appears. Clicking Restore My Active Desktop and then clicking Yes restores your Active Desktop settings, but the icons on the right side of the taskbar might be missing until you restart Windows.

This problem occurs when you have Naleco RADFind 96 version 1.0a installed and you are using a sound scheme that plays a Windows sound (.WAV) file for the Menu Popup and Windows Start events. The error message occurs if RADFind 96 is scanning your disk and the startup sound is playing when you click the Start button.

This problem might also occur during normal Windows operation if RADFind 96 is running and two system sounds are played at the same time. RADFind 96 is a file search program that scans your hard disk and indexes the files on the disk.

Solution One

Do not click the Start button until the Windows startup sound has finished playing or until RADFind 96 has finished scanning your drives.

Solution Two

Disable the sound for the Menu Popup event. To do this, follow these steps:

1. Click the Start button, choose Settings, and then click Control Panel.

2. Double-click the Sounds icon.

Figure 3-19.   *The Sound Properties dialog box.*

3. Select Menu Popup in the Events list box.

4. Select (None) in the Sound Name list box.

5. Click OK.

Solution Three

Uninstall RADFind 96. To do this, follow these steps:

1. Click the Start button, choose Settings, and then click Control Panel.

2. Double-click the Add/Remove Programs icon.

3. On the Install/Uninstall tab, click RADFind 96, and then click Add/Remove.

Related KB article   Q192847

Online Services Folder Setup Programs Don't Work

You attempt to use the Setup programs located in the ONLINE SERVICES folder on the desktop and see the following error message:

The item '<file>' that this shortcut refers to has been changed or moved.

The nearest match, based on size, date, and type, is:

'<nearest match>'. Do you want this shortcut to point to this item?

This can occur if the Setup files for the online service that you want to use have not been installed on your computer.

Solution

To resolve this problem, follow these steps:

1. Click the Start button, choose Settings, click Control Panel, and double-click the Add/Remove Programs icon.

2. On the Windows Setup tab, if the Online Services check box is selected, clear the Online Services check box, and then click Apply. If the Online Services check box is not selected, go to step 3.

3. On the Windows Setup tab, select the Online Services check box, and then click Apply.

4. Insert the Windows 98 CD-ROM into the CD-ROM drive when you are prompted to do so, click OK, and then click OK.

5. Double-click the Setup program for the online service you want to use in the ONLINE SERVICES folder on your desktop, and then follow the instructions on your screen.

Related KB article Q188072

Open and Explore Shortcut Commands Are Unavailable

You right-click the Start button and the Open and Explore shortcut menu commands are unavailable.

This problem occurs when you use the TweakUI tool to hide one or more drives.

Solution

Unhide any hidden drives. To do so, follow these steps:

1. Click the Start button, choose Settings, and then click Control Panel.

2. Double-click the TweakUI icon.

3. Select the My Computer tab, and then clear any check boxes.

4. Click Apply, and then click Close.

5. Restart your computer.

Related KB article Q188209

Program Shortcuts Don't Add to Start Menu

You try to add a program to the Start menu by dragging a program file to the Start button on the taskbar, but Windows displays the following message:

Unable to create a shortcut here. Do you want the shortcut to be placed on the desktop?

This occurs because the Start menu is damaged or has been deleted.

Solution One

Restart the computer. The system creates a new START MENU folder and reenables the Start menu.

Solution Two

Delete the START MENU folder. To do this, follow these steps:

1. Right-click the Start button, and choose Explore from the shortcut menu.

2. Display the contents of the WINDOWS folder.

3. Right-click the START MENU folder, and choose Delete from the shortcut menu.

4. Restart the system to reenable and re-create the Start menu.

Related KB article Q120357

Right-Dragging Start Menu Items Produces Unexpected Results

You use the right mouse button to drag items to different locations in the Start menu, and you experience unexpected results. For example, when you drop an object anywhere in the Start menu, a shortcut menu may open for the closest item. Afterward, you might be unable to open or close cascading menus on the Start menu or to close the Start menu itself. Microsoft has confirmed this to be a problem in Windows 98.

Solution

Close and reopen the Start menu. To do so, follow these steps:

1. Click the Start button, and then click Run.

2. Click Cancel.

3. Click the Start button to open the Start menu again. Use the left mouse button (instead of the right mouse button) to reorder the Start menu items.

Related KB article Q183961

Run Dialog Box Does Not Allow Extended Characters

You type commands in the Run dialog box, and you are not able to type some extended characters. A black line or box appears instead of some of the extended characters you type.

Solution

This problem occurs because Windows uses MS Sans Serif for its system font. This font does not include a complete set of extended characters.

Related KB article Q192109

Run Dialog Box Opens Wrong Folder

You type a path in the Open box to a folder or share, and the folder displayed is not the appropriate folder. This problem can occur if the folder contains a DESKTOP.INI file from the TEMPORARY INTERNET FILES, TASKS, MY BRIEFCASE, or FONTS folder.

Solution One

Delete the DESKTOP.INI file from the shared folder.

Warning If the folder is the Temporary Internet Files, Tasks, My Briefcase, or Fonts folder, do not delete the DESKTOP.INI file. Doing so will create additional problems.

Solution Two

If the problem occurs on a remote resource, you can map the network drive instead of connecting to it by typing the path in the Open dialog box.

The DESKTOP.INI file contains information regarding shell folders. This file contains a unique Class ID (CLSID) that identifies the portion of the shell it is in. If the CLSID line in the DESKTOP.INI file is removed or changed, the problem does not occur.

Note If you are using the Windows Desktop Update component, DESKTOP.INI files are created in customized folders. The problem does not occur unless the folder is the TEMPORARY INTERNET FILES, TASKS, MY BRIEFCASE, or FONTS folder.

Related KB article Q177615

Shortcut Missing

You try to modify a program shortcut in your STARTUP folder, and the shortcut is missing.

Solution

The program shortcut may be located in the WINDOWS\ALL USERS\START MENU\PROGRAMS\STARTUP folder. To work around this problem, use Windows Explorer to modify the shortcut in the WINDOWS\ALL USERS\START MENU\PROGRAMS\STARTUP folder.

Related KB article Q192338

Tweak UI Tool Removes Log Off Command

You attempt to use the Log Off command on the Start menu, and the Log Off command is missing.

Solution

The problem occurs when the TweakUI tool has been configured to remove the Log Off command from the Start menu. To use TweakUI to enable the Log Off command on the Start menu, follow these steps:

1. Click the Start button, choose Settings, click Control Panel, and then double-click the TweakUI icon.

2. Select the Internet Explorer 4 tab, clear the Allow Logoff check box, and then click OK.

3. Restart your computer.

Related KB article Q190644

Taskbar

Clock Loses Time

The clock on the taskbar and in the Date/Time tool in Control Panel experiences a loss of time. This problem may occur for any of the following reasons:

- You change the year in the Date/Time tool. When you click a different year in the Date/Time Properties dialog box, the clock stops. When you click Apply or OK, the clock starts again, but it does not compensate for the length of time it was stopped.

- You change the month or date in the Date/Time tool. When you click a different month or date in the Date/Time Properties dialog box, the current time is decreased by 5 to 10 seconds. Over time, this can result in a significant time loss.

- You are using a third-party program that synchronizes its clock with that of a server on the Internet (for example, Atomic Clock).

- You resize the taskbar. This can stop the clock until you restart your computer.

- You are using the Johnny Castaway screen saver. This screen saver can cause resource leaks, which can result in time loss.

Solution One

Use the Date/Time tool to set the correct time.

Solution Two

Determine if the time loss is a result of a weak computer battery. To do so, follow these steps:

1. Click the Start button, choose Programs, and then click MS-DOS Prompt.

2. At the command prompt, type *time* and then press the Enter key.

3. Compare this time with the time reported by the clock on the taskbar.

4. Type *exit*, and then press the Enter key.

5. Compare the computer's time and time on the clock. If they differ, your computer's battery is too weak to keep accurate time, and it should be replaced. For information about how to replace your computer's battery, refer to the documentation included with your computer.

Note This problem does not affect the clock in your computer's CMOS.

Related KB article Q189706

Date/Time Changes When Restarting Computer or Connecting to Network

You restart your computer or connect to your network, and the date or time changes if a program synchronizes your computer's clock with a computer clock on your network.

Solution

Set your computer clock to the correct date and time. To do this, follow these steps:

1. Click the Start button, choose Settings, and then click Control Panel. Double-click the Date/Time icon. On the Date & Time tab, click the correct date and time, and then click OK.

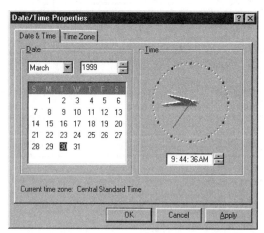

Figure 3-20. *The Date & Time tab of the Date/Time Properties dialog box.*

2. Restart your computer in Safe mode. To start in Safe mode, restart your computer, press and hold down the Ctrl key, and then choose Safe Mode from the Startup menu.

3. If the date and time are correct, continue to step 4. If the date or time is incorrect, a hardware issue is causing the problem. For example, the battery in your computer might need replacing.

4. Restart your computer normally, but do not log on to your network.

5. If the date and time are correct, continue to step 6. If the date or time is incorrect, a program that is not related to your network is changing the date or time. For more information about how to identify the cause of the date or time change, see KB article Q192926, "How to Perform Clean-Boot Troubleshooting for Windows 98."

6. Restart your computer normally, and log on to your network.

7. If the date and time are correct, something else is changing your computer date and time, such as Task Scheduler (Windows 98). If the date or time is incorrect, contact your network administrator to determine what program is changing your date or time. You can disable the program on your computer, or correct the date and time on the network computer.

Related KB article Q193912

Options Lost Starting Windows

You start Windows in Safe mode and then restart Windows, and your nondefault taskbar options are lost. For example, if you selected the Show Small Icons In Start Menu option, this option is no longer selected after you start Windows in Safe mode and then restart Windows normally.

Solution

After starting Windows in Safe mode and then restarting Windows, you must reselect any nondefault taskbar options.

Related KB article Q129417

Program Doesn't Appear on Taskbar

The Windows program you are using does not appear on the taskbar. This problem occurs when you are running Xerox's Text Bridge Instant Access OCR program.

Solution

Close Instant Access, and remove it from the STARTUP folder. To do this, follow these steps:

1. Press Ctrl+Alt+Delete to open the Close Program dialog box.

2. Click Instant Access (TBMENU.EXE), and then click End Task.

3. Click Cancel.

4. Click the Start button, choose Settings, and then click Taskbar & Start Menu.

5. Select the Start Menu Programs tab, and click Remove.

6. Double-click StartUp, and then click Instant Access.

7. Click Remove, click Close, and then click OK.

Related KB article Q139727

Shift+Tab Doesn't Go from Icons to Taskbar

In Windows 95, with no open windows on the desktop, pressing the Tab key cycles through the Start button, the taskbar, and a desktop icon, in that order. Pressing Shift+Tab reverses the cycle, going from the Start button, to a desktop icon, to the taskbar.

In Windows 98, the Tab key works similarly to the way it works in Windows 95 (although the Quick Launch toolbar and the Channel bar may be added to the cycle). The Shift+Tab key combination, however, does not go from a desktop icon to the taskbar as in Windows 95. Instead, Shift+Tab goes from a desktop icon to the Start button.

In other words, if you press Shift+Tab when there are no open windows, Windows 98 may not reverse the normal Tab key order—even though it should.

Solution

To work around this problem, press the Tab key until the appropriate item is active.

Related KB article Q191171

Start Button Menu Hidden by Office Shortcut Bar

You use the right mouse button to click the Start button, and part of the resulting context menu is hidden behind the Microsoft Office Shortcut bar.

This problem occurs when the Shortcut bar is positioned at the bottom of the screen and its Auto Hide option enabled. The Windows Shortcut bar has a higher display priority than the context menu.

Solution One

Move the Windows taskbar to a different place on the screen by clicking an empty space on the taskbar and dragging it to a different edge of the screen.

Solution Two

Disable the Auto Hide function of the Office Shortcut bar. To do so, follow these steps:

1. Right-click an empty space on the taskbar, and choose Properties from the shortcut menu.

Figure 3-21. *The Taskbar Properties dialog box.*

2. Clear the Auto Hide check box, and click OK.

Related KB article Q136012

System Clock Wrong When Computer Started at Midnight

You start your computer at midnight, but the date does not change or it is set two days ahead.

This problem can occur if you start your computer within seconds of midnight. The exact time is different on each computer, but there is less than a one-second window of time in which the date does not change. In an even smaller window of time, the date is incremented twice, which results in it being ahead by two days.

Note If you are setting the date and time in the AUTOEXEC.BAT file, the window of time may be larger.

Solution

To work around this issue, manually set the date using the Date/Time tool. To do so, follow these steps:

1. Click the Start button, choose Settings, and then click Control Panel.

2. Double-click the Date/Time icon.

3. On the Date & Time tab, click the correct date, and then click OK.

Related KB article Q191797

Taskbar Does Not Move

You try to reposition the taskbar to a new location, with Norton Navigator version 1.0 installed, and it covers up other icons, such as the Start button.

Solution

Uninstall Norton Navigator. For information about how to do so, contact Symantec, or view the documentation included with Norton Navigator.

Note Contact Symantec to inquire about the availability of a fix for this issue.

Related KB article Q188983

Taskbar Not Visible in Windows

You run Windows and the taskbar is not visible on the screen

This problem occurs if you have moved or resized the taskbar so that it is too small or is located in a position that is not visible.

Solution One

To resize the taskbar, follow these steps:

1. Press Ctrl+Esc to select the taskbar and display the Start menu.

2. Press the Esc key. The Start menu disappears, but the taskbar is still selected.

3. Press Alt+Spacebar, and click Size.

4. Move the taskbar where you would like it by using the mouse or one of the arrow keys.

Solution Two

You can restore the taskbar by rebooting the computer in Safe mode. To do this, follow these steps:

1. Restart your computer.

2. Press and hold down the Ctrl key after your computer completes the Power On Self Test (POST).

3. Choose Safe Mode from the Startup menu.

Related KB article Q134237

Windows Update

Blank Screen or Error Message Displays During Connection

You connect to the Microsoft Windows Update site, and you see only a blank white page, or you receive one of the following error messages:

You chose not to download the software controls or there was a problem with downloading the controls, in which case much of the Windows Update site will be unavailable to you. You would like to download the controls now, please click Try Again below.

Your Internet Explorer security settings are set to High. In order to use the Windows Update site, you need to set your security settings at medium. To change your security settings: From the View menu on the toolbar, choose Internet Options. Click the Security tab, and then select Internet zone in the drop-down box. Click Medium.

For more information on Internet Explorer security settings, see: http://www.microsoft.com/ie/ ie40/features/sec-zones.htm.

You click Try Again, and you continue to receive the error messages. This problem occurs when the Microsoft Active Setup or the Windows Update files are missing or damaged.

Solution

Remove and then reinstall the Active Setup and Windows Update files. To do so, follow these steps:

1. Click the Start button, choose Settings, and then click Control Panel.

2. Double-click the Internet icon.

3. On the General tab, click Settings, and then click View Objects.

4. Locate the following files (if they exist):

   - WUSYSINFO
   - WUREDIRINFORB
   - INSTALLENGINECTL OBJECT

5. Right-click one of the files, and then click Update. Repeat this step for each of the files that exists

6. If you are prompted to install Active Setup, click Yes.

7. Close the Downloaded Program Files window.

8. Click OK, and then click OK.

9. Restart your computer, and then connect to the Windows Update site to see if the problem is resolved.

Solution Two

If the problem persists, download the Microsoft Scripting Engine 3.1b for Internet Explorer from the following Microsoft web site: *http://www.microsoft.com/msdownload/vbscript/scripting.asp*

Related KB article Q192854

Connection to Site Fails

You connect to the Windows Update site, and you see one of the following:

- A blank web page
- A scripting error message
- Either of the following error messages:

    Error Installing Dependency

    An unknown error occurred

Or your computer stops responding (hangs) when you attempt to download a file.

These problems may be the result of a poorly written Java program, a damaged ActiveX control, a broken cookie, a damaged file in the TEMPORARY INTERNET FILES folder, or a nonregistered copy of Windows 98.

Solution One

Verify that your copy of Windows 98 is registered. To do so, follow these steps:

1. Click the Start button, choose Programs, choose Accessories, choose System Tools, and then click Welcome To Windows.

2. Click Register Now, and then follow the instructions on your screen. If Register Now is not listed, your copy of Windows 98 is already registered.

Solution Two

Remove any damaged or poorly written files downloaded from the Internet. To do this, follow these steps:

1. Click the Start button, choose Shut Down, click Restart In MS-DOS Mode, and then click OK.

2. At the command prompt, type the following commands, pressing the Enter key after each command and pressing the Y key if you are prompted to confirm folder deletion:

```
cd\windows

deltree cookies

deltree history

deltree downlo~1

deltree tempor~1

exit
```

Solution Three

If you have a cookie that stores a password for a particular web site, copy the contents of the COOKIES folder to a new folder instead of deleting the COOKIES folder. To do so, type the following commands at the command prompt, pressing the Enter key after each command:

```
md <new folder>

copy c:\windows\cookies\*.* c:\windows\<new folder>
```

Replace <new folder> with the name of the folder to which you want to copy the contents of the COOKIES folder.

Solution Four

Use the System Configuration Utility to determine if a file or program that is loaded into memory is preventing you from loading the Windows Update site. For information about clean-boot troubleshooting using the System Configuration Utility, see KB article Q192926, "How to Perform Clean-Boot Troubleshooting for Windows 98."

Solution Five

Use System File Checker to replace any changed or damaged system files. For information about how to replace altered files using System File Checker, see KB article Q129605, "How to Extract Original Compressed Windows Files."

Solution Six

Install the JAVA.INF file from the TOOLS\MTSUTIL folder on your Windows 98 CD-ROM. To do this, follow these steps:

1. With the Windows 98 CD-ROM in your CD-ROM drive, click the Start button, choose Find, and then click Files Or Folders.

2. In the Named box, type *java.inf,* select your CD-ROM drive in the Look In box, and then click Find Now.

3. Right-click the JAVA.INF file in the list of found files, and choose Install from the shortcut menu.

4. Close the Find dialog box.

5. Rename and then extract a new copy of the MSJAVA.DLL file from your Windows 98 CD-ROM into the WINDOWS\SYSTEM folder using the System File Checker tool.

Solution Seven

Delete the Internet Explorer 4.0 Setup files. To do this, follow these steps:

1. Click the Start button, choose Settings, and then click Control Panel.

2. Double-click the Add/Remove Programs icon.

3. In the list of installed programs, select Microsoft Internet Explorer 4.0 Setup Files.

4. Click Add/Remove, click Yes when you are prompted to remove the files, and then click OK.

If you install Internet Explorer 4.0 in Windows 95, save the uninstall information, and then upgrade to Windows 98, the INTERNET EXPLORER 4.0 SETUP files remain on your hard disk. Deleting these files resolves the *Error Installing Dependency* error message. For more information, see KB article Q179650, "Error Message: Error Installing Dependency."

Solution Eight

Obtain the latest version of the Microsoft Java VM from the Microsoft web site at *http://www.microsoft.com/java/*. Because the Microsoft web site is constantly updated, the site address may change without notice. In this case, link to the Microsoft home page at *http://www.microsoft.com/*.

Related KB article Q193657

Content Advisor Password Requested

You connect to the Windows Update web site, and you are prompted repeatedly for your Content Advisor password.

This problem occurs when you enable Content Advisor. The Windows Update web site is not a rated web page, and the Content Advisor does not allow you to view unrated web sites unless you provide a password.

Solution

Enable viewing of web pages that are not rated in the Content Advisor. To do so, follow these steps:

1. In Internet Explorer, choose Internet Options from the View menu.

2. Click the Content tab, and then click Settings.

3. Type your password, click OK, click the General tab, and then select the Users Can See Sites That Have No Rating check box.

4. Click OK, and then click OK again.

5. Close and reopen Internet Explorer.

Related KB article Q188207

NetZIP Causes Download Problems

You download a component from the Windows Update web site, and you see the following error message:

An unknown error has occurred during installation.

If you click Back and then click Download again, you might see this error message:

Explorer

This program has performed an illegal operation and will be shutdown.

And if you click Details, you see the following information:

Explorer caused an exception C0010000H in module MSJAVA.DLL at 015F:xxxxx.

When you click Close, EXPLORER.EXE reloads and all the icons on the right side of the taskbar disappear except for the Volume icon. You must restart your computer to regain full functionality.

These circumstances can occur if Software Builders International's NetZIP is installed and enabled.

Solution One

Temporarily disable NetZIP. To do this, follow these steps:

1. Right-click the NetZIP icon on the right side of the taskbar, and then click Disable.

2. Download the component you are interested in from the Windows Update web site.

3. After the download from the Windows Update site is finished, right-click the NetZIP icon on the right side of the taskbar, and then click Enable.

Solution Two

Uninstall NetZIP. To do this, follow these steps:

1. Click the Start button, choose Settings, and click Control Panel.

2. Double-click the Add/Remove Programs icon.

3. On the Install/Uninstall tab, click NetZIP, click Add/Remove, and then follow the instructions on the screen to uninstall NetZIP.

Related KB article Q191799

Start Menu Shouldn't Display Windows Update Tool

You use the Windows Update tool to download updated product features, device drivers, and system files from the Windows Update web site. Shortcuts to the Windows Update tool (WUPDMGR.EXE) appear in two locations on the Start menu; at the top of the Start menu and in the SETTINGS folder on the Start menu. The Windows Update Wizard is also available in the Update Device Driver Wizard in Device Manager. You can remove the shortcuts to Windows Update tool on the Start menu and the Windows Update Wizard check box in the Update Device Driver Wizard if you want.

Solution One

To remove the Windows Update shortcut at the top of the Start menu, right-click the shortcut, and then click Delete.

Solution Two

To remove the Windows Update shortcut from the SETTINGS folder on the Start menu, add the DWORD value NoWindowsUpdate to the following Registry key:

```
HKEY_LOCAL_MACHINE\Software\Microsoft\Windows\CurrentVersion\Policies\Explorer
```

Set the data value to 1. To do this, follow these steps:

Warning Please read the Introduction for information on how to safely edit the Registry.

1. Click the Start button, click Run, enter *Regedit* in the Run box, and click OK.

2. Navigate your way down through the folders in the left pane until you locate the key described above.

3. Add the DWORD value NoWindowsUpdate, and set the data value to 1.

4. Close Regedit.

5. Restart Windows.

Solution Three

To remove the Windows Update Wizard check box from the Update Device Driver Wizard, add the DWORD value NoDevMgrUpdate to this Registry key:

`HKEY_LOCAL_MACHINE\Software\Microsoft\Windows\CurrentVersion\Policies\Explorer`

Set the data value to 1.

Warning Please read the Introduction for information on how to safely edit the Registry.

1. Click the Start button, click Run, enter *Regedit* in the Run box, and click OK.

2. Navigate your way down through the folders in the left pane until you locate the key described above.

3. Add the DWORD value NoDevMgrUpdate, and set the data value to 1.

4. Close Regedit.

5. Restart Windows.

To restore the Windows Update tool in the SETTINGS folder on the Start menu, or the Update Device Driver Wizard in Device Manager, use Registry Editor to change the appropriate data values from 1 to 0.

Note When you add or remove the Windows Update shortcut on the Start menu, the change takes effect when you restart your computer. When you add or remove the Windows Update Wizard check box in the Update Device Driver Wizard in Device Manager, the change takes effect immediately.

Related KB article Q189525

Unknown Error During Installation

You try to download a component from the Windows Update page, and you receive the following error message:

An unknown error has occurred during installation.

If you click Back and then click Download Again, you receive the following error message:

Explorer: This program has performed an illegal operation and will be shutdown.

If you then click Details, you see the following information:

Explorer caused an exception C0010000H in module MSJAVA.DLL at 015F:xxxxx.

This problem can occur if the Microsoft Java Virtual Machine is damaged.

Solution

To resolve this problem, follow these steps:

1. Click the Start button, choose Programs, and then click Windows Explorer.

2. Double-click the WINDOWS folder, and then double-click the DOWNLOADED PROGRAM FILES folder.

3. Delete the following files by right-clicking them one at a time and choosing Remove from the shortcut menus:

   - DIRECTANIMATION JAVA CLASSES

   - INTERNET EXPLORER CLASSES FOR JAVA

   - MICROSOFT XML PARSER FOR JAVA

   - WIN32 CLASSES

   - INSTALLENGINECTL OBJECT

   - WUREDIRINFOB CLASE

4. Double-click the SYSTEM folder.

5. Delete the following files by right-clicking them one at a time, and choosing Remove from the shortcut menus:

   - ASCTRL.OCX

   - INSENG.DLL

   - WUDETECT.DLL

   - WUPDATTO.DLL

   - WUREDIRB.DLL

6. Restart your computer.

7. Insert your Windows 98 CD-ROM into your CD-ROM drive, click the Start button, choose Programs, and then click Windows Explorer.

8. Double-click the D:\TOOLS folder if your CD-ROM is drive D, and then double-click the MTSUTTIL folder.

9. Right-click the JAVA.INF file, and then choose Install from the shortcut menu.

10. Close Windows Explorer.

Related KB article Q193576

Web Help or Windows Update Displays Error Message

You try to use the Windows Update or Web Help feature and see an error message similar to one of the following messages:

The path 'http://windowsupdate.microsoft.com' does not exist or is not a directory.

The path 'http://windows.microsoft.com/isapi/redir.dll?OLCID=0x0409&0S=at&PRD=windows upddate' does not exist or is not a directory.

The path 'http://windows.microsoft.com/isapiredir.dll?OLCID=0x0409&CLCID=0x0409&OS =at&prd=support&ar=w98' does not exist or is not a directory.

This problem can occur if a program modifies the properties of the Internet Explorer icon on the desktop, which interferes with Windows Explorer's ability to identify a web address as a command line and display web content. Using System Policy Editor to enable the Hide Internet Explorer Icon policy is also known to cause this behavior.

Deleting the Internet Explorer icon from the desktop does not affect Windows Explorer's ability to recognize a web address as a command-line parameter.

The Run dialog box accepts both complete and abbreviated web addresses because Internet Explorer is able to interpret them correctly. For example, any of the following command lines should perform as expected in the Run dialog box:

```
www.microsoft.com

http:\\www.microsoft.com

iexplore http:\\www.microsoft.com

iexplore www.microsoft.com
```

Windows Explorer must have the complete web address to function correctly. You always receive an error message when you type the following command line in the Run dialog box:

```
explorer www.microsoft.com
```

If the Hide Internet Explorer Icon policy is enabled, you receive an error message when you type the following command line in the Run dialog box:

```
explorer http:\\www.microsoft.com
```

Solution One

To resolve this behavior, use System Policy Editor to disable the Hide Internet Explorer Icon policy. To do this, follow these steps:

Note System Policy Editor is available in the TOOLS\RESKIT\NETADMIN\POLEDIT folder on the Windows CD-ROM.

1. Click the Start button, and click Run.

2. Type *poledit* in the Open box, and click OK.

3. Choose either Open Policy or Open Registry, as appropriate, from the File menu.

4. Double-click the user's policy file or Local User, as appropriate.

5. Double-click the Desktop category to expand it, and then click Desktop Restrictions. (Click the words, not the check box.) You must have the SHELLM.ADM file as a current policy template to have Desktop Restrictions available.

6. Clear the Hide Internet Explorer Icon check box, and click OK.

7. Choose Save from the File menu, and then choose Exit from the File menu.

8. Restart Windows.

Solution Two

To disable the Hide Internet Explorer Icon policy using Registry Editor, delete the NoInternetIcon value from the following Registry key:

```
HKEY_CURRENT_USER\Software\Microsoft\Windows\CurrentVersion\Policies\Explorer
```

Warning Please read the Introduction for information on how to safely edit the Registry.

1. Click the Start button, click Run, enter *Regedit* in the Run box, and click OK.

2. Navigate your way down through the folders in the left pane until you locate the key described above.

3 Delete the NoInternetIcon value.

4. Close Regedit.

5. Restart Windows.

Related KB article Q190414

Windows Update Stops at Initializing Product Catalog

You visit the Windows Update web page, click Product Updates, and the update process does not continue, and you see the following message:

Please Wait: Windows Update is initializing the Product Catalog.

In addition, your computer might display the hourglass pointer. Although the update process might not continue, your computer might still respond normally, and you might still be able to browse other web pages.

Solution

The hard disk that contains the WINDOWS folder is incorrectly configured as removable. To reconfigure the hard disk, follow these steps:

1. Click the Start button, choose Settings, and then click Control Panel.

2. Double-click the System icon.

3. Click the Device Manager tab, and then double-click the Disk Drives branch to expand it.

4. Click your hard disk (for example, Generic IDE Disk Type01), click Properties, and then click the Settings tab.

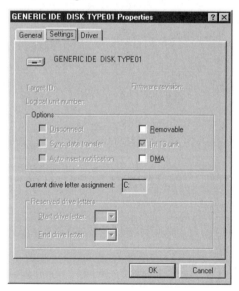

Figure 3-22. *The Generic IDE Disk Type01 Properties dialog box.*

5. Clear the Removable check box, and then click OK.

6. Repeat steps 4 and 5 for each hard disk, click Close, and then click Yes to restart your computer.

When you visit the Windows Update web page, and then click Product Updates, you normally expect to see a Windows Update dialog box with the following message:

> *This program can determine what components are installed on your computer, and whether new components, upgrades, or enhancements are available, specific to your computer. This check is done without sending any information to Microsoft. Would you like to check now?*

You do not see this dialog box if your computer has no fixed (nonremovable) disks.

Related KB article Q194174

CHAPTER 4

Disks and Controllers

CD-ROMs and DVDs

AST Advantage 828 Disables CD-ROM Changer

Your AST Advantage 828 computer contains a CD-ROM changer, and it does not work properly after you upgrade to Windows 98. Only a single CD-ROM drive is displayed in Device Manager, and the CD-ROM changer is displayed as Unknown Hardware under the Other Devices branch.

This problem occurs if SmartCD Manager is installed. The SCDMGRT3.VXD file located in the WINDOWS\SYSTEM\IOSUBSYS folder prevents Windows 98 from detecting the CD-ROM changer.

Solution

Move the SCDMGRT3.VXD file into a different folder, by following these steps:

1. Right-click the Start button, and choose Explore.

2. Choose Folder Options from the View menu.

3. Click the View tab, click the Show All Files option to select it, and click OK.

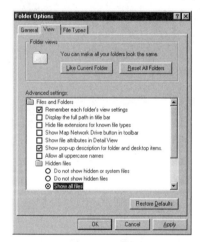

Figure 4-1.   *The Folder Options dialog box.*

4. Click the plus sign next to the WINDOWS folder.

5. Click the plus sign next to SYSTEM folder, and click the IOSUBSYS folder.

6. Click the SCDMGRT3.VXD file, and drag it to the MY DOCUMENTS folder.

Related KB article   Q188968

Audio CDs Play Automatically

You insert an audio CD, and Windows starts CDPLAYER.EXE by default, even though you don't want that to happen.

Solution

Associate another program with audio CDs, by following these steps:

1. Double-click My Computer.

2. Choose Folder Options from the View menu, and click the File Types tab.

3. Click AudioCD on the list of registered file types, and click Edit.

4. Click Play in the Action box, and click Edit.

Note If *Play* is not in bold letters, click Set Default.

5. In the Application Used To Perform Action box, enter the name of the program you want to run when you insert an audio CD, and click OK.

Note For additional information about the automatic playing of audio CDs in Windows, see KB article Q126025, "Preventing Windows 95 from Playing Audio CDs Automatically."

Related KB article Q154724

CD-ROM Causes Windows to Not Respond

You are copying a large folder structure from a CD-ROM drive to a local hard drive, and your computer stops responding.

Solution

To solve this problem, follow these steps:

1. Click the Start button, choose Settings, and click Control Panel.

2. Double-click the System icon.

3. Click the Performance tab, and click File System.

4. Click the CD-ROM tab.

5. In the Optimize Access Pattern For box, choose the setting that matches the CD-ROM drive you are using.

6. Click OK, and reboot your computer when prompted.

7. If steps 1–6 do not solve the problem, repeat steps 1–5. In the Optimize Access Pattern For box, click No Read Ahead.

8. Click OK, and reboot your computer.

Related KB article Q132882

CD-ROM Copies of Programs Don't Work Properly

You upgrade to Windows 98, and your CD-ROM copies of some programs do not work correctly. For example, you try to start a program, and you are prompted to insert the program's CD-ROM even though you have already inserted the copy of the program in the CD-ROM drive. Note that the program's original CD-ROM might still work correctly. Microsoft has confirmed that this behavior is not caused by a problem in Windows 98, but might be caused by design changes in Windows 98.

Solution One

Use the program's original CD-ROM.

Solution Two

Create a new copy of the program's original CD-ROM in Windows 98. For information, see the documentation included with your CD-ROM recording program.

Related KB article Q186297

CD-ROM Drive Causes Device, File, or Folder Errors

You try to use your CD-ROM drive and encounter one of the following problems:

- You cannot run executable (.EXE) files.

- You cannot view complete folder listings.

- You receive the following error message:

    Device not found.

This problem occurs when you are using an old version of the MSCDEX.EXE file that is not compatible with Windows 95 or Windows 98.

Solution

To solve this problem, follow these steps:

1. Click the Start button, choose Run, enter *sysedit* in the text box, and click in the C:\AUTOEXEC.BAT window.

2. Change the MSCDEX.EXE line so that it reads

    <drive>:\<windows>\command\mscdex.exe <parameters>

    where <drive> is the drive letter on which the WINDOWS folder is located, <windows> is the name of the folder in which Windows is installed, and <parameters> are the parameters from the original line containing MSCDEX.EXE.

Note To maintain compatibility with the installed CD-ROM driver, make sure to use all the parameters exactly as they are used in the original line.

---

3. Choose Save from the File menu, and close the program.

4. Reboot your computer.

Related KB article Q139428

CD-ROM Drive Inaccessible

You are unable to use your CD-ROM if your IDE (Integrated Device Electronics) controller cables are not properly connected. For example, your primary controller cable is incorrectly connected to your secondary controller.

Solution

Verify that your IDE controller cables are correctly connected. For information, see the documentation included with your motherboard or computer.

Related KB article Q193620

CD-ROM Drive Inaccessible When Windows Doesn't Start

Your computer stops responding (hangs), and you are not able to access your CD-ROM drive to extract files or reinstall Windows or Internet Explorer 4.0. This problem can also occur if you see an error message stating that you need to reinstall Windows.

Solution One

Restart your computer by using the Windows 98 Startup disk you created during setup. Choose the appropriate startup method from the StartUp menu.

Solution Two

1. Restart your computer. After your computer completes the Power On Self Test (POST), press and hold down the Ctrl key until you see the Windows 98 StartUp menu, and then choose Command Prompt Only.

2. Type each of the following lines, pressing Enter after each one:

```
cd\<windows>
edit system.ini
```

(where <windows> is the name assigned to your WINDOWS folder.)

3. Press Alt+S, press F, type *shell=* in the Find What box, and then press Enter.

4. Change the line to *shell=winfile.exe*. This step temporarily changes the shell to File Manager, available in Windows 98 for compatibility purposes.

Note File Manager is not recommended for normal use because it does not recognize and can damage long filenames if you change files or folders.

5. Press Alt+F, press S (to save), press Alt+F, and then press X (to exit).

6. Restart your computer.

Note You might not be able to use your CD-ROM drive if other core files (such as VMM32.VXD or WIN.COM) are damaged.

7. Use your CD-ROM to extract files, if necessary, or reinstall Windows or Internet Explorer 4.0.

8. Choose Run from the File menu, enter *sysedit* in the box, and click OK.

9. Choose SYSTEM.INI from the Window menu.

10. Change the shell= line to *shell=explorer.exe*.

11. Choose Save from the File menu, click Save, and then choose Exit from the File menu to restore the Windows Explorer shell.

12. Restart your computer.

Related KB article Q182090

CD-ROM Drive Unavailable After Installing Windows

You install Windows 98 and are unable to access your CD-ROM drive.

This problem occurs when you have a dual-channel integrated device electronics (IDE) controller installed in your computer or a hard disk that is on the second IDE channel.

Solution

To solve this problem, follow these steps:

1. Click the Start button, choose Settings, click Control Panel, and then double-click the System icon.

2. Click the Device Manager tab.

3. Click the Hard Disk Controllers branch to expand it, click your IDE controller, and click Properties.

4. Click the Settings tab.

5. In the Dual IDE Channel Settings box, click Both IDE Channels Enabled, and click OK.

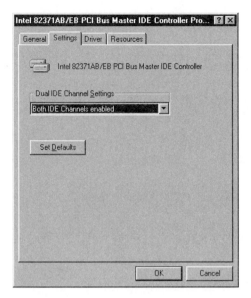

Figure 4-2. *The IDE Controller Properties dialog box.*

6. Click OK, and restart your computer.

Related KB article Q189526

CD-ROM Drive Uses Different Letter than Desired

Windows automatically assigns your CD-ROM drive a letter you don't want to use.

Solution

Change the drive letter of the CD-ROM drive, by following these steps:

1. Click the Start button, choose Settings, and click Control Panel.

2. Double-click the System icon, and click the Device Manager tab.

3. Click the plus sign next to the CD-ROM item.

4. Click the CD-ROM drive you want to change, and click Properties.

5. Click the Settings tab.

6. In the Reserved Drive Letters section, set Start Drive Letter and End Drive Letter to the drive letter you want the CD-ROM drive to use. Click OK until you return to Control Panel.

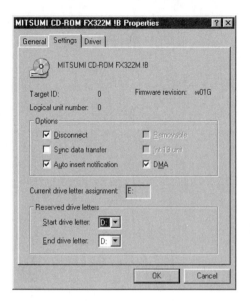

Figure 4-3.   *The Settings tab in the CD-ROM drive's Properties dialog box.*

7. Restart your computer.

Related KB article Q121244

Creative or MKE DVD Does Not Allow Write Access

You are using a first-generation Creative DVD kit or MKE DVD kit, and the kit doesn't work properly with Windows 98. For example, you're no longer able to write to the drive. These DVD kits rely on the Compact Disc File System (CDFS), and Windows 98 loads the Universal Disk Format file system (UDF) by default for DVD drives. This problem does not occur with later versions of Creative DVD kits. The DXR2 kit works correctly with UDF.

Solution

Disable UDF for DVD drives, by following these steps:

1. Click the Start button, choose Run, type *msconfig* in the Open box, and click OK.

2. Click Advanced.

3. Select the Disable UDF File System check box, and click OK.

4. Click OK. When you are prompted to restart your computer, click Yes.

When your computer restarts, UDF is disabled and the DVD kit should work as expected.

Related KB article Q188115

Formatting Re-Writable CD-ROM Drive Causes Errors

You try to format a blank CD-ROM disk with a CD-ROM Re-Writable (CD-RW) drive, and you receive the following error message:

Error: Write Data

Illegal Start Block Address. (0x4000004b)

You cannot read or write to disk through drive letter access.

This problem occurs because Advanced Power Management (APM) is enabled on your computer.

Solution One

Disable APM permanently on your computer if you do not want to use it, by following these steps:

1. Click the Start button, choose Settings, click Control Panel, and then double-click the Power Management icon.

2. In the System Standby box, click Never, click Never in the Turn Off Monitor box, and click Never in the Turn Off Hard Drive box.

3. Click Apply, click OK, and restart your computer.

Solution Two

If you do not want to permanently disable APM on your computer, you can temporarily disable it, use your CD-RW drive, and then reenable APM, by following these steps:

1. Click the Start button, choose Settings, click Control Panel, and double-click the Power Management icon.

2. Click Never in the System Standby box, click Never in the Turn Off Monitor box, and click Never in the Turn Off Hard Drive box.

3. Click Apply, click OK, and then restart your computer.

4. Use your CD-RW drive, and then restart your computer.

5. Click the Start button, choose Settings, click Control Panel, and then double-click the Power Management icon.

6. In the System Standby, Turn Off Monitor, and Turn Off Hard Drive boxes, click the appropriate time settings you want to use.

7. Click Apply, click OK, and then restart your computer.

Related KB article Q190922

Four CD-ROM Drives Displayed When Only One Is Present

You upgrade to Windows 98, and four CD-ROM drives are displayed in My Computer and Windows Explorer even though you have only one CD-ROM drive in your computer.

This problem occurs when you use an NEC 4X4, 4X6, 4X8, or 4X16 CD-ROM drive, and you installed an NEC Single CD in your earlier version of Windows.

Solution

Reinstall Single CD by using the disk included with your NEC 4X CD-ROM drive.

Related KB article Q189386

HP Re-Writable CD-ROM Causes Windows to Stop Responding

You install a Hewlett-Packard CD-ROM Re-Writable (CD-RW) drive in your Compaq Deskpro computer, and your computer stops responding when you try to view a window, such as My Computer or Windows Explorer, that points to the Hewlett-Packard CD-RW drive.

This problem can occur because Compaq uses a custom device driver CPQDFVS.VXD, located in the \WINDOWS\SYSTEM\IOSUBSYS folder, that can cause your computer to hang when you try to read from the CD-RW drive.

Solution One

Delete or rename the CPQDFVS.VXD file. For information about how to rename a file, click the Start button, choose Help, click the Index tab, type *renaming*, and then double-click the Renaming Files topic.

Solution Two

Contact Compaq to inquire whether it has a solution for this problem.

Related KB article Q186367

Philips or HP CD-R Drives Inaccessible

You upgrade Windows 95 to Windows 98, and you're unable to access your Philips CDD200 CD-R or Hewlett-Packard 4020i CD-R CD-ROM drive. This problem can occur if Corel CD Creator 2.0 is installed on your computer.

Microsoft has confirmed that this behavior is not caused by a problem in Windows 98, but might be caused by design changes in Windows 98.

Solution One

Use a different program, such as the latest version of Adaptec Easy CD Pro, to gain access to your CD-ROM drive.

Solution Two

Contact Philips or Hewlett-Packard to inquire about the availability of updated firmware.

Related KB article Q187695

Ricoh CD-RW Drive Causes Error Message

You attempt to erase, format, or copy data to a CD-ROM Re-Writable (CD-RW) CD using a Ricoh CD-RW drive and Adaptec Direct CD software, and you see this error message:

CD-RW is not under Direct CD's control

This problem can occur when the following conditions exist:

- Your Ricoh CD-RW drive has a firmware revision earlier than version 2.03.

- You are using Adaptec Direct CD version 2.0 or earlier.

Solution

Contact Adaptec and Ricoh to obtain updates.

Related KB article Q188165

Rock Ridge Formatted CD-ROMs Don't Read

Windows 98 does not support the Rock Ridge CD-ROM extensions. Rock Ridge is a method of storing POSIX file system extensions on a CD-ROM. Windows 98 uses the Joliet file system for deep subfolders and long filenames rather than the Rock Ridge CD-ROM extensions. Joliet permits the use of Unicode characters and clarifies some ambiguities in the ISO 9660 standard while providing some additional extensions.

Solution

If you need to read Rock Ridge-formatted CD-ROMs in Windows 98, use the Windows 98 version of MSCDEX.EXE and the MS-DOS device drivers provided by your CD-ROM drive's manufacturer.

Related KB article Q152200

Sanyo 3-D IDE CD-ROM Cannot Access More than One Disk

You use the Sanyo 3-D ATAPI (IDE) CD-ROM 3 disk changer, and although all three drives appear, only one disk is accessible.

Solution

Remove the REM command from the beginning of the MSCDEX line in your AUTOEXEC.BAT file, and disable the Windows 98 protected-mode disk driver, by following these steps:

1. Click the Start button, choose Settings, and click Control Panel.

2. Double-click the System icon, and click the Device Manager tab.

3. Select the View Devices By Connection option.

4. Locate the Sanyo drive.

5. Locate the parent controller.

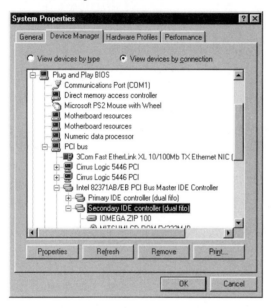

Figure 4-4. *The Device Manager tab in the System Properties dialog box.*

6. Select the controller, and click Properties.

7. Under Device Usage, select the Disable In This Hardware Profile check box.

This procedure enables access to all three drives from Windows 98 protected mode; however, your hard disk drive, CD-ROM, and any other devices under the controller will be accessed only through real-mode drivers.

For information about updating to a Windows 98 driver, contact your hardware vendor.

Related KB article Q191480 or HARDWARE.TXT in your WINDOWS folder

Sanyo 3CD Multidisk CD-ROM Assigns Three Drive Letters

You upgrade to Windows 98 and notice that your Sanyo 3CD multidisk CD-ROM drive now has three drive letters assigned to it. This problem occurs even though the Smart CD Manager program previously assigned only one drive letter to this drive.

This problem can occur because Windows 98 replaces the CDVSD.VXD and TORISAN3.VXD files included with the Smart CD Manager program. The updated versions of these files are not compatible with the Smart CD Manager program.

Solution

Reinstall the Smart CD Manager program.

Related KB article Q188110

Small Computer System Interface (SCSI) CD-ROM Drive Inaccessible

Windows 98 Setup restarts your computer for the first time, Setup is unable to gain access to your Small Computer System Interface (SCSI) CD-ROM drive, and you receive error messages stating that files cannot be found. The filenames vary depending on your computer's hardware. After setup is completed and you attempt to start Windows 98, your computer stops responding, and only a blinking cursor is displayed on a black screen.

This problem occurs when the HIDE120.COM file is being loaded from the AUTOEXEC.BAT file.

Solution

To solve this problem, follow these steps:

1. Restart your computer. After your computer completes the Power On Self Test (POST), press and hold down the Ctrl key until you see the Windows 98 StartUp menu, and then choose Safe Mode Command Prompt Only.

2. At the command prompt, type *edit autoexec.bat*, and press Enter.

3. Disable the following line in the AUTOEXEC.BAT file by typing *rem* at the beginning of the following line:

    <drive>:\lsl120\hide120.com

4. Press Alt+F, press S (to save), press Alt+F again, and then press X (to exit).

5. Restart your computer normally.

Some devices, such as your sound card or video adapter, might not work properly when you start Windows 98. To solve this problem, follow these steps:

1. Click the Start button, choose Settings, click Control Panel, double-click the System icon, and click the Device Manager tab.

2. Click a device that is not working properly (indicated by an exclamation point in a yellow circle next to the device), click Remove, and click OK to confirm device removal.

3. Repeat step 2 for each device that is not working properly.

4. Click Close, and then restart your computer. Windows 98 should detect the devices and install the appropriate drivers.

Related KB article Q189464

Sony CD-ROM Drive Not Detected During Setup

The Sony CD-ROM drive in your computer is not detected during the setup operation.

This problem occurs when the Sony CD-ROM drive is attached to a Media Vision sound card. Setup searches for the drives at several base I/O addresses, but it is not in the range of addresses that Setup checks.

Solution

Set up the CD-ROM drive in Windows manually, by following these steps:

1. Click the Start button, choose Settings, and click Control Panel.

2. Double-click the Add New Hardware icon, and click Next.

3. Click No, and click Next.

4. Click CD-ROM controllers, and click Next.

5. Choose Sony in the Manufacturers box, choose Sony Proprietary CD-ROM Controller in the Models box, and click Next.

6. Click Next, and click Finish.

7. When you are prompted to restart your computer, click No.

8. Click the Start button, choose Settings, and click Control Panel.

9. Double-click the System icon.

10. Double-click the CD-ROM Controllers branch on the Device Manager tab, and double-click Sony Proprietary CD-ROM Controller.

11. Click the Resources tab.

12. Click Basic Configuration 0 in the Settings Based On box.

13. Clear the Use Automatic Settings check box.

14. Use the Change Settings option to modify the resources to match the CD-ROM drive's settings.

Note If your Media Vision card is permanently set to use IRQ 5, do not select IRQ 5, or else Windows or the CD-ROM drive will not work correctly.

15. Click OK.

16. Reboot your computer when you are prompted.

Related KB article Q134532

Toshiba DVD Player Displays Error Message

You use Windows Explorer to eject a DVD movie that is being played by a Toshiba DVD player, and you see the following error message on a blue screen:

Re-insert the media and press any key to continue.

When you reinsert the DVD movie in the player and press a key, you receive the same error message and the movie is automatically ejected.

This problem can occur if you press a key before the DVD movie is fully spun up, or at normal rotational velocity.

Solution

Insert the DVD movie into the player, and then wait to press a key until the light on the Toshiba DVD player is turned off. This indicates that the DVD movie is fully spun up.

Related KB article Q188175

Two CD-ROM Drives Displayed When Only One Is Present

You upgrade to Windows 98, and two CD-ROM drives are listed in My Computer, even though you have only one physical CD-ROM drive in your computer. Also, if you look at the Performance tab under the System icon in Control Panel, the second drive is reported to be using MS-DOS Compatibility Mode Paging.

This problem can occur if you manually assign a drive letter to your CD-ROM drive on your Windows 95–based computer but you leave at least one unused drive letter. If you then upgrade to Windows 98, the unused drive letter and the original drive letter are mapped to the same CD-ROM drive.

Solution

To solve this problem, follow these steps:

1. Click the Start button, choose Settings, click Control Panel, and then double-click the System icon.

2. Click the Device Manager tab, and double-click the CD-ROM branch to expand it.

3. Click the second CD-ROM listed under the CD-ROM branch, click Properties, click the Settings tab, and then change the Start drive and End drive letters to the same as the drive letter for the first CD-ROM drive.

4. Click OK, click OK again, and then restart your computer.

Related KB article Q188723

Disk Controllers and Software

Adaptec EZ-SCSI 3.1 Does Not Install Correctly

You run EZ-SCSI 3.1 in Windows 98, and your CONFIG.SYS and AUTOEXEC.BAT files are not properly modified, possibly preventing the use of any SCSI devices you have.

Solution

Run EZ-SCSI for DOS. To do this, click the Start button, and choose Shut Down. Click the Restart In MS-DOS Mode option, and click OK. Run the EZ-SCSI program as described in your software documentation.

For information about Adaptec software products designed specifically for Windows 98, contact Adaptec directly, at 800-959-7274 or 408-945-8600 or at *http://www.adaptec.com.*

Related KB article Q188978 or PROGRAMS.TXT in your WINDOWS folder

Adaptec EZ-SCSI 4 Causes Invalid Page Fault After Reinstalling

You reinstall the Adaptec EZ-SCSI version 4.0x software and receive the following error message:

ADPST32 caused an invalid page fault in module MSCUISTF.dll at 015f:007dlbf7.

This problem can occur if the following conditions exist:

- An Adaptec 3940UW Dual Channel SCSI adapter is installed on your computer.

- You previously set the Write and Read Cache settings to Enable in SCSI Explorer (included with EZ-SCSI 4.0x).

- You uninstalled the EZ-SCSI software and then restarted your computer before attempting to reinstall the EZ-SCSI software.

Solution

To solve this problem, follow these steps:

1. Restart your computer. When you see the SCSI BIOS information, press Ctrl+A to start the SCSI setup program.

2. In the SCSI setup program, press the F6 key to restore the factory default settings. You must do this for both channels.

3. Turn your computer off and then back on.

4. Uninstall and then reinstall the EZ-SCSI software.

If these steps do not solve the problem, contact Adaptec for assistance.

Related KB article Q188827

FDISK Does Not Show Hard Disk Partitions

You run the FDISK command at a command prompt from within Windows, and you do not see any defined partitions on the hard disk.

This problem occurs when your computer contains a Phoenix Plus version 0.10 GLB01 BIOS and the Disable All 32-Bit Protected-Mode Disk Drivers check box is selected on the Troubleshooting tab in System Properties.

Solution

Either obtain an updated version of your computer's BIOS by contacting the manufacturer or enable 32-bit protected-mode disk drivers, by following these steps:

1. Click the Start button, choose Settings, and click Control Panel.

2. Double-click the System icon, and click the Performance tab.

3. Click File System, and click the Troubleshooting tab.

4. Clear the Disable All 32-Bit Protected-Mode Disk Drivers check box.

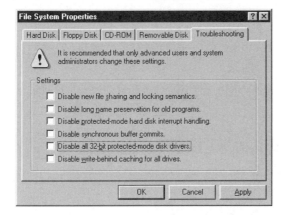

Figure 4-5. *The File System Properties dialog box.*

5. Click OK, and click Close.

6. Click Yes when you are prompted to restart your computer.

Related KB article Q139579

Gateway 2200 Solo Causes No Fixed Disk Error

You use a Gateway 2200 Solo laptop computer, and you receive an error message stating that no fixed disk is present when you start your computer.

This problem occurs when the Device Manager settings to disable the Integrated Device Electronics (IDE) controllers are enabled. The problem occurs because Device Manager writes to non-volatile RAM (NVRAM), resetting the Basic Input/Output System (BIOS) to disable IDE controllers.

Solution One

Do not disable the IDE controllers in Device Manager if the only bootable device is an IDE hard disk.

Solution Two

Reenable the IDE controllers in your computer's CMOS settings. For information about modifying your computer's CMOS settings, see your computer's documentation or contact the manufacturer.

When Windows 98 starts up, enable the IDE controllers in Device Manager. If you do not enable the IDE controllers in Device Manager, the problem reoccurs the next time you start your computer. To enable the IDE controllers in Device Manager, follow these steps:

1. Click the Start button, choose Settings, and click Control Panel.

2. Double-click the System icon, and click the Device Manager tab.

3. Double-click the Hard Disk Controllers branch to expand it.

4. Click an IDE controller, and click Properties.

5. Clear the Disable In This Hardware Profile check box.

6. Click OK.

7. Repeat steps 4–6 for each IDE controller.

8. Click OK.

Related KB article Q192987

Hard Disk Controller Doesn't Allow 32-Bit File Access

Your computer contains a PCI-IDE hard disk controller that employs serialization between the two IDE channels, and you experience the following:

- Thirty-two-bit file system access and 32-bit virtual memory are not available.

- Device Manager displays an exclamation point in a yellow circle for the primary and secondary IDE channels.

The protected-mode driver for the hard disk controller was not properly initialized when you previously started Windows. When this occurs, a NOIDE entry is placed in the Registry, and this entry prevents Windows from making any later attempts to initialize the protected-mode driver. Removing and reinstalling the hard disk controller does not solve this problem.

Solution

Make Windows attempt to reinitialize the protected-mode IDE driver, by removing the NOIDE entry from the following Registry key:

```
HKEY_LOCAL_MACHINE\System\CurrentControlSet\Services\VxD\IOS
```

Follow these steps:

1. Navigate your way to the TOOLS\MTSUTIL folder on the Windows 98 CD-ROM, right-click the NOIDE.INF file, and choose Install. This step should remove a NOIDE entry, if it exists.

2. Restart Windows.

Windows now attempts to initialize the protected-mode driver for the controller. If no problems are encountered, the file system and virtual memory operate in 32-bit mode, and Device Manager does not display an exclamation point in a yellow circle for the IDE channels.

If the protected-mode driver is not initialized properly, an error message is displayed and the NOIDE Registry entry is re-created. Windows uses the MS-DOS compatibility mode file system the next time you start your computer. This problem can occur with an IDE controller that requires serialization between the primary and secondary IDE channels. The protected-mode drivers for these IDE controllers can fail to be initialized if one of the following situations occurs:

- One IDE channel has a supported hard disk, and the second channel has a CD-ROM or other type of drive that requires real-mode drivers to be loaded. Because of the serialization between the two IDE channels, it is impossible to access the hard disk in protected mode and use the other device in real mode. This situation causes the protected-mode driver to fail initialization, and the NOIDE switch is placed in the Registry to prevent future errors. Both disk devices then operate in real mode.

- The driver for the IDE controller is manually removed from Device Manager and then reinstalled, or the protected-mode driver is disabled and then subsequently reenabled. Some PCI controller drivers are not designed for dynamic enabling and disabling and can cause the protected-mode driver to fail initialization.

The Windows device drivers for the following controllers are known to exhibit this behavior:

- CMD PCI-0640 PCI-IDE controller

- Standard Dual PCI-IDE controller

- Opti Dual PCI-IDE controller

Other PCI-IDE controllers that use serialization between the IDE channels might also exhibit this behavior.

Related KB article Q151911

Intel Bus Mastering Drivers Cause Errors

You upgrade to Windows 98 and experience one or more of the following situations:

- Device Manager reports resource conflicts with your hard disk controller.

- Your computer runs very slowly.

- You cannot gain access to your CD-ROM drive in Windows 98 or in MS-DOS using real-mode drivers.

This problem occurs when Intel bus mastering drivers are installed before you upgrade to Windows 98.

Solution

To solve this problem, follow these steps:

1. Restart your computer. After your computer completes the Power On Self Test (POST), press and hold down the Ctrl key until you see the Windows 98 StartUp menu, and then choose Safe Mode.

2. Click the Start button, choose Programs, and click Windows Explorer.

3. If the IDEATAPI.INF file in the WINDOWS\INF folder exists, rename the file.

Note The IDEATAPI.INF file is a hidden file. To be able to see hidden files, choose Folder Options from the View menu in Windows Explorer, click the View tab, click Show All Files, and click OK.

---

4. Rebuild the Windows 98 driver information database by renaming the DRVDATA.BIN and DRVIDX.BIN files located in the WINDOWS\INF folder.

5. Click the Start button, choose Settings, click Control Panel, and then double-click the System icon.

6. Click the Device Manager tab, and double-click the Hard Disk Controllers branch to expand it.

7. Click the hard disk controller, and click Remove.

8. If more than one hard disk controller is listed, repeat steps 6 and 7.

9. Click OK.

10. Restart your computer. Windows enumerates the hard disk controller and installs the correct drivers.

Note During enumeration, Windows 98 uses the IDEATAPI.INF file provided by Intel and the existing bus mastering drivers rather than the MSHDC.INF file and the drivers included with Windows 98.

Related KB article Q189518

Iomega Ditto Dash Doesn't Install

After you install Windows 98, Device Manager displays an exclamation point in a yellow circle next to Iomega Ditto Dash.

Solution

Use the Add New Hardware Wizard to manually install the drivers for your Iomega Ditto Dash card, by following these steps:

1. Click the Start button, choose Settings, and click Control Panel.

2. Double-click the Add New Hardware icon.

3. Click Next, and click Next again to search for Plug and Play devices.

4. Click No, The Device Isn't In The List, and click Next.

5. Click No, I Want To Select The Hardware From A List, and click Next.

6. Under Hardware Types, click Tape Drive Controllers, and click Next.

7. Under Manufacturers, click Iomega, and click Iomega Ditto Dash under Models.

8. Click Next, click Next again, and click Finish.

If an exclamation point in a yellow circle is still displayed next to Iomega Ditto Dash in Device Manager, you might have to change the card's resource settings. For information, see KB article Q133240, "Troubleshooting Device Conflicts with Device Manager."

Related KB article Q194533

MicroHouse EZ-Driver Is Not Compatible with Windows Drivers

You install Windows 98 on a computer with the MicroHouse EZ-Driver software, and Device Manager reports that some of your drives are using MS-DOS compatibility mode.

The MH32BIT.386 device driver that installs with EZ-Driver loads in the SYSTEM.INI file. This device driver is not compatible with the Windows protected-mode disk drivers and is not removed by Windows Setup.

Solution

Disable the line that loads the MH32BIT.386 device driver in the SYSTEM.INI file, by following these steps:

1. Use a text editor, such as Notepad, to open the SYSTEM.INI file in the WINDOWS folder.

2. Locate the line that loads the MH32BIT.386 device driver.

3. Place a semicolon (;) at the beginning of the line.

4. Save and close the SYSTEM.INI file.

5. Using the EZ.EXE program by MicroHouse, disable the Floppy Boot Protection option.

6. Restart Windows.

Note For additional information about the MH32BIT.386 device driver, see the documentation included with EZ-Driver or contact MicroHouse.

Related KB article Q137405

RAMDrive Does Not Copy File with Long Filename

You try to copy a file with a long filename to a RAMDrive larger than 10 megabytes (MB), and you receive the following error message:

The destination does not support long filenames. Please enter a name for this file.

If you try to rename this file, you are not able to use a long filename.

Solution One

Do not copy files with long filenames to a RAMDrive larger than 10 MB.

Solution Two

Reduce the size of the RAMDrive. A RAMDrive smaller than 10 MB should not exhibit this behavior. If possible, reduce the size of your RAMDrive until it is smaller than 10 MB.

Related KB article Q192927

Hard Drives

Disk Error Messages

You see any of the following error messages when you start or use your computer:

Serious Disk Error Writing Drive <X>

Data Error Reading Drive <X>

Error Reading Drive <X>

I/O Error

Seek Error - Sector not found

These error messages indicate either damaged data or physical damage on the hard disk.

Solution

Run ScanDisk. To run it from within Windows, follow these steps:

1. Click the Start button, choose Programs, click Accessories, click System Tools, and click ScanDisk.

2. Select the drive you want to examine for errors.

3. Click Thorough, and click the Start button.

Running ScanDisk with the Thorough option selected examines the hard disk for physical damage. If damaged data is detected, ScanDisk gives you the option to save the damaged data to a file or to discard the data. The ScanDisk surface scan might take a considerable amount of time on large hard disks.

To run ScanDisk from a command prompt outside Windows, follow these steps:

1. Click the Start button, choose Shut Down, click Restart In MS-DOS Mode, and click OK.

2. Type *scandisk <x>* at the command prompt (where <x> is the letter of the hard disk you want to check), and then press Enter.

3. When ScanDisk finishes its initial check, it prompts you to perform a surface scan on the drive. Click Yes or press Enter.

If ScanDisk is unable to repair damaged data or indicates that the hard disk has physical damage, you might need to have a qualified service professional check the disk.

Related KB article Q150532

DMA Check Box in Device Manager Doesn't Remain Selected

You enable DMA (direct memory access) support on the Settings tab in an IDE (Integrated Device Electronics) hard disk's properties, and the DMA check box in Device Manager does not remain selected even though the IDE controller reportedly supports bus mastering and DMA.

Solution

The hard disk might not support a multiple-word DMA protocol. Determine whether your primary IDE hard disk supports multiple-word DMA protocol, by following these steps:

1. Restart your computer. After your computer completes the Power On Self Test (POST), press and hold down the Ctrl key until you see the Windows 98 StartUp menu, and then choose Command Prompt Only.

2. At the command prompt, type *debug*.

3. At the hyphen prompt, type the following lines, pressing Enter after each line; do not type the semicolon (;) or the comment after the semicolon:

Note The first character of each line is the letter *o,* not the numeral 0.

```
o 1f6 a0 ; a0 (a-zero) is for a master drive, use b0 for a slave.
o 1f2 22 ; 22 is for DMA mode 2, use 21 for DMA mode 1.
o 1f1 03 ; 03 (zero-3) is to program the hard disk timing.
o 1f7 ef ; ef is the set feature command for the hard disk.
i 1f1    ; Reads in the error status; a value is returned.
```

4. To exit Debug, type *q* and press Enter.

If the number returned after entering *i 1f1* is 00, the hard disk accepts the DMA protocol timing you entered with the *o 1f2* statement and the hard disk supports DMA. A return value of 04 indicates that the hard disk does not support a DMA multiple-word protocol. If the value returned is not 00 or 04, you might not have typed the characters correctly, or you might have to exit Windows.

PIO mode 3 hard disks might support multiple-word DMA mode 1. PIO mode 4 hard disks should support multiple-word DMA mode 2. If you have a PIO mode 4 drive that does not support multiple-word DMA mode 2, the hard disk might have a firmware problem. Contact your hard disk's manufacturer, and verify the firmware version.

Test the secondary IDE drive, by following these steps:

1. Restart your computer. After your computer completes the Power On Self Test (POST), press and hold down the Ctrl key until you see the Windows 98 StartUp menu, and then choose Command Prompt Only.

2. At the command prompt, type *debug*.

3. At the hyphen prompt, type the following lines, pressing Enter after each line; do not type the semicolon (;) or the comment after the semicolon:

Note The first character of each line is the letter *o*, not the numeral 0.

```
o 176 a0 ; a0 (a-zero) is for a master drive, use b0 for a slave.

o 172 22 ; 22 is for DMA mode 2, use 21 for DMA mode 1.

o 171 03 ; 03 (zero-3) is to program the hard disk timing.

o 177 ef ; ef is the set feature command for the hard disk.

i 171    ; Reads in the error status; a value is returned.
```

4. To exit Debug, type *q* and press Enter.

If the number returned after entering *i 171* is 00, the hard disk accepts the DMA protocol timing you entered with the *o 172* statement and the hard disk supports DMA. A return value of 04 indicates that the hard disk does not support a DMA multiple-word protocol.

If your drive does support a DMA multiple-word protocol and the DMA check box does not remain selected, the IDE controller might not be compatible with the Microsoft IDE bus mastering driver.

DMA (also referred to as bus mastering) reduces CPU overhead by providing a mechanism for data transfers that do not require monitoring by the CPU. The transfer rate for a particular data transfer event does not noticeably increase. However, overall CPU overhead should be reduced using DMA mode.

A disadvantage of implementing DMA data-transfer operations has been that the PC/AT and IDE hard disk controller evolved around PIO data-transfer methods. As a result, the system Int 13h BIOS and native operating system device drivers evolved around PIO transfers rather than around DMA transfers. Modifications to the BIOS, as well as external device drivers, have been necessary to achieve the incremental performance that DMA offers.

Related KB article Q159560

Drive Unavailable After Hot Docking

You hot-undock (eject) and then hot-dock (insert) your laptop computer using a docking station containing a hard disk, and one or more hard disks or CD-ROM drives become unavailable to Windows. This problem can occur when Windows attempts to assign the same drive letter to one of the drives in the docking station and to an existing drive in the portable computer during the hot-docking operation.

Solution

Restore access to all drives installed in both your computer and the docking station, by shutting down and restarting Windows.

Related KB article Q193342

Hard Drive Doesn't Format

You try to format your hard disk, and you see the following error message:

Insufficient memory to load system files.

Format terminated.

This problem can occur if you attempt to format your hard disk by using the *format c: /q/u/s/v* command at a command prompt and your computer does not have enough free conventional memory to use the */s* parameter (switch).

The problem can also occur if you start your computer by using the Windows 98 startup disk and then attempt to format your hard disk.

Solution One

Do not use the */s* parameter (switch) with the FORMAT command. After the format process is finished, use the *SYS C:* command to transfer the system files to the hard disk.

Solution Two

Restart your computer by using the Windows 98 startup disk, choose Start Computer With CD-ROM Support from the StartUp menu, and then use the FORMAT command to format your hard disk.

Related KB article Q177864

Maximum Partition Size for Drive Larger than 8 GB Is Only 8 GB

You try to partition a drive that is larger than 8 GB (gigabytes), and the maximum partition size is 8 GB if the hard disk controller does not fully support the Interrupt 13 (Int 13) extensions. This information applies to both IDE and SCSI hard disk drives.

Solution

Contact your drive controller's manufacturer for information about a possible upgrade to a version of the BIOS that fully supports Interrupt 13 extensions.

For a hard disk that is larger than 8 GB and that uses the FAT32 file system to be fully addressed, the disk must support Interrupt 13 extensions. IO.SYS tests for the presence of Interrupt 13 extensions. If these extensions are not detected, the default CHS LBA (Logical Block Addressing) limit of 7.9 GB is used.

To determine whether your BIOS supports Interrupt 13 extensions, see your computer's documentation or contact your computer's manufacturer.

Related KB article Q153550

Performance

Bootup Takes a Long Time or Drives Use MS-DOS Compatibility Mode

You install the FAT32 file system on a drive that uses OnTrack Disk Manager version 6.03 or 7.04, and you find that all drives use MS-DOS compatibility mode or your computer seems to take an unusually long time to boot. Either situation occurs because Dynamic Drive Overlay is unable to find in the root folder the files it needs to start correctly.

Solution

Configure Disk Manager to avoid searching the root folder for overlay files, or upgrade Disk Manager to version 8.0 or later.

Note For information about or assistance with configuring Disk Manager, contact OnTrack Technical Support.

Dynamic Drive Overlay makes calculations for the starting root folder cluster based on FAT12 and FAT16 volumes and returns a value of zero for FAT32 volumes. This process occurs because of changes made in the root folder structure. The overlay software searches all possible clusters in the root folder for its overlay files.

Configuring the Disk Manager Dynamic Drive Overlay software to avoid searching the root folder causes Disk Manager not to hook the DOS Arena Chain, forcing Disk Manager to load low in conventional memory.

Related KB article Q152701

CD-ROM Program Doesn't Perform Well

You run a program that accesses a CD-ROM drive, and you notice that the program is not performing optimally. You notice slow data transfer in a business or reference program or skipping or slow audio and video in a multimedia program.

This problem occurs when the Supplemental Cache Size and Optimize Access Pattern For settings are not set correctly for your CD-ROM drive.

Solution

Improve your CD-ROM drive's performance, by following these steps:

1. Click the Start button, choose Settings, click Control Panel, and then double-click the System icon.

2. Click the Performance tab, and click File System.

3. Click the CD-ROM tab.

4. Move the Supplemental Cache Size slider to the right to allocate more random access memory (RAM) for caching data from the CD-ROM drive or to the left to allocate less RAM for caching data.

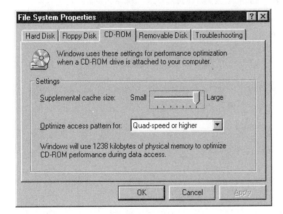

Figure 4-6. *The CD-ROM tab in the File System Properties dialog box.*

Note Many multimedia programs perform better with a smaller cache because these programs do not reuse data.

5. For reading continuous data, such as .AVI files, use a higher setting in the Optimize Access Pattern For box. For reading random data, increase the Supplemental Cache Size setting and decrease the Optimize Access Pattern For setting.

6. Click OK, and click Close.

7. Restart your computer when you are prompted.

Note If you are using real mode drivers for your CD-ROM drive, these settings have no effect.

Related KB article Q141368

PCI BusLogic SCSI Controller Performs Slowly

You try to use the PCI BusLogic SCSI controller, and the system performs slowly. Or Device Manager displays an exclamation point in a yellow circle next to the PCI BusLogic SCSI controller.

Solution

This problem occurs when the BusLogic card is not configured as a true PCI device. If the version number in the upper right corner of the card is -01-4.23K or later, the card is supported in true PCI mode and Microsoft recommends that you remove the jumpers in the bottom right corner of the card. However, if the version is earlier than -01-4.23K, do not remove the jumpers.

Related KB article Q132657

Removable Disks and Tape Drives

Copying Files to Floppy Displays Error Message

You try to copy one or more files to a double-density floppy disk after you format the disk, and you receive a Disk Copy error message on a blue screen.

Solution

Copy the file or files to the floppy disk in MS-DOS. For information about copying files in MS-DOS, click the Start button, choose Programs, click MS-DOS Prompt, type *copy /?*, and then press Enter.

Related KB article Q185702

Copying Floppy Disk Displays Error Messages

You use the DISKCOPY command at a command prompt in Windows 98, and you see the following error message:

Error: Unrecoverable write error on drive A Side <n>, track <n>

After you right-click the disk drive in Windows Explorer and choose Copy Disk, you see the following error message:

Error: Unable to write to the destination disk.

Check to make sure the disk is inserted properly in the drive, the drive door is closed, and the disk is not write-protected.

This problem can occur if the *target disk,* the floppy disk to which you are attempting to copy, is not formatted.

Solution One

Format the floppy disk before using the DISKCOPY command.

Solution Two

Use the DISKCOPY command in MS-DOS mode, by following these steps:

1. Click the Start button, and choose Shut Down.

2. Click Restart In MS-DOS Mode, and click OK.

3. At the command prompt, type the DISKCOPY command you want to use. For example, type *diskcopy a: b:*, and then press Enter.

4. When the copy operation is finished, type *exit* and press Enter.

Related KB article Q187692

DISKCOPY Causes Errors When Starting from Run Command Line

You try to run the DISKCOPY command by choosing the Run command from the Start menu to copy from one 3.5-inch floppy disk drive to another identical drive, and you see the following error message:

Unrecoverable read error on drive A: side 0, track 64

Unrecoverable write error on drive B: side 0, track 64

Target diskette may be unusable.

Note This problem does not occur on computers with one 3.5-inch floppy disk drive and one 5.25-inch floppy disk drive or on computers with two 5.25-inch floppy disk drives.

Solution One

Run the DISKCOPY command in MS-DOS mode, by following these steps:

1. Click the Start button, and choose Shut Down.

2. Click Restart In MS-DOS Mode, and click OK.

3. At the command prompt, type the DISKCOPY command. For example, type *diskcopy a: b:*, and then press Enter.

4. When the copy operation is finished, type *exit,* and then press Enter.

Solution Two

Disable protected-mode support for the floppy disk controller. This action causes the floppy disk drives to operate in MS-DOS compatibility mode. Follow these steps:

1. Click the Start button, choose Settings, click Control Panel, and double-click the System icon.

2. Click the Device Manager tab.

3. Click the Floppy Disk Controllers branch to expand it, and double-click Standard Floppy Disk Controller.

4. Select the Disable In This Hardware Profile check box, and click OK.

5. Restart your computer when you are prompted.

Solution Three

Manually copy the information from the source disk to the destination disk.

Related KB article Q150743

Drive Letter Changes Don't Remain

You change floppy disk drive letters in your computer's CMOS (complementary metal oxide semi-conductor) settings, and Windows continues to access the drives by using their original drive letters. This problem can occur if your computer's BIOS swaps the floppy disk drives in firmware, which Windows does not detect automatically. Most computers swap the drives electrically, which Windows can detect successfully.

Solution

Use Registry Editor to delete the following key from the Registry:

HKEY_LOCAL_MACHINE\Enum\Flop\GENERIC_NEC__FLOPPY_DISK_

Warning Please read the Introduction for information about how to safely edit the Registry.

1. Click the Start button, choose Run, and enter *regedit* in the Run box. Click OK.

2. Navigate your way through the folders in the left pane, and delete the appropriate key.

3. Restart Windows.

If Windows still accesses the floppy disk drives incorrectly, use the Add New Hardware icon in Control Panel to redetect your computer's hardware.

Related KB article Q145808

Folder Doesn't Copy to Floppy Disk

You try to copy a folder to a floppy disk, and you see the following error message:

The file being copied is too large for the destination drive.

If possible, insert a higher-capacity disk.

This problem occurs if the folder you are copying contains a file larger than the formatted capacity of the floppy disk. For example, after you format a 1.44 MB 3.5-inch floppy disk, it has only 1.38 MB of free disk space. If you try to copy to the floppy disk a folder that contains a file larger than 1.38 MB, you see the preceding error message. When the error message is displayed, the file information is displayed in the Copying dialog box.

Solution One

Move the file to another folder, and then try to copy the folder again. For information about how to move a file, click the Start button, choose Help, click the Index tab, enter *moving* in the box, and double-click the Moving Files Or Folders topic.

Solution Two

Use Microsoft Backup to back up the folder. To start Microsoft Backup, click the Start button, choose Programs, click Accessories, click System Tools, and click Backup.

Related KB article Q188128

Iomega Zip Drive or SyQuest Removable-Media Disk Drive Causes Windows to Stop Responding or Operate Slowly

You use an Iomega Zip drive or SyQuest removable-media disk drive, and Windows 98 operates slowly or your computer randomly stops responding (hangs). This problem occurs if the drive is attached to your computer's parallel port.

Solution One

If your Iomega Zip drive is connected to your computer's parallel port, update the driver for the drive, by following these steps:

1. Click the Start button, choose Settings, and click Control Panel.

2. Double-click the System icon, and click the Device Manager tab.

3. Double-click the Iomega device for which you are installing an updated driver, click the Driver tab, and click Update Driver.

4. Click Next.

5. Click Display A List Of All Drivers In A Specific Location So You Can Select The Driver You Want, and click Next.

6. Click Have Disk, click the drive containing the Windows 98 CD-ROM in the Copy Manufacturer's Files From box, browse to the DRIVERS\STORAGE\IOMEGA\PPA3 folder, click OK, and click OK again.

Solution Two

If your SyQuest removable-media disk drive is connected to your computer's parallel port, download and install the latest driver for your drive from the SyQuest web site.

Related KB article Q190639

MS-DOS Doesn't Read Floppy Disks

In several situations, MS-DOS does not successfully read a floppy disk. For example, if you use the MS-DOS directory command (DIR) to look at the contents of a standard floppy disk or a DMF floppy disk, the command results are unintelligible. If you switch floppy disks that are the same density but are formatted differently (for example, a 1.44-MB high-density disk is exchanged for a 1.68-MB high-density disk), MS-DOS also has trouble showing the disk contents or reading the disk.

Solution One

Contact your computer's manufacturer to ensure that your CMOS settings are correct. You should also run a virus-detection utility to determine whether your computer is infected with a virus.

Solution Two

Determine whether change-line support is the cause of your problem, by following these steps:

1. Restart your computer, and press the F4 key when you see the message *Starting Windows*.

2. Insert a non-DMF disk in drive A (assuming that drive a: is your 1.44MB floppy drive) and then type the following lines at the MS-DOS prompt, pressing the Enter key after each line:

   ```
   a:
   ```

   ```
   dir
   ```

3. If the preceding commands work successfully, insert a DMF disk and type *dir*.

4. If your floppy disk is a 1.44 MB A drive and the second DIR command fails, garbage characters appear onscreen, or subsequent reads of the floppy disk fail (during setup or otherwise), insert the statement *DRIVPARM=/d:0 /f:7* at the end of the CONFIG.SYS file and reboot your computer.

5. If your floppy disk is a 1.44 MB drive B and the second DIR command fails, garbage characters appear onscreen, or subsequent reads of the floppy disk fail (during setup or otherwise), insert the statement *DRIVPARM=/d:1 /f:7* at the end of the CONFIG.SYS file and reboot your computer:

6. If your CONFIG.SYS file contains a DRIVER.SYS line, disable it by typing *rem* immediately preceding the line.

7. Repeat steps 2 and 3. If the preceding steps work successfully, change-line support is not functioning properly—leave the DRIVPARM statement in your CONFIG.SYS file. If the preceding steps fail, remove the DRIVPARM statement from your CONFIG.SYS file and contact your computer's manufacturer to ensure that your CMOS settings are correct.

Related KB article Q118580

Removable Drive Ejection Causes Windows to Not Respond

You use a removable drive for the Windows paging drive (the location of the Windows swap file) and eject the drive while Windows is running, and either your computer stops responding (hangs) or you see a *Fatal Exception* error message. The drive containing the Windows swap file cannot be safely ejected while Windows is running. Windows does not prevent the paging drive from being ejected when you right-click the drive icon in Windows Explorer and choose Eject.

Solution One

Do not use Windows Explorer to eject the paging drive.

Solution Two

Set the paging file to a nonremovable drive, if one is available, by following these steps:

1. Click the Start button, choose Settings, and click Control Panel.

2. Double-click the System icon.

3. Click the Performance tab, and click Virtual Memory.

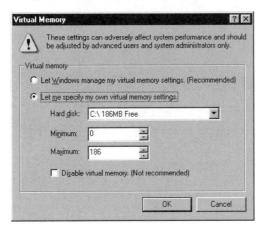

Figure 4-7. *The Virtual Memory dialog box.*

4. Click Let Me Specify My Own Virtual Memory Settings, and then select the paging file location and size. (The drive listed in the Hard Disk box is the current paging drive.)

5. Click OK twice.

You can also follow these steps to determine which drive is the current paging drive:

1. Click the Start button, choose Find, and click Files Or Folders.

2. Enter *win386.swp* in the Named box, click a drive in the Look In box, and click Find Now.

This file is the Windows paging file (or swap file), and the drive on which it is located is the paging drive. If your first search does not locate this file, repeat step 2 and click a different drive.

When a removable drive is used as the paging drive, Windows prevents the drive from being ejected through hardware. For example, pressing the eject button on the drive while Windows is running displays the following message:

Eject Request to Drive In Use. The drive cannot be ejected because it is in use by the system.

The only option is OK, and the drive is not ejected.

For more information about paging files or removable drives, see KB articles Q128327, "How Windows 95/98 Manages Virtual Memory," and Q163317, "MS-DOS Compatibility Mode When Booting from Removable Disk."

Related KB article Q179141

SyQuest EzFlyer 230 Disk Drive Is Not Accessible

You try to access a SyQuest EzFlyer 230 removable-media disk drive attached to your computer's enhanced parallel port (EPP) after you upgrade to Windows 98, and you see the following error message:

<drive letter> not accessible. The device is not ready.

Solution

Obtain and install the most current driver version for this drive. For information, contact SyQuest or see the documentation included with the SyQuest EzFlyer 230 removable-media disk drive.

Related KB article Q189328

CHAPTER 5

Internet

Connecting and Connections

America Online Doesn't Connect or Install

You attempt to connect to America Online or install the preview version of the America Online 4.0 software, and you can't.

This problem occurs when you're using an early version of the America Online software, which is incompatible with the version of Internet Explorer included with Windows 98.

Solution One

Install the version of the America Online software included on the Windows 98 CD-ROM. To do so, follow these steps:

1. Click the Start button, choose Settings, and then click Control Panel.

2. Double-click the Add/Remove Programs icon.

3. Click the Windows Setup tab.

4. Select Online Services, and then click Details.

5. Select the America Online check box, click OK, and then click OK again.

Figure 5-1.   *The Online Services dialog box.*

6. Double-click the Online Services folder on your desktop, and then double-click the America Online icon to start the installation process.

Solution Two

Obtain the latest version of the America Online 4.0 software from America Online's web site at *http://www.aol.com/*

Related KB article Q188654

America Online Preview Software Displays Error Message

You type your password to log on to America Online using the preview version of the America Online 4.0 software on the Windows 98 CD-ROM and see the following error message:

WAOL caused an invalid page fault in module MSVCRT.DLL at 015f:7800129a

This problem occurs with the incorrect version of the MSVCRT.DLL file. For instance, if you install a program that replaces the MSVCRT.DLL file with a later version of the file.

Solution

Obtain the latest version of the America Online 4.0 software from the America Online Web site at *http://aol.com*

Related KB article Q191621

AT&T WorldNet Launches Internet Explorer Automatically

You use AT&T WorldNet to connect to the Internet, and Internet Explorer starts automatically. This problem occurs because AT&T WorldNet starts Internet Explorer by default after each successful connection.

Solution

Configure AT&T WorldNet not to start Internet Explorer after each connection. To do so, follow these steps:

1. Start the AT&T WorldNet Connection Manager. To do this, double-click the Connect To AT&T WorldNet Service icon on the desktop.

2. Click Profile Properties.

3. Clear the Start The Internet Software After Connecting To AT&T WorldNet Service check box, and then click OK.

After you make this change, you must manually start Internet Explorer after you connect to AT&T WorldNet.

Related KB article Q188199

CompuServe Client Does Not Send E-Mail

You send mail using the Microsoft Exchange CompuServe client, and you receive the following error message:

Your message did not reach some or all of the intended recipients

This problem occurs when you send mail with the Rich Text Format (RTF) option enabled to an Internet client using the CompuServe Internet profile in Microsoft Exchange. Note than you cannot resend the same message with the RTF option disabled.

Solution

Disable the RTF option and copy the text of the message to a new message. To do so, follow these steps:

1. Choose Services from the Tools menu.

2. Click CompuServe Mail, and then click Properties.

3. Click the Default Send Options tab, and disable the Send Using Microsoft Exchange Rich Text Format option.

4. Click OK.

5. Create a new mail message and copy the text from the original message to the new message. Send the message.

Related KB article Q140013

Connecting to CompuServe Displays Error Message

You attempt to connect to CompuServe by double-clicking the CS3 Connection icon in Dial-Up Networking, and you see the following error message:

Error 691: The computer you are dialing in to cannot establish a Dial-Up Networking connection. Check your password, and then try again.

This problem occurs if you've set up the CompuServe service from the Online Services folder on the Start menu and haven't yet connected to CompuServe through the CompuServe software included in Windows 98. The CompuServe setup isn't complete until you connect to the service using the CompuServe software to set up the default dial-up setting.

Solution

Complete the CompuServe setup by connecting to CompuServe using the CompuServe software included in Windows 98. To do so, follow these steps:

1. Click the Start button, choose Programs, choose Online Services, choose CompuServe, and then click CompuServe 4.0.

2. Click Setup.

3. Enter your member name, member ID, and password, and then click OK.

4. Click Internet.

5. Click Yes when you are prompted to use Dial-Up Networking to connect to the Internet.

6. Click the appropriate country, and then click OK.

7. After you have connected to CompuServe, log off CompuServe, and then restart your computer.

Related KB article Q188120

Internet Connection Wizard Doesn't Connect

You use Internet Connection Wizard to sign up and configure your computer for a new Internet account, and your computer is unable to connect to the Microsoft Internet Referral Server, and you receive the following error message:

The Internet Connection Wizard could not establish a connection. Click Next to try again. Click Help for more information.

This problem occurs, because the Internet Connection Wizard does not correctly configure the Dial-Up Networking connection to the Microsoft Internet Referral Service when both of the following conditions exist:

- The area code that the Internet Connection Wizard is trying to call to connect to the Microsoft Internet Referral Server is different from your area code.

- The referral server uses the X.25 network protocol instead of Transport Control Protocol/Internet Protocol (TCP/IP).

The following countries use the X.25 network protocol:

Austria	Guam	Lithuania	Singapore
Belarus	Hong Kong	Luxembourg	South Africa
Belgium	Hungary	Malaysia	Spain
Brazil	Indonesia	Mexico	Sweden
Bulgaria	Ireland	Netherlands	Switzerland
Chile	Israel	New Zealand	Taiwan
Colombia	Italy	Norway	Ukraine
Denmark	Kazakhstan	Peru	Uzbekistan
Estonia	Korea (South)	Philippines	Venezuela
Finland	Kuwait	Portugal	
Greece	Latvia	Russia	

Solution

Manually select the correct X.25 script file for the Microsoft Internet Referral Service Dial-Up Networking connection. To do so, follow these steps:

1. Run the Internet Connection Wizard, and follow the instructions on the screen until you receive the following message:

    The Internet Connection Wizard could not establish a connection.

Note Do not click Cancel or close the Internet Connection Wizard because this deletes the Dial-Up Networking connection you are trying to configure.

2. Click the Start button, choose Programs, choose Accessories, choose Communications, and then click Dial-Up Networking.

3. Right-click the Microsoft Internet Referral Service connection, and choose Properties from the shortcut menu.

4. Click the Scripting tab, and then click Browse.

5. Navigate to the WINDOWS folder, select the ICW25<X>.SCP file (where <x> is the letter a, b, or c).

Note If there is more than one ICW25<X>.SCP file, close the Internet Connection Wizard, rename any ICW25<X>.SCP files in the WINDOWS folder, and then repeat steps 1–5.

6. Click Open, click OK, close the DIAL-UP NETWORKING folder, and then follow the instructions on the screen to finish the Internet Connection Wizard.

Related KB article Q188600

Internet Connection Wizard Encounters Problems

You experience some of the following problems while using the Internet Connection Wizard:

- A conflict occurs with another program running on your computer.
- Your modem may not be operational.
- The modem Setup program may not have finished successfully.
- You receive the following error message:

    The Internet Connection wizard could not detect your modem. It may be turned off, currently in use, or not installed properly. Click Help for more information.

Solution One

To solve these problems, follow these steps:

1. Close any open programs, especially all programs that might be using the same communications port as your modem, such as any fax program, HyperTerminal, or Phone Dialer.

2. In the Internet Connection Wizard, click Redial. To start the Internet Connection Wizard from Internet Explorer, choose Internet Options from the View menu, click the Connection tab, and then click Connect.

Solution Two

If you have an external modem, check the power to your modem. To do so, follow these steps:

1. While your computer is running, turn off your modem, and then turn it on again.

2. Check to make sure your modem is operational. For example, the CS or Clear To Send (CTS) indicator lights on your modem should be illuminated.

3. If your modem is operational, click Redial.

4. If you determine there is a problem with your modem, or you redial and it still does not work, your modem may not have initialized correctly. Completely shut down your computer, and then turn the computer back on while the modem is powered on.

Solution Three

From within the Internet Connection Wizard, verify the type of modem you are using by viewing the selection in the The Current Modem Is box. If your modem is set to Standard Modem or shows something other than the modem you are using, try choosing the correct modem from the list and then redialing. If this does not work, uninstall and then reinstall your modem. To do so, follow these steps:

1. Click the Start button, choose Settings, and then click Control Panel.

2. Double-click the Modems icon to open the Modems Properties dialog box.

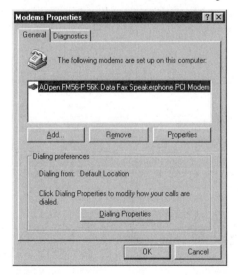

Figure 5-2. *The Modems Properties dialog box*

3. Select the modem, and then click Remove.

4. Click OK.

5. To reinstall the modem, repeat steps 1 and 2 if necessary to display the Modems Properties dialog box, click Add, and follow the onscreen instructions. If your current modem is not available in the modem list or is not detected, you may need to follow the instructions in the documentation provided by your modem manufacturer.

6. In the Could Not Connect dialog box, click Cancel.

To restart the Internet Connection Wizard, click the Start button, choose Programs, choose Internet Explorer, and click Connection Wizard. When the Choose Modem dialog box appears, follow the instructions for selecting your modem. If this fails to resolve the issue, continue to the next step.

Note If you still encounter problems, view the SUPPORT.TXT file for product support phone numbers in your area.

Related KB article Q169517

Internet Connection Wizard Repeatedly Restarts Computer

You attempt to create a new Internet account using the Internet Connection Wizard on a Compaq Presario computer, and you are repeatedly prompted to restart your computer. It appears that you are stuck in a continuous loop.

This problem occurs if your computer includes a preinstalled network client. The network client included with some newer Compaq Presario computers does not provide password caching.

The Internet Connection Wizard requires password caching but does not require a network logon. If you want to use the Microsoft Client for Microsoft Networks or the Microsoft Client for Novell Networks, and you are not connected to a local area network, change your primary network logon to Windows Logon.

Solution

Install a network client that provides password caching, such as the Microsoft Family Logon network client.

Note For information about how to install the Microsoft Family Logon network client, see KB article Q176057, "Description of the Microsoft Family Logon Client."

Related KB article Q191981

Internet Connection Wizard Text Illegible

You start the Internet Connection Wizard and are unable to read some of the text in the wizard. This can occur if the Use High Contrast option is enabled in the Accessibility Options tool in Control Panel.

Solution

Disable the Use High Contrast option in the Accessibility Options tool in Control Panel. To do so, follow these steps:

1. Click the Start button, choose Settings, and click Control Panel.

2. Double-click the Accessibility Options icon, and then clear the Use High Contrast check box on the Display tab.

3. Click OK.

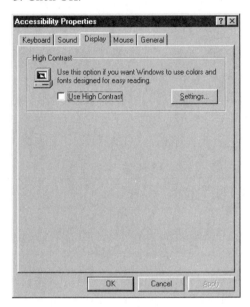

Figure 5-3. *The Accessibility Properties dialog box.*

Related KB article Q185968

Internet Connection Wizard Won't Start

You start the Internet Connection Wizard and see the following error message:

Failed to load the Internet Connection wizard helper component.

This occurs if the TAPI32.DLL file in the WINDOWS\SYSTEM folder is missing or damaged.

Solution

Extract a new copy of the TAPI32.DLL file from your Windows 98 CD-ROM to the WINDOWS\SYSTEM folder using the System File Checker tool. For information about how to do this, see KB article Q129605, "How to Extract Original Compressed Windows Files."

Related KB article Q193892

ISP Connection Fails After Upgrading from Windows 3.1x

You attempt to connect to your Internet service provider (ISP) after you upgrade to Windows 98 and you receive one of the following error messages:

Dial-in driver not loaded

PCTCPAPI083: 4.10 PC/TCP kernel and VxD not loaded. Your application would be adversely affected. DLL initialization failed.

This problem occurs when you upgrade from Microsoft Windows 3.1x or Microsoft Windows for Workgroups 3.1x to Windows 98. Windows 3.1x and Windows for Workgroups 3.1x are 16-bit operating systems. Windows 98 Setup cannot migrate Internet Explorer settings and ISP connections from a 16-bit operating system.

Solution

Run the Internet Connection Wizard to create a new ISP connection. To do this, click the Start button, choose Programs, choose Internet Explorer, click Connection Wizard, and then follow the instructions on your screen.

Related KB article Q188291

MSN Dials but Doesn't Connect

You try to connect to the Internet using MSN, The Microsoft Network, as your service provider, and Windows dials but is unable to connect to MSN, or you receive the following error message:

Member ID or password wrong

This problem occurs because the Dial-Up Networking connectoids that are created for The Microsoft Network's primary and backup telephone numbers contain incorrect logon information.

Solution One

Connect to The Microsoft Network by double-clicking the MSN icon on your desktop. This synchronizes the logon information in the Dial-Up Networking connectoids with the correct information in The Microsoft Network.

Solution Two

Double-click either of the icons for The Microsoft Network in the DIAL-UP NETWORKING folder, and then change the name and password as follows:

User name: *MSN/<user name>*

Password: *<password>*

(where <user name> is your member ID on The Microsoft Network, and <password> is your password.)

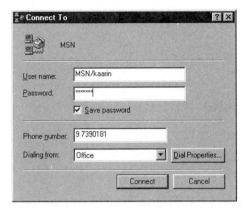

Figure 5-4. *The Connect To dialog box.*

After you add this information and connect to The Microsoft Network, the second connectoid is automatically updated.

Note If you do not enter *MSN/* before your user name, you cannot sign in to The Microsoft Network.

Related KB article Q136833

MSN Detected When You No Longer Use MSN

You connect to the Internet using an Internet service provider (ISP) other than MSN, The Microsoft Network, and you receive either of the following error messages when you start Internet Explorer:

Update MSN for Windows 98. We noticed that you are running MSN. Windows 98 provides you with a new improved version of MSN that will let you connect faster, with more capabilities.

We have detected that MSN has previously been installed on this computer. If you currently sub-scribe to MSN (or wish to), you must click "MSN Setup" below before you can connect to MSN via Internet Explorer. To continue using Internet Explorer for purposes other than accessing MSN, click "Internet Explorer" below.

This problem occurs when a shortcut to MSN Quick View is located in the STARTUP folder.

Solution

Remove the shortcut to MSN Quick View from the STARTUP folder. To do so, follow these steps:

1. Click the Start button, choose Settings, and then click Taskbar & Start Menu.

2. On the Start Menu Programs tab, click Remove.

3. Double-click the STARTUP folder.

4. Click MSN Quick View, and then click Remove.

5. Click Close, click OK, and then restart your computer.

Related KB article Q192815

MSN Doesn't Start

You double-click the MSN icon on the desktop, and MSN, The Microsoft Network, does not start. This problem occurs when you install Windows 98 from disks.

Solution One

Install MSN from an original Windows 98 CD-ROM. To do so, follow these steps:

1. Click the Start button, choose Settings, and then click Control Panel.

2. Double-click the Add/Remove Programs icon.

3. Click the Windows Setup tab.

4. Click Online Services, and then click Details.

5. Select The Microsoft Network check box, click OK, and then click OK again.

Figure 5-5.   *The Online Services dialog box.*

Windows 98 includes the following online services, each of which can be installed only from the CD-ROM version of Windows 98:

- America Online

- AT&T WorldNet Service

- CompuServe

- Prodigy Internet

- The Microsoft Network

Solution Two

Contact MSN Customer Service to obtain an MSN CD-ROM.

Related KB article Q188245

No Prompt to Disconnect from Internet

You connect to the Internet and then close your Internet browser program, and you aren't prompted to disconnect from the Internet. This problem occurs if Prodigy is your Internet service provider (ISP) and you aren't using the Prodigy software to establish your Internet connection.

Solution One

Use the Prodigy software to establish your connection to the Internet. For information about how to do so, contact Prodigy, or see the documentation included with the Prodigy software.

Solution Two

Manually disconnect from the Internet after you close your Internet browser program by right-clicking the modem icon on the taskbar, and then choosing Disconnect from the shortcut menu.

Related KB article Q193795

Winsock Program Doesn't Work in Windows

You upgrade to Windows 98 and install or try to use a Winsock program, but the program does not run, or you receive the following error message:

The following system files have been replaced with older versions by a program you recently ran. These files are currently in use and cannot be automatically repaired. Windows may not run properly until you exit and restart Windows so that these files can be automatically repaired.

C:\Windows\Winsock.dll

This problem occurs when you install Dial-Up Networking, TCP/IP, or the IPX/SPX-compatible protocol in Windows. Setup renames the existing WINSOCK.DLL file to WINSOCK.OLD and installs a new suite of Windows Sockets 1.1 interface files.

Current Winsock programs may not be compatible with the Windows WINSOCK.DLL file because of proprietary services in the program's version of the file.

If the program you try to run is not compatible with the installed version of the WINSOCK.DLL file, you may receive an error message, or the program may not run.

Solution One

Use Dial-Up Networking to connect to your Internet service provider. Dial-Up Networking provides support for 16-bit and 32-bit Windows Sockets programs.

Solution Two

Use both your current Winsock program and the Windows Winsock programs. To do so, follow these steps:

1. Copy the WINSOCK.OLD file from the WINDOWS folder or the WINDOWS\SYSTEM folder to the folder containing the program's executable file.

2. Rename the WINSOCK.OLD file in its new folder to WINSOCK.DLL.

The following Winsock programs may work if you place their version of the WINSOCK.DLL file in the program's folder:

- Chameleon
- CompuServe Internet Dialer or CompuServe Net Launcher
- FTP Software
- Internet in a Box
- Internet Office
- Mosaic in a Box
- NetCom Net Cruiser
- Pipeline
- Spry Air Series
- Trumpet

Solution Three

Contact the manufacturer of the Winsock program to obtain an update.

Related KB article Q139384

E-Mail and Outlook Express

Address Book Won't Import into Outlook Express

You attempt to import a Windows Messaging personal address book into Outlook Express and see the following error message:

The following unrecoverable error has occurred: The MAPISVC.INF file is missing. To exit, click Finish.

When you click Finish, you see the following message:

There are no profiles. Choose the Mail and Fax icon in the Control Panel to create a new profile.

When you click OK, you see the following message:

Address book import has completed successfully.

When you click OK, you are returned to the Address Book Import Tool dialog box, but the Windows Messaging personal address book is not imported into Outlook Express.

Note In this article, Windows Messaging refers to both Microsoft Exchange and Microsoft Windows Messaging.

This problem occurs if Windows Messaging is not installed on your computer.

Solution

Install Windows Messaging, and then import the Windows Messaging personal address book into Outlook Express. To do so, follow these steps:

1. Click the Start button, and then choose Run to open the Run dialog box.

2. Enter *D:\tools\oldwin95\message\us\wms.exe,* and click OK (assuming D is the drive letter of the CD-ROM drive containing your Windows 98 CD-ROM).

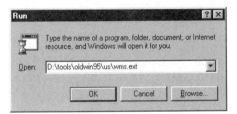

Figure 5-6. *The Run dialog box.*

3. Create a new Windows Messaging profile using the personal address book you want to import into Outlook Express. For information about how to do so, see KB article Q129211, "Frequently Asked Questions About Microsoft Exchange Profiles."

4. Import the Windows Messaging personal address book into Outlook Express. For information about how to do so, see KB article Q175017, "How to Import and Export Address Books in Outlook Express."

Windows Messaging is not included in Windows 98. If you upgrade from Windows 95 and had Windows Messaging installed, Windows Messaging is available in Windows 98.

Related KB article Q180506

Address Book Won't Open After Upgrading

You upgrade to Windows 98 and receive the following error message when you open the Windows Address Book:

Unable to open address book, a component is missing. You must reinstall Outlook Express.

You reinstall Microsoft Outlook Express and still receive the error message.

This problem occurs when you upgrade your computer to Windows 98 by running Windows 98 Setup from MS-DOS, and you have more than one folder whose name begins with "Outlook" in your PROGRAM FILES folder.

Solution

To solve this problem, follow these steps:

1. Click the Start button, choose Settings, and then click Control Panel.

2. Double-click the Add/Remove Programs icon, and then click the Windows Setup tab.

3. Clear the Outlook Express check box, and then click OK.

Figure 5-7.   *The Windows Setup tab of the Add/Remove Programs Properties dialog box.*

4. Click the Start button, choose Programs, and then click Windows Explorer.

5. Double-click the PROGRAM FILES folder.

6. Rename the Outlook Express folder to *Old Outlook Express,* and then click Yes when you are prompted to confirm that you want to rename the read-only folder.

7. Rename the !$!$!$!$.OER folder to *Outlook Express.*

8. Click the Start button, choose Settings, and then click Control Panel.

9. Double-click the Add/Remove Programs icon, and then click the Windows Setup tab.

10. Select the Outlook Express check box, and then click OK.

Related KB article Q192321

Address Book Won't Open in Outlook Express

You attempt to open the Address Book in Outlook Express, and because the long folder name for the OUTLOOK EXPRESS folder is missing, you see the following error message:

The Address Book could not be launched. A required component is missing, please re-install Outlook Express.

Solution

Restore the long folder name. To do so, follow these steps:

1. Click the Start button, choose Find, and then click Files Or Folders to open the Find window.

2. Enter *outloo* in the Named box, and then click Find Now.

3. In the list of found files, locate the OUTLOOK EXPRESS folder. It is usually in the PROGRAM FILES folder and may have a short folder name of OUTLOO~1.

4. Right-click the OUTLOOK EXPRESS folder, choose Rename from the shortcut menu, enter *Outlook Express*, and then press the Enter key.

5. When you are prompted to verify that you want to rename the read-only folder, click Yes.

6. Close the Find program.

Related KB article Q194463

Automatic Redial After Busy Signal Doesn't Work in Outlook or Outlook Express

You try to dial out in Outlook Express or Outlook 97, and both programs may not redial automatically after receiving a busy signal.

Solution One

After you receive a busy signal, try to dial again. Repeat this process until you connect.

Solution Two

Establish the connection, then start the e-mail program by following these steps:

1. Click the Start button, choose Programs, choose Accessories, choose Communications, and then click Dial-Up Networking to display the Dial-Up Networking window.

2. Double-click the connection you use for Outlook 97 or Outlook Express, and then follow the instructions on the screen to complete the connection.

Related KB article Q181815

Default Mail Program Can't Be Specified

You uninstall Outlook 97 and view the Mail and News settings for Internet Explorer, and you find you can't specify your mail program.

Solution

Reinstall Outlook Express or Internet Explorer. To reinstall Outlook Express, use the Add/Remove Programs tool in Control Panel. For more information, see KB article Q171229 "How to Add and Remove Internet Explorer 4.0 Components."

Reinstalling Internet Explorer restores Windows Messaging as a mail service option. For more information about Windows Messaging and installing Internet Explorer, see KB articles Q158435, "Windows Messaging Missing from Mail and News Options," and Q170993, "How to Install Internet Explorer and Troubleshoot Setup Problems."

For additional information, see KB articles Q154359, "How to Change Default Mail Client for Internet Explorer," and Q174431, "OFF97: Problems Occur After Removing MS Internet Explorer 4.0."

Related KB article Q176571

Dial-Up Networking Doesn't Attempt to Reconnect After Busy Signal

You attempt to connect to your Internet service provider (ISP) to check for new e-mail, and you receive a busy signal. Dial-Up Networking doesn't attempt to redial even though it is configured to do so, and you see the following error message:

Error 676: The line is busy. Try again later.

This problem occurs if you attempt to connect to your ISP using Microsoft Outlook Express, or if you double-click the Dial-Up Networking connection to your ISP.

Solution One

Connect to your ISP using Microsoft Internet Explorer, and then check for new mail using Outlook Express.

Solution Two

Click OK when you receive the error message, and then click Connect to attempt to connect again.

Related KB article Q187215

Messages Won't Download

You attempt to download your mail with Outlook Express and receive one of the following error messages:

An unknown error has occurred while attempting to receive mail. Please check your account settings, net connection, and TCP/IP configuration.

An attempt to allocate memory failed. The system is out of memory.

This problem occurs if there isn't enough free disk space to download your mail.

Solution

Increase the amount of free space on your hard disk by removing any unnecessary files.

Related KB article Q171276

Messages Won't Purge

You attempt to purge a deleted message from an Internet Message Access Protocol (IMAP) server following the instructions provided in Outlook Express Help, and the steps don't work.

Solution

Purge deleted messages from an IMAP server. To do so, follow these steps:

1. Select the message, and click the Delete toolbar button.

2. Choose Purge Deleted Messages from the Edit menu to remove the deleted messages from the folder.

Related KB article Q185411

Messaging Can't Connect to Post Office

You install Windows Messaging Service from the Windows 98 CD-ROM and aren't able to connect to a post office. This problem occurs if you install Windows Messaging after Microsoft Outlook Express has been installed.

Solution

Install Windows Messaging before Installing Outlook Express. To do so, follow these steps:

1. Click the Start button, choose Settings, and then click Control Panel.

2. Double-click the Add/Remove Programs icon.

3. On the Install/Uninstall tab, select Windows Messaging, and then click Add/Remove.

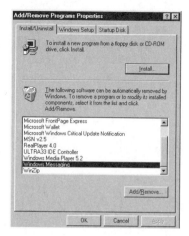

Figure 5-8. *The Install/Uninstall tab of the Add/Remove Programs Properties dialog box.*

4. Click No when you are prompted to restart your computer, and then click the Windows Setup tab.

5. Clear the Outlook Express check box, and then click OK.

6. Restart your computer.

7. Display the Control Panel window again, and double-click the Add/Remove Programs icon.

8. On the Install/Uninstall tab, click Install, and then click Next.

9. Insert your Windows 98 CD-ROM. Type *<drive>:\tools\oldwin95\message\us\wms.exe* in the Command Line For Installation Program box (where <drive> is the letter of your CD-ROM drive.)

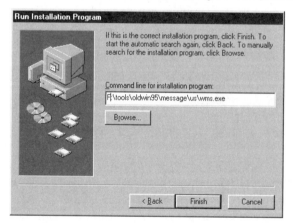

Figure 5-9. *The Run Installation Program dialog box.*

10. Click Finish.

11. Click Yes when you are prompted to restart your computer.

12. Display the Control Panel window again, double-click the Add/Remove Programs icon, and then click the Windows Setup tab.

13. Select the Outlook Express check box, and then click OK.

Related KB article Q191576

Microsoft Exchange Attachment Numbering Not Reset

You send messages as attachments using the Internet Mail information service in Microsoft Exchange (Windows Messaging), and the messages are numbered as MSG0001.TXT, MSG0002.TXT, MSG0003.TXT, and so on.

When you compose a new message, the numbering sequence does not start over, but instead continues with the next number. This could lead recipients to believe they have not received all the attachments.

Solution One

Reset the attachment counter by closing and restarting Microsoft Exchange.

Solution Two

Send the attachments using MIME instead of Uuencode. MIME displays the attachments correctly.

Solution Three

Move the information from the attachments into the body of the message.

Related KB article Q162351

Outlook and Outlook Express Don't Recognize .MBX Files

You copy .MBX files (with or without matching .IDX files) from Internet Mail and News or Outlook Express to the mail folder, and neither Outlook Express nor Outlook recognizes them.

With a new hierarchy in the Outlook Express and Outlook tree, you can no longer simply place .MBX stores (with or without matching .IDX files) in a user's mail folder and have Outlook Express or Outlook recognize them. The FOLDERS.NCH file keeps track of all the folders and their location in the hierarchy.

Solution

Rename or delete the FOLDERS.NCH file. Outlook Express or Outlook will then reenumerate the list of folders and create a new file. Re-creating this file places every folder at the root level. Once these are imported, you can drag folders to their appropriate location if you want to use nesting.

Rename or delete the FOLDERS.NCH file. To do so, follow these steps:

1. Close Outlook Express or Outlook.

2. Click the Start button, choose Find, and then click Files Or Folders to open the Find window.

3. In the Named box, enter *folders.nch,* and then click Find Now.

4. Select the FOLDERS.NCH file, and then choose Rename or Delete from the File menu.

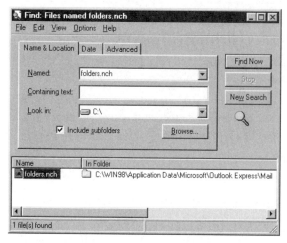

Figure 5-10.   *The Find window.*

Related KB article Q163845

Outlook Express Doesn't Display Reply Ticking

You reply to a message in Outlook Express and reply ticking doesn't appear. This problem occurs when you have your default mail message format set to HTML.

Indenting the previous text of a mail message with ticking, indicated by default with the ">" character, is disabled in HTML mode. This occurs even if you elected to send the initial mail message as plain text by overriding the default setting.

Solution

Set your default message format to Plain Text. To do so, follow these steps:

1. In Outlook Express, choose Options from the Tools menu.

2. Click the Send tab. In the Mail Sending Format box, click the Plain Text option button.

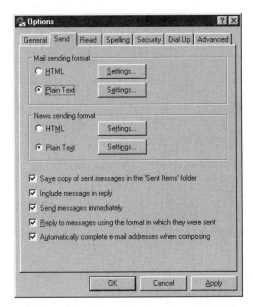

Figure 5-11. *The Send tab of the Options dialog box.*

3. If you want to customize the way your replies appear, click Settings. In the Plain Text Settings dialog box, you can select a different character to mark ticking, or you can turn the feature off. Click OK to accept these settings, and then click OK again.

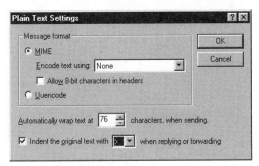

Figure 5-12. *The Plain Text Settings dialog box.*

Related KB article Q192316

Outlook Express Icon Starts Another Program

You uninstall Outlook Express, and the Outlook Express icon remains on the desktop. Double-clicking the icon may start Microsoft Paint, Microsoft Compression Agent, or another program.

This problem occurs if the Internet Connection Wizard installed the Outlook Express icon. When you uninstall Outlook Express, Outlook Express Setup does not remove the Outlook Express icon installed by the Internet Connection Wizard.

Solution

Delete the Outlook Express icon on your desktop. To do so, right-click the shortcut, choose Delete from the shortcut menu, and then click OK.

Related KB article Q193702

Outlook Express Stores Mail and News in Undesired Folder

You can change the default storage location of Outlook Express mail and news folders. By default, Outlook Express stores mail and news folders in the WINDOWS\APPLICATION DATA\ MICROSOFT\OUTLOOK EXPRESS folder (assuming Windows is the folder in which Windows 98 is installed). When user profiles are enabled, the default storage location is WINDOWS\PROFILES\<USERNAME>\APPLICATION DATA\MICROSOFT\OUTLOOK EX-PRESS (where <username> is the name you use to log on to Windows). However, if Microsoft Internet Mail And News was already installed on your computer when you upgraded to Outlook Express, the default storage location of Outlook Express mail and news folders is PROGRAM FILES\ INTERNETEXPLORER\INTERNET MAIL AND NEWS.

Solution

Change the storage location of Outlook Express mail or news by changing the Store Root value to the full path for the folder you want to use as your new storage location. This value is located in the following Registry key:

```
HKEY_CURRENT_USER\Software\Microsoft\Outlook  Express
```

The STORE ROOT folder contains a MAIL folder and a NEWS folder in which the data files for mail and news are located. If you install Outlook Express without upgrading Internet Mail And News, the Store Root is the OUTLOOK EXPRESS folder. If you include the MAIL folder in the Store Root path, a new MAIL AND NEWS folder is created in the existing MAIL folder. As a result, you cannot see the messages in the OUTLOOK EXPRESS\MAIL folder until you remove Mail from the Store Root path.

When you use user profiles, the Store Root value is located in this Registry key:

```
HKEY_USERS\<username>\Software\Microsoft\Outlook  Express
```

where <username> is the name you use to log on to Windows.

Warning Please read the Introduction for information on how to safely edit the Registry.

To change the Store Root value, follow these steps:

1. Click the Start button, choose Run, enter *Regedit* in the Open box, and then click OK.

2. Navigate your way down through the folders in the left pane.

3. Double-click the Store Root value, and change the path in the Value Data box.

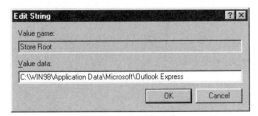

Figure 5-13. *The Edit String dialog box.*

4. Close Regedit.

5. Restart Windows.

Related KB article Q175037

Rich Text Format Not Enabled with Internet Mail Information Service

You try to send an e-mail message in Rich Text Format (RTF) with the Internet Mail information service for Microsoft Exchange, but the option is not enabled.

When sending mail using the Internet Mail information service, you must enable RTF for each individual recipient. You cannot enable RTF for all Internet Mail messages, or for an individual message. This behavior differs from that of the CompuServe Mail information service, which allows you to enable RTF for all messages, but does not allow you to enable RTF for an individual recipient or an individual message.

Solution One

Enable RTF for an individual Internet Mail recipient already listed in your personal address book. To do so, follow these steps:

1. In Microsoft Exchange, click the Address Book toolbar button.

2. Select the recipient from the list of addresses, and then choose Properties from the File menu.

3. Click the SMTP - Address tab.

4. Select the Always Send To This Recipient In Microsoft Exchange Rich-Text Format check box.

Solution Two

Enable RTF for an individual Internet Mail recipient not already listed in your personal address book by following these steps:

1. In Microsoft Exchange, click the Compose New Message toolbar button.

2. Enter the Internet address of the recipient in the To text box, and then choose Check Names from the Tools menu.

3. Double-click the Internet address that you typed, and then select the Always Send To This Recipient In Microsoft Exchange Rich-text Format check box.

4. Optionally, to add the recipient to your personal address book, click the Address Book toolbar button.

Solution Three

Enable the RTF option for all messages that you send using the CompuServe Mail information service. To do so, follow these steps:

1. In Microsoft Exchange, choose Services from the Tools menu.

2. Click CompuServe Mail, and then click Properties.

3. Click the Default Send Options tab.

4. Select the Send Using Microsoft Exchange Rich-Text Format check box.

Note For information about problems that can occur when you send messages using the CompuServe Mail information service after you enable the RTF option, see KB articles Q140013 and Q136101.

Related KB article Q142575

Scrolling Doesn't Work in Address Book

You attempt to change the display name of a Windows Address Book entry and are unable to scroll through the list of display names in the entry's Properties dialog box. This occurs if you use the Tab key to select the Display box, and then try to use the arrow keys to scroll through the list of display names.

Solution

Change the display name using the keyboard. To do so, follow these steps:

1. Press the Tab key to select the Display box.

2. Press Alt+Down arrow to view the list of display names.

3. Use the arrow keys to select a name, and then press the Enter key.

4. Use the Tab key to select OK, and then press the Enter key.

Related KB article Q191682

Signature File Too Large

You use a signature file with a mail or news message in Outlook Express and receive the following error message:

Warning: Your signature file is too large. It has been truncated, please make the file smaller.

This problem occurs when your signature file exceeds the 4K limit.

Solution

Make your signature file smaller, or use the text option rather than an HTML file.

Related KB article Q165806

Windows Address Book Can't Be Accessed in Outlook Express

You attempt to use the Windows Address Book (.WAB) in Outlook Express and receive the following error message:

Wab.exe is Linked to Missing Export Advapi32.dll

This problem occurs when the ADVAPI32.DLL file is the incorrect version or is damaged.

Solution

Extract a new copy of the ADVAPI32.DLL file using System File Checker. To start the System File Checker, click the Start button, choose Run, enter *sfc.exe* in the Open box, and then click OK.

Related KB article Q181685

General Web Browsing

ActiveX Controls Don't Work

Your ActiveX controls work incorrectly or not at all, because the Initialize And Script ActiveX Controls Not Marked As Safe option is disabled in Security Settings in Internet Properties.

This problem occurs when you upgrade from Internet Explorer version 4.0 or 4.01 to Windows 98 or Microsoft Internet Explorer Service Pack 1 and Internet Explorer is configured to use Medium Security.

Solution

Manually configure this option in Security Settings in Internet Properties. To do so, follow these steps:

1. Click the Start button, choose Settings, and then click Control Panel.

2. Double-click the Internet icon, and then click the Security tab.

3. Click the Custom (For Expert Users) option button, and then click Settings.

4. Click the Disable option button under Initialize And Script ActiveX Controls Not Marked As Safe, and then click OK.

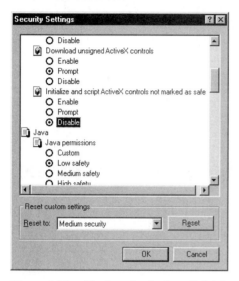

Figure 5-14. *The Security Settings dialog box.*

5. Click OK.

Related KB article Q185644

America Online Download Doesn't Complete

You attempt to download a file from America Online over a Dial-Up Networking TCP/IP Point-to-Point Protocol (PPP) Internet connection and receive the following error message:

(TCP/IP) Lost Connection

This problem occurs when you are using the America Online software configured to use a Transmission Control Protocol/Internet Protocol (TCP/IP) Winsock connection instead of a modem connection. This error message usually occurs when the download is approximately 50 percent finished, then the file transfer is halted, and you are disconnected from America Online.

Configure the America Online software to use a TCP/IP Winsock connection instead of a modem connection. This allows you to use an existing Dial-Up Networking TCP/IP Internet connection to connect to America Online.

Solution

Upgrade your America Online software to version 2.5 or later. For information about obtaining this software upgrade, please contact America Online Technical Support.

Related KB article Q132062

Cannot Access Secure Web Site

You attempt to view a web page using Internet Explorer and receive the following error message:

Cannot open Internet site https://<Web address>. A connection to the server could not be established.

This problem occurs for one of the following reasons:

- You have mismatched Windows Sockets dynamic-link library (DLL) files. For example, this occurs if you install the Windows Sockets (Winsock) 2.0 update for Windows 95 on a Windows 95–based computer, upgrade to Windows 98, and then attempt to revert to your previous version of Winsock by running the WS2BAKUP.BAT file.

- Your Dial-Up Networking (DUN) or Internet settings are incorrect.

The Winsock 2.0 update for Windows 95 includes the WS2BACKUP.BAT file for removing Winsock 2.0. If you attempt to remove the update on a computer you upgraded to Windows 98, the files restored from the WS2BACKUP.BAT file don't work properly.

Note For more information, see KB article Q177719, "How to Identify Winsock 2.0 Run-Time Components for Windows 95."

Solution One

Remove and reinstall the Transmission Control Protocol/Internet Protocol (TCP/IP). To do so, follow these steps:

1. Click the Start button, choose Settings, and then click Control Panel.

2. Double-click the Network icon.

3. On the Configuration tab, select TCP/IP, and then click Remove. Repeat this step for each instance of TCP/IP before continuing to step 4.

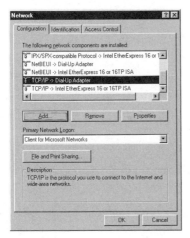

Figure 5-15. *The Configuration tab of the Network dialog box.*

4. Click OK, and then click Yes when you are prompted to restart your computer.

5. Click the Start button, choose Settings, and click Control Panel.

6. Double-click the Network icon.

7. Click Add, select Protocol, and click Add.

8. Select Microsoft in the Manufacturers list box and select TCP/IP. Click OK. If you receive version conflict error messages during this process, click No when you are prompted to keep a newer version of the file.

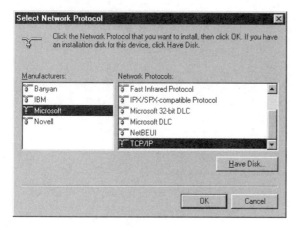

Figure 5-16. *The Select Network Protocol dialog box.*

9. Restart your computer.

Solution Two

Repeat the steps in Solution One, but remove and reinstall all installed network components.

Solution Three

Check with your Internet service provider to verify your Internet settings.

Related KB article Q188773

Cannot Open Internet Site Error Message

You attempt to view a web site, and Internet Explorer 4.0, 4.01, or 4.01 Service Pack 1 (SP1) intermittently returns one of the following error messages:

- *Internet Explorer cannot open the internet site URL:<site> the downloaded file is not available. This could be due to your security language setting or because the server was unable to retrieve the requested file.*

- *Internet Explorer cannot open the internet site URL:<site> the connection to the server was reset.*

Internet Explorer does not properly handle an HTTP/1.1 302 redirect returned from a proxy server or Internet server when the HTTP/1.1 302 redirect is sent to Internet Explorer in two separate TCP frames (one with the HTTP/1.1 302 redirect, and the other with a HTML body containing a page for the new location).

When Internet Explorer receives the first TCP frame with an HTTP/1.1 302redirect, Internet Explorer processes the redirect command and attempts to use the open socket connection to the server that sent the redirect. This occurs because Internet Explorer has not processed the second TCP frame containing the FIN or the "socket close connection" command, so Internet Explorer assumes that the current state of the socket connection is still open. This is an intermittent problem, because Internet Explorer may recognize that the socket connection was closed by the server and open a new socket connection to the server if Internet Explorer receives the TCP frames close enough together, or if no HTML body is sent at all.

Solution

A supported fix that corrects this problem is now available from Microsoft, but has not been fully tested and should be applied only to computers experiencing this specific problem. If you are not severely affected by this specific problem, Microsoft recommends that you wait for the next service pack that contains this fix.

To solve this problem immediately, contact Microsoft Product Support Services to obtain the fix. For a complete list of Microsoft Product Support Services phone numbers and information on support costs, please go to the following address on the World Wide Web:

http://support.microsoft.com/support/supportnet/default.asp

Related KB article Q193489

Cannot Open Secure Web Site Because of Missing Library File

You attempt to connect to a secure web site using Internet Explorer and receive the following error message:

Internet Explorer cannot open the Internet site HTTPS://<address>. One of the library files needed to run this application cannot be found.

You can receive this error message if the SCHANNEL.DLL file is missing or is damaged.

Solution

Restore the original SCHANNEL.DLL file to the WINDOWS\SYSTEM folder. To do so, follow these steps:

1. Click the Start button, choose Find, and then click Files Or Folders.

2. Enter *schannel.dll* in the Named box, and then click Find Now.

3. Right-click the SCHANNEL.DLL file in the WINDOWS\SYSTEM folder, and choose Rename from the shortcut menu.

4. Enter *schannel.old* in the text box, and then press the Enter key.

5. Use the System File Checker to extract the SCHANNEL.DLL file into the WINDOWS\SYSTEM folder.

Note For more information, see the System File Checker Tool section in KB article Q129605.

Related KB article Q188839

Cannot View Web Pages

After you install Microsoft Windows Media Player 5.2, you are unable to view some Web pages if they use the <Hidden=true> Hypertext Markup Language (HTML) tag with embedded media files.

Solution One

Obtain Windows Media Player 6.0 or later from the Microsoft web site at *http://www.microsoft.com/windows/mediaplayer*.

Solution Two

Contact the web page author (or the web server administrator) and request that the <Hidden=true> HTML tag be removed.

Related KB article Q193712

Cannot View Web Pages Because Program Not Found

You attempt to view an Internet or intranet web page and receive the following error message:

Program not found. Windows cannot find Program.exe. This program is needed for opening files of type 'URL:HyperText Transfer Protocol'.

This occurs when you use the Network TeleSystems TCP Pro TCP/IP network protocol, which doesn't make the Internet Connection Wizard start automatically the first time you try to access a web page. One of the Internet Connection Wizard's functions is to associate documents written in Hypertext Markup Language (HTML) with your web browser.

Solution

Run the Internet Connection Wizard manually. To do so, follow these steps:

1. Click the Start button, choose Run, enter *inetwiz* in the Open box, and then click OK.

2. Follow the instructions on the screen.

Note For information on resolving this issue, contact the program's manufacturer.

Related KB article Q189583

Error in Secured Channel Support

You use the 128-bit version of Internet Explorer 4.01 Service Pack 1 and receive the following error message:

> *Internet Explorer can not open the Internet site http://<site> an error occurred in secured channel support*

This problem occurs if you attempt to visit a web site with an invalid Secure Sockets Layer (SSL) certificate. When you are using the 128-bit SCHANNEL.DLL file, an error occurs during the secured channel handshake. Internet Explorer attempts to open the connection to the server and the server responds with an error, causing Internet Explorer to produce the error message.

Solution One

Disable PCT 1.0. To do so, follow these steps:

1. Choose Internet Options from the View menu in Internet Explorer.

2. Click the Advanced tab.

3. Under Security, clear the PCT 1.0 check box.

4. Click OK.

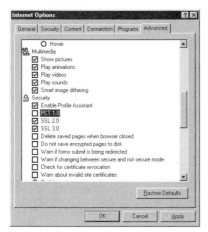

Figure 5-17.   *The Advanced tab of the Internet Options dialog box.*

5. Close Internet Explorer.

Solution Two

If you've disabled the PCT 1.0, SSL 1.0, and SSL 2.0 security options, restore the defaults by following these steps:

1. Choose Internet Options from the View menu in Internet Explorer.

2. Click the Advanced tab.

3. Click Restore Defaults, and then click OK.

4. Close Internet Explorer.

Related KB article Q192408

Home Page Appears Upside Down and Backwards

You try to customize your personalized start page at:

http://home.microsoft.com/personalizing.personalizing.asp

and the web page appears upside down and backwards.

This problem occurs if you use a Creative Graphics Blaster MA302 display adapter that is configured to use High Color (16 Bits) or higher resolution.

Solution One

Contact Creative Labs to inquire about the availability of a fix for this issue.

Solution Two

Change the Color Palette setting in Display Properties to 256 Color or lower by following these steps:

1. Click the Start button, choose Settings, and click Control Panel.

2. Double-click the Display icon, and then click the Settings tab.

3. Select 256 Colors from the Color list.

4. Click OK.

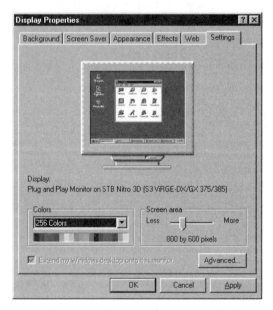

Figure 5-18.   *The Settings tab of the Display Properties dialog box.*

Related KB article   Q191069

Personal Web Server Pages Don't Display

You install Windows 98, and other users are not able to view your web pages that are hosted using Microsoft Personal Web Server. This problem occurs when you run the Internet Connection Wizard and your home page address in Personal Web Server is changed from your computer name to your user logon name.

Solution

Enter your computer name again in Network properties. To do so, follow these steps:

1. Click the Start button, choose Settings, click Control Panel, and then double-click the Network icon.

2. Click the Identification tab.

3. In the Computer Name box, enter your computer name again, and then click OK.

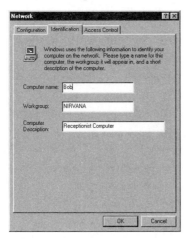

Figure 5-19. *The Identification tab of the Network dialog box.*

4. If you are prompted to restart your computer, do so.

Related KB article Q188198

Script Error Message When Attempting to View Web Page

You navigate to a web page and receive one or more of the following error messages:

An error has occurred on the script on this page. Line: 252 Char: 18 Error: Syntax error Code: 0

An error has occurred on the script on this page. Line: 500 Char: 4 Error: Expected Statement Code:0

An error has occurred on the script on this page. Line: 638 Char: 1 Error: Type mismatch: "FuncInitialize_Arrays" Code: 0

This problem occurs if you are using the WRQ @Guard program and the Eliminate Script-Based Popup Windows feature is enabled.

Solution

Disable the Eliminate Script-Based Popup Windows feature, and then empty your TEMPORARY INTERNET FILES folder. To do so, follow these steps:

1. Disable the Eliminate Script-Based Popup Windows feature. For information about how to do so, view the documentation included with @Guard, or contact WRQ.

2. Click the Start button, choose Settings, click Control Panel, and then double-click the Internet icon.

3. Click Delete Files, click OK, and then click OK.

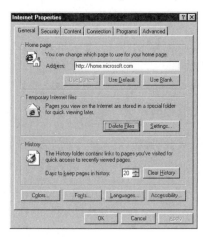

Figure 5-20. *The Internet Properties dialog box.*

Related KB article Q193359

Unable to Access Intranet Address

You access the Internet through a proxy server and are using the Personal Web Manager to create a web site or add pages to a web site, and you receive the following error message:

Internet Explorer cannot open the Internet site http://localhost/iisadmin/publish/welcome.asp

The server returned an invalid or unrecognized response.

The problem occurs because Internet Explorer is not configured to bypass the proxy server for local (intranet) addresses.

Solution

Configure Internet Explorer to bypass the proxy server for local (intranet) addresses. To do so, follow these steps:

1. In Internet Explorer, choose Internet Options from the View menu to open the Internet Options dialog box.

2. Click the Connection tab.

3. Select the Bypass Proxy Server For Local (Intranet) Addresses check box.

4. Click OK.

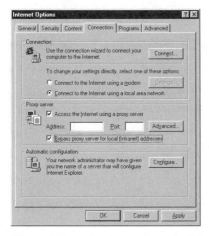

Figure 5-21. *The Connection tab of the Internet Options dialog box.*

Related KB article Q183636

Unable to Download File from the Internet

You try to download a file from the Internet and receive the following error message:

Internet Explorer could not download <filename> from <Internet site>. The downloaded file is not available. This could be due to your Security or Language Settings or because the server was unable to retrieve the requested file.

This problem occurs if the TEMPORARY INTERNET FILES folder is too full, or if the INDEX.DAT file in the TEMPORARY INTERNET FILES folder or the COOKIES folder has been marked with the Read Only attribute.

The INDEX.DAT file, a cache file used by Internet Explorer, may be marked as Read Only during an upgrade or when you install another program.

Note For more information, see KB articles Q178702, "Description of the MM256.DAT and MM2048.DAT Files," and Q181228, "Download of File from IIS 4.0 Fails on IE 4.01 Client."

When you download a file, Internet Explorer assigns the downloaded file a unique identification number and then searches the INDEX.DAT file for that identification number. If the downloaded file's identification number is found, the contents of the file are stored locally on your computer's hard disk, and Internet Explorer uses that locally stored content instead of downloading the information from the Internet. If the downloaded file's identification number is not found, the contents of the file must be downloaded from the Internet, and the INDEX.DAT file is updated with the file's identification number. If the INDEX.DAT file has the Read Only attribute, the file cannot be updated.

Solution

Change the Read Only attribute and delete unnecessary files from the Temporary Internet Files folder. To do so, follow these steps:

1. Click the Start button, choose Find, and then click Files Or Folders to open the Find window.

2. In the Named box, enter *index.dat.*

3. In the Look In box, type *c:\windows\temporary internet files; c:\windows\cookies* (assuming C is the drive on which you installed Windows and WINDOWS is the folder in which you installed Windows), and then click Find Now.

Figure 5-22. *The Find window.*

4. Right-click the INDEX.DAT file in the WINDOWS\TEMPORARY INTERNET FILES folder, and then choose Properties from the shortcut menu.

5. Clear the Read Only check box, and then click OK.

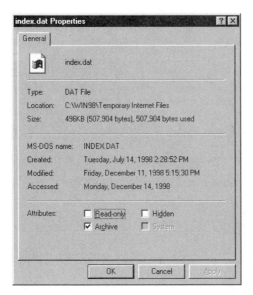

Figure 5-23. *The Properties dialog box for the INDEX.DAT file.*

6. Right-click the INDEX.DAT file in the COOKIES folder, and choose Properties from the shortcut menu.

Note If cookies are disabled, this file may not be present in the COOKIES folder. Skip to step 8.

7. Clear the Read Only check box, and then click OK.

8. Close the Find window, and then restart your computer.

9. Click the Start button, choose Settings, click Control Panel, and then double-click the Internet icon.

10. Click Delete Files, and then click OK.

Related KB article Q183506

Internet Explorer

Active Setup Goes to Wrong Web Site

You try to add a component to Internet Explorer by using Internet Explorer Active Setup, and Internet Explorer goes to a web site other than the Internet Explorer Addon page. This problem occurs if the Registry has an incorrect value for the Internet Explorer Addon page.

Solution

Use Registry Editor to add the Addon_URL value to the following Registry key if it does not already exist:

```
HKEY_LOCAL_MACHINE\SOFTWARE\Microsoft\Internet Explorer\Main
```

Modify the value data of the Addon_URL value to

`http://www.microsoft.com/ie/ie401/download/rtw/x86/en/download/addon98.htm`

by following these steps:

Warning Please read the Introduction for information on how to safely edit the Registry.

1. Click the Start button, choose Run, enter *Regedit* in the Open box, and then click OK.

2. Navigate your way down through the folders in the left pane until you locate the key described above.

3. Modify the value of Addon_URL as described above.

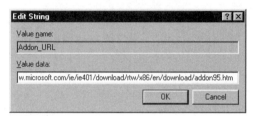

Figure 5-24. *The Edit String dialog box.*

4. Close Regedit.

5. Restart Windows.

Note This location is the default Internet location for updates. If you have a different local page for addons, you can place the appropriate local web address in the appropriate Registry key.

Related KB article Q192225

Channel Subscriptions Not Backed Up

You can back up your channel subscriptions if you wish. You can then restore them to your computer or to another computer.

Solution

To back up your channel subscriptions, use Registry Editor to export the following Registry keys:

`HKEY_CURRENT_USER\Software\Microsoft\Windows\CurrentVersion\NotificationMgr`

`HKEY_CURRENT_USER\Software\Microsoft\Windows\CurrentVersion\Taskman`

Warning Please read the Introduction for information on how to safely edit the Registry.

1. Click the Start button, choose Run, enter *Regedit* in the Open box, and then click OK.

2. Navigate your way down through the folders in the left pane until you locate the keys described above.

3. Click the folder to select its contents for export.

4. Choose Export Registry File from the Registry menu. Browse to a location to store the exported file, and then specify a name for this new file. The .REG filename extension is added automatically; you can edit this file using any text editor if you want.

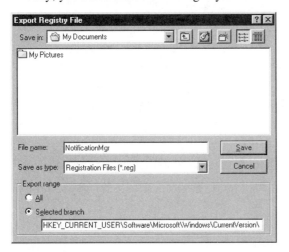

Figure 5-25. *The Export Registry Key dialog box.*

5. To import the .REG file back into the Registry, double-click it.

Related KB article Q189881

Content Advisor Error Message

You run Internet Explorer and receive the following error message:

Content Advisor configuration information is missing. Someone may have tried to tamper with it. You may wish to check the Content Advisor settings.

When you click OK, Internet Explorer can no longer access the Internet. This problem occurs when the ratings system has been enabled and the RATINGS.POL file is missing or damaged. Removing and reinstalling Internet Explorer does not resolve this issue.

Solution

Create a new RATINGS.POL file. To do so, follow these steps:

1. Close Internet Explorer.

2. Check your WINDOWS\SYSTEM folder to see if a RATINGS.POL file exists.

Note You must be able to view hidden files to view the RATINGS.POL file. To view hidden files in My Computer or Windows Explorer, choose Options from the View menu in My Computer or Windows Explorer, click the View tab, select Show All Files under Hidden Files, and then click OK.

3. If there is no RATINGS.POL file, skip to step 4. If there is a RATINGS.POL file, rename it to RATINGS.OLD.

4. Start Internet Explorer, and then choose Internet Options from the View menu to open the Internet Options dialog box.

5. Click the Content tab, and then click Settings in the Content Advisor area.

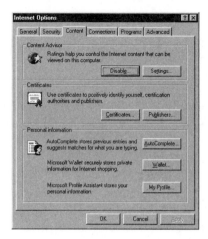

Figure 5-26. *The Internet Options dialog box.*

6. Type the Supervisor password, and then click OK.

Note If you do not know or have forgotten the Supervisor password, contact a Microsoft Technical Support Engineer for assistance. For information about how to contact a Microsoft Technical Support Engineer, visit the Microsoft web site at *http://support.microsoft.com/support/contact/default.asp.*

---

7. Select the Ratings options that meet your needs, and then click OK.

When you restart Internet Explorer, the changes take effect.

Related KB article Q154999

Credentials Requested More than Necessary

Internet Explorer prompts you for your credentials one more time than necessary. This problem occurs if you are using Windows NT Challenge/Response (NTLM) authentication on your proxy server when a remote Web server uses Basic authentication. This occurs with Internet Explorer 4.01 Service Pack 1 or the version of Internet Explorer included in Windows 98.

Solution

Contact Microsoft Technical Support for information about the availability of an update. An update to address this problem is now available but is not fully tested and should be applied only to computers experiencing this specific problem. Unless you are severely impacted by this specific problem, Microsoft does not recommend implementing this update at this time.

Related KB article Q189033

Downloading 128-Bit Internet Explorer Produces Error Messages

You attempt to download the 128-bit version of Internet Explorer and receive one of the following error messages:

Whois Timed Out

Invalid DNS entry

You may also see an error message indicating that you cannot be recognized as a U.S. or Canadian citizen, because your domain's physical location cannot be verified.

Your Internet service provider (ISP) may have assigned you an identifier that does not allow you to be recognized as a U.S. or Canadian citizen. InterNIC is an international organization responsible for registering each Internet site and assigning an identifier for it. Every ISP must register with InterNIC. InterNIC assigns an identifier using three settings:

- Domain Name Service (DNS) Internet Protocol (IP) address

- Domain Name

- Range of IP address that an ISP can assign to its clients

These settings identify you and the ISP to the 128-bit Internet Explorer download server. This server, before beginning the download, compares the identifier you have with the identifier InterNIC assigned to the ISP. If they don't match, Microsoft cannot identify you as a U.S. or Canadian citizen and must refuse the download. Microsoft is responsible for assuring that 128-bit encryption in Internet Explorer is available only to citizens of the United States and Canada.

You might also get these messages if you are part of a network using a proxy server to access the Internet. Depending on how the proxy server is configured, the identifier may not be available.

Solution

Contact your Internet service provider (ISP).

Related KB article Q175565

Downloading File Displays ActiveX Icon

You try to download a program (.EXE) or a Zip (.ZIP) file and Internet Explorer displays a blank web page with an ActiveX icon in the upper-right corner. If you click the ActiveX icon, you receive the following error message:

Error Locating Object Handler There is no viewer available for the type of object you are trying to open. The following information is available about this object:

Address of Object: <Web address of the file>

Content Type: <type of file>

Possible location of viewer: Microsoft ActiveX Gallery

Do you want to go to this location to download a viewer for this type of object?

This problem occurs if a plug-in or ActiveX control has been uninstalled or deleted from your computer but has left entries in the Registry. The following plug-ins and ActiveX controls have been known to cause this behavior:

- NetZip
- Cheyenne Web Browser Anti-Virus.

Solution

Delete the following Registry key:

```
HKEY_LOCAL_MACHINE\Software\Microsoft\Internet  Explorer\Plugins\Extension
```

Warning Please read the Introduction for information on how to safely edit the Registry.

1. Click the Start button, choose Run, enter *Regedit* in the Open box, and then click OK.

2. Navigate your way down through the folders in the left pane, and then delete the Registry key.

3. Close Regedit.

4. Restart Windows.

Note For more information, see KB article Q154036, "Troubleshooting Active Content in Internet Explorer."

Related KB article Q180553

Download Halts When Internet Explorer Is Closed

You close Microsoft Internet Explorer's parent window (the first instance of Internet Explorer when you are running multiple instances of Internet Explorer) while you are trying to download a .AVI, .MOV or .MPG file, and the file download stops. Microsoft has confirmed this to be a problem in Windows 98.

Solution

Don't close the parent window while downloading files of these types.

Related KB article Q187395

Folder Contents Missing from Menu in Internet Explorer

You add a folder to the Links toolbar in Internet Explorer and then click the folder, and the contents of the folder are missing from the menu that appears. Only the folder name may appear on the menu. This problem occurs if you copied or moved the folder to the Links toolbar.

The Links toolbar is designed to contain shortcuts to frequently used Web pages. Although you can copy or move a folder to the Links toolbar, you may be unable to view its contents when you click it.

When you add a web page to the Links toolbar, its shortcut is copied to the WINDOWS\ FAVORITES\LINKS folder (assuming Windows is the name of the folder in which Windows is installed). If user profiles are enabled on your computer, the web page shortcut is copied to the WINDOWS\PROFILES\<USERNAME>\FAVORITES\LINKS folder (where <username> is the name you use to log on to Windows).

Solution One

Create a shortcut to the folder on the Links toolbar. To do so, follow these steps in Internet Explorer:

1. Choose Organize Favorites from the Favorites menu.

2. Double-click the LINKS folder.

3. Right-click an empty area in the Organize Favorites dialog box, choose New from the shortcut menu, and then choose Shortcut from the submenu.

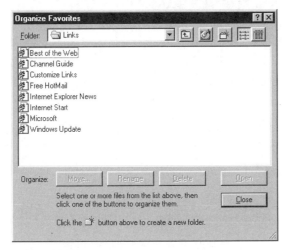

Figure 5-27. *The Organize Favorites dialog box.*

4. In the Command Line box, enter the path of the folder to which you want to create a shortcut, and then click Next.

5. Enter a name for the shortcut, and then click Finish.

6. Click Close.

Note When you click the shortcut to the folder on the Links toolbar, or when you choose Links from the Favorites menu and then choose the shortcut to the folder from the submenu, the folder is opened in a new window.

Solution Two

Add the folder to the Favorites menu in Internet Explorer. To do so, follow these steps:

1. Choose Organize Favorites from the Favorites menu.

2. Click the Start button, choose Programs, and then click Windows Explorer.

3. Locate the folder you want to add to the Favorites menu.

4. Drag the folder to the Organize Favorites window.

5. Click Close.

If the folder contains shortcuts to web pages or other files, you can view the shortcuts by choosing the folder from the Favorites menu. If the folder does not contain shortcuts, choose the folder from the Favorites menu to open the folder in a new window.

Note For more information, see KB article Q171228, "How to Customize the Links Toolbar in Internet Explorer 4.0."

Related KB article Q179232

FTP or Gopher Hangs Internet Explorer 4.0SP1

You try to use Internet Explorer version 4.0 with Internet Explorer Service Pack 1 installed to access a File Transfer Protocol (FTP) or Gopher site, and Internet Explorer stops responding. Also, you may see an error message similar to the following:

Internet Explorer cannot open the Internet site <Web address>.

Overlapped I/O operation is in progress.

This problem occurs if you are using a proxy autoconfiguration script. The following is an example of a proxy autoconfiguration script that may cause the error:

```
function FindProxyForURL(url, host)

    {

        if (isPlainHostName(host) || dnsDomainIs(host, ".msn.com"))

                return "DIRECT";

        else

                return "PROXY gproxy:80; DIRECT";

    }
```

The overlapped input/output error is caused by not transitioning properly from a PROXY attempt to a DIRECT attempt. Microsoft has confirmed this to be a problem in Windows 98.

Solution One

Contact Microsoft Technical Support to obtain a fix bundled in a self-extracting and installing executable file named 1916.EXE. The binary installed is WININET.DLL and should have the following time stamp and file size:

```
06/03/98  09:30p                    370,448 Wininet.dll
```

Solution Two

To solve this problem, follow these steps:

1. In Internet Explorer, choose Internet Options from the View menu.

2. Click the Connection tab.

3. Click Configure, delete the text in the URL box, and then click OK.

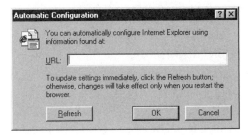

Figure 5-28. *The Automatic Configuration dialog box.*

4. Select the Access the Internet Using A Proxy Server check box, and then enter the proxy server address and port number. You can obtain this information from your network administrator.

5. Click OK.

A limitation still exists because File Transfer Protocol (FTP) and Gopher connections are unable to try a combination of proxies and DIRECT during the same download attempt. For FTP and Gopher scenarios, if FindProxyForUrl returns a list such as

```
PROXY proxy1; PROXY proxy2; ...; PROXY proxyN; DIRECT
```

and all N proxies do not connect, then Wininet does not correctly try the DIRECT case. You still receive an error message, but if you try the same Web address (URL) again, the DIRECT case is then tried. Ideally, requests normally go through a proxy server, so you are unlikely to experience this. This problem is not reproducible if DIRECT is used alone.

Related KB article Q187770

Installation Displays Error Messages

You install Internet Explorer and receive one of these error messages:

Load error #35: Cannot access bce server

Load error #5: Initialize failed

Load error #35: Couldn't register with bce server

Load error #5: Initialize failed

This problem occurs if you have Lexmark printer drivers installed.

Solution

Obtain the NEWBCE.EXE self-extracting file from Lexmark Technical Support.

Copy the NEWBCE.EXE file to the WINDOWS\SYSTEM folder. To do so, follow these steps:

1. In Windows Explorer, locate and double-click the NEWBCE.EXE file.

2. When you are prompted to replace the existing files, click Yes.

If you are prompted to connect to your Internet service provider (ISP) after you install the NEWBCE.EXE file and restart your computer, follow these steps:

Warning Please read the Introduction for information on how to safely edit the Registry.

1. Click the Start button, choose Run, enter *Regedit* in the Open box, and then click OK.

2. Navigate your way down through the folders and remove the LEXSTART.EXE string value from the following Registry key:

        HKEY_LOCAL_MACHINE\Software\Microsoft\Windows\CurrentVersion\Run

3. Delete the following Registry key:

        HKEY_LOCAL_MACHINE\Software\Lexmark\

4. Close Regedit.

5. Rename the LEXLMPM.DLL file. Click the Start button, choose Find, and then click Files Or Folders. In the Named box, enter *lexlmpm.dll* and then click Find Now. In the list of found files, right-click the LESLMPM.DLL file, and choose Rename from the shortcut menu. Type a new name for the LESLMPM.DLL file (such as LEXLMPM.XXX), and press the Enter key. Close the Find window.

6. Restart your computer.

Related KB article Q181669

Installation Incomplete

You try to install Internet Explorer and receive the following error message at the end of Active Setup:

Installation is incomplete.

The following Internet Explorer 4.0 components were not installed:

Internet Explorer 4.0 Web Browser, Windows Desktop Update, Microsoft Outlook Express.

For more information, click Help. Setup will now finish the installation for components that were installed successfully.

You click OK to continue, and then click OK to restart your computer, and you receive several of the following error messages when you log in to Windows 98:

An error occurred loading "C:\Windows\System\mlang.dll". The file may not have been installed or it has been corrupted.

Unable to call the function "DllInstall" in the file "C:\Windows\System\comctl32.dll" because that function does not exist or is not exported.

CAPI: The install program could not open signature file.

Unable to find the function "DllRegisterServer" in the file "C:\Windows\System\wintrust.dll."

Error loading IEDKCS32.DLL. The specified module could not be found.

Unable to install Java packages from C:\Windows\Java\classes\xmldso.cab. Unspecified error.

Error registering the OCX C:\Windows\System\webcheck.dll.

Internet Explorer is not currently your default browser. Would you like to make it your default browser?

After you see the error messages, the previously installed version of Internet Explorer may start automatically.

When you try to remove Internet Explorer using the Add/Remove Programs tool in Control Panel, you see the following error messages:

Setup Error 544. Setup is unable to open the data file 'C:\Program Files\Plus!\Microsoft Internet\Setup\SETUP.stf'; run Setup again from where you originally ran it.

Setup Error 723. Setup was unable to read configuration information from the first section of the setup file: C:\Program Files\Plus!\MicrosoftInternet\Setup\SETUP.stf.

Setup was not completed successfully.

You may also see other error messages. This behavior occurs if the WINHLP32.EXE file is not present in the Windows folder in Windows 98.

Solution

Extract a new copy of the WINHLP32.EXE file from your original Windows 98 disks or CD-ROM to the WINDOWS folder. For information about using the Extract tool, see KB article Q129605, "How to Extract Original Compressed Windows Files."

Related KB article Q179636

Install Fails on a Drive with More than 4 GB Free Space

You are unable to install Internet Explorer 4.01 Service Pack 1 (SP1) on a computer with a hard disk that has more than 4 gigabytes (GB) of available space.

Solution

Contact Microsoft Product Support Services to obtain an immediate fix. For a list of Microsoft Product Support Services phone numbers and information on support costs, go to the following address on the World Wide Web:

http://support.microsoft.com/support/supportnet/default.asp

Note This fix has not been fully tested and should be applied only to systems experiencing this specific problem. If you are not severely affected by this specific problem, Microsoft recommends that you wait for the next Internet Explorer service pack that contains this fix.

Related KB article Q192714

Internal Error in Windows Internet Extensions

You use Internet Explorer over a dial-up connection, and the following error message appears when you attempt to view a web site:

Internet Explorer cannot open the Internet site <site name>.

An internal error occurred in the Windows Internet Extensions.

When you click OK, the Navigation Canceled page appears in Internet Explorer.

This problem occurs for either of the following reasons:

- You start Net.Medic 1.x by VitalSigns Software after you establish a dial-up connection but before you start Internet Explorer.

- The incorrect version of the WSOCK32.DLL file is installed on your computer.

Solution One

If this problem occurs because you start Net.Medic 1.x by VitalSigns Software after you establish a dial-up connection but before you start Internet Explorer, follow these steps:

1. Restart the computer. When you see the Windows 98 startup screen, press and hold down the Shift key for the duration of Windows startup.

2. If you are prompted for a user name and password during startup, release the Shift key and enter your logon information normally. Before you click OK, press and hold down the Shift key once again.

3. Once you have verified that Net.Medic did not start, connect to the Internet and download the update from VitalSigns Software's web site at:

   http://www.vitalsigns.com/techsupport/indexes/nm_upgrades98_index.html

Solution Two

If the problem occurs because an incorrect version of the WSOCK32.DLL file is installed on your computer, follow these steps:

1. Click the Start button, and choose Shut Down. Click the Restart In MS-DOS Mode option button, and then click OK.

2. At the MS-DOS prompt, type *C:* and press the Enter key (assuming C is the letter of the drive on which Windows is installed. If not, type the correct drive letter.)

3. Type the following commands, pressing the Enter key after each one:

```
cd\windows\system

ren wsock32.dll wsock32.old

exit
```

4. Extract a new copy of the WSOCK32.DLL file to the WINDOWS\SYSTEM folder.

Note You can extract the WSOCK32.DLL file using the System File Checker tool. For more information, see KB article Q129605, "System File Checker Tool."

5. Restart your computer.

Related KB article Q188952

Internet Explorer 4 Quits While Viewing Web Page

Internet Explorer quits unexpectedly when you view a web page that contains a script written in JScript that uses the Window.External function with a very long string. It is difficult, but possible, for an individual to cause malicious code to be run on your computer as a result of this problem.

Additional information about this issue is available on the following Microsoft web sites:

http://www.microsoft.com/ie/security/jscript.htm

http://www.microsoft.com/security/bulletins/ms98-011.htm

Solution One

Obtain and install Windows Explorer's *Windows.External.Jscrpt* security update from the Windows Update service.

1. Click the Start button, and choose Windows Update.

Note You can also access the Microsoft Windows Update web site by displaying the web page at *http://windowsupdate.microsoft.com.*

---

2. Click the Products Updates hyperlink.

3. Select the Internet Explorer Window.External.Jscript Security Update check box, and then click Download.

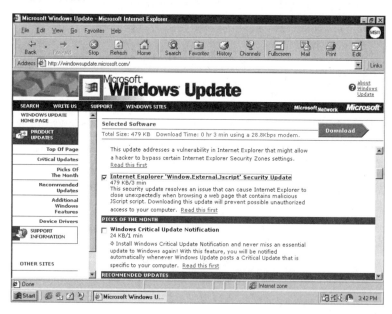

Figure 5-29. *The Product Updates web page of the Microsoft Windows Update web site.*

4. Follow the instructions onscreen to complete the download process, and restart your computer when prompted to do so.

The update file name is SCR.EXE. It includes the following files:

- JSCRIPT.DLL
- VBSCRIPT.DLL
- DISPEX.DLL
- SCRRUN.DLL

All of these files are dated 7/2/98 and are version 3.1.3101.

The Microsoft Scripting Engine version 4.0 (included with Microsoft Visual Studio 6.0) and version 5.0 (beta available for download) are not affected by this problem. If you attempt to install this update over version 4.x or 5.x of the Scripting Engines, you receive a version conflict message for the files being updated. Click Yes to keep your existing files.

Solution Two

If you are unable to apply the patch, you can reduce your risk of being affected by this problem by disabling Active Scripting in Internet Explorer. To do so, follow these steps:

1. Click the Start button, choose Settings, and then click Control Panel.

2. Double-click the Internet icon.

3. Click the Security tab.

4. Select Internet Zone from the Zone box.

5. Click the Custom (For Expert Users) option button, and then click Settings.

6. Under Scripting, click the Disable option in the Active Scripting section.

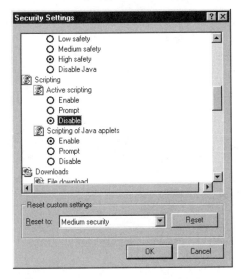

Figure 5-30. *The Security Settings dialog box.*

7. Click OK.

8. Select Restricted Sites Zone from the Zone box.

9. Repeat steps 5–7.

10. Click OK.

Related KB article Q191200

Internet Explorer Doesn't Connect to the Internet

You start Internet Explorer, and your modem doesn't dial your Internet Service Provider (ISP). You also see the following error message:

Internet Explorer could not open the Internet site http://<Web address>

A connection to the server could not be established.

If you check your connection settings by choosing Internet Options from the View menu and then clicking the Connection tab, you will see that the Connect To The Internet Using A Modem option is disabled and the Connect To The Internet Using A Local Area Network option is enabled. Changing these settings and then restarting Internet Explorer or your computer does not resolve this problem.

This problem occurs if PKWare PKZip for Windows version 2.60.01 (shareware version) is installed, and the TSADBOT.EXE program is running.

Some of the shareware versions of PKZip include TSADBOT.EXE, which displays advertisements for various web sites and is run every time you start your computer or PKZip. The version of PKZip on PKWare's web site does not include the TSADBOT.EXE program, and PKZip for Windows version 2.60 (retail version) does not exhibit this behavior.

Solution One

Stop the Tsadbot program from running by renaming the file. To do so, follow these steps:

1. Press Ctrl+Alt+Delete to open the Close Program dialog box, select Tsadbot from the list, click End Task, and then click End Task.

2. Click the Start button, choose Find, and then click Files Or Folders.

3. In the Named box, enter *tsadbot.exe*, and click Find Now.

4. In the list of found files, right-click the TSADBOT.EXE file, choose Rename from the shortcut menu, and then enter a new name for the file (such as TSADBOT.XXX). Press the Enter key.

5. Close the Find tool.

Solution Two

Note This method prevents the connection settings from being changed only when you start your computer. They are still changed when you run PKZip.

Using Registry Editor, delete the following Registry key:

```
HKEY_LOCAL_MACHINE\SOFTWARE\Microsoft\Windows\CurrentVersion\Run\TimeSink Ad Client
```

Warning Please read the Introduction for information on how to safely edit the Registry.

1. Click the Start button, choose Run, enter *Regedit* in the Open box, and then click OK.

2. Navigate your way down through the folders in the left pane until you locate the key described above.

3. Delete the key.

4. Close Regedit.

5. Restart Windows.

Related KB article Q191451

Internet Explorer Doesn't Disconnect Automatically

You close Internet Explorer and aren't prompted to disconnect.

This occurs if the EnableAutodisconnect value in the Registry is set to a data value of 00 00 00 00.

Solution

Modify the data value of the EnableAutodisconnect value in the following Registry key:

`HKEY_CURRENT_USER\Software\Microsoft\Windows\CurrentVersion\Internet  Settings`

Change the data value to 01 00 00 00 by following these steps:

Warning Please read the Introduction for information on how to safely edit the Registry.

1. Click the Start button, choose Run, enter *Regedit* in the Open box, and then click OK.

2. Navigate your way down through the folders in the left pane until you locate the key described above.

3. Modify the value of EnableAutodisconnect to 01 00 00 00.

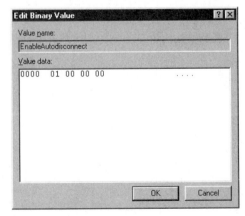

Figure 5-31. *The Edit Binary Value dialog box.*

4. Close Regedit.

5. Restart your computer.

Related KB article Q193555

Internet Explorer Doesn't Disconnect Automatically from MSN

You close Internet Explorer and aren't prompted to disconnect from MSN (The Microsoft Network).

This problem occurs when you connect to the Internet using Internet Explorer rather than by using the MSN or Quick Connect icon. When you connect with Internet Explorer, the Dial-Up Networking connection created by MSN Setup is used, but this connection does not automatically prompt you to disconnect when you close Internet Explorer.

Solution

Create a new connection icon for MSN using the settings in your current MSN connection, and then configure Internet Explorer to use the new connection. To do so, follow these steps:

1. Double-click My Computer, and then double-click Dial-Up Networking.

2. Right-click the MSN icon, choose Properties from the shortcut menu, and write down all the information in the connection. After you write down the information, click OK.

3. Double-click the Make New Connection icon. Enter a name for the new connection, and then click Next. Follow the prompts on the screen, entering the information you copied from the MSN connection. After the connection is created, a new icon appears in the DIAL-UP NETWORK-ING folder.

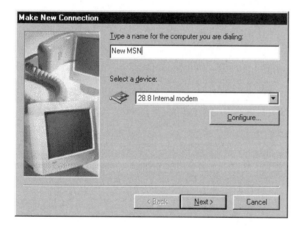

Figure 5-32. *The Make New Connection dialog box.*

4. Click the Start button, choose Settings, and then click Control Panel.

5. Double-click the Internet icon, and then click the Connection tab.

6. Verify that the Connect To The Internet Using A Modem option is selected. Click Settings. In the Use The Following Dial-Up Networking Connection box, select the new connection you created in step 3. Click OK, and then click OK.

7. Click OK.

Related KB article Q191876

Internet Explorer Doesn't Start

You double-click the Internet Explorer icon on the desktop and receive the following error message:

Windows cannot find Program.exe, which is needed for opening files of type "Internet Explorer".

This problem occurs if you are using MSN (The Microsoft Network) software when you upgrade to Windows 98, and the ONLINE SERVICES folder is missing or damaged. The Internet Explorer icon on the desktop references MSNMIG.EXE in the ONLINE SERVICES folder, and when Windows is unable to find this file, it generates the error message.

Solution

Extract the MSNMIG.EXE file to the PROGRAM FILES\ONLINE SERVICES folder, and then reinstall MSN.

Note For more information, see the System File Checker Tool section in KB article Q129605. For information about how to install MSN, see KB articles Q159037 and Q159870.

Related KB article Q188592

Internet Explorer Doesn't Start When Clicking on a URL

You click a web address in a document in a non-browser program such as an e-mail program, and Internet Explorer doesn't start, or you receive the following error message:

Cannot find program.exe needed for opening files of type URL_transfer protocol

This problem occurs if the URL:Hypertext Transfer Protocol file association is no longer associated with Internet Explorer.

Solution

Edit the URL:Hypertext Transfer Protocol file association to associate this type of file with Internet Explorer. To do so, follow these steps:

1. Click the Start button, choose Settings, and then click Folder Options.

2. Click the File Types tab, select URL:HyperText Transfer Protocol from the Registered File Types list, and then click Edit.

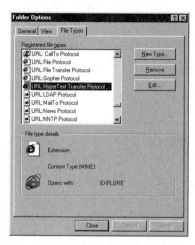

Figure 5-33. *The File Types tab of the Folder Options dialog box.*

3. In the Actions box, select Open, and then click Edit.

4. Click Browse, navigate to the \PROGRAM FILES\INTERNET EXPLORER folder, click the IEXPLORE.EXE file, then click Open.

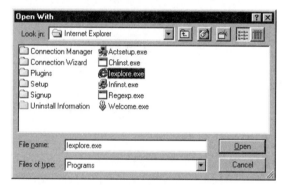

Figure 5-34. *The Open With dialog box.*

5. Click OK, click Close, and then click Close.

Related KB article Q191219

Internet Properties Dialog Box Stops Responding

You attempt to view the Security tab in the Internet Properties dialog box, and your computer stops responding or you see one of the following error messages:

An error occurred while Windows was working with the Control Panel file C:\WINDOWS\SYSTEM\INETCPL.CPL.

EXPLORER caused an invalid page fault in module INETCPL.CPL at <address>

When you click OK or Close, the Internet Properties dialog box closes. This problem occurs if a Registry key is damaged.

Solution

Use Registry Editor to remove the following Registry key:

```
HKEY_CURRENT_USER\Software\Microsoft\Windows\CurrentVersion\Internet
Setting\Zones
```

Warning Please read the Introduction for information on how to safely edit the Registry.

1. Click the Start button, choose Run, enter *Regedit* in the Open box, and then click OK.

2. Navigate your way down through the folders in the left pane until you locate the Registry key described above.

3. Delete the key.

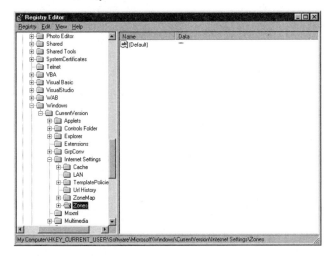

Figure 5-35. *The Registry Editor window.*

4. Close Regedit.

5. Restart your computer.

Related KB article   Q186890

Internet Site Cannot Be Opened

You start Internet Explorer and receive the following error message:

Internet Explorer cannot open the Internet site <address>. A connection with the server could not be established.

This error message occurs for either or both of the following reasons:

- Multiple copies of the WSOCK32.DLL file are installed on your computer.

- An incorrect version of the WSOCK32.DLL file is installed on your computer.

Solution One

Rename the additional WSOCK32.DLL files. To do so, follow these steps:

1. Click the Start button, choose Find, and then click Files Or Folders to open the Find window.

2. In the Named box, enter *wsock32.dll,* and then click Find Now.

3. Rename any copy of the WSOCK32.DLL file that is not in the WINDOWS\SYSTEM folder.

Solution Two

Replace the WSOCK32.DLL file. To do so, follow these steps:

1. Restart your computer. After your computer completes the Power On Self Test (POST), press and hold down the Ctrl key until you see the Windows 98 Startup menu, and then choose Safe Mode Command Prompt Only.

2. Rename the WSOCK32.DLL file in the WINDOWS\SYSTEM folder to WSOCK32.OLD by typing the following line, and then pressing the Enter key:

```
ren <drive>:\<windows>\system\wsock32.dll wsock32.old
```

(where <drive> is the letter of the drive on which the Windows folder is located, and <windows> is the name of the folder in which Windows is installed). For example:

```
ren c:\windows\system\wsock32.dll wsock32.old
```

Note This procedure assumes you do not already have a file named WSOCK32.OLD. If you do, use a filename extension that is not currently in use.

---

3. Restart Windows normally.

4. Click Start, choose Run, enter *sfc.exe* in the Open box, and then click OK to start the System File Checker tool.

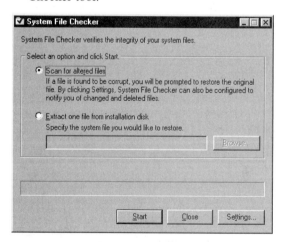

Figure 5-36. *The System File Checker dialog box.*

5. Extract a new copy of the WSOCK32.DLL file from your original Windows 98 CD-ROM into the WINDOWS\SYSTEM folder using the System File Checker tool. The Windows 98 WSOCK32.DLL file is 40K and has a date stamp of 5/11/98.

Note For more information, see KB article Q129605, "How to Extract Original Compressed Windows Files."

6. Restart your computer.

Note For more information, see KB article Q175039, "Err Msg: A Connection to the Server Could Not Be Established."

Related KB article   Q175722

Invalid DHCP Lease Error When Using Cable Modem

You attempt to view a web page in Internet Explorer using a cable modem, and you are unable to do so or receive the following error message:

Invalid DHCP lease

This problem occurs when your cable modem is configured to automatically obtain an IP address from a Dynamic Host Configuration Protocol (DHCP) server. Windows 98 automatically assigns an IP address if your adapter is unable to obtain one. Because a connection across a cable modem is slower than a connection across a network, Windows 98 may automatically assign an IP address before the cable modem is able to obtain one from the DHCP server. Since this automatically assigned IP address is not valid for the Internet service provider (ISP), you can not access resources on the Internet using the cable modem.

There are two types of cable modem services, one-way cable modems and two-way cable modems. One-way cable modems send information over the phone line and receive information over the cable. Two-way cable modems send and receive information over the cable.

When Windows 98 does not initially detect a DHCP service, it assigns an IP Autoconfiguration Address. If Windows 98 later detects a DHCP service on the network, Windows 98 switches from the IP Autoconfiguration Address to the address that is assigned by the DHCP server.

To disable IP Autoconfiguration Addressing, right-click the IPAC_OFF.INF file located in the TOOLS\MTSUTIL folder on the Windows 98 CD-ROM, and then click Install.

Note For more information, see KB article Q188480, "Windows 98 MTSUTIL.TXT File."

Solution One

For one-way cable modems, follow these steps:

1. Click the Start button, and then choose Run.

2. Enter *winipcfg* in the Open box, and press Enter.

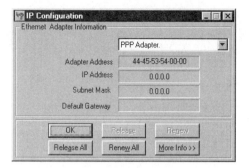

Figure 5-37. *The IP Configuration window.*

3. Select PPP Adapter from the list of adapters.

4. Verify that you have a Windows-assigned IP address by verifying that the IP Address box has the following address:

    169.254.x.x.

    (where x is any number between 0 and 255).

5. Click Release, and then click Renew.

6. Select the network adapter connected to your cable modem from the list of adapters.

7. Verify that you have a Windows-assigned IP address by verifying that the IP Address box has the following address

    169.254.x.x.

    (where x is any number between 0 and 255).

8. Click Release. The IP address should be 0.0.0.0.

Solution Two

For two-way cable modems, follow these steps:

1. Click the Start button, and then choose Run.

2. Enter *winipcfg* in the Open box, and press Enter.

3. Select the network adapter connected to your cable modem from the list of adapters.

4. Verify that you have a Windows-assigned IP address by verifying that the IP Address box has the following address:

    169.254.x.x.

    (where x is any number between 0 and 255).

5. Click Release, and then click Renew.

Related KB article Q189255

Invalid Page Fault in Module KERNEL32.DLL

You use Microsoft Internet Explorer to access the Internet and receive the following error message:

IEXPLORE caused an invalid page fault in module Kernel32.dll

This can be caused by any of the following situations:

- One or more dynamic link libraries (DLLs) are located on the desktop.

- Internet Explorer's internal Java Just-In-Time (JIT) compiler is enabled, and the web page you are loading contains a Java program that is incompatible with the compiler.

- Internet Explorer is configured to automatically use items that show active content, and the web page you are loading contains active content that is not functioning properly.

- The third-party display driver you are using is damaged or incompatible with Windows.

- You are using Active Server Pages (ASP) to perform an ODBC query on a database on an Internet Information Server (IIS), or you are running a large ASP file while Secured Sockets Layer (SSL) security is enabled.

Solution One

Configure Windows so that DLLs are not hidden, and then rename or move any DLLs located on the desktop. To do so, follow these steps:

1. Double-click My Computer.

2. Choose Folder Options from the View menu, and then click the View tab.

3. Under the heading Hidden Files, click the Show All Files option button, and then click OK.

4. To rename a file on the desktop, right-click the file, choose Rename from the shortcut menu, enter the new name you want to use for the file, and then press the Enter key.

5. To move a file, drag it from the desktop to a folder on your hard disk using My Computer or Windows Explorer.

Solution Two

Disable Internet Explorer's internal Java JIT compiler. To do so, follow these steps:

1. Choose Internet Options from the View menu in Internet Explorer, and then click the Advanced tab.

2. Clear the "Java JIT Compiler Enabled" check box.

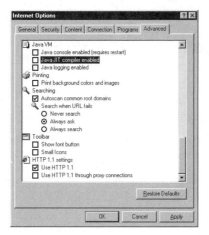

Figure 5-38. *The Internet Options dialog box.*

Solution Three

Configure Internet Explorer so that it does not automatically show active content, such as vertical marquees or animations. To do so, follow these steps:

1. Choose Internet Options from the View menu in Internet Explorer, and then click the Security tab.

2. Click the Custom (For Expert Users) option button, and click Settings.

3. Click the Disable option button under Run ActiveX Controls And Plug-Ins.

Note For more information, see KB article Q154036, "Troubleshooting Active Content in Internet Explorer."

Solution Four

Configure Windows to use the Standard Display Adapter (VGA) or Super VGA display adapter type. To do so, follow these steps:

1. Click the Start button, choose Settings, click Control Panel, and then double-click the Display icon.

2. Click the Settings tab, and then click Advanced.

3. Click the Adapter tab, click Change, click Next, and then click the second option button to show all devices.

4. Click Next, and click the Show All Hardware option button.

5. Select (Standard Display Types) from the Manufacturers box and Standard Display Adapter (VGA) or Super VGA from the Models box, and click Next.

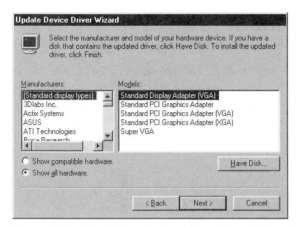

Figure 5-39. *The Update Device Driver Wizard dialog box.*

If the problem persists after performing these steps, the third-party display driver you are using may be damaged or incompatible with Windows. If the display driver is damaged, you may be able to work around the problem by reinstalling the driver from the disk provided by the hardware manufacturer. If the problem continues after reinstalling the driver, contact the driver's manufacturer and ask about protected-mode drivers for your display adapter.

Solution Five

Uninstall the Windows Desktop update component. For information about how to do this, see KB article Q165695, "How to Add or Remove Windows Desktop Update."

Solution Six

Change the value of the BufferingOn value to 1 in the following Registry key:

```
HKEY_LOCAL_MACHINE\System\CurrentControlSet\Services\W3SVC\ASP\Parameters
```

Warning Please read the Introduction for information on how to safely edit the Registry.

Follow these steps:

1. Click the Start button, choose Run, enter *Regedit* in the Open box, and then click OK.

2. Navigate your way down through the folders in the left pane.

3. Double-click the BufferingOn value, and change the value to 1.

4. Close Regedit.

5. Restart your computer.

Related KB article Q155116

Invalid Page Fault in Module MSAAHTML.DLL

You close Internet Explorer and receive the following error message:

Explorer caused an invalid page fault in module Msaahtml.dll at <address>.

Note The MSAAHTML.DLL file provides Microsoft Active Accessibility support in Internet Explorer. For information about Active Accessibility, visit the following Microsoft web site: *http://www.microsoft.com/enable/msaaintro.htm.*

When you reply to an e-mail message using Microsoft Outlook Express, you may receive the following error message:

Msimn caused an Invalid Page Fault in module msaahtml.dll at <address>.

This problem occurs if IBM ViaVoice 98 is installed on your computer.

Solution

To solve this problem, follow these steps:

1. Click the Start button, and choose Run.

2. In the Open box, type the following line:

    regsvr32 /u msaahtml.dll

3. Click OK, and then click OK again when you receive the following message:

    DllUnregisterServer in MSAAHTML.DLL succeeded.

Related KB article Q191607

Mosaic Launches Instead of Internet Explorer

You try to start Internet Explorer by double-clicking an Internet shortcut, and the NCSA Mosaic or SPRY Mosaic web browser program starts. This problem occurs if the Internet Shortcut file type is configured to start Mosaic instead of Internet Explorer.

Solution

Configure the Internet Shortcut file type to start Internet Explorer by following these steps:

1. Double-click My Computer, choose Folder Options from the View menu, and then click the File Types tab.

2. In the Registered File Types list box, select Internet Shortcut, and then click Edit.

3. In the Actions box, select Open, and then click Edit.

4. In the Application Used To Perform Action box, type *rundll32.exe shdocvw.dll,OpenURL %1.*

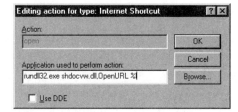

Figure 5-40. *The Editing Action For Type: Internet Shortcut dialog box.*

5. Click OK, click Close, and then click Close.

6. Restart your computer.

Related KB article Q193572

Personal Certificate Not Wanted in Internet Explorer

You need to remove a personal certificate from Internet Explorer version 4.0 or 4.01.

Solution

To solve this problem, follow these steps:

Warning Please read the Introduction for information on how to safely edit the Registry.

1. Click the Start button, choose Run, enter *Regedit* in the Open box, and then click OK.

2. Navigate your way down through the folders in the left pane until you locate the following Registry key:

   `HKEY_CURRENT_USER\Software\Microsoft\SystemCertificates\My\Certificates`

This Registry key contains the keys that represent your personal certificates. To remove a specific personal certificate, delete the corresponding Registry key.

3. Close Regedit.

4. Restart your computer.

Related KB article Q185059

PowerToys Zoom In/Zoom Out Feature Doesn't Work

You attempt to use the Internet Explorer 4.0 PowerToys Zoom In/Zoom Out feature after you install the Windows 98 PowerToys TweakUI tool and are unable to do so.

This problem occurs because the Zoom In/Zoom Out feature is not included with the version of PowerToys on your Windows 98 CD-ROM. It is installed when you install Internet Explorer 4.0 PowerToys. The Internet Explorer 4.0 PowerToys is designed only for Microsoft Windows 95–based and Microsoft NT–based computers.

Note For more information, see KB article Q188920, "Windows 98 Power Toys README.TXT file."

Solution

Install the Magnifier tool included with Windows 98. To do so, follow these steps:

1. Click the Start button, choose Settings, click Control Panel, and then double-click the Add/Remove Programs icon.

2. Click the Windows Setup tab, double-click Accessibility, and then select the Accessibility Tools check box.

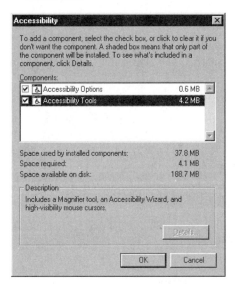

Figure 5-41. *The Accessibility dialog box.*

3. Click OK, click OK, insert the Windows 98 CD-ROM when you are prompted to do so, and then follow the instructions on the screen to finish the installation.

4. To use the Magnifier tool, click the Start button, choose Programs, choose Accessories, choose Accessibility, and then click Magnifier.

Related KB article Q190772

Runtime Error in Internet Explorer

You run Internet Explorer and receive the following error message:

Runtime Error 216 at 00009275.

This problem occurs if you are running the Oakley SmartWheel version 1.0 mouse driver.

Solution One

Contact Oakley Data Services about the availability of a fix to this problem.

Solution Two

Uninstall the Oakley SmartWheel version 1.0 mouse driver and install a Microsoft mouse driver. To do so, follow these steps:

1. Click the Start button, choose Settings, click Control Panel, and then double-click the Add/Remove Programs icon.

2. Select Oakley SmartWheel 1.0, click Add/Remove, and then click OK.

3. Install a Microsoft mouse driver. For information about how to do so, view the documentation included with your mouse or computer.

Solution Three

Change the screen area in the Display Properties dialog box to 800 by 600 pixels. To do so, follow these steps:

1. Click the Start button, choose Settings, click Control Panel, and then double-click the Display icon.

2. Click the Settings tab. Under Screen Area, move the slider to 800 by 600 Pixels.

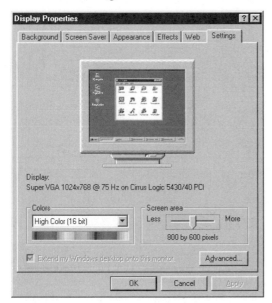

Figure 5-42. *The Display Properties dialog box.*

3. Click OK, click OK, and then click Yes.

Related KB article Q189989

Search Bar Doesn't Open Web Sites in Main Window

You click an item in the Search bar in Internet Explorer, and the web site opens in the Search bar instead of the right side of the window. This problem occurs if there is an invalid Search Bar value in the Registry.

Solution

Remove the invalid Search Bar value in the following Registry key

`HKEY_CURRENT_USER\Software\Microsoft\Internet Explorer\Main`

and verify that the data value for the Search Page and Default_Search_URL values match each other in the following Registry key:

`HKEY_LOCAL_MACHINE\Software\Microsoft\Internet Explorer\Main`

To solve this problem, follow these steps:

Warning Please read the Introduction for information on how to safely edit the Registry.

1. Click the Start button, choose Run, enter *Regedit* in the Open box, and then click OK.

2. Navigate your way down through the folders in the left pane until you locate the first key named above.

3. Delete the invalid Search Page value.

4. Navigate your way down through the folders in the left pane until you locate the second key named above.

5. Confirm that the data values for the Default_Search_URL matches that of the Search Page. If they don't, edit the incorrect one.

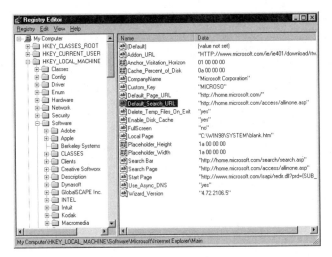

Figure 5-43. *The Registry Editor window.*

6. Close Regedit.

7. Restart your computer.

Related KB article Q191580

Search Bar Wrong Size

You can change the default Search bar size in Internet Explorer.

Solution

Modify the ExplorerBar value data in following Registry key

HKEY_CURRENT_USER\Software\Microsoft\Internet Explorer\Main

so that the second pair of values is one of the following values:

00 - normal screen

01 - normal screen

02 - half screen

03 - 3/4 screen

04 - full screen

For example, if you want to change the default Search bar size to half-screen, and the ExplorerBar value data is currently ff 01 00 00 61 93 45 00, change the 01 value to 02 so that the value data reads ff 02 00 00 61 93 45 00.

To solve this problem, follow these steps:

Warning Please read the Introduction for information on how to safely edit the Registry.

1. Click the Start button, choose Run, enter *Regedit* in the Open box, and then click OK.

2. Navigate your way down through the folders in the left pane until you locate the key described above.

3. Modify the ExplorerBar value data as described above.

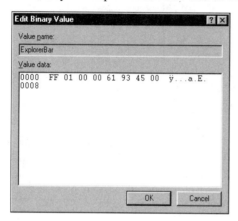

Figure 5-44. *The Edit Binary Value dialog box.*

4. Close Registry Editor.

5. Close Internet Explorer if it is running.

6. Restart your computer.

Related KB article Q192885

Subscriptions Can't Be Updated Using Schedules with AOL

You cannot use schedules to update subscriptions if America Online is your Internet service provider (ISP). To use schedules for subscription updates, you must use Dial-Up Networking as your dialer to establish a connection to your ISP. America Online uses a proprietary dialer.

Solution

Manually update your subscriptions. To do so, follow these steps:

1. Connect to America Online.

2. In Internet Explorer, choose Update All Subscriptions from the Favorites menu.

If you do not want to update all your subscriptions, choose Manage Subscriptions from the Favorites menu, right-click the subscription you want to update, and then choose Update Now from the shortcut menu.

Note For more information, see KB article Q171227, "How to Use Subscriptions in Microsoft Internet Explorer."

Related KB article Q174839

Subscriptions Don't Update Automatically

Your computer is unable to connect to the Internet to update subscriptions automatically. This problem occurs if your computer is configured to use Advanced Power Management (APM) features and is in a low-power state at the scheduled time for updating subscriptions.

Solution

Disable APM support. To do so, follow these steps:

1. Disable APM in your computer's Basic Input/Output System (BIOS). For information about how to do this, see the documentation included with your computer.

2. Click the Start button, choose Settings, and then click Control Panel.

3. Double-click the Power Management icon to open the Power Management Properties dialog box, and then clear the Allow Windows To Manage Power Use On This Computer check box.

4. Click OK, close Control Panel, and then restart your computer.

Related KB article Q180783

Web Pages Load Slowly

If you have a slow connection to the Internet, large pictures, sounds, videos, and other multimedia files take a long time to appear or play.

Solution

To improve browsing performance in Internet Explorer, you can prevent pictures, sounds, videos, and other multimedia files from appearing or playing automatically when you access web pages. To do so, follow these steps:

1. Start Internet Explorer, and then choose Internet Options from the View menu.

2. Click the Advanced tab, and then select one or more of the following check boxes in the Multimedia area to clear them and prevent their appearing or being played automatically:

   - Show Pictures
   - Play Videos
   - Play Sounds

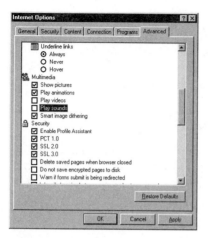

Figure 5-45. *The Advanced tab of the Internet Options dialog box.*

3. Click Apply.

4. Click the Security tab, click the Custom (For Expert Users) option button, and then click Settings.

5. Click Disable for one or more of the items in the following Active Content areas:

   - ActiveX Controls And Plug-ins (prevents Internet Explorer from automatically using items that show active content)

   - Java (prevents Internet Explorer from viewing Java programs automatically)

   - Scripting

6. Click OK.

Note For more information, see KB article Q153775, "How to Not Play Sounds and Videos in Internet Explorer."

Related KB article Q153790

Web Page Won't Load in Internet Explorer

You are unable to load a particular web page using Internet Explorer because the page contains active content, such as vertical marquees or animations.

To determine if the web page contains active content, follow the steps in the solutions below, and, after each series of steps, check to see if you can open the page. If you can open the page, contact the Web site's administrator to report the problem and inquire about additional ways to access the page.

While most active content contained in Web pages is safe, some Web pages contain active content that can potentially cause security problems on your computer. For example, an ActiveX control that runs automatically when you load a particular web page might damage your data or cause your computer to become infected with a virus. Internet Explorer uses safety levels for active content to help prevent this situation from occurring. Internet Explorer 4.0 provides four levels: High, Medium, Low, and Custom.

Solution One

Configure Internet Explorer so that it does not run ActiveX scripts automatically. To do so, follow these steps:

1. Choose Internet Options from the View menu to open the Internet Options dialog box.

2. Click the Security tab, click the Custom (For Expert Users) option button, and then click Settings.

3. Scroll down to the Scripting section, and then click the Disable option button under Scripting Of Java Applets and also under Active Scripting.

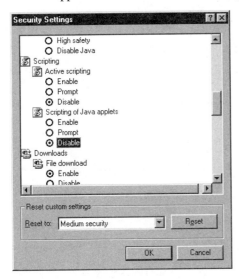

Figure 5-46. *The Security Settings dialog box.*

4. Click OK twice.

Note In Internet Explorer, ActiveX scripting refers to both Java scripting and Microsoft Visual Basic Scripting Edition. Clearing the Run ActiveX Scripts check box disables both types of scripts.

If you are now able to load the web page, the problem is being caused by an ActiveX script that the web page contains. The script most likely is written incorrectly or contains unsupported objects, properties, or elements.

Solution Two

Configure Internet Explorer so that it does not automatically use items that show active content, such as vertical marquees or animations. To do so, follow these steps:

1. Choose Internet Options from the View menu to open the Internet Options dialog box.

2. Click the Security tab, click the Custom (For Expert Users) option button, and then click Settings.

3. Click Disable under the following sections:

- Download Unsigned ActiveX Controls

- Script ActiveX Controls Marked Safe For Scripting

- Initialize And Script ActiveX Controls Not Marked As Safe

- Download Signed ActiveX Controls

- Run ActiveX Controls And Plugins

4. Click OK twice.

If you can now open the web page, the problem is being caused by active content that the web page contains.

Solution Three

Verify that Internet Explorer's internal Java Just-In-Time (JIT) compiler is disabled. To do so, follow these steps:

1. Choose Internet Options from the View menu to open the Internet Options dialog box.

2. Click the Advanced tab, and then clear the Java JIT Compiler Enabled check box under Java VM.

3. Click OK.

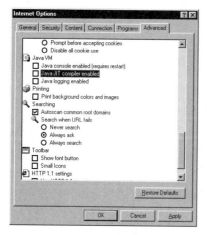

Figure 5-47. *The Advanced tab of the Internet Options dialog box.*

If the problem is caused by a Java program that the web page contains, and the problem still occurs when the Java JIT Compiler is disabled, the Internet Explorer status bar should display a message that provides additional information. If the message indicates that a particular class is not found, the appropriate class file may not exist on the server that contains the web page, or the server may be too busy.

Solution Four

Configure Internet Explorer so that it does not run Java programs automatically. To do so, follow these steps:

1. Choose Internet Options from the View menu to open the Internet Options dialog box.

2. Click the Security tab, click the Custom (For Expert Users) option button, and then click Settings.

3. Click Disable Java under Java Permissions, and then click OK twice.

If you can now open the web page, the problem is being caused by one or more Java programs that the web page contains.

Note For more information, see KB article Q174360, "How to Use Security Zones in Internet Explorer 4.0."

Related KB article Q154036

Window Too Small or Off Screen

You open a new window in Internet Explorer, and the window opens at the edge of the screen, with only a small section of the new window visible. This problem occurs if Registry key values for Internet Explorer are incorrect or damaged.

Solution

Use Registry Editor to remove the following Registry key values:

```
Hkey_Current_User\Software\Microsoft\Internet  Explorer\Main\window_placement
```

```
Hkey_Current_User\Software\Microsoft\internetexplorer\Desktop\Explorer\desktop\oldWorkAreas
\OldWorkAreaRects
```

To solve this problem, follow these steps:

Warning Please read the Introduction for information on how to safely edit the Registry.

1. Click the Start button, choose Run, enter *Regedit* in the Open box, and then click OK.

2. Navigate your way down through the folders in the left pane until you locate the keys described above.

3. Delete the key values.

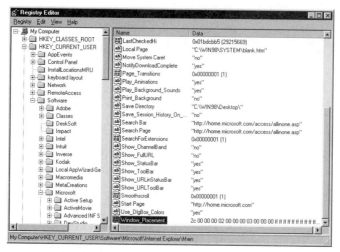

Figure 5-48. *The Registry Editor window.*

4. Close Regedit.

5. Restart your computer.

Related KB article   Q194759

NetMeeting

Audio Is Inaudible

You participate in a NetMeeting conference using audio and are unable to hear the other person, but he or she may be able to hear you (or vice versa).

This behavior occurs if any of the following conditions exists:

- The microphone is not working or is not properly connected to the sound card.

- The volume is turned off or set very low, or the speakers are not properly connected to the sound card.

- Both participants are not using full-duplex.

- You are using a Slirp dial-up connection or another emulated Transmission Control Protocol/Internet Protocol (TCP/IP) connection.

- You or your Internet service provider (ISP) are using a proxy server to connect to the Internet, and the ports used to send audio are closed (ports 1720 and 1731).

- Audio is disabled by a system policy.

Solution One

If the other person cannot hear you, determine whether your microphone works. To do so, follow these steps:

1. Click the Start button, choose Programs, choose Accessories, choose Entertainment, and then click Sound Recorder to open the Sound Recorder dialog box.

Note If Sound Recorder is not installed, install it using the Add/Remove Programs tool in Control Panel.

2. Click Record, and then speak into the microphone.

Figure 5-49. *The Sound Recorder window.*

If you cannot record a .WAV file, verify that the microphone is properly connected to the sound card and that the microphone settings are correct. To do so, double-click the Volume icon on the taskbar, and then verify that the Microphone slider is at the top and the Mute check box is not selected.

If there is no Volume icon on the taskbar, follow these steps:

1. Click the Start button, choose Settings, click Control Panel, and then double-click the Multimedia icon to open the Multimedia Properties dialog box.

2. Select the Show Volume Control On The Taskbar check box, and then click OK.

If you still cannot record a .WAV file, use another microphone.

Solution Two

If you cannot hear the other person, verify that you can hear .WAV files by following these steps:

1. Click the Start button, choose Programs, choose Accessories, choose Entertainment, and then click Sound Recorder to open the Sound Recorder dialog box.

2. Choose Open from the File menu.

3. Locate and click a .WAV file, and then click Open.

4. Click Play.

If you cannot hear the .WAV file, verify that the volume settings are correct. Double-click the Volume icon on the taskbar, and then verify that the Volume Control slider is at the top and that the Mute check box is not selected.

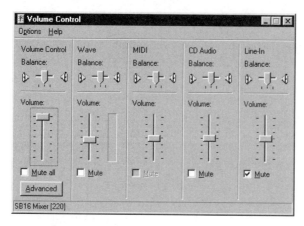

Figure 5-50. *The Volume Control window.*

If you are using amplified speakers, verify that they are properly connected to the sound card, that they are turned on, and that the volume control is turned up.

Solution Three

With full-duplex audio, you and the other person can speak (and hear) simultaneously. With half-duplex audio, you and the other person must take turns speaking. If you are using half-duplex sound card drivers and have a sensitive microphone, you may be the only person who can speak because you are continuously sending data.

Note For more information, see KB article Q155024, "Must Take Turns Speaking in NetMeeting."

NetMeeting 2.1 supports DirectSound. If your sound card supports full duplex audio and you are using half-duplex DirectSound drivers, contact your hardware vendor to inquire about the availability of updated drivers for your sound card or disable DirectSound support in NetMeeting.

Note For more information, see KB article Q179646, "NM: How to Disable DirectSound Support in NetMeeting."

Solution Four

If you're using a Slirp connection, see KB article Q155176, "Audio Connection Problems Using NetMeeting." Slirp is a TCP/IP emulator that enables you to create a serial line Internet protocol (SLIP) or Point-to-Point protocol (PPP) connection when you are logged on to a UNIX server. NetMeeting does not support the use of emulated TCP/IP connections.

Solution Five

If you're sending audio through a proxy server using NetMeeting, test the connection to the proxy server to make sure that ports 1720 and 1731 are open.

Note For more information, see KB article Q171648, "Troubleshooting Connections in NetMeeting Using Telnet."

If the audio ports are closed on the proxy server, contact your network administrator or ISP.

Note For more information, see KB article Q158623, "How to Establish NetMeeting Connections Through a Firewall."

Solution Six

Verify whether audio is disabled by a system policy by displaying the Tools menu in NetMeeting. If the Audio Tuning Wizard command is unavailable, and there is a sound card in your computer, audio may be disabled by a system policy. If this is the case, contact your network administrator.

Note For more information, see KB article Q165622, "NetMeeting Audio: Poor Quality, Distortion, Echoing, No Sound."

Related KB article Q174611

Audio or Video Unavailable in NetMeeting Conference

Audio or video may be unavailable during a NetMeeting conference if the conference was not established using Dial-Up Networking and Transmission Control Protocol/Internet Protocol (TCP/IP). NetMeeting audio and video capabilities are possible only when you are using TCP/IP.

Solution

Establish the conference with Dial-Up Networking, using TCP/IP, and then start NetMeeting.

Note You can install TCP/IP using the Network tool in Control Panel. (To access Control Panel, click the Start button, choose Settings, and then click Control Panel.)

When you use NetMeeting with TCP/IP, be sure that TCP/IP is installed and configured correctly. TCP/IP is not installed by default on a Windows-only local area network (LAN). When you install TCP/IP, you must manually configure IP addresses, LMHOSTS files for name resolution, and HOSTS files for domain name resolution.

Note For more information, see KB article Q139710, "How to Enable Dial-Up Networking Server Capabilities."

If you have another adapter that is not using TCP/IP, you may want to unbind TCP/IP for the adapter. To do so, follow these steps:

1. Click the Start button, choose Settings, and then click Control Panel.

2. Double-click the Network icon to open the Network Properties dialog box.

3. From the list of installed components, select the network adapter from which you want to unbind TCP/IP, and then click Properties.

4. Click the Bindings tab, and clear the TCP/IP check box.

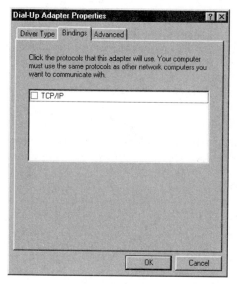

Figure 5-51. *The Bindings tab in the Dial-Up Adapter Properties dialog box.*

5. Click OK twice.

6. When Windows prompts you to restart the computer, click Yes.

When the computer restarts, TCP/IP will no longer be bound to that adapter.

Related KB article Q165611

Audio Problems in NetMeeting

You participate in an audio conference in NetMeeting and experience various audio problems, such as poor audio quality, voice distortion, echoing, or sound loss.

Solution One

Free up memory and available bandwidth or audio by

- Closing unnecessary programs that are running

- Reducing the number of shared programs

- Closing unnecessary windows (including Whiteboard and Chat)

- Postponing large file transfers

Solution Two

Run the Audio Tuning Wizard again. To do so, follow these steps:

1. In NetMeeting, choose Audio Tuning Wizard from the Tools menu.

2. Follow the instructions on the screen.

Note You cannot use the Audio Tuning Wizard during a conference. You must leave the conference, run the Audio Tuning Wizard, and then call the other conference participants back.

If the Audio Tuning Wizard indicates that your sound card is not supported, you may be able to use the audio features of NetMeeting, but you may experience poor sound quality. If your computer has more than one audio device, make sure that the audio devices selected in the Audio Tuning Wizard match the selections in the Multimedia tool in Control Panel.

Solution Three

Choppy full-duplex sound may indicate that the sound card cannot simultaneously send and receive audio signals. Try switching to half-duplex sound quality. To do so, follow these steps:

1. In NetMeeting, choose Options from the Tools menu.

2. Click the Audio tab, and then clear the Enable Full Duplex Audio check box.

If the sound continues to worsen, run the Audio Tuning Wizard again to reset your audio values.

Solution Four

Speak a little farther from the microphone or test to make sure the microphone sensitivity isn't set too high. To adjust microphone sensitivity, run the Audio Tuning Wizard again, or manually adjust the microphone sensitivity. To do so, follow these steps:

1. In NetMeeting, choose Options from the Tools menu to open the Options dialog box.

2. Click the Audio tab, and then in the Microphone Sensitivity area, click Adjust Sensitivity Automatically. If this option is already selected, click Let Me Adjust Sensitivity Myself.

3. Adjust the Sensitivity slider.

If you move the slider to the right, your voice will be transmitted earlier and will be less likely to cut out, but it might also transmit sound when you are silent. After you adjust the setting, speak a few sentences and wait for feedback from a conference participant before changing the setting again.

In addition, ask the other participant to move the microphone away from the speakers. Also, try decreasing the speaker volume.

Solution Four

Run NetMeeting in a quiet environment. If background noise levels have changed since you ran the Audio Tuning Wizard, run the Audio Tuning Wizard again.

Solution Five

If you have a computer with a slower processor, and you're running audio and video simultaneously, turn off video.

Solution Six

Be sure that TCP/IP is installed and configured correctly. When you use NetMeeting with TCP/IP, you must use a local area network (LAN) with TCP/IP, or you must establish the conference with Dial-Up Networking, using TCP/IP, and then start NetMeeting. You can install TCP/IP using the Network tool in Control Panel.

Solution Seven

Move your sound card to a slot away from video cards or fans; they may cause playback problems with sound codecs (compression technology). For information about your hardware devices, refer to your computer's documentation, or consult your hardware manufacturer.

Solution Eight

Avoid speaking while moving a shared program window. When you move a shared program window while talking to a NetMeeting participant, the available bandwidth is decreased.

Solution Nine

Determine if the Network Bandwidth is set too high. To do so, follow these steps:

1. Start NetMeeting, and then choose Options from the Tools menu to open the Options dialog box.

2. Click the General tab.

3. In the Network Bandwidth section, click a slower bandwidth than that currently selected.

4. Click OK, and then restart NetMeeting.

Related KB article Q165622

Can't Connect to Directory Server

When you are using NetMeeting and try to connect or reconnect to a Directory server using an Internet Locator server (ILS) or a User Location server (ULS), you may receive one or both of the following error messages:

The User Location Server could not be found. Your information will not be available to others.

There was a problem connecting to the Directory Server. Please choose another server.

You may be able to view the Directory server with your web browser.

Solution One

If your Directory server is down or busy, try again later, or use a different server. To determine if your Directory server is down, follow these steps:

1. Try to ping the server. While connected to your ISP, type *ping <name of the Directory server>* at a command prompt, and then press the Enter key.

2. If you do not get a reply, the Directory server may be down, or your Domain Name Service (DNS) configuration may be invalid.

3. If you get a reply, try using the Internet Protocol (IP) address as your Directory server.

Solution Two

If you're using a 16-bit Winsock connection, ask your ISP if a 32-bit version is available, or use Dial-Up Networking to establish the connection before you start NetMeeting. To determine if your connection is 16-bit or 32-bit, follow these steps:

1. When you are connected to your ISP, click the Start button, choose Run, enter *winipcfg* in the Open box, and then click OK to open the IP Configuration dialog box.

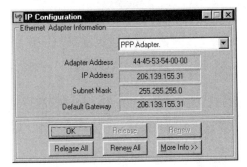

Figure 5-52. *The IP Configuration dialog box.*

2. If the fields display all zeros, you are probably using a 16-bit version of WINSOCK.DLL.

3. Check to see if your ISP can work properly with a 32-bit version of WINSOCK.DLL. If appropriate, upgrade to the 32-bit version. The Dial-Up Networking tool included with Windows 98 uses a 32-bit connection.

Note For more information about how to connect to the Internet using the Dial-Up Networking tool, see KB article Q138789, "How to Connect to the Internet in Windows 95/98." For more information about the Winipcfg tool, see KB article Q141698, "How to Use Winipcfg to View TCP/IP Settings." For more information about old Winsock programs, see KB article Q139384, "Programs Using Old WINSOCK.DLL File May Not Work in Windows."

Solution Three

If you are using a proxy connection, ask your network administrator to check the proxy settings. Use port 389 for ILS and port 522 for ULS.

- For information about how to determine if the ILS/ULS ports are open to the ILS server, see KB article Q171648, "Troubleshooting Connections in NetMeeting Using Telnet."

- If you can connect to the Microsoft ILS/ULS servers, but not to other ILS/ULS servers, see KB articles Q163444, "NetMeeting 2.0 Cannot Connect to ILS Server," and Q161643, "NetMeeting Clients Can't Connect to Multihomed ILS."

- For information about proxy configuration, see KB article Q158623, "How to Establish NetMeeting Connections Through a Firewall," and the NetMeeting Resource Kit, Chapter 4, "Firewall Configuration." The NetMeeting Resource Kit is available on the Microsoft Web site at *http://www.microsoft.com/netmeeting/reskit/*.

Solution Four

If you recently closed NetMeeting, wait a few minutes before attempting to reconnect to the Directory server. Your user name may remain listed as connected to the Directory server. NetMeeting sends a termination message to the Directory server when closing. This message notifies the server to remove your user name, a process that usually takes less than a minute. Because the server is receiving Transmission Control Protocol/Internet Protocol (TCP/IP) information, it may not recognize that NetMeeting has terminated. It is possible for your user name to remain listed for 5 minutes or more.

Related KB article Q154494

NetMeeting Hangs on Startup

You start NetMeeting and the main window stops responding (hangs). The next time you start NetMeeting, your computer may hang when the main NetMeeting window opens. The mouse pointer still moves, but pressing Ctrl+Alt+Delete does not open the Close Program dialog box.

This occurs if the Hewlett-Packard "Fonts for the Family" set of TrueType fonts is installed. Several of these fonts are incompatible with Windows 98. This behavior may also be caused by damaged TrueType fonts.

NetMeeting processes all the installed fonts when it starts. It does this so that it will know how to handle fonts that may not be installed on other computers when you share a program in a conference. Hewlett-Packard has confirmed that the following fonts are incompatible with Windows 98:

Artistik	Gallia	Snowdrift
Ashley Inline	Harlow	Stencil Sans
Boxed In	Holidays	Thunderbird
Broadway	ITC Pioneer	Torino Outline
Challenge Extrabold	Kidprint	Traffic
Creepy	Old English	Yearbook Outline
Eclipse	Party	

Solution

Remove the "Fonts for the Family" fonts from the WINDOWS\FONTS folder. You may want to drag these fonts into another folder, instead of deleting them, to verify that these fonts are the cause of the problem.

To open the Fonts folder, follow these steps:

1. Click the Start button, choose Settings, and then click Control Panel.

2. Double-click the Fonts icon to open the Fonts window.

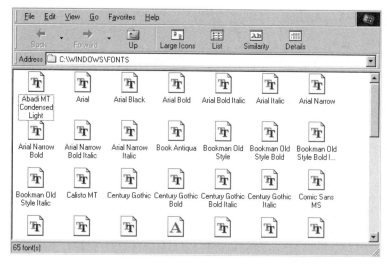

Figure 5-53. *The Fonts window.*

To make sure there are no damaged fonts, double-click each font in the FONTS folder. If your computer hangs when you double-click a font, that font may be damaged. If you find a damaged font, drag it from the FONTS folder into another folder. If the damaged font is a required font or a font you want to use, reinstall the font from the appropriate source.

Note For more information about the "Fonts for the Family" font set, see KB article Q149418, "Problems with HP 'Fonts for the Family' Font Package."

Related KB article Q156094

No Audio and Video Exchange in NetMeeting

You establish a NetMeeting conference in which both participants are capable of sending audio and video, and you are unable to exchange audio and video until you choose Switch Audio And Video from the Tools menu and then click the participant with whom you are conferencing. You may also experience poor audio and video quality, problems connecting to an Internet Locator Server (ILS) directory server, and problems listing the ILS directory. These problems result if the Internet Service Provider (ISP) that either participant is using does not support Internet Protocol (IP) header compression.

Solution

Disable IP header compression in the Dial-Up Networking connection you use to connect to your ISP. To do so, follow these steps:

1. Click the Start button, choose Programs, choose Accessories, choose Communications, and then click Dial-Up Networking to open the Dial-Up Networking window.

2. Right-click the dial-up connection you use to connect to your ISP, and then choose Properties from the shortcut menu to open the Properties dialog box.

3. Click the Server Types tab, and then click TCP/IP Settings to open the TCP/IP Settings dialog box.

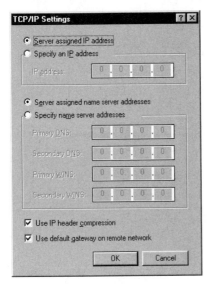

Figure 5-54. *The TCP/IP Settings dialog box.*

4. Clear the Use IP Header Compression check box, and then click OK.

5. Click OK, and then click OK again.

Related KB article Q174594

Parties Can't Speak Simultaneously

You start a conference in Microsoft NetMeeting, and both parties cannot speak simultaneously but have to take turns.

This problem occurs if you have half-duplex audio instead of full-duplex audio. Full-duplex audio allows you and the other person to talk (and hear) simultaneously, as in a normal telephone conversation. With half-duplex audio, you and the other person must take turns speaking, as in a two-way radio conversation.

The requirements for a full-duplex audio conversation are as follows:

- Full-duplex sound card

- Full-duplex sound card driver

- Full-duplex audio enabled in NetMeeting

- Both conference participants must also be full-duplex-audio capable

- Speakers or headphones and microphones

Solution One

Determine whether the sound cards and drivers are capable of full-duplex audio by following these steps:

1. Click the Start button, choose Programs, choose Accessories, choose Entertainment, and then click Sound Recorder to open the Sound Recorder window.

Figure 5-55.   *The Sound Recorder window.*

2. Repeat step 1 to start a second Sound Recorder session.

3. In the first Sound Recorder session, play a sound (.WAV) file that is at least 30 seconds long. Follow these steps:

   a. Choose Open from the File menu to open the Open dialog box.

   b. Locate and select an appropriate .WAV file.

   c. Click Open.

4. While the first session of Sound Recorder plays the .WAV file, switch to the second session of Sound Recorder, and record a .WAV file. To do so, click the Record button at the bottom of the Sound Recorder dialog box (the rightmost button with the red circle).

If you can record a .WAV file while another .WAV file plays, your sound card and the sound card drivers support full-duplex audio. If you cannot record a .WAV file while another .WAV file is playing, there is a problem in one of the following areas:

- The sound card does not support full-duplex audio.

- The sound card driver does not support full-duplex audio.

- The sound card or sound card driver is not properly configured to support full-duplex audio.

Solution Two

Verify that full-duplex audio is enabled in NetMeeting by following these steps:

1. In NetMeeting, choose Options from the Tools menu to open the Options dialog box.

2. Click the Audio tab, and then make sure the Enable Full Duplex Audio check box is selected.

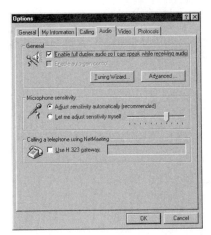

Figure 5-56.   *The Audio tab in the NetMeeting Options dialog box.*

Related KB article   Q155024

Screen Refresh Slow

The screen refresh is slow when you share a program in NetMeeting.

Solution One

Verify that NetMeeting is configured for the maximum speed your connection allows.

Note To determine the speed of your Internet connection, see the documentation for the hardware being used to connect your computer to the Internet (modem, ISDN, or network adapter).

Change the speed NetMeeting is configured. To do so, follow these steps:

1. In the NetMeeting window, choose Options from the Tools menu to open the Options dialog box.

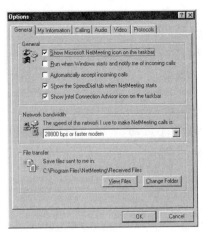

Figure 5-57.   *The Options dialog box in NetMeeting.*

2. Click the General tab, if necessary.

3. In the Network Bandwidth section, select the appropriate option for your connection: 14400 BPS Modem, 28800 BPS Or Faster Modem, ISDN, or Local Area Network.

4. Click OK.

Solution Two

Disable audio and video. To do so, follow these steps:

1. When you are connected during a call, click the Current Call tab.

2. Click the video icon next to the name of the person to whom you want to stop sending video, and then click Stop Sending Audio And Video.

Related KB article Q154354

Shared Program Discolored in NetMeeting

You use a shared program in a NetMeeting conference, and the shared program appears discolored. This occurs when the participating computers are using a color palette of more than 256 colors. NetMeeting supports sending a maximum of 256 colors across a network connection.

Solution

Change the Color Palette setting to High Color (16 Bit) or lower on the participating computers. To do so, follow these steps:

1. Click the Start button, choose Settings, click Control Panel, and then double-click the Display icon to open the Display Properties dialog box.

2. Click the Settings tab.

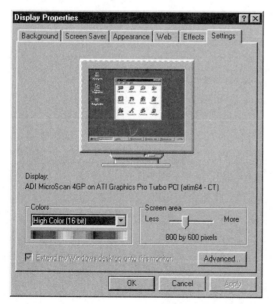

Figure 5-58. *The Settings tab of the Display Properties dialog box*

3. From the Color Palette box, select High Color (16 Bit) or a lower setting.

4. Click OK.

5. Restart your computer when you are prompted.

True Color-to-True Color video conferencing connections may lose video quality. Sixteen-bit color-to-16-bit color video conferencing connections have the best video quality.

Note For more information, see KB article Q165778, "Poor Video Image Quality in NetMeeting."

Related KB article Q176100

Sound Echoes Through Speakers or Headphone

During a NetMeeting conference, your voice echoes back through your speakers or headphones when you speak into a microphone to a participant who is using a full-duplex sound card.

One of the meeting participants may be listening to you with his or her microphone positioned too close to the speakers.

Solution

Request that the other NetMeeting participant try one of the following:

- Move his or her microphone away from the speakers.
- Decrease the volume of the speakers.
- Adjust the sensitivity of his or her microphone.
- Run the Audio Tuning Wizard.
- Disable the use of full-duplex audio drivers.
- Use headphones.

To run the Audio Tuning Wizard, follow these steps:

1. Choose Options from the Tools menu to open the Options dialog box.

2. Click the Audio tab.

3. Click Tuning Wizard, and then follow the instructions on the screen.

To disable the use of full-duplex audio drivers, follow these steps:

1. Choose Options from the Tools menu to open the Options dialog box.

2. Click the Audio tab.

3. Clear the Enable Full Duplex Audio check box.

To adjust microphone sensitivity, follow these steps:

1. Choose Options from the Tools menu to open the Options dialog box.

2. Click the Audio tab.

3. In the Microphone Sensitivity section, click the Let Me Adjust Sensitivity Myself check box.

4. Move the microphone sensitivity slider to the left to decrease the microphone's sensitivity,

5. Click OK.

Related KB article Q166038

Unable to Share Program in NetMeeting

You attempt to share a program in NetMeeting, and the Share button on the toolbar and the Share Application command on the Tools menu are unavailable. This occurs if any double-byte character set (DBCS) fonts are installed. NetMeeting does not support DBCS fonts.

Note DBCS fonts are usually indicative of Japanese or Chinese character sets.

Solution

Uninstall all DBCS fonts, then verify that the fonts are removed from the WINDOWS\FONTS folder. It may be necessary to manually delete the DBCS fonts from the Fonts folder.

Related KB article Q194984

Uninstall Doesn't Remove NetMeeting Folder

You uninstall NetMeeting, but the NetMeeting folder is not removed.

Solution

Delete the NetMeeting folder manually. To do so, follow these steps:

1. Click the Start button, choose Programs, and then click Windows Explorer.

2. Navigate to the PROGRAM FILES\NETMEETING folder, in which NetMeeting is stored by default.

3. Select the NETMEETING folder, and press the Delete key.

4. In the Confirm Folder Delete dialog box, click Yes.

Related KB article Q158677

Video Problems in NetMeeting

During a NetMeeting conference, participants see poor-quality images in the video window, or some areas of the video window contain incorrect colors.

Solution One

Close programs that you don't need to access during the meeting. This will increase processor speed.

Solution Two

Select a smaller image size. Smaller images are processed better than larger images on a computer with a slower processor. To change the image size, follow these steps:

1. Choose Tools from the Options menu to open the Options dialog box.

2. Click the Video tab.

3. In the Send Image Size section, click Small.

Solution Three

Increase video image quality. To do so, follow these steps:

1. Choose Options from the Tools menu to open the Options dialog box.

2. Click the Video tab.

3. In the Video Quality section, drag the selector toward Better Quality.

Solution Four

Increase camera lighting. When some cameras are used in a dark area, they may cause your computer to become extremely slow and unresponsive.

Related KB article Q165778

Video Screen Is Black

You see a black screen when you view the My Video window in NetMeeting, or you are unable to view live video from a video capture card.

This is caused by any of the following:

- The video capture card is configured to use an unsupported video format.

- The video capture card is using video overlay mode. (Video overlay mode is not supported by NetMeeting 2.0.)

- The video capture card does not support Microsoft Video 1.0 for Windows.

- Multiple video devices are installed on your computer.

Video overlay mode enables a video capture card to send video directly to the memory on the video capture card, bypassing the central processing unit (CPU) and reducing the processor overhead. NetMeeting 2.0 does not capture video from a video capture card in video overlay mode.

To determine if your video capture card supports preview mode or overlay mode, refer to the documentation that came with your video capture card, or contact the manufacturer of your video capture device.

Solution

Configure the video capture card to one of the video formats supported by NetMeeting and confirm that the video capture card supports Microsoft Video 1.0 for Windows. Currently, Microsoft NetMeeting supports the following video formats: RGB4, RGB8, RGB16, RGB24, and YVU9.

Related KB article Q166114

Other Internet Programs

Crescendo Internet Explorer Plug-In May Not Work Correctly

You try to use the Crescendo! plug-in for Internet Explorer, and it doesn't work correctly. This occurs under any of the following conditions:

- You upgrade Internet Explorer version 4.0 to 4.01.

- You upgrade Microsoft Windows 95 to Windows 98.

- You reinstall Internet Explorer version 4.0 or 4.01.

Solution

Reinstall the Crescendo! plug-in. For information about how to do so, contact Crescendo!

Related KB article Q187693

FrontPage Express Pastes RTF Text Incorrectly

You copy text formatted in Rich Text Format (RTF) and paste it into FrontPage Express, and odd characters are displayed.

The ability to convert Rich Text Format (.RTF) files is not included in FrontPage Express. The characters you see are American Standard Code for Information Interchange (ASCII) character codes.

Solution

To solve this problem, follow these steps:

1. Copy and paste your text into a non-RTF text editor such as Notepad to strip all formatting from the text.

2. Copy the text from Notepad, and then paste it into FrontPage Express.

3. Reapply any appropriate formatting

Related KB article Q166087

FTP Stops Responding

You start the FTP.EXE program in Windows 98, and the program stops responding. This occurs if the SocksCap32 program is installed on your computer.

Solution

To solve this problem, wait until the FTP.EXE program finishes starting.

Related KB article Q187348

Microsoft Chat Reports an Error Message When Loading a Rule Set

You attempt to open a saved rule set in Microsoft Chat and receive the following error message:

Load Rule Set: The rule set being loaded has the same name "<rule set name>" as an existing rule set.

You are then prompted to overwrite the existing rule set, rename the rule set being opened, or cancel the operation. If you choose to overwrite the existing rule set, you receive the same error message. If you choose to rename the rule set you opened, you receive the following error message:

The rule set "<rule set name>" already exists. Please choose another name.

This problem occurs if you delete a rule set with the same name using the Rule Sets tab in the Automations dialog box. Deleting a rule set in this manner does not remove the rule set (.CRS) file from the folder in which you saved it.

Solution

Create a new rule set using the same name as one you previously deleted. First delete the existing .CRS file. To do so, follow these steps:

Note By default, Microsoft Chat saves .CRS files in the MY DOCUMENTS folder.

1. Click the Start button, choose Find, and then click Files Or Folders.

2. Enter **.crs* in the Named text box, and then click Find Now.

3. In the list of found files, right-click the .CRS file with the same name as the rule set you are creating, and then choose Delete from the shortcut menu.

4. Choose Close from the File menu.

Note For more information, see KB article Q187754, "How to Create and Edit Rules."

Related KB article Q192403

Pingname and Pingnum Display Error Message

You run the PINGNAME.BAT or PINGNUM.BAT batch file from the WINDOWS\HELP folder at a command prompt and receive request-timed-out responses.

These two files are used to test your Internet connection. They ping *www.microsoft.com* (by name) and *ftp.microsoft.com* (by IP address). However, you receive request timed out responses because no computer in the *microsoft.com* domain responds to the ICMP requests.

Solution

To work around this issue, modify the PINGNAME.BAT file and change the names

```
www.microsoft.com
```

```
ftp.microsoft.com
```

to other names that do respond to the ping command. Modify the PINGNUM.BAT file and replace the IP addresses it contains with IP addresses that respond to the ping command.

Related KB article Q188173

RealPlayer Displays PNCRT.DLL Not Found Error Message

When you try to play a file using Real Networks RealPlayer program, or when you start your computer, you receive this error message:

A required .DLL file, PNCRT.DLL, was not found

You may then receive the following error message:

Access to the specified device, path, or file is denied.

This problem occurs if the PNCRT.DLL file is missing from the WINDOWS\SYSTEM folder.

Solution

Uninstall and then reinstall RealPlayer. To do so, follow these steps:

1. Click the Start button, choose Settings, click Control Panel, and then double-click the Add/Remove Programs icon.

2. On the Windows Setup tab, select Internet Tools (the words, not the check box), and then click Details.

3. Clear the Real Audio Player 4.0 check box, click OK, and then click Apply.

4. On the Windows Setup tab, select Internet Tools (the words, not the check box), and then click Details.

5. Select the Real Audio Player 4.0 check box, click OK, and then click OK.

6. Restart your computer.

Related KB article Q190898

TCP/IP Utility Doesn't Work When Not Connected to the Internet

If you are not connected to the Internet, and you try to use a Transmission Control Protocol/Internet Protocol (TCP/IP) utility, you may be unable to do so. For example, Personal Web Server and Telnet may not work correctly, and other TCP/IP utilities may generate error messages.

This problem occurs if your computer has a dynamically assigned Internet Protocol (IP) address from your Internet service provider (ISP). The TCP/IP stack will not load correctly without a specified web address. This behavior is implemented to free up system resources (or system memory) by not loading unneeded network components.

Solution One

Connect to your ISP before you use a TCP/IP utility.

Solution Two

Temporarily assign a static IP address to your computer.

Note For more information about how to temporarily assign a static IP address to your computer, see the "To Assign a Private IP Address for a Simple Network" topic in Windows Help.

After you temporarily assign a static IP address to your computer and are no longer using a TCP/IP utility, return your IP configuration to its original state to free up system resources (or system memory) by not loading unneeded network components.

Related KB article Q184603

CHAPTER 6

Laptops

PC Cards

Acer AcerNotes Emit a Low Tone When PC Cards Are Inserted

You insert a PC Card in an AcerNote after installing the 32-bit PC Card drivers and hear a low tone.

Solution One

1. Click the Start button, and click Run. Enter *sysedit* in the text box, and click OK.

2. Click the SYSTEM.INI window, and then find and disable the *EMMExclude* line by typing a semicolon (;) in front of it.

3. Click the CONFIG.SYS window, and delete any *X=A000h-FFFh* parameters after the device=c:\windows\emm386.exe command. For more information on the EMM386.EXE command, read the MSDOSDRV.TXT file in your \WINDOWS directory.

4. Close Sysedit, and click Yes when prompted to save SYSTEM.INI and CONFIG.SYS.

Solution Two

If you still hear a low tone after completing Solution One, follow these steps:

1. Click the Start button, choose Settings, and then click Control Panel.

2. Double-click the PC Card icon, click Global Settings, and then clear the Automatic Selection check box.

3. Set the valid range to start at 000D0000 and end at 000DFFFF.

4. Click OK.

Related KB article Q191480 or HARDWARE.TXT in your WINDOWS folder

Amacom Flip Disk PC Card Drive Inaccessible

You start your computer without the Amacom Flip Disk PC Card drive inserted in a PC Card slot and then insert this card after your computer starts, and you can't access the drive.

Solution

Insert the card before you start your computer.

Note To resolve this issue, install the most current version of driver for the Amacom Flip Disk PC Card. For information about how to do so, contact Amacom or view the documentation included with the PC Card.

Related KB article Q190155

CardBus Controller Behaves Unexpectedly

You upgrade a computer with a CardBus controller from Windows 95 to Windows 98, and the CardBus controller loses functionality, and you see the following status for the controller in Device Manager:

The device has been disabled in the hardware. In order to use this device, you must re-enable the hardware. See your hardware documentation for details. (Code 29.)

This behavior occurs if the PC Card controller is set to PCIC instead of CardBus in the computer's CMOS settings.

Solution

To solve this problem, follow these steps:

1. Click the Start button, choose Settings, click Control Panel, and then double-click the System icon.

2. Click the Device Manager tab.

3. Click the CardBus controller, and then click Properties.

4. Click Enable IRQ Steering, and then click OK.

If enabling IRQ steering doesn't resolve the issue, contact the computer's manufacturer for information about a possible BIOS update.

Related KB article Q188124

HP OmniBook 600C PCMCIA Cards or Mouse Don't Work

You install Windows 98 on an HP (Hewlett-Packard) OmniBook 600C, and the PCMCIA cards and/ or the mouse don't work.

The mouse on the HP OmniBook 600C requires a special driver which is not used if Windows 98 is installed on a clean system or in a different directory than the previous version of Windows. The PCMCIA controller requires special drivers located in the Windows Driver Library.

Solution One

To solve this problem, follow these steps:

1. Copy Hewlett-Packard's OBMOUSE.DRV into the WINDOWS 98\SYSTEM directory. (Search your hard drive if you don't know where this file is.)

2. Click the Start button, and click Run. Type *sysedit* in the text box, and click OK.

3. Click the SYSTEM.INI window, and then change the mouse.drv=mouse.drv line under the [boot] section to read mouse.drv=obmouse.drv, and change the mouse= line under the [386Enh] section to read *mouse – *.vmd*.

4. Choose Save from the File menu, close the program, and then restart Windows.

Solution Two

To use PC Cards, use the Windows Update tool to download drivers for your PCMCIA controller, or contact Hewlett-Packard for the drivers.

Related KB article Q191480 or HARDWARE.TXT in your WINDOWS folder

Megahertz Em1144T Modem Doesn't Work

You use the Megahertz Em1144T PCMCIA modem in a real-mode environment, and the modem doesn't work.

This is a known problem whereby this card enabler ignores the default values set for certain parameters.

Solution

Set the *COMIRQ* and *COMBASE* parameters explicitly in the Megahertz section of your PROTOCOL.INI file. To open your PROTOCOL.INI file, click the Start button, click Run, type *protocol.ini* in the text box, and click OK.

Related KB article Q191480 or HARDWARE.TXT in your WINDOWS folder

PC Card Intermittently Reports Modem Not Found Or Not Ready

You use PC Card Power Management, and your PC Card modem occasionally doesn't work or gives the *Modem not found or not ready* error message.

Solution

To solve this problem, follow these steps:

1. Click the Start button, click Run, type *regedit* in the text box, and click OK.

2. Go to HKEY_LOCAL_MACHINE\SYSTEM\CurrentControlSet\Services\Class\Modem.

3. Click the key for the modem you're trying to use.

4. Choose New from the Edit menu, and then choose DWORD Value from the submenu.

5. Type *ConfigDelay* in the Name text box.

6. Double-click the key, and enter *3000* for a 3-second delay.

7. Close Regedit.

Related KB article Q191480 or HARDWARE.TXT in your WINDOWS folder

PC Card Network Adapter Shows Error Code 10 Status

You install Windows 98 on a Digital HiNote Ultra II laptop, and Device Manager displays an exclamation point in a yellow circle next to the PC Card (PCMCIA) network adapter, with a status of *Error Code 10* in the adapter's properties. This problem occurs when the PC Card network adapter uses memory that the computer's Basic Input/Output System (BIOS) has reserved.

Solution

To solve this problem, follow these steps:

1. Click the Start button, choose Settings, and then click Control Panel.

2. Double-click the System icon.

3. On the Device Manager tab, double-click Computer.

4. Click the Reserve Resources tab, and then click Memory.

5. Click Add, type *CA000* in the Start Value box, and then type *CB000* in the End Value box.

Figure 6-1. *The Edit Resource Setting dialog box.*

6. Click OK, and then click OK.

7. Click the PC Card network adapter, and then click Remove.

8. Click OK, and then click Close.

9. Restart your computer.

Related KB article Q190841

PC Card (PCMCIA) Device Causes Computer to Stop Responding

You insert a PC Card (PCMCIA) device into a CardBus socket, and your computer stops responding, or you receive an error message that says the card was removed without pressing the Stop button.

This problem occurs when you are using a PC Card that is not CardBus aware. Some PC Card devices were developed before CardBus technologies were available and are unable to correctly identify themselves to a CardBus socket.

Solution

Contact the manufacturer of the PC Card to inquire about the availability of a fix for this issue.

Related KB article Q190695

PC Cards Don't Work in NEC Versa M and AT&T Globalyst

You have an NEC Versa M or AT&T Globalyst, with the PCMCIA Power setting in your BIOS set to Disabled, and your PC Cards don't work.

Solution

To solve this problem, follow these steps:

1. Restart your computer.

2. When the cursor changes to a rectangle, press F1.

3. Select Power in the BIOS configuration program, and then change the PCMCIA Power setting to Enabled.

4. Save the settings, and restart your computer. The PC Card Wizard should work normally now.

Related KB article Q191480 or HARDWARE.TXT in your WINDOWS folder

PC Controller Chip in Device Manager Displays Circled Exclamation Point

You install Windows 98 on an Acer AcerNote Light 35X notebook computer, and Device Manager displays an exclamation point in a yellow circle next to the PC Controller Chip (PCIC) device, with a status of *Error Code 10* in the PCIC device's properties. This occurs if the CardBus feature is disabled in the computer's CMOS (complementary metal-oxide semiconductor) settings.

Solution

Enable the CardBus feature in your computer's CMOS settings or contact the computer manufacturer about obtaining an update to address this issue. For information about modifying your computer's CMOS settings, see your computer's documentation.

For information about how to use a software method to enable the CardBus feature, see KB article Q188124, "Problem with CardBus Controller After Upgrading to Windows 98."

Related KB article Q194458

PCMCIA Card Doesn't Initialize

The PCMCIA card device in your laptop computer doesn't initialize properly.

Some PCMCIA devices require an upper memory area mapped to the PCMCIA socket for data buffering. If this memory region is in use by the computer's BIOS or a built-in device, the PCMCIA device does not respond when the Windows protected-mode socket driver tries to allocate the memory.

For example, if the computer's BIOS allocates memory for ROM shadowing in the upper memory area (UMA) and the socket driver tries to reallocate this memory, the PCMCIA device fails to initialize. A sample failure code for a PCMCIA network card experiencing this problem is *Problem 10*.

Solution

To solve this problem, follow these steps:

1. Click the Start button, choose Settings, and then click Control Panel.

2. Double-click the System icon.

3. Click the Device Manager tab, and then double-click Computer.

4. Click the Reserve Resources tab, click the Memory option button, and then click Add.

5. In the Start Value and End Value boxes, enter values for the start and end of the memory range you want to reserve.

6. Click OK.

After you restart your computer, Configuration Manager avoids using the reserved memory range when it allocates PCMCIA resources.

Related KB article Q129327

Suspended Computer Doesn't Recognize New PC Card

You remove a CardBus PC Card network adapter or CardBus PC Card ATA hard disk and insert another PC Card while your computer is suspended, and the new PC Card is not recognized when you resume the computer. While the computer is suspended, Windows doesn't remove the original PC Card, nor does it enumerate the new PC Card.

Solution

Resume the computer before switching PC Cards.

Related KB article Q188123

TI 1130 CardBus Controller Doesn't Work on NEC Versa 6030

You run Windows 98 on an NEC Versa 6030–series laptop computer with BIOS revision 1.18, and the TI 1130 CardBus controller doesn't work. NEC Versa 6030–series laptop computers may have BIOS revision 1.18 or 2.x.

Solution

Contact the manufacturer of your computer to obtain an updated version of your computer's BIOS.

Related KB article Q187221

Toshiba 3Com Multifunction PC Card Malfunctions

You upgrade Microsoft Windows 95 to Windows 98 on a Toshiba laptop computer, and your 3Com multifunction PC Card doesn't work correctly.

This problem occurs if the 3Com multifunction PC Card is in a PC Card slot when you install Windows 98.

Solution

Remove the 3Com multifunction PC Card from the PC Card slot, and then reinstall Windows 98.

Related KB article Q190421

TrueFFS Flash File System for PC Cards Doesn't Work

You use the MS-DOS or Windows 3.1 TrueFFS driver in Windows 98, and the TrueFFS PC Card doesn't work.

Solution

To solve this problem, follow these steps:

1. Click the Start button, choose Settings, and then click Control Panel.

2. Double-click the Add New Hardware icon, click Next, click Next again, click No, I Want To Select The Hardware From A List, and then click Next.

3. Click Hard Disk Controllers, and then click Next.

4. From the Manufacturers list, select M-Systems.

5. In the Models list, select your flash card, and then click Next. If M-Systems does not appear in the Manufacturers list, click Have Disk, insert the M-Systems Windows 98 installation disk in the CD-ROM or floppy disk drive, and then follow the instructions on your screen.

6. Follow the instructions on your screen.

Related KB article Q191480 or HARDWARE.TXT in your WINDOWS folder

Power Management

Advanced Power Management Support Device Shows Code 10

You view the Advanced Power Management (APM) Support device in Device Manager, and an exclamation point in a yellow circle is displayed for the device, and you receive the following status message:

This device is not present, not working properly, or does not have all the drivers installed. See your hardware documentation (Code 10.)

One of the following conditions causes this problem:

- APM support is disabled in the computer's BIOS.

- Your computer does not support Microsoft's implementation of APM.

Solution

To solve this problem, follow these steps:

1. Enable APM support in the computer's BIOS. For information about modifying your computer's BIOS settings, consult your computer's documentation or manufacturer.

2. If APM has been enabled, and the status remains unchanged, contact your computer's manufacturer for information regarding your motherboard's compatibility with Windows 98.

Related KB article Q188981

Advanced Power Management Turns Monitor Off

Your monitor is turned off by Advanced Power Management (APM), and you can't resume it. This problem occurs if any of the following conditions exists:

- The 3D Maze screen saver (3D MAZE.SCR) is currently running.

- Your display resolution is set to 800x600 or higher.

- You are using a Matrox MGA Impression Lite, Plus, Plus 220, or Ultima video adapter and driver.

Microsoft has confirmed this to be a problem in Windows 98.

Solution One

To change your screen saver to something other than the 3D Maze screen saver, follow these steps:

1. Press a key or move your mouse to disable the screen saver. If you are using a screen saver password, type the password, and then press Enter.

2. Press Ctrl+Esc to open the Start menu.

3. Press U to shut down Windows 98.

4. Press S to select Shut Down.

5. Press Enter to shut down your computer.

6. When your computer shuts down, power it back up, and, when Windows loads, change your screen saver. For information about how to do this, click the Start button, click Help, click the Index tab, type *screen*, and then find and double-click the Screen Savers help topic.

Solution Two

To change your display resolution to something other than 800 x 600, follow these steps:

1. Press Ctrl+Esc to open the Start menu.

2. Press U to shut down Windows 98.

3. Press S to select Shut Down.

4. Press Enter to shut down your computer.

5. When your computer shuts down, power it back up, and when Windows loads, change your display resolution. For information on how to do this, click the Start button, click Help, click the Index tab, type *display*, and then find and double-click the Resolution topic.

Solution Three

If you are using a Matrox MGA Impression Lite, Plus, or Plus 220 Video Adapter and Driver, contact Matrox to inquire about the availability of updated drivers.

Related KB article Q187727

Alarms Tab Settings Lost When Shutting Down Windows

You change settings on the Alarms tab in the Power Management tool, then change settings using the Power Meter icon on the taskbar, and the settings you just changed on the Alarms tab are lost when you shut down Windows. The alarm settings revert to the values saved from the previous Windows session. Microsoft has confirmed this to be a problem in Windows 98.

Solution

To solve this problem, follow these steps:

1. Right-click the Power Meter icon on the taskbar, and choose Adjust Power Properties from the shortcut menu.

2. Click the Power Meter tab, and select or clear the Show Details For Each Battery check box.

3. Click the Advanced tab, select or clear the Show Power Meter On Taskbar check box, and then click Apply.

4. If you want, select the Show Power Meter On Taskbar check box.

5. Click OK.

Related KB article Q192512

Cisco Suite 100 Doesn't Resume from Sleep Mode

You run the Cisco Suite 100 program and try to resume your computer from Sleep mode, and your computer doesn't resume. This occurs intermittently, but it occurs more often after the computer has been in Sleep mode for an extended period of time.

Cisco Suite 100 causes this problem because the Transmission Control Protocol/Internet Protocol (TCP/IP) included with this program is not compatible with the Advanced Power Management features in Windows.

Solution

To solve this problem, follow these steps:

1. Uninstall the TCP/IP protocol included with the Cisco Suite 100 program. For information about how to do so, view the documentation included with the Cisco Suite 100 program, or contact Cisco.

2. Click the Start button, choose Settings, click Control Panel, and then double-click the Network icon.

3. Click the Configuration tab, click Add, click Protocol, click Add, select Microsoft in the Manufacturers box, select TCP/IP in the Network Protocols box, and then click OK.

4. Click OK, and then restart your computer when you are prompted to do so.

Related KB article Q189861

Compaq 4700 Hangs When Sleep Is Pressed

You press the Sleep button on a Compaq 4700 series computer and see the following error message on a blue screen:

Invalid VxD dynamic link call from TRIVXD (01) 00000044 to device "0026", service 2. Your windows configuration is invalid. Run the windows setup program to correct this problem.

If you then press any key, your computer may stop responding (hang).

Solution

Disable Advanced Power Management in your computer's Basic Input/Output System (BIOS). For information about how to do so, see the documentation included with your computer, or contact Compaq.

Related KB article Q194369

Compaq Presario 4834 Turns Off When You Choose Standby

You use a Compaq Presario 4834 with a monitor other than a Compaq monitor with USB ports, and your computer turns off when you choose the Standby option in the Shutdown dialog box.

This occurs when your BIOS is configured for a Compaq monitor with USB ports, but you're using a different monitor.

Solution

Configure your BIOS to not use the Compaq monitor with USB ports, or contact Compaq for an updated BIOS.

Related KB article Q191480 or HARDWARE.TXT in your WINDOWS folder

Critical Battery Alarm Sound Doesn't Play

You configure a low or critical battery alarm to play a sound and display a text message, and the message is displayed when a low or critical battery condition occurs, but the sound doesn't play. However, the sound plays when you click OK to close the message window, or when the window closes automatically after a 5-minute delay. This problem also occurs when you configure the computer to perform an action, such as standing by or shutting down.

This problem occurs on computers that conform to the Advanced Configuration and Power Interface (ACPI) specification.

Solution

Don't configure any other type of notification or action except the sound alarm.

Related KB article Q190356

Critical Suspend Mode Causes Unexpected Results

Your computer goes into Critical Suspend mode, and you experience unexpected results when you resume. This occurs because Windows 98 does not support Critical Suspend/Critical Resume. Instead, Windows 98 sends power management notifications directly to individual device drivers. When your computer is put into Critical Suspend mode, the device drivers are not notified, and, as a result, they aren't properly resumed.

Solution One

Avoid using Critical Suspend mode in Windows 98. Because of the tighter integration of device drivers and the ability to send power management notifications, Windows 98 Advanced Power Management (APM) is more robust than Microsoft Windows 95 APM. The notification of device drivers is mandatory in ensuring a successful resume.

Solution Two

Windows 98 includes a Critical Battery Alarm that is set to 3 percent by default. When your computer reaches 3 percent, Windows 98 can suspend the computer normally, and you can switch batteries or plug your computer into a wall outlet using the AC adapter, and then resume from Suspend mode correctly.

If you need to implement a BIOS Critical suspend, set the BIOS trip point to 2 percent or less. This allows Windows 98 to suspend the computer correctly at the 3 percent Critical Battery Alarm.

Related KB article Q189194

Computer Doesn't Resume from Standby Mode

You attempt to resume your computer from Standby mode, and it stops responding, and only a blinking cursor is displayed on a black screen.

This occurs when all of the following conditions exist:

- You use the keyboard or a power management timer to put your computer into Standby mode.

- An MS-DOS Prompt window is open when your computer goes into Standby mode.

- Your computer uses Advanced Configuration and Power Interface (ACPI) features.

This problem occurs only when Standby mode is invoked using the keyboard or a power management timer. If you use your mouse to invoke Standby mode, you are able to resume properly.

Solution

Press Alt+Tab to resume your computer from Standby mode.

Related KB article Q190362

Device Driver or Program Disables Standby Mode

You attempt to put Windows 98 in Standby mode, and you receive the following error message:

Your computer cannot go on standby because a device driver or program won't allow it. Close all programs and try again.

You close all programs and attempt to put Windows 98 into Standby mode, and you receive the same error message.

This occurs when a program, driver, or hardware device is preventing Windows 98 from going into Standby mode. This is also referred to as a "veto" of the suspend command Windows 98 sends to the computer's BIOS.

Solution

Use the Power Management Trouble Shooter (PMTSHOOT.EXE) tool to determine which program, driver, or hardware device is preventing Windows 98 from going into Standby mode. For more information on using this tool, see KB article Q185949.

Related KB article Q188246

Digital HiNote Ultra 2000 Does Not Display Standby Option

When you click the Shutdown command from the Start menu, there is no Standby option on the Digital HiNote Ultra 2000.

Solution

Contact Digital for an updated BIOS with improved power management support.

Related KB article Q191480 or HARDWARE.TXT in your WINDOWS folder

Hibernation Mode Engages Instead of Standby Mode

You use a computer that conforms to the Advanced Configuration and Power Interface (ACPI) specifications and experience one of the following problems:

- You select the Standby action for the Power button on the Advanced tab of the Power Management tool in Control Panel, and the computer hibernates instead of standing by.

- You select Standby as the action taken when the lid of the portable computer is closed, and the computer hibernates instead of standing by when the lid is closed.

- You click the Start button, click Shut Down, and then click Stand By, and the computer hibernates instead of standing by.

This occurs on ACPI-compliant computers if the Enable Hibernation Support option is enabled on the Hibernate tab in the Power Management tool in Control Panel. Under this configuration, Windows 98 causes the computer to hibernate instead of standing by when you press the Power button.

Solution

Obtain the following updated files for Windows 98, as well as later versions of these files from Microsoft Technical Support.

Table 6-1. Updated Files for Windows 98

Filename	Version	Date created	Size
CONFIGMG.VXD	version 4.10.2101	dated 6/29/98 9:01pm	115,665 bytes
VPOWERD.VXD	version 4.10.210	dated 6/29/98 9:01pm	37,523 bytes
NTKERN.VXD	version 4.10.2102	dated 7/21/98 9:02pm	55,252 bytes

Related KB article Q190715

IBM ThinkPad 770 Doesn't Suspend

Your IBM ThinkPad 770 computer with an IBM 20H2999 PCI-to-PCI docking bridge has been in its docking station for a sufficient amount of time to go to Suspend mode, but it doesn't.

Solution

Obtain the following updated file for Windows 98 from Microsoft Technical Support:

PCI.VXD version 4.10.2016 dated 06/26/98 09:13am 65,895 bytes

Related KB article Q190089

NeoMagic 128XD Video Driver Causes Standby Mode to Not Engage

You attempt to put Windows 98 in Standby mode by clicking the Start button, clicking Shut Down, clicking Stand By, and then clicking OK, and Windows 98 won't go into Standby mode. If it does, you may be unable to resume. This occurs if you are using a NeoMagic 128XD video driver, which isn't supported in Windows 98. Gateway 2300x notebook computers contain a NeoMagic 128XD display adapter.

Solution

Contact NeoMagic Technical Support to inquire about the availability of an updated driver.

Related KB article Q187285

NetWare Client Causes Standby Mode to Not Engage

You try to suspend your computer (or place it in Standby mode) and see an error message similar to the following:

Your computer can't go on standby because a device program won't allow it.

Close all open programs, and then try again.

This behavior occurs if you install a real-mode Novell NetWare network client (such as NetX or VLM), which are continuously loaded in memory.

Solution One

Use a 32-bit NetWare network client.

Solution Two

Don't attempt to suspend your computer or place it in Standby mode.

Related KB article Q118118

Network Connection Disabled After APM Suspends Computer

If you run a network client program that connects to a network server program and your computer then suspends itself, the network client program may be unable to connect to the network server program again.

For example, if Microsoft Hearts runs on another computer, you play the game across a network connection. If your computer is suspended by Advanced Power Management (APM), Hearts generates the following error message when your computer resumes:

The dealer has left the game. Hearts will end.

When you click OK, restart Hearts, and choose to connect to the game on the other computer, you receive the following error message:

Unable to connect to the dealer. Hearts will end.

If you restart your computer, you are able to connect to the Hearts game across the network.

Hearts is a Network Dynamic Data Exchange (NetDDE) program. This same behavior also occurs if you run a NetDDE program across a network connection using a PC card network adapter, stop the PC card service, remove the network adapter, and then insert the network adapter again. NetDDE wasn't designed to communicate with APM services.

Solution

Restart your computer or disable APM. To disable APM, follow these steps:

1. Click the Start button, choose Settings, and then click Control Panel.

2. Double-click the System icon.

3. Click the Device Manager tab.

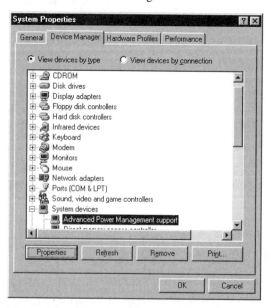

Figure 6-2. *The Device Manager tab in the System Properties dialog box.*

4. Double-click System Devices, and then double-click Advanced Power Management Support.

5. Click the General tab, and then select the Disable In All Profiles check box.

6. Click OK twice.

Related KB article Q182520

Power Management Settings Don't Work

Changing when your computer goes to sleep in the Control Panel's Power Management applet has no effect on the actual amount of time before your system goes into sleep mode.

Some computers won't let Windows have complete control of power management. If you find that changing your Power Management settings has no effect, your computer's own power management settings are overriding Windows' settings.

Solution

Open your computer's power management configuration program (most likely inside your BIOS settings) and disable any Standby, Suspend, Monitor, or Hard Drive time-out values.

Related KB article Q191480 or HARDWARE.TXT in your WINDOWS folder

Screen Saver Causes Standby Mode to Not Engage

Your computer has been inactive long enough for it to go to Standby mode, but it doesn't, and you receive a message which says your computer will stand by in 15 seconds, but it still doesn't go to Standby mode.

This occurs when one of the following Windows 98 screen savers is in use:

- 3D Flower Box
- 3D Flying Objects
- 3D Maze
- 3D Text
- Channel Screen Saver

This problem applies only to computers that support Advanced Power Management (APM) or the Advanced Configuration and Power Interface (ACPI) specification

Solution One

Configure your computer to use a screen saver that is not on the above list. To do this, follow these steps:

1. Right-click an empty area of the desktop, and choose Properties from the shortcut menu.

2. Click the Screen Saver tab, and select a different screen saver from the Screen Saver drop-down list.

Solution Two

Continue using one of the above screen savers, but reduce its complexity. To do this, follow these steps:

1. Click the Start button, choose Settings, click Control Panel, and then double-click the Display icon.

2. Click the Screen Saver tab, and then click Settings under Screen Saver. The settings you can change to reduce the complexity of the screen saver vary with different screen savers, but you may be able to disable, or slow down, one or more of the following settings:

   - Resolution

   - Size

   - Complexity

   - Speed

   - Surface Style

   - Smooth Shading

   - Full Screen

   - Maze Overlay

   - Image Quality

   - Textures

   If a setting has a slider that varies from Minimum to Maximum, try setting it to Minimum, or clear a setting's check box to totally disable it, or change a setting from High to Low. After you alter a setting, click OK to apply the change.

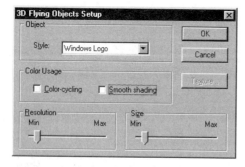

Figure 6-3.   *The 3D Flying Objects Setup dialog box.*

3. Test to determine if the issue is solved. If not, repeat steps 1–3, disabling more settings until the screen saver is usable.

Note If you perform all of these steps and the screen saver remains unusable, you'll need to discontinue use.

Related KB article Q189619

Standby Displays Error Message

You attempt to put Windows 98 in Standby mode by clicking the Start button, clicking Shut Down, clicking Stand By, and then clicking OK, and you see the following error message:

A device driver or program will not let your system enter Stand By mode.

This occurs if Diamond Multimedia/NetCommander ISDN adapter drivers are installed on your computer. These drivers prevent Windows 98 from going into Standby mode.

Solution

Contact Diamond Multimedia Technical Support to inquire about the availability of updated drivers.

Related KB article Q187323

Standby Mode Causes Windows to Stop Responding

You install Novell Client32 version 2.2.0 or earlier in Windows 98, then attempt to put Windows into Standby mode, and your computer stops responding.

Windows 98 includes the latest version of the VMLID.NLM file. If you upgrade Windows 95 with Novell Client32 to Windows 98, the VMLID.NLM file is updated. If you install Novell Client32 after Windows 98 is installed, the earlier version of the VMLID.NLM file is used.

Solution One

Use the System File Checker tool to extract an updated version of the VMLID.NLM file from your original Windows 98 disks or CD-ROM to the NOVELL\CLIENT32 folder.

Solution Two

Obtain the 952201.EXE patch from Novell Technical Support or Novell's web site.

Related KB article Q188100

Standby Option Missing from Shut Down Windows Dialog Box

You click the Start button and then click Shut Down, and the Standby option is missing from the Windows Shut Down dialog box. This issue can occur for any of the following reasons:

- When you received the following message, you clicked Yes:

  *The last few times your computer went on standby it stopped
  responding. Would you like to prevent your computer from going on
  standby in the future?*

- Your computer stopped responding while in Standby mode two consecutive times.

- Advanced Power Management (APM) is not configured properly in your computer's Basic Input/Output System (BIOS).

Solution

To solve this problem, follow these steps:

1. Click the Start button, choose Settings, click Control Panel, and then double-click the System icon.

2. Click the Device Manager tab, and then double-click the System Devices branch to expand it.

3. Verify that an Advanced Power Management Support entry is listed under the System Devices branch. If this entry is present, click it, click Remove, restart your computer, and then skip to step 6. If this entry is not present, use the following steps:

4. Click the Start button, choose Settings, click Control Panel, and then double-click the Add New Hardware icon.

5. Follow the instructions on the screen to finish the Add New Hardware Wizard. If this wizard successfully detects and installs support for APM, do not continue with the remaining steps in this article. If this wizard doesn't successfully detect and install support for APM, your issue may be related to problems with your hardware, and Microsoft recommends you contact your hardware manufacturer for further assistance.

6. Click the Start button, choose Settings, click Control Panel, and then double-click the Add New Hardware icon.

7. Follow the instructions on the screen to finish the Add New Hardware Wizard. If this wizard successfully detects and installs support for APM, continue to step 8. If this wizard does not successfully detect and install support for APM, your issue may be related to problems with your hardware, and Microsoft recommends you contact your hardware manufacturer for further assistance.

8. Restart your computer, and then test to determine if the issue is resolved by clicking the Start button and then clicking Shut Down. If the issue is resolved, do not continue with the remaining steps in this article. If the issue is not resolved, continue to step 9.

9. Click the Start button, choose Settings, click Control Panel, and then double-click the System icon.

10. Click the Device Manager tab, double-click the Floppy Disk Controllers branch to expand it, click Standard Floppy Disk Controller, and then click Remove.

11. Restart your computer. Note that when you do so, Windows automatically detects your floppy disk controller, and the SuspendFlag entries in the Registry are reset.

12. Test to determine if the issue is resolved by clicking the Start button and then clicking Shut Down. If the issue is resolved, do not continue with the remaining steps in this article. If the issue is not resolved, continue to step 13.

13. If you are on a network, contact your network administrator before performing the next step.

Warning Please read the Introduction for information on how to safely edit the Registry.

14. Click the Start button, click Run, enter *Regedit* in the Run box, and click OK.

15. Navigate your way down through the folders in the left pane until you locate the following Registry key:

```
HKEY_LOCAL_MACHINE\System\CurrentControlSet\Services\VXD\VPOWERD
```

16. Verify that a Flags value and a SuspendFlag value exist. If these values do not exist, close Registry Editor and contact your hardware manufacturer for further assistance. If these values do exist, verify that the data value of the Flags value is greater than or equal to 200. If it is, modify the data value of the Flags value by subtracting 200 from the current value. For example, if the value is currently 310, change it to 110. Change the data value of the SuspendFlag value to 0 if it is not already 0.

17. Close Regedit.

18. Restart Windows.

Related KB article Q188134

Standby or Suspend Mode Doesn't Engage

You attempt to enter Standby (or Suspend) mode, and an application or device driver prevents the computer from doing so.

Solution

Use PMTShoot to identify the application or device driver that prevents your computer from suspending.

As your system suspends and then resumes, you will see text displayed by PMTShoot. This text is grouped according to the phases that comprise the Suspend process. In many cases, you will find this grouping useful in diagnosing the cause of the Suspend failure.

Install PMTShoot on your computer. To do so, follow these steps:

1. Insert the Windows 98 CD-ROM in your CD-ROM drive

2. From Windows Explorer, navigate to the D:\TOOLS\MSTUTIL\PMTSHOOT directory, and then double-click PMTSHOOT.EXE (substitute "D" for the letter of your CD-ROM drive).

3. Click Yes when Setup asks if you would like to continue.

4. Click OK.

5. Click OK to restart your computer.

To use PMTShoot, follow these steps:

When you suspend your computer, PMTShoot displays all the activity on your computer. Note the text. You may need to scroll up or down to see all of it. If you don't see a vertical scroll bar, resize the window slightly to create one.

Take note of the information displayed in red. This is what PMTShoot considers to be most relevant to the suspend failure. Often, PMTShoot will display the name of the device and driver that caused the suspension to fail. With this information, you can make the necessary adjustments to resolve the problem.

To uninstall PMTShoot, follow these steps:

1. Click the Start button, choose Settings, and then click Control Panel.

2 Double-click the Add/Remove Programs icon.

3. Click PMTShoot - Power Management Trouble Shooter.

4. Click Add/Remove.

5. Click Yes to restart the computer.

Related KB article Q191493

Suspend Function Doesn't Initiate

You try to suspend your computer, and it continues to operate in its normal operating state.

This problem occurs for one of the following reasons:

- Your computer's Integrated Device Electronics (IDE) controller has a secondary channel, but does not have an IDE hard disk connected to it. (For example, this problem can occur with a laptop computer and its docking station if the bay in the docking station is normally occupied by the secondary IDE hard disk but is currently empty, or if a different drive type currently occupies it, such as a floppy disk drive or a CD-ROM drive.)

- The secondary IDE controller channels, or other devices, are marked as disabled in Device Manager.

Solution

Obtain the following updated Windows 98 file from Microsoft Technical Support:

CONFIGMG.VXD version 4.10.2016 dated 6/29/98 6:52pm 155,665 bytes

Related KB article Q189577

ThinkPad Stops Responding After Resuming from Standby

You place a Windows 98–based computer into Standby mode and then resume, and the computer stops responding (hangs). This problem has been reported for the following laptops: IBM ThinkPad 770E, IBM ThinkPad 770ED, IBM ThinkPad 600, IBM ThinkPad 560D, and IBM ThinkPad 380Z.

Solution

A supported fix that corrects this problem is now available from Microsoft in Service Pack 1. Contact Microsoft Technical Support to obtain the fix.

Related KB article Q193473

Toshiba 4500 Doesn't Suspend Properly

You shut down your Toshiba 4500 laptop computer in Suspend mode, or close the lid, and Windows appears to shut down successfully. However, when you resume Windows after a short delay, the computer reboots.

The Toshiba 4500 laptop computer requires an additional driver file to use Advanced Power Management (APM) features.

Solution

Obtain the WRESUME.386 file from Toshiba. To make it work on your system, follow these steps:

1. Click the Start button, click Run, enter *Sysedit* in the Open box, and click OK.

2. Choose the C:\WINDOWS\SYSTEM.INI window.

3. In the [386ENH] section of the file, enter the following line:

   device=<path>\wresume.386

   in which <path> indicates the path to the WRESUME.386 file. For example, if the WRESUME.386 file is located in your windows folder on drive C, add the line *device=c:\windows\wresume.386*

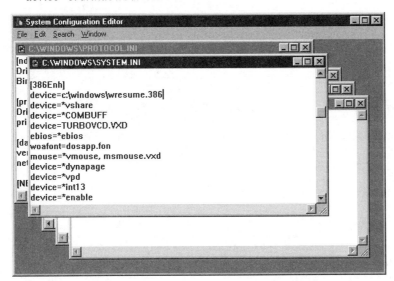

Figure 6-4. *The SYSTEM.INI file in the System Configuration Editor.*

4. Choose Save from the File menu, and close the program.

5. Reboot the computer.

Related KB article Q132333

Toshiba Laptop Doesn't Display Hard Disk

You resume your Toshiba laptop computer from Suspend mode while it is in the docking station, and hard disks attached to the AMD Small Computer System Interface (SCSI) controller are missing in My Computer and Windows Explorer.

The Advanced Power Management (APM) BIOS used by Toshiba laptop computers supports suspending and resuming while the computer is docked.

Solution

Obtain the TAP utility from Toshiba's web site. This utility prevents the computer from going into Suspend mode while it is docked.

Related KB article Q190368

Toshiba Laptop Doesn't Suspend Automatically

Windows does not automatically go into low-power suspended mode on a Toshiba laptop computer.

Solution

There is no way to cause the computer to suspend automatically. You must suspend it either by clicking the Start button and choosing Suspend or by using the hardware switch.

Related KB article Q132765

Toshiba Protege 300 Doesn't Allow CD-ROM Access

You resume your Toshiba Protege 300 series computer from Standby mode, and you are unable to gain access to your integrated drive electronics (IDE) CD-ROM drive, and Device Manager displays *Code 12* for your CD-ROM drive.

This occurs when you resume your computer from Standby mode twice in the same session.

Solution

Restart your computer. The IDE controller normally uses interrupt request (IRQ) 15, but when you resume your computer a second time, IRQ 15 is used by "Unknown Device."

Related KB article Q188203

Toshiba T2150 Stops Responding After Suspending

You suspend your Toshiba 2150, or attempt to resume after suspending it, and the computer stops responding.

Solution

Comment out the line in your CONFIG.SYS file that loads the TOSCDROM.SYS driver. To do so, follow these steps:

1. Click the Start button, click Run, type *notepad c:\config.sys* in the Open box, and click OK.

2. Type *rem* in front of the line device=c:\cddrv\toscrdrom.sys. (Your line might be slightly different.)

3. Choose Save from the File menu, close Notepad, and then restart your computer.

Related KB article Q191480 or HARDWARE.TXT in your WINDOWS folder

Toshiba Tecra Displays Six Extra Drive Letters

You resume your Toshiba Tecra laptop computer from Suspend mode, and then view your local drives, and you notice that six new extra drive letters are visible.

This problem occurs when you use a Toshiba Tecra laptop computer with a Small Computer System Interface (SCSI) hard disk attached to an American Micro Devices (AMD) SCSI controller built into a docking station. Some Toshiba Tecra laptop computers come with preinstalled software that disables suspend-and-resume functionality while your computer is in a docking station.

Solution

Contact Toshiba to inquire about a fix for this problem.

Related KB article Q188332

Unplugging and Plugging Computer Causes Errors

You plug and unplug the power cord on a battery-powered computer that conforms to the Advanced Configuration and Power Interface (ACPI) specification, and one of the following problems occurs:

- Your computer stops responding (hangs).

- You receive a *Fatal Exception 0E* error message.

Your computer might appear to retain some degree of functionality after you experience one of these symptoms, but certain ACPI functions, such as thermal management, are disabled. This can cause the computer's internal temperature to reach dangerously high levels and render Windows 98 unable to activate the appropriate cooling methods to reduce the temperature.

Solution

Shut down and restart your computer. If you are unable to shut down Windows properly, turn your computer off and then back on.

Note To prevent this problem from occurring, don't plug and unplug the power cord repeatedly or in rapid succession.

Related KB article Q190508

Specific Models

Compaq Armada Doesn't See Floppy Disk Drive

You use a Compaq Armada expansion base, and the floppy disk drive in the expansion base is not displayed in My Computer or Windows Explorer.

Solution

This problem occurs if Windows doesn't detect the floppy disk drive in the Compaq Armada expansion base or if the expansion base contains an earlier Basic Input/Output System (BIOS) that is not fully compatible with Windows 98. To resolve this issue, please contact Compaq for information on how to update the BIOS on your expansion base.

Related KB article Q190919

Compaq Presario PC Card Slot Stops Responding

You upgrade a Compaq Presario1610, 1615, 1620, 1680, 1681, or 1682 computer to Windows 98, and the PC Card (PCMCIA) slot stops responding (hangs).

Solution

Upgrade the Compaq Presario's Basic Input/Output System (BIOS) before you upgrade to Windows 98. Please contact Compaq for a Softpaq update, or download Softpaq file *SP5138* from the following Compaq web site: *http://www.compaq.com/athome/win98/1610.html*.

If you have already installed Windows 98, install the BIOS update and then run Windows 98 Setup again.

Related KB article Q192581

Fujitsu Lifebook Stops Responding

You use a 700 series Fujitsu Lifebook computer with an integrated 56KflexDSVD LTModem controllerless Peripheral Component Interconnect (PCI) modem and disconnect a dial-up networking connection, and your computer stops responding.

This occurs because the modem driver provided by Fujitsu doesn't work correctly with Windows 98 power management.

Solution One

Contact Fujitsu to obtain an updated modem driver.

Solution Two

Disable power management for your computer's COM port by using Registry Editor to modify the following Registry key:

```
Hkey_Local_Machine\System\CurrentControlSet\Services\VxD\VCOMM
```

Change the value of the EnablePowerManagement key from 01 00 00 00 to 00 00 00 00. To do so, follow these steps:

Warning Please read the Introduction for information on how to safely edit the Registry.

1. Click the Start button, click Run, enter *Regedit* in the Run box, and click OK.
2. Navigate your way down through the folders in the left pane until you locate the specified Registry key.
3. Modify the value of the EnablePowerManagement key from 01 00 00 00 to 00 00 00 00.
4. Close Regedit.
5. Restart Windows.

When you change this value in the Registry, you may experience the following:

- Internal modems in your computer are not power manageable, so they are always on (at a D0 state).
- Any Personal Computer Memory Card International Association (PCMCIA) modem or external modem attached to a COM port on your computer stays on (at a D0 state).
- If your computer is in a docking station that has a Peripheral Component Interconnect (PCI) or an Industry Standard Architecture (ISA) modem, they are always on (at a D0 state).

Related KB article Q185358

Gateway 2000 Solo 2100 or 2200 Do Not Produce Modem Sounds

You use a PC Card modem with a Gateway 2000 Solo 2100 or 2200 laptop computer, and you don't hear modem sounds when the computer is attached to a Gateway Solo Mini-Dock docking station.

Solution

Remove the computer from the docking station. If you need to hear modem sounds while the computer is docked, use an external modem.

Related KB article Q189157

IBM ThinkPad 701c Causes Illegal Operation

You try to install Windows 98 on your IBM ThinkPad 701c computer and receive the following error message:

GRPCONV has performed an illegal Operation

Explorer caused an Invalid Page Fault in Module KERNEL32.DLL at 015F:BFF72825

Turning the computer off and back on may allow Setup to finish, but you continue to receive similar error messages.

The IBM ThinkPad 701c was designed for Microsoft Windows 3.1. This computer requires a BIOS upgrade to be compatible with Plug and Play before it can be upgraded to Windows 95. IBM doesn't recommend installing Windows 98 on this computer.

Solution

Don't install Windows 98 on this computer.

Related KB article Q192157

IBM ThinkPad 750 and 755 Power Management, Mwave and/or Docking Doesn't Work

Power management works incorrectly on ThinkPad models 750. On ThinkPad models 755cd, cx, ce, cse, cdv (but not 755c), Mwave may be lost if you have more than 8MB of RAM, or, if you install Windows 98 to a different folder, the infrared port doesn't work properly, docking isn't supported, and power management doesn't work correctly. These problems are caused by problems with the drivers and BIOS.

Solution

Download fixed drivers from IBM.

Related KB article Q191480 or HARDWARE.TXT in your WINDOWS folder

IBM ThinkPad 770 Stops Responding

You try to start your IBM ThinkPad 770 laptop computer, and your computer stops responding.

This problem occurs when the CSMAPPER.SYS file loads from the CONFIG.SYS file. The CSMAPPER.SYS file prevents the use of linear-flash and synchronous random-access memory (SRAM) Personal Computer Memory Card International Association (PCMCIA) cards that use MS-DOS real-mode drivers. This problem occurs because your computer is unable to access this type of memory.

Solution

Remove the real-mode drivers, and then install protect-mode drivers. To do this, follow these steps:

1. Restart your computer. After your computer completes the Power On Self Test (POST), press and hold down the Ctrl key until you see the Windows 98 Startup menu, and then choose Command Prompt Only.

2. Type *edit CONFIG.SYS*, and then press Enter.

3. Type *rem* at the beginning of the lines that reference the CSMAPPER.SYS and CARDDRV.EXE files.

4. Press Alt+F, press S, press Alt+X, and then press Enter.

5. Restart your computer.

6. Insert your Windows 98 CD-ROM in your CD-ROM drive.

7. Click the Start button, choose Find, and then click Files Or Folders.

8. Select your CD-ROM drive in the Look In drop-down list box, and then click Find Now.

9. Right-click the TRUEFFS.INF file, and then choose Install from the shortcut menu.

Related KB article Q188690

IBM ThinkPad 770 Ultra Bay Hot Swap Doesn't Work

The IBM ThinkPad 770 Ultra Bay hot swap virtual device driver under Windows 95 provides the user the ability to hot swap disk drives, CD-ROM and DVD-ROM drives, or a secondary battery.

When you upgrade to Windows 98, your original Ultra Bay hot swap driver doesn't allow you to use the suspend/resume power management feature.

Solution

After you install Windows 98, replace the existing file (IBMBAY.VXD) with the one included in the DRIVERS\PWRMGMT\IBM\ folder. To do so, follow these steps:

1. Make a backup of the IBMBAY.VXD file located in the SYSTEM subfolder of your WINDOWS folder.

2. Copy the IBMBAY.VXD in the DRIVERS\PWRMGMT\IBM\ folder to the SYSTEM subfolder of your WINDOWS folder.

3. Restart your computer. The suspend/resume feature will now work.

Note This file replacement is required only for ThinkPad 770 systems with Windows 95 preloaded.

Related KB article Q191532

IBM ThinkPad Device Doesn't Work

You enable a device on your IBM ThinkPad computer using ThinkPad Configuration Utility (TPW.EXE) or Device Manager, and the device doesn't work. This occurs if the device is enabled only in ThinkPad Configuration Utility or only in Device Manager; the device must be enabled in both to work properly.

Solution

Enable the device in both Device Manager and ThinkPad Configuration Utility. To do so, follow these steps:

1. For information on how to enable the device using ThinkPad Configuration Utility, contact IBM Technical Support.

2. Restart your computer.

3. Click the Start button, choose Settings, and click Control Panel.

4. Double-click the System icon, and then click the Device Manager tab.

5. Click the disabled device, and then click Properties.

6. On the General tab, clear the Disable In This Hardware Profile check box, click OK, and then click Close.

If the device still doesn't work, try enabling it again using ThinkPad Configuration Utility.

Related KB article Q188191

IBM ThinkPad Doesn't Display Plug and Play BIOS

Your IBM ThinkPad (360/750/755 series) dockable notebook computer is equipped with Plug and Play BIOS, but you see no Eject PC command on the Start menu when it is docked in a docking station, and no Plug and Play BIOS node is displayed in System Devices in the Device Manager.

Solution

Early versions of dockable notebook computers with a Plug and Play BIOS are not compatible with Windows. To make your computer compatible with Windows, contact the manufacturer and obtain the most recent Plug and Play BIOS. A Plug and Play BIOS dated after 7/1/95 is normally compatible with Windows.

Related KB article Q134468

IBM ThinkPad Freezes When Docked in ThinkPad Dock II

You start your IBM ThinkPad while docked in the ThinkPad Dock II, and your computer freezes repeatedly.

The freeze is caused by the Adaptec 1530P SCSI controller's BIOS interfering with normal system operation.

Solution One

Disable the SCSI BIOS. To do so, follow these steps:

1. Restart your computer while it is docked.

2. Press Ctrl+A to start the Adaptec SCSISelect utility.

3. Choose Configure/View Host Adapter Settings.

4. Choose Advanced Configuration Options.

5. Change the setting for Host Adapter BIOS to Disabled.

6. Press Esc until you are prompted to exit the utility. When you exit, the computer will restart.

Note The Adaptec controller works fine in Protected mode even without the BIOS enabled, so you should not lose access to any SCSI devices.

Solution Two

Disable the BIOS completely, thus enabling the adapter to run completely in Plug and Play mode. The BIOS resources are allocated dynamically at Windows 98 startup. However, this solution requires that you change a DIP switch inside the dock station. For details about disabling the SCSI adapter BIOS, refer to your Dock II manual.

Related KB article Q191480 or HARDWARE.TXT in your WINDOWS folder

Jetbook 7050 Laptop Reports Error Message

You install or upgrade to Windows 98 on a Jetbook 7050 laptop computer and receive the following error message:

A Fatal Exception 006 has occurred at 0000:0000007.

Solution

This problem occurs if the Basic Input/Output System (BIOS) revision of the laptop computer is earlier than 1.06a. To resolve this problem, contact the computer's manufacturer for information about how to upgrade the BIOS to revision 1.06a or later.

Related KB artiolc Q191539

Toshiba Laptop Does Not Allow Alt+Tab Command During Setup

You try to install Windows 98 on your Toshiba laptop computer, and you receive a message that recommends you close all running programs before you continue with Setup. However, when you try to view all running programs by pressing Alt+Tab, you don't see any.

This occurs when your Toshiba laptop computer is running the Toshiba Application Controller program. You can't use Alt+Tab to view this program when it is running.

Solution

Disable the Toshiba Application Controller program before you run Windows 98 Setup. For information about how to do so, view the documentation included with your computer, or contact Toshiba.

Related KB article Q188229

Toshiba Laptops Malfunction with Windows

The following Toshiba laptop computers may not function correctly with Windows and may lock up, fail to boot, and display the general protection (GP) fault error messages:

- 400CS/CDT
- 610CT
- T2100 mono
- T2100CS/CT
- T2110CS
- T2130CS/CT
- T2150CDS/CDT
- T2400CS/CT
- T2450CT
- T3600CT
- T4700CS/CT
- T4800CT
- T4850CT
- T4900CT

Solution

Upgrade to BIOS version 5.0. To obtain an upgrade, or for information about the BIOS upgrade process, contact Toshiba.

Related KB article Q151434

Toshiba Protege 300 Mouse Buttons Don't Work Together

You try to use two of your mouse buttons simultaneously on your Toshiba Protege 300 series computer and can't. This is because Toshiba installs a proprietary mouse driver, TMOUSE.VXD, which prevents two-button simultaneous operation of your mouse.

Solution One

Contact Toshiba to ask about a fix for this issue.

Solution Two

Use Registry Editor to remove the Tmouse value from the Registry key. To do so, follow these steps:

Warning Please read the Introduction for information on how to safely edit the Registry.

1. Click the Start button, click Run, enter *Regedit* in the Run box, and click OK.

2. Navigate your way down through the folders in the left pane until you locate the following key:

   `HKEY_LOCAL_MACHINE\System\CurrentControlSet\Services\VXD3`

3. Remove the key.

4. Close Regedit.

5. Restart Windows.

Related KB article Q188180

Toshiba Satellite Pro 400 CDT Laptop Doesn't Start Windows

You attempt to start Windows on a Toshiba Satellite Pro 400 CDT laptop computer with a Personal Computer Memory Card International Association (PCMCIA or PC Card) device installed and the computer stops responding. This occurs if the Toshiba Satellite Pro 400 CDT laptop computer has an older BIOS version installed.

Solution

Update the BIOS on your laptop computer to version 5.60 or later, and then reinstall Windows. For information about how to update the BIOS on your laptop computer, please contact Toshiba.

Related KB article 188097

Toshiba Tecra 750CDT Won't Resume

If your Toshiba Tecra 750CDT laptop computer goes into Suspend mode while it is in a docking station, you can't resume it.

This behavior occurs if the docking station contains an ATI video adapter and is configured to use multiple monitors. The Peripheral Component Interconnect (PCI) bridge in the docking station turns off the power to the ATI video adapter when the laptop computer goes into Suspend mode.

Solution One

Undock the computer, resume it from Standby mode, and then dock it again.

Solution Two

Disable Advanced Power Management (APM) support in the docked hardware profile. To do so, follow these steps:

1. Click the Start button, choose Settings, and then click Control Panel.

2. Double-click the System icon, and then click the Device Manager tab.

3. Double-click the System Devices branch to expand it.

4. Click Advanced Power Management Support, and then click Properties.

5. Click the General tab, select the Disable In This Hardware Profile check box, and then click OK.

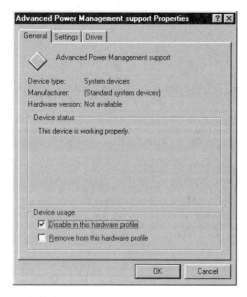

Figure 6-5.   *The Advanced Power Management support Properties dialog box.*

6. Click OK, and then click Yes when you are prompted to restart your computer.

Related KB article Q191884

Toshiba Tecra 8000 DVD Causes Windows to Stop Responding

You use a Toshiba Tecra 8000 DVD, with a DVD drive left open, and a few minutes after starting, Windows stops responding.

Solution One

Close the drive tray while Windows is starting or within 1 minute thereafter.

Solution Two

Disable auto insert notification or DMA access for the DVD drive or CD-ROM drive. To do this, follow these steps:

1. Click the Start button, choose Settings, and click Control Panel.

2. Double-click the System icon, and then click the Device Manager tab.

3. Click the CD-ROM branch to expand it, select your CD-ROM drive or DVD drive, and then click Properties.

4. Click the Settings tab, clear the Auto Insert Notification or DMA check boxes if they are checked, and click OK.

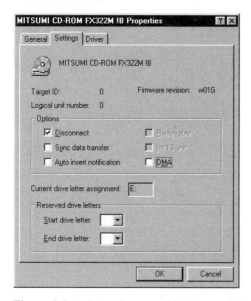

Figure 6-6.   *The DVD or CD-ROM Properties dialog box.*

5. Click OK, and then restart your computer.

Related KB article Q192713

Zenith NoteFLEX 486DX Doesn't Detect PC Cards, PCMCIA Hard Disks, and/or Flexshow Docking Station CD-ROM

Zenith NoteFLEX 486DX cannot detect PC Cards, and/or PCMCIA hard drives, and/or the built-in CD-ROM in the Flexshow Docking Station.

Solution

The HARDWARE.TXT file located in your WINDOWS folder describes specific steps that you can take to solve these problems. To view the HARDWARE.TXT file, click the Start button, click Run, type *HARDWARE.TXT* in the Open box, and click OK.

Related KB article Q191480 or HARDWARE.TXT in your WINDOWS folder

CHAPTER 7

Modems and Dial-Up Communications

Dial-Up Networking

All Modems Configure with Extra Settings

You configure a Dial-Up Networking connection to use extra settings, and all subsequent connections you create for that modem are automatically configured with the same extra settings.

This problem occurs because Dial-Up Networking updates the MODEM.CPL file when you create a connection with extra settings. When you create a new connection for the same modem, the extra settings are automatically applied to the new connection.

Solution

Manually install another copy of the same modem driver, and configure the extra settings separately. To do so, follow these steps:

1. Click the Start button, choose Settings, click Control Panel, and then double-click the Modems icon.

2. Click Add.

3. Select the Don't Detect My Modem; I Will Select It From A List check box, and then click Next.

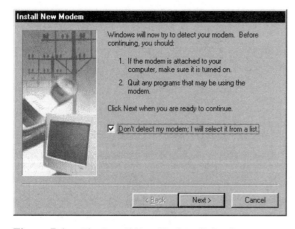

Figure 7-1.   *The Install New Modem dialog box.*

4. Click the appropriate manufacturer and model, and then click Next.

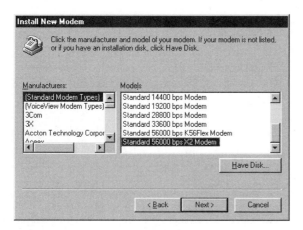

Figure 7-2. *Choosing a modem from the Install New Modem dialog box.*

5. Click the appropriate communications port, click Next, and then click Finish.

6. Click the appropriate modem, and then click Properties.

7. On the Connection tab, click Advanced, enter the new extra settings in the Extra Settings box, click OK, click OK again, and then click Close.

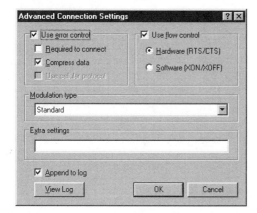

Figure 7-3. *The Advanced Connection Settings dialog box.*

Related KB article Q188301

Client Doesn't Connect to a Windows 98 NWSERVER

You are unable to connect to a Windows 98 Dial-Up Networking server when you're running a Windows for Workgroups Remote Access Service (RAS) client, Windows NT 3.1 RAS client, Windows 98 Dial-Up Networking client, or Windows NT 3.5 RAS client.

This problem can occur if the Dial-Up Networking server to which you want to connect is a Windows 98 computer set up as an NWSERVER and the Dial-Up Networking client you're using is using the RAS drivers rather than the Point-to-Point Protocol (PPP) drivers. The server is unable to get the plain-text version of the client password. The plain-text password is necessary in order to do user-level security with a NetWare server. User-level security is enabled by definition if you are running NWSERVER.

Solution

Use the Windows 98 Dial-Up Networking client in PPP mode or the Windows NT 3.5 RNA client in PPP mode.

To tell the Windows 98 Dial-Up Networking client to use the PPP mode, follow these steps:

1. Click the Start button, choose Programs, choose Accessories, choose Communications, and click Dial-Up Networking.

2. Right-click the connection you're trying to make, and choose Properties from the shortcut menu.

3. Click the Server Types tab.

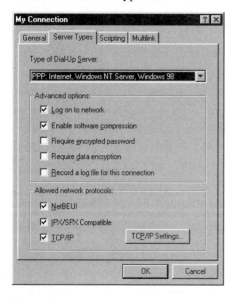

Figure 7-4.   *The Server Types tab in the My Connection dialog box.*

4. Select PPP: Internet, Windows NT Server, Windows 98 from the Type Of Dial-Up Server drop-down list.

5. Click OK.

Related KB article Q122143

Connection Fails

You try to connect by using a Dial-Up Networking connection and receive an error message stating that the modem does not exist, is not plugged in, or is out of service. You receive this message even though a modem is attached and working correctly.

This problem occurs if you select a modem for Dial-Up Networking connections, later remove the modem, and then add another modem.

Solution

To solve this problem, follow these steps:

1. Double-click My Computer on the desktop.

2. Double-click the Dial-Up Networking icon.

3. Right-click the connection icon.

4. Choose Properties from the shortcut menu, and then select the new modem.

Related KB article Q132781

Connection Fails Using Country and Area Codes

You attempt to use a Dial-Up Networking connection with country code and area code information, and you see the following error message:

Dial Up Networking could not establish a connection with <server>.

If you click Cancel while your modem is dialing, you notice that the phone number contains extra digits. If you view the connection properties, the correct dialing information is displayed. If you create a new connection, it also dials the extra numbers.

Solution

Typing the entire phone number in the Area Code box in the connection's properties can damage connection information in the Registry. Use Registry Checker (SCANREG.EXE) to restore an undamaged copy of the Registry. Follow these steps:

1. Restart your computer. After your computer completes the Power On Self Test (POST), press and hold down the Ctrl key until you see the Windows 98 StartUp menu, and then choose Command Prompt Only.

2. At the command prompt, type *scanreg /restore*, and then press the Enter key.

3. Follow the instructions on your screen to restore a copy of the Registry that was created before the error message occurred.

Note For more information about how to use Registry Checker, see KB article Q184023, "Command-Line Switches for the Registry Checker Tool."

4. Restart your computer normally, and then try to use the Dial-Up Networking connection again. If you still receive the error message, continue with step 5.

5. Right-click the connection you want, and then choose Properties from the shortcut menu.

6. Clear the Use Area Code And Dialing Properties check box.

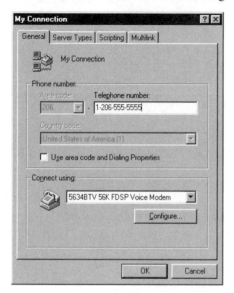

Figure 7-5.   *The General tab in the My Connection dialog box.*

7. In the Telephone Number box, enter the complete phone number, including the area code, and then click OK.

Related KB article   Q194804

Connection Information Lost

After you upgrade to Windows 98 from Windows 3.x or Windows for Workgroups 3.x, Dial-Up Networking does not contain any of the previous connection information.

Solution

Windows 3.x and Windows for Workgroups 3.x Dial-Up Networking connections cannot be automatically migrated to Windows 98. You must manually re-create your Dial-Up Networking connections. Follow these steps:

1. Double-click My Computer, and then double-click Dial-Up Networking.

2. Double-click Make New Connection, and then follow the instructions onscreen to create a new connection.

3. Repeat steps 1 and 2 until you re-create the connections you want, close Dial-Up Networking, and then close My Computer.

Related KB article   Q183207

Dialing Properties Can't Be Modified

You attempt to modify a Dial-Up Networking connection's dialing properties, and the Dial Properties option is unavailable if the Use Area Code And Dialing Properties check box is not selected in the Dial-Up Networking connection's properties.

Solution

To solve this problem, follow these steps:

1. Double-click the My Computer icon on the desktop, and then double-click Dial-Up Networking.

2. Right-click the connection you want to modify, and then click Properties.

3. Click the General tab, select the Use Area Code And Dialing Properties check box, and then click OK.

Related KB article Q194710

Dial-Up Adapter Installation Causes Errors

You restart your computer following the installation of the Dial-Up Adapter and receive the following error messages:

Cannot find a device file that may be needed to run Windows or a Windows application.

The Windows Registry or SYSTEM.INI file refers to this device, but the device file no longer exists . . .

If you still want to use the application associated with this device file, try reinstalling that application to replace the missing file.

The following files are listed as missing:

- VNETSUP.VXD
- NWLINK.VXD
- NWREDIR.VXD
- NSCL.VXD
- VREDIR.VXD
- NDIS.VXD
- NDIS2SUP.VXD
- VNETBIOS.VXD

Two additional dialog boxes appear, informing you that the following two files cannot be found:

- NWNP32.DLL
- MSNP32.DLL

After you acknowledge these error messages, Windows starts normally but without Dial-Up Networking functionality.

This problem can occur if you install Dial-Up Networking or the dial-up adapter and then cancel Setup while the Copying Files dialog box is displayed. The Dial-Up Networking files are not copied to the hard disk, although the filenames are added to the Windows Registry. When the computer is restarted, the files are requested and cannot be found.

Solution

Note If you have previously set up Dial-Up Networking and have added items such as phone numbers, TCP/IP settings, and other protocols, record the information before you remove the dial-up adapter. Do the same for network adapter properties information if a network adapter is listed under Network Properties.

Remove and then reinstall Dial-Up Networking by following these steps:

1. In Control Panel, double-click the Add/Remove Programs icon.

2. Click the Windows Setup tab, and then click Communications.

3. Click Details.

4. Clear the Dial-Up Networking check box.

Figure 7-6. *The Communications dialog box.*

5. Click Close, and then click OK.

6. When you are prompted to restart Windows, do so.

7. In Control Panel, double-click the Add/Remove Programs icon.

8. Click the Windows Setup tab, and then click Communications.

9. Click Details.

10. Select the Dial-Up Networking check box.

11. Click Close, and then click OK.

12. When you are prompted to restart Windows, do so.

If any additional protocols are needed, add the protocols by using the Network icon in Control Panel.

Note Check with your system administrator or Internet service provider to determine the required settings for Dial-Up Networking and TCP/IP. For additional information about configuring Dial-Up Networking to work with an Internet service provider, see KB article Q133219, "Connecting to the Internet Using a Service Provider."

If you cancel the Dial-Up Adapter installation while the Copying Files dialog box is displayed, the installation proceeds and returns the following message:

You must now restart your computer before the new settings will take effect. Do you want to restart your computer now?

Because the files were not copied to the hard disk, you see the error messages listed at the beginning of this article. Completing the installation of the files as just outlined solves the problem.

Note For information about similar startup problems, see KB articles Q140010, "Microsoft Plus! Setup Inadvertently Installs NetWare Client," and Q137454, "Err Msg: Cannot Find a Device File, VNETSUP.VXD."

Related KB article Q166832

Dial-Up Adapter Malfunctions

You upgrade your Windows 3.1x-based computer running the Novell NetWare VLM network client with a dial-up adapter installed, and this adapter does not work correctly.

This problem occurs because Windows 98 Setup installs a dial-up adapter if it is not already installed during an upgrade.

Solution One

Remove the dial-up adapter by following these steps:

1. Click the Start button, choose Settings, click Control Panel, and then double-click the Network icon.

2. Click Dial-Up Adapter, click Remove, and then click OK.

3. Restart your computer.

Solution Two

If you want to use the dial-up adapter and TCP/IP is not installed, you can install this protocol by following these steps:

1. Click the Start button, choose Settings, click Control Panel, and then double-click the Network icon.

2. Click Protocol, click Add, select Microsoft in the Manufacturers box, click TCP/IP, and then click OK.

3. Restart your computer.

Related KB article Q190692

Digital Signature Warning During Installation

You install Dial-Up Networking (DUN) or Virtual Private Networking (VPN) by using the Add/Remove Programs icon in Control Panel, and you receive one of the following warning messages:

Caution: Microsoft has not digitally signed the software you want to install: <device> Do you want to continue the installation?

Caution: Microsoft has not digitally signed the software you want to install: <device>

This problem occurs when you use system policies and you have enabled the Digital Signature Check policy. The warning message you receive depends on the level of security specified in the policy. When you install a program by using the Add/Remove Programs icon and the Digital Signature Check policy is enabled, SETUPX.DLL expects a full path statement to verify that drivers have been properly signed. When you install DUN or VPN by using the Add/Remove Programs icon, SETUPX.DLL receives a filename rather than the full path statement, causing the warning message to appear.

Solution

When you receive the warning message, click Yes if you have an option to continue. If you do not have that option, contact your system administrator to lower the security setting for the Digital Security Check policy.

Related KB article Q188563

DNS Settings Incorrect After Batch Windows Installation

During an automated (or batch) installation of Windows 98, Domain Name Service (DNS) settings for the TCP/IP protocol are not added to the Windows 98 configuration, even though the correct DNS settings are specified in the [MSTCP] section of the batch (.INF) file.

This problem can occur if Dial-Up Networking is selected as an optional component to be installed during the automated installation. If Dial-Up Networking is installed during an automated installation, any DNS settings specified in the batch .INF file are not saved to the Windows configuration.

Solution

A supported fix that corrects this problem is now available from Microsoft but has not been fully regression-tested and should be applied only to computers experiencing this specific problem. To solve this problem immediately, contact Microsoft Technical Support to obtain the fix. If you are not severely affected by this specific problem, Microsoft recommends that you wait for the next service pack that contains this fix.

For a complete list of Microsoft Technical Support phone numbers and information about support costs, please go to this address on the World Wide Web: *http://support.microsoft.com/support/supportnet/default.asp.*

Related KB article Q192117

Error 630 Error Message Displayed

You attempt to use Dial-Up Networking and receive the following error message:

Error 630: The computer is not receiving a response from the modem. Check that the modem is plugged in, and if necessary, turn the modem off, and then turn it back on.

This error message can occur if the modem is using a new serial port assignment because of new devices installed by Windows 98 hardware detection.

Solution One

Change the properties of the Dial-Up Networking connection to use the new modem settings:

1. Double-click My Computer, and double-click Dial-Up Networking.

2. Right-click the Dial-Up Networking connection you want to use, and then choose Properties from the shortcut menu.

3. Select the correct modem from the Connect Using drop-down list, and then click OK.

Solution Two

Programs in the STARTUP folder can also cause this error message. Temporarily disable programs in the STARTUP folder by following these steps:

1. Click the Start button, choose Programs, choose Accessories, choose System Tools, and then click System Information.

2. Choose System Configuration Utility from the Tools menu.

3. Click the Startup tab.

4. Clear the check box next to any program that might access your modem. If you are unsure whether a specific program should be disabled, clear all the check boxes except for ScanRegistry, TaskMonitor, SystemTray, and LoadPowerProfile.

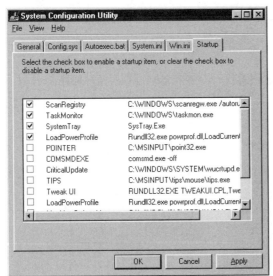

Figure 7-7. *The System Configuration Utility dialog box.*

5. Click OK, and reboot your system. If the modem works, turn back on each startup one by one, restarting and testing your modem each time, until you identify the program that is causing the problem. (Leave that one turned off, turn the rest on, and select Normal Startup on the General tab.)

Related KB article Q190554

Error 633 Error Message Displayed

You attempt to use Dial-Up Networking, and you receive the following error message:

Error 633: The modem is not installed or configured for Dial-Up Networking. To check your modem configuration, double-click the Modems icon in Control Panel.

This error message can occur if the TELEPHON.INI file is missing or damaged.

Solution

To solve this problem, follow these steps:

1. Click the Start button, choose Find, and then click Files Or Folders.

2. Enter *telephon.ini* in the Named text box, and then click Find Now.

3. If you do not find the TELEPHON.INI file, skip to step 4. If you do find the TELEPHON.INI file, right-click it, choose Rename, type *telephon.old*, and then press the Enter key.

4. Close Find, click the Start button, choose Run, type *tapiini.exe*, and then press the Enter key.

5. Restart your computer.

This program runs very quickly; nothing seems to happen. If you are not sure that the program ran, display the contents of the WINDOWS folder again to verify that the program created a new TELEPHON.INI file.

Related KB articles Q190554, Q189388, Q120221

Error 745 Error Message Displayed

You try to connect to a remote computer by using Dial-Up Networking, and you see the following error message:

Error 745: An essential file is missing.

Re-install Dial-Up Networking.

This error message can occur when a Dial-Up Networking dynamic-link library (DLL) file is missing or damaged.

Solution

Remove and reinstall Dial-Up Networking:

1. Click the Start button, choose Settings, and click Control Panel.

2. Double-click the Add/Remove Programs icon.

3. Click the Windows Setup tab, click Communications, and then click Details.

4. Clear the Dial-Up Networking check box, click OK, and then click OK again.

5. Restart your computer.

6. Open Windows Explorer.

7. If the RASAPI32.DLL file exists in the WINDOWS\SYSTEM folder, rename the file.

8. Extract a new copy of the RASAPI32.DLL file from your original Windows 98 CD-ROM or floppy disks to the WINDOWS\SYSTEM folder by using System File Checker. To start System File Checker, click the Start button, choose Run, enter *sfc.exe* in the Open box, and then click OK.

Warning Please read the Introduction for information on how to safely edit the Registry.

---

9. Click the Start button, choose Run, enter *regedit* in the Run box, and then click OK.

10. Navigate your way down through the folders in the left pane, and then delete the SMM_Files key under the following Registry key:

    `HKEY_LOCAL_MACHINE\System\CurrentControlSet\Services\RemoteAccess\Authentication`

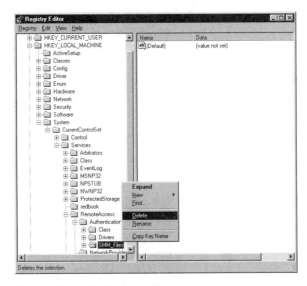

Figure 7-8. *The Registry Editor.*

11. Close Regedit.

12. Click the Start button, choose Settings, and click Control Panel. Double-click the Add/Remove Programs icon.

13. Click the Windows Setup tab, click Communications, and then click Details.

14. Select the Dial-Up Networking check box, click OK, and then click OK again.

15. When you are prompted to restart your computer, click Yes.

To determine the DLL file Dial-Up Networking uses, view the Path value under this Registry key:

```
HKEY_LOCAL_MACHINE\System\CurrentControlSet\Services\RemoteAccess\Authentication\
SMM_Files\PPP
```

The default value is RASAPI32.DLL. If Dial-Up Scripting is installed in Windows 95, this value might be SMMSCRPT.DLL.

Related KB article Q174579

Folder Doesn't Open

You try to open the DIAL-UP NETWORKING folder and it does not open. The folder appears briefly or not at all. Reinstalling Windows does not solve the problem. Missing or damaged files might cause this problem.

Solution

To solve this problem, follow these steps:

1. Restart your computer. After your computer completes the Power On Self Test (POST), press and hold down the Ctrl key until you see the Windows 98 StartUp menu, and then choose Command Prompt Only.

2. Rename the WSOCK32.DLL, WSOCK32N.DLL, RNAUI.DLL, MSVCRT20.DLL, and RASAPI32.DLL files in the WINDOWS\SYSTEM folder (if the files are there). To do this, enter the following lines at the C: prompt, and press the Enter key after each line:

```
cd \
cd windows\system
ren wsock32.dll wsock32.xxx
ren wsock32n.dll wsock32n.xxx
ren rnaui.dll rnaui.xxx
ren msvcrt20.dll msvcrt20.xxx
ren rasapi32.dll rasapi32.xxx
```

3. Reboot the computer.

4. Extract a new copy of the WSOCK32.DLL, WSOCK32N.DLL, RNAUI.DLL, MSVCRT20.DLL, and RASAPI32.DLL files from the Windows disks or CD-ROM.

Related KB article Q142806

Modem Doesn't Respond

You run Dial-Up Networking and receive the following error message:

The computer is not receiving a response from the modem. Check that the modem is plugged in, and if necessary, turn the modem off, and then turn it back on.

You run HyperTerminal or MSN (The Microsoft Network), and you get disconnected immediately after you click Connect.

This problem can occur if you have an invalid command in the Extra Settings box in the Advanced Connection Settings dialog box or if your modem is trying to connect too quickly.

Solution

To solve this problem, follow these steps:

1. In Control Panel, double-click the Modems icon.

2. Click the General tab, select your modem, and then click Properties.

3. Click the Connection tab, and then click Advanced.

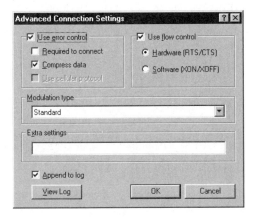

Figure 7-9. *The Advanced Connection Settings dialog box.*

4. Verify or remove the setting in the Extra Settings box.

5. Click OK or Close until you return to Control Panel.

Test to determine whether the problem is solved. If it is not, follow these steps:

1. In Control Panel, double-click the Modems icon.

2. Click the General tab, select your modem, and then click Properties.

3. Click the Connection tab, and then click Advanced.

4. Add an *&F* setting to the Extra Settings box, and then click OK or Close until you return to the desktop.

Related KB article Q151165

Modem Missing in Dial-Up Networking

You create a new Dial-Up Networking connection, and your modem is missing from the Select A Device box. Also, when you try to use an existing Dial-Up Networking connection, you see the following error message:

Dial-Up Networking

Error 633: The modem is not installed or configured for Dial-Up Networking.

To check your modem configuration, double-click the Modems icon in Control Panel.

If you test your modem by clicking More Info on the Diagnostics tab under the Modems icon in Control Panel, your modem responds normally and seems to be working correctly.

This problem can occur if the Telephony Application Programming Interface (TAPI) service provider entry in the Registry is missing or has been altered.

Solution

Use Registry Editor to view the following Registry key:

```
HKEY_LOCAL_MACHINE\Software\Microsoft\Windows\Current  Version\Telephony\Providers
```

```
Then modify the value of ProviderFilename0 to "TSP3216L.TSP", without quotations.
```

Here are the steps:

Warning Please read the Introduction for information on how to safely edit the Registry.

---

1. Click the Start button, choose Run, enter *regedit* in the Run box, and then click OK.

2. Navigate your way down through the folders in the left pane until you locate the key just described.

3. Modify the value of ProviderFilename0.

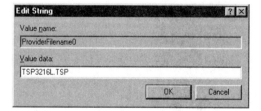

Figure 7-10. *The Edit String dialog box.*

4. Close Regedit.

5. Restart Windows.

Related KB article Q191444

Password Doesn't Save

You try to save your password by selecting the Save Password check box when you are making a Dial-Up Networking connection, and your password is not saved. This problem can occur even when you connect successfully to the server and your password has not changed. Any of the following situations can cause this problem:

- Password caching is disabled.

- One or more of the files associated with Dial-Up Networking is missing or damaged.

- Your password list (.PWL) file is damaged.

- The RNA.PWL file (if it exists) is damaged.

- Automatic logon is enabled.

Solution

Warning Please read the Introduction for information on how to safely edit the Registry.

To solve this problem, follow these steps:

1. Verify that password caching is enabled. To do so, click the Start button, choose Run, enter *regedit* in the Run box, and then click OK.

2. Navigate your way down through the folders in the left pane until you locate the DisablePwdCaching string value in the following Registry key:

   ```
   HKEY_LOCAL_MACHINE\Software\Microsoft\Windows\CurrentVersion\Policies\Network
   ```

   If password caching is disabled, the DisablePwdCaching string value has a value data of 1. To enable password caching, change the value data to 0. Close Regedit.

3. Remove Dial-Up Networking. Click the Start button, choose Settings, click Control Panel, and then double-click the Add/Remove Programs icon. Click the Windows Setup tab. Click Communications, and then click Details. Clear the Dial-Up Networking check box, click OK, and then restart your computer if you are prompted to do so.

4. Reinstall Dial-Up Networking. Click the Start button, choose Settings, click Control Panel, and then double-click the Add/Remove Programs icon. Click the Windows Setup tab. Click Communications, and then click Details. Select the Dial-Up Networking check box, click OK, and then restart your computer if you are prompted to do so.

5. Rename your .PWL file by typing the following line at a command prompt and then pressing the Enter key:

   ```
   ren c:\<windows>\<username>.pwl <username>.xxx
   ```

   where <windows> is the name of your WINDOWS folder and <username> is the user name you use to log on to Windows. After renaming your .PWL file, restart Windows.

   When the Enter Network Password or Welcome To Windows dialog box appears, type your usual password, and click OK. When you are prompted to confirm your password, type your password again in the Confirm New Password box, and click OK.

> **Note** If no .PWL files are on the drive (for example, you press the Esc key when prompted for a password as Windows starts), password caching will not be enabled. You must first log on to the network in order to create a .PWL file.

6. Rename the RNA.PWL file in the WINDOWS folder by typing the following line at a command prompt and then pressing the Enter key:

```
ren c:\<windows>\rna.pwl rna.xxx
```

where <windows> is the name of your WINDOWS folder. After renaming the RNA.PWL file, restart Windows.

> **Note** The RNA.PWL file might not exist on your computer. This file is not required in all configurations.

7. Disable automatic logon. Use Regedit to delete the AutoLogon string value from this Registry key:

```
HKEY_LOCAL_MACHINE\Software\Microsoft\Windows\CurrentVersion\Network\Real Mode
Net
```

8. Close Regedit.

9. Restart Windows.

Related KB article Q148925

Password Required to Browse Other Computer

You use Dial-Up Networking to connect from a Windows 98 computer to a Windows NT 4.0 Workstation-based computer, and you connect, but you receive the following message when you attempt to browse:

> *Enter network password. You must provide a password to make this connection. Resource:* *<computername>\ipc$*

You use Dial-Up Networking to connect from a Windows 98 computer to another Windows 98 computer, and you connect, but you receive the following message when you attempt to browse the host computer:

> *Enter network password. You must provide a password to make this connection. Resource:* *<computername>\ipc$*

You are unable to browse for any of the following reasons:

- The Windows 98 computer is not a client of a domain environment but the Log On To Windows NT Domain option is enabled.

- The user name and password you are using to log in to the Windows 98 computer are not contained in the local user accounts database of the Windows NT computer you are attempting to browse.

- The Windows 98 host is configured with user-level authentication to an NT domain.

This problem can occur when the workgroup name is entered for the domain name. When Windows 98 Dial-Up Networking initially makes the connection, it prompts you for the domain name and caches this information. The error message occurs because the Windows NT computer cannot validate you.

When you connect to a Windows NT Remote Access Service (RAS) server, you are prompted to provide a user name and password to make the RAS connection. When the connection is successful, the user name and password you used to log on to Windows 98 are used to determine whether you have permission to access the Windows NT computer you are attempting to browse. If the user name and password do not exist in the local user accounts database of the Windows NT computer, you are unable to browse or access resources on that computer.

Solution One

Disable the Log On To Windows NT Domain option on the Windows 98 client computer, by following these steps:

1. Click the Start button, choose Settings, click Control Panel, and then double-click the Network icon.

2. On the Configuration tab, click Client For Microsoft Networks, and then click Properties.

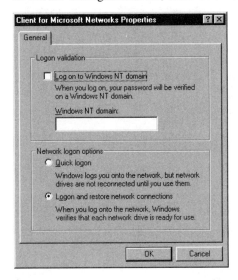

Figure 7-11. *The Client For Microsoft Networks Properties dialog box.*

3. In the Logon Validation section, clear the Log On To Windows NT Domain check box.

4. Click OK.

Solution Two

Log on to Windows 98 with a valid Windows NT user account:

1. Save and close any open work on your computer.

2. Click the Start button, and then click Log Off <username>; where <username> is the name of the user logged on to the computer.

3. Click Yes.

4. When you are prompted, log on with a user name and password contained in the local user accounts database of the Windows NT–based computer you are attempting to browse.

Solution Three

Use User Manager to set up user accounts in the local accounts database of the Windows NT–based computer you are attempting to browse. These user accounts must contain the same logon information (user name and password) that are used when a user logs on to his or her computer.

Solution Four

Disable user-level authentication on the Windows 98 host by following these steps:

1. Save and close any open work on your computer.

2. Click the Start button, choose Settings, click Control Panel, and double-click the Network icon.

3. Click the Access Control tab.

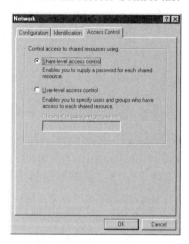

Figure 7-12.   *The Access Control tab in the Network dialog box.*

4. Click the Share-Level Access Control option button, and click OK.

5. Restart the computer as prompted.

Related KB article Q162325

Point-to-Point Tunneling Protocol Disconnects All Dial-Up Networking Connections

You disconnect a Point-to-Point Tunneling Protocol (PPTP) connection, and all current Dial-Up Networking connections are also disconnected. This problem can occur if MSN (The Microsoft Network) version 2.5, 2.51, or 2.52 is installed.

Solution

Prevent this problem from occurring by exiting from MSN Quick View before you disconnect your PPTP connection:

1. Click the MSN Quick View icon on the taskbar.

2. Choose MSN Options, and then click Close.

Related KB article Q186227

Point-to-Point Tunneling Protocol Doesn't Connect

You attempt to make a Virtual Private Networking (VPN) connection by using Point-to-Point Tunneling Protocol (PPTP), and you receive the following error message:

The Microsoft Dial-Up adapter is in use or not responding properly.

Disconnect other connections and then try again. If this problem persists, shut down and restart your computer.

You click OK, and you can connect to the Internet, but you are unable to establish a PPTP connection.

This problem can occur if Dial-Up Adapter #2 (VPN Support) is not installed in the network properties.

Solution

Remove and then reinstall Virtual Private Networking by using the Add/Remove Programs icon in Control Panel:

1. Click the Start button, choose Settings, and click Control Panel.

2. Double-click the Add/Remove Programs icon.

3. Click the Windows Setup tab.

4. Click Communications, and then click Details.

5. Clear the Virtual Private Networking check box, click OK, and then click Apply.

6. Restart Windows.

7. Click the Start button, choose Settings, and click Control Panel.

8. Double-click the Add/Remove Programs icon.

9. Click the Windows Setup tab.

10. Click Communications, and then click Details.

11. Select the Virtual Private Networking check box, click OK, and then click Apply.

12. Restart Windows.

If you remove and then reinstall Microsoft Virtual Private Networking Adapter in the network properties, Dial-Up Adapter #2 (VPN Support) is not reinstalled.

Related KB article Q188141

Protocol Error During Connection

You use Dial-Up Networking to connect to an Internet service provider. The connection is not successful, and you receive the following error message:

Dial-Up Networking could not negotiate a compatible set of protocols

When you open the PPPLOG.TXT file, you see the following line:

IPCP: No addresses negotiated

This problem occurs because the IP address has not been preset for this connection to your Internet service provider.

Solution

First, obtain an IP address from your Internet service provider. Then, set the provider's IP address on your computer:

1. Double-click My Computer on the desktop.

2. Double-click the Dial-Up Networking icon.

3. Right-click the icon for the Internet service provider you are trying to connect with.

4. Choose Properties from the shortcut menu.

5. Click the Server Type tab, and click TCP/IP Settings.

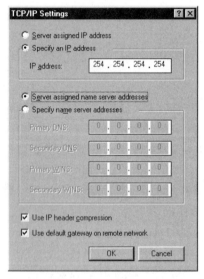

Figure 7-13. *The TCP/IP Settings dialog box.*

6. Type the new IP address in the space provided, and click OK.

Related KB article Q134588

RAS Server Connection Fails

You use Dial-Up Networking to dial in to a Point-to-Point Protocol (PPP) or Remote Access Service (RAS) server that uses callback security, and the connection fails.

This problem occurs because Windows 98 is not configured for call-back security. (It's a Windows NT function.)

Solution

Adjust your modem settings to support the Callback CP (control protocol) for processing server callback security:

1. Click the Start button, choose Settings, and click Control Panel.

2. Double-click the Modems icon, and select the modem you are using.

3. Click Properties, click the Connection tab, and then click Advanced.

4. Enter *AT S0=1* in the Extra Settings text box, and click OK.

Related KB article Q137941

Virtual Private Network Adapter Removal Doesn't Remove Dial-Up Adapter

You remove the Virtual Private Network (VPN) adapter in the Add/Remove Programs icon in Control Panel, and the Dial-Up Adapter is not removed. This behavior is by design.

Solution One

Uninstall Dial-Up Networking by following these steps:

1. Click the Start button, choose Settings, click Control Panel, double-click the Add/Remove Programs icon, and then click the Windows Setup tab.

2. Click Communications (the word *Communications,* not the check box), click Details, and then clear the Dial-Up Networking check box.

3. Click OK, click OK again, and then click Yes when you are prompted to restart your computer.

Solution Two

Remove the dial-up adapter:

1. Click the Start button, choose Settings, click Control Panel, double-click Network, and then click the Configuration tab.

2. Click Remove, and then click Yes when you are prompted to restart your computer.

Related KB article Q186243

Winsock Program Doesn't Automatically Connect

Winsock-based programs do not automatically start a Dial-Up Networking connection. This problem can occur if the Autodial settings in the Registry are missing or damaged or have been replaced by third-party values.

Solution

Modify the following Registry settings to reflect the values shown:

`HKEY_LOCAL_MACHINE\System\CurrentControlSet\Services\Winsock\Autodial`

Modify AutodialDllName32 to the value *wininet.dll*, and modify AutodialFcnName32 to a value of *InternetAutodialCallback.*

`HKEY_LOCAL_MACHINE\System\CurrentControlSet\Services\Winsock\Parameters`

Delete the MSTCP Value data (so the data box is blank).

Here are the steps:

Warning Please read the Introduction for information on how to safely edit the Registry.

---

1. Click the Start button, choose Run, enter *regedit* in the Run box, and then click OK.

2. Navigate your way down through the folders in the left pane until you locate the keys just described.

3. Right-click the value name, choose Modify, and enter the new data values.

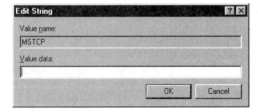

Figure 7-14. *The Edit String dialog box.*

4. Close Regedit.

5. Restart Windows.

Note These settings affect all programs, including third-party programs, that use the Winsock automatic dialing function.

Related KB article Q190921

Workgroup Name Change Isn't Detected

You change the workgroup name on the Identification tab in the network properties and try to use a previously created Dial-Up Networking connection, and you are not authenticated correctly. Instead, you are prompted to enter your name, domain, and password.

This problem occurs when you dial in to a Windows NT server that uses Microsoft Challenge-Handshake Authentication Protocol (MSCHAP) for authentication. Dial-Up Networking caches workgroup information separately for each connection. If your computer is not set to log on to a domain, Dial-Up Networking sends the workgroup name to the Dial-Up server as the domain name. This protocol is by design.

Solution

Enter the correct information when you are prompted for your name, domain, and password. This action updates the cache for future connections. You must do this for each connection that was created before you changed the workgroup name.

Related KB article Q129811

Faxing

Dial-Up Networking Server Intercepts Fax Transmission

Because Dial-Up Networking Server answers incoming calls on the first ring, other fax and communications programs are unable to answer incoming calls when Dial-Up Networking Server is installed and configured to allow caller access.

Solution

Allow other fax or communications programs to answer incoming calls by following these steps:

1. Click the Start button, choose Programs, choose Accessories, choose Communications, and then click Dial-Up Networking.

2. Choose Dial-Up Server from the Connections menu.

3. If only one modem is installed, skip to step 4. If more than one modem is installed, click the tab that corresponds to the modem being used with Dial-Up Networking Server.

4. Click the No Caller Access option button, and then click OK.

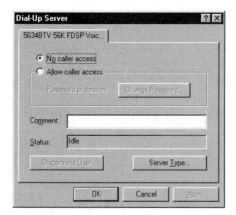

Figure 7-15.   *The Dial-Up Server dialog box.*

Note For information about other problems with Microsoft Fax and other communications programs that can be configured to answer incoming calls automatically when you use Dial-Up Networking Server, see KB article Q137641, "Microsoft Fax Modem Answers but Cannot Establish Link."

Related KB article Q153102

Document Doesn't Arrive in Your Exchange Inbox

Although Windows successfully receives an incoming fax, the fax is not delivered to your Exchange Inbox. This problem can occur for the following reasons:

- The fax message was larger than 1 MB.

- Transmission errors occurred during reception of the fax.

- Line noise occurred in a high-speed transmission.

Solution

Make sure that the fax was received, and then check the WINDOWS\SPOOL\FAX folder for a file named RCV<nnnnn>.MG3 or RCV<nnnnn>.EFX. If this file exists, you can force delivery to your Inbox. To do so, follow these steps:

1. Close Exchange.

2. Note the names of the .MG3 or .EFX files in the WINDOWS\SPOOL\FAX folder. These files represent received faxes that were not delivered to your Inbox.

3. Back up the files you found in step 2 by copying them to another folder.

4. Use Registry Editor to modify the following Registry key:

```
HKEY_LOCAL_MACHINE\Software\Microsoft\At Work Fax\Local Modems\Received
```

This key can have several string values in the form R<nn> and F<nn>, where <nn> is a two-digit decimal number. These entries must be numbered consecutively, starting with 00. The F<nn> entry holds the fax filename string value (for example, RCV<nnnnn>.MG3 or RCV<nnnnn>.EFX). The R<nn> entry contains the result code for the fax transmission. Because a value of 001 indicates that the fax was successfully received, this value should always be set to 001. The following example represents entries for two files:

```
F00=RCV3edd0.MG3

R00=001

F01=RCV4bd10.EFX

R01=001
```

Warning Please read the Introduction for information on how to safely edit the Registry.

5. Click the Start button, choose Run, enter *regedit* in the Run box, and then click OK.

6. Navigate your way down through the folders in the left pane until you locate the RECEIVED folder. Add a new Registry value for F<nn> with a string value equal to the fax filename. Make sure to create a new Registry value for the corresponding R<nn> entry with a value of 001.

7. Repeat step 6 for each of the fax files.

8. Start Exchange again. The fax messages should now appear in your Inbox.

Related KB article Q136897

Fax Transmission Isn't Received

You attempt to use Microsoft Phone version 1.0 to receive incoming faxes using Microsoft Fax, you see an *initializing modem* message, and then nothing happens. This problem can occur if you are using a Sound III 336SP modem on a Packard Bell computer.

Solution

Install the original OEM drivers for your modem. To obtain them, contact Packard Bell or visit the Packard Bell web site, at *http://www.packardbell.com.*

Note By default, Microsoft Fax is not installed in Windows 98. However, it is available in the following folder on the Windows 98 CD-ROM: <drive>:\TOOLS\OLDWIN95\MESSAGE\US, where <drive> is the drive letter of your CD-ROM drive.

Related KB article Q186239

Incoming Fax Appears Garbled

You receive a fax in Exchange, the fax seems to be garbled, and when you open the fax in Fax Viewer, the output looks like a bar code or appears to contain empty pages. This problem can occur because some Class 2 fax modems reverse the bit order of incoming faxes.

Solution

Reverse the bit order for incoming faxes by following these steps:

> **Warning** Please read the Introduction for information on how to safely edit the Registry.

1. Exit and log off Exchange.

2. Click the Start button, choose Run, enter *regedit* in the Run box, and then click OK.

3. Navigate your way down through the folders in the left pane until you locate the Registry key:

   `Hkey_Local_Machine\Software\Microsoft\At Work Fax\Local Modems\TAPI0001<xxxx>`

   where <xxxx> is a unique TAPI identifier for the fax modem.

4. Using Registry Editor, add the string value CL2SWBOR to the Registry key.

5. Set the string value for CL2SWBOR to 1.

6. Close Regedit.

7. Restart Windows.

Related KB article Q148877

Modem Answers but Doesn't Establish a Connection

You use Microsoft Fax to receive a fax and the modem answers but does not negotiate a successful link.

This problem occurs because another program that answers the phone first or Microsoft Fax is not set to answer the phone.

Solution

Disable the Auto Answer mode in the program that is answering the phone. Or set the program to answer the phone after a greater number of rings, and set Microsoft Fax to answer the phone.

Related KB article Q137641

ScanDisk Disables Automatic Incoming Fax Reception

You use the Microsoft Fax information service with Exchange to automatically receive faxes, and faxes are not received automatically if ScanDisk is performing a surface scan and is the active program. This problem does not occur if the desktop is the active program.

Solution

Do not perform a surface scan when you want faxes to be received automatically. Microsoft does not recommend running other programs while performing a surface scan with ScanDisk.

Note Exchange and the Microsoft Fax information service are not included with Windows 98. No faxing service is included with Windows 98. Exchange and the Microsoft Fax information service are included with Windows 95. If you upgrade from Windows 95 to Windows 98, you can continue to use Exchange and the Microsoft Fax information service if they are already installed when you upgrade.

Related KB article Q178998

General Modem Issues

Compaq Computer Doesn't Detect Modem

After you install Windows 98 on a Compaq computer that contains an internal 33.6 or 56 kilobits per second (Kbps) modem, your modem is not listed under the Modems icon in Control Panel. Running the Add New Hardware Wizard does not detect the modem. This problem can occur if you installed Windows 98 (either the upgrade or the full version) in a folder other than the existing WINDOWS folder.

Solution One

Contact Compaq Computer Corporation.

Solution Two

To work around this problem, install the Compaq modem drivers from the DRIVERS\ MODEM\COMPAQ folder on the Windows 98 CD-ROM. Follow these steps:

1. Click the Start button, choose Settings, and then click Control Panel.

2. Double-click the Add New Hardware icon to start the Add New Hardware Wizard.

3. Click Next, click Next again, and then click Next again.

4. Click Search For The Best Driver For Your Device (Recommended), and then click Next.

5. Select the Specify A Location check box, and clear all other check boxes.

6. Click Browse, navigate to the DRIVERS\MODEM\COMPAQ folder on the Windows 98 CD-ROM, and then click OK.

7. Click Next, and then click Finish.

8. After the modem is installed, restart your computer.

You might see additional dialog boxes if your modem includes other telephony capabilities (such as speaker phone, caller ID, and telephone answering). In that case, follow the instructions on your screen. If you are prompted for additional files, make sure that Windows 98 is searching for files in the DRIVERS\MODEM\COMPAQ folder on the Windows 98 CD-ROM.

This problem is known to occur with the Presario series 1000, 2000, 3000, 4000, and 6000 and with the Armada 1500.

You cannot install the modem drivers from the Compaq Presario recovery CD-ROM without first formatting your hard disk and installing Windows 98 or installing Windows 98 on a new hard disk.

For additional information about Windows 98 drivers for Compaq modems, see the README.TXT file in the DRIVERS\MODEM\COMPAQ folder on the Windows 98 CD-ROM.

Related KB article   Q193896

Connection Disconnects When 20 Digits Are Dialed

You dial an international or a credit card call through a PBX phone system, and the connection is lost when you have dialed 20 digits.

This problem occurs because most PBX telephone systems have a 20-digit dialing limit. If you dial more than 20 digits, the call is terminated.

Solution

Contact your PBX administrator, and inquire about changing the 20-digit dialing limit.

Related KB article   Q136103

Could Not Open Port Error Message

You try to use your modem and receive the *Could not open port* error message.

This error message is typically the result of a resource conflict or a program loading from the STARTUP folder that opens a communication port.

Solution

Use the troubleshooting steps in the following article "Modem Doesn't Dial Out" to resolve this error message if it is caused by a resource conflict. Try the following technique first, though.

To temporarily disable programs in the STARTUP folder, follow these steps:

1. Click the Start button, choose Programs, choose Accessories, choose System Tools, and then click System Information.

2. Choose System Configuration Utility from the Tools menu.

3. Click the Startup tab.

4. Clear the check box next to any program that might access your modem. If you are unsure whether a specific program should be disabled, clear all the check boxes except for ScanRegistry, TaskMonitor, SystemTray, and LoadPowerProfile.

Figure 7-16. *The Startup tab in the System Configuration Utility.*

5. Click OK, and reboot your system. If the modem works, turn back on each startup one by one, re-starting and testing your modem each time, until you identify the program causing the problem. (Leave that one turned off, turn the rest back on, and select Normal Startup on the General tab.)

Related KB article Q190554

High-Speed Modems Detected at Lower Speed

High-speed modems (faster than 28.8 Kbps) are detected as 28.8-Kbps modems if Windows does not contain any hardware information about newer, faster modems.

Solution

Consult the manufacturer's documentation regarding the Windows installation instructions. The manufacturer might provide a disk with your 33.6-Kbps or higher-speed modem; this disk should contain the necessary .INF file for a successful installation. If no disk is provided, contact your hardware manufacturer.

Related KB article Q165886

Install New Modem Icon Does Not Detect Modem Correctly

You use the Install New Modem Wizard, and Windows does not detect the exact manufacturer, make, and model of your modem. This problem occurs even though your modem is listed in the Manufacturers box in the Install New Modem Wizard and under the Modems icon in Control Panel.

This problem can occur if your modem uses a driver that is compatible with a variety of modems rather than a unique driver.

Solution

Use the driver provided by the modem manufacturer if the driver is Windows 98 compatible. For information about how to install the driver, refer to the documentation included with your modem or contact the manufacturer. If your modem is listed in the Manufacturers box under the Modems icon, you can manually install the modem rather than attempt to detect it. Windows 98 automatically identifies, configures, and installs Plug and Play devices, including internal and PC card modems.

Related KB article Q187630

Logon History Isn't Found

You try to verify a modem logon or view modem logon history, but no file is created to save this information.

This problem occurs when the MODEMLOG.TXT file is not created.

Solution

Create the MODEMLOG.TXT file by following these steps:

1. Click the Start button, choose Settings, and click Control Panel.

2. Double-click the Modems icon.

3. Choose the modem for which you want to create a log file, and click Properties.

4. Click the Connection tab, and click Advanced.

5. Select the Append To Log check box, and click OK.

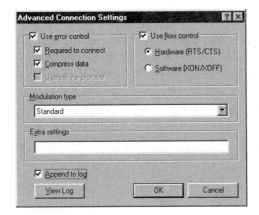

Figure 7-17. *The Advanced Connection Settings dialog box.*

6. Click OK, and close the program.

Note Programs that are not TAPI-enabled do not log information in the MODEMLOG.TXT file.

Related KB article Q142730

Modem Doesn't Dial Out

You are unable to dial out using your modem in Windows 98.

Solution One

If Windows 98 detected your modem, verify that the installed driver is the correct driver for your modem. To do so, click the Start button, choose Settings, and click Control Panel. Double-click the Modems icon, and then verify that the modem listed on the General tab is the correct modem.

If no modem is listed or if the modem is listed incorrectly, update the modem driver by following these steps:

1. Click the Start button, choose Settings, and click Control Panel.

2. Double-click the System icon, and then click the Device Manager tab.

3. Double-click the Modem branch to expand it, if it exists. If the Modem branch does not exist, look for an Other Devices branch, and then double-click the branch to expand it.

4. Double-click your modem (or other device), click the Driver tab, and then click Update Driver.

5. Use the Update Device Driver Wizard to search for the best driver, or manually select your driver from a list. Drivers for some additional modems are included in the DRIVERS\MODEM folder on the Windows 98 CD-ROM.

If your modem still does not work properly, see the following solutions.

Solution Two

If you have a 3Com USRobotics WinModem (check the documentation included with your modem or computer), Windows 98 did not detect it, and the WinModem drivers were previously installed and removed, follow these steps to remove any remaining Registry entries:

1. Insert your Windows 98 CD-ROM, and then double-click the WMREGDEL.EXE program in the DRIVERS\MODEM\3COM-USR\WINMODEM folder on the Windows 98 CD-ROM. This step clears all WinModem-related Registry entries.

2. Restart your computer, and then click the Start button, choose Settings, and click Control Panel.

3. Double-click the Modems icon, and then click Add to use the Install New Modem Wizard to detect your modem and install its drivers. Additional drivers for your WinModem might exist in the DRIVERS\MODEM folder on the Windows 98 CD-ROM, or you can download updated versions from your manufacturer.

If Windows 98 still does not detect your WinModem, the WMREGDEL.EXE program might not have removed all the necessary Registry entries. Contact 3Com USRobotics to inquire about the availability of a solution for this problem. Alternatively, something might be physically wrong with the WinModem, or a resource conflict might exist. Contact 3Com USRobotics for the procedure to test your hardware, or see Solution Four for information about resolving a hardware conflict.

For more information about the WinModem and how to troubleshoot it, obtain the USRobotics WinModem FAQ from the 3Com USRobotics web site.

Solution Three

If you have a standard modem (not a WinModem) and you cannot dial out, follow these steps to test a direct communication to the COM port:

1. Click the Start button, choose Programs, and click MS-DOS Prompt.

2. Type the following command at the command prompt: *echo ATM1L3X0DT12345 > COM2* if COM2 is the serial port number to which the modem is connected. The modem should dial the touch-tone digits *12345*.

3. To hang up the modem, type *echo ATH0 > COM2* if COM2 is the serial port to which your modem is connected.

4. Restart your computer in MS-DOS mode by clicking the Start button, clicking Shutdown, and then clicking the Restart In MS-DOS Mode option button and clicking OK. Repeat steps 2 and 3, and type *exit* when you're finished.

If the modem does not respond with a dial tone or communication signal in MS-DOS mode, something might be physically wrong with either the modem or the COM port. To determine whether this is the case, contact your modem manufacturer or computer manufacturer to verify the functionality of your hardware.

If the modem does not respond with a dial tone or communication signal in Windows 98 but does respond in MS-DOS mode, Windows 98 might not be communicating correctly with your COM port. Follow these steps to detect or fix your COM port:

1. Click the Start button, choose Settings, and click Control Panel.

2. Double-click the Add New Hardware icon, and then follow the instructions onscreen to detect your COM port.

3. After running the Add New Hardware Wizard, click the Start button, choose Settings, and click Control Panel.

4. Double-click the System icon, and then click the Device Manager tab.

5. Double-click the Ports branch, and verify that the port your modem is connected to is listed and has no errors. If the port has a resource conflict (double-click Port, click the Resources tab, and then check for conflicts), see Solution Four for information about resolving hardware conflicts.

6. If the port has driver errors or your modem still doesn't work properly (double-check to make sure that your modem is connected to the correct port and has the proper drivers installed), use System File Checker to verify the integrity of the SERIAL.VXD, VCOMM.VXD, and SERIALUI.DLL serial port drivers.

Solution Four

If your modem is set to use the same resources as another device in your computer, a resource conflict exists, and either one or both of the devices will not work. Standard modems use an input/output (I/O) address and interrupt request (IRQ). In addition, the WinModem frequently uses a direct memory access (DMA) setting.

Use Device Manager to determine whether a resource conflict exists:

1. Click the Start button, choose Settings, and click Control Panel.

2. Double-click the System icon, and then click the Device Manager tab.

If a resource conflict prevents one device from working, an exclamation point in a yellow circle is normally displayed for the device. In some cases, however, a WinModem that conflicts with another device might not have an exclamation point in a yellow circle. In that case, *you* must determine whether a conflict exists.

To view the resource settings your modem uses, follow these steps:

1. On the Device Manager tab, double-click the Modem branch to expand it.

2. Double-click your modem, and then click the Resources tab.

Note If the Resources tab does not exist, Windows 98 cannot configure your modem's resources. To determine the resources your modem is using, consult the documentation included with your modem.

3. Note the resource settings your modem uses, and then click OK.

4. Double-click Computer to view all the resource settings in use on your computer, listed by resource. Click each resource setting to determine whether another device is using any of the same settings your modem is using. Note that you can disregard hardware labeled IRQ Holder For PCI Steering; even though this entry shares an IRQ with one other piece of hardware, it does not cause a conflict.

If another device is using any of the same settings as your modem, you have to change the setting for that device or your modem. If the device is a Plug and Play device, you might be able to do this on the Resources tab in Device Manager, although some devices might require you to change jumper pins or dip switches on the device. To determine the best way to change resource settings for the device, consult the documentation included with either the device or your computer.

Solution Five

If your modem passes a diagnostics test, the problem is usually with the specific program or component you are trying to use and not with your modem or the modem driver. To verify whether the modem passes a diagnostics test, follow these steps:

1. Click the Start button, choose Settings, and then click Control Panel.

2. Double-click the Modems icon, and then verify that your modem is listed on the General tab. If your modem is not listed, the driver is not installed properly or at all, and your modem cannot be tested. If this is the case, follow the steps in Solution One to install the modem driver.

3. Click Diagnostics, click the COM port to which your modem is attached, and then click More Info.

If the More Info dialog box appears without an error message and displays a series of *AT* commands and responses, the modem has passed a diagnostics test. Double-check the program you are having trouble with to see whether you have the modem properly set up within your program.

If your modem passes a diagnostics test but is not available in HyperTerminal, Dial-Up Networking, or Phone Dialer, the problem might be with TAPI, or the TELEPHON.INI file might be missing or damaged. To solve this problem, please see "Error 633 Error Message Displayed." (Also see Solution Six.)

Solution Six

If the modem passes a diagnostics test and works with some programs but not with others, the problem is probably specific to the program.

If the modem works with HyperTerminal, Dial-Up Networking, and Phone Dialer but not with another third-party 32-bit communications program, the problem is with the third-party program. For information about how to solve the problem, contact the program's manufacturer.

Sixteen-bit programs access the COM port directly. To test whether direct communication with the COM port exists, follow these steps:

1. Click the Start button, choose Programs, choose Accessories, choose Communications, and then click HyperTerminal. If HyperTerminal is not installed, install it by using the Windows Setup tab under the Add/Remove Programs icon in Control Panel.

2. Double-click Hypertrm, enter *test* in the Name text box, and then click OK.

3. Select Direct To Com2 (if your modem is set up on COM2) from the Connect Using drop-down list, and then click OK.

4. Select 9600 from the Bits Per Second drop-down list, and then click OK. You should see a *Connected h:mm:ss* message on the status bar (in the bottom-left corner of the HyperTerminal window).

5. Type *at*, and then press the Enter key. *OK* should be displayed.

If *OK* is displayed, HyperTerminal is accessing the COM port directly, in the same manner as a 16-bit program. If your 16-bit program still cannot communicate with the modem on that COM port, contact the program's manufacturer.

Related KB articles Q190363, Q129605, Q84279, Q188601, Q189388, Q12022, Q120221, Q174579, Q188125, Q190554

Modifications Cause Problems

You modify your modem's properties and experience one of the following problems:

- The Configure option is unavailable in HyperTerminal or Dial-Up Networking.

- After you double-click the Modems icon in Control Panel and then click Properties on the General tab of the Modems Properties dialog box, you receive the following error message:

   The modem properties cannot be displayed because the modem information is corrupt.

- Removing and reinstalling the modem does not correct the problem.

These problems can occur if the MODEMUI.DLL file is damaged.

Solution

Repair the damaged file by following these steps:

1. In Windows Explorer or My Computer, rename the MODEMUI.DLL file in the WINDOWS\ SYSTEM folder to *modemui.xxx*.

2. Extract a new copy of the MODEMUI.DLL file to your WINDOWS\SYSTEM folder. The MODEMUI.DLL file is in the WIN98_55.CAB file on the Windows 98 CD-ROM.

Note For information about using Extract, type *extract* at a command prompt, or see KB article Q129605, "How to Extract Original Compressed Windows Files."

3. Restart Windows.

These problems can also occur if an incorrect version of the UMDM16.DLL file is installed in the WINDOWS\SYSTEM folder. To install the correct version, rename the UMDM16.DLL file, and then extract a new copy of the file from your original Windows disks or CD-ROM.

Related KB article Q148781

NDISWAN TAPI or Unimodem Driver Doesn't Change

You try to add or remove a Telephony driver and receive the following error message:

The telephony system cannot perform that function at this time.

Please try again later.

This message can occur if you try to add or remove one of the following Telephony drivers by using the Telephony icon in Control Panel:

- NDISWAN TAPI service provider
- Unimodem service provider

This behavior is by design.

Solution

You cannot remove these drivers or their associated functionality from your computer.

Related KB article Q191468

No Dial-Tone Error Reported When Using Calling Card

You use a Telephony API (TAPI) program such as Dial-Up Networking, Phone Dialer, or HyperTerminal, and you see the following error message:

There is no dial-tone. Make sure your modem is connected to the phone line.

This error message occurs when you are trying to dial by using a calling card and you have enabled the Wait For Dial Tone Before Dialing option.

Solution

To solve this problem, follow these steps:

1. Click the Start button, choose Settings, and click Control Panel.

2. Double-click the Modems icon, and select the modem you are using.

3. Click Properties, and click the Connection tab.

4. Clear the Wait For Dial Tone Before Dialing check box.

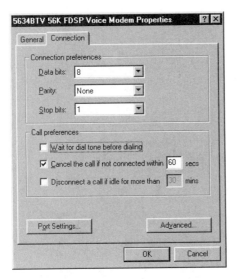

Figure 7-18. *The Connection tab in the Modem Properties dialog box.*

5. Click OK, and then click OK again.

Related KB article Q140260

WinModem Not Found

You upgrade to Windows 98, double-click the WinModem icon in Control Panel, and receive the following error message:

> *Error: There is no WinModem found in your computer, but some corrupted files were found and they have been cleaned.*

When you view your modem in Device Manager, you notice multiple WinModem entries.

This problem occurs when your WinModem is not using the most current .INF file or device driver.

Solution

Uninstall the WinModem drivers, remove the multiple WinModem entries in Device Manager, and then reinstall the most current WinModem drivers. To do so, follow these steps:

1. Uninstall the WinModem drivers. To do so, click the Start button, choose Settings, click Control Panel, double-click the WinModem icon, and then click Uninstall.

Note Test to determine whether the uninstall process was successful. To do so, see whether the WinModem icon is still in Control Panel. If the WinModem icon is gone, the uninstall process was successful, and you should continue to step 2. If the WinModem icon is still visible, the uninstall process was not successful, and you should contact USRobotics for additional assistance.

2. Remove the WinModem entries in Device Manager by continuing to steps 3 and 4.

3. Right-click My Computer, click Properties, and then click the Device Manager tab.

4. Double-click the Modem branch to expand it, click a WinModem entry, and then click Remove. Continue this process until all WinModem entries are removed, and then click OK.

Note If no Modem branch is in Device Manager, continue to step 5.

5. Reinstall the most current WinModem drivers. For information about how to do so, contact USRobotics, or view the documentation included with your WinModem.

Related KB article Q188601

Specific Problems

AT&T Globalyst Does Not Detect TPC Modems

Windows 98 does not detect TPC modems properly in certain AT&T Globalyst computers.

All AT&T Globalyst computers with model numbers in the *3348-23xx-xxxx* series require updated drivers to operate correctly with Windows 98.

Solution

Contact AT&T Technical Support for updated drivers for the TPC modem.

Related KB article Q146202

Cordes Comspeed Displays Error Message

You upgrade to Windows 98 or you install Cordes Comspeed version 2.14, and you receive a *fatal exception* error message on a blue screen. This message is repeated when you restart your computer. Windows 98 is not compatible with the type of .VXD file this program uses.

Solution One

Upgrade to Cordes Comspeed version 2.15 or later.

Solution Two

To work around this problem, follow these steps:

1. Restart your computer. After your computer completes the Power On Self Test (POST), press and hold down the Ctrl key until you see the Windows 98 StartUp menu, and then choose Safe Mode Command Prompt Only.

2. Enter the following lines, and press the Enter key after each line:

```
cd windows\system\iosubsys

ren comspeed.vxd comspeed.old
```

3. Restart your computer.

4. Click the Start button, choose Programs, click Startup, right-click Comspeed, and then choose Delete.

Related KB article Q186203

Hayes Accura 56K+FAX Modem Detected As Rockwell 333 DPF Modem

Windows 98 Setup detects your Hayes Accura 56K+FAX external modem as a Rockwell 333 DPF external PnP modem.

This problem occurs because the Hayes Accura 56K+FAX external modem contains an alternate identification string identifying it as a Rockwell 333 DPF External PnP modem. Because Windows 98 does not include a setup information file (.INF) for a Hayes Accura 56K+FAX external modem, the alternate identification string is used. This behavior is by design.

Solution

Contact Hayes Microcomputer Products to inquire about the availability of an updated .INF file. After you obtain the file, follow these steps to install your Hayes Accura 56K+FAX External modem:

1. Click the Start button, choose Settings, and then click Control Panel.

2. Double-click the System icon.

3. Click the Device Manager tab.

4. Double-click the Modem branch, click Rockwell 333 DPF External PnP, and then click Properties.

5. On the Driver tab, click Update Driver, click Next, click Search For A Better Driver Than The One Your Device Is Using Now, and then click Next.

6. In the Specify A Location box, enter the full path to the .INF file.

7. Click Next, and then click Finish.

Related KB article Q189123

Intel DSVD Modem Not Detected on Sony Computer

If you have a Sony PCV70, PCV90, PCV100, or PCV120 computer, the Intel DSVD modem included with your computer is not detected by Windows 98. This problem happens because the Intel DSVD modem uses two communications (COM) ports. If both COM1 and COM2 ports are already enabled, the Intel DSVD modem is configured for COM3 and COM5. This results in Windows 98 being unable to detect the modem.

Solution

Disable the COM1 or COM2 port on your computer. For information about how to do so, contact Sony Technical Support.

If you are required to reinstall the Intel DSVD device drivers, you must use your Sony Recovery CD-ROM because the modem drivers are not available anywhere else. The Sony web site contains only updates to device drivers, not complete device drivers. If you do not have the Sony Recovery CD-ROM, you can request one from Sony by calling 1-888-476-6972.

Related KB article   Q191665

Racal Modem Doesn't Respond

You use the Install New Modem Wizard and allow it to attempt to detect your modem, and your Racal modem stops responding.

Solution

Rather than try to detect your modem in the Install New Modem Wizard, select the Don't Detect My Modem check box, click Next, and then select one of the standard modem types from the list. If you already ran detection, turn your modem off and then back on again, run the Install New Modem Wizard, select the Don't Detect My Modem check box, click Next, and then select your modem from the list.

Related KB article   Q191480 or HARDWARE.TXT in your WINDOWS folder

Sierra 33600 Modem Detected As Sierra 28800 Modem

You install a Sierra 33600 Plug and Play SQ3465 modem, and Windows 98 detects and installs a Sierra 28800 Plug and Play SQ3465 modem.

The newer Sierra 33600 modem uses the same Plug and Play identifier as the older Sierra 28800 modem.

Solution

No change is necessary. The modem should function correctly.

Related KB article   Q192195

Sound 4 WinModem Causes Error Messages

After you install Windows 98 on an NEC or Packard Bell computer that includes a Sound 4 WinModem, you experience one or more of the following symptoms:

- The modem does not appear in Device Manager.

- You run the diagnostics utility by using the Modems icon, and you receive the error message *Port already open.*

- Dial-Up Networking programs cannot gain access to the modem.

- You start Windows and receive the following error message:

  Cannot find a device file that may be needed to run Windows or a Windows application.

The Windows Registry or SYSTEM.INI file refers to this device file, but the device file no longer exists.

If you deleted this file on purpose, try uninstalling the associated application using its uninstall program or setup program.

If you still want to use the application associated with this device file, try reinstalling that application to replace the missing file, TURBOVBF.VXD.

Solution

Contact your computer's manufacturer.

Related KB article Q192798

Speed Decreases and Modem Randomly Disconnects

You connect to your Internet service provider by using a USRobotics 56K WinModem, and you experience either of the following symptoms at connection speeds higher than 33.6 kilobits per second (Kbps) if line noise exists or a resource conflict exists between the WinModem and another device in your computer:

- The modem randomly disconnects from your ISP.

- You download files, and the connection speed decreases and does not resume its original speed during the session.

Solution One

If line noise is preventing consistent connections to your ISP, follow these steps:

1. Click the Start button, choose Settings, and then click Control Panel.

2. Double-click the Modems icon.

3. Click the General tab, click your modem, and then click Properties.

4. Click the Connection tab, and then click Advanced.

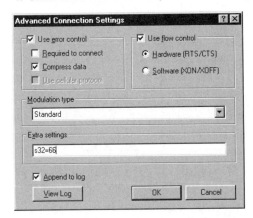

Figure 7-19. *The Advanced Connection Settings dialog box.*

5. In the Extra Settings box, enter one of the following modem initialization strings:

    s32=66

    s32=34

Note The s32=66 initialization string disables support for the V.90 standard, and the s32=34 initialization string disables support for the X2 standard. For additional information about the V.90 standard, see KB article Q192326, "Information About V.90 Modem Connectivity."

6. Click OK, click OK again, and then click Close.

7. If the problem is not solved, repeat steps 1 through 6, using the other modem initialization string in step 5.

Solution Two

For information about troubleshooting resource conflicts between modems and other hardware devices, see KB article Q190554, "Troubleshooting Modem Problems in Windows 98."

Related KB article Q193962

Speed Slows After Upgrading Windows

You are running Windows, and it reports that it is communicating at a slower speed than your previous version of Windows reported.

This problem occurs when new versions of Windows report the actual speed at which the information is being transmitted over the modem line, whereas older versions of Windows report the speed at which the computer is communicating with its modem. Although you cannot adjust the speed at which your modem communicates over the line, you can change the speed your communications program reports.

Solution

To solve this problem, follow these steps:

1. Click the Start button, choose Settings, and click Control Panel.

2. Double-click the Modems icon.

3. Select the modem you are using, and click Properties.

4. Click the Connection tab, and click Advanced.

5. Enter *S95=0* in the Extra Settings text box, and click OK.

6. Click OK, and then click Close.

Related KB article Q139952

Sportster 28.8 Modem Loses Connection Speed

You use a 3Com USRobotics Sportster 28.8 modem in Windows, and it begins to lose characters per second or bits per second after extended use.

USRobotics has confirmed that Sportster 28.8 modems with a firmware revision earlier than 4/18/95 experience this problem.

Solution

Obtain from 3Com USRobotics a firmware revision dated 4/18/95 or later. You can order the revision by calling (847) 982-5151. Have the UPC bar code and serial number of the modem available.

Related KB article Q131613

USRobotics WinModem Isn't Detected

Your USRobotics WinModem is not detected when Windows 98 starts up and is not listed in Device Manager (on the Modem branch or Other Devices branch). This problem occurs even if the modem was working properly in Windows 95.

Solution

Use the WMREGDEL.EXE program on the Windows 98 CD-ROM to clear all WinModem-related Registry entries, and then restart your computer. Follow these steps to use WMREGDEL.EXE:

1. Insert your Windows 98 CD-ROM, and then double-click the WMREGDEL.EXE program located in the DRIVERS\MODEM\3COM-USR\WINMODEM folder on the Windows 98 CD-ROM. This step clears all WinModem-related Registry entries.

2. Restart your computer, and then click the Start button, choose Settings, and click Control Panel.

3. Double-click the Modems icon, and then click Add to use the Install New Modem Wizard to detect your modem and install its drivers. Additional drivers for your WinModem might be in the DRIVERS\MODEM folder on the Windows 98 CD-ROM, or you can download updated versions from your manufacturer.

If Windows 98 still does not detect your WinModem, the WMREGDEL.EXE program might not have removed all the necessary Registry entries. Contact 3Com USRobotics to ask about the availability of a solution for this problem. Alternatively, something might be physically wrong with the WinModem, or a resource conflict might exist. Contact 3Com USRobotics for the procedure to test your hardware.

Related KB article Q190554

USRobotics WinModem Repeatedly Prompts Restarts During Uninstall

After you uninstall a USRobotics WinModem by using Device Manager or the Modems icon in Control Panel and then restart your computer, Windows tries to install the modem and prompts you to restart your computer. After you do so, Windows prompts you to restart your computer again, and this behavior continues indefinitely.

Solution

Use the WinModem utility to uninstall your WinModem rather than use Device Manager or the Modems icon. Follow these steps:

1. Restart your computer. After your computer completes the Power On Self Test (POST), press and hold down the Ctrl key until you see the Windows 98 StartUp menu, and then choose Safe Mode.

2. Click the Start button, choose Settings, and then click Control Panel.

3. Use the WinModem utility to uninstall your WinModem. For information about how to do so, see the documentation included with your WinModem.

4. Restart your computer normally, and if you are prompted to install your WinModem again, use the software included with your modem to do so.

The WinModem is manufactured by USRobotics, a vendor independent of Microsoft; Microsoft makes no warranty, implied or otherwise, regarding this product's performance or reliability.

Related KB article Q183074

Zoom Comstar 14.4 or 28.8 Plug and Play Modem Does Not Install

You attempt to install a Zoom Comstar 14.4 or 28.8 Plug and Play modem in Windows and experience one of the following problems:

- The modem is configured to use the COM5 port if the COM1 and COM2 ports are already in use when you install the modem. This problem can occur even when the COM3 and COM4 ports are not already installed.

- You install the modem, and the serial port the modem is configured to use is not listed in Device Manager.

- You are unable to communicate with the modem by using the ECHO command from a command prompt in Windows unless the real-mode drivers that came with the modem are installed in the AUTOEXEC.BAT and CONFIG.SYS files.

- You are unable to establish a connection by using the modem with HyperTerminal, Dial-Up Networking, Phone Dialer, or any other 32-bit communications program.

Solution

Contact Zoom Telephonics.

Related KB article Q146639

Zoom V.34I Modem Detected As Standard Modem

You run the Add New Hardware Wizard, and the Zoom V.34I modem is detected as a standard modem, even though the modem is included on the hardware list. This situation happens because the Zoom V.34I modem included on the hardware list is not a 28.8-Kbps modem and the actual installed modem is a 28.8-Kbps modem.

Solution

Install the modem by using the manufacturer's driver disk and follow these steps:

1. Click the Start button, choose Settings, and then click Control Panel.

2. Double-click the Modems icon.

3. Click Add to start the Install New Modem Wizard.

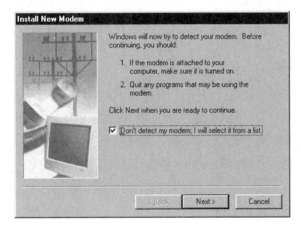

Figure 7-20. *The Install New Modem Wizard.*

4. Select the Don't Detect My Modem; I Will Select It From A List check box, and then click Next.

5. Click Have Disk.

6. In the Install From Disk dialog box, enter the path to the disk in the Copy Manufacturer's File From box, and then click OK.

7. Follow the instructions onscreen.

If you don't have the manufacturer's driver disk, contact the manufacturer to obtain the appropriate drivers. These drivers are available as a file named MUUPG.EXE from the Zoom web site, at *http://www.zoomtel.com/files/drivers.html*.

Related KB article Q178353

CHAPTER 8

Monitors, Video Adapters, and Display

Display Adapters

3DFX-Based Adapter Hardware Acceleration Features Unavailable

After you perform a clean installation of Windows 98 (by installing on an empty hard disk or a new folder), you're unable to use the hardware acceleration features of your 3DFX adapter. This situation can occur because Windows 98 does not provide Glide drivers. To work correctly, programs written to utilize the 3DFX chip set might require additional support from Glide drivers.

Solution

Download and then install the latest 3DFX Glide drivers (GETVGR.EXE) from your 3DFX adapter manufacturer's web site.

Related KB article Q186578

ATI 3D Rage Pro Video Adapter Games Won't Run

After you install Windows 98, you can't run some of the games included with the ATI 3D Rage Pro video adapter. When you try to run these games, some of them display only the starting screen and then return to the preceding screen.

Windows 98 uses its own video drivers for the 3D Rage Pro video adapter. In order to work properly, some of the games included with the 3D Rage Pro video adapter require dynamic-link library (DLL) files that are available only with the ATI-supplied drivers.

This problem has been noted with the following software:

- MechWarrior 2 ATI 3D Rage Edition
- Psygnosis Formula 1 for ATI 3D Rage Pro

Solution

Reinstall the drivers provided by ATI, specifically the ATI3DCIF.DLL and ATI3DCOR.DLL files.

Related KB article Q187343

ATI All-In-Wonder Pro Driver Causes Fatal Exception

You install the ATI All-In-Wonder Pro video adapter drivers version 5.0 or later provided by ATI, and you receive the following error message on a blue screen:

A Fatal Exception 0D has occurred. Press any key to continue.

This problem occurs when either of the following conditions exists:

- You are using a program written to use features of the Windows 3.x 16-bit video device drivers that are no longer available in the 32-bit video device drivers used in Windows 98.
- You are using a program that installs an older version of a multimedia program.

Solution One

Contact ATI Technical Support to obtain the appropriate drivers for your ATI All-In-Wonder Pro video adapter.

Solution Two

Contact the program's manufacturer to inquire about a possible update to address this problem.

Solution Three

Work around this problem by following these steps:

1. Restart your computer. After your computer completes the Power On Self Test (POST), press and hold down the Ctrl key until you see the Windows 98 Startup menu, and then choose Safe Mode.

2. Click the Start button, click Run, type *msconfig,* and then click OK.

3. Click the SYSTEM.INI tab, double-click the [boot] branch to expand it, and then right-click DISPLAY.DRV=PNPDRVR.DRV.

Figure 8-1. *The System Configuration Utility dialog box.*

4. Click Clear, click OK, and then click Yes when you are prompted to restart your computer.

5. Repeat steps 2 and 3.

6. Click Select, click OK, and then click No when you are prompted to restart your computer.

7. Click the Start button, choose Settings, and then click Control Panel.

8. Double-click the Display icon, click the Settings tab, and then click Advanced.

9. Click the Adapter tab, click Change, click Next, and then click Display A List Of All The Drivers In A Specific Location, So You Can Select The Driver You Want.

10. Click Next, click the ATI All-In-Wonder Pro dated 5/11/98.

11. Click Next, click Next, and then click Finish.

12. Click Apply, click Close, and then restart your computer.

Related KB article Q192803

ATI All-In-Wonder Driver Detects As ATI Rage II+ Adapter

You remove the ATI All-In-Wonder or ATI All-In-Wonder Pro display adapter driver, and Windows 98 redetects the display adapter as an ATI Rage II+ display adapter.

This problem occurs when you are using an older version of the ATI All-In-Wonder or ATI All-In-Wonder Pro display adapter containing incorrect BIOS information.

Solution

Manually install the correct display adapter drivers by following these steps:

1. Click the Start button, choose Settings, click Control Panel, and then double-click the System icon.

2. On the Device Manager tab, double-click the Display Adapters branch to expand it, and then double-click ATI Rage II+.

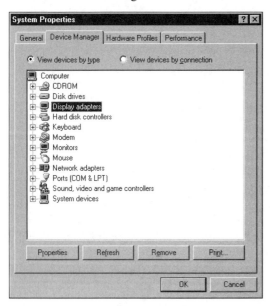

Figure 8-2. *The Device Manager tab in the System Properties dialog box.*

3. On the Driver tab, click Update Driver, click Next, click Display A List Of All The Drivers In A Specific Location, So You Can Select The Driver You Want, and then click Next.

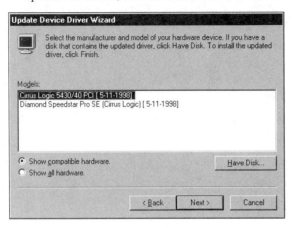

Figure 8-3. *The Update Device Driver Wizard.*

4. Click the appropriate display adapter driver, click Next, click Next, click Finish, and then click Yes to restart your computer.

Related KB article Q185603

Avance Logic Adapter Does Not Set Higher than 640 x 480

You're using an Avance Logic PCI video adapter, and you cannot change your display settings to a resolution higher than 640 x 480 with 16 colors. If you view the Settings tab by using the Display icon in Control Panel, the tab reports that you have an unknown monitor on an unknown device. If you then view Display Adapter Properties in Device Manager, it reports that a Windows 3.1 driver is in use.

Windows 98 does not include drivers for this video adapter, so when Setup detects this adapter, it installs a standard VGA driver, and this driver is not capable of displaying a resolution that is higher than 640 x 480 with 16 colors.

Solution

Contact Avance Logic to inquire about the availability of a video adapter driver.

Related KB article Q193508

Colors and Screen Area Settings Don't Change

You attempt to modify the Colors or Screen Area setting by using the Display icon in Control Panel, and the settings have no effect, even though Windows displays the Windows Will Now Resize Your Desktop dialog box.

This behavior can occur if you are using a Diamond Stealth II S220 video adapter, you have installed the latest drivers for this video adapter (including the Diamond InControl Tools software) from the Diamond Multimedia web site, and you are logged on to Windows.

Solution One

Do not log on to Windows before changing the display settings. When you restart your computer, click Cancel when you are prompted to log on. This problem does not occur if you are not logged on to Windows.

Solution Two

Use the Diamond InControl Tools software rather than the Display icon in Control Panel to change the display resolution and color depth. For information about using the Diamond InControl Tools software, contact Diamond Multimedia or refer to the program's documentation.

Related KB article Q193549

Cyrix MediaGX Display Behaves Unexpectedly

You install Windows 98 on a Cyrix MediaGX–based computer with an integrated display adapter and your display works correctly, but you see the following error message whenever you restart your computer:

Your display adapter is not configured properly.

This problem occurs because the integrated display adapter in the Cyrix MediaGX–based motherboard uses a proprietary driver not included in Windows 98. This issue is specific to new installations of Windows 98 and does not occur if you upgrade from Windows 95; in this case, Setup keeps the existing display adapter driver.

Solution

Install the most current version of display adapter driver for the integrated display adapter in your Cyrix MediaGX–based motherboard. To do so, obtain the most current version of display adapter driver from Cyrix, and then follow these steps:

1. Click the Start button, choose Settings, click Control Panel, and double-click the Display icon.

2. On the Settings tab, click Advanced, click the Adapter tab, click Change, click Next, click Display A List Of All Drivers, click Have Disk, and then navigate your way to the disk containing the driver for your display adapter.

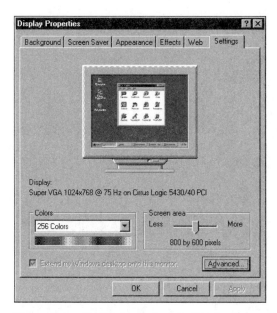

Figure 8-4. *The Settings tab of the Display Properties dialog box.*

3. Follow the instructions on the screen to install the new driver, and restart your computer when you are prompted.

Related KB article Q188169

Diamond Fire GL 1000 Pro Video Adapter Causes Errors

After you install the drivers (version 1.02) included with your Diamond Fire GL 1000 Pro video adapter in Windows 98, you see the following error message on a blue screen when you attempt to place your computer in Standby mode:

Invalid VxD dynamic link call from VPOWERD(06) + 00000BD9 to device VMCPD Service C

If you press Y to continue, your computer continues functioning normally.

The Diamond Setup program replaces the VMCPD.VXD file with version 1413 by calling the DirectX installation without checking the installed version of the file first. Removing the driver or changing to another driver does not resolve the issue.

Solution

Use System File Checker to extract a new copy of the VMCPD.VXD file to the WINDOWS\SYSTEM\VMM32 folder. For information about how to do this, see KB article Q129605, "How to Extract Original Compressed Windows Files."

Related KB article Q194999

Diamond Multimedia Stealth II S220 Causes Windows to Stop Responding

You try to use a Diamond Stealth II S220 display adapter with Windows 98, and your computer stops responding.

This problem occurs most frequently when you start the Add New Hardware Wizard while the drivers for the Diamond Stealth II S220 included with Windows 98 are installed. In this situation, your computer might hang. If the standard VGA video driver is installed, the Add New Hardware Wizard runs successfully.

Solution

Obtain and install the most current version of driver for this display adapter. To do this, contact Diamond Multimedia or view the documentation included with your display adapter.

Related KB article Q190646

Display Adapters Branch Missing in Device Manager After Upgrade

You upgrade Windows 95 to Windows 98, and the Display Adapters branch is missing in Device Manager.

This problem occurs when your video adapter uses the nVidia RIVA 128 chip set and is unable to acquire an interrupt request line (IRQ) during the Plug and Play detection portion of Windows 98 Setup.

Solution One

Assign an IRQ to your video adapter. In your computer's Basic Input/Output System (BIOS), enable the Assign IRQ To VGA option.

Note The BIOS of some computers does not have this option.

See the documentation included with your computer or motherboard, or consult your computer's manufacturer for information about changing settings in the BIOS.

Solution Two

Disable the PCI bus IRQ steering in Device Manager. For information about how to do this, please see KB article Q182628, "How to Disable PCI Bus IRQ Steering in Windows."

Related KB article Q189235

IBM Aptiva Stealth Display Device Doesn't Function

Windows doesn't use display devices contained on some bridged display devices, such as the STB MVP/3D 4-port card. The onboard display adapter is used instead. In some IBM Aptiva Stealth models, the BIOS improperly configures PCI bridges. In addition, the system design does not allow the onboard display adapter (on the motherboard) to be disabled. This results in a resource conflict. The virtual display device (VDD) does not allow secondary display adapters to be started if a resource conflict is detected.

Solution

Contact IBM Technical Support for a BIOS update for your specific Aptiva Stealth model.

Related KB article Q188156

ISA Display Adapter Doesn't Upgrade Correctly

You experience one or more of the following problems after you install Windows 98:

- A Peripheral Component Interconnect (PCI) display adapter appears as a disabled device in Device Manager, and your Industry Standard Architecture (ISA) display adapter does not appear in Device Manager.

- When you start Windows 98, you receive the following error message:

  Your display adapter is not configured properly.

  To correct this problem, start the Hardware Installation Wizard.

- When your computer automatically restarts for the second time during Windows 98 Setup but before Windows 98 is completely started, the information displayed on the screen appears distorted. Even though you might be unable to read the information on the screen, Windows 98 starts successfully.

This behavior can occur because ISA display adapters might not be detected properly when you upgrade a Windows 95–based computer with an integrated PCI display adapter.

Solution

Verify that your integrated PCI display adapter is disabled, and then reinstall your ISA display adapter; follow these steps:

1. Verify that your integrated PCI display adapter is disabled. For information about how to do so, view the manufacturer's documentation included with your integrated PCI display adapter.

2. Click the Start button, choose Settings, click Control Panel, and then double-click the Add New Hardware icon.

Figure 8-5. *The Add New Hardware Wizard.*

3. Follow the instructions on the screen to finish installing your ISA display adapter.

Related KB article Q185220

OpenGL-Based Program Does Not Work Correctly

You upgrade to Windows 98, and your OpenGL-based programs no longer work correctly or do not work at all.

This problem occurs when you use an nVidia RIVA 128-based display adapter. The Windows 98 drivers for the nVidia RIVA 128-based display adapter do not support OpenGL.

Solution

Contact the manufacturer of your display adapter to inquire about the availability of a display adapter driver that supports OpenGL.

Related KB article Q189979

PCI Display Card Works Only in VGA Mode

You use a PCI display card that is configured by the BIOS to use a specific IRQ and you also use the secondary PCI IDE controller in your computer, but your display card works only in VGA mode.

Solution One

Disable the secondary PCI IDE controller by following these steps:

1. Disable the secondary PCI IDE controller in your BIOS. (Refer to your computer's manual for instructions on changing your BIOS settings.)

2. Click the Start button, choose Settings, and click Control Panel.

3. Double-click the System icon.

4. Click the Device Manager tab, and then click the plus sign next to Hard Disk Controllers to display the Secondary IDE controller.

5. Right-click your Secondary IDE controller, and then select Properties from the shortcut menu.

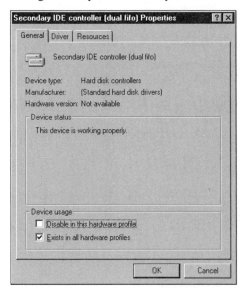

Figure 8-6. *The Secondary IDE Controller Properties dialog box.*

6. Select the Disable In This Hardware Profile check box, and clear the Exists In All Hardware Profiles check box.

7. Click OK, restart your system, and then install your Windows 98 display card drivers.

Solution Two

Disable the IRQ of the PCI display adapter in your BIOS so that your PCI IDE controller does not try to use it (not all BIOSes support this option).

Related KB article Q191480 or HARDWARE.TXT in your WINDOWS folder

S3 Virge PCI Adapter Detected When Diamond Stealth 3D Is Present

Windows 98 Setup detects that you are using an S3 Virge PCI display adapter, even though you are actually using one of the following video adapters:

- Diamond Stealth 3D 2000

- Diamond Stealth 3D 2000 Pro

- Diamond Stealth 3D 3000 Pro

This problem occurs when Windows 98 Setup detects the S3 Virge chip set on the video adapter.

Solution One

Obtain the latest video adapter driver from the manufacturer. To obtain the latest driver, please visit the Diamond Multimedia web site, at the following location:

http://www.diamondmm.com

Solution Two

Change to the appropriate video adapter by following these steps:

1. Click the Start button, choose Settings, and then click Control Panel.

2. Double-click the Display icon, click the Settings tab, and then click Advanced.

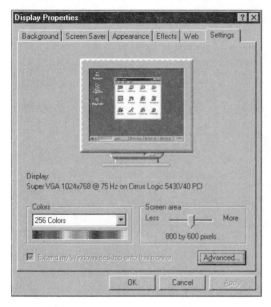

Figure 8-7. *The Settings tab in the Display Properties dialog box.*

3. Click the Adapter tab, and then click Change.

4. Click Next, click Display A List Of All The Drivers In A Specific Location, So You Can Select The Driver You Want, and then click Next.

5. Click Show All Hardware.

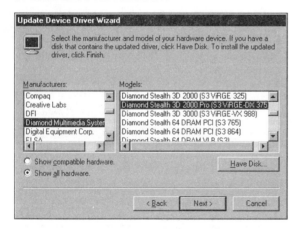

Figure 8-8. *The Update Device Driver Wizard.*

6. In the Manufacturers box, select the manufacturer of your video adapter.

7. In the Models box, select the appropriate model, and then click Next.

8. If you receive an Update Driver Warning dialog box, click Yes.

9. Click Next, click Finish, and then click Yes to restart your computer.

Related KB article Q192271

STB TV Display Distorts or Full Screen Mode Doesn't Work

When you're using an STB TV PCI adapter, you experience the following symptoms if you are using a Riva 128–based video adapter with Windows 98 drivers:

- If you move the STB TV window, your screen becomes distorted.

- If you try to change the STB TV window to full-screen mode, you are unable to expand the window larger than 640 x 480 pixels, and the remaining portion of the screen turns bright pink. If you restore the window to its original size, your screen becomes distorted.

Solution One

Obtain the latest Windows 98 drivers for your Riva 128–based video adapter from the manufacturer. An alternative solution is to use the Windows 95 drivers for your display card.

Solution Two

Follow these steps to refresh the desktop:

1. Click the Minimize button (the first button in the upper right corner of the STB TV window).

2. Click a blank area of the desktop, and then press the F5 key to refresh the desktop.

3. Click each desktop icon to refresh it.

4. Right-click STB TV on the taskbar, and then click Restore.

Related KB article Q193435

Unknown Monitor Error Message

You create a new hardware profile by starting your computer in a new docking state or by copying an existing hardware profile in the System Properties dialog box, and the first time you start your computer you receive the following message:

Unknown Monitor

The monitor type is not maintained as part of a hardware profile, so when you create a new hardware profile, the existing monitor settings are not copied.

Solution

Reselect the monitor type when you start the computer in the new hardware profile by following these steps:

1. Click the Start button, choose Settings, and then click Control Panel.

2. Double-click the Display icon.

3. Choose the Settings tab, and then click Advanced.

4. Choose the Monitor tab, and then click Change.

5. Click Next, click Display A List Of All The Drivers In A Specific Location, So You Can Select The Driver You Want, and click Next.

6. Click Show All Hardware, and select the manufacturer of your monitor in the Manufacturers box.

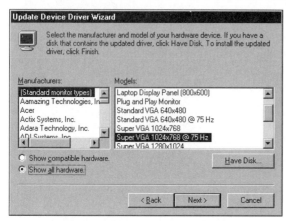

Figure 8-9.   *The Update Device Driver Wizard.*

7. Select the monitor you are using in the Models box, click Next, and then click Next.

8. Close the program.

Related KB article   Q132839

Zoomed Video PC Card Fails After Upgrade to Windows 98

You upgrade Windows 95 or Windows 95 OEM Service Release 1, 2, 2.1, or 2.5 to Windows 98, and you can't use your Zoomed Video PC Card device (or devices). Here are some possible causes:

- The display adapter driver was not updated properly, or an updated driver is required.

- The Zoomed Video PC Card is not in the correct slot.

- The Zoomed Video device requires third-party socket services.

Solution One

Contact the manufacturer of the Zoomed Video device or your original equipment manufacturer (OEM) for updated drivers.

Solution Two

Make sure that the Zoomed Video PC Card is in the correct slot.

Note Some PC Card controllers enable only one of two sockets. You might need to check the manufacturer's documentation to see whether one or both sockets enable Zoomed Video support.

Solution Three

Enable your third-party PC Card socket services. Check the manufacturer's documentation for information about how to do this.

Windows 98 supports Video Port Extension (VPE) drivers, and a Video Port Manager (VPM) driver might be installed. Some VPM drivers might still function with Windows 98, but might need an updated VPE driver.

Related KB article Q180154

Display Settings

Advanced Display Properties Does Not Function Properly

You click the Settings tab in Display properties, click Advanced, and then press Alt+A, and either of the following symptoms occurs:

- The Apply The New Color Settings Without Restarting option receives the focus (the dotted-line box) but is not selected.

- The Apply button is pressed.

This problem occurs because two items are associated with the Alt+A key combination:

- The Apply The New Color Settings Without Restarting option

- The Apply button

Solution One

If you can use the mouse or another pointing device, click Apply or Apply The New Color Settings Without Restarting, as appropriate.

Solution Two

If you cannot use the mouse or another pointing device and you want to click Apply, press the Tab key until the Apply button has the focus (has a dotted-line box around it), and then press the Enter key. If you cannot use the mouse or another pointing device and you want to click Apply The New Color Settings Without Restarting, follow these steps:

1. Press the Tab key until one of the After I Change Color Settings options has the focus (has a dotted-line box around it).

2. Press the Up arrow key or Down arrow key to select Apply The New Color Settings Without Restarting.

Related KB article Q192755

ATI Display Adapters Limit Resolution and Colors

After you install an ATI Mach 64 display adapter as the primary display device and install an ATI Rage II display adapter as the secondary display device in your computer, the only screen resolution available is 640 x 480 and the only color palette available is 16 colors. This problem can occur if a resource conflict exists with your ATI Mach 64 and ATI Rage II display adapters.

Solution

To solve this problem, follow these steps:

1. Click the Start button, choose Settings, click Control Panel, and double-click the System icon.

2. On the Device Manager tab, double-click the Display Adapters branch to expand it, and then double-click ATI Mach 64.

3. On the Resources tab, select the Use Automatic Settings check box.

4. Click OK, and then click OK.

5. Restart your computer when you are prompted to do so.

Related KB article Q187681

Desktop Color Doesn't Change

You attempt to change the color of your desktop by using the Display icon in Control Panel, and your desktop color does not change. This can occur if all the following conditions exist:

- The Windows Desktop Update component is installed, and you are viewing your desktop as a web page.

- Your desktop wallpaper contains a .JPG or .GIF graphics file.

- Your desktop wallpaper is stretched.

Solution

To solve this problem, follow these steps:

1. Click the Start button, choose Settings, and then click Control Panel.

2. Double-click the Display icon, and click the Web tab.

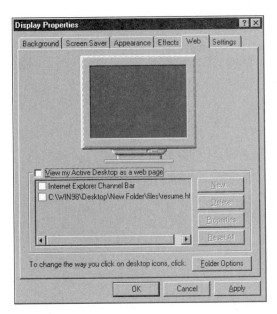

Figure 8-10.   *The Web tab in the Display Properties dialog box.*

3. Clear the View My Active Desktop As A Web Page check box, and then click Apply.

4. Click Yes when you receive the following prompt:

>*The wallpaper you selected can be shown on the desktop only if Active Desktop is enabled.*
>
>*Do you want to enable it?*

5. Click OK.

These steps change the color only around the names of desktop icons. Your desktop wallpaper is retained. To remove the desktop wallpaper so that your background is displayed as a solid color, click No in step 4.

Related KB article Q188086

Display Options Unavailable

You try to change the Desktop Area setting in the Display Properties dialog box, and some options the video adapter is capable of providing aren't available. For example, a video adapter that can display 1024 x 768 x 256 resolution offers only 640 x 480 x 256 and 800 x 600 x 16 as the resolution options.

Solution One

If your computer is a PCI system, verify that the Monitor Timing settings in the system BIOS match the capabilities of the display monitor, as described in your monitor documentation. Refer to the documentation for your computer system to obtain information about how to make the necessary changes to the Monitor Timing settings.

Solution Two

If the monitor you are using doesn't match the monitor type Windows thinks you're using, you can specify the correct monitor. You can see on the Settings tab of the Display Properties dialog box which monitor Windows thinks you're using.

To change the monitor type, follow these steps:

1. Click the Start button, choose Settings, and click Control Panel.

2. Double-click the Display icon, and click the Settings tab.

3. Click Advanced.

4. Click the Monitor tab of your display adapter's Properties dialog box, and click Change. This step starts the Update Device Driver Wizard.

5. Click Next to begin.

6. Click the second option button, and click Next.

Note Click the first option button to search for updated drivers for your monitor.

---

7. If your monitor is not listed, click Show All Hardware, and then select your monitor manufacturer from the Manufacturers list and the model from the Models list. If you can't find your model, select Standard Monitor Types from the Manufacturers list, and then select the Standard setting that corresponds to the capabilities of your monitor.

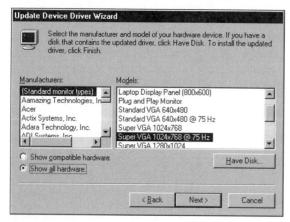

Figure 8-11. *The Update Device Driver Wizard.*

8. Select the Device you are using in the Models box, click Next, and then click Next.

9. Close the program.

Solution Three

If you are confident that the display and video adapter are capable of a higher resolution, the problem might be that the Windows display driver does not support the display mode you are trying to use. Change the display adapter driver by following these steps:

1. Click the Start button, choose Settings, and click Control Panel.

2. Double-click the Display icon, click the Settings tab, and click Advanced.

3. Click the Adapter tab, and click Change. This step starts the Update Device Driver Wizard.

4. Click Next to begin.

5. Click the second option button, and click Next.

Note Click the first option button to search for updated drivers for your display adapter.

6. If your adapter is not listed, click Show All Hardware, select Standard Display Types from the Manufacturers list, and then select one of the high-resolution generic (Super VGA) modes from the Models list.

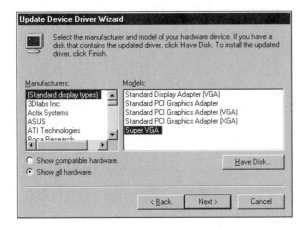

Figure 8-12.   *The Update Device Driver Wizard.*

Note This might not function correctly depending on your configuration.

7. Select the device you are using in the Models box, click Next, and then click Next.

8. Close the program.

Solution Four

If you are using a Windows 3.1 display driver, the Desktop Area and Color Palette settings are not changeable in the Display Properties dialog box. To change the resolution, you must click Change Display Type and change the Adapter Type to the Windows 3.1 display driver you want to use.

Related KB article Q121319

Display Properties Dialog Box Replaces Effects Tab with Plus! Tab

You view the Display Properties dialog box, and the Effects tab is missing or you see a Plus! tab even if Microsoft Plus! for Windows 98 is not installed on your computer.

This problem occurs because Windows 95 font smoothing is installed on your computer. Windows 98 includes font-smoothing components. Installing Windows 95 font smoothing in Windows 98 results in the deletion of these font-smoothing components.

Solution

Uninstall Windows 95 font smoothing, and then reinstall the Windows 98 version. To uninstall Windows 95 font smoothing, follow these steps:

1. Click the Start button, choose Settings, and then click Control Panel.

2. Double-click the Add/Remove Programs icon, and click the Install/Uninstall tab.

3. In the list of installed programs, click Windows 95 Font Smoothing (Uninstall Only), and then click Add/Remove.

4. Click Yes when you are prompted to restart your computer.

Related KB article Q194148

Maximum Screen Area Doesn't Display

You try to increase the screen area in the Display Properties dialog box and are unable to choose a higher screen area. For example, your monitor supports a maximum screen area of 1600 x 1200 pixels, but this setting is missing from the Screen Area box. If your monitor's Extended Identification Data (EDID) contains incorrect information about your monitor, you must install your monitor manually.

Solution

To solve this problem, follow these steps:

1. Click the Start button, choose Settings, click Control Panel, and then double-click the Display icon.

2. Click the Settings tab, and then click Advanced.

3. Click the Monitor tab, clear the Automatically Detect Plug And Play Monitors check box, and then click Apply.

4. Click Change, click Next, click Display A List Of All The Drivers In A Specific Location, So You Can Select The Driver You Want, and then click Next.

5. Click Show All Hardware, and then follow the instructions on the screen to finish installing your monitor.

Related KB article Q182595

Monitor Type Not Retained by Setup

You upgrade to Windows 98 from an earlier version of Windows or you reinstall Windows 98, and Setup does not retain your monitor type. The Display Properties dialog box and Device Manager list the monitor type as Unknown Monitor.

Solution

Select the correct monitor type by following these steps:

1. Click the Start button, choose Settings, and then click Control Panel.

2. Double-click the Display icon to open the Display Properties dialog box.

3. Click the Settings tab, and then click Advanced to open the Properties dialog box.

4. Click the Monitor tab, and then click Change to start the Update Device Driver Wizard.

5. Click Next, click Display A List Of All The Drivers In A Specific Location, So You Can Select The Driver You Want, and click Next.

6. Click Show All Hardware.

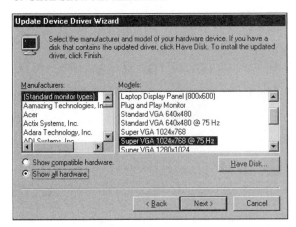

Figure 8-13. *The Update Device Driver Wizard.*

7. In the Manufacturers box, select the manufacturer of your monitor.

8. In the Models box, select the model of the monitor you are using.

9. Click OK, and then click OK.

Related KB article Q195044

NEC 4FG Monitor Display Distorts

You are using an NEC 4FG monitor and you change the display resolution to 1280 x 1024 pixels or higher, and then your screen becomes distorted. This problem can occur if you are using a video adapter that defaults to a refresh rate of 60 Hz.

Some video adapters, such as the Diamond Stealth 64 Video 2001 and S3 Trio 64V+ video adapters, default to a refresh rate of 60 Hz. NEC 4FG monitors can support only refresh rates of less than 60 Hz at a resolution of 1280 x 1024 or higher.

Solution

Optimize the refresh rate of your video adapter before you change the display resolution. To do so, follow these steps:

1. Click the Start button, choose Settings, and click Control Panel.

2. Double-click the Display icon.

3. Click the Settings tab, and click Advanced.

4. Click the Adapter tab, and then click Optimal in the Refresh Rate box.

5. Click OK, and then click OK when you receive the following message:

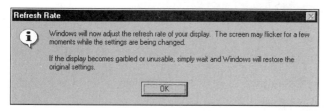

Figure 8-14. *The Refresh Rate dialog box.*

6. Click Yes when you are prompted to keep this setting, and then click OK.

Related KB article Q187622

Resolution or Color Palette Doesn't Change

You attempt to change your display resolution or color palette, and the only resolution available is 640 x 480 and the only color palette available is 16 colors. This behavior can occur when you install Windows 98 on a computer with an AST Ascentia P video adapter. Windows 98 does not support the AST Ascentia P video adapter.

Solution

Contact AST Technical Support to inquire about a possible update.

Related KB article Q187216

Screen Savers Don't Work

You upgrade from Windows 95 to Windows 98 and then uninstall Windows 98, but Windows 98 screen savers remain on the list of available screen savers. You try to select one of these screen savers, and nothing happens.

Solution

Ignore the extra Windows 98 screen savers that appear on the list of available screen savers.

Related KB article Q187275

VGA Mode Is Monitor's Only Functioning Mode

You cannot change your display to a higher resolution or color depth than 640 x 480 at 16 colors. When you use a PCI display adapter configured by your BIOS to use IRQ 15 and you have a functioning secondary PCI IDE disk controller also configured to use IRQ 15 (by default), Windows 98 assigns IRQ 15 to the IDE disk controller, forcing your display adapter to use VGA mode. This prohibits you from achieving higher resolutions or color depths.

Solution

To load the accelerated Windows 98 driver for your display adapter, eliminate the resource conflict.

You can do this by disabling the secondary PCI IDE controller in the BIOS, if your BIOS allows, and disabling the secondary PCI IDE controller in Device Manager under System Properties.

Or, if your BIOS allows, disable the IRQ of the display adapter or manually reconfigure the display adapter to use a different IRQ setting.

Obtain a BIOS upgrade from your hardware vendor if your BIOS doesn't provide the necessary tools to solve this problem.

Related KB article Q188481 or DISPLAY.TXT in the WINDOWS folder

Fonts

Enabling Font Smoothing Doesn't Smooth Fonts

You enable font smoothing when multiple monitors are connected to your computer, and screen fonts do not appear to be smoother on any of the monitors if any display adapter in your computer is using 256 colors or a lower color depth.

Solution

Set the color depth for all display adapters to High Color (16 bit) mode.

To enable font smoothing, follow these steps:

1. Click the Start button, choose Settings, and then click Control Panel.

2. Double-click the Display icon to open the Display Properties dialog box.

3. Click the Effects tab, select the Smooth Edges Of Screen Fonts check box, and then click OK.

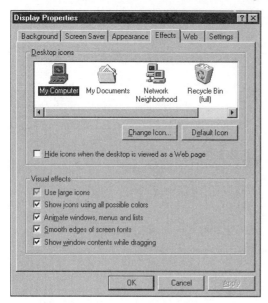

Figure 8-15.   *The Effects tab in the Display Properties dialog box.*

Windows 98 supports the use of multiple monitors to expand your desktop area. To use multiple monitors, you need a supported Peripheral Component Interconnect (PCI) or Accelerated Graphic Port (AGP) video adapter for each monitor and DirectX 5-compliant video drivers.

Note A Permedia video adapter other than a Permedia NT or Permedia-2 cannot be used as your primary video adapter.

Related KB article Q182445

Euro Symbol Doesn't Insert into Document

You are using a TrueType font that includes the euro symbol (a *C* with two horizontal lines through the center), and nothing happens when you attempt to insert the euro symbol into a document. (Character Map incorrectly states that Ctrl+2 is the key combination for the euro symbol.)

Solution

Press Alt+0128 to insert the euro symbol into the document.

Related KB article Q186169

Program Displays Blank Character As Date

Some programs display unintelligible or blank characters for the date. This includes dates displayed in the program and also in printed output.

This problem occurs when regional setting information for displaying date formats is damaged or incorrect in the Registry.

Solution

Change the regional setting information by following these steps:

1. Click the Start button, choose Settings, and then click Control Panel.

2. Double-click the Regional Settings icon.

3. On the Date tab, select the appropriate date format settings.

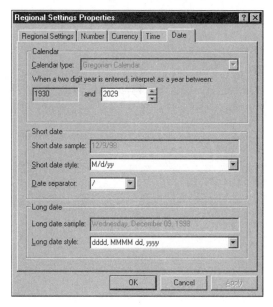

Figure 8-16.   *The Date tab in the Regional Settings Properties dialog box.*

4. Click OK.

5. Restart your computer.

Related KB article Q192317

TrueType Fonts Don't Work

You can't select TrueType fonts in WordPad or Microsoft Word, even though you can select TrueType fonts in Microsoft Excel and you can view TrueType fonts in your FONTS folder.

Word and WordPad check the capabilities of the default printer to determine how to display the document as it will be printed. Excel does not limit the fonts that can be selected, because many customers use Excel to view and manipulate spreadsheets without printing.

This problem occurs because the default printer is set to a printer that does not support TrueType fonts (such as the Generic/Text Only printer).

Solution

Change the default printer by following these steps:

1. Click the Start button, choose Settings, and then click Control Panel.

2. Double-click the Printers icon.

3. If you have a printer installed that supports TrueType fonts, right-click the printer, and then choose Set As Default from the shortcut menu.

4. If you do not have another printer installed that supports TrueType fonts, double-click Add Printer to start the Add Printer Wizard and install the driver for your printer. Follow the instructions on the screen.

Related KB article Q169330

TrueType Fonts Missing

You notice one or more of the following problems:

- TrueType fonts are not present in the FONTS folder.

- You receive this error message if you try to add a TrueType font:

     The <fontname> TrueType font is already installed. To install a new version, first remove the old version.

- TrueType fonts are not listed in any program.

- Documents you created previously are now printed differently, or the formatting is changed when you view the document.

- Your custom desktop settings have changed fonts.

This problem is caused because the Windows Registry key that lists TrueType fonts is damaged or missing.

Solution One

Use the Fontreg tool to add a Registry key to allow the installation of TrueType fonts; follow these steps:

1. Click the Start button, and then click Run.

2. Type *Fontreg* in the Open box, and then click OK.

3. Click the Start button, choose Settings, click Control Panel, and double-click the Fonts icon.

4. Choose Install New Font from the File menu.

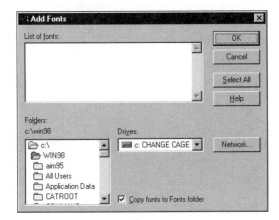

Figure 8-17. *The Add Fonts dialog box.*

5. In the Folders box, select the folder that contains the TrueType fonts; it's usually the WINDOWS\FONTS folder.

6. Click Select All, and then click OK.

7. If your documents are still not printed as you expect, remove and reinstall the appropriate printer driver.

Solution Two

Warning Please read the Introduction for information about how to safely edit the Registry.

Follow these steps to replace a missing or damaged Fonts key in the Registry:

1. Move the contents of the FONTS folder to an empty folder.

2. Click the Start button, click Run, and enter *Regedit* in the Run box. Click OK.

3. If the Fonts key exists in the following Registry setting, delete the Fonts key and then add it again:

   `HKEY_LOCAL_MACHINE\Software\Microsoft\Windows\CurrentVersion`

   If the Fonts key does not exist in the Registry setting just listed, add the following key:

   `Fonts`

4. Click the Start button, choose Settings, click Control Panel, and double-click the Fonts icon.

5. Choose Install New Font from the Fonts menu.

6. In the Folders box, select the folder you moved the fonts to in step 1.

7. Click Select All, and then click OK.

8. If your documents are still not printing as expected, you must remove and reinstall the appropriate printer driver.

Note Windows 98 has a limit of approximately 1,000 fonts. For more information about this limitation, see KB article Q131943, "TrueType Font Limits in Windows 95/98."

Related KB article Q133732

Multiple Monitors

ATI Rage II PCI Adapter Does Not Work As Secondary Display Adapter

You use the ATI Rage II PCI video adapter as a secondary display adapter on a computer with multiple monitors, and the secondary display adapter does not work properly. When you view the ATI Rage II PCI Properties dialog box in Device Manager, you see the following message:

Multiple Display Support cannot start this device. The area of memory normally used by video is in use by another program or device. To enable Multiple Display Support, remove EMM386 or other memory managers from CONFIG.SYS and restart your computer.

Solution One

Add an *EMMExclude* entry to the SYSTEM.INI file by following these steps:

1. Using any text editor (such as Notepad), open the SYSTEM.INI file. By default, the SYSTEM.INI file is located in the WINDOWS folder.

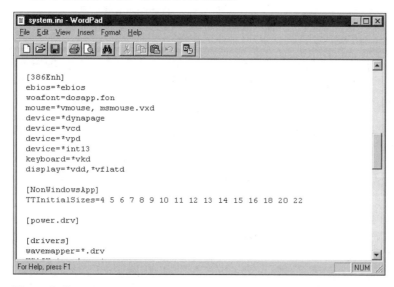

Figure 8-18. *The SYSTEM.INI file.*

2. Add the following line to the [386enh] section of the SYSTEM.INI file:

```
emmexclude=c000-cfff
```

3. Save and then close the SYSTEM.INI file.

4. Restart Windows.

Solution Two

Add a line in the CONFIG.SYS file to load EMM386.EXE by following these steps:

1. Using any text editor (such as Notepad), open the CONFIG.SYS file. The CONFIG.SYS file is located in the root folder.

2. Add the following lines:

```
device=<windows>\himem.sys

device=<windows>\emm386.exe x=c000-cfff
```

where <windows> is the path to the folder in which Windows is installed.

3. Save and then close the CONFIG.SYS file.

4. Restart Windows.

Solution Three

Disable the line in the CONFIG.SYS file that loads EMM386.EXE by following these steps:

1. Using any text editor (such as Notepad), open the CONFIG.SYS file. It's located in the root folder.

2. Disable the following line by typing the word *rem* followed by a space at the beginning of the line:

```
device=<windows>\emm386.exe
```

where <windows> is the path to the folder in which Windows is installed.

3. Save and then close the CONFIG.SYS file.

4. Restart Windows.

Related KB article Q187510

ATI Video Adapter Requires Multiple Monitor Reconfiguring

You reinstall Windows 98 on a computer that contains multiple monitors using ATI video adapters, and you have to reconfigure some monitors after Setup is completed.

Windows 98 disables Plug and Play functionality for ATI video adapters because they do not handle Plug and Play correctly.

Solution

Manually set each monitor connected to an ATI video adapter by following these steps:

1. Click the Start button, choose Settings, and then click Control Panel.

2. Double-click the Display icon.

3. Click the Settings tab.

4. In the Display box, click the adapter you want, and then click Advanced.

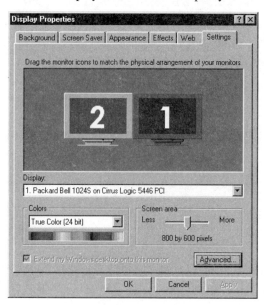

Figure 8-19. *The Settings tab in the Display Properties dialog box.*

5. On the Monitor tab, click Change.

6. Click Next, click Display A List Of All The Drivers In A Specific Location, So You Can Select The Driver You Want, and then click Next.

7. Click Show All Hardware.

8. Click the appropriate manufacturer and model of your monitor, click Next, and then click Finish.

9. Click Close, and then click OK.

Repeat steps 4 through 9 for each video adapter for which you have to set a monitor.

Related KB article Q188243

Horizontal Line Displays on One or More Monitors

Multiple monitors are connected to your computer, and a horizontal line continually scrolls down the screen of one or more monitors. This behavior can occur if your monitors are too close to a fluorescent light source or if an unshielded monitor is placed too close to another monitor.

Solution One

Move the unshielded monitor away from any monitors or fluorescent light sources.

Solution Two

Place a shield (for example, a cookie sheet) between the unshielded monitor and any monitors it interferes with.

Note For additional information about how to shield an unshielded monitor, contact the manufacturer of the unshielded monitor.

Most early monitors are unshielded, which means that they do not confine the magnetic field they emit. Later monitors are shielded so that most of the magnetic field they emit is confined within the monitor. If you place an unshielded monitor too close to another monitor, the magnetic field emitted by the unshielded monitor might interfere with the other monitor.

Windows 98 supports the use of multiple monitors to expand your desktop area. To use multiple monitors, you need a supported Peripheral Component Interconnect (PCI) or Accelerated Graphic Port (AGP) video adapter for each monitor that is connected to your computer, and you need DirectX 5–compliant video drivers.

Note For information about how to use multiple monitors in Windows 98, see the "Multiple Display Support" topic in the Windows help system.

Related KB article Q178594

Mouse or Windows Hangs While Playing Game

You are using a mouse to navigate through a playing field in a Windows game, and the mouse or Windows stops responding (hangs) if you are using multiple monitors and the game is not designed to run on a computer using multiple monitors.

Solution

Contact the manufacturer of the game about obtaining an update.

Some Windows games have a playing field that can be scrolled or navigated through by moving the mouse pointer toward the edge of the screen. If there is no secondary monitor, the mouse pointer stops at the edge of the screen. If a secondary monitor is added, you might inadvertently overshoot the edge of the screen by moving the mouse pointer to the secondary monitor.

Related KB article Q181924

Mouse Pointer Appears on Multiple Monitors

You have multiple monitors connected to your computer, and you move the mouse pointer from the primary to the secondary monitor. A copy of the mouse pointer remains on the primary monitor. This behavior can occur if either or both of the following conditions exist:

- You are using an unsupported video adapter as the primary video adapter.

- You are using an unsupported vendor-provided video adapter driver for the primary video adapter.

Solution

Use only a supported PCI video adapter and driver as the primary video adapter. To determine whether your primary video adapter and driver are supported for use with a multiple-monitor configuration, view the DISPLAY.TXT file located in the WINDOWS folder.

To use multiple monitors in Windows 98, you need a supported Peripheral Component Interconnect (PCI) or Accelerated Graphic Port (AGP) video adapter for each monitor connected to your computer. Using an unsupported PCI video adapter as the primary video adapter might work, but you might experience video problems.

For additional information about using multiple monitors in Windows 98, click the Start button, click Help, click the Index tab, type *multiple,* and then double-click the Multiple Display Support topic.

Related KB article Q187579

Mouse Works Only on Primary Monitor

You have multiple monitors connected to your computer, and you can use the mouse only with the primary monitor if you are running an MS-DOS program in full-screen mode.

Solution

Minimize the MS-DOS program by pressing Ctrl+Esc, or run the MS-DOS program in a window by pressing Alt+Enter.

If the mouse pointer is not in the primary monitor when you minimize the MS-DOS program or run it in a window, a mouse pointer might appear on the primary monitor and on the monitor where the actual mouse pointer is located. To resolve this behavior, move the mouse pointer to the primary monitor.

Related KB article Q180652

MS-DOS Program Runs Only on Primary Monitor

You have multiple monitors connected to your computer, and an MS-DOS program in full-screen mode runs only with the primary monitor.

Solution

Press Alt+Enter to run the program in a window. Windows 98 runs full-screen MS-DOS-based programs only on the primary monitor.

Related KB article Q180944

NBA Hang Time Program Window Doesn't Display on Second Monitor

You are playing NBA Hang Time on a computer with multiple monitors and try to move the program window to the second monitor. The program isn't visible, and the screen displays garbled characters.

Solution

Because NBA Hang Time is not totally compatible with multiple monitors, do not try to move the program window to the second monitor.

Related KB article Q194730

Program Doesn't Display on Multiple Monitors

You run a program on a computer using multiple monitors, and the program's dialog boxes, short-cut menus, and message boxes aren't displayed or are displayed on the primary monitor even though the program is displayed on a different monitor.

Solution

Because the program is not designed to run on a computer using multiple monitors, contact the manufacturer of the program about obtaining an update to address this issue.

Some programs center dialog boxes and message boxes so that they appear exactly in the middle of the screen. For compatibility reasons, Windows 98 reports that the screen size is the size of only the primary monitor's screen. When a program determines where to display a dialog box or message box in this manner, the dialog box or message box is displayed on the primary monitor.

Some programs use predetermined coordinates to determine where to display dialog boxes and message boxes. Therefore, the dialog boxes and message boxes are always displayed on the primary monitor.

Related KB article Q180177

Programs Appear Off Screen

You disable multiple display support, and some programs are displayed off the screen if the program was displayed on a monitor other than the primary monitor before you disabled multiple display support. This behavior can also occur if you change the arrangement of the monitors on the Settings tab in the Display Properties dialog box.

Solution One

1. Start the program.

2. Right-click the program on the taskbar, and then choose Maximize from the shortcut menu.

3. Right-click a blank area of the taskbar, and then choose Cascade Windows from the shortcut menu.

4. Resize the program's window as appropriate.

Solution Two

1. Start the program.

2. Right-click the program on the taskbar, and then choose Move from the shortcut menu.

3. Move the mouse pointer to the middle of the screen.

4. Use the arrow keys to move the program window to a viewable area on the screen.

5. Press the Enter key.

6. Resize the window if necessary.

Solution Three

1. Click the Start button, choose Programs, click Control Panel, and then double-click the Display icon to open the Display Properties dialog box.

2. Click the Settings tab.

3. In the Display box, click the secondary display adapter.

4. Select the Extend My Windows Desktop Onto This Monitor check box, and then click OK.

Related KB article Q181691

Screen Saver Runs Only on Primary Monitor

You are using multiple monitors, and your screen saver runs only on your primary monitor if the screen saver was not designed to work with multiple monitors.

Solution

Use a screen saver designed to work with multiple monitors.

The following screen savers are included with the Windows 98 desktop themes and are not designed to work with multiple monitors:

- Dangerous Creatures

- Inside Your Computer

- Leonardo da Vinci

- Mystery

- Nature

- Science

- Sports

- The '60s USA

- The Golden Era

- Travel

The following screen savers are included with Windows 98 and are not designed to work with multiple monitors:

- Baseball

- Jungle

- Space

- Underwater

- Windows 98

Related KB article Q178690

Suspend Command Does Not Function on Multiple Monitors

You use the Suspend command on the Shut Down menu, the primary monitor is not powered off, and a flashing cursor appears in the upper left corner of the monitor.

This problem occurs when the Basic Input/Output System (BIOS) setting that controls power management for the display adapter is incorrect.

Solution

Consult the computer's manufacturer or documentation to change the settings stored in the computer's BIOS.

Related KB article Q189748

Wallpaper Displays Incorrectly on Multiple Monitors

You use multiple monitors in Windows 98, and one monitor displays your desktop wallpaper incorrectly on the Windows logon screen. After you log on to Windows 98, the desktop wallpaper is displayed correctly.

This problem occurs when all the following conditions exist:

- You use a Matrox Millenium video adapter as your primary adapter, and it is set to a resolution of 1152 x 864 pixels and a color depth of 65,536 colors.

- You use an S3 Trio 64V+ (Diamond Stealth Video 2001) video adapter as your secondary adapter, and it is set to a resolution of 1024 x 768 pixels and a color depth of 256 colors.

- You use a pattern as your desktop wallpaper.

Solution

Use the same color depth for all video adapters.

Related KB article Q189757

Window Doesn't Drag from One Monitor to Another

Multiple monitors are connected to your computer, and you can't drag a window from one screen to another if the window is maximized or your monitors are not positioned correctly.

Solution One

Restore the window before you drag it by clicking Restore.

Solution Two

Verify your monitor's position. For information about how to do so, see the "Arranging Monitors" topic in the Windows help system.

Windows 98 supports the use of multiple monitors to expand your desktop area. To use multiple monitors, you need a supported Peripheral Component Interconnect (PCI) or Accelerated Graphic Port (AGP) video adapter for each monitor that is connected to your computer, and you need DirectX 5–compliant video drivers. For information about how to use multiple monitors in Windows 98, see the "Multiple Display Support" topic in the Windows help system.

Note Currently, a Permedia video adapter cannot be used as your primary video adapter (excludes the Permedia NT and Permedia-2).

Related KB article Q177895

Screen Element Appearance

Animate Windows, Menus And Lists Check Box Doesn't Deselect

You clear the Animate Windows, Menus And Lists check box on the Effects tab in the Display Properties dialog box, and the check box isn't selected again when you restart your computer. This behavior can occur if user profiles are enabled on the computer, and the Animate Windows, Menus And Lists check box is selected for the default user.

Solution One

Disable User Profiles. For more information, please see KB article Q156826, "How to Disable and Delete User Profiles."

Solution Two

Disable the animation of windows, menus, and lists for the default user by following these steps:

Note The following steps might change this setting for all users of the computer.

Warning Please read the Introduction for information about how to safely edit the Registry.

1. Click the Start button, click Run, and enter *Regedit* in the Run box. Click OK.

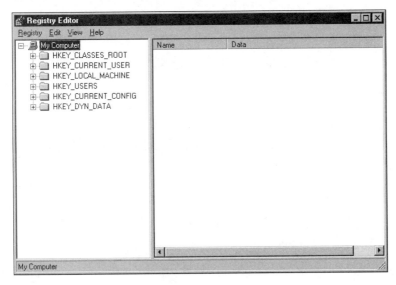

Figure 8-20. *The Registry Editor.*

2. Navigate your way down through the folders in the left pane.

3. Note the data value of the UserPreferencemask binary value in the following Registry key:

`HKEY_CURRENT_USER\Control Panel\Desktop`

For example, the data value might be the following value:

`a0 00 00 00`

4. Change the UserPreferencemask binary value to the data value you noted in step 3 in the following Registry key:

`HKEY_USERS\.Default\Control Panel\Desktop`

5. Close the Regedit.

6. Restart Windows.

Related KB article Q187222

Bitmap Image Displays Incorrectly in Quick View

You right-click a Windows bitmap (BMP) file and then click Quick View, and unintelligible characters are displayed rather than the BMP image if the BMP image was created using Imaging.

Solution

Save the file as 16-color bitmap by following these steps:

1. Open the BMP file by using Microsoft Paint.

2. Choose Save As from the File menu.

3. In the Save As Type box, click 16 Color Bitmap (*.BMP, *.DIB).

4. In the File Name box, type a new name for the file. For example, if the filename is IMAGE.BMP, type *imagex.bmp*.

5. Click Save.

6. Right-click the BMP file you saved in step 4, and then click Quick View.

Related KB article Q183072

Dialog Box or Message Box Malfunctions

You try to use Windows, and it displays one of the following problems:

■ The background of a dialog box is not displayed correctly.

■ The area under the dialog box contains multicolored bits of garbled information.

■ Messages in Microsoft Exchange are not displayed correctly.

You can solve this problem either by increasing the graphics acceleration setting or by modifying the SYSTEM.INI file.

Solution One

Increase the graphics acceleration setting by following these steps:

1. Right-click My Computer on the desktop, and choose Properties from the shortcut menu.

2. Click the Performance tab, click Graphics, and then move the Hardware Acceleration slider all the way to the right.

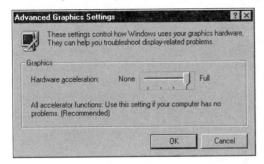

Figure 8-21. *The Advanced Graphics Settings dialog box.*

3. Click OK, and then click Close.

4. Click Yes when you are prompted to restart your computer.

Solution Two

Modify the SYSTEM.INI file by following these steps:

1. Click the Start button, and choose Run.

2. Enter *System.ini* in the Open text box, and click OK.

3. Add the line *LockCursor=1* to the [display] section of the SYSTEM.INI file.

4. Choose Save from the File menu, and then click Exit.

Related KB article Q132792

Error Messages or Message Boxes Aren't Visible

You run a program that opens a message box, and you do not see the message box on the desktop while you run other programs. For example, if your computer is part of a network, you do not see a pop-up message from your network administrator. Or, if you run a debugger program, set a break point in your program code, and then run other programs, the debug terminal window does not appear in the foreground when the break point is reached.

This behavior can occur if the program in the foreground uses one of these Application Programming Interface (API) methods:

- SetForegroundWindow()
- SetActiveWindow()
- SetFocus()

Windows 98 might return a value of FALSE to a program when these API methods are used.

The following programs might demonstrate this behavior:

- Blue Sky Software RoboHelp 5.0
- Borland Turbo Debugger
- IBM Global Network Dialer
- Setup programs that use InstallShield, by InstallShield Software
- Watcom Debugger version 11.0a
- Windows 98 Infrared Monitor Control Panel tool

Solution One

Add a compatibility entry for each program to the [Compatibility95] section of the WIN.INI file, the [Compatibility32] section of the WIN.INI file, or both sections. For example, Microsoft Visual C++ has the following entry in the [Compatibility95] section of the WIN.INI file:

```
MSDEV=0x00000002
```

Watcom Debugger 11.0a requires the following entry in the [Compatibility95] section of the WIN.INI file:

```
WDW=0x00000002
```

Contact the software manufacturer for the appropriate compatibility entry.

To work around this behavior, add a ForegroundLockTimeout Binary value with a data value of 00 00 00 00 to the following Registry key:

```
HKEY_CURRENT_USER\Control Panel\Desktop
```

Warning Please read the Introduction for information about how to safely edit the Registry.

Follow these steps:

1. Click the Start button, click Run, and enter *Regedit* in the Run box. Click OK.
2. Navigate your way down through the folders in the left pane until you locate the folder.
3. Create the new Binary value as just described.
4. Close Regedit.
5. Restart Windows.

Warning This alters the behavior of Windows 98 and all your programs and can lead to unexpected results.

Solution Two

Work around this behavior by pressing Alt+Tab to switch between programs in the foreground or minimize other programs on the desktop.

Related KB article Q185244

Ghost Rectangle Displays When Dragging Window

You enable the Show Window Contents While Dragging feature, and Windows shows a ghost rectangle rather than the contents of the window while dragging the window.

Solution

Many programs simulate window dragging by drawing a ghost rectangle and then moving the window when the mouse button is released. These programs override the Show Windows Contents While Dragging feature and function as they were originally written. This behavior is by design and is not changeable in Windows.

Related KB article Q132606

Monitor Displays Garbled Image

You're using Windows, and the monitor displays an image, but it is weird or garbled.

Solution

Follow this procedure to correct this problem: if you cannot see the screen well enough to perform the steps, restart your system. After your computer completes the Power On Self Test (POST), press and hold down the Ctrl key until you see the Windows 98 Startup menu, and then choose Safe mode.

1. Right-click a blank area of your desktop, and choose Properties from the shortcut menu.

2. In the Display Properties dialog box, click the Settings tab.

3. Click Advanced, and then click the Performance tab.

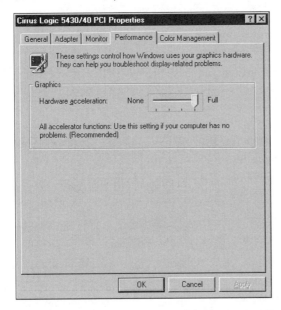

Figure 8-22. *The Performance tab in the monitor Properties dialog box.*

4. Move the Hardware Acceleration slider one notch to the left. If this step doesn't fix it, repeat until corrected.

Related KB article Q188481 or DISPLAY.TXT in the WINDOWS folder

Num Lock Indicator Light Does Not Light

Your computer resumes from Standby mode, and you notice that the Num Lock indicator light on your keyboard does not light, although the Num Lock key still works correctly.

This problem occurs when your computer's Basic Input/Output System (BIOS) does not respond correctly to the Windows 98 instruction to relight the Num Lock key.

Solution

Press the Num Lock key twice. Contact the manufacturer of your computer's motherboard to inquire about the availability of an updated BIOS that resolves this problem.

Related KB article Q188416

Program Files Folder Displays Incorrectly As Web Page

You view the PROGRAM FILES folder as a web page on a Windows 98 computer using a Windows 95 or Windows NT computer with Internet Explorer 4.0 or later installed; the file's folder is displayed incorrectly, and you see the following message:

Warning

Modifying the contents of this folder may cause your programs to stop working correctly.

To add or remove programs, click the Start button, choose Settings, click Control Panel, and then click Add/Remove Programs.

The Windows 95 and Windows NT computers do not have the WEBVIEW.CSS file installed. This file is needed to correctly display the default Windows 98 PROGRAM FILES folder in Web view.

Solution

Copy the WEBVIEW.CSS file to the PROGRAM FILES folder, and then modify the FOLDER.HTT file in the PROGRAM FILES folder by following these steps:

1. The WEBVIEW.CSS and FOLDER.HTT files have the hidden attribute. Verify that you can view hidden files on your Windows 98 computer. For information about how to do so, see KB article Q141276, "How to View System and Hidden Files in Windows."

2. Copy the WEBVIEW.CSS file to the PROGRAM FILES folder.

3. Click the Start button, choose Programs, click Windows Explorer, and then double-click the PROGRAM FILES folder.

4. Choose Customize This Folder from the View menu to start the Customize This Folder Wizard.

5. Click Next, and then click Next to open the file in Notepad.

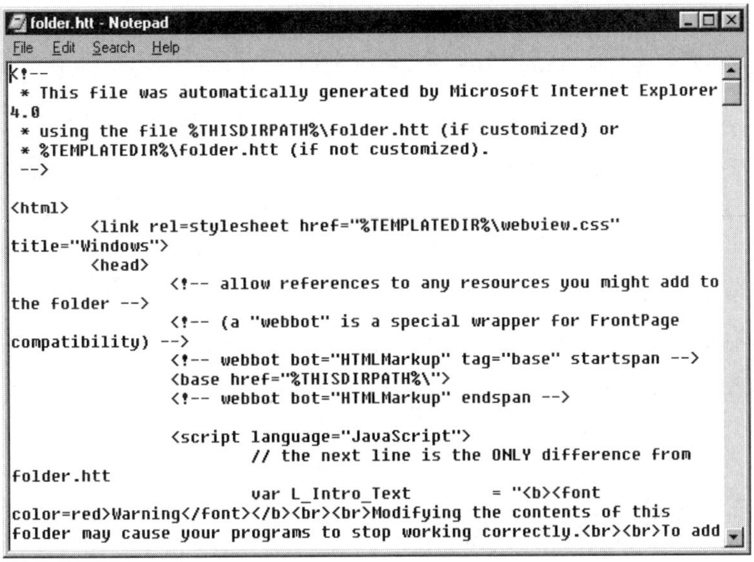

```
folder.htt - Notepad
File Edit Search Help
<!--
 * This file was automatically generated by Microsoft Internet Explorer
4.0
 * using the file %THISDIRPATH%\folder.htt (if customized) or
 * %TEMPLATEDIR%\folder.htt (if not customized).
 -->

<html>
        <link rel=stylesheet href="%TEMPLATEDIR%\webview.css"
title="Windows">
        <head>
                <!-- allow references to any resources you might add to
the folder -->
                <!-- (a "webbot" is a special wrapper for FrontPage
compatibility) -->
                <!-- webbot bot="HTMLMarkup" tag="base" startspan -->
                <base href="%THISDIRPATH%\">
                <!-- webbot bot="HTMLMarkup" endspan -->

                <script language="JavaScript">
                        // the next line is the ONLY difference from
folder.htt
                        var L_Intro_Text        = "<b><font
color=red>Warning</font></b><br><br>Modifying the contents of this
folder may cause your programs to stop working correctly.<br><br>To add
```

Figure 8-23. *The PROGRAM FILES folder open in Notepad.*

6. Remove the %TEMPLATEDIR%\ entry from the following line:

```
<link rel=stylesheet href=?%TEMPLATEDIR%\webview.css? title=?Windows?>
```

7. Choose Save from the File menu, close Notepad, click Finish, and then close Windows Explorer.

Related KB article Q184785

Screen Colors Change Incorrectly

You change the color of a button, and other colors also change. For example, if you change the color of the scroll bar button to blue, all other buttons (such as the caption buttons), the message box, the scroll bar, the inactive caption, the inactive border, the active border, and the menu bar also change to blue.

Solution

To solve this problem, follow these steps:

1. Change the button color to what you want it to be. (Changing the color of one button changes the color for all buttons. You cannot change them individually.)
2. Change the message box, scroll bar, inactive caption, inactive border, and active border items to the colors you want them to be. (Although you can change the inactive and active borders' colors, the entire border color does not change. Only a thin strip of the new color that's selected appears on the border.)

Related KB article Q119598

Title Bar Doesn't Display Fading Effect

A window's title bar (the bar at the top of the window) doesn't display a fading effect between two colors (a gradient fill) if your display adapter is configured to use a color palette of 256 colors or fewer.

Solution

Configure your display adapter to use a color palette of more than 256 colors by following these steps:

1. Click the Start button, choose Settings, click Control Panel, and then double-click the Display icon to open the Display Properties dialog box.

2. Click the Settings tab.

3. In the Colors section, click High Color (16 bit), and then click OK.

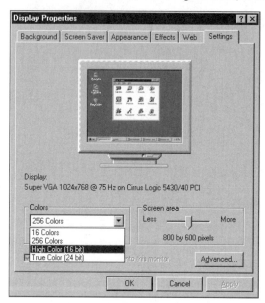

Figure 8-24.   *The Settings tab in the Display Properties dialog box.*

4. Restart your computer when you are prompted.

Related KB article Q184604

ToolTips Should Not Be Displayed

You can turn off the ToolTips that are displayed when you move the mouse pointer over the Minimize, Maximize, or Close buttons.

Solution

Use the Registry Editor to modify the UserPreferencemask value in the following Registry key:

```
HKEY_CURRENT_USER\Control Panel\Desktop
```

Follow these steps:

1. Click the Start button, click Run, and enter *Regedit* in the Run box. Click OK.

2. Navigate your way down through the folders in the left pane until you locate the indicated folder.

3. Make a note of the current value in the UserPreferencemask entry. (For example: ae 00 00 00).

4. Double-click the UserPreferencemask entry to open the Edit Binary Value dialog box. Under Value Data, the cursor is located in front of the first value (for example from above: ae). For the first number or letter, see below for the correct value to use in the next step (the second number or letter remains the same):

   - If the first character is e, use 6.

   - If the first character is a, use 2.

   - If the first character is c, use 4.

   - If the first is character 8, use the number 0.

   Type the correct first number, and then type the second number or letter. The original first value is moved to the right. Press the Delete key to remove the original value. For example: ae 00 00 00 becomes 2e 00 00 00.

5. Close Regedit.

6. Restart Windows.

Note If Profiles are enabled, the UserPreferencemask value for the Default user might also need to be changed. The key containing this is HKEY_USERS\.Default\Control Panel\desktop.

Related KB article Q186385

CHAPTER 9

Networks

Adapters

3Com Plug and Play Adapter Detected As IBM Token Ring

A 3Com Tokenlink Velocity Plug and Play (3c319) network adapter is detected as an IBM Token Ring (all types) network adapter if the 3Com adapter is in ISA/EISA (non-Plug and Play) mode.

This behavior occurs regardless of whether the network adapter is in 3Com mode or IBM mode. Even if the 3Com Tokenlink Velocity network adapter is detected correctly, it might not work properly in ISA/EISA mode. Manually installing the 3c319 driver does not work.

The IBM Token Ring (all types) network adapter driver uses I/O port A240 and Interrupt IRQ9, and these resources cannot be modified.

Solution

Use this network adapter in Plug and Play mode only. For information about how to set this network adapter to Plug and Play mode, contact 3Com Corporation.

Related KB article Q177858

Adaptec ANA-69111A/TX Network Adapter Misidentified

You have an Adaptec ANA-6911A/TX network adapter, and the Windows 98 hardware detection process incorrectly identifies it as a PCI Fast Ethernet DEC 21143-based adapter.

This behavior occurs if the network adapter responds during the hardware-detection process with an identification code that matches the PCI Fast Ethernet DEC 21143-based adapter.

Solution

Remove the PCI Fast Ethernet DEC 21143-based adapter, and then use the Adaptec installation software included with the network adapter to install the correct network adapter drivers.

To remove the PCI Fast Ethernet DEC 21143-based adapter, follow these steps:

1. Click the Start button, choose Settings, and click Control Panel.

2. Double-click the Network icon.

3. On the Configuration tab, click PCI Fast Ethernet DEC 21143 Based Adapter, and then click Remove.

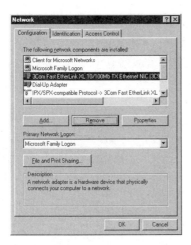

Figure 9-1. *The Network dialog box.*

4. Click OK.

Related KB article Q191033

ArcNet ISA Adapter Removes Computer from Network

You start Windows, and your computer no longer appears on the network.

The Thomas Conrad TC6245 ArcNet ISA network adapter requires a memory exclusion to prevent other devices from using its address space.

Solution One

To solve this problem, follow these steps:

1. Click the Start button, choose Run, and enter *Sysedit* in the text box.

2. Choose the C:\WINDOWS\SYSTEM\INI window.

3. In the [386Enh] section of the file, enter the line *EMMExclude=DC00-DFFF.*

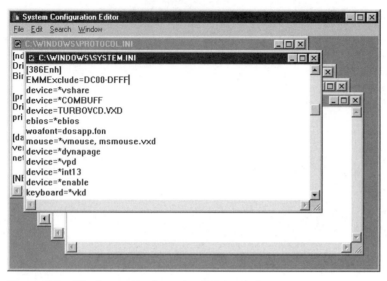

Figure 9-2.   *The System Configuration Editor window.*

4. Choose Save from the File menu and close the program.

5. Restart your computer.

Solution Two

If you are already loading EMM386.EXE in your CONFIG.SYS file, follow these steps:

1. Click the Start button, choose Run, and enter *Sysedit* in the text box.

2. Choose the C:\CONFIG.SYS window.

3. Add *X=DC00-DFFF* to the end of the line loading EMM386.EXE. For example, the line might read device=c:\windows\emm386.exe noems x=dc00-dfff.

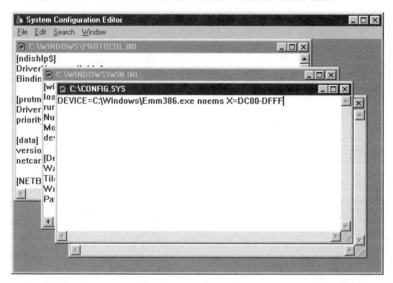

Figure 9-3.   *The CONFIG.SYS file.*

4. Restart your computer.

Note You might have to use different values for the exclusion. Make sure to exclude the actual memory range the card is using.

Related KB article Q132386

Dell Optiplex Computer Causes DIBEngine Error

Windows reports a random DIBEngine error messages using a Dell Optiplex 486 DX computer with a Phoenix BIOS.

This problem occurs when the network card is sharing a slot with another card.

Solution

Move the network card to a different ISA slot.

Related KB article Q132795

Error Code 8 Appears in Device Manager

You install Windows on a computer running real-mode networking software (such as Novell's VLM or NETX). Device Manager displays an exclamation point in a yellow circle next to the network adapter, and displays *Error Code 8* in the network adapter's properties. The real-mode network components function correctly.

This error code is generated by Configuration Manager when it tries to access the NDIS.VXD file but is unable to locate it. There actually are no problems with your networking functions.

Solution

Remove the error indicators by installing a protected-mode NDIS protocol such as NetBEUI; follow these steps:

1. Click the Start button, choose Settings, and click Control Panel.

2. Double-click the Network icon.

3. Click Add, select Protocol, and then click Add.

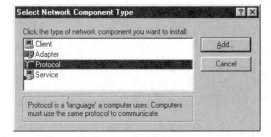

Figure 9-4. *The Select Network Component Type dialog box.*

4. Select Microsoft in the Manufacturers box, select NetBEUI from the Network Protocols list, and then click OK.

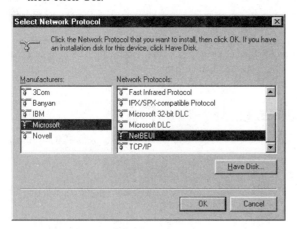

Figure 9-5.   *The Select Network Protocol dialog box.*

5. Double-click your network adapter, click the Bindings tab, and verify that the NetBEUI protocol is not bound to the adapter.

6. If the NetBEUI check box is selected, clear the check box.

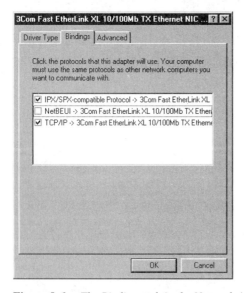

Figure 9-6.   *The Bindings tab in the Network Adapter Properties dialog box.*

7. Click OK.

Note It is not necessary to bind the NetBEUI protocol to an adapter or client because NDIS.VXD is loaded if a protected-mode NDIS protocol is present.

Related KB article Q138606

IBM Token Ring PCMCIA Network Card Does Not Connect

You use an IBM 16/4 Token Ring PCMCIA network adapter in MS-DOS mode and the adapter does not function, so the computer does not connect to the network.

This network adapter requires an IBM enabler to work properly in MS-DOS mode. The device works properly when using the 32-bit Windows drivers.

Solution

Follow these steps to load the real-mode enabler in the CONFIG.SYS file:

1. Click the Start button, and click Run.

2. Enter *Sysedit* in the text box, and click OK.

3. Choose the C:\CONFIG.SYS window, and add the following line to the CONFIG.SYS file:

   ```
   device=<path>:\pointtr.sys
   ```

   where <path> is the path to the POINTTR.SYS file.

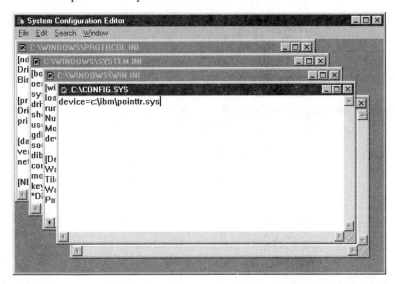

Figure 9-7. *The CONFIG.SYS file.*

Note This line should be the first line in the CONFIG.SYS file. Do not load real-mode card service drivers or socket service drivers in the CONFIG.SYS file.

4. Remove any other socket or card drivers you might have installed with your PCMCIA cards, because they are not compatible with the IBM driver. If you are unsure of which lines to remove, consult the documentation included with your PCMCIA hardware or contact the hardware manufacturer.

5. Choose Save from the File menu, and then close the program.

6. Reboot your computer.

Related KB article Q134486

Industry Standard Architecture (ISA) Network Adapter Causes Errors

You install an Industry Standard Architecture (ISA) network adapter in the docking station of a portable computer using Advanced Configuration and Power Interface (ACPI) features, and the network adapter appears in both the docked and undocked hardware profiles. If you remove the ISA network adapter from the undocked hardware profile, the computer stops responding. When this occurs, pressing Ctrl+Alt+Delete results in the following error message:

MSGSRV32 not responding.

After you receive this error message, your computer becomes unstable.

Solution

To solve this problem, follow these steps:

1. Shut down and undock the computer, and then start the computer.

2. While your computer starts, press and hold down the Ctrl key until the Windows 98 Startup menu appears.

3. Choose Safe Mode from the Startup menu, and then press the Enter key.

4. Click the Start button, choose Settings, and click Control Panel.

5. Double-click the System icon, and then click the Device Manager tab.

6. Double-click the Network Adapters branch to expand it.

Figure 9-8.   *The Device Manager tab in the System Properties dialog box.*

7. Click the ISA network adapter, and then click Remove.

8. Restart your computer normally.

Related KB article   Q190027

Multiple IP Addresses Desired for Computer with Single Network Adapter

You can use more than one IP address on a computer even though the computer has only a single network adapter.

Solution

Use Registry Editor to edit the following Registry section so that you can add additional IP addresses:

Warning Please read the Introduction for information about how to safely edit the Registry.

To do this, follow these steps:

1. Click the Start button, click Run, and enter *Regedit* in the Run box. Click OK.

2. Navigate your way down through the folders in the left pane to the following Registry section:

   `HKEY_LOCAL_MACHINE\System\CurrentControlSet\Services\Class\NetTrans\`

   You will see multiple subkeys with values of 0000, 0001, and so on. If your computer has only one network adapter, choose the 0000 entry. You should then see a value named IPAddress and a value named IPMask in the right pane. For each additional IP address, the IPAddress value should contain the current IP addresses, a string of IP addresses separated by commas with no embedded spaces. The IPMask value should be a list of comma-separated subnet masks with no embedded spaces.

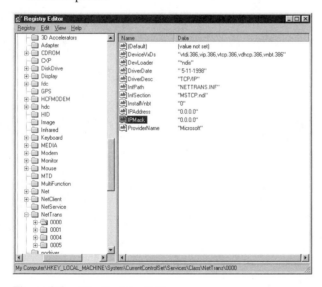

Figure 9-9. *The Registry Editor.*

3. Add a mask value for each IP address by double-clicking the key, entering the appropriate value in the Value Data text box, and then clicking OK.

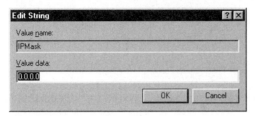

Figure 9-10. *The Edit String dialog box.*

4. Close Regedit.

5. Restart Windows.

Related KB article Q156772

Realtek Network Adapter Sends Corrupt Data Packet

You use a Realtek network adapter, and it sends an occasional corrupt data packet.

This problem occurs when you are using the RTL8029.SYS driver included with Windows 98.

Solution

Download the updated driver for your Realtek network adapter from the following Realtek web site:

http://www.realtek.com.tw/cn/NEW/doc/8029-driver.htm

Related KB article Q189778

Direct Cable Connection

Direct Cable Connection Doesn't Work with IR Port

When you attempt to connect two computers by using the Direct Cable Connection tool, you might have the option to select an LPT port. If you select an LPT port and it is an infrared (IR) port, the connection does not succeed and you receive either of the following error messages:

Waiting to connect via cable on LPT<n>. Is the host computer running?

Cannot connect to the host computer. Make sure you have Direct Cable Connection on the host computer and you have connected your cable to both computers.

Solution

Use an IR COM port rather than an IR LPT port for IR communication between computers.

Related KB article Q193587

Direct Cable Connection Won't Connect

You try to establish a connection between a Windows 95 and a Windows 98 computer using Direct Cable Connection, and you are unable to connect. By default, Windows 95 installs the NetBEUI protocol and the IPX/SPX protocol. However, Windows 98 installs only Transport Control Protocol/Internet Protocol (TCP/IP), and because Direct Cable Connection requires that the same protocol be installed on both computers, you are unable to connect.

Solution

To connect and share resources between two computers running Windows 95 or Windows 98 using Direct Cable Connection, you should have the following components installed:

- Client for Microsoft Networks

- File and Printer Sharing for Microsoft Networks

- The same protocol installed on both computers

To add Client for Microsoft Networks, follow these steps:

1. Click the Start button, choose Settings, and click Control Panel.

2. Double-click the Network icon.

3. On the Configuration tab, click Add.

4. Select Client from the list box, and then click Add.

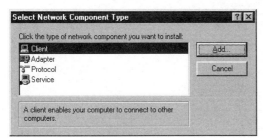

Figure 9-11. *The Select Network Component Type dialog box.*

5. In the Manufacturers box, select Microsoft. In the Network Clients box, select Client For Microsoft Networks, click OK, and then click OK again.

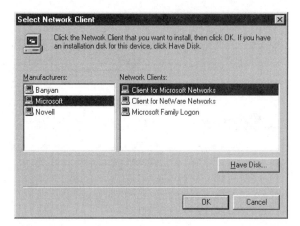

Figure 9-12. *The Select Network Client dialog box.*

6. Restart your computer when you are prompted to do so.

To add File and Printer Sharing, follow these steps:

1. Click the Start button, choose Settings, and click Control Panel.

2. Double-click the Network icon.

3. On the Configuration tab, click Add.

4. Select Service from the list box, and then click Add.

5. In the Models box, select File And Printer Sharing For Microsoft Networks, and then click OK.

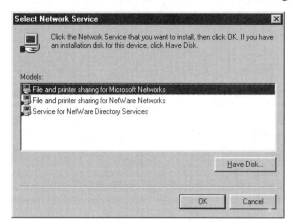

Figure 9-13. *The Select Network Service dialog box.*

6. Click OK.

7. Restart your computer when you are prompted to do so.

To add a protocol, follow these steps:

1. Click the Start button, choose Settings, click Control Panel, and double-click the Network icon.

2. Click Add, click Protocol, and then click Add.

3. In the Manufacturers box, click Microsoft. In the Network Services box, select a protocol. Be sure that at least one common protocol is installed on both computers.

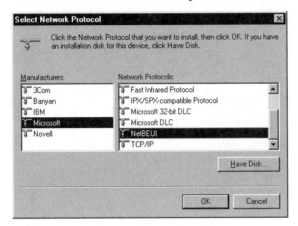

Figure 9-14. *The Select Network Protocol dialog box.*

4. Click OK, and then click OK again.

5. Restart your computer when you are prompted to do so.

Related KB article Q188167

Shared Resources Can't Be Viewed on Guest Computer

You are unable to view shared resources on a computer you are connected to using the Direct Cable Connection (DCC) tool if you are trying to use the host computer to view shared resources on the guest computer. The guest computer can view shared resources on the host computer, but the host computer cannot view shared resources on the guest computer.

Solution

Set the host as the computer whose resources you want to view. For information about how to do so, see the "Setting Up" topic in the Windows help system.

Related KB article Q194709

Drive Mapping

Cheyenne ARCSOLO 3.02 Cannot Connect to Network Drives

ARCSOLO 3.02 cannot connect to network drives mapped through Client for NetWare Networks and Client for Microsoft Networks when the drives are already mapped.

Solution

Follow these steps to add a line to your SYSTEM.INI file:

1. Click the Start button, and click Run.

2. Enter *sysedit* in the Open box, and click OK.

3. Click the SYSTEM.INI tab.

4. Enter *network.drv=commctrl.dll* on a new line under the [boot] section.

Figure 9-15. *The SYSTEM.INI window in the System Configuration Editor.*

5. Choose Save from the File menu, close the program, and then restart your computer.

Note To disable this line in your SYSTEM.INI file, type a semicolon in front of it in the System Configuration Utility.

Related KB article Q188978 or PROGRAMS.TXT in your WINDOWS folder

Mapped Network Drives Unavailable After Upgrading to Windows 98

After you upgrade Microsoft Window 3.x to Windows 98, some of your mapped network drives are unavailable. They appear in My Computer with an *X,* indicating that they are disabled. This behavior can occur if the Internetwork Packet Exchange/Sequenced Packet Exchange (IPX/SPX) protocol was the only protocol installed in Windows 3.x when you upgraded to Windows 98.

Solution

Disconnect and then reconnect the network drive by following these steps:

1. Right-click My Computer, and then choose Disconnect Network Drive from the shortcut menu.

2. Select the drive you want to disconnect, and then click OK.

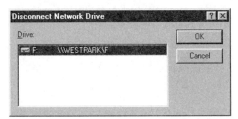

Figure 9-16. *The Disconnect Network Drive dialog box.*

3. Right-click My Computer, and then choose Map Network Drive from the shortcut menu.

4. Select a drive letter from the Drive box.

5. Enter the path to the network drive in the Path box, and then click OK.

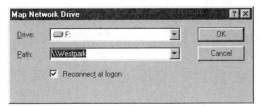

Figure 9-17. *The Map Network Drive dialog box.*

6. Repeat steps 1 through 5 for each disabled mapped network drive.

Related KB article Q191063

NET USE Command Displays Error Message

You use the NET USE command to delete a mapped network drive, and you see the following error message:

The drive letter you specified is the current drive of a command prompt. Be sure the drive you are trying to delete is not the current drive in any of your sessions.

Do you want to continue this operation? (Y/N) [N]:

This occurs even though no other command prompt is currently using the mapped network drive you are attempting to delete.

Solution

Type *y*, and then press the Enter key to delete the mapped network drive.

Related KB article Q187271

Network Shortcut to MS-DOS Program Doesn't Remap Drive

You map a network drive with Windows Explorer, create a shortcut to an MS-DOS-based program on the mapped drive, and then disconnect the mapped drive, and the drive is not reconnected automatically when you try to use the shortcut. Instead, you receive the following error message:

Cannot find the working folder for this program. The program may have difficulty locating its files and documents. Make sure that the working folder is specified correctly in the property sheets for the program and any shortcuts to it.

Do you wish to run the program anyway?

You click Yes and receive the following message:

Cannot find the file '<drive>:\<path>\<program filename>.' Make sure the file exists on your system and that the path and filename are correct.

Solution One

Click the Reconnect At Logon check box when you map the network drive. This option remaps the drive every time you start Windows. Do not disconnect the drive manually.

Figure 9-18.   *The Map Network Drive dialog box.*

Solution Two

Use a Universal Naming Convention (UNC) name in the MS-DOS-based program's command line in the shortcut.

Related KB article   Q134845

Windows 98 Computer Doesn't Allow Network Access

You try to use a Windows NT computer to connect to a share on a Windows 98–based computer and are unable to do so. When you try to map a drive, you receive the error message *Error 53 - Network name not found.* However, other Windows 95 and Windows 98 clients can view and connect to the share.

Solution One

If you are using the File And Printer Sharing for NetWare Networks service on the Windows 98–based computer and SAP advertising is not enabled, enable SAP advertising by following these steps:

1. Click the Start button, choose Settings, and click Control Panel.

2. Double-click the Network icon.

3. Select the File And Print Sharing For NetWare Networks service, and then click Properties.

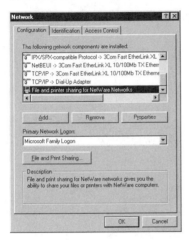

Figure 9-19. *The Configuration tab in the Network dialog box.*

4. In the Property box, select SAP Advertising. In the Value box, select Enabled.

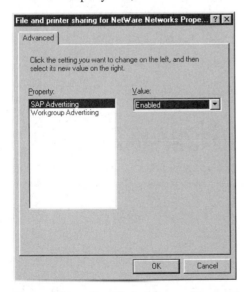

Figure 9-20. *The File And Printer Sharing For NetWare Networks Properties dialog box.*

5. Click OK, and then click OK.

Solution Two

If you are using the Internetworking Packet Exchange/Session Packet Exchange (IPX/SPX) protocol and do not have the Network Basic Input/Output System (NetBIOS) layer enabled on the Windows 98–based computer, enable NetBIOS Over IPX/SPX. To do this, follow these steps:

1. Click the Start button, choose Settings, and click Control Panel.

2. Double-click the Network icon.

3. Select the IPX/SPX-Compatible Protocol, and then click Properties.

4. Click the NetBIOS tab, and then select the I Want To Enable NetBIOS Over IPX/SPX check box.

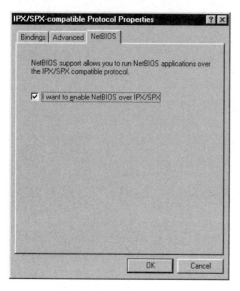

Figure 9-21. *The IPX/SPX-Compatible Protocol Properties dialog box.*

5. Click OK.

Related KB article Q190827

Windows Explorer Does Not Connect to Network Drive

You receive one of the following error messages when Windows tries to reconnect a mapped network drive or when you try to map a drive to a network resource in Windows Explorer:

> *The following error occurred while reconnecting X: to \\<server>\<share> Invalid local device. Do you want to restore this connection the next time you log on?*

> *The following error occurred while reconnecting X: to \\server\sys Permanent connection not available. Do you want to restore this connection the next time you log on?*

> *The following error occurred while trying to connect X: to \\<server>\ <share> Invalid local device.*

> *The following error occurred while trying to connect X: to \\server\sys Device not connected.*

where \\\<server>\\\<share> is a shared Microsoft resource and \\server\sys is a shared resource on a NetWare server.

This error occurs when the drive letter you are trying to map is higher than the last drive available to Windows. The last drive available to Windows is defined in the lastdrive= statement in the CONFIG.SYS file. For example, this error occurs if you try to map drive Q, but the CONFIG.SYS file contains the statement lastdrive=p.

Solution One

Remove the lastdrive= statement from the CONFIG.SYS file. To do this, follow these steps:

1. Click the Start button, and click Run.

2. Enter *notepad c:\config.sys* in the Open box, and click OK.

3. Type rem in front of the lastdrive= line.

Figure 9-22.   *The CONFIG.SYS file inNotepad.*

4. Choose Save from the File menu, close Notepad, and then restart your computer.

Solution Two

Modify the lastdrive= statement in the CONFIG.SYS file so that the last drive available to Windows is greater than the last drive letter you want to map.

Solution Three

Map a drive letter that is less than the last drive available to Windows rather than the drive letter you are trying to map. For example, if the last drive letter available to Windows is drive P, map drive O to the network resource.

Related KB article Q130077

File Sharing

Accessing Shared Folder Displays Error Message

You attempt to connect to a shared folder by clicking Start, clicking Run, entering the Universal Naming Convention (UNC) path to the folder in the Open box, and then clicking OK; then you see the following error message:

> *MPREXE caused an invalid page fault in module <unknown> at <address>.*

This error message can occur if the share name of the folder to which you are attempting to connect contains more than 46 characters.

Solution

Rename the folder's share name by using less than 46 characters, or contact your network administrator.

Related KB article Q187525

File or Printer Sharing Doesn't Work

You start your computer and see the following error message:

> *Cannot find a device file that may be needed to run Windows or a Windows Application. The Windows Registry or SYSTEM.INI file refers to this device file, but the file no longer exists. If you deleted this file on purpose, try uninstalling the associated application using its uninstall or setup program. If you still want to use the application associated with this device file, try reinstalling the application to replace the missing file, Vserver.vxd.*

A computer attempts to reconnect a mapped network drive to your computer, and the following error message is displayed on that computer:

> *The following error occurred while reconnecting <drive>: to \\<computername>\<sharename>. Permanent connection not available. Do you want to restore this connection the next time you log on?*

If someone attempts to access shared files on your computer using a Universal Naming Convention (UNC) connection, that person sees the following error message:

> *\\<computername> The network connection cannot be found.*

These error messages might appear even though file and printer sharing for Microsoft Networks is installed and enabled on your computer.

This behavior can occur if either of the following conditions exists:

- The VSERVER.VXD file is missing or damaged in the WINDOWS\SYSTEM folder.

- The DeviceVxds value with a value data of VSERVER.VXD is missing or damaged in the following Registry key:

```
HKEY_LOCAL_MACHINE\System\CurrentControlSet\Services\Class\NetService\0000
```

Solution One

Using System File Checker, extract a new copy of the VSERVER.VXD file from your original Windows CD-ROM to the <drive>:\<windows>\SYSTEM folder (<drive> is the drive on which Windows is installed, and <windows> is the folder in which Windows is installed). For information about how to replace altered files by using System File Checker, see KB article Q129605, "How to Extract Original Compressed Windows Files."

Solution Two

Follow these steps:

1. Click the Start button, choose Settings, and then click Control Panel.

2. Double-click the Network icon to open the Network dialog box.

3. Click the Configuration tab, and then click File And Print Sharing to open the File And Print Sharing dialog box.

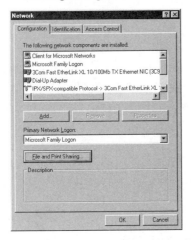

Figure 9-23. *The Configuration tab in the Network dialog box.*

4. Clear the I Want To Be Able To Give Others Access To My Files and the I Want To Be Able To Allow Others To Print To My Printer(s) check boxes.

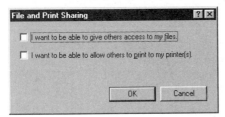

Figure 9-24. *The File And Print Sharing dialog box.*

5. Click OK, click OK again, and then restart your computer when you are prompted to do so.

6. Repeat steps 1 through 5, selecting the I Want To Be Able To Give Others Access To My Files and the I Want To Be Able To Allow Others To Print To My Printer(s) check boxes in step 4.

Related KB article Q194990

Network Doesn't Work

When Windows 98 is used on a network, a variety of hardware and software-related problems can cause one or more computers to lose the capability to browse or communicate with other computers. These problems range from no network functionality to random error messages when transmitting data across the network.

Before you begin troubleshooting your network connectivity problem, consider the following questions:

- Has this configuration ever worked before, or did this just start happening? If it just started, what has changed between the time this configuration was working and the time it stopped working?

- Has new hardware, cabling, or software been added? If this new addition is removed, does the problem go away?

- Is this problem occurring on one computer, several, or all of them? If the problem is happening on all computers, it might be cabling or connector related. If the problem is happening on only one or a few computers, it might be software or hardware related.

- Is the connection to the computer active (if the network adapter has transmit/receive data lights, are they blinking)?

To troubleshoot network connectivity problems, attempt each solution, and then attempt to connect to the computer again. If you are still unable to connect to the computer, proceed to the next solution.

Note Before you begin troubleshooting, make backup copies of the following system configuration files: CONFIG.SYS, AUTOEXEC.BAT, SYSTEM.INI, WIN.INI.

If you are receiving a network-related error message when you start your computer, look in the table of contents or index of this book, or query in the Microsoft Knowledge Base for the exact error message you experience.

Solution One

Verify that your computer and the computer you are trying to view has file and print sharing installed; follow these steps on both computers:

1. Click the Start button, choose Settings, and then click Control Panel.

2. Double-click the Network icon.

3. Verify that File And Printer Sharing For Microsoft Networks is on the list of installed network components. If it is not installed, continue with step 4. If it is installed, see Solution Two.

4. Click File And Print Sharing, select the I Want To Be Able To Give Others Access To My Files check box, and then click OK.

Figure 9-25. *The File And Print Sharing dialog box.*

5. Click OK, and then restart your computer.

Solution Two

Verify that the network adapter settings are correct and that no conflicts with other hardware devices exist. Follow these steps:

1. Click the Start button, choose Settings, and then click Control Panel.

2. Double-click the System icon, and then click the Device Manager tab.

3. If an exclamation point in a yellow circle is displayed next to the network adapter, continue with step 6.

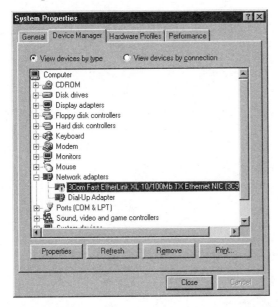

Figure 9-26. *The Device Manager showing a disabled network adapter.*

4. If a red *X* is displayed next to the network adapter, enable the network adapter by double-clicking on it, clearing the Disable In This Hardware Profile check box, and then clicking OK.

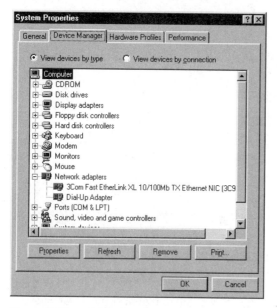

Figure 9-27. *The Device Manager showing a network adapter with a resource conflict.*

5. Click Close, and then restart your computer if you are prompted to do so. If you see an exclamation point in a yellow circle displayed next to the network adapter in Device Manager, or the network is still unavailable, continue with step 6. Otherwise, go to Solution Three.

6. Double-click the network adapter, and then click the Resources tab.

7. Verify that the resource settings are correct for your network adapter and are not conflicting with another device (see the Conflicting Device List part of the screen). To determine whether your network adapter is physically configured to use these settings, refer to the documentation included with it.

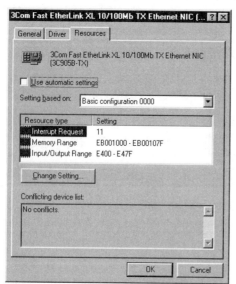

Figure 9-28. *The Resources tab in the Network Adapter Properties dialog box.*

8. To change the resource settings (if the settings don't match your hardware or are conflicting with another device), clear the Use Automatic Settings check box.

9. Specify different resource settings for the network adapter. You might need to try several settings if you do not know the settings used by other hardware devices.

10. Click OK, and then click No when you are prompted to restart your computer.

11. Click the Start button, click Shut Down, click the Shut Down option, and then click OK.

12. Turn off your computer for 10 to 15 seconds, and then turn it back on.

Continue trying different resource settings until you no longer have any hardware conflicts. If you still have network problems, see Solution Three.

Solution Three

Use System File Checker to verify that no Windows 98 networking files are damaged or replaced. For information about using System File Checker, see KB article Q185836, "Description of the System File Checker Tool (SFC.EXE)." For information about how to replace altered files using System File Checker, see KB article Q129605, "How to Extract Original Compressed Windows Files."

Note If you apply a fix provided by Microsoft, some networking files might be replaced with updated versions. To prevent further problems from occurring, do not replace these updated files.

Solution Four

Use System Configuration Utility to disable all non-essential drivers and programs that might be preventing network drivers from loading properly; follow these steps:

1. Click the Start button, choose Programs, choose Accessories, choose System Tools, and then click System Information.

2. Choose System Configuration Utility from the Tools menu.

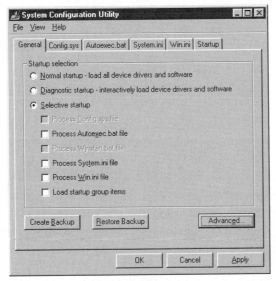

Figure 9-29.   *Using the System Configuration Utility to disable drivers at startup.*

3. On the General tab, click Selective Startup, and then clear the following check boxes: Process CONFIG.SYS File, Process AUTOEXEC.BAT File, Process WINSTART.BAT File, Process SYSTEM.INI File, Process WIN.INI File, Load Startup Group Items.

4. Click OK, and then close the System Information tool.

5. Restart your computer.

If you can access the network, selectively add back the startup items you disabled until you have pinned down the problem, and then systematically troubleshoot the file preventing you from accessing the network for the line or lines causing your problem.

Solution Five

Attempt to view other computers on the network by using a Universal Naming Convention (UNC) connection; follow these steps:

1. Click the Start button, and then click Run.

2. In the Open box type, type \\<*computername*> where <computername> is the name of the computer to which you are trying to connect, and then click OK.

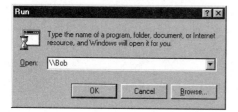

Figure 9-30.   *The Run dialog box.*

If you can view other computers using only a UNC connection, the following causes are indicated:

- A browse server may not be selected on the network. In a Windows 98 network, a computer that maintains a list of workgroup servers is selected. It can take anywhere from 5 to 15 minutes to establish a browse server. If no browse server exists, you cannot browse computers on the network. Wait a few minutes, and then try again.

- There might be a network cabling problem or a problem with the other computer's network adapter configuration. This can be the case only if the local computer appears in Network Neighborhood.

Solution Six

Verify that the network cabling and connectors are working properly and that the network cabling is connected to your computer and the computer to which you are trying to connect.

If the network cabling is Thin Ethernet, connect two computers with a single cable, T-connectors, and terminators that are known to work properly. If the network cabling is twisted-pair (RJ-45), you must use a hub or concentrator. Windows 98 does not support direct connections of RJ-45 cable between computers. This check isolates possible cabling or connector problems that might not be clearly visible.

Note It might also be necessary to reroute network cabling away from sources of electrical interference, such as fluorescent lights, radios, and cordless telephones.

If the network topology is 10Base2 (Thin Ethernet or Thinwire), place a 50-Ohm terminator on the network adapter. If the local computer name now appears in Network Neighborhood but does not appear when the regular cabling is attached, a cabling or connector problem exists. Examples of cabling and connector problems include an electrical short in the cabling, improper termination, and the use of the wrong type of cabling. Ensure that each computer's T-connector is secured on each network adapter, that 50-Ohm terminators are at each end of the network segment, and that RG-58 cabling (not RG-59 or RG-62 cabling) is being used.

If the local computer does not appear in Network Neighborhood, the problem might be with the local network adapter's hardware or software configuration. To determine whether this is the case, refer to Solution Nine.

Solution Seven

There might be a problem with the network redirector. The following test uses the Windows 98 network components to generate a NetBIOS name conflict on the network (each computer must have a unique computer name on the network). To perform this test, set two computers to use the same computer name and check to see whether an error message is generated. If an error message is displayed, the computers are communicating. If no error message occurs, a hardware problem exists on the network.

To test the network redirector, change the computer name to the name of the computer to which you are trying to connect; follow these steps:

1. Click the Start button, choose Settings, and then click Control Panel.

2. Double-click the Network icon.

3. Click the Identification tab, and then, in the Computer Name text box, type the name of the computer to which you are trying to connect.

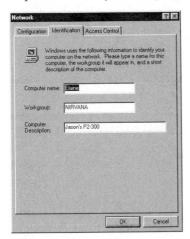

Figure 9-31. *The Identification tab in the Network dialog box.*

4. Click OK, and then click Yes when you are prompted to restart your computer. You should receive the following error message when your computer is starting up:

The following error occurred while loading protocol number 1. Error 38: The computer name you specified is already in use on the network. To specify a different name, double-click the Network icon in Control Panel.

If you receive this error message, the two computers are communicating. If you do not receive this error message, one of the following hardware problems might exist:

- The network adapter's configuration (hardware, I/O address, IRQ, and memory conflict, for example) is incorrect on one or more of the computers. For information about how to change network adapter settings, refer to Solution Two.

- One or more of the network adapters is malfunctioning. If your network adapter includes a diagnostic utility, run the utility to determine whether the network adapter is functioning properly.

- There is a problem with the cabling or connectors. This could be an electrical short or interference or a cable, connector, or terminator that is not the correct specification for your network.

    To troubleshoot electrical shorts and interference problems, either test the cabling with a testing device, or replace it with cables and connectors that are known to work correctly.

5. Repeat steps 1 through 3, changing the computer name back to its original, unique name in step 3.

Note Steps 6 through 10 are not possible unless real mode drivers for the network are loading.

---

6. Restart your computer. After your computer completes the Power On Self Test (POST), press and hold down the Ctrl key until you see the Windows 98 Startup menu, and then choose Command Prompt Only.

7. Start the real-mode redirector. To do so, type *net start workstation* at the command prompt, and then press the Enter key.

8. Try to view another computer on the network by typing *net view \\<computer name>* at the command prompt, where <computername> is the name of the computer to which you are trying to connect, and then pressing the Enter key.

9. Stop the real-mode redirector by typing *net stop* at the command prompt and then pressing Enter.

10. Restart your computer normally.

If you can connect to the computer in step 8, the problem might be caused by an upper memory block (UMB) conflict, a hardware conflict, or a virtual device driver (VxD) that is interfering with Windows 98 networking functionality. See Solution Eight for more information.

Solution Eight

Use the System Configuration Utility to exclude upper memory to determine whether a UMB conflict is causing the problem; follow these steps:

1. Click the Start button, choose Programs, choose Accessories, choose System Tools, and click System Information.

2. Choose System Configuration Utility from the Tools menu.

3. Click Advanced.

4. Select the EMM Exclude A000-FFFF check box, and then click OK.

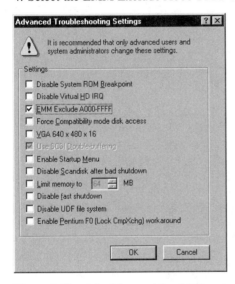

Figure 9-32. *The Advanced Troubleshooting Settings dialog box.*

5. Click OK, click OK again, and then click Yes when you are prompted to restart your computer.

6. Double-click the Network Neighborhood icon on the desktop.

If you are able to view other computers in Network Neighborhood, the network adapter's memory address needs to be excluded by using a UMB provider (such as EMM386.EXE) or by adding an EMMEXCLUDE line in the [386Enh] section of the SYSTEM.INI file.

For example, if the network adapter uses a memory address in the C800-CFFF range, use a text editor (such as NOTEPAD.EXE) or System Configuration Editor to add the following line to the [386Enh] section of SYSTEM.INI: *emmexclude=C800-CFFF*.

If you are unable to view other computers in Network Neighborhood but you are able to view them using the real-mode redirector in MS-DOS, consider the following possible causes:

■ A resource conflict exists between the network adapter and another hardware device.

■ The settings in Network properties do not match the actual settings on the network adapter.

For information about how to resolve either of these possible causes, refer to Solution Two.

Solution Nine

Remove and reinstall the network adapter drivers by following these steps:

1. Click the Start button, choose Settings, and then click Control Panel.

2. Double-click the Network icon.

3. In the list of installed network components, select your network adapter, and then click Remove.

4. Select Client For Microsoft Networks, and then click Remove.

5. Click OK, and then click Yes when you are prompted to restart your computer.

6. Repeat steps 1 and 2.

7. On the Configuration tab, click Add.

8. Select Adapter, and then click Add.

9. In the Manufactures box, select the network adapter's manufacturer, and then select the appropriate model in the Network Adapters box.

10. Click OK, click OK again, and then click Yes when you are prompted to restart your computer.

Note If the network adapter is hardware configurable (uses jumpers or switches), the settings on the network adapter and in Device Manager must match. To determine the settings for the network adapter, refer to the documentation included with the adapter or contact the network adapter's manufacturer. If the network adapter is software configurable, you might need to specify different resources in Device Manager. For example, some hard disk controllers are configured to use an I/O address of 300h by default, which is also the default for some network adapters. To change the network adapter's resource settings in Device Manager, refer to Solution Two.

---

11. Try to connect to the computer using its UNC name. For information about how to do so, refer to Solution Five.

12. If you are unable to connect to the computer using its UNC name, double-click the Network Neighborhood icon on the desktop to see whether the local computer is listed.

If you are still unable to view the local computer in Network Neighborhood or connect to other computers using the real-mode redirector, there are several other possible causes:

- The wrong network adapter driver is being used. If the adapter is emulating another adapter (such as the NE2000), it might be necessary to change jumpers or switches on the adapter for the driver to work properly. For more information about configuring the network adapter or obtaining updated drivers, contact the network adapter's manufacturer.

- The network adapter is in a slot that is not functioning correctly. To verify this, put the network adapter in another slot in the computer or install the network adapter in another computer to determine whether the adapter itself is defective.

- The network adapter is malfunctioning. Try using a different network adapter, or run a diagnostic test if one is included with the adapter.

- The bus speed on the computer is too fast for the network adapter. Most network adapters are designed to work at Industry Standard Architecture (ISA) bus speed, which is 8.33 megahertz (MHz). Setting the bus speed any faster might result in unreliable performance. The bus speed setting is usually changed in the computer's CMOS. Try lowering the computer's bus speed if intermittent problems occur.

- There is a bad or missing connection. Some network adapters, such as the Intel EtherExpress 16, include a utility that checks the integrity of wiring and connectors between two computers. If one of these utilities is available, use it to determine whether the two computers are physically connected.

Solution Ten

Run a diagnostic test on the network adapter to ensure that it is functioning correctly. Some network adapter diagnostic programs can also test communication between computers (this tests the network adapter and cabling). If this test works, Windows 98 should also work, as long as you're using the correct drivers. If this low-level test does not allow two network adapters to communicate, some type of hardware problem exists with a network adapter, the cabling, or the connectors. Contact your hardware vendor if either the network adapter diagnostic test or the network test fails.

Windows 98 includes the NET DIAG utility, which you can use to perform a low-level communications test between two computers. To perform this test, follow these steps:

1. On one computer, click Start, choose Programs, and click MS-DOS Prompt.

2. At the command prompt, type *net diag* and press the Enter key. If a NetBIOS-capable protocol (such as NetBEUI or TCP/IP) and IPX/SPX are both installed, press I (for IPX) or N (for NetBIOS) to test the network connection using that particular protocol. When you receive the following prompt:

    IPX and NetBIOS have been detected. Press I to use IPX for diagnostics, N to use NetBIOS, or E to exit this program.

    NET DIAG searches for a diagnostics server and should display the following prompt:

    No diagnostic servers were found on the network. Is Microsoft Network Diagnostics currently running on any other computers on the network?

3. Press N (for No). This step causes the computer from which you are running NET DIAG to be a diagnostic server until you press a key.

4. On another computer, click Start, choose Programs, and then click MS-DOS Prompt.

5. At the command prompt, type *net diag* and press the Enter key. If a NetBIOS-capable protocol (such as NetBEUI or TCP/IP) and IPX/SPX are both installed, you receive the following prompt:

    IPX and NetBIOS have been detected. Press I to use IPX for diagnostics, N to use NetBIOS, or E to exit this program.

6. Press I (for IPX) or N (for NetBIOS) to test the network connection using the protocol you set your first computer to use.

If you are unable to communicate with the diagnostic server using the protocol you chose, try the other protocol on both computers.

If you are able to communicate with the diagnostic server using one protocol but not the other, the network is working properly. For the protocol you are unable to communicate with, verify that it is installed correctly on both computers, and then run NET DIAG again.

If you are unable to communicate with the diagnostic server using either protocol, run NET DIAG again, but this time reverse the role of each computer.

If you are still unable to establish a connection between the two computers, continue with step 7.

7. Click the Start button, choose Programs, choose Accessories, choose System Tools, and then click System Information.

8. Choose System Configuration Utility from the Tools menu.

9. On the General tab, clear the Process CONFIG.SYS File and Process AUTOEXEC.BAT File check boxes.

10. Click OK, and then close the System Information tool.

11. Restart your computer. After your computer completes the Power On Self Test (POST), press and hold down the Ctrl key until you see the Windows 98 Startup menu, and then choose Command Prompt Only.

Note Make sure that a diagnostic server is currently running on the network.

---

12. At the command prompt, type *net diag* and press the Enter key. If a NetBIOS-capable protocol (such as NetBEUI or TCP/IP) and IPX/SPX are both installed, you receive the following prompt:

    IPX and NetBIOS have been detected. Press I to use IPX for diagnostics, N to use NetBIOS, or E to exit this program.

13. Press I (for IPX) or N (for NetBIOS) to test the network connection using the protocol you set your first computer to use.

14. Restart your computer normally. In the System Configuration Utility, click the Normal Startup button to allow your computer to boot normally again.

If you are unable to communicate with the diagnostic server using either protocol, some type of hardware problem exists with a network adapter, network cabling, or the connectors.

If your network adapter is not on the supported network adapter list, you might want to contact the network adapter manufacturer for information about the correct emulation or for an updated network adapter driver. The manufacturer might also have information about jumpers and switches that might need to be reconfigured for a particular emulation mode (for example, NE2000 emulation).

For more information about diagnosing problems with your network adapter or cabling, contact the hardware vendor.

Related KB article Q192534

Opening File on Shared Network Drive Fails

When you attempt to connect to a shared network drive on a Windows 98 computer, you receive the following error message:

Access to the specified device, path or file is denied.

Or you connect to the shared network drive, but the files on the drive are incorrect. Either can happen if the shared network drive is a removable drive that is not currently in the computer or if the shared network drive is partitioned using a non-MS-DOS file system.

Solution

Ask your network administrator to reconfigure the remaining drives so that the correct share names and access permissions are used for each drive.

In a networking environment, every shared resource has a share name that is linked to the drive letter on which the resource is located. This drive letter is associated with a logical drive on the computer. If a shared logical drive becomes unavailable, its drive letter, share name, and access permissions are assigned to a different logical drive.

For example, drive 1 is a removable drive shared with full access permissions, and drive 2 is a fixed hard disk shared with read-only access permissions. If drive 1 is not in the computer when you attempt to connect to it, you instead connect to drive 2 and have full access permissions to it. If you attempt to connect to drive 2, you receive the error message.

This problem also occurs if a shared network drive is converted to a non-MS-DOS file system. For example, drive 1 is a fixed hard disk shared with full access permissions, and drive 2 is a fixed hard disk that is not shared. If your computer is configured as a dual-boot system (that is, it is configured to run both Windows 98 and Windows NT 4.0) and you convert drive 1 to an NTFS file system, drive 2 inherits the drive letter, share name, and access permissions of drive 1 when you start Windows 98.

Related KB article Q178372

Removing Distributed File System Client Causes Problems

You upgrade a Windows 95–based computer on which the Distributed File System (DFS) client is installed in Windows 98, and the DFS service is still listed on the Configuration tab in Network properties. If you remove the DFS client in Network properties, you experience the following symptoms:

- You receive the following error message when you double-click the Network icon in Control Panel:

  Your network is not complete. Do you want to continue?

- When you restart your computer, Windows detects new hardware and attempts to install software for it.

- You lose network connectivity.

In Windows 95, you must install the DFS service separately to gain access to DFS shares on a Windows NT server. In Windows 98, this service is included in the Client for Microsoft Networks, and no separate service is required. However, Windows 98 Setup only updates the DFS components; it does not remove the separate DFS client.

Solution

If you have removed the DFS service, follow these steps:

1. Click the Start button, choose Settings, and click Control Panel.

2. Double-click the Network icon. If the error message listed above appears, click Yes.

3. On the Configuration tab, select Client For Microsoft Networks, click Remove, click OK, and then restart your computer when you are prompted.

4. Click the Start button, choose Settings, and click Control Panel.

5. Double-click the Network icon.

6. Click Add, select Client, and then click Add.

7. In the Manufacturers box, select Microsoft.

8. In the Network Clients box, select Client For Microsoft Networks, and then click OK.

9. Click OK, and then restart your computer when prompted. When your computer restarts, you should have access to DFS shares even though no DFS service is listed in Network properties.

Related KB article Q188196

Windows NT Client Does Not Connect to Windows 98 Server

You try to connect a Microsoft Windows NT workstation to a shared folder on a Windows 98 computer, and it does not connect. This problem occurs because the password encryption method used by Windows NT is different from the method used by Windows 98.

Solution

Use all uppercase or all lowercase characters in the Windows 98 shared folder password. Or you can remove password protection from the shared folder. Or you can use user-level access control rather than share-level access control.

Related KB article Q131675

Logon

Cannot Log On or Error Message at Startup

You start Windows 98, and you do not see a Windows or Network logon dialog box. You also see one of the following error messages:

No network provider accepted the given network path.

The operation being requested was not performed because the user has not logged on to the network. The specified service does not exist.

In addition, the Change Passwords tab is missing from the Passwords Properties dialog box.

This behavior can occur if the AutoLogon entry appears in the following Registry key:

```
HKEY_LOCAL_MACHINE\SOFTWARE\MICROSOFT\WINDOWS\CURRENTVERSION\NETWORK\REAL MODE
NET AUTOLOGON=<SOME NUMBER> AutoLogon=<some number>
```

Solution

Remove the AutoLogon entry from the Registry by following these steps:

1. Select AUTOLOG.INF found in the \TOOLS\MTSUTIL folder on the Windows 98 CD.

2. Right-click AUTOLOG.INF, and choose Install from the shortcut menu.

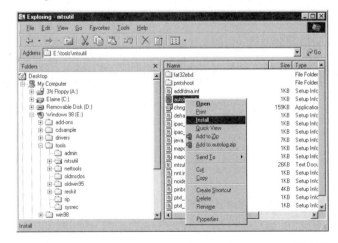

Figure 9-33. *Windows Explorer showing the contents of the Windows 98 CD-ROM.*

3. Restart your system.

Related KB article Q188480 or MTSUTILS.TXT in the TOOLS\MTSUTIL folder on the Windows 98 CD-ROM

Domain Controller Unavailable to Validate Logon

You attempt to log on to your network; then you see the following error message and are unable to view or use network resources:

No domain server was available to validate your logon

This can occur if you connect to your network by using an infrared device (not a fast infrared device) and your computer is configured to use only the IPX/SPX protocol.

Solution

Install another network protocol that is in use on your network. Find out from you network administrator which protocol to use, and then follow these steps:

1. Click the Start button, choose Settings, and click Control Panel.

2. Double-click the Network icon.

3. Click Add, select Protocol, and then click Add.

4. In the Manufacturers box, select Microsoft, and then select the appropriate network protocol in the Network Protocols list box.

5. Click OK, click OK, and then restart your computer.

Related KB article Q193670

Domain Controller Unavailable to Validate Password

You use Connection Manager to connect to a Point-to-Point Tunneling Protocol (PPTP) server over a Remote Access Services (RAS) connection, and you receive the following error message:

No domain controller was available to validate your password. You may not be able to gain access to some network resources.

When you use a Dial-Up Networking connection to connect, the error message does not occur.

Solution One

Cancel the first prompt for Windows domain logon. When Windows prompts you for a password the first time, click Cancel. When the PPTP connection connects, you are prompted for a password. Enter the password at this time.

Solution Two

Disable the Microsoft Client binding on the PPP adapter by following these steps:

1. Click the Start button, choose Settings, and click Control Panel.

2. Double-click the Network icon, and then click the Configuration tab.

3. Select TC/PIP->Dial-Up Adapter, and then click Properties.

4. Click the Binding tab, and then clear the Client For Microsoft Networks check box.

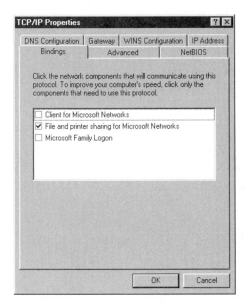

Figure 9-34. *The TCP/IP Properties dialog box.*

5. Click OK.

6. Close the Network control panel, and then restart your computer when you are prompted.

Related KB article Q193105

Error Message Prevents Network Logon

You start Windows, and you receive the following error message:

> *Unable to update configuration from <path> Error 5:Access is denied. You may need to contact your administrator.*

The system policy for your computer has an incorrect entry for the Path For Manual Update option.

Solution

Edit the Registry by using System Policy Editor (POLEDIT.EXE); check with your network administrator before you make any changes. The System Policy Editor is available in the TOOLS\RESKIT\NETADMIN folder on the Windows 98 CD-ROM. Use the Add/Remove Programs tool in the Control Panel to install System Policy Editor.

Follow these steps to edit the Registry by using System Policy Editor:

1. Click the Start button, and click Run.

2. In the Open box, enter *poledit*, and click OK.

3. Choose Open Policy from the File menu, and then double-click the policy being used.

4. Double-click the computer you want to change.

5. Double-click the Network icon, and then double-click Update.

6. Select the Remote Update check box, and then enter the path for manual update using this syntax:

For a CONFIG.POL file stored on another computer:

`\\<computername>\<sharename>\config.pol`

For a CONFIG.POL file stored locally:

`<drive letter>:\<path>\config.pol`

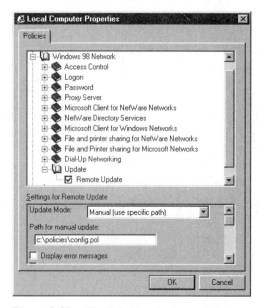

Figure 9-35. *The Policies tab.*

7. Select Manual from the Update mode drop-down list box.

8. Use Save or Save As on the File menu to save your changes, and then close System Policy Editor.

9. Restart Windows.

Note This error can also occur if you do not have the primary network login set correctly and you try to log in to the wrong server first.

Related KB article Q139705

Logon Attempt Displays Error Message

You attempt to connect to a Samba server or a LanManager server from your Windows 98–based client computer, and the following error message is displayed:

Incorrect Password.

This error message occurs even though you provide the correct user account and password.

This problem occurs because Windows 98 does not send plain text passwords to Server Message Block (SMB) servers by default.

Solution One

Configure the Samba server to support Challenge Handshake Authentication Protocol (CHAP) password encryption. Please refer to your Samba documentation for information about how to configure a Samba SMB server.

Note This method is preferred because it is more secure than sending unencrypted passwords over the network.

Solution Two

Enable Password Authentication Protocol (PAP) plain text password use in Windows 98 by following these steps:

Warning If you enable plain text password use in Windows 98, all passwords are sent on the network in an unencrypted format. These passwords might be viewed by anyone using a network monitoring program. If security is a concern for your network environment, do not enable plain text passwords.

1. Insert your Windows 98 CD-ROM in the CD-ROM drive.

2. Click the Start button, and then click Run.

3. In the Open box, type *<drive>:\tools\mtsutil*, where <drive> is the letter of the CD-ROM drive that contains the Windows 98 CD-ROM, and then click OK.

4. Right-click the PTX_ON.INF file, and then choose Install from the shortcut menu.

5. Restart your computer.

Solution Three

Use the following solution only if you do not have access to the Windows 98 CD-ROM. These steps enable PAP password use without the CD-ROM, as mentioned in Solution Two.

Warning Please read the Introduction for information about how to safely edit the Registry.

1. Click the Start button, click Run, and enter *Regedit* in the Run box. Click OK.

2. Locate the following key in the Registry:

   HKLM\System\CurrentControlSet\Services\VxD\VNETSUP

3. Change the data value for the EnablePlainTextPassword value to 1.

4. Close Regedit.

5. Restart Windows.

Related KB article Q187228

Logon to Network or Network Access Impossible

You are unable to log on to your network or gain access to network resources in Windows 95/98.

This behavior can occur if you bind the same protocol to a single network adapter multiple times. Windows 95 and Windows 98 do not detect that the protocol is already bound to the network adapter, which results in your being able to add multiple instances of the protocol to the network adapter.

Solution

Remove all duplicate entries for the protocol in Network Properties by following these steps:

1. Click the Start button, choose Settings, and click Control Panel.

2. Double-click the Network icon.

3. In the list of installed network components, select a duplicate entry for the protocol, and then click Remove. Repeat this step for each duplicate entry in the list.

4. Click OK, and then restart your computer when you are prompted to do so.

Related KB article Q191291

Logon to Novell NetWare Server Displays Error Message

You attempt to log on to a Novell NetWare server using the Novell Client32 network client, and you see the following error message:

> *Login-4.20.42-870: An unknown error was returned during LOGIN's attempt to attach. Error code: 8805.*

When this occurs, you might not be able to connect to any resources on the network. This behavior can occur if you also have the Banyan VINES 16-bit network client installed. Using both 16-bit and 32-bit clients simultaneously might result in impaired network connectivity.

Solution

Upgrade the VINES client to the 32-bit VINES client. For information about how to do this, please contact Banyan.

Related KB article Q188073

NetWare Bindery Server Doesn't Let You Log In

When you attempt to log in to a NetWare bindery server, you see the following error message:

> *The server name you specified is not valid or server is not available.*

Solution

Because this behavior can occur if your user name contains a space, replace the space with an underscore (_).

Related KB article Q190829

Network Access Denied Because User Name or Password Invalid

You attempt to establish a Dial-Up Networking (DUN) connection with another Windows computer, and a User Logon dialog box prompts you for a user name, a password, and a domain name.

Note In the Novell environment, the domain name prompt is replaced with a preferred server prompt.

You click OK and see the following message, and then your connection is terminated:

> *The computer you have dialed in to has denied access because the username and/or password is invalid on the domain.*

You are being denied access because the user name, password, domain name, or preferred server name you are using is incorrect or because the password cache files have become damaged. This can happen if the Windows Dial-Up Networking Server is

- Connected to a LAN (local area network) that uses a Microsoft Windows NT or Novell NetWare server for user validation
- Not connected to a LAN and does not use a Windows NT or NetWare server for user validation

Solution One

In the first situation, if user-level security is enabled, the DUN Server provides pass-through user validation to a Windows NT or NetWare server. In this case, correcting the erroneous user name, password, domain name, or preferred server name solves the problem.

Note When user-level security is enabled, a user must have a valid account on the network and must be added to the DUN Server's access list in order to access the network.

Solution Two

If share-level security is enabled, the server can be password-protected. In this case, the DUN Server does not provide pass-through user validation, and access to the network might be denied for the following reasons:

- There is a password for the server, but you are using an incorrect password.
- There is no password for the server, but you are providing a password.
- The RNA password list cache (.PWL) file is damaged.

If you are providing a password when one is not needed, remove the password from the Dial-Up Networking connection you are using. If you do not know whether a password is needed for the server, if you have forgotten the password, or if the .PWL files are damaged, follow these steps on both the client and server computers:

1. Close all open programs.

2. Restart your computer. After your computer completes the Power On Self Test (POST), press and hold down the Ctrl key until you see the Windows 98 Startup menu, and then choose Command Prompt Only.

Note For more information about Windows 98 startup, see KB article Q178548, "No 'Starting Windows 98' Message at Startup."

Warning You must restart your computer to a command prompt to follow these steps correctly. If you rename the RNA.PWL file in an MS-DOS session within Windows, the cached copy of the file is flushed back to disk when you shut down and restart your computer.

3. Type the following line, and press the Enter key:

```
cd <windows>
```

where <windows> is your WINDOWS folder.

4. Type the following line, and then press the Enter key:

```
ren rna.pwl rna.xxx
```

Renaming the RNA.PWL file resets the password settings for Dial-Up Server and Direct Cable Connection.

5. Restart your computer.

When you start Dial-Up Networking or when the DUN Server loads, you see an error message stating that the password list file is damaged or missing. Acknowledge this message to continue. A new RNA.PWL file is created automatically.

Related KB article   Q148899

Networking Components Can't Be Used over the Internet

You are connected to the Internet through an Internet service provider (ISP) and are not able to log in to a Windows NT Domain or use Microsoft Networking functionality to connect to another Windows NT or Windows 95/98 computer on the Internet. This might be the case even though you have been able to do so in the past.

Solution

A number of ISPs have disabled User Datagram Protocol (UDP) ports 137 and 138 and Transmission Control Protocol (TCP) port 139 on their routers to reduce network traffic and to provide protection against out-of-band (OOB) data attacks on servers. Microsoft Networking components rely on these ports (especially TCP port 139) for NetBIOS communication.

If you could previously use Microsoft Networking components over the Internet but no longer can, contact your ISP to determine whether UDP port 137 or 138 or TCP port 139 has been disabled on the ISP's routers.

It should be noted however, that this method of connecting to a Windows NT domain over the Internet is not a secure configuration and is not recommended by Microsoft. However, you can use the Point-to-Point Tunneling Protocol (PPTP) as an alternative method for communicating with your network over the Internet. PPTP is a networking technology that supports multiprotocol virtual private networks (VPNs), enabling remote users to access corporate networks securely across the Internet. Using PPTP, remote users can use Windows NT Workstation, Windows 95/98, and other point-to-point protocol (PPP)-enabled computers to dial in to a local Internet service provider to connect securely to their corporate networks using the Internet.

For more information, see the following KB articles:

- Q161410, "How to Set Up a Private Network Over the Internet Using PPTP"

- Q154062, "Using PPTP Over a Non-PPTP Enabled Internet Provider"

- Q142027, "Troubleshooting NET USE Failure (When PING NetBIOS Name Works)"

- Q143478, "Stop 0A in TCPIP.SYS When Receiving Out Of Band (OOB) Data"

- Q168747, "Update to Windows 95 TCP/IP to Address Out-of-Band Issue"

- Q139608, "SMB Traffic During Windows NT Domain Login"

Related KB article Q170998

Network Logon Displays Loading System Policies Error Message

You log on to the network and briefly see this message:

loading system policies

even though system policies are not implemented on the network. This occurs because Windows is configured to download a policy file automatically if one exists on the network. Windows displays the error message while it is searching the network for a policy file.

Solution

Use System Policy Editor to disable the update policy by following these steps:

1. Install System Policy Editor if it is not already installed. For information about how to do so, follow the instructions in the POLEDIT.TXT file located in the TOOLS\RESKIT\NETADMIN\ POLEDIT folder on the Windows CD-ROM.

2. Click the Start button, and click Run.

3. Type *poledit* in the Open box, and then click OK.

4. Choose Open Registry from the File menu.

5. Double-click Local Computer, double-click Windows 98 Network, and then double-click Update.

6. Clear the Remote Update check box, and then click OK.

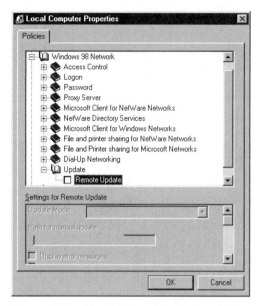

Figure 9-36. *The Policies tab in the Local Computer Properties dialog box.*

7. Choose Save from the File menu, and then exit the program.

8. Restart Windows.

Related KB article Q194094

Network Resource Access Denied Because of Cached Password

You try to access a network resource while password caching is enabled, and access to the network resource is denied.

This problem occurs when Windows caches your passwords in the password list file when you connect to a password-protected network resource.

Solution

Remove entries in the password list (.PWL) file by using Password List Editor (PWLEDIT.EXE.) To do this, you must be logged on using the computer that has the problem. To install Password List Editor, follow these steps:

1. Click the Start button, choose Settings, and click Control Panel.

2. Double-click the Add/Remove Programs icon, and click the Windows Setup tab.

3. Click Have Disk.

4. In the Copy Manufacturer's Files From box, Enter *<CDROM drive>:tools\reskit\netadmin\ pwledit* (where <CDROM drive> is the drive letter of the CD-ROM drive containing the Windows 98 CD-ROM).

5. Click OK.

6. Click Password List Editor, and then click Install.

7. After installation is complete, click Start, choose Programs, choose Accessories, choose System Tools, and click Password List Editor.

8. To remove a password entry, select the entry from the list, and then click Remove.

Related KB article Q147833

No Logon Server Available

You attempt to connect to a share on a Windows-based computer that is using a Windows NT domain to provide user-level security, and you receive the following error message:

There are currently no logon servers available to service the logon request.

This problem occurs regardless of which users have been given access to the share you are connecting to and which access rights each user has been given. This problem does not occur when the Windows-based computer you are connecting to is configured for share-level security.

This problem can occur when your user account is configured so that you can log on to certain computers in the domain. If your user account is configured in this manner and the Windows-based computer you are attempting to connect to is not one of the specified computers, you are unable to connect to resources on that computer. This can also occur on a peer-to-peer network when the computer you are trying to connect to is configured for user-level security.

Solution

Configure the Windows-based computer you are attempting to connect to for share-level security, or contact your network administrator. To configure a Windows-based computer for share-level security, follow these steps:

1. Click the Start button, choose Settings, and then click Control Panel.

2. In Control Panel, double-click the Network icon to open the Network dialog box.

3. Click the Access Control tab.

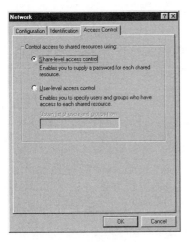

Figure 9-37. *The Access Control tab in the Network dialog box.*

4. Click Share-Level Access Control, click OK, and then restart your computer when you are prompted to do so.

Note After you change the type of access control, any resources that were shared on that computer are no longer shared. You must share the resources again to allow other people to access them.

If the Windows-based computer you are attempting to connect to cannot be configured for share-level security, ask your network administrator about additional workarounds that will allow you to access resources on that computer.

Related KB article Q157063

No Network Access Using Domain Name

Using the TCP/IP protocol, you are unable to access network resources using a domain name. You can access the resource using an IP address. Or, when you try to ping a host name, you receive the following error message:

Bad IP address

Solution

Rename or delete the WIN.COM file in the root folder of the boot drive. Windows cannot use WINS, DNS, or HOSTS files for name resolution when a WIN.COM file is in the root folder of the boot drive. In this case, the WINDOWS folder, rather than the WINDIR folder, becomes the root folder, and Windows cannot locate files in the SYSTEM folder.

This problem can occur if the WIN.COM file is in any folder listed before the WINDOWS folder in the PATH environment variable.

Related KB article Q162811

Password List Does Not Save Passwords

You select the Save This Password in Your Password List check box in a logon dialog box, and you are prompted for your password the next time you log on, even though your password has not changed.

This problem occurs when the password list file is damaged.

Solution

Delete or rename your password list file by following these steps:

1. Click the Start button, and click Find.

2. Enter in the text box the user name you use to log on, and select drive C: from the Look In drop-down list.

3. Click Find Now.

4. Right-click the file that has your user name with the .PWL file extension.

5. Choose Delete or Rename from the shortcut menu.

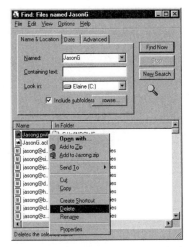

Figure 9-38. *The Find: Files dialog box.*

6. After deleting or renaming the file, restart Windows.

Related KB article Q135197

Real-Mode Networking Services Loads Incorrect Network Redirector

You start the Windows real-mode networking services, and the commands NET LOGON or NET START WORKSTATION load the incorrect network redirector.

The NET.EXE file contains two redirectors: VREDIR for the Microsoft Client, and NWREDIR for the NetWare Client. Windows determines which redirector to load by checking the Preferredredir key in the Registry. If this key is not set, VREDIR is loaded by default.

Solution

Check the Primary Network Logon setting to ensure that the desired client is selected. To check the Primary Network Logon setting, follow these steps:

1. Click the Start button, choose Settings, and then click Control Panel.

2. Double-click the Network icon.

3. In the Network dialog box, select the desired client from the Primary Network Logon drop-down list box, and then click OK. This setting automatically makes the appropriate changes to the Registry.

The NET LOGON command does not work with NWREDIR. The NET LOGON command is not supported with NetWare NCP servers. If you use this command with NWREDIR, you receive the following error message:

Error 50: You attempted an operation that cannot be performed from your computer or that is not supported on the specified server.

Related KB article Q134595

Unable to Log On to TCP/IP Network

You install Windows 98 on a computer participating in a Transmission Control Protocol/Internet Protocol (TCP/IP) network, and you see the following error message when you attempt to log on to the network:

Invalid VxD dynamic link call from VNBT(01) 0000F4aa. This was called from VTDI, service E.

This behavior can occur if the VTDI.386 file is in a folder other than the WINDOWS\SYSTEM folder.

Solution

Rename the files by following these steps:

1. Click the Start button, choose Find, and then click Files Or Folders to open the Find dialog box.

2. In the Named box, enter *vtdi.386*, and then click Find Now.

3. In the list of found files, right-click a VTDI.386 file that is not in the WINDOWS\SYSTEM folder, and then choose Rename from the shortcut menu.

4. Type a new name for the VTDI.386 file (such as *VTDI.xxx*), and press the Enter key.

5. Repeat steps 3 and 4 for each VTDI.386 file that is not in the WINDOWS\SYSTEM folder.

6. Close the Find tool, and then restart your computer.

Related KB article Q194536

Unable to Log On to Windows NT Domain

If the Client for Microsoft Networks is installed and configured to log on to a Windows NT domain, you see the following error message when you attempt to log on to the domain as part of the Windows startup and logon process:

No domain server was available to validate your password. You may not be able to gain access to some network resources.

In addition, if you attempt to use Dial-Up Networking to connect to your Windows NT network, the following situations occur, even though the Log On To Network option is selected in the Dial-Up Networking connection you are using:

- You have a Windows NT login script configured, and your login script is not processed when you connect to the network using Dial-Up Networking.

- User profiles and system policies, if so configured, are not updated or downloaded from the network server.

These symptoms might occur if a network adapter is in the computer, but the computer is not physically connected to the local area network (LAN). This might be the case when you are logging on from a remote location with a portable computer that contains a PC Card network adapter but is not currently connected to the LAN.

When Windows starts, it checks for the presence of a network adapter. If one is found, it attempts to log on to the Windows NT domain, if so configured, when you first log on to Windows. Regardless of whether this initial attempt succeeds, Windows attempts to log on to the domain only once during your Windows session.

If Windows does not detect the presence of a network adapter in the computer when you start Windows, it does not attempt to log on to the Windows NT domain when you first log on to Windows. If you later connect to the network by using Dial-Up Networking and have the Log On To Network option enabled, Windows attempts to log on to the Windows NT domain and process your login script. Again, this occurs only once during your Windows session; if you disconnect your Dial-Up Networking connection and then later reconnect without either restarting Windows or logging off and logging on again, Windows does not repeat your domain logon and does not process your login script again.

Solution One

Before you log on to Windows on a computer that is not connected to the LAN, remove the network adapter from the computer. This prevents Windows from attempting to log on to the Windows NT domain when you first log on to Windows. Later, when you connect to your network by using Dial-Up Networking, Windows attempts to log you on to the Windows NT domain and process your login script (if any).

Solution Two

Create a separate hardware profile for when you want to work while not connected to the LAN. In the new hardware profile, disable the network adapter in Device Manager. When you start the computer, you can choose between the two hardware profiles you created. When your computer is not connected to your LAN, choose the hardware profile in which the network adapter is disabled.

Note For additional information, see KB articles Q141600, "How to Manually Create Hardware Profiles for Laptop Computers," and Q128919, "Resources for Disabled Devices Not Freed Up."

If your computer has a docking station you always use when it's connected to your LAN, and that you never use when you are not connected to the LAN, you can disable the network adapter in the Undocked hardware profile rather than create a new profile.

If the network adapter can be installed in the docking station rather than in the laptop computer itself, you can install the network adapter in the docking station rather than manually disable it in the Undocked profile.

Solution Three

When your computer is not connected to the LAN, you might be able to bypass the initial Windows logon screen by clicking Cancel in the Windows logon dialog box. In this case, you are not logged on to the network or to the Windows NT domain unless and until you log on using Dial-Up Networking. However, if user profiles are enabled for your installation of Windows, you should not use this method because you may not receive your user-specific settings unless you are logged on to Windows as yourself.

Related KB article Q193937

User Name Can't Be Found

You type a valid user name followed by one or more spaces in the login dialog box, and you see the following error message:

The username cannot be found

The name appears correct because the spaces are not displayed.

Solution

Because Windows treats any space (whether leading or trailing) as a valid character, avoid typing leading or trailing spaces in the User Name box on the login screen. To determine whether leading or trailing spaces exist, select the name with the mouse to see whether the spaces are highlighted.

Related KB article Q193615

User's Profile Has Different User's Settings

You log on to a Windows workstation that has user profiles enabled and you get a previous user's settings.

This problem occurs when the home directory for the domain server is set to a local default directory and Windows assumes that all users want to share settings.

Solution

To solve this problem, follow these steps:

1. Go to the Windows NT domain controller computer.

2. Click the Start button, choose Programs, choose Administrative Tools (Common), and click User Manager for Domains.

3. Double-click a user's icon, and then click Profile.

4. Verify that the Connect option is selected and the text box contains a valid network path; for example, *<logon server>\Home\username*.

5. Repeat steps 3 and 4 for each user on the domain network.

Related KB article Q132818

Users with Identical User Names Have Identical Settings

Users with the same user name on different servers or domains appear to be the same user to Windows and use the same user profile.

Windows identifies a user's profile by user name only. When a user logs on, if the profile on the workstation is newer than the profile on the server, the profile is copied to the server. This behavior is by design for mobile computing because the user might have changed the profile while not connected to the network.

Solution

To solve this problem, follow these steps:

1. Have users with the same user names on different servers or domains change their user names so that they are not identical.

2. When another user with the same user name logs on in the future, have that user click No when prompted with this message:

   You have not logged on at this computer before. Would you like this computer to retain your individual settings for use when you log on here in the future?

3. Rename the user profiles with this problem from USER.DAT to USER.MAN in the user's home directory. This step prevents Windows from copying the profile back to the server and forces the user to use the profile.

Related KB article Q135211

Validating Server Information Not Displayed

Windows doesn't display a dialog box that lists the server which validates a Windows client logging on to a Microsoft Windows NT or LAN Manager domain. This information can be very useful if you are troubleshooting network problems.

Solution One

Use System Policy Editor, available in the TOOLS\RESKIT\NETADMIN\POLEDIT folder on the Windows 98 CD-ROM, to edit the Registry. Follow these steps:

1. Click the Start button, and then choose Run.

2. In the Open box, type *poledit* and click OK.

3. From the File menu, choose Open Registry, and then double-click Local Computer.

4. Double-click the Network icon, and then double-click Microsoft Client For Windows Networks.

5. Select the Log On To Windows NT check box.

6. In the Settings For Log On To Windows NT section, select the Display Domain Logon Confirmation check box, and then click OK.

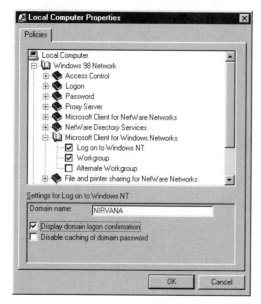

Figure 9-39. *The Policies tab in the Local Computer Properties dialog box.*

7. Save your changes, and close System Policy Editor.

8. Restart Windows.

Solution Two

Follow these steps to edit the Registry by using Registry Editor:

Warning Please read the Introduction for information about how to safely edit the Registry.

1. Click the Start button, click Run, and enter *Regedit* in the Run box. Click OK.

2. Navigate your way down through the folders in the left pane until you locate the following Registry key:

```
HKEY_LOCAL_MACHINE\Network\Logon
```

3. Use Registry Editor to add a DWORD value named DomainLogonMessage to this Registry key.

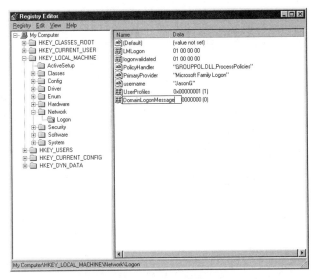

Figure 9-40. *The Registry Editor window.*

4. Set the data value for DomainLogonMessage to 1.

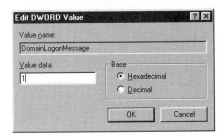

Figure 9-41. *The Edit DWORD Value dialog box.*

5. Close Regedit, and restart Windows.

Related KB article Q150898

Network Neighborhood

Folder Is Not Accessible Using Remote Computer

You attempt to access a folder on a remote Windows computer and receive one of the following error messages:

Folder <Folder Name> does not exist

The folder (path) does not exist

This error occurs when the name of the remote folder is identical to the volume label of the remote drive that contains the folder or if the Network Neighborhood icon is hidden by using the TweakUI PowerToy.

Solution

To solve this problem, use one of the following methods:

- Change the volume label of the remote drive.

- Rename the remote folder.

- Use TweakUI to unhide the Network Neighborhood icon.

- Share the folder directly. Access the folder by using a \\<computername>\<foldername> \\<comp>\driveshare>\<folder> naming convention.

Note You cannot make either of the first two changes locally. You must make them at the remote computer.

Related KB article Q130597

Network Neighborhood Does Not Display Computers

You double-click the Network Neighborhood icon to browse computers on your network, and Network Neighborhood searches endlessly without displaying any computers. This behavior can occur if NetSoft NS/Portfolio for AS/400 with SNA Client 2.11 is installed on your computer.

Solution

Contact NetSoft to inquire about the availability of an updated version of NS/Portfolio.

Related KB article Q188142

Unable to Browse Network

You attempt to browse computers on your network by using Network Neighborhood, but only the Entire Network icon is displayed. When you double-click Entire Network, you see the following error message:

> *Unable to browse the network. The network is not accessible. For more information, look in the Help Index, at the topic 'Network Troubleshooter.'*

This can occur if a Peripheral Component Interconnect (PCI) network adapter is being used on one of the computers on the network. If the network adapter is in PCI slot 1 and an Accelerated Graphic Port (AGP) video adapter is installed, a conflict between the network adapter and the AGP video adapter can occur and prevent you from browsing the network.

Solution One

Verify that resources are being assigned automatically to the network adapter by following these steps:

1. Click the Start button, choose Settings, and then click Control Panel.

2. Double-click the System icon to open the System Properties dialog box.

3. Click the Device Manager tab, click the Network Adapters branch to expand it, click your network adapter, and then click Properties to open the Properties dialog box.

4. Click the Resources tab, click the Use Automatic Settings check box, click OK, and then click OK again.

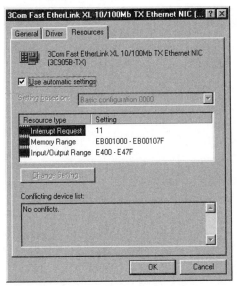

Figure 9-42. *The Resources tab in the Network Adapter Properties dialog box.*

Solution Two

Move the network adapter from slot 1 to another available PCI slot. For information about how to do so, see the documentation included with the computer, or contact the computer's manufacturer.

Solution Three

Disable PCI bus IRQ steering. For information about how to do so, see KB article, Q182628, "How to Disable PCI Bus IRQ Steering in Windows."

Solution Four

In the computer's Basic Input/Output System (BIOS), change the shared interrupt request line (IRQ) to Industry Standard Architecture (ISA) so that it cannot be assigned by PCI bus IRQ steering. For information about how to change BIOS settings, see the documentation included with the computer, or contact the computer's manufacturer.

Solution Five

Verify that a resource conflict does not exist between the network adapter and another device in the computer. If a resource conflict exists between the network adapter and another device, it might not be apparent in Device Manager. For information about how to troubleshoot resource conflicts, see KB article Q192534, "Troubleshooting Windows 98 Network Connection Problems."

For information about how to contact the computer's manufacturer, see one of the following KB articles: Q65416, "Hardware and Software Third-Party Vendor Contact List, A-K"; Q60781, "Hardware and Software Third-Party Vendor Contact List, L-P"; or Q60782 "Hardware and Software Third-Party Vendor Contact List, Q-Z."

Related KB article Q193938

Novell Networks

Error Message After Upgrading NetWare Client32

You upgrade your Windows 98–based computer from the Novell Client32 version 2.11 or 2.12 program to version 2.20 and then restart your computer, and you see the following error message:

Windows Networking: The following error occurred while restoring <drive letter>: to <server and share name> Permanent connection not available. Do you want to restore this connection the next time you log on?

You are also unable to access or view a resource on a persistent-mapped Windows NT network drive, although other methods of accessing this Windows NT network drive might still work.

Solution

Manually re-create persistent-mapped network connections to the appropriate Windows NT network drives after you upgrade to Novell Client32 version 2.20. Note that when you map a network drive, to make the connection "persistent," you must select the Reconnect At Logon check box in the Map Network Drive dialog box.

Related KB article Q188722

IntraNetWare Login Shortcut Does Not Appear on Start Menu

You perform a custom installation of the Novell Client32 network client, and the IntraNetWare Login shortcut does not appear on the Start menu.

This problem occurs when you install both the Novell NetWare/IP protocol and the Novell IPX/IP Gateway service. Installing both the NetWare/IP protocol and the IPX/IP Gateway service is not a recommended configuration.

Solution

Uninstall and then reinstall the Novell Client32 client. For information about uninstalling and re-installing Novell Client32, consult the documentation included with the Novell Client32 client, your network administrator, or Novell.

Related KB article Q188333

Microsoft Client for NetWare Networks Prevents Network Access

If you have Microsoft Service for NetWare Directory Services installed and remove the Client for NetWare Networks, you see the following error message and then are unable to access the network correctly:

The NetWare-compatible shell is not available. Contact your network administrator.

The Microsoft Service for NetWare Directory Services is still installed. Removing the Client for NetWare Networks before removing the Microsoft Service for NetWare Directory Services deletes Registry information that other programs might require.

Solution

Reinstall the Client for NetWare Networks by following these steps:

1. Click the Start button, choose Settings, and click Control Panel.

2. Double-click the Network icon to open the Network dialog box.

3. Click the Configuration tab, and then click Add to open the Select Network Component Type dialog box.

4. Select Client, and then click Add to open the Select Network Client dialog box.

5. From the Manufacturers list, select Microsoft, and from the Network Clients list, select Client For NetWare Networks.

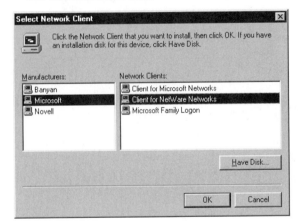

Figure 9-43. *The Select Network Client dialog box.*

6. Click OK, and then restart Windows.

Now follow these steps to remove the Microsoft Service for NetWare Directory Services:

1. Click the Start button, choose Settings, and click Control Panel.

2. Double-click the Network icon to open the Network dialog box.

3. Select Service For NetWare Directory Services, and then click Remove.

4. Select Client For NetWare Networks, and then click Remove.

5. Click OK.

6. Restart Windows.

Related KB article Q148729

MPREXE.EXE Causes Invalid Page Fault

A program that uses the old GetOpenFileName() API is logged on to a Novell Network, and the following error message occurs:

MPREXE.EXE caused an invalid page fault in module KERNEL32.DLL

This error message occurs as a result of a problem with the Client for NetWare Networks and the Microsoft Service for NetWare Directory Services (MSNDS) network clients.

Solution

Contact Microsoft Technical Support to obtain the fix for this problem. A supported fix that corrects this problem should be applied only to computers experiencing this specific problem. If you are not severely affected by this specific problem, Microsoft recommends that you wait for the next service pack that contains this fix.

For a complete list of Microsoft Technical Support phone numbers and information about support costs, please go to the following address on the World Wide Web:

http://support.microsoft.com/support/supportnet/default.asp

Related KB article Q192249

NetWare 4.xx Server Hyperlink Does Not Work

You click an embedded hyperlink that points to an object on a Novell NetWare 4.xx server and nothing happens. The error message you receive varies depending on which program is used to create the document containing the hyperlink. If Microsoft WordPad is used, the error message is as follows:

Failed to create the object. Make sure the application is entered in the system Registry.

If Word or Excel is used, the error message is as follows:

Cannot open the specified file.

This problem occurs when the Client for NetWare Directory Services (NDS) installs and the file being linked is located on a NetWare 4.xx server running NDS. Windows 98 treats the NDS and Bindery systems as separate file systems. Network Neighborhood displays both the server and an NDS tree that represent the two file systems. To create a hyperlink to a document, you must choose the appropriate file system. Mapped drives do not fully implement the NDS file system.

Solution

Use a Universal Naming Convention (UNC) path traversing the NDS tree to the target file to link a path to the object by following these steps:

1. Click the Start button, choose Programs, choose Accessories, and click WordPad.

2. On the Insert menu, click Object.

3. Click Create From File.

4. Click the Link check box to select it.

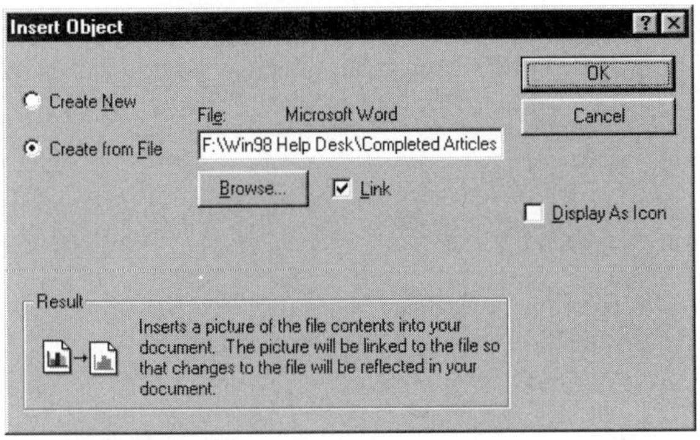

Figure 9-44. *The Insert Object dialog box.*

5. Click Browse.

6. In the Look In box, select Network Neighborhood.

7. Locate the folder, not the server name, containing the object.

8. Double-click the object.

9. Click OK.

Related KB article Q192332

NetWare Administrator Program Causes Error Messages

You run the Novell NetWare Administrator program (NWADMIN.EXE) on a computer running Windows configured with the Client for NetWare Networks, and an MS-DOS window opens and displays the following error message:

> *This program must be run under Microsoft Windows*

The reason is that the NetWare Administrator program (NWADMIN.EXE) works only with Novell VLM (the NetWare MS-DOS requester) and not with the Client for NetWare Networks.

When you run NWADMIN.EXE on a computer running Windows configured with the Microsoft Service for NetWare Directory Services (NDS), you might receive one of the following error messages:

> *Invalid Context*

> *Unknown Object Type*

> *Cannot read object's information*

> *Program Error: Your program is making an invalid dynamic link call to a .DLL file.*

These error messages might occur when you run Microsoft Service for NetWare Directory Services (NDS) and NETWARE.DRV, NWADMIN.EXE, and all the required .DLL files do not match.

Solution One

If you're using Client for NetWare Networks, use the real-mode VLM instead in order to use the NetWare Administrator program. Contact Novell Technical Support if you need technical assistance configuring VLM.

Solution Two

If you're using Microsoft Service for NetWare Directory Services (NDS), follow these steps to run NWADMIN.EXE:

1. Make sure that the NETWARE.DRV file you are using is the one included with the Microsoft Service for NetWare Directory Services (NDS).

2. Make sure that you have at least version 4.10.2 of NWADMIN.EXE and its required .DLL files. These .DLL files are supplied by Novell and should be located in the public folder from which you are running NWADMIN.EXE.

3. Make sure that you have in your WINDOWS\SYSTEM subfolder the latest .DLL files from NWDLL2.EXE. You can display the WINDOWS\SYSTEM subfolder in Windows Explorer by clicking the Start button, choosing Programs, and clicking Windows Explorer. Display the contents of your hard drive by clicking the plus sign next to your hard drive in the folder list. Then click the plus sign next to the WINDOWS folder and click the SYSTEM folder to select it. The most recent version of NWADMIN.EXE is in NWAMN2.EXE and is available on the Novell FTP site. You can use Internet Explorer to access the FTP site by clicking Launch Internet Explorer on the Quick Launch toolbar and entering *ftp://ftp.novell.com* in the Address box. NWDLL2.EXE is also available at this location.

Related KB article Q124712

NetWare Client Hangs Computer or Reboots at Shutdown

Novell NetWare Client version 4.10 (VLM.EXE) causes your computer to stop responding (hang) or restart when you shut down your computer.

Solution

Obtain the latest version of NetWare redirector from Novell.

Related KB article Q132776

NetWare Directory Services Causes Errors

You run a NetWare Directory Services (NDS) tool, and you receive one of the following error messages:

Unicode not loaded

Can't set context

This problem occurs because your NetWare client does not have access to Unicode tables.

Solution

Map a search drive to the PUBLIC\NLS directory on your NetWare server. To do so, you can either use a search drive mapping or set the local path environment variable. Consult your NetWare documentation to learn how to do this.

Related KB article Q138047

NetWare Driver Does Not Load

You start Windows and receive the following error message:

Cannot load a device file that is specified in the SYSTEM.INI. The performance of Windows should not be affected without this file NWREDIR.VXD. Press a key to continue.

You press any key and receive the following error message:

Invalid VxD dynamic link call from NWREDIR(04) + 000000B9 to device "0487," service 6. Your Windows configuration is invalid.

This problem occurs when you load a real-mode NetWare redirector (NETX or VLM) while the Client for NetWare Networks (NWREDIR) loads for the same network card. This problem can also occur if the real-mode protocol driver IPXODI.COM (or any other ODI driver) is being bound to the network adapter before NWREDIR is loaded, even if either NETX or VLM is being used.

Solution One

Remove the real-mode NetWare driver from the AUTOEXEC.BAT file by following these steps:

1. Click the Start button, and select Run.

2. Enter *Sysedit* in the text box, and click OK.

3. In the AUTOEXEC.BAT window, delete any line that contains STARTNET.BAT, NETX.EXE, or VLM.EXE.

4. Close the window, and reboot the computer.

Solution Two

Remove the Client for NetWare Networks and add the correct driver for the NetWare shell you are using by following these steps:

1. Click the Start button, choose Settings, and click Control Panel.

2. Double-click the Network icon.

3. Select Microsoft Client For NetWare Networks, and then click Remove.

4. Click Add, click Client, and then click Add.

5. In the Manufacturers box, select Novell. In the Network Clients box, select the appropriate client for the NetWare shell you are using. (If you do not know which NetWare shell you are using, contact your network administrator.)

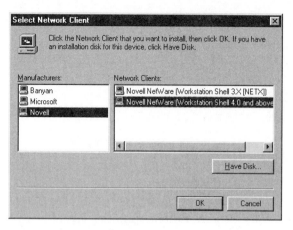

Figure 9-45. *The Select Network Client dialog box.*

6. Click OK, and then click OK again.

7. Insert the appropriate Windows 98 disk as required.

8. Insert the appropriate Novell workstation disk as required.

Related KB article Q129389

NetWare Filenames Truncated

You view a Novell NetWare volume using the DIR command or the VOL command at an MS-DOS prompt in Windows, and only the first eight characters of the volume name are displayed. This can occur when you use Client for NetWare Networks or Microsoft NetWare Directory Services (MSNDS).

Solution One

View the NetWare volume in Windows Explorer.

Solution Two

Use the MAP command at an MS-DOS prompt to display the list of mapped drives and their volume names. To do so, type the following command at the MS-DOS prompt, and then press the Enter key:

```
map
```

Related KB article Q185785

NetWare Networks Makes AUTOEXEC.BAT File Inaccessible

When you install the Client for NetWare Networks as the network services provider, drives that are mapped and printers that are captured in the AUTOEXEC.BAT file are no longer available.

This occurs if Novell NetWare version 3.x or 4.x real-mode drivers were being loaded from the AUTOEXEC.BAT file before you installed the Client for NetWare Networks. The Client for NetWare Networks uses NWREDIR rather than NETX or VLM as the network redirector. NWREDIR is a 32-bit protected-mode redirector that is loaded when Windows is loading. The AUTOEXEC.BAT file is processed before NWREDIR is loaded. Because the AUTOEXEC.BAT file is processed before network services are started, network drives cannot be mapped and network printers cannot be captured in the AUTOEXEC.BAT file.

Solution One

Rather than map network drives in the AUTOEXEC.BAT file, reconnect each network drive in Windows 98 as a persistent connection. To do this, follow these steps:

1. Start Windows Explorer.

2. Choose Map Network Drive from the Tools menu.

3. In the Drive box, click the drive letter you want for the connection.

4. In the Path box, enter the path for the network connection.

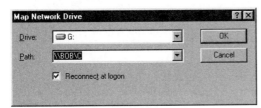

Figure 9-46. *The Map Network Drive dialog box.*

5. Select the Reconnect At Logon check box.

6. Click OK.

7. Repeat steps 2 through 6 for each network drive.

8. Remove the Map commands from the AUTOEXEC.BAT file. The network connections will be available each time you start Windows.

Solution Two

Rather than capture network printers in the AUTOEXEC.BAT file, follow these steps:

1. Click the Start button, choose Settings, and then click Printers.

2. Double-click the Add Printer icon to start the Add Printer Wizard.

3. When you are asked *How is this printer attached to your computer?* click Network Printer, and then click Next.

4. In the Network Path Or Queue Name box, enter the correct path or queue name for the network printer. If you print from MS-DOS-based applications as well as from Windows-based applications, click Yes underneath the Do You Print From MS-DOS-Based Programs? prompt. Click Next.

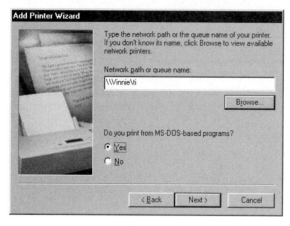

Figure 9-47. *The Add Printer Wizard.*

5. Click Next.

6. Click Finish.

7. Repeat steps 2 through 6 for each network printer.

8. Remove the capture commands from the AUTOEXEC.BAT file. The network printer connections will be available each time you start Windows.

Related KB article Q125433

NetWare NWADMIN3X.EXE Displays Error Message

You attempt to run the Novell NetWare NWADMIN3X.EXE administration utility and see the following error message displayed:

Cannot find Prtwin16.dll. Windows needs this file to run Nwadmin3x.exe.

This error message occurs because NWADMIN3X.EXE is the 16-bit version of the utility that is designed to work with Windows 3.1.

Solution

Use NWADMIN95.EXE rather than NWADMIN3X.EXE. Or manually copy the necessary files to the local hard disk. For information about how to use these methods, contact your network administrator or Novell.

Related KB article Q187495

NetWare Server Connection Is Disabled

You shut down Windows and log on as a different user, and persistent connections to a NetWare server are disabled. This is evident because they appear in My Computer with an *X*. When this occurs, mapped drives are not available until you double-click the drive in Windows Explorer.

Note This problem does not occur with drives mapped to Windows NT or Windows 95/98 servers, or with UNC connections to NetWare servers.

This problem occurs because you use the same user name and password for both the Windows NT and NetWare domains and your primary network logon is set to the Client for Microsoft Networks.

Solution

Either change your user name on one of the domains or set your primary network logon to the Client for NetWare Networks. To do this, follow these steps:

1. Click the Start button, choose Settings, and click Control Panel.

2. Double-click the Network icon.

3. Select Client For NetWare Networks from the Primary Network Logon box.

4. Click OK, and then click Yes when you are asked to restart your computer.

Related KB article Q142234

NetWare Server Does Not Allow File Renaming

You try to rename a file on a Novell NetWare server, and you are unable to do so.

This occurs when the new filename and the old filename have the same MS-DOS 8.3 filename. For example, the FILE 123.TXT file has an MS-DOS 8.3 filename of FILE123.TXT. When you try to rename the FILE 123.TXT file to FILE123.TXT by removing the space in the filename, you are trying to choose a name that is a duplicate of the existing MS-DOS 8.3 filename.

Solution

Rename the file to a name that is completely different from the current filename, and then rename the file to the name you want.

Related KB article Q189298

Network Functionality Lost When Upgrading to Windows 98

When you upgrade your computer to Windows 98, network functionality is lost if your computer is running the Novell NetWare Client32 for MS-DOS network client.

Solution

Manually remove the NetWare Client32 for MS-DOS network client before you upgrade to Windows 98. For information about how to do so, contact Novell or consult the documentation included with the program.

Related KB article Q178054

Notebook Computer Does Not Reestablish NetWare Network Connections

If you disconnect from your network by undocking your laptop computer or removing a Personal Computer Memory Card International Association (PCMCIA) network adapter and then establish network connectivity again, network connections based on your NetWare login script are unavailable.

This problem can occur if you do not run your NetWare login script when you establish network connectivity again. By default, your NetWare login script is not run when you establish network connectivity again. This behavior is by design.

Solution

Run your NetWare login script when you establish network connectivity again. For information about how to do so, review your NetWare documentation, contact your system administrator, or contact Novell.

Related KB article Q191481

Novell Client32 Behaves Unexpectedly

You install Windows 98 on a computer on which Novell Client32 for Microsoft Windows 95 version 2.2.0 or earlier is installed or you reinstall Novell Client32 after Windows 98 is installed, and the following symptoms occur:

- You receive a Fatal Exception 0E error message on a blue screen while Windows 98 Setup is searching for Plug and Play devices.

- Novell's 32-bit ODI drivers do not work after Setup is completed.

If the ODI drivers are reenabled using the Automatic Skip Driver Agent (ASD.EXE) tool, they are disabled the next time you start your computer.

This behavior can occur if you run Windows 98 Setup from MS-DOS because the VMLID.NLM and ODILOAD.VXD files are not updated. Windows 98 Setup automatically updates the VMLID.NLM and ODILOAD.VXD files if Setup is run from within Windows 95.

Solution

Extract the updated versions of the VMLID.NLM and ODILOAD.VXD files from the BASE5.CAB cabinet file on your original Windows 98 CD-ROM or disks. Extract the VMLID.NLM file to the NOVELL\CLIENT32 folder, and extract the ODILOAD.VXD file to the WINDOWS\SYSTEM folder. For information about using the Extract tool, type *extract* at a command prompt, or see KB article Q129605, "How to Extract Original Compressed Windows Files."

Related KB article Q188168

Novell Client32 Does Not Install Successfully

You install the Novell Client32 NetWare client from a NetWare source and receive a page fault error message. When this occurs, the client installation is not successful, and all .INF files in the WINDOWS\INF folder are unavailable. You cannot add any new network clients because all the .INF files are unavailable.

This problem occurs because the Novell SETUP.EXE program calls a function that modifies some of the .INF files and then renames the WINDOWS\INF folder to WINDOWS\INFFNI after it has finished uninstalling all NetWare components. During this renaming process, the Microsoft NETDI.DLL experiences a minor fault and the renaming of the WINDOWS\INFFNI folder to WINDOWS\INF does not occur.

Solution

Obtain the following updated file for Windows 98 from Microsoft Technical Support, or wait for the next service pack containing this file:

Netdi.dll dated 5-12-98, version 4.10.2029.16 317,840 bytes

Related KB article Q190656

Novell Client Removal Produces Unexpected Results

You attempt to remove the Novell 32-bit network client (Client32) from Windows by using the Network tool in Control Panel, and you experience unexpected results.

Solution

Use the UNC32.EXE tool to properly remove Client32. To obtain the UNC32.EXE tool, contact Novell Technical Support or download it from the Novell web site.

Related KB article Q188144

Novell NDS Server Does Not Log On

After you successfully log on to a Novell NDS server from a command prompt and then start Windows, if you right-click Network Neighborhood and then click WHOAMI, you do not appear to be logged in.

This problem occurs when you do not have a search drive mapped to a public directory on the Novell NDS server. This can occur when you do not have Read and Filescan permissions to a public directory or when a *no_default* statement is in your login script.

Solution One

If you do not have Read and Filescan Right permissions to a public directory, contact your network administrator to request these permissions.

Solution Two

If a *no_default* statement is in your login script, map a search drive to a public directory on the Novell NDS server before you start Windows. For information about how to do this, contact your network administrator, or contact Novell.

Related KB article Q190694

NWADMIN Displays Error Message

When you attempt to use the NWADMN3X.EXE utility, you see the following error message:

> *NWADMIN: This program has performed an illegal operation and will be shut down. If the problem persists, contact the program vendor.*

This can occur if Microsoft Service for NetWare Directory Services (MSNDS) is installed on the computer. When MSNDS is installed, the NWADMN3X.EXE utility is unable to locate all the files required to run.

Solution

Do not use the NWADMN3X.EXE utility on a computer on which MSNDS is installed.

Related KB article Q188192

Other Software

Banyan VINES 32-Bit Client Does Not Reinstall

If you uninstall and then attempt to reinstall the client by clicking Add, clicking Client, clicking Add, clicking Vines32, and then clicking OK in the Network tool in Control Panel, you receive the following error message:

> *Failed to load resource DLL*

This problem occurs because the Banyan VINES setup information files (INFs) are not correctly identified when you attempt to reinstall the Banyan VINES 32-bit client.

Solution

To solve this problem, follow these steps:

1. Click the Start button, choose Settings, click Control Panel, and then double-click the Network icon.

2. Click Add, click Client, click Add, and then click Have Disk.

3. Click the folder in which the Banyan VINES client files are located.

4. Click OK, and then restart your computer when prompted.

Related KB article Q189001

Banyan VINES Client Loses Network Access

After you upgrade to Windows 98 over a Windows 95 installation running the 16-bit Banyan VINES client, you do not have access to the Banyan VINES network.

This behavior can occur because Windows 98 Setup disables the following lines in the CONFIG.SYS file:

```
Device=c:\Banfiles\protman.dos  /i:c:\banfiles
```

```
Device=c:\Banfiles\epro.dos (or current real-mode adapter driver)
```

and adds the following line to the AUTOEXEC.BAT file:

```
c:\windows\net start
```

Solution

To restore network connectivity using the Banyan VINES 16-bit client, follow these steps:

1. Click the Start button, and click Run.

2. Enter *Sysedit* in the Open box, and then click OK.

3. Select the CONFIG.SYS window.

4. Remove the *REM-by Windows Setup* text from the following lines:

```
Device=c:\Banfiles\protman.dos  /i:c:\banfiles
```

```
Device=c:\Banfiles\<network adapter driver>
```

Figure 9-48. *The CONFIG.SYS file in the System Configuration Editor.*

5. Verify that the CONFIG.SYS file still shows the following entries:

    ```
    Device=c:\Banfiles\protman.dos  /i:c:\banfiles
    ```

    ```
    Device=c:\Banfiles\epro.dos (or current real mode nic driver)
    ```

6. Select the AUTOEXEC.BAT window.

7. Type *REM* followed by a space at the beginning of the following line:

    ```
    c:\windows\net start
    ```

8. Verify that the AUTOEXEC.BAT file still contains the following VINES stack:

    ```
    c:\windows\net initialize
    ```

    ```
    cd banfiles
    ```

    ```
    ban /nc
    ```

    ```
    ndisban
    ```

    ```
    redirall
    ```

    ```
    netbind
    ```

    ```
    arswait
    ```

    ```
    z:\login
    ```

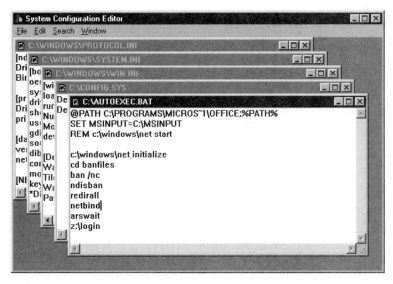

Figure 9-49. *The AUTOEXEC.BAT file in the System Configuration Editor.*

9. Choose Exit from the File menu.

10. Click Yes when you are prompted to save the CONFIG.SYS and AUTOEXEC.BAT files.

11. Restart your computer.

Related KB article   Q190911

Banyan VINES Components Do Not Appear in Network Tool

You upgrade your Banyan VINES 32-bit network client software by using the Banyan NEWREV tool, and the upgraded VINES components do not appear in the Network tool in Control Panel. You also can no longer access the VINES network. When this occurs, you receive one or more of the following error messages:

16 IPOPEN returned 105

Newrev error: Newrev failed to install the new client. Newrev has failed. You will need to reinstall your client.

This problem occurs because the Banyan Newrev tool does not function properly with Windows 98.

Solution

Use the latest VINES 32-bit client that matches your VINES server version, by removing the existing 32-bit client and upgrading to the latest client version. Refer to the Banyan VINES user documentation for assistance, or contact your network administrator.

Related KB article   Q189652

Banyan VINES Network Client Removal Causes Error Message

When you remove the Banyan VINES 32-bit network client for Windows, you see the following error message:

Failed to load resource DLL (VNSNDIR.DLL)

When you remove the Banyan VINES 32-bit client using the Network tool in Control Panel, the Banyan VINES protocol is not removed automatically before the computer is restarted. If the Banyan VINES protocol is not removed from the Network tool, it does not appear in the Network tool after you restart your computer, but an error message occurs every time you double-click the Network tool.

Solution

Install the Banyan VINES network client from the original installation location, and then immediately remove the Banyan VINES client and protocol from the Network tool in Control Panel.

Related KB article Q178133

Banyan VINES Network Does Not Allow Print Service Installation

You attempt to install a print service on a Banyan VINES network by clicking the Start button, clicking Run, entering the Universal Naming Convention (UNC) path to the print service in the Open box, and then clicking OK, and you see the following error message:

\\streettalk\<printer>@<server>@<servers> is not accessible

This problem occurs because the print service must be installed using the Printers icon in Control Panel.

Solution

To solve this problem, follow these steps:

1. Click the Start button, choose Settings, and then click Printers.

2. Double-click Add Printer.

3. Click Next, click Network Printer, and then click Next.

4. In the Network Path or Queue Name box, type the full path to the print service, click Next, and then proceed through the Add Printer Wizard.

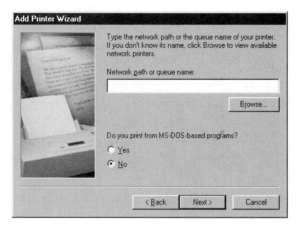

Figure 9-50. *The Add Printer Wizard.*

Related KB article Q189223

Frontier Technologies Network Server Appears Disconnected

You map a drive to your Frontier Technologies Network File System (NFS) server, log off, log on, and then view the mapped network drive icon; your mapped drive appears to be disconnected because the network icon has a red circle with a slash through it.

Solution

Refresh the icon by pressing F5 or choosing Refresh from the View menu.

Related KB article Q190896

IBM Client Access/400 Doesn't Run

IBM Client Access/400 doesn't work in Windows 98.

Solution

Obtain a patch from IBM by using the SNDPTFORD command through Electronic Customer Support (ECS), and then ask for APAR II08704.

Or you can call (800) 274-0015 and press 1 for the support line. Enter your customer number, and then press 1 for a new call. Press 6 for PTF, and ask for APAR II08704.

Related KB article Q188978 or PROGRAMS.TXT in your WINDOWS folder

Removal of Networking Components Produces Startup Errors

When you restart your computer after removing all networking components, you see the following error message:

Invalid VxD dynamic link call from BANCOM(01) + 000169B0 to device "0028," service 800A. Your Windows configuration is invalid. Run the Windows Setup program again to correct this problem.

To continue running Windows, press Y or Enter. To quit the current program press N. If you continue running Windows, your system may become unstable. Do you want to continue? Press Y for Yes or N for No.

If you press Y, your computer either restarts or stops responding (hangs), requiring a reset or power down, and then your computer starts in Safe mode. If you press N, you see the following error message:

While initializing device BANCOM: Invalid VxD dynamic link call to device 28, service E8 service 74 for Windows 98. Your Windows configuration is invalid. Run the Windows Setup program again to correct this problem. Press any key to continue.

When you press a key, the Shut Down screen appears or your computer shuts down.

This behavior can occur if you remove all networking components in Network properties. When you do this, the Banyan VINES protocol may still be installed, even though it is not listed in Network properties.

Solution

Add and remove the Banyan VINES client by following these steps:

1. Restart your computer.

2. After your computer completes the Power On Self Test (POST), press and hold down the Ctrl key until you see the Windows 98 Startup menu, and then choose Safe Mode.

Note For more information about Windows 98 startup, see KB article Q178548, "No 'Starting Windows 98' Message at Startup."

---

3. Click the Start button, choose Settings, click Control Panel, and then double-click the Network icon to open the Network dialog box.

4. Click Add to open the Select Network Component Type dialog box.

5. Click Client, and then click Add to open the Select Network Client dialog box.

6. Click Have Disk to open the Install From Disk dialog box.

7. Enter the path to the Banyan VINES client files in the Copy Manufacturer's File From box, and click OK.

8. Click the network adapter that is installed in your computer.

Note You might be prompted to install the network adapter as many as three times, and you might not be able to access your CD-ROM drive in Safe mode. When you are prompted for files during installation, click Skip.

---

9. Restart your computer when you are prompted.

10. Click the Start button, choose Settings, click Control Panel, and then double-click the Network icon to open the Network dialog box.

11. Click Yes when you receive the following prompt:

    Your network is not complete. Do you want to continue?

12. Click Add to open the Select Network Component Type dialog box.

13. Click Client, and then click Add to open the Select Network Client dialog box.

14. Click Have Disk to open the Install From Disk dialog box.

15. In the Copy Manufacturer's Files From box, type the path to the Banyan VINES client files.

16. Click OK.

17. When you are prompted, restart your computer.

18. Click the Start button, choose Settings, click Control Panel, and then double-click the Network icon to open the Network dialog box.

19. Click the Banyan VINES client for Windows 95, and then click Remove.

20. When you are prompted to confirm the removal, click Yes.

21. Click the Banyan VINES protocol for Windows 95, and then click Remove.

22. Click OK.

23. When you are prompted, restart your computer.

You might receive the following error message before you remove all the network components:

Failed to Load Resource DLL (VNSNDIR.DLL)

For more information about this error message, see KB article Q178133, "Error Message: Failed to Load Resource DLL (VNSNDIR.DLL)."

Related KB article Q178470

Rumba Office 2.0 Installation Has Problems

You install Rumba Office 2.0 with the shared folders functionality on, and you experience installation problems.

Solution

Turn off shared folders when you install Rumba, by following these steps:

1. Select Custom.

2. Select AS/400.

3. Clear the Shared Folders and Client API check boxes.

4. Continue the installation process.

Related KB article Q188978 or PROGRAMS.TXT in your WINDOWS folder

Small Business Server Client Disk Causes General Protection Fault

You set up the client disk on your computer, and you receive a general protection (GP) fault error in SETUP.EXE from source IPDETECT while installing the networking options.

This problem occurs when the following options are not installed:

- TCP/IP
- File and Print Sharing for Microsoft Networks
- Microsoft Family logon service

Solution

Set up the following options:

- Verify that the TCP/IP protocol is installed with no other protocols installed.
- Verify that the File and Print Sharing for Microsoft Networks service is installed.
- Remove the Microsoft Family logon service.

After you set up all these options, restart your computer and rerun the client setup disk.

If your setup attempt fails and you have checked the preceding information (and the client applications still do not install correctly), follow these steps on your server:

1. In Manager Server Console, click More Tasks, and then click Manage Computers.

2. Select the Windows 98 computer you are installing.

3. Click Add Software.

4. Select the user who will be using this computer.

5. Select all the applications you want to install.

6. Log off the client computer, and log back on as the user. The client application should install correctly now.

Related KB article Q189849

Protocols

Cannot Connect to Resources Because of Invalid IP Addresses

You can't view or connect to any shared resources on a network that uses the Transport Control Protocol/Internet Protocol (TCP/IP), even though your network adapter and network server settings are working correctly.

This problem can occur if you change the Internet Protocol (IP) address for your computer to any of the following IP addresses in the TCP/IP Properties dialog box:

0.0.0.0

127.<x>.<y>.<z>

255.0.0.0

255.255.0.0

255.255.255.0

255.255.255.255

To specify any of these addresses, you must click Specify An IP Address on the IP Address tab in the TCP/IP Properties dialog box, type the invalid TCP/IP address, click OK, click OK when you receive the following message, and then click Cancel:

The specified IP address is not valid. Please check that the value you typed is correct. If you believe the value is correct but you still receive this message, check with your network administrator.

In a TCP/IP network, each computer has a unique IP address that determines its identity. Certain IP addresses are reserved for specific uses and cannot be assigned to a computer on your network; for example, the 127.0.0.1 IP address is reserved for testing the network with the Ping command. The following table lists reserved IP addresses that should not be used for a computer; <x.y.z> is a range of numbers from 0 to 254:

Table 9-1.   Reserved IP Addresses

IP address	Reserved usage
127.0.0.1	Loopback/LocalHost address
255.0.0.0	Class A subnet mask
255.255.0.0	Class B subnet mask
255.255.255.0	Class C subnet mask
225.<x.y.z> - 239.<x.y.z>	Class D address (multicast only)
240.<x.y.z> - 254.<x.y.z>	Class E address (reserved)
255.255.255.255	Broadcast address

If you use any of the addresses listed in the table as the IP address for a computer, no other computer can communicate with it successfully.

A *subnet mask* is an address for a subnetwork used to expand the range of possible IP addresses on the network. A subnet mask acts to identify an IP address on different subnetworks. TCP/IP uses the binary format to resolve an IP address and subnet mask.

Both the IP address and the subnet mask use binary format for each octet. An IP address consists of four octets. The portion of the octet in binary format that is not used by the subnet mask becomes the portion of the IP address that differentiates it from other IP addresses on the same subnetwork. The assigned IP address and the subnet mask are combined in binary format to create the resolved IP address in a TCP/IP network. If the resolved IP address in binary format is all zeroes or ones (for example, 11111111, or decimal 255), it is an invalid IP address.

Solution

Change the IP address to a valid IP address by following these steps:

1. Click the Start button, choose Settings, click Control Panel, and then double-click the Network icon.

2. On the Configuration tab, double-click either TCP/IP or TCP/IP-><network adapter>, where <network adapter> is the name of your network adapter.

3. On the IP Address tab, type a valid IP address in the IP Address box, and then click OK. If you do not know a valid IP address for your computer, contact your network administrator.

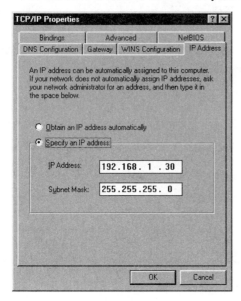

Figure 9-51.   *The TCP/IP Properties dialog box.*

4. Click OK, and then click OK.

For information about troubleshooting TCP/IP, see KB article Q172218, "Microsoft TCP/IP Host Name Resolution Order."

Related KB article Q185753

DNS Settings Changes Can't Be Canceled

When you click the Enable DNS or Disable DNS option on the DNS Configuration tab in the TCP/IP Properties dialog box, the settings do not revert to the previous settings if you click Cancel and then click OK in the Network dialog box.

Solution

Click Cancel rather than OK in the Network dialog box.

Related KB article Q194561

IP Address Can't Be Canceled Once Added

When you add an Internet Protocol (IP) address to the Installed Gateways list on the Gateway tab in the TCP/IP Properties dialog box and then click Cancel, the IP address may not be removed from the list, and it may be changed to a different, invalid address if you click Cancel on the Gateway tab and then click OK in the Network dialog box.

Solution

Click Cancel rather than OK in the Network dialog box.

Related KB article Q194667

IPX/SPX Bound to Dial-Up Adapter Multiple Times

When you view the list of installed network components in Network properties, the Microsoft IPX/SPX-compatible protocol shows up as bound to the Dial-Up Adapter multiple times. This can occur if you install the Microsoft IPX/SPX-compatible protocol before installing the Client for NetWare Networks.

Solution

Remove all duplicate entries by following these steps:

1. Click the Start button, choose Settings, click Control Panel, and then double-click the Network icon.

2. On the Configuration tab, select IPX/SPX-Compatible Protocol->Dial-Up Adapter, and then click Remove. Repeat this step for all duplicate IPX/SPX-compatible Protocol->Dial-Up Adapter entries.

3. Click OK, and then click Yes when you are prompted to restart your computer.

Related KB article Q193455

Microsoft IPX/SPX-Compatible Protocol Displays Error Message on Novell Network

You are using a Novell NetWare network, and you install the Microsoft IPX/SPX-compatible protocol in Network properties. You experience the following symptoms:

- A loss of connectivity to your NetWare network resources

- The following error message:

    Invalid VxD dynamic link call from VREDIR(01) + 00006F4A to device '0487', service 4. Your Windows configuration is invalid. Run the Windows Setup program again to correct this problem.

When you install the Microsoft IPX/SPX-compatible protocol over the Novell 32-bit IPX protocol, the StaticVxD setting in the Registry changes from NWLINK2.VXD (the Novell setting) to NWLINK.VXD.

Solution One

Reinstall the Novell Client32 software.

Solution Two

Change the data value of the StaticVxD value in the following Registry key to NWLINK2.VXD:

HKEY_LOCAL_MACHINE\System\CurrentControlSet\Services\VxD\NWLink

Warning Please read the Introduction for information about how to safely edit the Registry.

Follow these steps:

1. Click the Start button, click Run, and enter *Regedit* in the Run box. Click OK.

2. Navigate your way down through the folders in the left pane until you locate the key described above.

3. Modify the value of StaticVxD to NWLINK2.VXD.

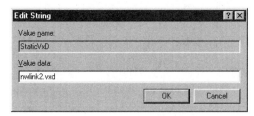

Figure 9-52. *The Edit String dialog box.*

4. Close Regedit.

5. Restart Windows.

Related KB article Q189221

NetBIOS Support for IPX/SPX-Compatible Protocol Not Added

You see the NetBIOS Support for IPX/SPX-Compatible Protocol component in Network properties; however, you cannot add it by using Add.

Solution

You cannot add this component by using Add. If you select the I Want To Enable NetBIOS Over IPX/SPX check box on the NetBIOS tab in IPX/SPX-Compatible Protocol properties, you see an entry for the NetBIOS Support for IPX/SPX-Compatible Protocol component in Network properties. This component should not be displayed. You can install this component only by selecting the I Want To Enable NetBIOS Over IPX/SPX check box.

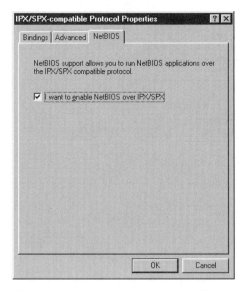

Figure 9-53. *The IPX/SPX-Compatible Protocol Properties dialog box.*

Related KB article Q134507

Network Component Missing from Network Tool

When you try to add a network component in the Network tool in Control Panel, the protocol, client, or service is missing. This can occur if one or more of the following files is missing or damaged:

- NETTRANS.INF
- NETCLI.INF
- NETSERVR.INF

Solution

Determine which files are missing or damaged and then extract a new copy of the file by following these steps:

1. Click the Start button, choose Settings, and then click Control Panel.

2. Double-click the Network icon to open the Network dialog box.

3. Click the Configuration tab, and then click Add to open the Select Network Component Type dialog box.

4. Click Protocol, and then click Add to open the Select Network Protocol dialog box.

5. If any of the following protocols is missing, extract a new copy of the NETTRANS.INF file to the WINDOWS\INF folder:

Table 9-2.   Protocols Contained in the NETTRANS.INI File

Manufacturer	Network protocol
Banyan	Banyan VINES ethernet Protocol
Banyan	Banyan VINES token ring Protocol
IBM	Existing IBM DLC Protocol
Microsoft	ATM Call Manager
Microsoft	ATM Emulated LAN
Microsoft	ATM LAN Emulation Client
Microsoft	Fast Infrared Protocol
Microsoft	IPX/SPX-compatible Protocol
Microsoft	Microsoft 32-bit DLC
Microsoft	Microsoft DLC
Microsoft	Microsoft NetBEUI
Microsoft	TCP/IP
Novell	Novell IPX ODI Protocol

Note For information about how to extract files, see KB article Q129605, "How to Extract Original Compressed Windows Files."

6. Click Cancel, click Client, and then click Add. If any of the following clients is missing, extract a new copy of the NETCLI.INF file to the WINDOWS\INF folder:

Table 9-3.   Clients Contained in the NETCLI.INF File

Manufacturer	Network clients
Banyan	Banyan DOS/Windows 3.1 Client
Microsoft	Client for Microsoft Networks
Microsoft	Client for NetWare Networks
Microsoft	Microsoft Family Logon
Novell	Novell NetWare (Workstation Shell 3.X [NETX])
Novell	Novell NetWare (Workstation Shell 4.0 and above [VLM])

7. Click Cancel, click Service, and then click Add. If any of the following services is missing, extract a new copy of the NETSERV.INF file to the WINDOWS\INF folder:

   ▪ File and printer sharing for Microsoft Networks

   ▪ File and printer sharing for NetWare Networks

   ▪ Service for NetWare Directory Services

8. Close the Network tool, and then close Control Panel.

Related KB article Q193637

Network Protocols Missing

After you upgrade a Windows 3.1x–based computer running the NetBEUI or IPX/SPX protocol to Windows 98, these protocols are missing from the list of installed network components, and the Transmission Control Protocol/Internet Protocol (TCP/IP) can now be installed.

Solution

Reinstall any missing protocol you want to use by following these steps:

1. Click the Start button, choose Settings, click Control Panel, and then double-click the Network icon.

2. Click Add, click Protocol, and then click Add.

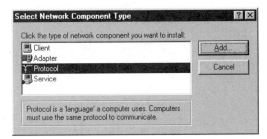

Figure 9-54. *The Select Network Component Type dialog box.*

3. Select Microsoft, select the protocol you want to add, and then click OK.

4. Repeat steps 2 and 3 to add any other protocols you want, and then click OK.

Related KB article Q187677

Property Changes Remain in Effect After You Click Cancel

You change your domain in the properties for the Client for Microsoft Networks network client or change your preferred server in the properties for the Client for NetWare Networks network client, click OK, and then click Cancel, and your changes remain in effect.

This behavior can occur if you have either an Intel EtherExpress 16 or Intel EtherExpress Pro 10 network adapter and the following network protocols installed:

- Network Basic Input/Output System Enhanced User Interface (NetBEUI)

- Internetworking Packet Exchange/Session Packet Exchange (IPX/SPX)

- Transmission Control Protocol/Internet Protocol (TCP/IP)

Solution

Type your original domain or preferred server information in the properties for the network client, click OK, and then click OK.

Related KB article Q179231

Sony VAIO PCV 70/90 TCP/IP Does Not Function Properly

You upgrade to Windows 98 on a Sony VAIO Model PCV 70/90 computer running Windows 95 OEM Service Release version 2.0, and the Transport Control Protocol/Internet Protocol (TCP/IP) does not function correctly.

You experience one or more of the following symptoms:

- You are able to connect to your Internet service provider (ISP) by using Dial-Up Networking, but you are unable to browse the Internet. Also, you receive the following error message when you try to access a web address:

  Internet Explorer can not open the Internet Site HTTP://?. *A connection with the server could not be established.*

- If your computer is part of a network, TCP/IP-based connectivity no longer functions properly. For example, if your computer was configured to use TCP/IP to access a network printer, you are unable to do so now. Note that the functionality of other network protocols installed on your computer remains unaffected.

This problem occurs when the value of the CompatIDs key in your Registry is incorrectly set to TCP/IP rather than MSTCP. Windows 98 Setup does not properly upgrade some of your computer's TCP/IP-related files because of this problem.

Solution

Uninstall and then reinstall TCP/IP by following these steps:

1. Click the Start button, choose Settings, click Control Panel, and then double-click the Network icon.

2. On the Configuration tab, select TCP/IP, and then click Remove. Repeat this step for each instance of TCP/IP on the Configuration tab before continuing to step 3.

3. Click OK, and then click Yes when you are prompted to restart your computer.

4. Click the Start button, choose Settings, click Control Panel, and then double-click the Network icon.

5. Click Protocol, click Add, select Microsoft in the Manufacturers box, click TCP/IP, and then click OK.

Note You might receive version-conflict error messages during this process. If this happens, click No when you are prompted to keep a newer version of each file.

---

6. Restart your computer.

Related KB article Q185533

TCP/IP Installation Produces Error Message

You attempt to install Transmission Control Protocol/Internet Protocol (TCP/IP), and you see the following message if you install Personal Web Server 1.0a, remove TCP/IP, restart your computer, and then attempt to add TCP/IP:

A file being copied is older than the one currently on your system.

The file is the SVRAPI.DLL file.

Solution

Click No when you receive this message. This allows the correct file to be copied.

Related KB article Q194758

Windows 98 Has a Compatibility Problem with a Network Adapter, Protocol, or Client

When running Windows 98, you have a problem with one or more of the following:

- Changing a network adapter to 16-bit ODI or NDIS drivers
- Client for NetWare
- Installation of MS-DLC with Windows 98
- Intel EtherExpress 16 network cards and PCI computers
- Miramar Systems' PC MacLAN Appletalk connectivity
- ODI device drivers and MS TCP/IP
- Plug and Play network cards and 16-bit real-mode drivers
- Printing to PostScript printers over a NetWare network
- Real-mode protocols: warning icons on your network adapter
- Samba and Windows 98
- Using COMPSEC variables pointing to network COMMAND.COM files
- Using an IBM ThinkPad with a Dock II
- Using user profiles over the network

Solution

The NETWORK.TXT file located in your WINDOWS folder describes these problems and ways to avoid them as well as specific steps you can take to solve some of these problems. To view the NETWORK.TXT file, click the Start button, click Run, type *network.txt* in the text box, and click OK.

Related KB article Q191518 or NETWORK.TXT in your WINDOWS folder

C H A P T E R   1 0

Peripherals

Cameras

Kodak DC25 Camera Works When Disabled in Device Manager

You disable the Kodak DC25 Camera device in Device Manager, and the camera continues to function and download images.

Solution

This behavior is by design. Kodak Imaging uses TWAIN_32.DLL and the Kodak DC25 data source files to communicate with this device and has no hardware dependencies other than a functional communications port.

Related KB article Q189226

Kodak DC25 Files Can't Be Opened

You attempt to open a saved Kodak DC25 (.K25) file using the Scan New command in Imaging for Windows, and you receive the following error message:

The target file must be a DC20 or DC25 native file.

Solution

Connect your Kodak DC25 camera to your computer, or turn the camera on before you start Imaging for Windows.

Related KB article Q190914

USB Camera Degrades System Performance

You use a USB camera with certain PCI video cards, and performance is reduced or your computer seems to stop responding (hangs). Video playback is also affected. Certain PCI video cards do not work well with isochronous transactions, which USB cameras require. The video card might require several attempts to complete an operation.

Solution

To solve this problem, follow these steps:

1. Click the Start button, choose Settings, click Control Panel, and double-click the Display icon.

2. Click the Settings tab, and then click Advanced.

3. Click the Performance tab, and then move the Hardware Acceleration slider to None.

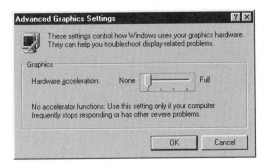

Figure 10-1. *The Advanced Graphics Settings dialog box.*

4. Click OK until you return to Control Panel.

5. When you are prompted to restart the computer, do so.

Related KB article Q164305

Infrared

Fast Infrared Device Does Not Work on Gateway 2000 Solo 9100

You install Windows 98 on a Gateway 2000 Solo 9100 computer that came with Windows 95 with Fast Infrared support installed, and the infrared device does not work. Also, Device Manager lists more than one Fast Infrared device.

This problem occurs because Windows 98 Setup does not detect or replace the original Fast Infrared drivers installed on the computer. When Setup finishes, two sets of Fast Infrared drivers are installed. The two sets of drivers cause a conflict, which does not allow the infrared device to work.

Solution

Remove all the Fast Infrared drivers, by following these steps:

1. Click the Start button, choose Settings, and click Control Panel.

2. Double-click the System icon, and then click the Device Manager tab.

3. Click the first infrared device listed under the Infrared Devices branch, click Remove, and then click OK to confirm the device removal.

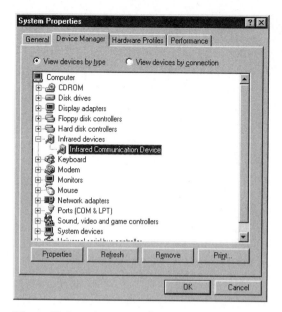

Figure 10-2. *The Device Manager tab in the System Properties dialog box.*

4. Repeat step 3 for each additional device listed under the Infrared Devices branch.

5. Double-click the Network Adapters branch to expand it. If a Fast Infrared port is listed, click the port, click Remove, and then click OK.

Note This device might not be listed in some cases.

---

6. Click OK to close Device Manager, and then restart your computer. When the computer restarts, Windows 98 detects the Fast Infrared device and installs the appropriate drivers.

Related KB article Q189151

IR Searching Doesn't Stop or Doesn't Start

If IR (infrared) communication is enabled and you select the Search For And Provide Status For Devices Within Range check box, searching does not start, or you see the following error message:

Cannot search for devices because other infrared devices are operating nearby.

If IR communication is enabled and you clear the Search For And Provide Status For Devices Within Range check box, searching does not stop.

Solution

Enable or disable IR communication and the Search For And Provide Status For Devices Within Range check boxes at the same time. To enable IR searching, follow these steps:

1. Click the Start button, choose Settings, and then click Control Panel.

2. Double-click Infrared, and then click the Options tab.

3. Select the Enable Infrared Communication check box, select the Search For And Provide Status For Devices Within Range check box, and then click Apply.

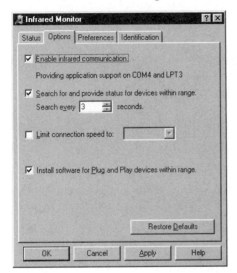

Figure 10-3. *The Options tab in the Infrared Monitor dialog box.*

4. Click OK.

To disable IR searching, repeat steps 1 through 4, clearing both check boxes in step 3.

Related KB article Q194964

Input Devices

Game Port Is Not Removed

You remove both a sound card from your computer and the sound card in Device Manager, and the game (joystick) port on the sound card still appears in Device Manager.

Solution

Remove the game port in Device Manager by following these steps:

1. Right-click My Computer on the desktop, choose Properties, and click the Device Manager tab.

2. Double-click Sound, Video, And Game Controllers, and double-click the Joystick icon.

Figure 10-4. *The Game Controllers dialog box.*

3. Click Remove, and close the program.

Related KB article Q132517

Game Port Stops Working

If you remove the SideWinder Game Device 2.0 software from a computer running Windows 98, the game port on the computer does not function properly. This problem can occur if you install the SideWinder Game Device software on a computer running Windows 95, upgrade to Windows 98, and then remove the SideWinder Game Device software. The program files for the SideWinder Game Device software have the same filenames as the standard game port driver files in Windows 98. When you remove the SideWinder Game Device software, you also remove the Windows 98 game port drivers.

Solution

Download and install the latest version of the SideWinder Game Device software from this Microsoft web address: *http://www.microsoft.com/sidewinder*.

Related KB article Q187546

Input Devices Menu Is Empty

You install a Microsoft input device driver, and the MICROSOFT INPUT DEVICES folder is empty. All other aspects of Setup are completed successfully.

Solution

Manually add the missing shortcuts to the MICROSOFT INPUT DEVICES folder: WINDOWS\ START MENU\PROGRAMS\MICROSOFT INPUT DEVICES.

Tables 10-1 through 10-4 list the shortcut names and locations for the shortcuts.

Table 10-1.   IntelliPoint Shortcuts and Their Associated Filenames

Shortcut name	Filename and location
Tools and Controls	C:\MSINPUT\MOUSE\MOUSEX32.EXE
Tool Bar	C:\MSINPUT\MOUSE\INBAR32.EXE
Readme	C:\MSINPUT\MOUSE\README.TXT
Online User's Guide_Help	C:\MSINPUT\MOUSE\IPOINT.HLP
Uninstall	C:\MSINPUT\MOUSE\UNINSTAL.EXE

Table 10-2.   IntelliType Shortcuts and Their Associated Filenames

Shortcut name	Filename and location
Manager	C:\WINDOWS\KBDX.EXE
Readme	C:\MSINPUT\KEYBOARD\README.TXT
Online User's Guide_Help	C:\MSINPUT\KEYBOARD\ITYPE.HLP
Uninstall	C:\MSINPUT\KEYBOARD\UNINSTAL.EXE

Table 10-3.   EasyBall Shortcuts and Their Associated Filenames

Shortcut name	Filename and location
Properties	C:\MSINPUT\EASYBALL\EZBALX32.EXE
Pointerland	C:\MSINPUT\EASYBALL\PTRLND16.EXE
Readme	C:\MSINPUT\EASYBALL\README.TXT
Online User's Guide_Help	C:\MSINPUT\EASYBALL\EZBALL.HLP
Uninstall	C:\MSINPUT\EASYBALL\UNINST32.EXE

Table 10-4.   SideWinder 3D Pro Shortcuts and Their Associated Filenames

Shortcut name	Filename and location
Readme	C:\MSINPUT\JOYSTICK\SIDEWNDR\README.TXT
Online User's Guide_Help	C:\MSINPUT\JOYSTICK\SIDEWNDR\SIDEWNDR.HLP
Uninstall	C:\MSINPUT\JOYSTICK\SIDEWNDR\UNINSTAL.EXE

Related KB article Q142422

IntelliMouse Wheel Does Not Scroll Web Page Frame

You use the IntelliMouse wheel to attempt to scroll through a web page frame that is not the active frame, and you receive either of the following error messages:

Explorer caused a stack fault in module <filename> at <address>

Explorer caused an invalid page fault in module <filename> at <address>

Internet Explorer then exits, or your computer stops responding (hangs).

Solution

Click inside the frame before you attempt to scroll through it.

Related KB article Q194359

Mouse or EasyBall Isn't Detected

You connect a Microsoft Plug and Play serial mouse, Microsoft EasyBall, or IntelliMouse to your computer, and Windows does not detect the new device, and running the Add New Hardware Wizard does not correct the problem. The reason is that the Registry entries for your previous mouse were not removed properly. This problem can occur when your previous pointing device was a Microsoft, Microsoft-compatible, or Logitech mouse.

Solution

Use Registry Editor to remove the Registry entries for your previous pointing device by following these steps:

Warning Please read the Introduction for information on how to safely edit the Registry.

1. Click the Start button, choose Run, enter *regedit* in the Run box, and then click OK.

2. Remove the following Registry keys:

   HKEY_LOCAL_MACHINE\System\CurrentControlSet\Services\Class\Mouse\<nnnn>

   where <nnnn> is an incremental 4-digit number starting at 0000.

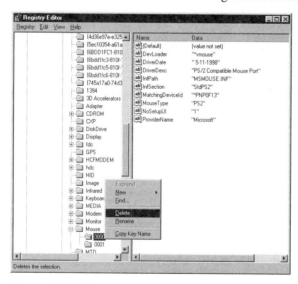

Figure 10-5. *The Registry Editor.*

3. Remove the following Registry keys, if they exist:

   `HKEY_LOCAL_MACHINE\Enum\Root\Mouse\<nnnn>`

   where <nnnn> in an incremental 4-digit number starting at 0000.

4. Remove all Registry keys under the following Registry key, if they exist:

   `Hkey_Local_Machine\Enum\Serenum`

5. Remove the following Registry key, if it exists:

   `HKEY_LOCAL_MACHINE\Software\Logitech\Mouseware`

6. Close Regedit.

7. Right-click My Computer on the desktop, and then choose Properties.

8. Click the Device Manager tab.

9. Click each mouse or serial pointing device, click Remove, and then click OK.

10. Restart Windows. When you restart Windows, your mouse or other pointing device is detected automatically and the appropriate drivers are installed for you.

Related KB article Q142405

Mouse Pointer Moves Uncontrollably

You move the mouse rapidly while the computer is in the process of resuming from Standby mode, or immediately after docking or undocking a portable computer, and the mouse pointer behaves erratically. The mouse pointer displays the following actions:

- It moves in a direction and speed different from the mouse.

- Windows and other objects behave as though they have been clicked, even if no mouse buttons are clicked.

- Other uncontrolled mouse actions occur.

When the computer is resuming from Standby (Suspend) mode, the mouse driver does not synchronize properly with the mouse if the mouse is moved rapidly. As a result, movement information from the mouse is misinterpreted as different movement or as button clicks, and button click information from the mouse is misinterpreted as movement.

Solution

Contact Microsoft Technical Support to obtain a fix for this problem. If you are not severely affected by this specific problem, Microsoft recommends that you wait and obtain the next service pack that contains this fix.

Related KB article Q192845

Pointer Trails Not Displayed on STB Velocity 128 Display Card

You enable the Show Pointer Trails option in the mouse properties in Windows 98, and pointer trails do not appear when you move the mouse if you are using an STB Velocity 128 video adapter with the video adapter drivers included with Windows 98. Pointer trails are provided by the video adapter driver, and the Windows 98 driver for this video adapter does not include this feature.

Solution

Contact the video adapter's manufacturer to determine whether the manufacturer has an available driver that provides pointer trail functionality.

Related KB article Q192720

Serial Mouse Does Not Work

You change the resources for a COM port to which a serial mouse is connected, and the mouse stops working.

You also see an exclamation point in a yellow circle in Device Manager with the following message when you view the properties for the mouse:

This device is either not present, not working properly, or does not have all the drivers installed. (Code 24).

This problem occurs when you change the resources for a COM port to which a serial mouse is connected to nonstandard settings. The standard resource settings for COM ports are listed in Table 10-5.

Table 10-5. Standard Resource Settings for COM Ports

I/O address	IRQ
03F8	4
02F8	3
03E8	4
02E8	3

Solution One

Remove the serial mouse and COM port in Device Manager, and then restart the computer. To do so, follow these steps:

1. Click the Start button, choose Settings, click Control Panel, and then double-click the System icon.

2. Click the Device Manager tab.

3. Click the serial mouse, and then click Remove.

4. Double-click the Ports (COM & LPT) branch to expand it.

5. Click the COM port to which the mouse is connected, and then click Remove.

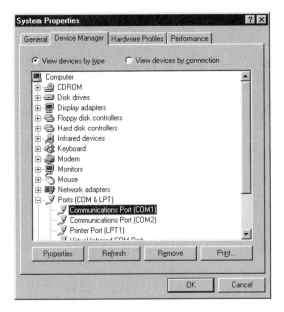

Figure 10-6. *The Device Manager tab in the System Properties dialog box.*

6. Click OK.

7. Restart the computer.

Solution Two

Set the COM port back to its original resource settings.

Related KB article Q188572

Web Pages Scroll by Themselves

You click and then release a scroll arrow, and the document or web page through which you were scrolling continues to scroll. This problem can occur if Logitech MouseWare is installed on your computer and the Event Macro Executive utility is being loaded when Windows starts.

Solution

Using Registry Editor, remove the *Em_exec.exe* string value from the following Registry key:

`HKEY_LOCAL_MACHINE\Software\Microsoft\Windows\CurrentVersion\Run`

Follow these steps:

Warning Please read the Introduction for information on how to safely edit the Registry.

1. Click the Start button, choose Run, enter *regedit* in the Run box, and then click OK.

2. Navigate your way through the folders in the left pane until you locate the key just described.

3. Delete the *Em_exec.exe* string value.

4. Close Regedit.

5. Restart Windows.

Related KB article Q193210

Winbook XP Keyboard Functions Incorrectly

You use the keyboard on a Winbook XP, and the keyboard behaves improperly.

Solution

Disable the Windows 98 power status polling by following these steps:

1. Click the Start button, choose Settings, and click Control Panel.

2. Double-click the System icon, and then click the Device Manager tab.

3. Click the plus sign (+) next to System Devices.

4. Select Advanced Power Management Support, and then click Properties.

5. Click the Settings tab, and then select the Disable Power Status Polling check box.

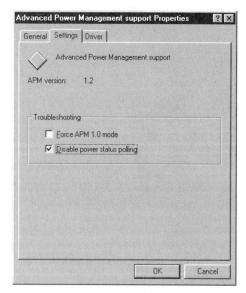

Figure 10-7. *The Advanced Power Management Support Properties dialog box.*

6. Click OK to save your changes.

Related KB article Q191480 or HARDWARE.TXT in your WINDOWS folder

Palmtop PCs

Handheld PC Doesn't Synchronize with Desktop Computer

You change the Bits Per Second port setting for the communications port to which your Handheld PC (H/PC) is connected, and you're unable to synchronize your H/PC with your desktop computer. Direct Cable Connection installs a driver for each port with a default baud rate of 115,200 bits per second (bps), and H/PC devices that use Direct Cable Connection default to a connection speed of 19,200 bps.

Solution

Restart your desktop computer after you change port settings.

Related KB article Q193807

Serial Device Isn't Compatible with Windows Programs

If you attach your Handheld PC (H/PC) and another serial device to a serial switch box connected to your desktop computer, Windows programs are unable to use the serial device.

Solution

Start and then stop ActiveSync Service Manager. Communications (COM) ports that are in use when you start ActiveSync Service Manager are reset. For example, if you are connected to your Internet service provider using a modem on a different COM port, the modem is disconnected from your ISP when you start ActiveSync Service Manager.

Related KB article Q194534

Scanners

Epson ES-600C Scanner Causes Error

You use an Epson ES-600C scanner with an Adaptec AHA-2940 Small Computer System Interface (SCSI) adapter, and you experience the following problems:

- You start your computer, and it stops responding during the Power On Self Test (POST).

- You try to load drivers for an Epson ES-600C scanner in Windows 98, and your computer prematurely restarts during device enumeration and then hangs during the POST.

Solution

Contact Epson Technical Support.

Related KB article Q192757

HP ScanJet 5P Scanner Doesn't Function

After you upgrade to Windows 98, your Hewlett-Packard (HP) ScanJet 5P scanner does not function. The HPSJUSD.DLL file provided by HP is not compatible with Windows 98.

Solution

Extract to the WINDOWS\SYSTEM folder a new copy of the HPSJUSD.DLL file from your original Windows 98 CD-ROM. If the scanner is connected to a SCSI adapter, also extract a copy of the SCSIMAP.SYS file to the WINDOWS\SYSTEM folder.

Related KB articles Q191530, Q129605

HP ScanJet 5100C Software Requires Windows 95

You attempt to install the Hewlett-Packard (HP) ScanJet 5100C scanner software, and you receive the following error message:

This software does not support Windows 98 and Windows NT. It requires Windows 95.

When you click Next, the HP ScanJet 5100C Setup program closes.

Solution

Contact Hewlett-Packard to obtain an updated version of the software program.

Related KB article Q188865

HP Scanner Software Displays Error Message

You install the Hewlett-Packard (HP) 4P scanner software and then use the HP scanner software to test the scanner, and you see the following error message:

Error Starting Program

The HPSCNTST.DLL file is linked to missing export HPSJ32.DLL:35

You click OK and see this error message:

C:\SCANJET\SCANTEST.EXE

A device attached to the system is not functioning.

This problem can occur when the HP 4P scanner software replaces the Windows 98 version of the HPSJ32.DLL file in the WINDOWS\SYSTEM folder. The Windows 98 HPSJ32.DLL file is 36K in size and has a date stamp of 5/11/98.

Although you receive the preceding error message when you attempt to use the HP scanner software to test the scanner, you can still use the HP 4P scanner using the HP software or Windows 98 Imaging.

Solution One

Extract to the WINDOWS\SYSTEM folder a new copy of the HPSJ32.DLL file from your original Windows 98 CD-ROM. The HPSJ32.DLL file is located in the DRIVER12.CAB cabinet file. For information about how to use Extract, type *extract* at a command prompt.

Solution Two

Use Device Manager to redetect your scanner by following these steps:

1. Click the Start button, choose Settings, and click Control Panel.

2. Double-click the System icon, and then click the Device Manager tab.

3. Double-click the SCSI Devices branch to expand it, and then click HP C1130A Imaging Device.

4. Click Remove, and then click Refresh.

You might need to restart your computer if the scanner does not appear in Device Manager when you click Refresh.

Solution Three

Use the Windows 98 scanner and camera test rather than the HP scanner software's test:

1. Click the Start button, choose Settings, and click Control Panel.

2. Double-click Scanners And Cameras, and then double-click HP Scanner 4P.

3. Click Test Scanner Or Camera.

Related KB article Q187319

Microtek ScanWizard 2.0b7 Doesn't Install Properly

Microtek ScanWizard 2.0b7 installs incorrectly or not at all.

Solution

To solve this problem, follow these steps:

1. Click the Start button, and then click Run.

2. Enter *msconfig* in the Open text box, and click OK.

3. Click the Win.ini tab in System Configuration Utility.

4. Select the [Compatibility] folder.

5. Click the New option button, and then enter *DSHELL=0x00400000.*

Figure 10-8.   *The WIN.INI tab in the System Configuration Utility.*

6. Click OK, restart your computer, and then reinstall Microtek ScanWizard.

7. Follow steps 1 through 4 after you're finished installing your program, and clear the check box next to the line you added.

Related KB article   Q188978 or PROGRAMS.TXT in your WINDOWS folder

Visioneer PaperPort Displays Error Messages

You close the Visioneer PaperPort version 5.0 program and see a general protection (GP) fault error message in EXPLORER.EXE. This problem can occur because PaperPort version 5.0 installs versions of the TWAIN.DLL and TWAIN_32.DLL files that are older than the Windows 98 versions of these files.

Solution

Restore the original versions of these files. To do so, use System File Checker in Windows 98 to replace the TWAIN.DLL and TWAIN_32.DLL files. For information about using System File Checker to extract files, see KB article Q129605, "How to Extract Original Compressed Windows Files."

Related KB article   Q187399

USB

Device Doesn't Function

You experience problems in using USB devices on some computers or hubs.

Solution

View the HARDWARE.TXT file located in your WINDOWS folder. The file describes many of the problems you might encounter with USB devices in addition to specific actions you can take to avoid many of them. Click the Start button, choose Run, enter *hardware.txt* in the text box, and then click OK.

Related KB article Q191480 or HARDWARE.TXT in your WINDOWS folder

Device Is Not Recognized

You connect a Universal Serial Bus (USB) device to your computer while the computer is in Standby mode, and the computer does not resume from Standby mode to process the USB device connection and immediately recognize the new USB device. The computer remains in Standby mode and does not recognize the USB device after it resumes.

If you disconnect and then reconnect the USB device after the computer has resumed operating, the USB device will be correctly recognized.

Solution

Obtain from Microsoft Technical Support the following updated files for Windows 98:

- Openhci.sys version 4.10.2018 dated 7/6/98 8:18pm 21,904 bytes

- Usbd.sys   version 4.10.2018 dated 7/6/98 8:18pm 17,568 bytes

- Usbhub.sys version 4.10.2018 dated 7/6/98 8:18pm 27,136 bytes

Related KB article Q189591

Digital Camera Does Not Appear in Device Manager

After you connect your Universal Serial Bus (USB) digital camera to your USB port, you're unable to view this device in Device Manager if you disabled it in Device Manager before disconnecting it.

Solution

Click Refresh in Device Manager.

Related KB article Q193607

Port or Device Malfunctions

You run Windows 98 on a computer with an Intel 82371SB PCI to USB universal host controller, and Universal Serial Bus (USB) ports and devices do not function properly if you are using an early version of the Intel 82371SB PCI to USB universal host controller chip set.

Solution

Contact the manufacturer of your motherboard to inquire about the availability of an update. Windows 98 does not support early versions of the Intel 82371SB PCI to USB universal host controller chip set. To determine whether you are using an early version of this controller chip set, follow these steps:

1. Click the Start button, choose Settings, and then click Control Panel.

2. Double-click the System icon, and then click the Device Manager tab.

3. Double-click the Universal Serial Bus Controller branch to expand it.

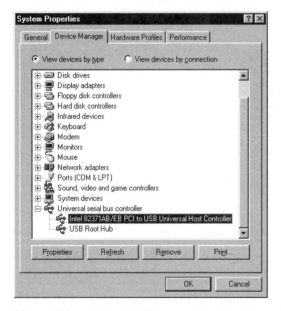

Figure 10-9.   *The Device Manager tab in the System Properties dialog box.*

4. Double-click Intel 82371SB PCI to USB Universal Host Controller, and then click the General tab.

5. If the Hardware Version line indicates that the version of the USB controller is 000, you have an early version of the USB controller chip set.

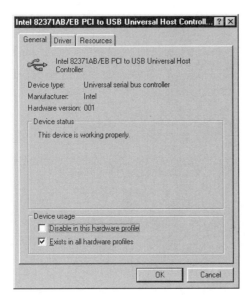

Figure 10-10. *The Properties dialog box for the Intel USB controller.*

Note This problem has also been reported to occur if the version of the USB controller is 001.

Related KB article Q181250

Toshiba Infinia Causes General Protection Fault Error

You install Windows 98 on a Toshiba Infinia computer that uses a Universal Serial Bus (USB) In Touch module, and you receive the following error message:

(unknown) caused a General Protection Fault in module URM.EXE at 015F:00000055

This problem occurs when the revision of the In Touch module is not compatible with the revision of the Toshiba Infinia. Several revisions of the Toshiba Infinia and the USB In Touch module exist. If you use an In Touch module on a Toshiba Infinia model other than that for which it is designed, this error message occurs. It happens when you repair or upgrade the In Touch module.

Solution

Disconnect the In Touch module. To solve this problem, contact Toshiba to ask about a possible update to solve this problem.

Related KB article Q188413

C H A P T E R   1 1

Printers

Fonts and Characters

Black Background Is Only Printed When Printing White Text

You attempt to print to a Hewlett-Packard (HP) printer an Adobe Acrobat (.PDF) document with white text on a black background from any version of Acrobat Reader, and only the black background is printed if your HP printer uses a Printer Control Language (PCL) driver. This limitation is in the HP PCL drivers and does not occur with PostScript drivers.

Solution One

Contact Hewlett-Packard about the availability of an updated PCL driver for your printer.

Solution Two

To solve this problem, follow these steps:

1. Click the Start button, choose Settings, and click Printers.

2. Right-click the printer you want, and choose Properties from the shortcut menu.

3. Click the Graphics tab, and click Use Raster Graphics.

4. Click OK, and close the PRINTERS folder.

Related KB article Q194708

Euro Symbol Doesn't Print

You print a document that contains the euro symbol, and the symbol is not printed if the font used to format it is not available on the computer that prints the document or if the printer driver substitutes a font that does not support the symbol. This problem has been observed with the following printers and drivers:

- Hewlett-Packard LaserJets 4, 5, and 6, using Printer Control Language (PCL)

- Hewlett-Packard LaserJets 4, 5, and 6, using PostScript (PS)

- Lexmark Optra C PS

Solution One

Format the euro symbol by applying a common TrueType font that contains the euro symbol, such as Arial, Courier New, Tahoma, or Times New Roman.

Solution Two

Configure your printer driver to use TrueType fonts by following these steps:

1. Click the Start button, choose Settings, and click Printers.

2. Right-click the printer you want to modify, and choose Properties from the shortcut menu.

3. Click the Fonts tab, and click a different TrueType font option.

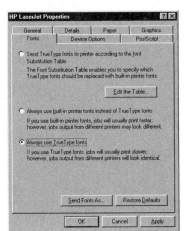

Figure 11-1.   *The Fonts tab of the Printer Properties dialog box.*

4. Click OK, and close the PRINTERS folder.

5. Test to determine whether the problem has been solved. If the problem persists, repeat steps 1–4, and choose a different font option in step 3.

Note To insert the euro symbol in a document, press Alt+0128 (use the numeric keypad), or use Character Map (CHARMAP.EXE).

Related KB article Q195041

Euro Symbol Prints As Black Dot or Blank Space

You print to a Hewlett-Packard (HP) LaserJet 5Si or 5Si/5Si MX PS printer a document that contains the euro symbol, and it prints as a black dot or blank space if TrueType fonts are not sent to the printer as bitmap soft fonts.

Solution

Send TrueType fonts to the printer as bitmap soft fonts by following these steps:

1. Click the Start button, choose Settings, and click Printers.

2. Right-click your HP LaserJet 5Si or 5Si/5Si MX PS printer, and choose Properties.

3. Click the Fonts tab.

4. For HP LaserJet 5Si/5Si MX PS printers, click Always Use TrueType Fonts, click Send Fonts As, select Bitmaps under TrueType Fonts, click OK, and click OK again.

Figure 11-2.   *The Send Fonts As dialog box.*

5. For HP LaserJet 5Si printers, click Download TrueType Fonts As Bitmap Soft Fonts, and then click OK.

Related KB article Q193935

HP LaserJet 4 Driver Doesn't Have TrueType Fonts

You install Windows 98, and your printer driver doesn't have TrueType fonts.

Solution

Hewlett-Packard TrueType screen fonts are available to LaserJet 4 printer users so that they can match their internal printer fonts. To obtain these fonts, contact Hewlett-Packard.

Related KB article Q189672

HP LaserJet 4Si, 4L, 4P, 4 Plus, 4V, 5, or 5P Printer Driver Doesn't Have TrueType Fonts

You install Windows 98, and your printer doesn't print TrueType fonts.

You need the Hewlett-Packard TrueType screen fonts to match your internal printer fonts.

Solution

Install HP TrueType fonts by following these steps:

Note If you cannot find your software disks, contact your Hewlett-Packard Driver Distribution Center.

1. Insert in the appropriate floppy disk drive Disk 1 of the HP LaserJet Printing System disk set.

2. Click the Start button, and choose Run.

3. Enter *a:\setup* in the Run dialog box.

4. Click Custom Installation, and click the appropriate HP LaserJet printer.

5. Click HP TrueType Screen Fonts. Clear the Printer Driver, Status Window, and Travel Guide check boxes.

6. Click OK, and follow the onscreen instructions.

Related KB article Q189672

International Font Prints As ASCII Font

You print to a PostScript printer in an international version of Windows, and you encounter one of the following problems:

- High-byte glyphs (non-ANSI glyphs) are printed as ASCII characters rather than as the appropriate international characters.

- TrueType fonts (such as Arial, Times New Roman, and Courier) are printed as U.S. ASCII characters rather than as Hebrew or Arabic characters.

This problem occurs because TrueType font substitution is enabled.

Solution

Configure your printer to always use TrueType fonts by following these steps:

1. Click the Start button, choose Settings, and click Printers.

2. Right-click the PostScript printer icon, and choose Properties from the shortcut menu.

3. Click the Fonts tab, and click Always Use TrueType Fonts.

4. Click OK.

Related KB article Q135228

TrueType Font Doesn't Print

You print to an inkjet printer with low resolution (75 to 150 dpi) or to a printer using a Generic/Text Only printer driver, and TrueType fonts do not print. TrueType fonts are not usually available on inkjet printers with lower resolutions (75 to 150 dpi).

Solution One

Select a different printer to print the document, if a different one is available, by following these steps:

1. Click the Start button, choose Settings, and click Printers.

2. Right-click a different printer, and choose Set As Default.

3. If no other printers are available in the Printers dialog box but you are connected to a network that contains other printers, double-click the Add Printers icon and follow the wizard's steps.

Solution Two

If you are using a Generic/Text Only printer driver, use the Add Printer Wizard as discussed in Solution One to find a more appropriate printer driver. To find a more appropriate driver, see your printer's documentation or contact the manufacturer.

Note This limitation does not apply to laser and dot-matrix printers.

Related KB article Q189672

General Errors

Astound 2.X Prints Incorrectly

You have problems when you print in Astound 2.X using a printer that uses the EMF (Enhanced Metafile Format) data format to spool its data.

Solution

Change the data format your printer uses to spool to RAW by following these steps:

1. Click the Start button, choose Settings, and click Printers.

2. Right-click your printer name, and choose Properties from the shortcut menu.

3. Click the Details tab, and click Spool Settings.

4. Select RAW from the Spool Data Format drop-down list box, and click OK.

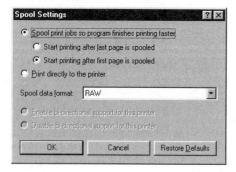

Figure 11-3. *The Spool Settings dialog box.*

Related KB article Q188978 or PROGRAMS.TXT in your WINDOWS folder

Dot-Matrix Printer Prints Slowly

You upgrade Windows, and your dot-matrix printer prints slowly. Or the printer prints only as the print head passes in one direction, not as the print head passes in both directions.

Solution One

Use printer fonts rather than TrueType fonts in your documents. Printer fonts on font lists have a printer icon next to their name, and TrueType fonts have a *TT* next to their name.

Solution Two

Configure your printer to use a lower print resolution, or a lower-quality printer font, by following these steps:

1. Click the Start button, choose Settings, and click Control Panel.

2. Double-click the Printers icon, right-click the printer you want to configure, and choose Properties from the shortcut menu.

3. Click the Graphics tab to modify the print resolution or the Device Options tab to modify the print quality, and then click OK.

Solution Three

Configure your print drivers to print directly to the printer, rather than spool print jobs to your hard disk, by following these steps:

Note Although this process speeds data to your printer, it slows the response of the program from which you are printing.

1. Click the Start button, choose Settings, and click Control Panel.

2. Double-click the Printers icon.

3. Right-click the printer you want to configure, and choose Properties from the shortcut menu.

4. Click the Details tab, click Spool Settings, click Print Directly To The Printer, and click OK. Click OK again.

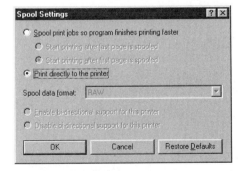

Figure 11-4. *The Spool Settings dialog box.*

Related KB article Q148348

Erratic Printing and Error Messages

The WIN.INI file has the read-only attribute on, and you experience the following situations:

- Although you cannot print from Windows-based programs, you can print from MS-DOS-based programs, such as EDIT.COM.

- You attempt to print from WordPad, and you receive the following error message:

  The printer could not be found.

- The Print command on the File menu in Notepad is unavailable.

- You try to print, and you receive any of the following error messages:

  An error occurred during this operation

  Could not start print job

  Windows was unable to print the test page. Would you like to begin troubleshooting now?

Note that this problem might occur after you upgrade to Windows 98.

Solution

Remove the read-only attribute from the WIN.INI file, and install the printer driver again to update the WIN.INI file, by following these steps:

1. Click the Start button, choose Find, and click Files Or Folders.

2. Type *win.ini* in the Named box, and click Find Now.

3. Right-click the WIN.INI file in the list of files, and choose Properties.

4. Clear the Read-Only check box, and click OK.

5. Close Find, and restart your computer.

6. Click the Start button, choose Settings, and click Printers.

7. Right-click your printer, and choose Properties.

8. Click New Driver on the Details tab, and click Yes.

9. Select your printer's manufacturer on the Manufacturers list, and select the appropriate model on the Models list.

10. Click OK, and click OK again.

Related KB article Q191516

Not Enough Memory to Render Page Error Message

You print to a printer with bidirectional support and receive the following error message:

Not enough memory to render page

Either the printer driver determines the amount of printer memory incorrectly, or your printer does not have enough memory to support your current printer resolution.

Solution One

Redetect the printer memory by following these steps:

1. Verify that the printer is connected and ready to print.

2. Click the Start button, choose Settings, and click Printers.

3. Right-click the Printer icon, and choose Properties from the shortcut menu.

4. Click the Device Options tab, and click Restore Defaults.

5. Click OK.

Solution Two

Try printing the page at a lower resolution by following these steps:

1. Verify that the printer is connected and ready to print.

2. Click the Start button, choose Settings, and click Printers.

3. Right-click the icon for your printer, and choose Properties from the shortcut menu.

4. Click the Graphics tab, click the arrow next to Resolution, choose a setting lower than your current resolution, and click OK.

5. Restart your computer, and try printing again.

Related KB article Q134540

Printers Folder Doesn't Display Job Progress in Desired Terms

If the Spool Data Format option is set to EMF (Enhanced Metafile) and you are printing to a local printer, the size of the job (in kilobytes [KB] or megabytes [MB]) is unknown; therefore, the progress is displayed in terms of pages printed.

A print job's status is displayed in kilobytes or megabytes when at least one of the following conditions is met:

- The Spool Data Format option is set to RAW.

- You are printing to a PostScript printer. (PostScript printers cannot print in EMF format; progress to a PostScript printer can be reported in size only.)

Solution One

Change the Spool Data Format option by following these steps:

1. Click the Start button, choose Settings, and click Printers.

2. Right-click the appropriate printer icon, and choose Properties from the shortcut menu.

3. Click the Details tab, and click Spool Settings.

4. Change the Spool Data Format from RAW to EMF.

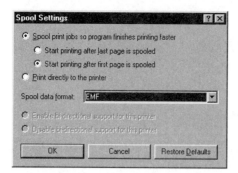

Figure 11-5. *The Spool Settings dialog box.*

5. Click OK.

Solution Two

Print to something other than a PostScript printer.

Related KB article Q122868

SPOOL32 Returns Error Message

The following error messages are displayed when you attempt to print or perform a printer-related action:

>*SPOOL32 caused a General Protection Fault in module Kernel32.dll at <address>.*

>*SPOOL32 caused an Invalid Page Fault in module Kernel32.dll at <address>.*

>*SPOOL32 caused a Stack Fault in module Kernel32.dll at <address>.*

The SPOOL32.EXE file is a 32-bit Windows 98 component that manages the spooling of print jobs. Spooling allows your computer's processor to quickly process a print job by temporarily storing it on the hard disk before sending it to the printer. This allows the processor to return control to the program from which you are printing at a much faster rate than if it processed the entire print job and then sent it directly to the printer. Spool32 error messages can occur if something is preventing the print job from being spooled properly.

Note To troubleshoot the error messages just described, try each of the following solutions, and then attempt to print again. If you still receive the error message, continue to the next solution.

Solution One

Disable all nonessential drivers and programs, and perform a clean boot of your computer. The clean-boot process eliminates the possibility of an antivirus program or other utility causing the error message. You should also disable any third-party printing software, such as Hewlett-Packard Port Monitor or Epson Spooler. To clean-boot your computer, follow these steps:

1. Click the Start button, choose Programs, click Accessories, click System Tools, and click System Information.

2. Choose System Configuration Utility from the Tools menu.

3. On the General tab, click the Selective Startup option button and then clear the following check boxes:

   ■ Process CONFIG.SYS File

   ■ Process AUTOEXEC.BAT File

   ■ Process WINSTART.BAT File (if you cannot clear this box, it means that you do not have a WINSTART.BAT file)

   ■ Process SYSTEM.INI File

   ■ Process WIN.INI File

   ■ Load Startup Group Items

Note If you cannot clear a check box, either you don't have the file or the file is empty.

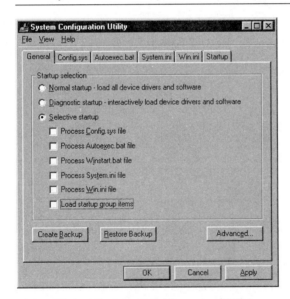

Figure 11-6. *The System Configuration Utility.*

4. Click OK, and exit System Information.

5. Restart your computer. If the error goes away, selectively check the boxes you cleared until the problem appears again. Then check all boxes and troubleshoot the file you last selected for the program or command causing the problem.

Solution Two

Change the spooling format from Enhanced Metafile (EMF) to RAW, and attempt to print directly to the printer rather than spool the print job, by following these steps:

1. Click the Start button, choose Settings, and click Printers.

2. Right-click the printer you are using, and choose Properties.

3. Click Spool Settings on the Details tab.

4. Click Print Directly To The Printer.

5. Click RAW in the Spool Data Format box.

6. Click OK, click OK again, and close the Printers window.

Solution Three

Some printer drivers have a coding error that can cause one of these error messages to occur. To determine whether that is the case, update or change the printer driver by following these steps:

1. Click the Start button, choose Settings, and click Printers.

2. Right-click the icon for your printer, choose Properties from the shortcut menu, click the Details tab, and click New Driver.

3. Choose the manufacturer and model for your printer, and click OK. Insert your Windows 98 CD-ROM when prompted.

4. Try to print from your application with this driver.

5. If this step does not work, contact your printer's manufacturer for a different driver. Repeat steps 1 and 2. If you are using a driver from a floppy disk or CD-ROM or a file downloaded from the Internet, click Have Disk, and navigate to the location of the driver. After your new driver is installed, try printing again.

Solution Four

A terminate-and-stay-resident (TSR) or other program might prevent SPOOL32.EXE from being run when Windows 98 starts up. To work around this problem, use one of the following methods:

- Create a shortcut to the <windows>\SYSTEM\SPOOL32.EXE file in the STARTUP folder, where <windows> is the folder in which Windows 98 is installed. For information, click the Start button, choose Help, click the Index tab, enter *shortcuts*, and double-click the Creating topic.

- Using a text editor (such as Notepad), add the line <drive>:\<WINDOWS>\SYSTEM\SPOOL32.EXE to the Load= or Run= line in the [Windows] section of the WIN.INI file where <drive> is the drive on which Windows 98 is installed and <windows> is the folder in which Windows 98 is installed.

Related KB article   Q191949

Hewlett-Packard Printers

HP 5Si or 5Si MX PS Causes Errors When Printing Acrobat PDF Files

You try to print Adobe Acrobat (.PDF) documents in duplex from Acrobat Reader version 3.01 to a Hewlett-Packard 5Si/5Si MX PS, your printer stops responding, and you see the following error message:

79 SERVICE (0142)

TRAP:0D   ADR:007D1588

Solution

Download and install the most current version of the printer driver from Hewlett-Packard.

Related KB article Q186064

HP Color LaserJet Printer Doesn't Print

You install or upgrade to Windows 98, and you cannot print to your Hewlett-Packard Color LaserJet printer or the printer does not print TrueType fonts.

Solution One

Install the PostScript support for your HP Color LaserJet. Use the printer drivers from the disks supplied with your printer by following these steps:

Note If you cannot find the disks, contact your Hewlett-Packard Driver Distribution Center.

1. Insert in the appropriate floppy disk drive the HP Color LaserJet Printer disk, Windows 3.1 PostScript 2.1.1.

2. Click the Start button, choose Settings, and click Printers.

3. Click Add Printer, and follow the onscreen instructions.

4. Click Have Disk. If you are prompted to replace or update the driver, click Yes.

Solution Two

To print using TrueType fonts, install drivers for your HP Color LaserJet printer from the Windows 98 CD-ROM.

1. Click the Start button, choose Settings, and click Printers.

2. Right-click the icon for your printer, and choose Properties from the shortcut menu. Click the Details tab, and click New Driver.

3. Select HP in the Manufacturers box, select the model for your printer, and click OK. Insert your Windows 98 CD-ROM when prompted. Complete the installation by following the prompts.

Related KB article Q189672

HP DeskJet 340, 1000c, 1100c, or 1120c Doesn't Work Properly

You print to a Hewlett-Packard DeskJet 340, 1000c, 1100c, or 1120c, and some aspect of functionality does not work correctly.

Solution

Install a Windows 98-compatible printer driver to make full use of the capabilities of your DeskJet 340, 1000C, 1100C, or 1120C. To obtain a Windows 98–compatible printer driver, visit the HP web site, at *http://www.hp.com/cposupport/escheme.html,* and then install the appropriate driver.

Related KB article Q189672

HP DeskJet 400 Doesn't Print Multiple Copies

You attempt to print multiple copies of a document to a Hewlett-Packard DeskJet 400 printer, and the Number Of Copies box is unavailable in the Print dialog box. The Collate check box is also unavailable.

Solution One

Print one copy of the document at a time.

Solution Two

Change the driver used by your Hewlett-Packard DeskJet 400 printer by following these steps:

Note Following these steps might change some capabilities of your Hewlett-Packard DeskJet 400 printer.

1. Click the Start button, choose Settings, and click Printers.

2. Right-click your Hewlett-Packard DeskJet 400 printer, and choose Properties.

3. Click New Driver on the Details tab, and click Yes when you are prompted to continue.

4. Select HP in the Manufacturers box, and select a different Hewlett-Packard DeskJet driver (such as HP DeskJet 500) in the Models box.

5. Click OK, and click OK again.

Related KB article Q187247

HP DeskJet 660C Printer Doesn't Print Duplex

You cannot print in duplex to a Hewlett-Packard DeskJet 660C printer in Windows 98, even though the printer normally supports this capability. If you attempt to use the Hewlett-Packard DeskJet 660C printer driver included with Windows 95, you receive the following error message:

Printer Driver Problem

Data needed by the printer driver cannot be found or has been corrupted.

Restart Windows and try printing again.

This problem occurs because the Hewlett-Packard DeskJet 660C printer driver included with Windows 98 does not support duplex printing and the version of the driver included with Windows 95 (version 9.02) is incompatible with Windows 98.

Solution

Contact Hewlett-Packard to inquire about the availability of an updated driver.

Related KB article Q188085

HP DeskJet 1200C or 1600C Misprints Colored Text

You send colored text or graphics images to a Hewlett-Packard DeskJet 1200C or 1600C printer, and some text or graphics do not print in the exact color in which they appear onscreen or they do not print at all. The reason is a limitation of the UNIDRV.DLL file and dithering limitations of the HP DeskJet 1200C and 1600C printers. In addition, the HP DeskJet 1200C printer uses the HPPCL5MS.DRV printer driver included with Windows 98. Other Hewlett-Packard DeskJet color printers that use the HPPCL5MS.DRV printer driver do not exhibit this behavior.

Solution One

If you are using an HP DeskJet 1200C printer, install the Windows 3.1 printer driver included with the printer by following these steps:

1. Click the Start button, choose Settings, and click Printers.

2. Double-click the Add Printer icon, and click Next.

3. Click either Local Printer or Network Printer, and click Next.

4. Click Have Disk.

5. In the Copy Manufacturer's Files From box, enter the drive and path for the HP DeskJet 1200C printer, and click Next.

6. Click the driver you want to install, and click OK.

Solution Two

If you are using HP DeskJet 1600C, disable dithering by following these steps:

1. Click the Start button, choose Settings, and click Printers.

2. Right-click your HP 1600C printer, and choose Properties from the shortcut menu.

3. Click the Graphics tab.

Figure 11-7. *The Graphics tab of the Printer Properties dialog box*

4. Click None in the Dithering section, and click OK.

Related KB article Q177840

HP DeskJet Printer Doesn't Print

You upgrade to Windows 98, and you cannot print to your Hewlett-Packard DeskJet printer. You experience one or more of the following situations:

- You try to print to the DeskJet printer or to a file, and you receive *Out of memory* or *Not enough memory* error messages.

- You try to print to the DeskJet printer, and you receive an error message that the printer is offline.

- You try to install the HP DeskJet printer drivers included with Windows 98, and you see an error message that UNIDRV.DLL is already in use.

- You print to a Hewlett-Packard Color DeskJet 5xx-series printer, and you receive the error message *Cannot print to device LPT1*.

- You try to print from WordPad, and you receive the error message *Could not start print job*.

- You try to print to the DeskJet printer, and your entire document is printed as random or unintelligible characters.

- You try to print to the DeskJet printer, and graphics images are printed but text is not.

- You try to print to the DeskJet printer, and text is printed but graphics images are not.

The Windows 3.1 drivers for the HP DeskJet printer were not successfully upgraded to the Windows 98 versions. If you can successfully print to a file, however, the problem is likely not caused by the drivers for the HP DeskJet printer. (To configure the drivers to print to a file, double-click the Printers icon in Control Panel, right-click the printer name, choose Properties from the shortcut menu, click the Details tab, and then click FILE (Creates A File On Disk) in the Print To The Following Port box.

Solution

To solve this problem, follow these steps:

1. Click the Start button, choose Settings, click Control Panel, and double-click the Printers icon.

2. Right-click the HP DeskJet printer, and choose Delete from the shortcut menu.

3. If more than one HP DeskJet printer is in the PRINTERS folder, repeat step 2 for each HP DeskJet printer.

4. Locate and remove the DESKJET.INI and DESKJETC.INI files in the WINDOWS folder.

Note Your computer might have only one of these files or both.

5. Locate and remove the following files in the WINDOWS\SYSTEM folder (to avoid deleting files that might be crucial to other HP components, delete only these files):

DESKJETC.DRV

HPDSKJET.DRV

HPSETUP3.DLL

HPV1284.DLL

HPV500.HPC

HPV500C.HPC

HPV510.HPC

HPV520.HPC

HPV540_A.HPC

HPV540_B.HPC

HPV550C.HPC

HPV560C.HPC

HPV660C.HPC

HPVBG.EXE

HPVCM.HPM

HPVCNFIG.EXE

HPVDOS.DLL

HPVDSM.EXE

HPVEXT24.DLL

IIPVIIT.DLL

HPVMLC.DLL

HPVMLCH.EXE

HPVMON.DLL

HPVPML.DLL

HPVQP.DLL

HPVRES.DLL

HPVTTPCL.DLL

HPVUI.DLL

HPVWCPS.DLL

HPVWIN.DLL

SCONFIG.DLL

TBKBASE.DLL

TBKCOMP.DLL

TBKNET.EXE

TBKUTIL.DLL

TBOOK.EXE

6. Rename all the OEM<n>.INF files in the WINDOWS\INF folder, where <n> is an incremental number starting at 0.

Note Do not use the OEM*.INF wildcard to rename files. Doing so might cause the wrong files to be renamed.

---

7. Remove the HP DeskJet Status Monitor if it is in the Startup group, by following steps 8–12.

8. Right-click the taskbar, and choose Properties from the shortcut menu.

9. Click the Start Menu Programs tab, and click Remove.

10. Double-click the Startup branch to expand it.

11. Click the HP DeskJet Status Monitor shortcut, and click Remove.

12. Click Close, and restart your computer.

13. Use the Add Printer Wizard to reinstall the HP DeskJet printer. Make sure to select the DeskJet driver included with Windows 98, not the Windows 3.x HP printer driver. If the new DeskJet printer does not show up on the Add New Hardware list, remove the DRVIDX.BIN and DRVDATA.BIN files from the WINDOWS\INF folder. This action causes the Add New Hardware Device Database list to be updated with the new printer.

Related KB article Q137996

HP DeskJet Printer Doesn't Print Correctly

You upgrade from Windows 3.x to Windows 98 and print to a Hewlett-Packard DeskJet printer, and you experience poor print quality or the printer loses some functionality.

Solution One

Delete your HP DeskJet printer driver by following these steps:

1. Click the Start button, choose Settings, and click Printers.

2. Click your printer to select it, and press Delete.

3. Follow the onscreen instructions.

4. Obtain and install the latest driver for your HP DeskJet printer by using one of the following methods:

   ■ Download the latest driver for your printer from *http://www.hp.com/cposupport/eschome.html*, and follow the installation instructions on the web site.

   ■ If you have an HP DeskJet model number 660C, 68XC, 69XC, 850C, 855C, or 870C and are using the U.S. version of Windows 98, install the drivers from your Windows 98 CD in the DRIVERS\PRINTERS folder.

Note The drivers in this folder are English-only and might not work properly on some localized versions of Windows 98.

Solution Two

The Windows 98 printer driver shipped with your printer also functions correctly. The simplest and most complete method of installing a driver is to run the SETUP.EXE program that comes with it. For more information, see the instructions included with the driver.

Related KB article Q189672

HP JetAdmin Service Causes Errors

You install the Hewlett-Packard JetAdmin service, and you are unable to see properties for any of your printers. Also, you right-click a printer icon in the PRINTERS folder, and you receive the following error message:

EXPLORER caused an invalid page fault in module KERNEL32.DLL at 015f:bffabea

When you click Close and click Properties, you see the following error message:

RUNDLL32 caused an invalid page fault in module KERNEL32.DLL at 015f:bff8abea

When you click Close, you can see properties for your printer.

This problem occurs when you have installed the Windows 98 HP JetAdmin drivers version 2.54 from the Windows 98 CD-ROM and you then install the Hewlett-Packard HP JetAdmin service.

Solution

Uninstall the Hewlett-Packard HP JetAdmin service, and then reinstall it, by following these steps:

1. Click the Start button, choose Settings, click Control Panel, and double-click the Network icon.

2. If an HP JetAdmin entry is on the list of installed network components, skip to step 4. If no HP JetAdmin entry is on the list of installed network components, click Add, and then click Service.

3. Click Hewlett-Packard, click HP Jet Admin, and click Cancel while the files are being copied. Restart your computer.

4. Click the Start button, choose Settings, click Control Panel, and double-click the Network icon.

5. Click HP JetAdmin, click Remove, and restart your computer.

6. Install the HP JetAdmin service. Run Setup from the <drive>:\DRIVERS\PRINTERS \JETADMIN\DISK1 folder on your Windows 98 CD-ROM, where <drive> is the drive that contains the Windows 98 CD-ROM.

Related KB article Q190628

HP JetAdmin Service Does Not Add

You try to add the Hewlett-Packard JetAdmin service in Windows 98 by double-clicking the Network icon in Control Panel, clicking Add, clicking Services,.and clicking Add; and the HP JetAdmin service is missing.

Or the HP JetAdmin service appears on the list of network services available to install, and you see the following error message when you attempt to add the HP JetAdmin service:

The file 'hpnetprn.inf' on the Windows 98 CD-ROM could not be found. Insert Windows 98 CD-ROM in the selected drive, and click OK.

This problem occurs because the HP JetAdmin service is not installed as a network service in Windows 98. The HP JetAdmin service is available on the Windows 98 CD-ROM.

Note If the HP JetAdmin service was installed in Windows 95 before you upgraded to Windows 98, the service still functions correctly. However, Microsoft recommends that you upgrade to the latest version of the HP JetAdmin service, available on the Windows 98 CD-ROM.

Solution

Install the HP JetAdmin service by running Setup from the <drive>:\DRIVERS\PRINTERS \JETADMIN\DISK1 folder on your Windows 98 CD-ROM, (where <drive> is the drive that contains the Windows 98 CD-ROM.

Related KB article Q188201

HP LaserJet 3 or 4 Causes Error Message When Printing Astound Sample Files

You print one of the sample files included with Astound (from Gold Disk, Inc.), and you see the following general protection (GP) fault error message:

<Program> caused a general protection fault in module <xxxxxx> at <address range>

This problem can occur if you try to print the sample file by using a Hewlett-Packard LaserJet 4-series (or later) printer driver or if you are using an HP LaserJet 3–series printer driver on an LPT printer port.

Solution

Print the sample file by using an HP LaserJet 3-series printer driver. Make sure that the printer is not connected to an LPT port.

Related KB article Q187328

HP LaserJet 5L, 5MP, 6L, 6P, or 6MP Printer Driver Doesn't Print TrueType Fonts

You install Windows 98, and your printer doesn't print TrueType fonts.

You need the Hewlett-Packard TrueType screen fonts to match your internal printer fonts.

Solution

Install HP TrueType fonts by following these steps:

Note If you cannot find your software disks, contact your Hewlett-Packard Driver Distribution Center.

1. Insert in the appropriate drive the HP LaserJet Printing System Disk 1.

2. Click the Start button, and choose Run.

3. Type *a:\setup*.

4. Select Typical Installation, and follow the onscreen instructions.

Related KB article Q189672

HP LaserJet Printer Doesn't Print

You try to print to a Hewlett-Packard LaserJet printer, and it doesn't print.

Solution

Disable the bidirectional support for the printer by following these steps:

1. Click the Start button, choose Settings, and click Printers.

2. Right-click the icon that represents your printer, and choose Properties.

3. Click Spool Settings on the Details tab.

4. Select the Disable Bidirectional Support For This Printer option, and click OK.

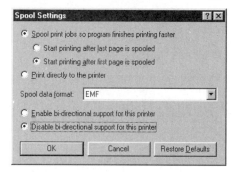

Figure 11-8. *The Spool Settings dialog box.*

5. Click OK again to exit.

Try your print job again. If you get an *Error 21 – print overrun* message on your LaserJet printer, follow these steps:

1. Click the Start button, choose Settings, and click Printers.

2. Right-click the icon that represents your printer.

3. Click Device Options, and clear the Page Protection check box.

4. If you have a LaserJet 3 printer, you have to set this option directly on the printer's front panel.

5. If you are using a LaserJet 4 printer and the Page Protection option is not available, try changing the printer driver to Raster mode rather than Vector mode on the Graphics tab in the Printer Properties dialog box.

6. Try your print job again.

If you still have problems, you can sometimes solve this problem by reducing the complexity of the page. Graphics images, such as pictures and drawings, create a heavy load on a print job and should be avoided whenever possible.

Related KB article Q189672

HP OfficeJet 500 or 600 Series Printer Doesn't Print Properly

You upgrade from Windows 3.1 to Windows 98, and your Hewlett-Packard OfficeJet Series 500 or 600 printer does not print properly.

Solution

Contact Hewlett-Packard for assistance. To locate the nearest Hewlett-Packard Support Center, see the documentation included with your printer.

To determine whether software updates are available for the HP OfficeJet (Series 500 and 600) products, visit the Hewlett-Packard web site, at *http://www.hp.com/go/all-in-one,* or contact the nearest Hewlett-Packard Support Center for more information.

Note You should uninstall the HP OfficeJet Series 500 and 600 printer drivers before you upgrade to Windows 98.

Related KB article Q189672

Hp OfficeJet Pro 1150c Does Not Function Correctly

You install or upgrade to Windows 98, and your Hewlett-Packard OfficeJet Pro 1150C printer does not function properly.

Solution One

If you upgraded to Windows 98 from Windows 3.1, first uninstall your HP OfficeJet Pro driver software.

1. Click the Start button, choose Settings, and click Printers.

2. In the PRINTERS folder, delete the icon for your HP OfficeJet Pro 1150C printer.

Install the Windows 95 driver that shipped with your HP OfficeJet Pro 1150C (its Windows 95 driver is compatible with Windows 98) by following these steps:

1. Click the Start button, choose Settings, click Control Panel, and double-click the Printers icon.

2. Double-click Add Printer, and follow the instructions that appear in the Add Printer Wizard.

3. Click Have Disk, and select the CD-ROM drive or the path where you saved the downloaded driver.

Note If you do not have the CD that came with your printer, you can download the latest Windows 95 driver from the Hewlett-Packard web site, at *http://www.hp.com/go/officejet-pro.*

Solution Two

If you upgraded to Windows 98 from Windows 95, the Scan Picture function of your HP OfficeJet Pro 1150C doesn't work with some applications. Delete the Microsoft OfficeJet Pro 1150C printer driver from the PRINTERS folder by following these steps:

1. Click the Start button, choose Settings, and click Printers.

2. In the PRINTERS folder, delete the icon for your HP OfficeJet Pro 1150C printer.

Install the Windows 95 driver that shipped with your OfficeJet Pro 1150C by following these steps:

1. Click the Start button, choose Settings, click Control Panel, and double-click the Printers icon.

2. Double-click Add Printer, and follow the instructions that appear in the Add Printer Wizard.

3. Click Have Disk, and select the CD-ROM drive or the path where you saved the downloaded driver.

Note If you do not have the CD that came with your printer, you can download the latest Windows 95 driver from the Hewlett-Packard web site, at *http://www.hp.com/go/officejet-pro*.

Solution Three

If you installed the Windows 98 default drivers, you lose scanning functionality on your OfficeJet Pro 1150C. Delete the OfficeJet Pro 1150C printer driver from the PRINTERS folder by following these steps:

1. Click the Start button, choose Settings, and click Printers.

2. In the PRINTERS folder, delete the icon for your HP OfficeJet Pro 1150C printer.

Install the Windows 95 driver that shipped with your OfficeJet Pro 1150C by following these steps:

1. Click the Start button, choose Settings, click Control Panel, and double-click the Printers icon.

2. Double-click Add Printer, and follow the instructions that appear in the Add Printer Wizard.

3. Click Have Disk, and select the CD-ROM drive or the path where you saved the downloaded driver.

Note If you do not have the CD that came with your printer, you can download the latest Windows 95 driver from the Hewlett-Packard web site, at *http://www.hp.com/go/officejet-pro*.

Related KB article Q189672

HP Photosmart Photo Printer Doesn't Print

You upgrade to Windows 98 from Windows 3.1, and your Hewlett-Packard Photosmart Photo printer doesn't print.

Solution

Delete the Photosmart Photo printer driver from the PRINTERS folder, and install the Windows 98 driver that came with your Windows 98 CD-ROM.

Note If you do not have the Windows 98 CD, you can download the latest driver from the Hewlett-Packard web site, at *http://www.hpcc920.external.hp.com/cposupport/indexesl/photprd.html*.

Use the SETUP.EXE program to install the driver software from either the driver software CD or the temporary location of the downloaded web version. Do not use the or Add Printer Wizard or install the drivers when Windows automatically detects the printer.

If you get a message that begins *Error finding LST file*, click Ignore and complete the installation. Because of changes to the Windows 98 file system, you can't access the multimedia presentation without getting a newer version of the driver.

If you get a message that reads *The file or folder 'REMIND.EXE' cannot be found*, click the OK button and complete the installation.

Related KB article Q189672

HP Printer/Scanner/Copier Series 300 Doesn't Function Properly

You upgrade to Windows 98 from Windows 3.1, and your Hewlett-Packard printer/scanner/copier Series 300 doesn't run properly.

Solution

Contact Hewlett-Packard for assistance. See either the documentation included with your product, or visit the Hewlett-Packard web site, *http://www.hp.com/go/all-in-one,* for software updates.

Note You should uninstall the HP printer scanner software before you upgrade to Windows 98.

Related KB article Q189672

Network

Client for NetWare Networks Displays Error Message

You try to print to a printer or a print queue configured to use the Microsoft Client for NetWare Networks and the Microsoft IPX/SPX-compatible protocol, and you receive the following error message:

There was an error writing to <\\servername\sharename> for printer <printername>.

The network printer is no longer available. Contact your system administrator, or try using a different printer. This printer will be set to work offline. To save your print job in the local printer queue, click OK.

Solution One

This problem is solved by the following updated file for Windows 98:

```
NWPP32.DLL   version 4.00.954   dated 05/28/98   9:54am   43,520 bytes
```

Install the latest Windows 98 Service Pack that addresses this problem. An update to address this problem is now available but is not fully regression tested and should be applied only to computers experiencing this specific problem. Unless your computer is severely affected by this specific problem, Microsoft does not recommend implementing this update at this time. Contact Microsoft Technical Support for additional information about the availability of this update.

Solution Two

Contact Novell for a copy of the Novell NetWare Client32 update for Windows 98.

Related KB article Q186322

LANtastic Network Printer Does Not Print

You try to print to a LANtastic network printer, and you receive the following error message:

Spool32 caused an invalid page fault in module WNPP32.DLL

This error occurs for one of the following reasons:

- The real-mode LANtastic driver uses the wrong syntax to capture a printer port.

- You need to update the LANTNET.DRV file from Artisoft.

Solution

Edit the STARTNET.BAT file in the LANTASTIC folder, and disable the *net use lptx* statement, by following these steps:

1. Click the Start button, choose Find, and click Files Or Folders.

2. Enter STARTNET.BAT in the Named text box, and select C: from the Look In drop-down list.

3. Click the file to open it.

4. Type *rem* at the beginning of the *Net Use LPT1* line.

5. Choose Save from the File menu, and close the program.

6. Reboot your computer.

Note To obtain the updated LANTNET.DRV file, download the LANT6X.EXE file from the Artisoft BBS.

Related KB article Q143394

Network Printer Does Not Print

You try to print to a network printer, and you receive one of the following error messages:

Cannot open printer driver

Cannot connect to printer. Check printer setup.

This problem occurs when the name of the shared network server or printer model you are using contains spaces. Some programs incorrectly use shortened versions for the name and location of network printers.

Solution One

Remove the spaces from the name of the print server or shared printer.

Solution Two

Capture a parallel port to the shared printer, and install the printer to that port.

Note For more information about capturing printer ports, see the topic "Capturing Printer Ports" in the Windows help system.

Related KB article Q130650

Network Printer Does Not Print When Using Dial-Up Networking

You try to print a web page to a network printer while you are using Dial-Up Networking to connect to another computer, and you are unable to print successfully. Also, the printer status is listed as User Intervention Required – Use Printer Offline.

This problem occurs for one of the following reasons:

- You cannot print to a network printer that is on a subnet different from the subnet of your Dial-Up Networking connection.

- Your printer is set to Offline mode.

Solution

To solve this problem, follow these steps:

1. Navigate to the appropriate web site, and print the web page or pages you want on your network printer.

Note Click OK if you receive any printing error messages.

2. Close your Dial-Up Networking connection.

3. Click the Start button, choose Settings, and click Printers.

4. Right-click the network printer, and clear the Use Printer Offline check mark.

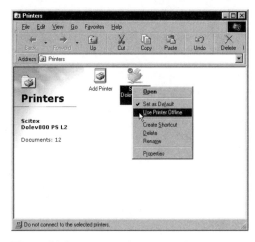

Figure 11-9. *A network printer's shortcut menu.*

5. Press F5 to refresh your printer's status, and close the PRINTERS folder.

Related KB article Q189104

PostScript Printer Doesn't Print over a NetWare Network

You cannot print to a PostScript printer over a NetWare network because banner pages are incorrectly configured on the NetWare server. Unless banner pages are correctly configured on the NetWare server, they cause errors and nothing prints.

Solution One

Ask your network administrator to correctly configure banner pages on the NetWare server for a PostScript printer.

Solution Two

Disable banner pages by clearing the Banner Pages check box in the Printer Properties dialog box, by following these steps:

1. Click the Start button, choose Settings, and click Printers.

2. Right-click the NetWare printer to which you are printing, and choose Properties.

3. Clear the Clear Banner Pages check box.

Solution Three

If you clear the Banner Page setting as just described and you still receive unwanted banner pages when you print from MS-DOS programs, change the port designation for the printer from the network path (UNC) name to the captured port by following these steps:

1. Click the Start button, choose Settings, and click Printers.

2. Right-click the icon for the printer you are using, and choose Properties.

3. On the Details tab, click the Print To The Following Port down arrow. Look for an entry that displays LPTx:. This Is The LPT Port You Have Captured.

4. Select LPTx: (\\SERVER\PRINTQUEUE), and click Apply.

5. Click Capture Printer Port, and click OK.

6. Disable the Banner Page setting as described in Solution Two.

Related KB article Q189672

Printing Lists from Windows Tools

Device Manager File Contains No Readable Text

You print the contents of Device Manager to a file, and the file does not contain readable information.

By default, Windows does not support the printing of Device Manager information to a text file. When Windows prints it to a file, Windows uses printer-specific language rather than plain text.

Solution

To print Device Manager information to a readable text file, install and use the Generic/Text Only printer. To install it, follow these steps:

1. Click the Start button, choose Settings, and click Printers.

2. Double-click the Add Printer icon.

3. Click Next.

4. When you see the message *How is this printer attached to your computer?* click Local Printer, and then click Next.

5. Select Generic in the Manufacturers box. In the Printers box, select Generic/Text Only, and click Next.

6. Select File in the Available Ports box, and click Next.

7. When you see the message *Do you want your Windows-based programs to use this printer as the default printer?* click No, and then click Next.

8. When you see the *Would you like to print a test page?* message, click No, and then click Finish.

To print the contents of Device Manager to a file, follow these steps:

1. Right-click My Computer, and choose Properties from the shortcut menu.

2. Click the Device Manager tab, and click Print.

3. In the Report Type box, click the option button for the report you want.

Note To print the Selected Class Or Device report, you must first click the class or device you want on the Device Manager tab.

4. Click Setup.

5. In the Specific Printer box, select Generic/Text Only On File, and then click OK.

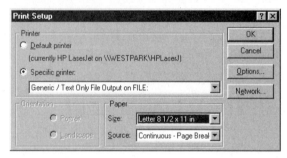

Figure 11-10. *The Print Setup dialog box.*

6. Click OK.

7. Type in the File Name box the path and name you want to use for the file, and click OK.

Related KB article Q127156

Device Manager Report Doesn't Print

You attempt to print a Device Manager report to a file, the report does not print, and you do not receive an error message if Microsoft Fax is set as the default printer.

Solution

Change the default printer by following these steps:

1. Click the Start button, choose Settings, and click Printers.

2. Right-click a printer other than Microsoft Fax, and choose Set As Default from the shortcut menu.

Note If you do not have another printer connected to your computer to set as the default, install any printer by clicking Add Printer, and then step through the Add Printer Wizard.

Related KB article Q177331

HISTORY or TEMPORARY INTERNET FILES Folder Contents Don't Print

You cannot print the contents of your Internet Explorer HISTORY or TEMPORARY INTERNET FILES folder.

Note You can see or print the contents of the HISTORY or TEMPORARY INTERNET FILES folders for only the user who is logged on to the computer. If you attempt to open another user's HISTORY or TEMPORARY INTERNET FILES folder, the contents of the logged-on user's HISTORY or TEMPORARY INTERNET FILES folder are displayed rather than the contents of the user's folder you selected.

Solution One

To print the contents of the HISTORY folder, follow these steps:

1. Click the Start button, choose Find, and click Files Or Folders.

2. Enter *history* in the Named box, and click Find Now.

3. Double-click the HISTORY folder.

Note If you find more than one HISTORY folder, open the folder that has Url History Folder listed as its type.

4. Look at the entries you want to print, and print the contents of the screen.

For information about how to print the contents of the screen, see the topic "To Copy the Window or Screen Contents" in the Windows help system.

Solution Two

To print the contents of the TEMPORARY INTERNET FILES folder, follow these steps:

1. Click the Start button, choose Find, and click Files Or Folders.

2. Enter *temporary internet files* in the Named box, and click Find Now.

3. Double-click the TEMPORARY INTERNET FILES folder.

4. Look at the entries you want to print, and print the contents of the screen.

A user can manually empty the HISTORY and TEMPORARY INTERNET FILES folders; therefore, the contents of these folders are not a reliable way of tracking web sites accessed by Internet Explorer. Proxy servers or stand-alone tracking software provides a more reliable way of tracking a user's access to web sites.

Related KB article Q182592

MSInfo Sections Don't Print

You attempt to print information selected in System Information (MSInfo), and the Selection option is unavailable in the Print dialog box.

Note Although MSInfo contains a print command, you might not want to use it; the printout of an MSInfo report consists of the entire contents of the System Information, Hardware Resources, Components, and Software Environment nodes and commonly prints more than 75 pages.

Solution

To print individual sections, follow these steps:

1. Select the information you want to print, by either using the mouse or holding down the Shift key while pressing the arrow keys.

2. Press Ctrl+C to copy the selected section to the Clipboard.

3. Open a text editor, such as Notepad, and press Ctrl+V or choose Paste from the Edit menu to paste the contents of the Clipboard into the text editor.

4. Print the information from the text editor.

Note To move between the left and right panes in MSInfo without a mouse, press F6. If the right pane is divided into two sections, press the Tab key to move between them.

Related KB article Q180739

Specific Printers

Canon Color Bubble Jet Prints Differently After Upgrade

You upgrade to Windows 98 from an earlier version of Windows, and you notice printing differences in the Windows 98 drivers for the Canon Color Bubble Jet (BJC) printers. As part of the Windows 98 installation, drivers are automatically upgraded to Windows 98 because earlier versions do not work under Windows 98. This statement applies to the following printers:

- BJC-70

- BJC-600

- BJC-600e

- BJC-800

- BJC-4000

Solution

Contact your local Canon representative (or see the section "Where to Find More Help" in your printer's manual) for information about the availability of updated drivers.

Related KB article Q189672

Canon LBP-8IV Printer Doesn't Print All Pages of a Document

You print a document to a Canon LBP-8IV printer, and the first few pages print correctly, although the remaining pages are blank. This problem can occur if the printer is attached to the computer with a parallel cable more than four feet long. The blank pages occur because the printer defaults to a 30-second time-out. This setting cannot be changed.

Solution

Connect the printer to the computer by using a parallel cable shorter than four feet. This length is recommended in the Canon LBP-8IV printer documentation.

Related KB article Q120680

Canon MultiPASS Multifunction Printer Produces Error Messages

You attempt to print to a Canon MultiPASS Multifunction printer, and you receive one of the following error messages:

SPOOL32 caused a General Protection Fault in module <unknown> at <address>.

SPOOL32 caused an Invalid Page Fault in module <unknown> at <address>.

SPOOL32 caused a Stack Fault in module <unknown> at <address>.

These error messages can occur if the Exclusive Port Control check box is selected in the Canon MultiPASS Desktop Manager.

Solution One

Clear the Exclusive Port Control check box by following these steps:

1. Click the Start button, choose Programs, and click MultiPASS Desktop Manager.

2. Choose Preferences from the File menu.

3. Clear the Exclusive Port Control check box, and click OK.

4. Restart your computer.

Solution Two

Disable Enhanced Metafile (EMF) spooling by following these steps:

1. Click the Start button, choose Settings, and click Printers.

2. Right-click your Canon printer, and choose Properties.

3. Click the Details tab, and click Spool Settings.

4. Select RAW in the Spool Data Format box.

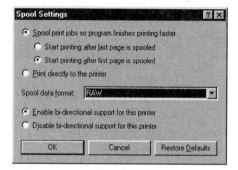

Figure 11-11. *The Spool Settings dialog box.*

5. Click OK, and click OK again.

Related KB article Q190825

Epson Action Laser 1600 Makes Computer Run Slowly

You send a print job from your Windows 98–based computer to an Epson Action Laser 1600 printer, and your computer runs slowly and your print job does not complete successfully. This problem can occur if you are using an older Epson printer driver. If so, it prevents the installation of a newer driver.

Solution

Rename the following files to a .OLD file extension, and restart your computer:

EPHPW.DRV

EPHEW.PRD

SID2BIDW.DLL

SID2BMGW.DLL

SID2BMGW.EXE

SID2BRDW.DLL

SID2BRFW.DLL

SID2CTLW.DLL

SID2DATW.DLL

SID2DLGW.DLL

SID2LIBW.DLL

SID2SFMW.DLL

SID2WST1.ITD

SID2OVL.ISD

SID2OVL.ITD

When you restart your computer, Windows 98 detects your printer and starts the Add New Printer Wizard. Follow the prompts to install the Windows 98 drivers for this printer.

Related KB article Q192444

Epson Stylus Color 500 Printer Cannot Be Installed

You attempt to install the Easy Setup Software (EASY500.EXE) program for your Epson Stylus Color 500 printer, and you see the following error message:

> *EPSIN500 caused a general protection fault in module EPSIN500.EXE at 0003:00000068.*

Solution

Install version 2.2AE or later of the Epson Stylus Color 500 printer drivers. For information about how to obtain updated printer drivers, contact Epson Technical Support.

Related KB article Q193910

Fargo Primera or Primera Pro Printer Doesn't Print Properly

You print to a Fargo Primera or Primera Pro, and the printer does not print correctly.

Some older versions of the Fargo Primera and Primera Pro printer drivers do not operate correctly under Windows 98. The Fargo Primera requires version 4.3 or later, and the Primera Pro requires version 2.7 or later.

Solution

To obtain either of these drivers, contact the Fargo BBS or Fargo Technical Support at the numbers listed in your printer documentation.

Related KB article Q189672

HP or Canon Inkjet Printer Causes Error

You print a black-and-white document (such as a fax or scanned image) using Imaging for Windows, and the document prints in all black or you receive the following error message:

Color management options are missing or unavailable

This problem occurs when an Image Color Matching (.ICM) profile has not been associated with the printer.

Solution

Associate an Image Color Matching profile with your printer by following these steps:

1. Click the Start button, choose Settings, and click Printers.

2. Right-click the printer, and choose Properties.

3. Click the Color Management tab.

4. Click Add.

5. In the Add Profile Association dialog box, click the appropriate .ICM file for your printer. To determine which profile to use, contact your printer's manufacturer.

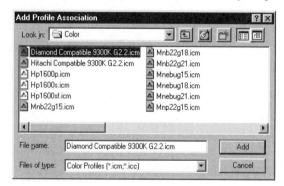

Figure 11-12. *The Add Profile Association dialog box.*

Note Most Canon color printers should use a profile that begins with BJC. Most Hewlett-Packard color printers should use the Diamond-Compatible 9300k G2.2 profile.

6. Click Add, and click OK.

Related KB article Q189764

LaserMaster Printer Doesn't Print

You upgrade to Windows 98 from Windows 3.1, and your LaserMaster printer drivers do not allow the printer to print.

The Windows 3.1 printer driver for LaserMaster products does not function under Windows 98.

Solution

Contact LaserMaster Technical Support at the phone number listed in your printer's documentation to obtain drivers compatible with Windows 98.

Related KB article Q189672

Lexmark MarkVision or Custom Printer Doesn't Work

Some early versions of MarkVision and the Lexmark custom printer drivers are incompatible with Windows 98. To avoid a problem with your system, Windows 98 disables these components when you upgrade from Windows 95 if you have LEXBCE version 1.03 or earlier. If you have a version later than LEXBCE 1.03, Lexmark software works correctly in Windows 98.

Solution

Determine which version of LEXBCE you have by following these steps:

1. Click the Start button, choose Programs, and click Windows Explorer.

2. Navigate to your WINDOWS\SYSTEM folder.

3. Right-click LEXBCE.DLL, and choose Properties.

4. Click the Version tab, and locate the file version information.

You can obtain a newer version of the software from the Lexmark Technical Support Center or on the World Wide Web, at *http://www.lexmark.com*.

Related KB article Q189672

Lexmark Medley Printer Does Not Print in Landscape Orientation

You try to print a document in landscape orientation on a Lexmark Medley printer using Lexmark Medley monochrome printer driver version 5.09.95, and the document prints in portrait orientation. Also, the landscape orientation option is not available in the Page Setup dialog box in WordPad.

Solution

Install the IBM/Lexmark ExecJet 4076 II printer driver included with Windows to print monochrome documents in landscape orientation by following these steps:

1. Click the Start button, choose Settings, and click Printers.

2. Double-click the Add New Printer icon, and click Next.

3. Click Next, select IBM/Lexmark in the Manufacturers box, and select IBM ExecJet 4076 II in the Printers box.

4. Click Next, click Next again, click Yes, and click Next.

5. Click Finish.

Related KB article Q142349

NEC SilentWriter SuperScript 610 Printer Doesn't Print

You upgrade to Windows 98 from Windows 3.1, and your NEC SilentWriter SuperScript 610 printer drivers do not allow the printer to print.

The Windows 3.1 printer driver for the SilentWriter SuperScript 610 does not function under Windows 98.

Solution

Contact NEC Technical Support at the phone number listed in your printer's documentation to obtain drivers compatible with Windows 98.

Related KB article Q189672

Panasonic KX-P 6100, KX-P 6300, or KX-P 6500 Causes Unknown Windows Version Error Message

You install the driver software for a Panasonic KX-P 6100, KX-P 6300, or KX-P 6500 printer, and you see the following error message:

Unknown Windows Version

Some versions of the installation software do not operate correctly under Windows 98.

Solution

Contact Panasonic to obtain an updated driver.

Related KB article Q189672

QMS JetScript Board Doesn't Print

You try to print with QMS JetScript boards using Windows 98, and the printer doesn't print.

Solution

Create a port named LPTx.DOS (where LPTx is LPT1, LPT2, or LPT3, depending on how the JetScript board is configured).

If you have the printer driver installed, skip to step 3. If you don't have the printer driver installed, begin with step 1:

1. Click the Start button, choose Settings, click Printers, and double-click Add Printer.

2. Follow the Add Printer Wizard's steps to add the printer.

3. Click the Start button, choose Settings, click Printers, right-click the icon for the QMS JetScript printer, and choose Properties.

4. Click Details, and click Add Port.

5. Click Other, and click Local Port.

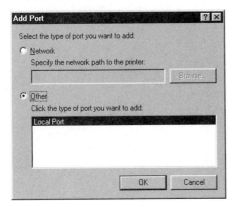

Figure 11-13. *The Add Port dialog box.*

6. Click OK, and enter the name of the port you want to add (for example, LPT1.DOS).

7. Click OK, and click OK again to close the Printer Properties dialog box.

Related KB article Q189672

C H A P T E R   1 2

Setup

General Errors

Application Error Message After Entering Product Key

You install Windows 98 and receive the following error message when you type your Product Key and then click OK:

Application Error

SUWIN caused a General Protection Fault in module PIDGEN.DLL @ 0001:5F2C

This might also occur if you start your computer with a Windows 98 Startup disk and then try to install Windows 98 from the CD-ROM.

This problem can occur for either of the following reasons:

- You are running Setup from the floppy disk version of Windows 98 and you typed the incorrect Product Key.

- Your computer's date is set incorrectly.

Solution One

Type the correct Product Key or, if you have misplaced your Product Key, contact Microsoft Technical Support to obtain the correct Product Key.

Solution Two

Reset you computer's date to the correct date. To do so, follow these steps:

1. Click the Start button, choose Settings, click Control Panel, and then double-click the Date/Time icon.

2. Adjust the date to the correct date, and then click OK.

Related KB article Q187268

Call to Undefined Dynalink Error Message

When Windows Setup verifies the available disk space, or when you are prompted to save your system files, you receive the following error message:

Call to Undefined Dynalink

Solution

This problem occurs when you have America Online (AOL) software installed, and you are installing Windows 98 from MS-DOS. To solve this problem, run Windows 98 Setup from within your current version of Windows. If you receive the same error message, rename the AOLNDI.DLL file in the WINDOWS\SYSTEM folder, and then run Setup from MS-DOS. To rename the AOLNDI.DLL file, follow these steps:

1. Restart your computer. After your computer completes the Power On Self Test (POST), press and hold down the Ctrl keyuntil you see the Window 98 Startup menu,and then choose Safe Mode Command Prompt Only.

2. Type the following lines, and press Enter after each line:

```
cd\<windows>\system
ren aolndi.dll *.old
```

where <windows> is the name of your WINDOWS folder.

3. Restart your computer, and then run Windows 98 Setup again.

4. Reinstall your America Online software.

Related KB article Q188970

Compaq Presario 4540 Problems with Windows 98

After you install Windows 98 on a Compaq Presario 4540 computer, you encounter any of the following problems:

- Printing problems (such as no printout at all)
- Modem does not function
- CD-ROM drive does not function
- Sounds are not played

These problems can occur if your computer does not have the required Compaq Softpaq updates that ensure compatibility with Windows 98.

Solution

Contact Compaq Computer for the required Softpaqs (Compaq's updated file and information packages) that ensure Presario 4540 compatibility with Windows 98.

Related KB article Q191097

Decoding Errors During Windows 98 Installation

You try to install Windows 98, or install a component that requires copying files from the original Windows disks or CD-ROM, and you receive an error message similar to one of the following messages:

Setup has detected the following decoding error: "Could not decode this setup (.CAB) file." Setup will attempt to recover from this situation, click OK to continue.

Setup (.cab) file error:

Setup has detected the following decoding error:

Setup has detected a corrupt setup (.cab) file. Setup will attempt to recover from this situation.

You click OK, and Setup either proceeds or generates the same error message again.

This behavior occurs for any of the following reasons:

- Your CD-ROM drive is not functioning properly. The CD-ROM may vibrate too much for the laser to accurately read the data. With the higher spin rates of modern CD-ROM drives, slight damage to a CD-ROM can affect the CD-ROM drive's ability to read a CD-ROM properly.

- Your computer is over-clocked. Extracting files from the Windows 98 cabinet files is memory intensive. If your computer is over-clocked beyond the default settings, it can contribute to decoding errors. Computers that are not over-clocked but are having a cooling problem can also experience decoding errors.

- Your computer has bad or mismatched RAM or cache. Even if Windows seems to be running without problems, the additional stress of extracting files and accessing the disk may contribute to decoding errors.

- Your computer has Bus Mastering or Ultra DMA enabled in the BIOS and in Device Manager. The data may be moving too quickly for the system to keep up.

- You are using a third-party memory manager.

- There is a virus on your computer.

- Your Windows 98 CD-ROM or disks are damaged.

Windows 98 Setup attempts to recover from the decoding error by re-seeking the CD-ROM and attempting to extract the files to a different location. Setup tries up to 128 times to re-seek on a random location on the CD-ROM to start the file copy process again. This is logged in the SETUPLOG.TXT file and you may notice CD-ROM and hard disk activity, but very little progress during Setup. If Setup is unable to extract the files after 128 retries, the decoding error message is displayed again.

Any of the following solutions may work. They are arranged from easiest to hardest. To minimize your effort, we recommend that you try these solutions in order.

Solution One

Remove the CD-ROM from the CD-ROM drive, rotate it one-quarter to one-half a turn, reinsert the CD-ROM into the drive, and then click OK.

Solution Two

Use real-mode CD-ROM drivers. If you are unable to locate the real-mode CD-ROM drivers for your CD-ROM drive, try using the CD-ROM drivers on the Windows 98 Startup disk. The Windows 98 Startup disk provides support for most types of CD-ROM drives, including integrated device electronics (IDE) and small computer system interface (SCSI) CD-ROM drives. Run Windows Setup from MS-DOS.

Solution Three

Slow down your computer by changing any of the following settings:

- CMOS settings

- Bus mastering

- External/internal cache

- RAM settings/timings

- Other settings that contribute to the speed at which your computer runs

Consult your computer's documentation for information on changing these settings.

Solution Four

Copy the contents of the WIN98 folder on the CD-ROM to an empty folder on your hard disk, and then run Windows Setup from that folder. If you are unable to copy the WIN98 folder on the CD-ROM to your hard disk, the CD-ROM might be damaged.

Solution Five

Follow these steps:

1. Restart your computer. After your computer completes the Power On Self Test (POST), press and hold down the Ctrl key until you see the Windows 98 Startup menu, and then choose Step-By-Step Confirmation.

2. Press the Y key at each prompt, except for the following prompts:

```
Process your startup device drivers (CONFIG.SYS)?

Process your startup command file (AUTOEXEC.BAT)?
```

If this solution solves the problem, you have a conflict with a terminate-and-stay-resident (TSR) program or real-mode device driver. Isolate the problem using the Step-by-Step Confirmation function.

Solution Six

Check your computer for a virus using virus-detection software.

Solution Seven

Run Windows 98 Setup using the following command at the C prompt:

```
setup /c
```

This switch bypasses running SMARTDrive.

Solution Eight

Use an MS-DOS text editor such as EDIT.COM to view the contents of SETUPLOG.TXT (located in the root of your boot drive). Look for the line that refers to the cabinet file (.CAB) that was accessed, and manually extract all the files from that cabinet file to an empty folder on the hard drive. Then copy any remaining files from the WIN98 folder on the CD-ROM to the same folder on the hard drive.

Usually, there are many duplicate entries in SETUPLOG.TXT that resemble the following:

CAB-Ben->CloseCabinet on ERROR 8 SUMB:Setup (.CAB) File Error:Setup has detected the following decoding error 'Setup has detected a corrupt Setup (.CAB) file.'. Setup will attempt to recover from this situation. Click OK to continue. OK DCE:F:\WIN98\\WIN98_37.CAB=13 DCE:remaining=0

Solution Nine

If you still receive a decoding error in Windows 98, you can manually extract all the Windows 98 files from the Windows 98 cabinet files on the CD-ROM to your hard disk, and then run Windows 98 Setup from the hard disk. It requires approximately 300 MB of hard disk space to extract the Windows 98 files. You can use the EXT.EXE utility to extract the Windows 98 files. This utility is located on the Windows 98 Startup disk and in the \OLDMSDOS folder on the Windows 98 CD-ROM. To manually extract the Windows 98 files, follow these steps:

1. Insert your Windows 98 Startup disk in the floppy disk drive, and then restart your computer. If you do not have a Windows 98 Startup disk, obtain one from any functioning Windows 98 computer by completing steps 2 and 3. If you have a Windows 98 Startup disk, continue to step 4.

2. Use a properly functioning Windows 98 computer and click the Start button, choose Settings, click Control Panel, and then double-click the Add/Remove Programs icon.

3. Click the Startup Disk tab, click Create Disk, follow the instructions on the screen, and use this disk on your nonfunctioning machine.

4. At the command prompt, type *ext*.

5. When you are prompted for the location of the cabinet files, type the path to the folder that you created in Solution Four.

6. When you are prompted for the files to extract, type *.* to extract all files.

7. When you are prompted for the location to which the files are to be extracted, type the path to the folder you created in Solution Three. Setup is designed to look for the existence of a file before it is extracted from the cabinet file.

Note This process does not extract the files in the PRECOPY1.CAB and PRECOPY2.CAB cabinet files.

8. After all the files have been extracted, run Setup from MS-DOS in the folder that contains the setup files.

Related KB article Q140901

Disk Write Fault Error Message

During Windows 98 Setup, you receive the following error message:

Setup had trouble copying a file Disk Write Fault error #1d.

You might also receive any of the following error messages while working in Windows or an MS-DOS session:

Invalid Device Request writing\reading device...

Duplicate filename or file in use

Cannot (copy\rename\delete) Cannot find the specified file.

cannot Create or Access...

Access Denied

This problem can occur if you try to access a file that has the same name as a terminate-and-stay-resident (TSR) device driver ID on your computer or the same name as a hardware port on your computer. For example, if your computer uses a CD-ROM driver with the device ID MSCD001, you would be unable to access any file named MSCD001.

Solution

To resolve this problem, run ScanDisk, which renames the interfering files that have the same name as the driver ID or hardware port. To do this, follow this step:

1. Click the Start button, choose Programs, choose Accessories, choose System Tools, and then click ScanDisk.

Related KB article Q185209

Error # 5 Occurs on Computer with Magic Folders

When you install Windows 98 and RSE Software Magic Folders is installed on your computer, you see the following error message when Setup attempts to copy the CHKDSK.EXE file:

Setup Error # 5, Access is denied

Because Magic Folders hides files and folders from the operating system, you should not run Chkdsk while Magic Folders is running. Chkdsk is unable to recognize files and folders hidden by Magic Folders and may incorrectly report them as errors. If you repair these errors, the files and folders may be damaged during the process.

Solution

Use ScanDisk if you need to use a disk utility. ScanDisk can safely find and repair disk problems while Magic Folders is running.

To resolve the problem and then install CHKDSK.EXE (in steps 2 and 3), follow these steps:

1. Click Skip File to allow Setup to continue without copying the CHKDSK.EXE file.

2. After Setup has finished, open Magic Folders, and choose Temporarily Enabling Chkdsk Access from the Utilities menu.

3. Extract a new copy of the CHKDSK.EXE file using the System File Checker tool. To start System File Checker, click the Start button, click Run, type *sfc.exe* in the Open box, and then click OK.

Related KB article Q181339

Fatal Exception Error Message

You receive the following error message while using Windows.

Fatal Exception Error 0x:xxxxxxxx

There are a number of reasons why this error occurs. Most are related to differences in the way that Windows 98 uses memory as compared to Windows 3.x. You might have a problem with your hardware memory that Windows 3.x did not detect. All 32-bit code in Windows 3.x runs in the first 4 MB of RAM, enabling it to run even if the rest of the RAM is partially faulty.

Solution One

Restart Windows in Safe mode to see if the error persists. If it does not, your memory could be OK; the problem could be in software or drivers. For more information on how to troubleshoot using Safe mode, see KB article Q156126, "Troubleshooting Windows 95 Using Safe Mode."

Solution Two

Disable the motherboard L2 cache. (For information about how to disable your motherboard LT cache, please view your computer documentation or contact your hardware manufacturer.)

Solution Three

Alter the CMOS settings, such as Memory Wait States. (For information about how to edit CMOS settings, see your computer documentation or contact your hardware manufacturer.)

Solution Four

Replace the RAM and/or system board (motherboard).

Related KB article Q138788

Filename or Directory Error Messages

Windows is installed to the root folder of your hard disk and when you try to use your computer, you see one of the following error messages:

> *Error Renaming File*

> *Cannot Rename <file or folder name>. Access is denied.*

> *Make sure the disk is not full or write protected and that the file is not currently in use.*

You might see the following message at a command prompt:

> *Cannot make directory entry <file name>*

You might see the following message when starting your computer at a command prompt:

> *Duplicate file name or File in use*

The number of files and folders in the root folder of the hard disk exceeds the limitations of the file allocation table 16 (FAT16) file system. This can happen after any of the following:

- You install Windows in the root folder with a large number of options.

Note By design, you are not normally able to install Windows in the root folder. You can do so only if you incorrectly type the path to the root folder. If you type the correct path to the root folder, you receive an error message. When you run Windows 98 Setup from an MS-DOS prompt, Setup is programmed to prevent you from specifying the root folder of a disk as the installation folder.

- You install additional software that adds files to the WINDOWS folder, which in this case is the root folder.

- Other computer usage creates additional files in the root folder.

The root folder on your hard disk can contain a maximum of 512 entries (files or folders). The folder might be full even if it contains fewer than 512 entries because long filenames require additional entries in the file allocation table. This limitation applies to computers using a file allocation table 16 (FAT16) file system. For more information about the root folder limitation, see KB article Q120138, "Errors Creating Files or Folders in the Root Directory."

Initially, Windows may function correctly because you have not exceeded the root folder entry limitation. As you install additional software and use your computer, however, the number of files in the root folder may increase and eventually exceed the root folder entry limitation.

Microsoft has confirmed this to be a problem in Windows 98.

Solution

Reduce the number of files and folders in the root folder, and then reinstall Windows in a folder other than the root folder.

To reinstall Windows to a new folder, follow these steps:

1. Start your computer with your Windows 98 Startup disk. If you do not have a Windows 98 Startup disk, obtain one from any functioning Windows 98 computer by completing steps 2 and 3. If you have a Windows 98 Startup disk, continue to step 4. If you do not have one, you might be able to create one on any computer that has a CD-ROM drive. For more information about how to do so, see KB article Q187632, "How to Create a Windows 98 Startup Disk that Supports FAT32."

2. Click the Start button, choose Settings, click Control Panel, and then double-click the Add/Remove Programs icon.

3. Click the Startup Disk tab, click Create Disk, follow the instructions on the screen, and use this disk on your nonfunctioning machine.

4. Choose Start Computer With CD-ROM Support, and press Enter.

5. At the command prompt, type *<CD-ROM letter>:\win98\setup* (where <CD-ROM letter> is the drive letter assigned to your CD-ROM drive), and then press Enter.

6. When you are prompted for a location in which to install Windows, choose a new folder. Do not reinstall Windows in the root folder of a hard disk.

For more information about installing Windows, see KB article Q193902, "How to Install Windows 98 into a New Folder," and KB article Q188881, "How to Install Windows 98: Helpful Tips and Suggestions."

Related KB article Q194361

General Protection Fault Error Message After Accepting License Agreement

You install Windows and receive a general protection (GP) fault error message after you accept the End User License Agreement. The error reads similarly to the following:

Suwin caused a GPF in 256_1280.drv at 0002:0D7B

This problem can occur if any of the following conditions exist:

- Your memory management software is incorrectly configured.

- Your computer has a GSI BIOS.

- Double buffering is required for your hard disk, but it is not enabled.

- You have a Cirrus Logic video card driver installed that is incompatible with the Windows Setup program.

- There is an antivirus setting enabled in your computer's CMOS settings.

Solution One

You can solve this problem by reconfiguring the memory management software so that Windows Setup finishes successfully. Refer to the memory management software's documentation for assistance.

Solution Two

If you have a GSI BIOS, contact the computer's manufacturer or your hardware vendor for more information.

Solution Three

You can enable double buffering for your hard disk. If required, contact your computer's manufacturer for assistance.

Solution Four

You can solve this problem by restarting the computer and running the Windows Setup program from MS-DOS.

Solution Five

Some computers include an antivirus feature that prevents programs from writing to the boot sector of the hard disk. Such features may be set in your computer's CMOS settings. To solve this problem, disable the antivirus feature in your computer's CMOS settings, and then run Setup again. After you have done this, you can reenable the antivirus feature. For more information about changing CMOS settings on your computer, contact your computer's manufacturer.

Related KB article Q135162

General Protection Fault When Starting Setup

You start Windows 98 Setup and see the following error message:

W98Setup caused a general protection fault in module w98setup.bin at 0003:00000856.

Setup cannot continue.

This problem can occur if you start Setup from a network resource whose Universal Naming Convention (UNC) path contains more than 240 characters. Setup uses a string buffer for installation with a character limit of 240 characters. If you try to run Setup from a path that exceeds this limit, the error message will be displayed.

Solution

Place the Windows 98 installation files in a folder whose UNC path contains fewer than 240 characters.

Related KB article Q187511

Micron M5-PI Series BIOS Corrupted After Installing Windows

You install Windows 98 on a Micron M5-PI Series (P-60, P-66) computer with the BIOS read/write jumper set in the read/write position, and your BIOS is corrupted.

Solution

Before you install Windows 98, make sure the BIOS read/write jumper (W22) is set to the read-only position. For more information, contact Micron Technologies.

Related KB article Q191480 or HARDWARE.TXT in your WINDOWS folder

Micron P90/P100 Has Installation or Operating Problems

You install Windows 98 on a Micron P90 or P100 computer with a BIOS version N14 or earlier and encounter problems.

Solution

Install BIOS version N15 or later. For more information, contact Micron Technologies.

Related KB article Q191480 or HARDWARE.TXT in your WINDOWS folder

Micronics Motherboard Flash BIOS Corrupted After Installing Windows 98

You install Windows 98 on a computer with a Micronics motherboard with a Flash BIOS with the read/write jumper set in the read/write position, and your BIOS is corrupted.

Solution

Set the BIOS read/write jumper to the read-only position before installing Windows 98. For more information, contact your computer manufacturer.

Related KB article Q191480 or HARDWARE.TXT in your WINDOWS folder

MPREXE Not Responding Error Message

After you install Windows, your password list (.PWL) file is damaged and you receive the following error message:

MPREXE not responding

Your computer stops responding (hangs). Microsoft has confirmed this to be a problem in Windows 98.

Solution

Re-create your password list file. To do so, follow these steps:

1. Click the Start button, choose Find, and then click Files Or Folders.

2. In the Named box, type *.pwl, and then click Find Now.

3. Right-click the <username>.PWL file, and then click Rename (where <username> is the name you use to log onto Windows).

4. Rename the <username>.PWL file to <username>.OLD, and then press Enter.

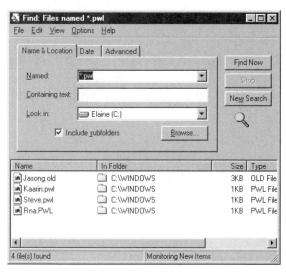

Figure 12-1. *The Find dialog box.*

5. Restart Windows.

When your computer restarts, you are prompted for a user name and password. If you want, you can choose to create a null password so that you are no longer prompted to log on when Windows starts. To create a null password, leave the Password box blank, click OK, and then click OK to confirm the password.

Note For more information about MPREXE.EXE issues, see KB article Q151708, "XCLN: Page Fault in Mprexe.exe When Starting Client," and KB article Q154092, "Err Msg: MPREXE Caused an Invalid Page Fault in Kernel32.dll."

Related KB article Q178084

Network Connectivity Lost After Windows 98 Installation

After you install Windows 98 by using an MSBATCH.INF file, your computer does not have network connectivity.

Solution

This problem can occur if both of the following conditions exist:

- The MSBATCH.INF file specifies static Transmission Control Protocol/Internet Protocol (TCP/IP) addressing.

- The MSBATCH.INF file is configured to install Dial-Up Networking.

To work around this issue, click OK during Setup when you receive a message that says you do not have network connectivity, click the Configuration tab, click Dial-Up Adapter, click Remove, and then click OK.

To prevent this problem from occurring the next time you use the MSBATCH.INF file, edit the MSBATCH.INF file to not install Dial-Up Networking.

Related KB article Q190954

Not Enough Disk Space Error Message on DriveSpace Compressed Drive

You try to install Windows 98 on a computer using DriveSpace compression and receive an error message similar to the following:

Not Enough Disk Space

There is not enough space on one or more of your drives to set up Windows 98. Setup may need to copy some files to your compressed drive's host drive or to your startup drive.

To set up Windows 98 on drive C:, quit Setup and free some space on the following drive. For more information, see Setup.txt on Setup Disk 1 or the Windows 98 compact disk.

Disk H: only has 0.0 MB of free space. You will need 1.5 MB to set up Windows 98.

This problem can be caused by insufficient free disk space on the DriveSpace host drive. Setup might require as much as 7 megabytes (MB) of free space on the host drive.

Solution

To resolve this problem, increase the amount of free disk space on the host drive, or resize the host drive.

For information about how to delete files and folders in Windows 98, click the Start button, click Help, click the Index tab, type *delete*, and then double-click the Deleting Files, Folders topic.

For information about how to resize the host drive, click the Start button, click Help, click the In-dex tab, type *reallocating*, double-click the Reallocating Free Disk Space topic, and then click Reallocate Free Space On A Compressed Or Host Drive.

Related KB article Q191369

Registration Wizard Fails When WebTV Is Damaged

You try to run the Windows 98 Registration Wizard, but your installation of WebTV for Windows is damaged and you see an error message similar to the following:

This program has performed an illegal operation and will be shut down. If the problem persists, contact the program vendor. REGWIZ caused an invalid page fault in module REGWIZC.DLL at 0257:10014da0.

Solution

Uninstall and then reinstall WebTV for Windows before you run the Windows 98 Registration Wizard. To do this, follow these steps:

1. Click the Start button, choose Settings, click Control Panel, and then double-click the Add/Re-move Programs icon.

2. Click the Windows Setup tab, clear the Web TV for Windows check box, and then click OK.

3. Restart your computer.

4. Click the Start button, choose Settings, click Control Panel, and then double-click the Add/Re-move Programs icon.

5. Click the Windows Setup tab, select the WebTV For Windows check box, and then click OK.

6. Restart your computer.

7. To run the Registration Wizard, click the Start button, click Run, type *regwiz /r* in the Open box, and then click OK.

Related KB article Q194904

Setup Not Successful Because of Swap File Problems

You run Windows 98 Setup as an upgrade to Windows 95 or Windows 3.x, but it does not complete successfully.

This problem can occur because of any of the following swap file problems:

- Setup might require 25 megabytes (MB) of extra space on the drive containing the swap file to account for growth during Setup. This can happen with dynamic or permanent swap files. For example, if you have a 100 MB drive or partition dedicated to support a 100 MB permanent swap file, Setup might be unable to continue until you reduce the size of the swap file.

- If you run Windows 98 Setup from within Windows 3.1x or Windows for Workgroups 3.1x, a swap file is required.

- If multiple installations of Windows exist, Setup searches through all SYSTEM.INI files to look for the paging drive (the drive with your swap file). This might cause Setup to incorrectly identify your paging drive or incorrectly detect multiple paging drives.

Solution One

Find which disk contains the swap file, then check the drive for at least 25 MB of free disk space and increase free disk space as necessary. For more information about how to free space on your paging drive, see Windows Help.

If you are upgrading from Windows 95, follow these steps to find which disk contains your swap file:

1. Click the Start button, choose Settings, click Control Panel, and then double-click the System icon.

2. Click the Performance tab, and then click Virtual Memory. If the Let Windows Manage My Virtual Memory Settings (Recommended) option is selected, then the disk that contains the WINDOWS folder also contains the swap file. If the Let Me Specify My Own Virtual Memory Settings option is selected, then the Hard Disk box displays the swap file disk. Make sure that the Minimum and Maximum boxes contain values at least 25 MB less than the amount of free space available on the drive. Click OK if you made any changes.

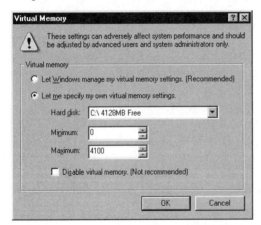

Figure 12-2.   *The Virtual Memory dialog box.*

3. Click Cancel, and then click Cancel.

If you are upgrading from Windows 3.1x and Windows for Workgroups 3.1x, follow these steps to find which disk contains your swap file:

1. In Program Manager, choose Main from the Window menu, and then double-click Control Panel.

2. Double-click Enhanced, and then click Virtual Memory. If the value in the Type box is None, then there is no swap file. If the value in the Type box is Temporary or Permanent, then the Drive box displays the swap file disk.

3. Click Cancel, and then click Cancel.

If you are upgrading from Windows 3.x, follow these steps to find which disk contains your swap file:

1. In Program Manager, choose Run from the File menu.

2. Type *sysedit*, and then click OK.

3. Click the SYSTEM.INI window, and then examine the [386Enh] section. If there is a PagingDrive= or PagingFile= line, then you can determine the disk that contains the swap file. If there are no such lines, then the disk that contains the WINDOWS folder also contains the swap file.

4. Choose Exit from the File menu.

Solution Two

If you are running Windows 98 Setup from within Windows 3.1x or Windows for Workgroups 3.1x, follow these steps to see whether your computer is using a swap file:

1. In Program Manager, choose Main from the Window menu, and then double-click Control Panel.

2. Double-click Enhanced, and then click Virtual Memory.

3. Examine the Type box, click Cancel, and then click Cancel. If the type is Temporary or Permanent, then your computer is using a swap file. If the type is None, then your computer is not using a swap file. For Windows 98 Setup to complete, you must enable a swap file.

To enable your computer to use a swap file, follow these steps:

1. In Program Manager, choose Main from the Window menu, and then double-click Control Panel.

2. Double-click Enhanced, and then click Virtual Memory.

3. Click Change. The new swap file settings should default to drive C with a type of Permanent. (Note that you can specify a type of either Temporary or Permanent.)

4. Click OK, click Yes, and then click OK to restart Windows.

Solution Three

Determine whether your paging drive is different from the drive to which Windows is installed. To do so, follow these steps:

Search your hard disk(s) for copies of the SYSTEM.INI file. Examine each SYSTEM.INI file for the PagingDrive=<drive x> line, where <drive x> is the drive containing the swap file. If this line exists and is set to an unexpected drive letter, delete or rename the file, or delete the line and change the drive letter, or create additional free disk space on the paging drive (the drive containing the swap file).

Related KB article Q192336

Startup Disk Creation Prompted for Nonexistent Drive

You install Windows 98 on a portable computer with no floppy disk drive, but you are prompted to create a Windows 98 Startup disk in the nonexistent A drive because the floppy disk controller is not disabled in your computer's Basic Input/Output System (BIOS).

Solution One

Disable the floppy disk controller in the computer's BIOS before running Setup. For information about how to do this, see the documentation included with your computer or contact the manufacturer.

Solution Two

Disable the floppy disk controller in Device Manager. To do this, follow these steps:

1. Click the Start button, choose Settings, and then click Control Panel.

2. Double-click the System icon.

3. Click the Device Manager tab, and then click the Floppy Disk Controllers branch to expand it.

4. Click Floppy Disk Controller, and then click Properties.

5. Select the Disable In This Hardware Profile check box.

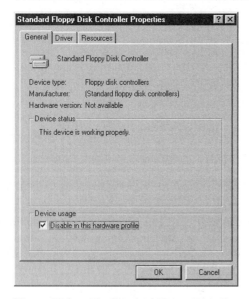

Figure 12-3.   *The Standard Floppy Disk Controller Properties dialog box.*

Note If more than one floppy disk controller is listed, repeat this step for each device listed.

6. Click OK, click Close, and then click Yes if you are prompted to restart your computer.

Related KB article Q194032

SU0013 Error Message on Toshiba Tecra Computer

You run Windows 98 Setup on a Toshiba Tecra computer and receive the following error message:

SU0013

Setup could not create files on your startup drive and cannot set up

Windows. If you have HPFS or Windows NT file system, you must create

an MS-DOS boot partition. If you have LANtastic server or SuperStor

compression, disable it before running Setup.

Some Toshiba Tecra computers were shipped with incorrect information in the hard disk partition table. As a result, Setup detects a problem with the hard disk. In this case, the partition table indicates that extended INT13 calls are not available. Regular INT13 calls work only in real (or MS-DOS) mode.

Solution

Run Windows 98 Setup from MS-DOS.

Related KB article Q188166

System Files Error Message

You attempt to install Windows 98 and see the following error message from Registry Checker (SCANREG.EXE):

Windows found an error in your system files and was unable to fix the problem.

Try deleting some files to free up disk space on your Windows drive.

If that doesn't work then you will need to install Windows to a new directory.

However, if you attempt to install Windows 98 in a different folder, you might receive the same error message and Setup might not finish. This problem can occur if you have a damaged Registry. Microsoft has confirmed this to be a problem in Windows 98.

Registry Checker is a Windows 98 tool that checks the Registry and attempts to repair it if it is damaged. Registry Checker runs as a normal part of Windows 98 Setup. Each time Windows 98 starts after Setup is complete, Registry Checker scans the Registry for corruption and creates a backup of the Registry if one has not been made for that date.

Warning Using either of the solutions causes Windows to lose information about third-party drivers, customized features, installed programs, and e-mail and Internet settings. After you use either of these methods, you must reconfigure all settings and reinstall all programs. Before you run Windows 98 Setup, you may want to back up all your data by using an MS-DOS-based backup program or by copying your most important data files to floppy disks.

Solution One

Two solutions are available: You can rename the WINDOWS folder, or you can rename the Registry files. To work around this problem by renaming the WINDOWS folder, follow these steps:

1. Restart your computer. After your computer completes the Power On Self Test (POST), press and hold down the Ctrl key until you see the Windows 98 Startup menu, and then choose Safe Mode Command Prompt Only.

2. Type the following line, and then press Enter:

```
ren c:\<windows> c:\oldwin
```

where <windows> is the name of your Windows folder.

3. Rerun Setup.

Solution Two

To work around this problem by renaming the Registry files, follow these steps:

1. Restart your computer. After your computer completes the Power On Self Test (POST), press and hold down the Ctrl key until you see the Windows 98 Startup menu, and then choose Safe Mode Command Prompt Only.

2. Type the following lines, and press Enter at the end of each line:

```
cd\<windows>

attrib -h -r -s system.dat

attrib -h -r -s user.dat

ren system.dat system.old

ren user.dat user.old
```

where <windows> is the name of your WINDOWS folder.

Related KB article Q183091

Time Zone Information Requested After Copying Files

You install Windows 98 and are prompted for your time zone. This might occur after Setup begins copying files—at this point, however, you do not normally have to provide any more input for the installation to finish.

If you perform a clean install or install to a folder different from your existing Windows 95 folder, there is no existing Registry that contains this information. Therefore, Setup is unable to determine the time zone.

Solution One

Install Windows 98 using Windows 95 instead of installing from a command prompt. If you want to install from a command prompt, install to the folder where your Windows 95 system is installed.

Solution Two

Install Windows 98 using an MSBATCH.INF file that contains the proper value for TimeZone in the [System] section of the file. For information about using an MSBATCH.INF file, see Appendix D in the Microsoft Windows 95 Resource Kit.

Related KB article Q182747

VFAT Device Error Message

You install Windows 98 and receive the following error message:

VFAT Device Initialization Failed

A device or resource required by VFAT is not present or is unavailable. VFAT cannot continue loading.

System halted.

This problem occurs when the SystemSoft CardWorks software installs on your computer during Windows 98 Setup. CardWorks also prevents IFSHLP.SYS from loading from the CONFIG.SYS file.

The following computers have exhibited this problem:

- IBM ThinkPad model 380 and 385
- Toshiba model 465CDX
- Toshiba 460CDT Pentium 166

Solution

Uninstall the CardWorks software. For information about how to do so, contact your computer's manufacturer.

Related KB article Q190110

Hangs

Ascentia M-Series Computer Hangs After Being Suspended

While you are installing Windows 98, your computer stops responding with 13 minutes of Setup remaining. This problem can occur if you have an AST Ascentia M-series computer that is suspended and then resumed during Windows 98 Setup.

Solution One

To work around this problem, restart your computer, run Setup again, and then choose Smart Recovery when you are prompted to do so. Do not suspend your computer until Windows 98 Setup is completed.

Solution Two

To resolve this problem, contact AST Technical Support to inquire about the availability of an updated BIOS.

Related KB article Q188109

Computer with 3Com Fast EtherLink XL PCI Hangs

You install Windows 98, and your computer stops responding during hardware detection or when your computer is restarted for the first time.

This problem occurs when a 3Com Fast EtherLink XL PCI network adapter is installed in your computer.

Solution

To work around this problem, follow these steps:

1. Turn off your computer, and then turn it back on to continue Windows 98 Setup.

2. After Setup has completed, click the Start button, choose Settings, and then click Control Panel.

3. Double-click the System icon.

4. Click the Device Manager tab, and then double-click the Network Adapters branch to expand it.

5. Click 3Com Fast EtherLink XL PCI Ethernet Adapter, and then click Remove.

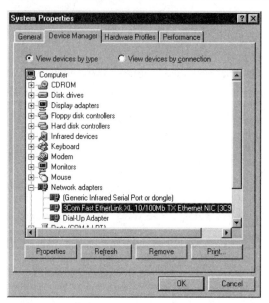

Figure 12-4.   *The Device Manager tab of the System Properties dialog box.*

6. Click Yes when you are prompted to restart your computer. Windows 98 should identify and install your network adapter.

Related KB article   Q188415

Hitachi Flora Computer Causes Screen Text to Flash

While you are installing Windows 98 on a Hitachi Flora M-series or NM-series computer, the screen switches to flashing colored text and your computer stops responding after the file copy stage of Setup is finished. If you try to start Windows 98 in Safe mode, your computer stops responding when the desktop is loaded.

This behavior can occur if your computer has more than 16 megabytes (MB) of memory installed or double buffering is being loaded in the MSDOS.SYS file. There may be an incompatibility between your computer's BIOS and the DBLBUFF.SYS file.

Solution One

To resolve this problem, contact Hitachi about obtaining a BIOS update for your computer.

If you cannot obtain a BIOS update for your computer, you may be able to work around this issue by not loading double buffering. Note that some computers, especially those that use a SCSI hard disk, might require double buffering to work properly. If you are not sure whether your computer requires double buffering, contact your computer's manufacturer. To avoid loading double buffering, use one of the following methods.

Solution Two

Use the Step-By-Step Confirmation startup method to avoid loading double buffering. To do so, follow these steps:

1. Restart your computer. After your computer completes the Power On Self Test (POST), press and hold down the Ctrl key until you see the Windows 98 Startup menu, and then choose Step-By-Step Confirmation.

2. Press the N key when you are prompted to load the DBLBUFF.SYS file. Press the Y key for all other prompts.

3. Restart Windows.

Solution Three

Edit the MSDOS.SYS file to prevent double buffering from being loaded. To do so, follow these steps:

1. Restart your computer. After your computer completes the Power On Self Test (POST), press and hold down the Ctrl key until you see the Windows 98 Startup menu, and then choose Safe Mode Command Prompt Only.

2. Type the following lines, and press Enter at the end of each line:

```
attrib -s -h -r msdos.sys

edit msdos.sys
```

3. In the [Options] section of the MSDOS.SYS file, locate the line that reads DoubleBuffer=<n>. If this line is not present, add it. Add the following line in the [Options] section:

```
DoubleBuffer=0
```

4. Change the DoubleBuffer= line to read:

```
DoubleBuffer=0
```

5. Save and then close the MSDOS.SYS file.

6. Restart Windows.

Related KB article Q188184

Slower Computer with Office Installed Runs Setup Slowly

During Windows 98 Setup, your computer appears to stop responding (hang). This problem can occur if Microsoft Office 95 or Office 97 is installed on your computer. Setup optimizes these files using the Winalign program, and on slower computers, this optimization can cause your computer to seem to hang or run slowly.

Solution

To resolve this issue, wait at least 5 minutes before you restart your computer. If no disk activity has occurred after 5 minutes or more, restart your computer.

Related KB article Q191391

Sound Files Cause Setup to Hang

You try to install Windows 98 and your computer stops responding (hangs).

Solution

Run Setup again. Sounds will not play, but Windows 98 should be successfully installed. This behavior can occur if Setup is unable to play a test sound file. If Setup is unable to play a test sound file, it does not play sounds during subsequent Setup attempts.

Because this behavior might be related to sound problems present before you ran Setup, you might be able to solve this problem by solving whatever prior sound problem exists.

If you manage to solve your prior sound problem, you can enable sound during Windows 98 Setup by deleting the following Registry key:

```
HKEY_LOCAL_MACHINE\SOFTWARE\Microsoft\Windows\CurrentVersion\Setup\NoMusic
```

Warning Please read the Introduction for information on how to safely edit the Registry.

Related KB article Q191257

Hardware and Hardware Detection

Fatal Error Message During Hardware Detection

With a SyQuest SparQ drive connected to a parallel port on your computer, you receive a Fatal Error message during the hardware detection portion of Windows 98 Setup. This problem can occur if you are using version 1.29 of SyQuest's EPATHD.MPD driver. The issue does not occur with version 1.3 of this driver.

Solution

To resolve this problem, contact SyQuest to obtain the EPATHD.MPD driver, version 1.3 or later. If you can't obtain the appropriate version of this driver, disconnect the SparQ drive from the parallel port. The error message will not occur if the drive is not connected.

Related KB article Q188147

Fatal Error 0E Error Message During Plug and Play Hardware Detection

You are upgrading from Windows 95 to Windows 98, with the Novell intraNetWare Client version 2.2 for Windows 95 (also known as Client32) installed, and Setup stops responding during the Plug and Play hardware detection process. When this occurs, you receive the following error message and Setup cannot continue:

Fatal Error 0E

Solution

To solve this problem, contact Novell to obtain an updated NWSIPX32.DLL file.

Related KB article Q189185

Hardware Doesn't Work with Windows 98

You obtain hardware but are unsure about whether it is compatible with Windows 98. In addition, you might need to install drivers for your new hardware.

To verify that your hardware is compatible with Windows 98, visit the Windows Hardware Quality Labs web site at *http://www.microsoft.com/hwtest/* and view the Hardware Compatibility List.

If your hardware is listed and you need to install drivers to run your device, you can either load the drivers from the Windows CD-ROM or disk or you can download a driver from an online service.

Solution One

Load a driver from the Windows CD-ROM or disk. To do so, follow these steps:

1. Install the device on your system.

2. Insert the CD-ROM or floppy disk.

3. Click the Start button, choose Settings, and then click Control Panel.

4. Double-click the Add New Hardware icon.

5. Follow the Add New Hardware Wizard's instructions.

Solution Two

Install drivers from an online service. To do so, follow these steps:

1. Download the driver to a disk from the online service.

2. Click the Start button, choose Programs, and then click Windows Explorer.

3. Double-click the file you downloaded from the online service.

4. Click the Start button, choose Settings, and then click Control Panel

5. Double-click the Add New Hardware icon. When you are asked, *Do you want Windows to search for your new hardware?* choose No.

6. Select the hardware type for the driver you are installing.

7. Click the Have Disk button.

8. Enter the location of the driver file.

9. Follow the Add New Hardware Wizard's instructions.

Related KB article Q131900

KSCLOCKF.AX Error Message During Plug and Play Hardware Detection

You upgrade from Microsoft Windows 95 and receive the following error message during the Plug and Play hardware detection process:

Cannot find the file KSCLOCKF.AX. Please insert the Windows 98 CD and click OK.

This problem can occur if you are upgrading from an Original Equipment Manufacturer (OEM) version of Windows 95 to Windows 98 and your computer has an ESS Technology ES1878 sound card.

Solution

To resolve this problem, copy the following cabinet files from your Windows 98 media to the WINDOWS\SYSTEM\PRECOPY folder, and then click OK to continue Setup:

- DRIVER11.CAB

- DRIVER12.CAB

- DRIVER14.CAB

- DRIVER15.CAB

- DRIVER17.CAB
- DRIVER20.CAB

Related KB article Q192394

Math Coprocessor Error Message During Setup

You install Windows 98 on a computer that contains a math coprocessor and receive the following error message:

Windows 98 requires a computer with a math coprocessor.

This problem occurs when math coprocessor support is disabled in Device Manager.

Solution

To solve this problem, follow these steps:

1. Click the Start button, choose Settings, and then click Control Panel.

2. Double-click the System icon.

3. Click the Device Manager tab, and double-click the System Devices branch to expand it.

4. Click Numeric Data Processor, and then click Properties.

5. On the Settings tab, select the Always Use The Numeric Data Processor check box, and then click OK.

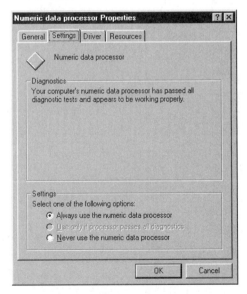

Figure 12-5. *The Numeric Data Processor Properties dialog box.*

6. Restart your computer when you are prompted to do so.

Related KB article Q189670

Plug and Play Hardware Detection Causes Setup to Hang

You attempt to install Windows 98, but Setup stops responding (hangs) during the Plug and Play hardware detection process. When you restart your computer, Setup hangs at the same point. This problem can occur if the SYSTEM.INI file contains the Display.drv=pnp.drv line.

Solution

Disable the Display.drv=pnp.drv line in the SYSTEM.INI file. To do so, follow these steps:

1. Restart your computer. After your computer completes the Power On Self Test (POST), press and hold down the Ctrl key until you see the Windows 98 Startup menu, and then choose Safe Mode.

Note For more information about Windows 98 Startup, see KB article Q178548, "No 'Starting Windows 98' Message at Startup."

2. Click the Start button, choose Programs, choose Accessories, choose System Tools, and then click System Information.

3. Choose System Configuration Utility from the Tools menu.

4. On the System.ini tab, click [Boot].

5. Clear the Display.drv=pnp.drv check box, click OK, and then click Yes when you are prompted to restart your computer.

Figure 12-6. *The System.ini tab in the System Configuration Utility.*

6. After Setup is completed, repeat steps 2–5, selecting the Display.drv=pnp.drv check box in step 5.

Some video adapters, such as Creative Labs PCI 3D video adapters, might replace the Display.drv=pnpdrvr.drv line with the Display.drv=pnp.drv line. This can prevent Plug and Play hardware detection from working properly.

Related KB article Q194721

Video Adapters Detected Incorrectly

You install Windows 98 on a computer with multiple video adapters, but Setup does not detect your video adapters correctly.

Solution

To resolve this problem, run Setup with only one video adapter in your computer. After Setup is finished, reinstall your additional video adapters, and then enable multiple display support. If your computer has an onboard video adapter, you should run Setup using only the onboard adapter.

Related KB article Q191622

Windows 98 Hangs While Setting Up Hardware Devices

After you install Windows 98, you receive the following message when you start your computer:

Windows 95 is now setting up your hardware and any plug and play devices.

This message stays on the screen indefinitely, and there is no way to close the message box.

You may also notice several conflicts in Device Manager, which vary from computer to computer.

Solution

To resolve this problem, follow these steps:

1. Click the Start button, click Run, type *sfc.exe* in the Open box, and then click OK.

2. Click Extract One File From Installation Disk.

3. In the Specify The System File You Would Like To Restore box, type *sysdm.cpl*, and then click the Start button.

4. In the Restore From box, select the drive from which you installed Windows 98.

5. In the Save File In box, type *c:\windows\system*, and then click OK.

6. Click OK, and then click Yes to restart the computer.

Related KB article Q191798

Zip Drive Not Detected When Installing Windows 98 from Zip Drive Connected to Parallel Port

When you attempt to install Windows 98 from a Zip drive connected to a parallel port, you may be prompted for the following files after Setup restarts your computer the first time:

- BIOS.VXD

- ISAPNP.VXD

- PCI.VXD

- PCIMO.PCI

- POWER.DRV

- VPOWERD.VXD

- WFM0200.ACV

You can skip installing all these files except the WFM0200.ACV file. For this file, you must click Cancel. After bypassing all these files, your Zip drive does not appear in My Computer or Windows Explorer.

Solution

Windows 98 cannot be installed from a Zip drive connected to a parallel port. To cause your Zip drive to appear in My Computer and Windows Explorer, follow these steps:

1. Click the Start button, choose Settings, and then click Control Panel.

2. Double-click the Add New Hardware icon to start the Add New Hardware Wizard.

3. Click Next, and then click Next.

4. Click No, I Want To Select The Hardware From A List, and then click Next.

5. In the Hardware Types box, select SCSI Controllers, and then click Next.

6. Insert your Iomega Zip drive installation disk in the floppy disk drive, click Have Disk, and then click OK.

7. Click Iomega Parallel Port Adapter, and then click OK.

8. After the controller is installed, reinstall the Iomega Guest 95 software.

9. Reinstall Windows 98 from the original Windows 98 CD-ROM to replace the missing files.

Related KB article Q194946

Network

Banyan Protocol Not Present in Network Properties

The Banyan DOS/Windows 3.1 Client and Banyan VINES protocol is missing from Network properties after you install Windows 98 from a shared network drive on a Banyan VINES network.

This problem occurs when you start your computer using a Banyan VINES boot disk, and then install Windows 98 from a shared network drive to a new folder on your hard disk.

Solution

Install and configure the Banyan VINES 16-bit network client and the appropriate protocol after Windows 98 is installed. To install the Banyan VINES 16-bit network client, follow these steps:

Chapter 12 Setup 689

1. Click the Start button, choose Settings, and then click Control Panel.

2. Double-click the Network icon.

3. Click the Configuration tab, and click Add.

4. Click Client, and then click Add.

5. In the Manufacturers box, select Banyan. In the Network Clients box, select Banyan DOS/ Windows 3.1 Client, and then click OK.

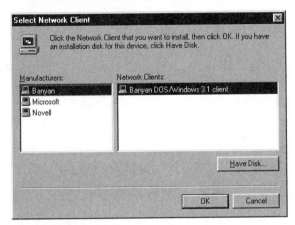

Figure 12-7. *The Select Network Client dialog box.*

6. Click the Configuration tab, and click Add.

7. Click Protocol, and then click Add.

8. In the Manufacturers box, select Banyan. In the Network Protocols box, select Banyan VINES Ethernet Protocol or Banyan VINES Token Ring Protocol, and then click OK.

9. Click OK, and then restart your computer when you are prompted to do so.

To configure the Banyan VINES 16-bit network client, follow these steps:

The following sections list the entries required in the AUTOEXEC.BAT, CONFIG.SYS, and PROTOCOL.INI files to use the Banyan VINES 16-bit network client in Windows 98. There are separate lists for when Banyan VINES is installed as the primary network client (connecting to a Banyan VINES server) or when it is installed with the Microsoft Client for Microsoft Networks. If there are multiple entries on the same line, use the first entry if your computer is on an Ethernet network. Use the second entry if your computer is on a Token Ring Network.

Note These entries apply only to Network Device Interface Specification (NDIS) drivers. If you are using monolithic Banyan VINES drivers, you must use Banyan's PCConfig utility to change Banyan drivers to NDIS drivers. Make sure the section name in the PROTOCOL.INI file matches the driver name.

- Banyan VINES as the Primary Network Client:

  The AUTOEXEC.BAT file should contain the following lines:

  ```
  cd \banfiles
  ```

  ```
  ban
  ```

  ```
  ndisban (If you are on an Ethernet Network); ndtokban (If you are on a  token
  ring network-in either case, do not include the words in parentheses in the
  file.)
  ```

  ```
  redirall
  ```

  ```
  netbind
  ```

  ```
  arswait
  ```

  ```
  z:login
  ```

  ```
  c:
  ```

  ```
  cd\
  ```

  The CONFIG.SYS file should contain the following lines:

  ```
  device=c:\banfiles\protman.dos  /i:c:\banfiles
  ```

  ```
  device=c:\banfiles\ndis2driver eg: exp16.dos
  ```

  The PROTOCOL.INI file should contain the following lines:

  ```
  [PROTOCOL MANAGER]
  ```

  ```
  drivername=protman$
  ```

  ```
  [VINES_XIF]
  ```

  ```
  drivername=ndisban$ ; (If you are on a token ring network, substitute
  ndtokban$ for ndisban$)
  ```

  ```
  bindings=MS$EE16
  ```

  ```
  [MS$EE16]
  ```

  ```
  drivername=EXP16$
  ```

  ```
  interrupt=5
  ```

  ```
  ioaddress=0x300
  ```

  ```
  iochrdy=late
  ```

■ Banyan VINES with Microsoft Client for Microsoft Networks:

The AUTOEXEC.BAT file should contain the following lines:

```
c:\windows\net initialize

cd \banfiles

ban

ndisban (If you are on an Ethernet Network); ndtokban (If you are on a token
ring network-in either case, do not include the words in parentheses in the
file.)

redirall

c:\windows\net start

arswait

z:login

c:

cd\
```

The CONFIG.SYS file should contain the following lines:

```
rem device=c:\banfiles\protman.dos /i:c:\banfiles

rem device=c:\banfiles\ndis2driver eg: elnkii.dos
```

The PROTOCOL.INI file should contain the following lines:

```
[NDISBAN$] ; NDTOKBAN$ for token ring

drivername=NDISBAN$ ; NDTOKBAN$ for token ring

bindings=ELNKII$


[NWLINK$]

drivername=NWLINK$

frame_type=4

cachesize=0

bindings=ELNKII$


[NETBEUI$]

drivername=NETBEUI$

lanabase=0
```

```
sessions=10

ncbs=12

bindings=ELNKII$


[ELNKII$]

drivername=ELNKII$

transceiver=external

interrupt=2

ioaddress=0x280

maxtransmits=12

datatransfer=pio_word

xmitbufs=2


[PROTMAN$]

priority=ndishlp$

drivername=protman$


[NDISHLP$]

drivername=ndishlp$

bindings=ELNKII$
```

Related KB article Q190417

Connection to Network Lost During Installation

You install Windows from a network drive, and then during the installation you lose your connection to the network drive. This problem might occur because of a memory-resident program.

Solution One

To determine whether a memory-resident program launched from your Startup folder or the Registry is interfering with your installation, follow these steps:

1. Click the Start button, click Run, type *msconfig* in the Open box, and click OK.

2. Click the Startup tab, click the Selective Startup option button, and then clear each check box.

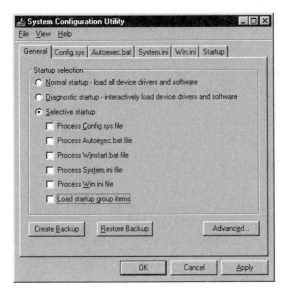

Figure 12-8. *The System Configuration Utility.*

3. Click OK, and then restart your computer and attempt to connect to your network drive.

Note For more information on clean booting using the System Configuration Utility, see KB article Q192926, "How to Perform Clean-Boot Troubleshooting for Windows."

If the problem is resolved, follow these steps:

1. Click the Start button, click Run, type *msconfig* in the Open box, and click OK.

2. Click the Startup tab, and select the first check box in the list.

3. Restart your computer and attempt to connect to your network drive.

If the problem is still resolved, repeat steps 1–3, but select the next check box in the list. When the problem returns, the file next to the last check box you selected is loading a program that is preventing Windows 98 Setup from completing. After you identify the file with the problem, continue with Solution Two. If the problem is in the Load Startup Groups option, use the Startup tab to identify which program is causing the problem, and then delete that program from the Startup folder on the Start menu.

Solution Two

A program loaded in the WINSTART.BAT (if available), AUTOEXEC.BAT, WIN.INI, SYSTEM.INI, or CONFIG.SYS files might be interfering with your Windows installation. To determine whether this is happening, follow these steps:

1. Click the Start button, click Run, type *msconfig* in the Open box, and click OK.

2. Click the Selective Startup option button, and then clear the Process Winstart.bat check box. (If this check box is gray, you do not have a WINSTART.BAT file.)

3. Click OK, and then restart your system and continue your installation.

4. If this solution allows you to complete the Windows 98 installation, you can reenable your WINSTART.BAT file.

5. If this solution did not resolve your problem, a program or device driver loaded from your CONFIG.SYS or AUTOEXEC.BAT file might be interfering with your network connection. Repeat steps 1–3 for these files instead of WINSTART.BAT. If you find that the problem file is CONFIG.SYS or AUTOEXEC.BAT, continue on to Solution Three. Otherwise, repeat this process with the WIN.INI and SYSTEM.INI files.

Solution Three

To isolate the line in the AUTOEXEC.BAT or CONFIG.SYS file that is causing the problem, follow these steps:

1. Click the Start button, click Run, type *msconfig* in the Open box, and click OK.

2. Click the Autoexec.bat tab. Clear the check boxes adjacent to all nonessential programs.

3. Click OK, and then restart your computer when you are prompted to do so.

If the problem is resolved, follow these steps:

1. Click the Start button, click Run, type *msconfig* in the Open box, and then click OK.

2. On the Autoexec.bat or Config.sys tab, select the first check box in the list.

3. Click OK, and then restart your computer when you are prompted to do so.

4. If the problem is still unresolved, repeat steps 1–3, but select the next check box in the list. When the problem returns, the last check box you selected is loading the memory-resident program that is causing the problem. Select all check boxes and then use Notepad to type *rem* in front of the line causing the problem, or contact the manufacturer of the program for further assistance.

Solution Four

If you are unable to start Windows 98 to use the above solutions, restart your computer using the Windows 98 Startup disk, and use real-mode network or CD-ROM drivers to gain access to the drive from which you are installing Windows 98. Then continue your Windows installation.

Related KB article Q191827

Error Message Accessing Setup Files Across Network After Second Reboot

You install Windows from a network drive using real mode network drivers and then receive an error message after Setup restarts your computer for the second time. This situation might occur because when Setup transitions from real-mode to protect-mode drivers, the domain information is not retained, causing you to lose your ability to access the Setup files.

Solution

To add the appropriate domain information to your network settings, follow these steps:

1. Click the Start button, choose Settings, and click Control Panel.

2. Double-click the Network icon, and click the Access Control tab.

3. Make sure that the User-Level Access Control option is selected and that the correct domain controller appears in the Obtain List Of Users And Groups From text box.

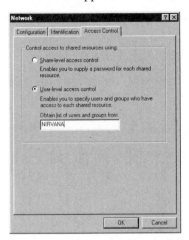

Figure 12-9. *The Access Control tab in the Network dialog box.*

4. Click the Configuration tab, select Client For Microsoft Networks, and then click Properties.

5. Under Logon Validation, verify that the Log On To Windows NT Domain check box is selected and the correct domain controller appears in the Windows NT Domain box.

6. Click OK, and then click OK again.

7. Click Yes to restart your computer. Setup should attempt to log you on to the network and continue the installation process.

Related KB article Q191827

Unable to Access the Network to Complete Installation

You install Windows 98 from a network drive and receive the following error message:

Setup cannot access the network to complete installation. Do you want to: Disable autologon, Reboot (recommended if you skipped autologon), Change network settings, Continue without access to the setup files (not recommended).

This error message can occur if any of the following are true:

- You are upgrading from Windows 95 by connecting to a network CD-ROM or a password-protected network drive or CD-ROM, but you don't map a drive letter to the network device.

- You are upgrading from Windows 3.1 by connecting to a password-protected network drive, but you aren't configured to connect to your Windows NT server.

- You are upgrading from MS-DOS with Windows 3.1 by connecting to a password-protected share that contains the Windows 98 Setup files, but you were unable to properly configure your networking components.

- Windows 98 Setup is unable to correctly detect or configure your network adapter.

Solution One

If you need to map a network drive, click the error message *Continue without access to the setup files (not recommended)* when you are prompted to do so, and then follow these steps:

1. Right-click Network Neighborhood, and then choose Map Network Drive from the shortcut menu.

2. Type the full path to the network drive in the Path text box.

3. Select the Reconnect At Logon check box, and then click OK.

4. Run SETUP.EXE from the mapped network drive containing the Windows 98 Setup files.

Solution Two

If your network settings are incorrect, configure your network settings to install Windows 98. To do this, follow these steps:

1. When you receive the error message during setup, enter your user name and password (if necessary), and then press Enter.

2. If you need validation by a domain, click Change Network Settings. Click the appropriate network client on the Configuration tab, and then click Properties.

3. Type the appropriate changes, and then click OK. For example, for the Client For Microsoft Networks, select the Log On To Windows NT Domain check box, enter the name of the domain in the Windows NT Domain text box, and then click OK.

4. If necessary, change the computer name and workgroup. To do so, click the Identification tab, type the appropriate information in the Computer Name text box and the Workgroup text box, and then click OK.

5. Click OK, and then click Yes when you are prompted to restart your computer.

6. Click Continue Without Access To The Setup Files if you receive an error message listed above.

7. If necessary, type your password when you are prompted to do so, and then click OK.

Solution Three

If you see the *Setup has trouble copying a file...* error message after verifying your network settings in Windows 98 and you are upgrading over MS-DOS and Windows 3.1, enable your real-mode network drivers, copy the Windows Setup files to your hard drive, and then finish your Windows installation. When you see the error message again, specify the folder on your hard drive to which you copied the Windows Setup files.

Related KB article Q188313

Reinstalling and Uninstalling

Display Settings Reset to VGA After Restoring Windows 95

You uninstall Windows 98 and restore Windows 95, but your display is reset to standard VGA.

Solution

If your display settings have been changed to standard VGA, reset your display adapter settings. To do so, follow these steps:

1. Click the Start button, choose Settings, and click Control Panel.

2. Double-click the Display icon, and then click the Settings tab.

3. Change the appropriate settings, and then click OK.

If you cannot change your display settings, you might need to reinstall the appropriate device driver for your video adapter. To do so, follow these steps:

1. Click the Start button, choose Settings, and click Control Panel.

2. Double-click the System icon, and then click the Device Manager tab.

3. Double-click the Display Adapters branch to expand it.

4. Select your display adapter, and then click Properties.

5. Click the Driver tab, click Update Driver, and then follow the instructions on the screen for locating and installing the correct driver for your display adapter.

Related KB article Q190672

Low Hard Disk Space Error Message When Running Setup in Windows 98

You run Windows 98 Setup from within Windows 98 and receive the following error message or one similar to it:

Hard Disk is Low on Disk Space

You are running out of disk space on drive C.

To free space on this drive by deleting old or unnecessary files, click Disk Cleanup.

You might receive this message even if you have sufficient free space on your hard disk.

This problem can occur when Setup is copying files to your computer and the free disk space on your computer reaches the low disk space notification threshold associated with the Disk Cleanup utility.

Solution

To work around this problem, either click Cancel in the Hard Disk Is Low On Disk Space dialog box or disable Disk Cleanup before running Setup.

To disable Disk Cleanup before running Setup, follow these steps:

1. Click the Start button, choose Programs, choose Accessories, choose System Tools, and then click Disk Cleanup.

2. Click the drive where Windows is installed, and then click OK.

3. Click the Settings tab, clear the If This Drive Runs Low On Disk Space, Automatically Run Disk Cleanup option button, and then click OK.

4. When you receive the Are You Sure You Want To Delete Files prompt, you can click Yes or No. If you click Yes, Disk Cleanup deletes files as specified on the Disk Cleanup tab. If you click No, the files are not deleted. Either choice closes Disk Cleanup.

Related KB article Q191489

MSYCRT.DLL Not Found Error Message After Uninstalling

After you uninstall Windows 98 and then restart your computer, you see the following error message:

A required .dll file, Msvcrt.dll, was not found.

This problem can occur if a shortcut to MSN Quick View is located in the StartUp folder.

MSN Quick View relies on the MSVCRT.DLL file for some of its functionality. When you uninstall Windows 98, the MSVCRT.DLL file is removed, but the shortcut to MSN Quick View remains in the STARTUP folder. As a result, when MSN Quick View is started, it cannot locate the MSVCRT.DLL file.

Solution

To resolve this problem, remove the shortcut to MSN Quick View from the STARTUP folder. To do so, follow these steps:

1. Click the Start button, choose Settings, and click Taskbar & Start Menu.

2. On the Start Menu Programs tab, click Remove.

3. Double-click the STARTUP folder.

4. Click MSN Quick View, and then click Remove.

5. Click Close, and click OK.

6. Restart your computer.

Related KB article Q187513

OEM Version Reinstallation of Windows Produces Error Messages

You attempt to reinstall an Original Equipment Manufacturer (OEM) version of Windows and see one of the following error messages:

INVALID PRODUCT IDENTIFICATION NUMBER

The number you entered is not valid. Please make sure you typed the correct number of digits, including dashes if appropriate.

CERTIFICATE OF AUTHENTICITY

The Certificate of Authenticity number you entered is not valid. Number entered: <number you entered> You cannot complete Setup without it. To return to the previous screen and retype the number, click on the re-enter button.

You did not enter the product ID correctly, or the product ID originally entered on the computer does not match the number being entered.

Solution One

Type the OEM Product ID number from the Certificate of Authenticity correctly. This number is on the front of the Windows booklet included with your computer. Enter the number as follows:

xxxxx-OEM-xxxxxxx-xxxxx

The Certificate of Authenticity is your assurance that the software you purchased with your computer system is legally licensed from Microsoft. If you have any concerns regarding the legitimacy of your Certificate of Authenticity (or if you do not have one), call the Microsoft Piracy Hotline 1-800-RU-Legit (in the United States or Canada), or contact your local Microsoft subsidiary.

Solution Two

When your computer was manufactured, your manufacturer entered a Certificate of Authenticity number other than the one printed on your Certificate of Authenticity. Therefore, the numbers do not match, and the software cannot be reinstalled. The only way to solve this conflict is to enter the number that the manufacturer used instead of the one printed on your Certificate of Authenticity. To do this, follow these steps:

1. Restart the computer.

2. After your computer completes the Power On Self Test (POST), press and hold down the Ctrl key until you see the Windows 98 Startup menu, and then choose Safe Mode Command Prompt Only.

3. Right-click My Computer, and then choose Properties from the shortcut menu.

The number should be listed. If you can no longer start Windows, contact your computer's manufacturer.

Related KB article Q162453

Program Disabled After Uninstalling Windows 98

After uninstalling Windows 98, you can no longer run a program that you could in Windows 98 or Windows 95. When you upgrade from Windows 95, Windows 98 might remove or change the settings of certain programs. Uninstalling Windows 98 might not restore the original Windows 95 settings for these programs.

Solution

Reinstall the program.

Related KB article Q190672

Safe Recovery Error Message in Reinstallation

You upgrade a Windows 95–based computer running Internet Explorer version 4.0 or 4.01 to Windows 98, uninstall Windows 98, and then reinstall Windows 98, and then see the following error message:

Safe Recovery

Setup encountered a problem or did not complete a previous installation. If you click Use Safe Recovery, Setup will restart file copying where it left off.

Not selecting Safe Recovery will restart the file copy process from the beginning.

You are then prompted to choose either Use Safe Recovery or Do Not Use Safe Recovery.

Solution

To continue the Windows 98 Setup program, you can choose either Use Safe Recovery or Do Not Use Safe Recovery. Under these conditions, the Safe Recovery error message does not indicate a problem, it does not affect the functionality of the Setup program, and therefore it can be safely ignored.

Related KB article Q186738

Short Filenames After Uninstalling Windows 98

You uninstall Windows 98, and the long filenames on the Start menu are replaced with MS-DOS-compatible (short) filenames in 8.3 format. For example, the ACCESSORIES folder on the Start menu might be displayed as follows:

Access~1.

This problem occurs when the Windows 98 uninstall procedure does not finish successfully.

Solution

To solve this problem, use the SULFNBK.EXE utility to restore your long filenames. To do this, follow these steps:

1. Click the Start button, choose Find, and then click Files Or Folders.

2. In the Named box, type *winlfn.ini*, and then click Find Now.

3. Note the location of the WINLFN.INI file. By default, the WINLFN.INI file is located in the root folder of drive C.

4. Click the Start button, and then click Run.

5. In the Open box, type *win.ini*, and then press Enter.

6. Click once in the space to the right of the [windows] section header, and then press Enter.

7. Type the following line, and then press Enter:

```
run_restore_lfn=
```

8. Type the following line, and then press Enter:

```
uninstallpath=<path>
```

where <path> is the path to the folder where the WINLFN.INI file is located.

9. Choose Save from the File menu, and then choose Exit from the File menu.

10. Click the Start button, click Run, type *sulfnbk* in the Open box, and then press Enter.

Note If the WINLFN.INI file does not exist on your computer, you can rebuild the Start menu manually.

Related KB article Q190418

SUWIN Warning Error Message in Reinstallation

You attempt to reinstall Windows 98 and see the following error message:

SUWIN Warning SU0167, the specified directory contains a directory named desktop that you must move or rename before Setup can continue.

For more information, see SETUP.TXT on Setup Disk 1 or the Windows CD-ROM.

This problem can occur if you upgrade to Windows 98 from Windows 3.1x, uninstall Windows 98, and then reinstall Windows 98. The error message occurs if you create files or folders on the desktop in Windows 98 before you uninstall Windows 98. If you do so, the DESKTOP folder is left in the WINDOWS folder when you uninstall Windows 98. You receive the error message because Windows 98 Setup cannot create a DESKTOP folder if one already exists.

Solution

To resolve this problem, rename the WINDOWS\DESKTOP folder to WINDOWS\DESKTOP.OLD before you reinstall Windows 98. After Windows 98 Setup is finished, you can move your files or folders from the WINDOWS\DESKTOP.OLD folder to the WINDOWS\DESKTOP folder. To rename the WINDOWS\DESKTOP folder at a command prompt, type the following lines, and press Enter after each line:

```
cd\windows

move desktop desktop.old
```

Related KB article Q187580

System Agent Disabled or Windows 98 Plus! Files Not Removed After Uninstalling Windows 98

You uninstall Windows 98, and the System Agent tool included with Microsoft Plus! for Windows 95 does not work or the Windows 98 Plus! files aren't removed.

Solution

To fix this problem, follow these steps:

1. Delete the PROGRAM FILES\PLUS! folder.

2. Install Microsoft Plus! for Windows 95 again.

To retain your existing scheduled tasks, save a copy of the SAGE.DAT file before you delete the Plus! folder. The SAGE.DAT file is located in the PROGRAM FILES\PLUS!\SYSTEM folder. After installing Plus!, copy the SAGE.DAT file back into the PROGRAM FILES\PLUS!\SYSTEM folder.

Related KB article   Q190672

Uninstall Displays Error Messages

You run UNINSTAL.EXE in real mode and see the following error messages:

The file Winundo.dat is missing or invalid

Restoring disk partition table

Restoring master disk partition table

WARNING: Uninstall should be run from within Windows 98 to insure that all the information on your disk(s) is properly restored.

Are you sure you want to continue? (Y/N)

Whether you choose Yes or No, when you restart your computer, you then see the following error message:

Invalid system disk

This problem can occur if you run the Drive Converter (FAT32) tool to convert drive C to the FAT32 file system and then run UNINSTAL.EXE in real mode. This problem does not normally occur because the Drive Converter (FAT32) tool removes UNINSTAL.EXE. However, if you manually restored the UNINSTAL.EXE file or run the UNINSTAL.EXE file from a Windows 98 Beta Startup disk after you converted a drive to the FAT32 file system, you might encounter this problem.

Note that this problem can also occur if you install Windows, run a third-party disk-partitioning tool, and then run UNINSTAL.EXE. Programs that change the partition structure can affect multiple drives. For example, if you use the PowerQuest Partition Magic tool to change your partition structure after you install Windows and then run UNINSTAL.EXE, all drives that were changed by Partition Magic are affected.

Microsoft has confirmed this to be a problem in Windows 98.

Solution

After this problem occurs, you cannot recover the information on drive C. You must run FDISK.EXE to re-create drive C, and then format drive C. After the format is complete, you can install Windows and reinstall programs on drive C.

If you own a copy of the upgrade edition of Windows 98, you need to have the Windows 3.1 or Windows 95 disks available when you are prompted for an alternate location for a qualifying product.

You must install Windows 95 OEM Service Release 2 or Windows 98 to have access to other drives that you converted to the FAT32 file system.

Related KB article Q187582

Uninstall Program Quits After Drives Checked

You attempt to run the Windows 98 Uninstall program (UNINSTAL.EXE), but the uninstall process quits after your drives are checked. This problem can occur if the WINUNDO.DAT file is located on a small computer system interface (SCSI) drive that requires real-mode drivers, and the drivers are not loaded. As a result, UNINSTAL.EXE cannot obtain the uninstall information from the WINUNDO.DAT file.

Solution

To resolve this problem, load the real-mode drivers for the SCSI drive, verify that you can gain access to the drive on which the WINUNDO.DAT file is located, and then run the UNINSTAL.EXE file located in the WINDOWS\COMMAND folder.

Related KB article Q188181

Windows NT Won't Boot After Uninstalling Windows 98

After you uninstall Windows 98 from a dual-boot computer with Windows 95 and Windows NT Workstation 4.0, you are unable to successfully start Windows NT Workstation because Setup deletes the Windows NT BOOT.INI file. This file is needed by NTLDR to start Windows NT successfully.

Solution

To resolve this problem, use the Windows NT Emergency Repair Disk to replace the missing files.

Related KB article Q188761

Restarting and First Run

Cannot Find Internet Explorer Files After First Restart

You install Windows 98 and receive the following error message after Windows 98 Setup restarts your computer for the first time:

Cannot find the file C:\Progra~1\Intern~1\chlinst.exe (or one of its components). Make sure the path and filename are correct and that all the required libraries are available.

You click OK, and Setup continues normally. After Windows 98 Setup is completed, you might experience the following problems:

- The Channel bar is empty.

- When you double-click the Internet Explorer icon on the desktop, you receive the following error message:

    Windows cannot find Iexplore.exe.

    This program is needed for opening files of type 'Internet Explorer.'

- A default Windows icon appears on the Quick Launch toolbar where the Internet Explorer icon normally appears.

- When you start the Internet Connection Wizard, you receive the following error message:

    The item 'ICWCONN1.EXE' that this shortcut refers to has been changed or moved. The nearest match, based on size, date, and type, is 'C:\PROGRA~1\!$!$!$!$.ier\CONNEC~1\ ICWCONN1.EXE'.Do you want this shortcut to point to this item?

- You view the contents of the PROGRAM FILES folder and see a !$!$!$!$.IER folder containing a folder beginning with INTERN and the Internet Explorer files.

- You install MSN, The Microsoft Network, from the Windows 98 CD-ROM, and receive the following error message:

    Cannot install Connection Manager. You must install Microsoft Internet Explorer 3.0 or later on your computer before installing Connection Manager.

These problems occur when you upgrade Windows 95 by running Windows 98 Setup in MS-DOS with more than one subfolder in the PROGRAM FILES folder that begins with INTERN (e.g., INTERNET EXPLORER and INTERNATIONAL FILES). When Setup is run in MS-DOS, it is a 16-bit program that can use only short filenames. The short filenames are converted to long filenames when Setup restarts your computer for the first time. If two or more short filenames are trying to use the same long filename, you experience the problems described above.

Solution

To solve these problems, follow these steps:

1. Click the Start button, choose Programs, and then click Windows Explorer.

2. Double-click the PROGRAM FILES folder.

3. Rename the INTERNET EXPLORER folder to OLD INTERNET EXPLORER. Click Yes when you are prompted to rename the read-only folder.

4. Rename the !$!$!$!$.IER folder to INTERNET EXPLORER.

5. Right-click the INTERNET EXPLORER folder, click Properties, verify the MS-DOS name is INTERN~1, and then click OK.

Note If the MS-DOS name is not INTERN~1, rename the INTERNET EXPLORER folder to something other than INTERNET EXPLORER, and then rename it back to INTERNET EXPLORER. Repeat step 5 to verify the MS-DOS name is INTERN~1.

6. Rename the PROGRAM FILES\INTERNET EXPLORER\CONNEC~1 folder to CONNEC~2. Click Yes when you receive the following prompt:

   This change could impact one or more registered programs. Do you want to continue?

7. Rename the CONNEC~2 folder to CONNECTION WIZARD.

8. Right-click the CONNECTION WIZARD folder, click Properties, verify the MS-DOS name is CONNEC~1, and then click OK.

Note If the MS-DOS name is not CONNEC~1, repeat steps 6–8.

9. Double-click the CHLINST.EXE file in the INTERNET EXPLORER folder to install the Channel bar.

10. Restart your computer so that Windows 98 can set up the Channel bar.

11. Double-click the default Windows icon on the taskbar, and click Yes when you receive the following prompt:

    The item 'IEXPLORE.EXE' that this shortcut refers to has been changed or moved. The nearest match, based on size, date, and type, is 'C:\Progra~1\Internet Explorer\iexplore.exe'. Do you want this shortcut to point to this item?

Note If the Internet Connection Wizard starts, click Cancel, and then click Yes. If it appears to start and then stops responding (hangs), repeat steps 6–8.

12. Click the Start button, choose Programs, and click Internet Explorer. Click Yes when you receive the following prompt:

    The item 'IEXPLORE.EXE' that this shortcut refers to has been changed or moved. The nearest match, based on size, date, and type, is 'C:\Progra~1\Internet Explorer\iexplore.exe'. Do you want this shortcut to point to this item?

At this point the Channel bar, Internet Explorer, and the Internet Connection Wizard are restored to full functionality. To recover the data from the original folder that began with INTERN, follow these steps:

1. Click the Start button, choose Programs, and then click Windows Explorer.

2. Double-click the PROGRAM FILES folder.

3. Create a new folder with the same name as the original INTERN folder.

4. Copy the files in the Internet Explorer folder to the folder you created in step 3.

Note In some cases, it might be necessary to reinstall the affected program.

Related KB article Q189168

Cannot Write to Drive C Error Message on Hewlett-Packard Vectra P6/200

You install Windows 98 on a Hewlett-Packard Vectra P6/200 computer with a BIOS version earlier than GG.06.11 and Setup restarts your computer after it finishes copying files. When the computer restarts, you receive the following error message:

Cannot write to drive "C". Press any key to continue.

Solution One

Press Enter. This often allows Setup to continue. You might encounter more than one error message; press Enter for each occurrence of an error message. After Setup finishes, ScanDisk starts when you next start the computer. If ScanDisk prompts to perform a thorough disk check, allow ScanDisk to do so. If you do not, you will receive the prompt each time you start the computer.

Solution Two

Upgrade the computer's BIOS. For information about obtaining and installing a BIOS upgrade, consult your computer's documentation or Hewlett-Packard.

Related KB article Q188200

CONFIGMG Windows Protection Error Message

After you run Windows 98 Setup, your computer restarts and you see the following error message:

While Initializing device CONFIGMG: Windows Protection Error. You need to restart your computer.

This problem can occur because Windows Setup flushes the L2 Cache as it initializes the PCI-to-AGP Bridge on a Micro-Star International MSI-5169 motherboard.

Solution One

To resolve this problem, contact your computer manufacturer to inquire about the availability of a possible BIOS upgrade.

Solution Two

Disable the external (CPU or L2) cache in the CMOS. For information about how to do so, refer to the documentation included with your computer or contact your hardware manufacturer.

Solution Three

If you are using an Accelerated Graphics Port (AGP) video adapter, try replacing the AGP video adapter with a Peripheral Component Interconnect (PCI) video adapter.

Related KB article Q187612

CSMAPPER Blue Screen Error Message

You install Windows 98 and see the following error message on a blue screen when you restart your computer:

Invalid VxD dynamic link call from CSMAPPER(01)+000003B4 to device "O97C", service 1

This problem can occur if there is a conflict between the CSMAPPER.SYS file and the Phoenix Card Manager program. The Phoenix Card Manager (PCM) program is included on some laptops with CardBus controllers that shipped with a version of Windows 95 that did not support CardBus. PCM is removed during Setup, so this issue should not reoccur if you reinstall Windows 98.

Solution

To resolve this problem, press Enter so Windows 98 Setup can continue.

Related KB article Q188116

Fatal Exception Error Message After Last Restart with Corel CD Creator 2.0

You are installing Windows, and when Setup restarts your computer for the last time, you see the following error message on a blue screen:

A fatal exception 0E has occurred at 0028:C02A0201 in VXD IOS(04)+00001FC9.

This problem can occur if Corel CD Creator 2.0 is installed on your computer. Windows is incompatible with the CDRASPI.VXD file installed by Corel CD Creator 2.0.

Solution

To resolve this problem, follow these steps:

1. Restart your computer. After your computer completes the Power On Self Test (POST), press and hold down the Ctrl key until you see the Windows 98 Startup menu, and then choose Safe Mode.

2. Click the Start button, choose Find, and then click Files Or Folders.

3. In the Named box, type *cdraspi.vxd,* and then click Find Now.

4. In the list of found files, right-click the CDRASPI.VXD file, and then click Rename.

5. Type a new name for the CDRASPI.VXD file (such as *CDRASPI.XXX*), and then press Enter.

6. Restart your computer normally.

For more information about this issue, please contact Corel Technical Support.

Related KB article Q187214

Fatal Exception Error Message in Module ASPIIF.EXE

You restart your computer after upgrading to Windows 98 from Windows 3.1x and receive a fatal exception error message in module ASPIIF.EXE and your drives go to MS-DOS Compatibility mode. This problem occurs if you continue to use the Windows 3.1x drivers for your Microtek Pagewix parallel port scanner.

Solution

To resolve this problem, obtain and install the most current drivers for your scanner. For information about how to do so, contact Microtek, or view the documentation included with your scanner.

Related KB article Q188802

Fatal Exception Error Message When Symantec Program Is Installed

After installing Windows 98, you receive the following error message when Windows 98 starts:

A Fatal Exception 0E has occurred at 0028:XXXXXXXX in VXD

SYMEvent(02)+XXXXXXXX.

This problem can occur if an older version of a Symantec program (such as Norton AntiVirus) is installed.

Solution

To resolve this problem, disable the Symantec SYMEVNT.386 file. To do so, follow these steps:

Warning Please read the Introduction for information on how to safely edit the Registry.

1. Click the Start button, click Run, type *Regedit* in the Open box, and click OK.

2. Navigate your way down through the folders in the left pane, and delete the following key if it exists:

   `HKEY_LOCAL_MACHINE\System\CurrentControlSet\Services\VxD\SymEvnt`

3. Close Regedit.

4. Click the Start button, click Run, type *sysedit* in the Open box, and click OK.

5. Choose SYSTEM.INI from the Window menu.

6. Choose Find from the Search menu.

7. In the Find box, type *symevnt.386*, and then press Enter. The SYMEVNT.386 file is part of the Symantec Event Handler, which is actually a set of files named SYMEVNT.386, SYMEVNT1.DLL, and S32EVNT1.DLL. These Norton files monitor system information and report that information to Norton AntiVirus and other Symantec utilities.

8. Type a semicolon (;) at the beginning of the line that contains *symevnt.386*.

9. Choose Save from the File menu, and then choose Exit from the File menu.

10. Restart your computer.

11. After Setup has finished successfully, reinstall the Symantec program. If the problem continues to occur, contact Symantec for additional information.

Related KB article 189655

Java Package Manager Stops Windows Installation

Your computer restarts for the first time during the installation of Windows 98, and you see a Java Package Manager dialog box with only an OK button in it. You click OK, and the message disappears, but Setup does not continue. Or, when you try to install the JAVA.INF file, you receive the following error message:

> *Unable to install java package from c:\windows\java\classes\win32ie4.cab.*

When you receive this error message, the installation process stops.

Solution

End the Java Package Manager task, finish Setup, and then install the JAVA.INF file manually. To do so, follow these steps:

1. Press Ctrl+Alt+Delete, click Java Package Manager, and then click End Task.

2. When you are prompted, click End Task again.

3. After Setup finishes and before you remove the Windows 98 CD-ROM from your CD-ROM drive, click the Start button, choose Find, and then click Files Or Folders.

4. In the Named box, type *java.inf*, select your CD-ROM drive in the Look In box, and then click Find Now.

5. Right-click the JAVA.INF file in the list of found files, and then choose Install from the shortcut menu.

6. Close Find.

7. Test to determine if the problem is resolved, and if it is not, delete the WINDOWS\JAVA folder, and then reinstall the JAVA.INF file again.

Related KB article Q185614

NTKERN Windows Protection Error Message After First Restart

You are installing Windows 98, and when your computer restarts for the first time, you receive the following error message:

> *While initializing device NTKERN: Windows Protection Error. You need to restart your computer.*

You might have defective RAM in your computer.

Solution One

If you have more than 16 MB of RAM on your computer, you might be able to work around this problem. Use the System Configuration tool to limit the amount of RAM available to Windows. To do so, follow these steps:

1. Restart your computer. After your computer completes the Power On Self Test (POST), press and hold down the Ctrl key until you see the Windows 98 Startup menu, and then choose Safe Mode.

2. Click the Start button, choose Programs, choose Accessories, choose System Tools, and then click System Information.

3. Choose System Configuration Utility from the Tools menu.

4. On the General tab, click Advanced.

5. Select the Limit Memory To <n> MB check box (where <n> is a number), and then set the memory limit value to 16 MB.

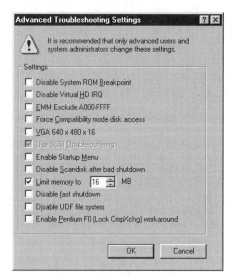

Figure 12-10.   *The Advanced Troubleshooting Settings dialog box.*

6. Click OK, click OK, and then restart your computer.

Solution Two

To resolve this issue, remove or replace memory chips in your computer to eliminate bad memory. For information about how to remove or replace your memory chips, please consult your hardware documentation or manufacturer.

Related KB article Q192397

Setup Hangs After First Restart

When you install Windows 98, setup hangs (stops responding) when your computer restarts for the first time. This can occur for the following reasons:

- The video adapter driver might not be the correct driver, or it might not be configured correctly.

- You are upgrading from Microsoft Windows 3.1 and might have a damaged Windows 3.1x group (.GRP) file.

- A program on your computer might not be totally compatible with Windows 98.

Solution One

To fix a video adapter driver conflict, start your computer in Safe mode, and then run Setup. To do this, follow these steps:

1. Restart your computer. After your computer completes the Power On Self Test (POST), press and hold down the Ctrl key until you see the Windows 98 Startup menu, and then choose Safe Mode.

2. Right-click in a blank part of the desktop, and choose Properties from the shortcut menu.

3. Click the Settings tab, and then click Advanced.

4. Click the Adapter tab, and then click Change.

5. Click Next, click the Display A List Of All The Drivers In A Specific Location option button, and then click Next.

6. Click the Show All Hardware option button, and then select Standard Display Types from the Manufacturers list box.

7. In the Models box, select Standard Display Adapter (VGA), click OK, and then click Next.

8. Click Next, click Next, and then click Finish.

9. Click Close, click Close, and then click Yes to restart your computer.

10. Run Windows 98 Setup.

Solution Two

Find and load an updated video driver for your display adapter, if available. Consult the manufacturer of your display adapter (graphics card) if required.

Solution Three

Warning Using Solutions Three and Four causes Windows to lose information about third-party drivers, customized features, installed programs, and e-mail and Internet settings. After you use either of these methods, you must reconfigure all settings and reinstall all programs.

If you have a damaged group file, use the Group Converter tool to re-create the groups. To do so, follow these steps:

1. Turn off your computer for at least 10 seconds, and then restart your computer.

2. Click the Start button, click Run, enter *grpconv.exe* in the Open box, and then click OK.

Solution Four

If you are running a program that is not totally compatible with Windows 98 (such as a utility program that scans Windows system files and is unable to correctly identify Windows 98 files) and Windows 98 Setup is able to identify this program, Setup generates an error message that includes instructions about resolving the issue. If Windows 98 Setup cannot detect the reason for the issue, you might receive the *Windows 98 Setup has failed* error message and then be prompted to restart your computer.

If you do not receive an error message, or you are unable to find specific troubleshooting information from other articles or the Knowledge Base, follow these steps:

1. Turn off your computer, wait at least 10 seconds, and then restart your computer.

2. Run Windows 98 Setup. When Windows 98 Setup determines that an error has occurred, you receive the Safe Recovery screen. Click Use Safe Recovery (Recommended), and then continue with Windows 98 Setup.

If you are still unable to complete Windows 98 Setup, use clean-boot troubleshooting. To do so, follow these steps:

1. Click the Start button, click Run, type *msconfig.exe* in the Open box, and then click OK.

2. On the General tab, click Selective Startup, and then clear the following check boxes:

   - Process Config.sys File

   - Process Autoexec.bat File

   - Process Winstart.bat File (if available)

   - Process System.ini File

   - Process Win.ini File

   - Load Startup Group Items

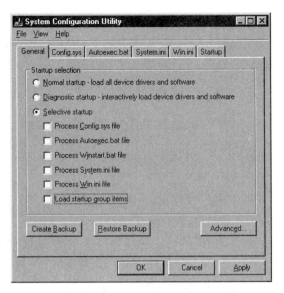

Figure 12-11. *The System Configuration Utility.*

3. Click OK, and then restart your computer when you are prompted to do so.

4. If Setup proceeds normally, you can return to msconfig, select one of the check boxes that you cleared in step 2, and repeat step 3. When you find the file that is causing the problem, you can use a similar process for the commands within that file. Their commands are available through tabs in msconfig. After you identify the problem, enable all check boxes and then use a text editor to comment out the line causing the problem.

Solution Five

If you cannot get Windows installed using the above solutions, install Windows 98 from MS-DOS mode. To do so, follow these steps:

1. Start your computer with your Windows 98 Startup disk. You can create a Windows 98 Startup disk on a computer on which Windows 98 has been successfully installed.

2. Choose Start Computer With CD-ROM Support, and then press Enter.

3. At the command prompt, enter *d:\win98\setup,* if your CD-ROM drive is letter E, and then press Enter. If your CD-ROM drive is a different letter, substitute accordingly.

4. When you are prompted for a location to install Windows, choose a new folder, and then complete Setup normally.

Related KB article Q193156

Setup Hangs After First Restart on Computer with SCSI Hard Disk

If your computer has only Small Computer System Interface (SCSI) hard disks, the installation process can stop after the first restart when installing Windows 98 if your computer's Basic Input/ Output System (BIOS) internal cache is set to Write Back.

Solution

Configure your computer's BIOS internal cache to Write Through. For information about how to do so, contact the manufacturer of your computer or motherboard, or see the documentation included with your computer or motherboard.

For more information about troubleshooting SCSI issues, see KB article Q133285, "SCSI Setup & Basic SCSI Troubleshooting in Windows."

Related KB article Q194836

SYSTEM.INI File Device Error Message After First Reboot

On the first reboot after installing Windows, you see the following error message:

A device has been specified more than once in the SYSTEM.INI file, or a device specified in SYSTEM.INI conflicts with a device which is being loaded by an MS-DOS device driver or application or a device loaded from the registry file. Remove the duplicate entry from the SYSTEM.INI file, and then restart Windows.

Duplicated device: int13

Press a key to continue

When you press a key, Windows loads normally. A device driver in the SYSTEM.INI file is loading the same services as Int13 (hard disk access). Windows 98 Setup parses the SYSTEM.INI file looking for these types of drivers and disables any it recognizes, although it doesn't recognize all problems.

Solution

You need to remove the drivers that are causing the problem. Open your SYSTEM.INI file in any text editor. Either comment out or delete lines that include any of the following drivers:

- ALIHDD.386
- ALIINT13.386
- INT13DT.386
- MAXI13.386
- PRO13.386
- SYMEVNT.386
- TRIINT13.386
- VPMTD.386
- WDCTRLDT.386

The drivers listed above are not recognized as Int13 service providers and are not normally removed by Windows 98 Setup.

Related KB article Q154273

Toshiba Tecra or Protege Stops Responding During Windows 98 Setup

You perform a "clean" installation of Windows 98 on your Windows 95–based Toshiba Tecra or Protege laptop computer, and your computer stops responding with a black screen the second time Windows 98 Setup restarts your computer. After this problem occurs, you can start your computer only in Safe mode. (A clean installation of Windows 98 means either installing Windows 98 on a blank hard disk or installing Windows 98 in a folder other than the folder in which Windows 95 is installed.)

This problem occurs because direct memory access (DMA) is enabled by default for Integrated Drive Electronics (IDE) drives in the upgrade version of Windows 98. Toshiba Tecra and Protege computers are not compatible with the Windows 98 DMA drivers. These computers use Toshiba's own bus-mastering DMA drivers.

Solution

Contact Toshiba for information about how to solve this problem.

Related KB article Q189113

VXD Error Message When Windows 98 Starts First Time on NEC Versa Laptop

You install Windows 98 and see the following error message when Windows 98 starts for the first time:

Invalid VxD dynamic link call from VXD(03) + <address> to device "0026," service 9.

Your Windows configuration is invalid.

Run the Windows Setup program again to correct this problem.

To continue running Windows press Y or ENTER. To quit the current program press N.

If you continue running Windows, your system may become unstable.

Do you want to continue?

This problem can occur if you are using a NEC Versa laptop computer with the NEC VersaGlide touchpad drivers installed. The VersaGlide drivers included with some NEC Versa laptop computers make an invalid call to the VPOWERD.VXD file during Setup.

Solution

To continue running Windows 98 Setup, press Enter. This behavior does not affect the functionality of Windows 98 or the use of the VersaGlide touchpad.

Related KB article Q188146

Windows Does Not Run on MS-DOS 7.00 or Earlier Error Message

You receive the following error message when the computer first restarts during the Windows 98 Setup:

This version of Windows does not run on MS-DOS 7.00 or earlier.

This error message can occur for any of the following reasons:

- Your computer is running antivirus software that protects the system files.

- The system files that were extracted during Setup may be damaged.

Solution One

To prevent this problem from occurring, disable your antivirus software before you install Windows 98. If you already installed Windows, disable your antivirus software and run Setup again. For information about how to disable your antivirus software, please consult the program's documentation or manufacturer.

Solution Two

If you suspect that your system files may be damaged, to copy intact system files to your hard disk. To do so, follow these steps:

1. Insert your Windows 98 Startup disk in the floppy disk drive, and then restart your computer. If you do not have a Windows 98 Startup disk, you need to obtain one from any Windows 98–based computer.

2. At the command prompt, type *sys a: c:*, and then press Enter.

Note If your hard disk is compressed, transfer the system files to the host drive for the compressed drive. Typically, the host drive for a compressed drive C is drive H.

---

3. Remove the Windows 98 Startup disk from the floppy disk drive, and then restart your computer. Windows 98 Setup should continue normally.

Related KB article Q188795

Windows Protection Error Causes Toshiba Libretto Computer to Turn Off

After you upgrade Windows 95 to Windows 98 and restart your computer, you see the following error message:

Windows Protection Error

You must restart your computer

Your computer might then turn off automatically.

This problem can occur when all of the following conditions exist:

- You have installed Windows 98 on a Toshiba Libretto 50CT, 70CT or 100CTcomputer.

- Your computer has a standard port replicator.

- You have a serial mouse attached to the standard port replicator.

The Windows 98 serial port driver (SERIAL.VXD) conflicts with Toshiba's power management driver (PWRSAVE.VXD).

Solution One

To resolve this problem, obtain the latest power management drivers for your computer from Toshiba's web site. These drivers are available as L50PWSAVE.EXE, L70PWSAVE.EXE, and L100PWSAVE.EXE.

Solution Two

To work around this issue, follow these steps:

1. Restart your computer. After your computer completes the Power On Self Test (POST), press and hold down the Ctrl key until you see the Windows 98 Startup menu, and then choose Safe Mode Command Prompt Only.

2. Use any text editor (such as EDIT.COM) to open the SYSTEM.INI file in the WINDOWS folder.

3. Locate the device=pwrsave.vxd line in the [386enh] section of the SYSTEM.INI file, and then disable it by placing a semicolon (;) at the beginning of the line.

4. Save and then close the SYSTEM.INI file.

5. Restart your computer.

Related KB article Q187212

Windows Won't Start After Setup on Computer with QEMM

You upgrade to Windows 98 on a computer with QEMM 7.01 – 8.01, and Windows fails to start after Setup finishes.

Solution

Refer to the \MANUAL\TECHNOTES\README.TXT file (packaged with QEMM) for information about specific software and hardware incompatibilities with QEMM software, and then follow these steps:

1. Restart your computer. After your computer completes the Power On Self Test (POST), press and hold down the Ctrl key until you see the Startup menu, and then choose Safe Mode Command Prompt Only.

2. Type *edit c:\config.sys* at the command prompt, and press Enter.

3. Change ST:M to *ST:F* on the Qemm386.sys line in the CONFIG.SYS file, choose Save from the File menu, and then restart your computer. If Windows 98 fails again, delete the ST:M or ST:F from the Qemm386.sys line in the CONFIG.SYS file, and then restart your computer.

4. Run QSETUP, and turn off DOS-UP, Quickboot, and Stealthing Options (see step 5).

5. Run the OPTIMIZE program.

Note If DOS-UP or Stealthing is enabled in QSETUP, OPTIMIZE adds them to the CONFIG.SYS file. Currently, Windows 98 may fail to start with DOSDATA.SYS and DOS-UP.SYS installed in the CONFIG.SYS file.

---

6. When the OPTIMIZE program is finished, restart your computer per step 1.

7. If the option is available, select Previous Version Of MS-DOS.

8. If you see Starting Windows 98 again, press F4.

Note DOSDATA.SYS, a portion of the DOS-UP features of QEMM, causes the Windows 98 multiboot feature to attempt to start Windows 98 even after you select the Previous Version Of MS-DOS option. To correct this problem permanently, start Windows and remove DOSDATA.SYS and DOS-UP.SYS from the CONFIG.DOS file.

Related KB article Q188978 or PROGRAMS.TXT in your WINDOWS folder

Windows Won't Start on Computer with 386MAX 7.0

You install Windows 98 on a computer with 386MAX 7.0 installed, and the operating system does not start after running Setup.

Solution

If Windows 98 fails to start after Setup, refer to the \MANUAL\README.TXT file (packaged with 386MAX) for information about specific software and hardware incompatibilities with the 386MAX software, and then follow these steps:

1. Run the MAXIMIZE program.

2. After MAXIMIZE restarts your computer for the first time, press the Ctrl key when you see the message BIOS Installed Successfully!

3. Choose Safe Mode Command Prompt Only.

4. Type *edit c:\config.sys* at the command prompt, and press Enter.

5. Delete the following lines in your CONFIG.SYS file:

```
Device=\386MAX\ExtraDOS.max  pro=\386MAX\ExtraDOS.pro

Install=\386MAX\ExtraDOS.max
```

6. Choose Save from the File menu, and then choose Open from the File menu. Open your 386MAX.PRO file, which is located in the folder where 386MAX is installed, and delete any lines beginning with PRGREG, HPDAREG, or STACKREG.

7. Restart your computer.

8. Press the Ctrl key when you see the message BIOS Installed Successfully!

9. Choose Command Prompt Only. MAXIMIZE should continue setting up.

10. Each time the computer restarts, repeat steps 8 and 9 until MAXIMIZE has finished.

Note If the message ExtraDOS Error appears, click OK.

Related KB article Q188978 or PROGRAMS.TXT in your WINDOWS folder

---

Upgrading

Cannot Load s3_95.dll Error Message

You install the updated Windows 3.x video driver for the S3 ViRGE 325 Peripheral Component Interconnect (PCI) display adapter, upgrade to Windows 98, and then receive the following error message:

> *Cannot load s3_95.dll correctly!*

Solution

To work around this problem, uninstall the updated Windows 3.x video driver for the S3 ViRGE 325 PCI display adapter. For information about this process, consult the documentation included with your display adapter, or contact the manufacturer of your display adapter.

Related KB article Q185044

Compaq Presario 1065 Doesn't Successfully Upgrade

After you upgrade Windows 95 OEM Service Release 2 (OSR2) to Windows 98 on a Compaq Presario 1065 computer, you experience any of the following problems:

- The Presario 336-vsc modem included with the computer does not work properly, and Device Manager displays a *Code 25* error message for the modem.

- The computer stops responding (hangs) when starting Windows 98.

- A mouse connected to the COM1 port stops responding.

Solution

To work around the problem, install the Presario 336-vsc modem driver included on the Compaq Quick Restore CD-ROM. To do so, follow these steps:

1. Click the Start button, choose Programs, and then click MS-DOS Prompt.

2. Insert the Compaq Quick Restore CD-ROM in the CD-ROM drive, and insert a blank, formatted disk in the A drive.

3. At the command prompt, type the following lines and press Enter after each line:

```
<cdrom>:

cd\cpqdrv\ccsd

qurst5

a:setup

exit
```

where <cdrom> is the drive letter of your CD-ROM drive.

Related KB article Q190815

Conventional Memory Error Message

You upgrade Windows 95 to Windows 98 and see the following error message displayed during the ScanDisk portion of Windows 98 Setup:

> *Setup cannot check your hard disks for errors because there is not enough conventional memory available, free more conventional memory and rerun Setup.*

Solution One

Increase the amount of free conventional memory, and then run Windows 98 Setup again. Using a text editor (such as Notepad), add the following lines to the CONFIG.SYS file, and then restart your computer:

```
device=c:\windows\himem.sys

device=c:\windows\emm386.exe noems

dos=high,umb
```

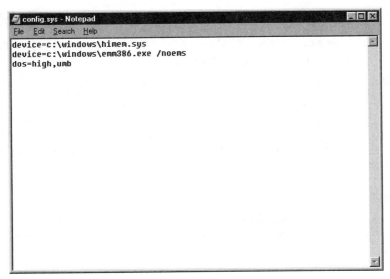

Figure 12-12.   *The CONFIG.SYS file in Notepad.*

Solution Two

Using a text editor (such as Notepad), disable all nonessential drivers and programs in the CONFIG.SYS and AUTOEXEC.BAT files, and then restart your computer. To disable a driver or program, type *rem* followed by a space at the beginning of the line. Make sure to disable any real-mode driver for which there is a protected-mode equivalent.

After Windows 98 is installed, you can reenable any lines in the CONFIG.SYS or AUTOEXEC.BAT file that you disabled.

Related KB article Q188140

Detection Manager API Error Message

You upgrade Windows 95 to Windows 98 using the setup /p command with additional detection switches and see the following error message:

Detection returned the following error: Invalid parameter while calling

Detection Manager API.

When Setup is complete, only Dial-Up Adapter appears in Device Manager.

This problem can occur if you use an invalid detection switch with the setup /p command. An invalid detection switch prevents hardware detection from being run during Setup.

Solution

To resolve this problem, run the Add New Hardware Wizard in Windows 98. To do so, follow these steps:

1. Click the Start button, choose Settings, and click Control Panel.

2. Double-click the Add New Hardware icon, and then follow the instructions on your screen.

Related KB article Q188177

Disk Write Error Message When Using Linksys Network Adapters

You upgrade your computer to Windows 98 when you have a Linksys EtherFast 10/100 network adapter installed and receive the following error messages:

Disk write error, unable to write to disk in drive C, data or files may be lost

An exception 0E has occurred @ 0028:C0035A67 in vxd ifsmgr (01)

After receiving these error messages, your computer stops responding.

This problem occurs because the EtherFast network adapter causes a resource conflict with Windows 98 PCI Steering.

Solution One

Modify the resources of the EtherFast network adapter so that it no longer conflicts with Windows 98 PCI Steering. To modify the resources of your EtherFast network adapter, consult the adapter's documentation or contact Linksys for more information.

Solution Two

Disable the EtherFast network adapter. To do this, follow these steps:

1. Restart your computer. After your computer completes the Power On Self Test (POST), press and hold down the Ctrl key until you see the Windows 98 Startup menu, and then choose Safe Mode.

2. Click the Start button, choose Settings, and then click Control Panel.

3. Double-click the System icon.

4. Click the Device Manager tab, and then double-click the Network Adapters branch to expand it.

5. Right-click the EtherFast adapter, and then choose Properties from the shortcut menu.

6. On the General tab, select the Disable In This Hardware Profile check box.

7. Click OK, and then click Close.

8. Restart your computer.

Note After you disable your network adapter, you cannot use any shared network programs, files, or printers.

Related KB article Q192844

DllInstall Error Message

During Windows 98 Setup, you see the following error message:

An error occurred calling DllInstall in C:\Windows\System\Shdocvw.dll (HRESULT=80004005)

This error message can occur if you installed Microsoft Internet Explorer 4.0 on your previous version of Windows and saved the Internet Explorer uninstall information. Windows 98 Setup attempts to register the uninstall information but cannot because Internet Explorer cannot be removed from Windows 98.

Solution

The error message under these conditions does not indicate a problem, and it does not affect the functionality of the Setup program. You can ignore the error message.

Related KB article Q191707

Errors Not Found After Setup Recommends Running ScanDisk

You try to upgrade from Windows 3.x to Windows 98, Setup quits, and then recommends that you run ScanDisk to repair your hard disk. However, after you run ScanDisk, no errors are found. This problem can occur if your Windows 3.x–based computer is configured to use a network server for virtual memory. Microsoft has confirmed this to be a problem in Windows 98.

Solution

To work around this problem, run Windows 98 Setup with the /is parameter. For example, type the following:

```
setup /is
```

This parameter runs Setup normally, but skips ScanDisk.

Related KB article Q185857

Fatal Exception Error Message When Using DMI Start Utility

You start your computer after upgrading to Windows 98 and receive the following error message:

Fatal Exception 0E at 0028:c028bac6 in VXD Vwin32 05 +000281a

You may also receive a series of *Invalid page fault* error messages in files with the ._AC extension. This behavior can occur if your computer automatically starts the third-party Desktop Management Interface (DMI) Start utility.

Solution

To work around this issue, disable the DMI Start utility. To do so, follow these steps:

1. Restart your computer. After your computer completes the Power On Self Test (POST), press and hold down the Ctrl key until you see the Windows 98 Startup menu, and then choose Safe Mode.

2. Click the Start button, choose Programs, choose Accessories, choose System Tools, and then click System Information.

3. Choose System Configuration Utility from the Tools menu.

4. On the Startup tab, clear the check box next to DMIStart.

5. Click OK. When you are prompted to restart the computer, click Yes.

Related KB article Q190915

Hard Disk and CD-ROM Drive Problems After Upgrading to Windows 98

You upgrade to Windows 98, with Helix Hurricane for Microsoft Windows 95 installed on your computer, and you encounter the following problems:

- You cannot gain access to your CD-ROM drive.

- Hard disks connected to the integrated drive electronics (IDE) controller are using MS-DOS Compatibility mode.

- An additional drive appears in My Computer and Windows Explorer that is approximately 13 megabytes (MB) in size.

Solution One

Remove Hurricane using the Hurricane Uninstall tool. To do this, follow these steps:

1. Restart your computer. After your computer completes the Power On Self Test (POST), press and hold down the Ctrl key until you see the Windows 98 Startup menu, and then choose Safe Mode Command Prompt Only.

2. Run the Uninstall tool in the folder in which Hurricane is installed.

Solution Two

If the Uninstall tool is not available, disable Hurricane. To do so, follow these steps:

1. Use a text editor (such as Notepad) to open the AUTOEXEC.BAT file.

2. Disable the line containing *qwatch.com* in the AUTOEXEC.BAT file. To disable the line, type *rem* followed by a space at the beginning of the line.

3. Save and then close the AUTOEXEC.BAT file.

4. Use a text editor to open the SYSTEM.INI file.

5. Disable the following lines in the [386Enh] section of the SYSTEM.INI file by placing a semicolon (;) at the beginning of each line:

```
device=<path>\arpl.386

device=<path>\Winsa.386

device=<path>\Winguard.386

device=<path>\vxmsems.386

device=<path>\windrv.386
```

```
device=<path>\vcache16.386

device=<path>\vsectd.386

device=<path>\heapx.386
```

6. Change the following lines in the [Boot] section of the SYSTEM.INI file:

From	To
system.drv=<path>\sysdrv.drv	system.drv=System.drv
display.drv=<path>\winsa256.drv	display.drv=Pnpdrvr.drv

Note If your original display driver was not PNPDRVR.DRV, start Windows in Safe mode and change the display driver to the appropriate driver.

7. Save and then close the SYSTEM.INI file.

8. Restart your computer.

Note If you continue to have problems, or for specific instructions about using the Hurricane uninstall tool, contact Helix Software.

Related KB article Q189092

HP Computer Hangs After Upgrading from Windows 95

Your Hewlett-Packard (HP) computer stops responding (hangs) when you select text or when you connect to a web site with numerous graphics images. This can happen if you use an HP 8175 or 8176 computer with an ATI 3D Rage II+ PCI video adapter and you upgraded from Windows 95.

Solution

Install the ATI Rage II+ PCI video adapter driver from the Windows 98 CD-ROM, or contact the manufacturer about obtaining an updated video adapter driver.

To install the ATI Rage II+ PCI video adapter driver from the Windows 98 CD-ROM, follow these steps:

1. Click the Start button, choose Settings, and then click Control Panel.

2. Double-click the Display icon.

3. Click the Settings tab, and then click Advanced.

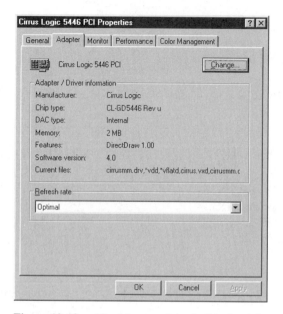

Figure 12-13. *The Adapter tab in the Display Adapter Properties dialog box.*

4. Click the Adapter tab, and then click Change to start the Update Device Driver Wizard.

5. Click Next, and then click Display A List Of All The Drivers In A Specific Location, So You Can Select The Driver You Want.

6. Click Next, click Have Disk, and then click Browse.

7. In the Drives box, select the CD-ROM drive that contains the Windows 98 CD-ROM.

8. In the Folders box, double-click the DRIVERS folder, and then double-click the DISPLAY folder.

9. Double-click the ATI folder, click OK, and then click OK.

10. Click the ATI Rage II+ Pro video adapter driver, and then click OK.

11. Click OK, and then click Next.

12. Click Next, and then click Finish.

13. Restart your computer.

Related KB article Q194064

Log On Prompts New Users to Personalize Settings

You upgrade a computer running Windows 95 with user profiles enabled to Windows 98, or you install Windows 98 using a scripted installation that uses user profiles, and each new user that logs on to Windows 98 for the first time is prompted to personalize his or her settings. This problem occurs because the default user profile is not personalized during Setup.

New user profiles are created from the default user profile unless an existing roving user profile already exists. Personalizing the default user profile increases the startup time of Windows 98 when a new user logs on for the first time. However, it prevents Windows 98 from prompting new users to personalize their settings.

Solution

To resolve this issue, follow these steps:

1. Restart the computer.

2. When you are prompted to log in, click Cancel. This logs you in as the default user.

3. Personalize the Windows 98 default user profile settings that you want to be the same for all new users.

Do not personalize any programs that retain user information unless the user information is a service account that is common to all computers.

Related KB article Q188111

Microsoft Mail Password Lost on Upgrade

You upgrade from Windows for Workgroups 3.11 to Windows 98, and your Microsoft Mail password is not retained.

Solution

Complete the upgrade, start Microsoft Mail, and type your password. Click the Save Your Password option, and click OK.

Related KB article Q190308

Mouse Power Driver Message

You start your computer after you upgrade your Windows 3.x–based computer to Windows 98 and receive the following error message:

Mouse Power driver not loaded - Check the driver setting in SYSTEM.INI.

This problem can occur because Mouse Power makes changes to your computer's system files or folders.

Solution

To resolve this issue, remove the references to Mouse Power from your system files. To do this, follow these steps:

1. Use a text editor (such as Notepad) to edit the SYSTEM.INI file, and edit the mouse.drv= line in the [boot] section to read *mouse.drv=mouse.drv*. If you are using a Logitech mouse, edit the line to read *mouse.drv=lmouse.drv*.

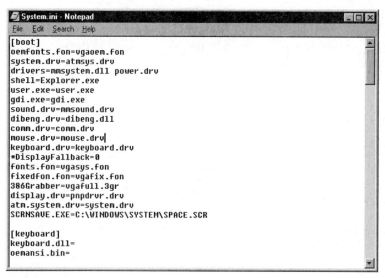

Figure 12-14.   *The SYSTEM.INI file in Notepad.*

2. Save the SYSTEM.INI file, and then restart your computer.

Related KB article Q185045

Problems Detected in ScanDisk

You are installing Windows 98 and see the following error message during the ScanDisk portion of Setup:

Setup checked the hard disks on your computer and found that there may be problems.

You need to check all of your drives before continuing Setup.

This problem can occur if you are using a real-mode Novell NetWare client and there is not enough free conventional memory to continue with Windows 98 Setup.

Solution One

Increase the amount of free conventional memory, and then run Windows 98 Setup again. To increase the amount of free conventional memory, use either or both of the following methods:

- Using a text editor (such as Notepad), add the following lines to the CONFIG.SYS file, and then restart your computer:

  ```
  device=c:\windows\himem.sys

  device=c:\windows\emm386.exe noems

  dos=high,umb
  ```

- Using a text editor (such as Notepad), disable all nonessential drivers and programs in the CONFIG.SYS and AUTOEXEC.BAT files, and then restart your computer. To disable a driver or program, type *rem* followed by a space at the beginning of the line. Make sure to disable any real-mode driver for which there is a protected-mode equivalent.

Solution Two

Use ScanDisk to thoroughly check your hard disk for errors. If you are upgrading from MS-DOS, follow these steps:

1. Type *scandisk* at a command prompt.

2. When you are prompted to perform a surface scan, press the Y key.

If you are upgrading from Windows 95, follow these steps:

1. Click the Start button, and then click Run.

2. In the Open box, type *scandskw*, and then click OK.

3. Click Thorough, and then click Start.

When you have finished checking your hard disk, run Windows 98 Setup using the setup /is command-line switch to skip the ScanDisk portion of Setup.

Related KB article Q188096

Program Group Conversion Fails

Windows uses groups and group items represented by icons to provide access to programs. The default groups for Windows 3.x are Main, Accessories, Games, and StartUp. An example of an item within the Main group is Control Panel. Windows 95/98 uses folders and links to provide the same functionality as groups and items in previous versions of Windows.

To facilitate the upgrade from Windows to Windows 95/98, an executable file named GRPCONV.EXE is included with Windows 95/98. This file provides the translation of groups and group items to folders and links. Each group is converted to a folder, and its items are converted to shell links, which are placed within that particular folder.

In some cases, however, the program group conversion experiences difficulties.

Solution

If a group fails to be converted or if an error is displayed during conversion, follow these steps:

1. Test GRPCONV.EXE by using it to convert a group file (.GRP) that was previously converted successfully. If this fails, GRPCONV.EXE has been corrupted, and you must replace this file with the GRPCONV.EXE file from your original Windows 98 CD-ROM. If this step is successful, continue with step 2.

2. Run the PROGMAN.EXE file that ships with Windows 98. This is the Windows 98 version of Program Manager. View the group that did not convert. If it displays and acts correctly in Program Manager, create a new group and copy (do not move) the items from the original group to the new one.

3. Close Program Manager, and run GRPCONV.EXE in interactive mode (grpconv /m) to convert the newly created group. If this step fails, continue with step 4.

4. Run Program Manager, delete the items in the newly created group, and copy a few of the items from the original group into the new group. If this fails, repeat this step with different items until you have determined which item is causing the failure.

Note It is also possible for a virus to cause conversion failure. You may therefore also want to use an antivirus utility to explore whether the failed program group conversion stems from a virus.

Related KB article Q119941

ScanDisk Hangs

You install Windows 98 and Setup stops responding (hangs) while ScanDisk is running.

Solution

To work around this behavior, run ScanDisk at a command prompt before you install Windows 98. To do so, follow these steps:

1. Restart your computer. After your computer completes the Power On Self Test (POST), press and hold down the Ctrl key until you see the Windows 98 Startup menu, and then choose Command Prompt Only.

2. At the command prompt, type *scandisk*, and then press Enter.

3. Click Yes, or press the Y key, when you are prompted to perform a surface scan.

4. When ScanDisk finishes, restart your computer normally, and then run Windows 98 Setup using the command setup /is. The /is command-line switch causes Setup to bypass ScanDisk.

Note If you want to run ScanDisk in the foreground during Windows 98 Setup so that you can view the ScanDisk results, run Windows 98 Setup using the setup /ih command.

Related KB article Q191366

Short Filenames with Numeric Tails Error Message

You upgrade from Windows 95 to Windows 98 and see the following error message:

Setup must be able to create short filenames with numeric tails for files with names longer than 8 characters. Enable this option and try running Setup again.

This error message can occur if the NameNumericTail string value with a data value of 0 exists in the following Registry key:

```
HKEY_LOCAL_MACHINE\System\CurrentControlSet\Control\FileSystem
```

Solution

Follow these steps:

Warning Please read the Introduction for information on how to safely edit the Registry.

1. Click the Start button, click Run, enter *Regedit* in the Open box, and click OK.

2. Navigate your way down through the folders in the left pane.

3. Delete the NameNumericTail string value in the following Registry key:

   `HKEY_LOCAL_MACHINE\System\CurrentControlSet\Control\FileSystem`

4. Close Regedit.

5. Restart your computer.

6. Run Windows 98 Setup.

The NameNumericTail=0 value causes the 8.3 alias for long filenames not to use a numeric tail (a tilde [~] followed by a digit at the end of the filename). For example, if you add the NameNumericTail=0 value to the Registry, the 8.3 alias for the PROGRAM FILES folder may be changed from Progra~1 to Programf. This can cause problems if you attempt to run or install a program that uses the PROGRAM FILES folder.

Related KB article Q179370

Su0358 Error Message

You attempt to install Windows 98 and receive the following error message:

SU0358

Setup detected one or more MS-DOS-based programs running on your computer. Close your MS-DOS programs, and then click OK to continue. Or, click Cancel to quit Setup.

This problem occurs when you upgrade Windows 3.1 to Windows 98 on an AST computer that is using AST's DESKTOP.EXE program instead of Program Manager as the interface (or shell).

If you attempt to close the DESKTOP.EXE program using Task Manager by pressing Ctrl+Esc, clicking DESKTOP.EXE, and then clicking End Task, Windows 3.1 attempts to close. This behavior occurs because you are using the DESKTOP.EXE program as the Windows 3.1 interface (or shell).

Solution

To solve this problem, follow these steps:

1. Click Cancel to close Setup.

2. Using a text editor (such as Notepad), open the SYSTEM.INI file. By default, the SYSTEM.INI file is located in the WINDOWS folder.

3. Locate the shell=<path>\desktop.exe line in the [Boot] section of the SYSTEM.INI file, and then disable it by placing a semicolon (;) at the beginning of the line.

4. Add the line shell=progman.exe beneath the line you disabled in step 3.

5. Save and then close the SYSTEM.INI file.

6. Restart Windows 3.1, and then run Setup again.

Related KB article Q185354

Windows 3.0 Upgrade Causes Errors in Licensing

You attempt to install Windows 98 on a computer on which Windows 3.0 is installed and receive the following error message after you type your Product Key and click OK:

Setup has searched the specified directory, but cannot find any qualifying products.

You are not a licensed user of one of the qualifying products, you must use the full version of Windows 98. Microsoft grants you no license rights to use this upgrade version, and the End User License Agreement included in this package is void.

You are a licensee of a qualifying product and are having problems, do not exit Setup. Either try Setup again or call Microsoft Product Support Services at the telephone number listed in your manual.

This problem occurs because Windows 98 is not designed to upgrade Windows 3.0.

Solution

Contact Microsoft Technical Support for assistance with this problem.

Related KB article Q188334

Windows 3.0 Upgrade Displays Error Message

You attempt to upgrade to Windows 98 from within Windows 3.0 using the full retail version of Windows 98 and see the following error message:

Windows 98 Setup requires Microsoft Windows version 3.1 or later. Quit Windows and type Setup /D at the MS-DOS command prompt.

This message is displayed because Setup requires Windows version 3.1 or later to upgrade from within the Windows graphical user interface (GUI). To upgrade Windows 3.0, you must run Windows 98 Setup from MS-DOS.

Solution

To resolve this issue, close Windows 3.0 and type *setup /d* at the MS-DOS command prompt. When you use the /d switch, Windows 98 Setup does not use the current Windows settings in the WIN.INI and SYSTEM.INI files. If you have programs that write information to these files, those programs may not work correctly after you install Windows 98, and it may be necessary to reinstall these programs.

Related KB article Q186832

Windows 3.1 Upgrade Displays Error Message

You attempt to upgrade Windows 3.1 to Windows 98 and see the following error message:

SUWIN

An error has occurred in your application. If you choose ignore you should save your work in a new file. If you choose close, your application will terminate.

When you click Close, you might see the following error message:

Application Error

SUWIN caused a general protection fault in module setupx.dll @ 0012:1346

This problem can occur if you disable virtual memory in Windows 3.1 before you run Windows 98 Setup.

Solution

To resolve this problem, enable virtual memory in Windows 3.1 before running Windows 98 Setup. To do this, follow these steps:

1. In the Main group, double-click 386 Enhanced.

2. Click Virtual Memory, and then click Change.

3. In the Type box, select Permanent or Temporary, and then click OK.

Related KB article Q188107

Windows 95 Programs Don't Work After Upgrading Windows

If you upgraded to Windows 98 from Windows 95 and you did not install Windows in the same directory as your old version of Windows, your old programs will not work because the Windows 98 Registry will not have the proper information about your programs.

Solution

Reinstall your programs. (Do not simply copy them.)

Related KB article Q188978 or PROGRAMS.TXT in your WINDOWS folder

Windows 98 CD

Discover Windows 98 Tour Causes Error Message

You click Discover Windows 98 on the Welcome To Windows 98 screen to start the Windows 98 Tour and receive the following error message:

> *The Windows 98 Tour ('Discover.exe') was not found. Please insert your Windows 98 CD or verify your network connection is still active. Windows 98 was installed from '<drive:>\<flat directory>'.*

This problem occurs when you copy the WIN98 folder (but not the WIN98\TOUR subfolder) from the Windows 98 CD-ROM to your hard disk and then install Windows 98 from the folder on your hard disk. The Setup source path specifies to retrieve files from the hard disk instead of the Windows 98 CD-ROM. The Discover Windows 98 tour files are located in the WIN98\TOUR folder on the Windows 98 CD-ROM.

Solution One

You can solve this problem by changing the Windows 98 Setup source path to retrieve files from the Windows 98 CD-ROM. To do so, follow these steps:

1. Click the Start button, click Run, type *poledit* in the Open box, and then click OK to start System Policy Editor. (If necessary, you can install the System Policy Editor through the Add/Remove Programs icon in Control Panel.)

2. Choose Open Registry from the File menu, and then double-click Local Computer.

3. Click the plus sign (+) next to Windows 98 System.

4. Click Network Path For Windows Setup, and then type the new source path.

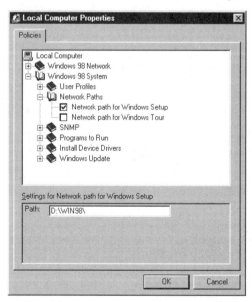

Figure 12-15. *The Local Computer Properties dialog box in the System Policy Editor.*

5. Save the changes to the Registry, close System Policy Editor, and then restart your computer.

6. Extract a new copy of the LAYOUT.INF file from the PRECOPY2.CAB file on your new Windows media to the WINDOWS\INF folder on the hard disk. For example, if you are changing the Setup source path because you switched from Windows disks to a Windows CD-ROM, extract the LAYOUT.INF file from the WIN98 folder on the Windows 98 CD-ROM to the WINDOWS\INF folder on the hard disk. For information about using the Extract tool, type *extract* at a command prompt.

Solution Two

You can solve this problem by copying the WIN98\TOUR folder, including all folders in the WIN98\TOUR folder, from the Windows 98 CD-ROM to the folder from which you installed Windows. To do this, follow these steps:

1. Right-click the Start button, and choose Explore from the shortcut menu.

2. Click the plus sign (+) next to the CD-ROM drive icon.

3. Click the WIN98\TOUR folder, and drag it to the folder from which you installed Windows.

4. Restart your computer.

Related KB article Q189307

Path to Windows Files Incorrect

If you originally installed Windows from floppy disks, and then bought a Windows CD-ROM, you can change the source path so that Setup retrieves files from your CD drive rather than from your floppy disk drive.

Solution

To change the Setup source path, you must use Registry Editor to modify the following Registry key:

`HKEY_LOCAL_MACHINE\Software\Microsoft\Windows\CurrentVersion\Setup\SourcePath`

Warning Please read the Introduction for information on how to safely edit the Registry.

To do so, follow these steps:

1. Click the Start button, click Run, enter *Regedit* in the Open box, and click OK.

2. Navigate your way down through the folders in the left pane until you locate the SETUP folder.

3. Double-click the SETUP folder, and in the right pane, locate SourcePath.

4. Right-click SourcePath, and choose Modify from the menu. Enter a new value, and then click OK. For example, if your CD drive is D, you would enter *D:\WIN98*.

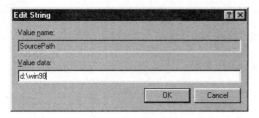

Figure 12-16.   *The Edit String dialog box.*

5. Close Regedit.

6. Restart your computer.

After you update the Registry, extract a new copy of the LAYOUT.INF file from the PRECOPY2.CAB file on your new Windows media to the WINDOWS\INF folder on your hard disk. For example, if you are changing the Setup source path because you switched from Windows floppy disks to a Windows CD-ROM, extract the LAYOUT.INF file from the WIN98 folder on the Windows 98 CD-ROM to the WINDOWS\INF folder on your hard disk. For information about using the Extract tool, type *extract* at a command prompt. For information on extracting files using the System File Checker, see KB article Q129605, "How to Extract Original Compressed Windows Files."

Related KB article Q131652

Setup Asks for Windows 98 CD-ROM

You upgrade from Windows 95 OEM Service Release 2 to Windows 98 on a hard disk that has been compressed with DriveSpace 3 and see an error message asking you to insert the Windows 98 CD-ROM even though it is already inserted. Microsoft has confirmed this to be a problem in Windows 98.

Solution

Click OK, and Setup continues normally. The error message might occur more than once during the Windows 98 installation.

Related KB article Q186938

Windows 98 CD Interactive Demos Causes Error Message(s)

You attempt to run the interactive demonstrations on the Windows 98 CD-ROM, and you experience one of the following problems:

- You click Interactive CD Samplers on the Windows 98 CD-ROM screen, and you receive the following error message:

    MS-SMPLR caused an invalid page fault in module OLEPRO32.dll @   015f:f308742

- You attempt to run Setup for the Dilbert's Desktop Games demonstration by double-clicking the DILBERT.EXE file in the CDSAMPLES\DEMOS\DIB folder on the Windows 98 CD-ROM, and you receive the following error message:

  Could not create a destination file c:\windows\temp\~IS_CMPX.~~~   Error number: 2

a You click OK, and receive the following error message:

  InstallShield Self-extracting EXE: Extract failed: return from extract=-8

These problems occur when your WINDOWS\TEMP folder is missing.

Solution One

Shut down and restart your computer. The WINDOWS\TEMP folder is re-created when you restart your computer.

Solution Two

Re-create the TEMP folder in the WINDOWS folder.

Related KB article Q189886

Windows 98 CD Not Found

You try to install Windows 98 and receive the following error message:

Please insert the following disk in drive D (or your CD-ROM drive):

Windows 98 boot disk or CD-ROM

When you are ready to continue, press ENTER

When you press Enter, you may receive the same message again, and this behavior may occur every time you press Enter.

This problem can occur if you are trying to install Windows 98 to a computer with two unformatted Integrated Device Electronics (IDE) hard disks.

Warning Do not carry out this solution if you have important data on your hard drives. Performing this procedure will delete all files on your hard drive; back up your data first!

Solution

To work around this problem, follow these steps:

1. With the message visible on the screen and the Windows 98 Startup Disk in the drive, press F3, and then press F3 again. Note that this closes Setup.

2. Type the following commands at the command prompt, and press Enter after each command:

```
a:

extract ebd.cab format.com /1 a:\

format c:
```

3. After the format process is complete, type the following command at the command prompt, and then press Enter:

```
format d:
```

4. After the format process is complete, restart your computer.

Related KB article Q190984

Windows Program File Extracting

Cabinet Files Aren't Saved on Hard Disk

You have all the Windows 98 cabinet files located on CD-ROM, and you need to copy them to your hard disk.

Solution

Use the Extract tool to copy cabinet files from the CD-ROM to your hard disk.

Note If you do not have a Startup disk, see the article titled "Windows Startup Disk Needs Creating" later in this chapter.

The Extract tool has only a command-line interface (not a GUI interface). Because Windows does not allow you to delete or overwrite a file that is in use, you might have to restart your computer in Command Prompt Only mode before you can use the Extract tool. If you receive an *Access denied* error message when you try to delete a file before using the Extract tool, or when you use the Extract tool to overwrite an existing file, follow these steps to restart your computer in Command Prompt Only mode and then use the Extract tool:

1. Click the Start button, and then click Shut Down.

2. Click the Restart In MS-DOS Mode option button, and then click OK.

Figure 12-17. *Restart the computer in MS-DOS mode.*

3. At the command prompt, type Extract, and press Enter to see specifications for the Extract tool.

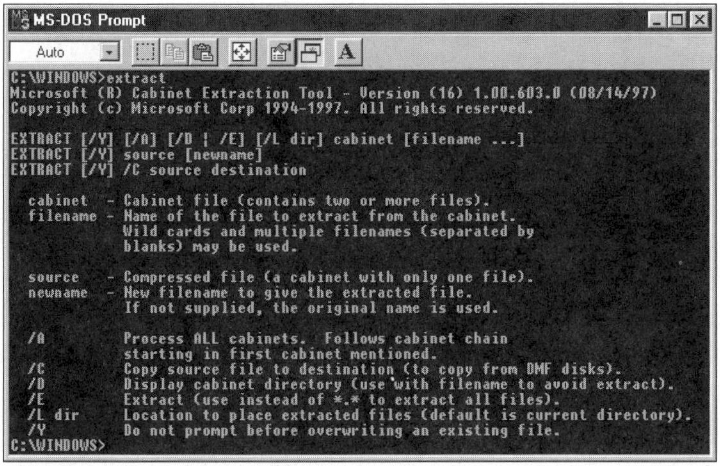

Figure 12-18. *The Extract tool.*

To use the Extract tool to copy cabinet files from the CD-ROM to your hard disk, use the following syntax in the Extract tool at the command prompt:

```
extract /c <cabinet> <destination>
```

For example, to copy the BASE4.CAB file from your Windows 98 CD-ROM in drive D to the WINDOWS\OPTIONS folder on drive C, use the following command:

```
extract /c d:\win98\base4.cab c:\windows\options
```

Note You cannot use the /a and /c switches at the same time. Therefore, you cannot copy all the cabinet files using a single command.

Other Optional Switches:

- Use the /y switch to cause the Extract tool to not prompt you before overwriting an existing file. If you use this switch when you are extracting a file, any file in the destination folder with the same name as the file you are extracting is automatically overwritten.

For example, to extract the UNIDRV.DLL file from the DRIVER13.CAB file on the Windows 98 CD-ROM in drive D to the WINDOWS\SYSTEM folder on drive C and automatically overwrite any existing UNIDRV.DLL file that is already there, use the following command:

```
extract /y /a d:\win98\driver13.cab unidrv.dll /l c:\windows\system
```

- Use the /e switch in place of the "*.*" wildcard designation when you are extracting or finding multiple files. For example, to extract all the files from the DRIVER13.CAB file on the Windows 98 CD-ROM in drive D to the WINDOWS folder on drive C, use either of the following commands:

```
extract /e  d:\win98\driver13.cab /l c:\windows
```

```
extract  d:\win98\driver13.cab *.* /l c:\windows
```

For a complete list of the command-line switches for the Extract tool, type extract at a command prompt.

Related KB article Q129605

CD-ROM Support Needs Initiating

You need to extract a file from the Windows 98 CD-ROM, but you are unable to use System File Checker, and you cannot access your CD-ROM drive from the command prompt.

Solution

To start your computer with CD-ROM support and then extract files, follow these steps:

1. Insert the Windows 98 Startup disk in drive A, and then restart your computer.

2. When the Microsoft Windows 98 Startup menu appears, choose Start Computer With CD-ROM Support.

3. Insert the Windows 98 CD-ROM in the CD-ROM drive.

4. To extract files at the command prompt, use the Extract tool. Or you can use the Extract Command Line Helper tool. To use Extract Command Line Helper, type *ext* at the command prompt, and then follow the instructions on the screen. The EXT.EXE tool builds a command line for the EXTRACT.EXE tool. For more information on the Extract tool, see KB article Q129605, "How to Extract Original Compressed Windows Files."

Related KB article Q129605

Contents of Cabinet Files Unknown

You have the CD-ROM that contains the Windows 98 program files and you need to know the contents of all the cabinet files.

Solution One

Use the Extract tool to display the contents of a cabinet file.

Note If you do not have a Startup disk, see the article "Windows Startup Disk Needs Creating" later in this chapter.

The Extract tool has only a command-line interface (not a GUI interface). Because Windows does not allow you to delete or overwrite a file that is in use, you might have to restart your computer in Command Prompt Only mode before you can use the Extract tool. If you receive an *Access denied* error message when you try to delete a file before using the Extract tool, or when you use the Extract tool to overwrite an existing file, follow these steps to restart your computer in Command Prompt Only mode and then use the Extract tool:

1. Click the Start button, and click Shut Down.

2. Click the Restart In MS-DOS Mode option button, and then click OK.

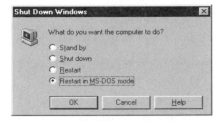

Figure 12-19. *Restart the computer in MS-DOS mode.*

3. At the command prompt, type *Extract*, and press Enter to see specifications for the Extract tool.

```
MS-DOS Prompt
Auto

C:\WINDOWS>extract
Microsoft (R) Cabinet Extraction Tool - Version (16) 1.00.603.0 (08/14/97)
Copyright (c) Microsoft Corp 1994-1997. All rights reserved.

EXTRACT [/Y] [/A] [/D | /E] [/L dir] cabinet [filename ...]
EXTRACT [/Y] source [newname]
EXTRACT [/Y] /C source destination

  cabinet  - Cabinet file (contains two or more files).
  filename - Name of the file to extract from the cabinet.
             Wild cards and multiple filenames (separated by
             blanks) may be used.

  source   - Compressed file (a cabinet with only one file).
  newname  - New filename to give the extracted file.
             If not supplied, the original name is used.

  /A         Process ALL cabinets. Follows cabinet chain
             starting in first cabinet mentioned.
  /C         Copy source file to destination (to copy from DMF disks).
  /D         Display cabinet directory (use with filename to avoid extract).
  /E         Extract (use instead of *.* to extract all files).
  /L dir     Location to place extracted files (default is current directory).
  /Y         Do not prompt before overwriting an existing file.
C:\WINDOWS>
```

Figure 12-20. *The Extract tool.*

Use the Extract tool to list the contents of cabinet files without actually extracting any files.

To display the contents of a cabinet file, use the following syntax:

```
extract /d <cabinet>
```

Solution Two

To display the contents of all the cabinet files in a cabinet chain, starting with the specified cabinet file, use the following syntax:

```
extract /a /d <cabinet>
```

For example, to display the contents of all the Windows 98 cabinet files starting with the BASE4.CAB file, use the following command:

```
extract /a /d d:\win98\base4.cab
```

Note The /a switch causes the Extract tool to list the contents of all the cabinet files in the cabinet chain, starting with the first cabinet file mentioned.

Related KB article Q129605

Internet Explorer 4.0 or 4.01 Files Need Extracting

You need to extract the Internet Explorer 4.0 or 4.1 files from you Windows 98 CD-ROM.

Internet Explorer 4.0 and 4.01 files are stored in cabinet files within cabinet files. Individual files are stored in the IE4_1.CAB through IE4_5.CAB files. The IE4_1.CAB through IE4_5.CAB files are included in the IE4_S1.CAB through IE4_S5.CAB files.

Solution

To extract individual files, you must first extract the IE4_<n>.CAB file. To do this, type the following command at a command prompt, and then press Enter:

```
extract ie4_s<n>.cab /e
```

where <n> is the number of the cabinet file you want to extract.

To extract individual Internet Explorer 4.0 or 4.01 files, follow the appropriate procedure explained elsewhere in this chapter, or see KB article Q129605, "How to Extract Original Compressed Windows Files."

Related KB article Q129605

Windows 98 System Files Need Extracting

You have corrupted or missing system files.

Solution One

Use the Extract tool to extract the files from your Windows 98 CD-ROM.

Note If you do not have a Startup disk, see the article "Windows Startup Disk Needs Creating" later in this chapter.

The Extract tool has only a command-line interface (not a GUI interface). Because Windows does not allow you to delete or overwrite a file that is in use, you might have to restart your computer in Command Prompt Only mode before you can use the Extract tool. If you receive an *Access denied* error message when you try to delete a file before using the Extract tool, or when you use the Extract tool to overwrite an existing file, follow these steps to restart your computer in Command Prompt Only mode and then use the Extract tool:

1. Click the Start button, and click Shut Down.

2. Click the Restart In MS-DOS Mode option button, and then click OK.

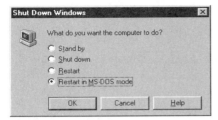

Figure 12-21. *Restart the computer in MS-DOS mode.*

3. At the command prompt, type *Extract*, and press Enter to see specifications for the Extract tool.

```
MS-DOS Prompt                                    _ □ ×
Auto        ▼   □ ▤ ▩ ⊞ ▣ ▤  A
C:\WINDOWS>extract
Microsoft (R) Cabinet Extraction Tool - Version (16) 1.00.603.0 (08/14/97)
Copyright (c) Microsoft Corp 1994-1997. All rights reserved.

EXTRACT [/Y] [/A] [/D | /E] [/L dir] cabinet [filename ...]
EXTRACT [/Y] source [newname]
EXTRACT [/Y] /C source destination

  cabinet  - Cabinet file (contains two or more files).
  filename - Name of the file to extract from the cabinet.
             Wild cards and multiple filenames (separated by
             blanks) may be used.

  source   - Compressed file (a cabinet with only one file).
  newname  - New filename to give the extracted file.
             If not supplied, the original name is used.

  /A         Process ALL cabinets. Follows cabinet chain
             starting in first cabinet mentioned.
  /C         Copy source file to destination (to copy from DMF disks).
  /D         Display cabinet directory (use with filename to avoid extract).
  /E         Extract (use instead of *.* to extract all files).
  /L dir     Location to place extracted files (default is current directory).
  /Y         Do not prompt before overwriting an existing file.
C:\WINDOWS>
```

Figure 12-22. *The Extract tool.*

Extract the system files from the cabinet file located on the Windows 98 CD-ROM to the appropriate location on your hard drive. All of the cabinet files are located in the WIN98 folder. For example, if you want to extract the UNIDRV.DLL file from the DRIVER13.CAB file, and the CD-ROM drive is drive D and your WINDOWS\SYSTEM directory is on drive C, you would type the following:

```
extract d:\win98\driver13.cab unidrv.dll /l c:\windows\system
```

Solution Two

Windows 98 includes a System File Checker tool, and you can use this tool to verify the integrity of your operating system files, to restore them if they are damaged, or to extract compressed files from the Windows 98 CD-ROM. To do this using System File Checker, follow these steps:

1. Click the Start button, choose Programs, choose Accessories, choose System Tools, and click System Information.

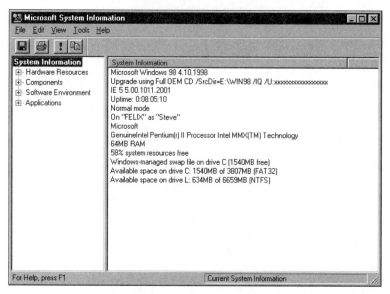

Figure 12-23. *The System Information window.*

2. Choose System File Checker from the Tools menu.

3. Click Extract One File From Installation Disk, enter the name of the file you want to extract in the Specify The System File You Would Like To Restore box, and then click Start.

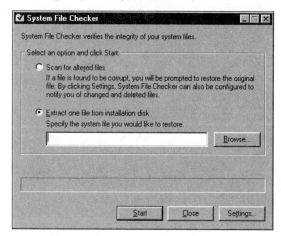

Figure 12-24. *The System File Checker tool.*

4. In the Restore From box, type the path to the WIN98 folder on the Windows 98 CD-ROM, type the destination folder in the Save File In box, if necessary, and then click OK.

5. Click OK, click OK, and then click Yes when you are prompted to restart your computer.

If you do not specify a source cabinet (.CAB) file in the Restore From box, System File Checker first searches for the file you are extracting in the specified folder (outside of a cabinet file). System File Checker then searches all cabinet files, sorted by MS-DOS directory order, in the specified folder. System File Checker extracts the first instance of the file it finds. To determine the order in which System File Checker searches cabinet files, type *dir* at a command prompt in the specified folder.

Windows Startup Disk Needs Creating

You need to create a Windows 98 Startup disk.

A feature included in the Windows 98 Startup disk is support for CD-ROM drives. This might be of benefit if you need to extract a file from the Windows 98 CD-ROM but you are unable to use System File Checker. (For example, if your computer does not start properly.)

Solution

Note The Windows 98 Startup disk provides support for most types of CD-ROM drives, including IDE and SCSI CD-ROM drives, but it might not support your particular CD-ROM drive.

To create a Windows 98 Startup disk, follow these steps:

1. On any Windows 98 computer, click the Start button, choose Settings, click Control Panel, and then double-click the Add/Remove Programs icon.

Figure 12-25. *The Startup Disk tab of the Add/Remove Programs Properties dialog box.*

2. Select the Startup Disk tab, click Create Disk, and then follow the instructions on the screen.

Figure 12-26. *The Insert Disk dialog box.*

Windows System File Extraction Location Unknown

You want to extract a Windows file from a cabinet file but the location of the Windows file you want to extract is unknown.

Solution

Use the Extract tool to extract the files from your Windows 98 Startup disk.

Note If you do not have a Startup disk, see the previous article, "Windows Startup Disk Needs Creating."

The Extract tool has only a command-line interface (not a GUI interface). Because Windows does not allow you to delete or overwrite a file that is in use, you may have to restart your computer in Command Prompt Only mode before you can use the Extract tool. If you receive an *Access denied* error message when you try to delete a file before using the Extract tool, or when you use the Extract tool to overwrite an existing file, follow these steps to restart your computer in Command Prompt Only mode and then use the Extract tool:

1. Click the Start button, and then click Shut Down.

2. Click the Restart In MS-DOS Mode option button, and then click OK.

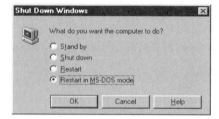

Figure 12-27. *Restart the computer in MS-DOS mode.*

3. At the command prompt, type *Extract*, and press Enter to see specifications for the extract tool.

```
MS-DOS Prompt                                          _ □ ×
Auto        ▼   □ 🖻 🖺   ⊞   🖼 🖨   A

C:\WINDOWS>extract
Microsoft (R) Cabinet Extraction Tool - Version (16) 1.00.603.0 (08/14/97)
Copyright (c) Microsoft Corp 1994-1997. All rights reserved.

EXTRACT [/Y] [/A] [/D | /E] [/L dir] cabinet [filename ...]
EXTRACT [/Y] source [newname]
EXTRACT [/Y] /C source destination

  cabinet  - Cabinet file (contains two or more files).
  filename - Name of the file to extract from the cabinet.
             Wild cards and multiple filenames (separated by
             blanks) may be used.

  source   - Compressed file (a cabinet with only one file).
  newname  - New filename to give the extracted file.
             If not supplied, the original name is used.

  /A         Process ALL cabinets.  Follows cabinet chain
             starting in first cabinet mentioned.
  /C         Copy source file to destination (to copy from DMF disks).
  /D         Display cabinet directory (use with filename to avoid extract).
  /E         Extract (use instead of *.* to extract all files).
  /L dir     Location to place extracted files (default is current directory).
  /Y         Do not prompt before overwriting an existing file.
C:\WINDOWS>
```

Figure 12-28. *The Extract tool.*

If you do not know which cabinet file contains the Windows file you want to extract, use the following command to search all the cabinet files in sequential order and then extract the file after it is found:

```
extract /a <cabinet> <filename> /l <destination>
```

For example, to extract the UNIDRV.DLL file from the Windows 98 CD-ROM in drive D into the WINDOWS\SYSTEM folder on drive C, use the following command:

```
extract /a d:\win98\base4.cab unidrv.dll /l c:\windows\system
```

The /a switch causes the Extract tool to search all the cabinet files starting with the first cabinet file mentioned on the command line (in this example, BASE4.CAB). You must modify the <cabinet> parameter accordingly to reflect the actual location of the cabinet files.

If the Extract tool cannot find the specified Windows 98 file in any of the cabinet files, the file might be located in the MINI.CAB, PRECOPY1.CAB, or PRECOPY2.CAB cabinet file. Use the following two commands to search these cabinet files:

```
extract /a d:\win98\precopy1.cab <filename> /l <destination>
```

```
extract d:\win98\mini.cab <filename> /l <destination>
```

The first command searches the PRECOPY1.CAB and the PRECOPY2.CAB cabinet files. The second command searches the MINI.CAB cabinet file. When you extract from a CD-ROM, you must modify the <cabinet> parameter in these commands accordingly.

To extract multiple files, use the same syntax as above, but use a wildcard designation for the <filename> parameter. For example, to extract all the Windows 98 files with a .TXT extension from the Windows 98 CD-ROM in drive D to the WINDOWS folder on drive C, use the following command:

```
extract /a d:\win98\base4.cab *.txt /l c:\windows
```

You can also use the Extract tool to determine which cabinet file contains a particular Windows file without actually extracting the file. When you use this syntax, the Extract tool searches the cabinet files but does not extract the file once it is found:

```
extract /a /d <cabinet> <filename>
```

For example, to find the Windows 98 UNIDRV.DLL file, starting with the BASE4.CAB file and with the Windows 98 CD-ROM in drive D, use the following command:

```
extract /a /d d:\win98\base4.cab unidrv.dll
```

Related KB article Q129605

Windows System Files Need Extracting from Known Cabinet File

You need to extract Windows 98 system files from your Windows 98 CD-ROM, and you know the location of the cabinet.

Solution One

Use the Extract tool to extract the files from your Windows 98 Startup disk.

Note If you do not have a Startup disk, see the article "Windows Startup Disk Needs Creating"earlier in this chapter.

The Extract tool has only a command-line interface (not a GUI interface). Because Windows does not allow you to delete or overwrite a file that is in use, you might have to restart your computer in Command Prompt Only mode before you can use the Extract tool. If you receive an *Access denied* error message when you try to delete a file before using the Extract tool, or when you use the Extract tool to overwrite an existing file, follow these steps to restart your computer in Command Prompt Only mode and then use the Extract tool:

1. Click the Start button, and then click Shut Down.

2. Click the Restart In MS-DOS Mode option button, and then click OK.

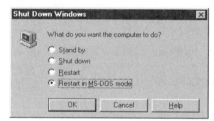

Figure 12-29. *Restart the computer in MS-DOS mode.*

3. At the command prompt, type *Extract*, and press Enter to see specifications for the Extract tool.

```
C:\WINDOWS>extract
Microsoft (R) Cabinet Extraction Tool - Version (16) 1.00.603.0 (08/14/97)
Copyright (c) Microsoft Corp 1994-1997. All rights reserved.

EXTRACT [/Y] [/A] [/D | /E] [/L dir] cabinet [filename ...]
EXTRACT [/Y] source [newname]
EXTRACT [/Y] /C source destination

  cabinet  - Cabinet file (contains two or more files).
  filename - Name of the file to extract from the cabinet.
             Wild cards and multiple filenames (separated by
             blanks) may be used.

  source   - Compressed file (a cabinet with only one file).
  newname  - New filename to give the extracted file.
             If not supplied, the original name is used.

  /A         Process ALL cabinets. Follows cabinet chain
             starting in first cabinet mentioned.
  /C         Copy source file to destination (to copy from DMF disks).
  /D         Display cabinet directory (use with filename to avoid extract).
  /E         Extract (use instead of *.* to extract all files).
  /L dir     Location to place extracted files (default is current directory).
  /Y         Do not prompt before overwriting an existing file.
C:\WINDOWS>
```

Figure 12-30. *The Extract tool.*

If you want to extract only a single file and you know which cabinet file contains the file you want to extract, use the following syntax to extract the file:

```
extract <cabinet> <filename> /l <destination>
```

For example, if you want to extract the Windows 98 UNIDRV.DLL file from the DRIVER13.CAB file, and your Windows 98 CD-ROM is in drive D and your WINDOWS\SYSTEM folder is on drive C, use the following command:

```
extract d:\win98\driver13.cab unidrv.dll /l c:\windows\system
```

Solution Two

If you want to extract multiple files and you know which cabinet file contains the files you want to extract, use the same syntax as above, but use a wildcard designation for the <filename> parameter. For example, to extract all the Windows 98 files that have a .TXT extension from the WIN98_47 cabinet file on your Windows 98 CD-ROM in drive D to the WINDOWS folder on drive C, use the following command:

```
extract d:\win98\win98_47.cab *.txt /l c:\windows\
```

Related KB article Q129605

CHAPTER 13

Sound and Video

MIDI and .WAV Files

Default MIDI Output Device Missing

You view your Windows 98–based computer's Musical Instrument Device Interface (MIDI) output devices in Multimedia properties and find a default MIDI output device missing from the Single Instrument box. Despite this, you might still be able to play MIDI files.

This problem occurs if you replace the Windows 98 Windows Driver Model (WDM) driver for your sound card with a virtual device driver (VxD).

Solution

Manually configure your default MIDI output device. To do so, follow these steps:

1. Click the Start button, choose Settings, and then click Control Panel.

2. Double-click the Multimedia icon.

3. Click the MIDI tab. In the Single Instrument list, select the MIDI playback device you want to use as the default device, click Apply, and then click OK.

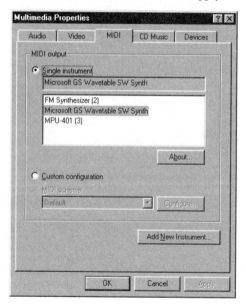

Figure 13-1. *The MIDI tab in the Multimedia Properties dialog box.*

Related KB article Q191249

MIDI File Causes Computer to Stop Responding

If a Musical Instrument Device Interface (MIDI, or .MID) file is played continuously, your computer stops responding (hangs) or performs sluggishly for a short time after you stop playing the file. Some third-party programs, such as screen savers and games, invoke repeated MIDI playback and are susceptible to this problem.

Solution

The MIDI sequencer (MCISEQ.DRV) loses a small amount of memory for each successive playback of a MIDI file. Closing and then reloading a file releases the lost memory.

Related KB article Q190927

MIDI File Makes No Sound

If you play a Musical Instrument Device Interface (MIDI) file, and you do not hear any sound even though the volume settings are correct, it may be that the GM.DLS file is missing or damaged.

Solution

To solve this problem, use the System File Checker tool to extract a new copy of the GM.DLS file from your Windows 98 CD-ROM into the WINDOWS\SYSTEM32\DRIVERS folder.

Related KB articles Q193255, Q129605

MIDI File Produces Static or Computer Hangs

You try to play a Musical Instrument Device Interface (MIDI) file on your computer, and you hear static, and your computer stops responding.

This problem occurs when your computer has a slow Central Processing Unit (CPU) and has a sound card that uses a Windows Driver Model (WDM) driver. When Windows 98 installs WDM sound card drivers, it also installs the Microsoft GS Synthesizer tool. This tool is very CPU intensive and may not perform well if you have a slow CPU.

Solution

To solve this problem, follow these steps:

1. Click the Start button, choose Settings, click Control Panel, and then double-click the Multimedia icon.

2. Click the MIDI tab.

3. Under Single Instrument, select a device other than the Microsoft GS Synthesizer, and then click OK.

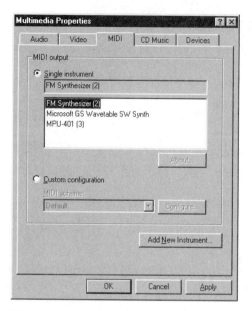

Figure 13-2. *The MIDI tab in the Multimedia Properties dialog box.*

Related KB article Q188511

MIDI File Sound Quality Poor

You play a Musical Instrument Device Interface (MIDI) file after installing Windows 98, and the sound quality is poor because of changes to the MIDI settings. Instead of sounding like actual musical instruments, for example, the playback may sound artificial or synthesized. This can happen if your default instrument has been changed from a high-quality wavetable synthesizer to a low-quality FM synthesizer.

Solution

To change the MIDI playback device settings, follow these steps:

1. Click the Start button, choose Settings, and then click Control Panel.

2. Double-click the Multimedia icon, and then click the MIDI tab.

3. In the MIDI Output box, select the MIDI playback device you want to use. If you don't know which device to select, consult your sound card's documentation or manufacturer.

4. Click OK.

Related KB article Q190824

MIDI Sound Pauses Video and Program

During a video sequence, you play a Musical Instrument Device Interface (MIDI) sound using the Microsoft GS Wavetable Synth playback device, and the video (and the rest of the program) pauses.

Certain programs open and close the MIDI port repeatedly. Windows 98 includes a high-quality software-based synthesizer that opens a large file of instrument sounds (GM.DLS). This can take a few moments, and, if done repeatedly, can cause delays in program flow. This is a problem because the 3.4 MB GM.DLS file (which houses all the MIDI samples for the GS Wavetable Synth device) is opened and closed each time.

Solution

Change the MIDI device to another device, such as the FM Synth or MPU-401 device. To do so, follow these steps:

1. Click the Start button, choose Settings, and then click Control Panel.

2. Double-click the Multimedia icon, and then click the MIDI tab.

3. In the MIDI Output box, select the MIDI playback device you want to use.

4. Click OK.

Related KB article Q191080

.WAV File Causes Errors

You use Windows and experience one of the following problems:

- You play a Windows Sound (.WAV) file and hear static.

- You play a .WAV file, and your computer restarts.

- You play a .WAV file, and your computer stops responding (hangs).

- You play a .WAV file, and you hear no sound at all.

- You enable a 16-bit sound scheme (for example, Robotz or Utopia), and Windows stops responding (hangs).

- When the Windows Start sound event is played during startup, you receive a *Fatal exception 0E* error message.

- After playing the Windows startup sound, your computer reboots .

Any of these problems can be caused by a lack of support for 16-bit direct memory access (DMA) on your computer.

Solution One

If the sound card in your computer is set for a 16-bit DMA channel (5, 6, or 7), use Device Manager to change the card's configuration to an 8-bit DMA channel (0, 1, or 3). If the sound card is set for an 8-bit DMA channel, change it to a 16-bit DMA channel. You may also need to run the configuration tool that is shipped with the sound card to change its DMA channel to match the Device Manager setting. If no configuration tool is shipped with the sound card, you may need to change jumpers on the card.

To change the DMA channel setting for the sound card in Device Manager, follow these steps:

1. Click the Start button, choose Settings, and then click Control Panel.

2. Double-click the System icon.

3. Click the Device Manager tab, and then double-click Sound, Video, and Game Controllers.

4. Double-click the sound card that is installed in your computer.

5. Click the Resources tab.

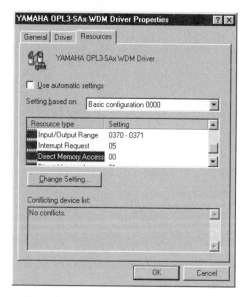

Figure 13-3.   *The Resources tab of the Driver Properties dialog box.*

6. Clear the Use Automatic Settings check box.

7. Double-click Direct Memory Access, and then change the DMA setting to the setting you want.

8. Click OK. When you are prompted to do so, restart your computer.

Solution Two

If 16-bit wave files are causing the problems, you can set the sound card to use single DMA mode only. For example, the Sound Blaster family of sound cards is software-configurable and can be set to single DMA mode with Device Manager. To do so, follow these steps:

1. Click the Start button, choose Settings, click Control Panel, and then double-click the System icon.

2. Click the Device Manager tab, double-click Sound, Video, and Game Controllers, and then double-click your sound card.

3. Click the Resources tab, and clear the Use Automatic Settings check box.

4. Select a configuration that includes only a single DMA setting (such as Basic Configuration 7) in the Settings Based On box.

5. Click OK or Close until you return to Control Panel.

Note This information applies only to sound cards that support single DMA operation and are software configurable. If yours is not, run the configuration utility included with your sound card to set it to single DMA mode (if single DMA mode is supported).

Related KB article Q127022

.WAV File Makes No Sound

You try to play a .WAV file and don't hear any sound. This problem occurs if you are using a Digital ES1888 sound card, which may cause a DMA conflict in your computer.

Solution

Contact Digital to inquire about the availability of a fix for this problem or to ask for an updated Basic Input/Output System (BIOS) for your sound card.

Related KB article Q188161

.WAV Files Don't Play or Multimedia Tool Displays Unusual Characters

You try to use Wave (.WAV) files, but they won't play in Windows. Also, when you view Multimedia properties (using the Multimedia Control Panel), unusual characters might be displayed. This behavior can be caused by VxD files installed by FreeTel.

Solution

To enable Windows sounds, follow these steps:

1. In any text editor (such as Notepad or Sysedit), open the SYSTEM.INI file, which is in the WINDOWS folder.

2. Locate the following lines in the [386ENH] section of the file:

```
Device=c:\Freetel\Freetel1.vxd

Device=c:\Freetel\Freetel2.vxd
```

3. Disable these lines by preceding each with a semicolon (;).

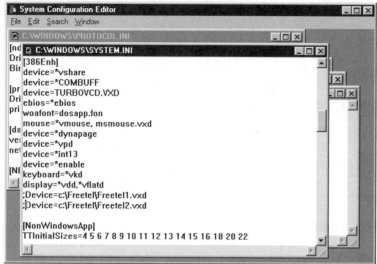

Figure 13-4.   *The SYSTEM.INI file in the System Configuration Editor.*

Warning Disabling these lines may affect the functionality of the FreeTel program. Contact FreeTel for information.

4. Save and then close the SYSTEM.INI file.

5. Shut down and restart Windows.

Related KB article Q164233

.WAV Files Don't Play or Play Choppy

After you upgrade to Windows 98, you try to play a Windows sound (.WAV) or other audio file, and the sound is choppy or won't play at all. This behavior is caused by using an incorrect or outdated driver for the sound card. This problem can also stem from a resource conflict (such as a direct memory access [DMA], input/ouput [I/O] address, or interrupt request line [IRQ] conflict).

Solution One

Replace or upgrade an incorrect or old device driver. To do so, follow these steps:

1. Click the Start button, choose Settings, click Control Panel, and then double-click the System icon.

2. Click the Device Manager tab, and then double-click the Sound, Video, And Game Controllers branch to expand it.

3. Click your sound card, and then click Properties.

4. Click the Driver tab, click Update Driver, and then click Next.

5. Click Display A List Of All The Drivers, and then click Next.

6. Click Show All Hardware, select the appropriate manufacturer and model in the Manufacturers and Models boxes, and then click Next. If the appropriate device is not listed, click Have Disk, and install the correct driver from the manufacturer's installation disk. If you receive a message stating that the current driver may be a closer match for your hardware than the driver you have selected, click Yes.

7. Click Next, click Finish, and then click Yes to restart your computer.

Solution Two

Sound problems might also result from resource conflicts. You may be able to resolve such conflicts by following the troubleshooting information in KB article Q184075, "Description of Microsoft System Information (MSINFO32.EXE) Tool."

Related KB article Q192046

Sound Cards

Acer FX-3D Sound Card Behaves Unexpectedly

You upgrade Microsoft Windows 3.1 to Windows 98, and your Acer FX-3D sound card doesn't work. You might also see the following error message when you start Windows 98:

Wave Audio Driver

Alert: The driver 15_16W95.vxd is out of date.

This occurs because the Windows 3.1 sound card drivers are still being loaded from the SYSTEM.INI file. The manufacturer's sound card installation program does not remove these drivers.

Solution

Remove the Windows 3.1 drivers. To do so, follow these steps:

1. Run the FX-3D uninstall program to remove the Windows 3.1 drivers.

2. Click the Start button, choose Settings, and then click Control Panel.

3. Double-click the System icon, and then click the Device Manager tab.

4. Double-click the Sound, Video, And Game Controllers branch to expand it, and then click FX-3D or AD1816. If FX-3D or AD1816 are not listed in the Sound, Video, And Game Controllers branch, check the Other Devices branch.

5. Click Remove.

6. Install the Windows 95 drivers using the disk included with your sound card.

These steps can be applied to any AD1816-based sound card.

Reinstalling the manufacturer-provided Windows 3.1 drivers for the Acer FX-3D sound card doesn't work, because they don't function correctly in Windows 98.

The Acer FX-3D is an Analog Devices AD1816A-based sound card named AcerMagic FX-3D. The FX-3D sound card includes both Windows 3.1 and Windows 95 drivers.

If you perform a clean installation of Windows 98, the sound card is detected as an Analog Devices sound card and is added to the Other Devices branch in Device Manager because Windows does not include drivers for it. If that happens, install the manufacturer-provided Windows 95 drivers.

Related KB article Q188171

AWE Control Tool Doesn't Display .SBK or .SF2 Sound Files

You attempt to open a sound bank (.SBK) or sound font (.SF2) file using the AWE Control tool by clicking SFont Bank (*.SBK, *.SF2) in the List Files Of Type box and then clicking the drive or folder in which the file is located, and the file isn't displayed. This can happen if you are using the AWE Control tool included with a Creative Labs Sound Blaster AWE64, Sound Blaster AWE64 Gold, Sound Blaster AWE64 Value, or Sound Blaster AWE32 sound card. Microsoft has confirmed that this behavior is not caused by a problem in Windows 98, but may be caused by design changes in Windows 98.

Solution

Click All Files (*.*) in the List Files Of Type box.

Related KB article Q186744

Aztech Rocky II Sound Card Wrongly Identified

You run the Add New Hardware Wizard to install an Aztech Rocky II sound card, and the sound card is incorrectly detected as a Sound Blaster Pro sound card. This occurs because the Aztech Rocky II sound card is Sound Blaster–compatible in MS-DOS. Because of this, Windows might incorrectly detect it as a Sound Blaster Pro (or compatible) and install the Sound Blaster Pro drivers.

Solution

To solve this problem, follow these steps:

1. Click the Start button, choose Settings, click Control Panel, and then double-click the System icon.

2. Click the Device Manager tab, double-click the Sound, Video, And Game Controller branch, click Sound Blaster Pro, and then click Properties.

3. Click the Driver tab, click Update Driver, and then click Next.

4. Click Display A List Of All The Drivers In A Specific Location, So You Can Select The Driver You Want, and then click Next.

5. Click Show All Hardware, select Aztech Labs in the Manufacturers box, select Aztech 2316 Compatible Legacy Audio (WDM) in the Models box, and then click Next.

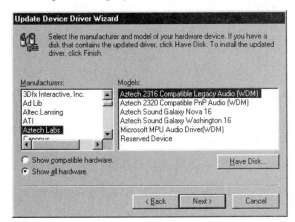

Figure 13-5. *The Update Device Driver Wizard dialog box.*

Note If you receive a message stating that the driver that you are installing was not written specifically for the selected hardware, click Yes.

6. Click Next, click Finish, and then click Yes to restart your computer.

Related KB article Q185793

CD Sound Quality Is Poor

You listen to a sound file or a CD on Windows, and the sound quality is poor.

Windows sets the detected sound card as the preferred device by default, but this device might not deliver the best sound quality.

Solution

Change the device that Windows uses to play sounds. To do so, follow these steps:

1. Click the Start button, choose Settings, and click Control Panel.

2. Double-click the Multimedia icon.

3. Click the Audio tab, and select the device you want in the Preferred Device boxes.

4. Select the Use Only Preferred Devices check box.

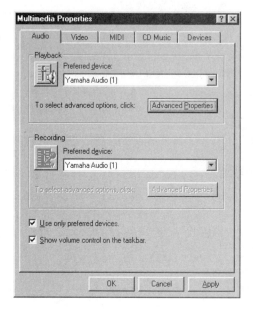

Figure 13-6. *The Multimedia Properties dialog box.*

5. Click OK.

Related KB article Q142006

ES1788 or ES688 Sound Card Not Detected

You install an ES1788 or an ES688 sound card, but Windows doesn't detect it, because it's not a Plug and Play device.

Solution

Use the Add New Hardware tool in Control Panel to manually install the device. To do so, follow these steps:

1. Click the Start button, choose Settings, and then click Control Panel.

2. Double-click the Add New Hardware icon to start the Add New Hardware Wizard.

3. Click Next, and then click Next.

4. Click No, I Want To Select The Hardware From A List, and then click Next.

5. In the Manufacturers box, select ESS Technology, Inc.

6. In the Models box, select ESS AudioDrive, click Next, and then click Next.

7. Restart Windows when you are prompted.

Related KB article Q181748

Media Vision 3D Sound Card Mixer Settings Do Not Work

You try to adjust volume settings in the sound mixer, but the Media Vision 3D sound card does not respond to slider movements.

Solution

Change the I/O address for the sound card to 220. To do this, contact the manufacturer or read the sound card's documentation. After you change the I/O address, remove the sound card in Device Manager, and then use the Add New Hardware Control Panel to redetect the sound card.

To remove the sound card in Device Manager, follow these steps:

1. Click the Start button, choose Settings, and then click Control Panel.

2. Double-click the System icon, and click the Device Manager tab.

3. Click Media Vision 3D sound card, and click Remove.

4. Click OK, and close the program.

To add the sound card, follow these steps:

1. Click the Start button, choose Settings, and then click Control Panel.

2. Double-click the Add New Hardware icon.

3. Follow the wizard's steps.

Related KB article Q137642

Multimedia Tool Displays Device Driver Information Instead of Settings

You attempt to view the settings for a device in the Multimedia tool, and driver information is displayed instead of the device settings. For example, if you click a device on the Devices tab in the Multimedia Properties dialog box, click Properties, and then click Settings, you might see the following information:

Creative Audio Driver (English)

Version 4.31.00

Copyright (c) Creative Technology Ltd 1994-1996

Audio Driver Team

This problem occurs if you are using Sound Blaster or Sound Blaster–compatible sound card drivers, and you attempt to view the settings for a device located under any of the following branches:

- Audio Devices

- MIDI Devices and Instruments

- Mixer Devices

- Line Input Devices

Microsoft has confirmed this to be a problem in Windows 98.

Solution

View the settings for your sound card using Device Manager. To do so, follow these steps:

1. Click the Start button, choose Settings, and click Control Panel.

2. Double-click the System icon, and then click the Device Manager tab.

3. Double-click the Sound, Video, And Game Controllers branch to expand it, click your sound card, and then click Properties. Each tab displays different settings for your sound card.

Related KB article Q185831

Mwave Device Doesn't Work Properly

You use a computer or peripheral based on the IBM Mwave chip and experience trouble with features supplied by the chip.

Solution

The HARDWARE.TXT file located in your WINDOWS folder describes specific steps you can take to solve these problems. To view the HARDWARE.TXT file, click the Start button, click Run, enter *Hardware.txt* in the text box, and then click OK.

Related KB article Q191480 or HARDWARE.TXT in your WINDOWS folder

Roland RAP-10 Sound Card Not Detected

Windows Setup does not detect a Roland RAP-10 sound card configured for base I/O address 330h.

The RAP-10 sound card has additional features not supported by standard Windows drivers. Either manually install the device by using the Add New Hardware tool in Control Panel, or change the device's base address and then run the Add New Hardware Wizard to detect and install the device.

Solution One

To manually install the device, follow these steps:

1. Click the Start button, choose Settings, and then click Control Panel.

2. Double-click the Add New Hardware icon.

3. Click Next, click No, and then click Next.

4. Double-click the Sound, Video, and Game Controllers icon.

5. Click Have Disk.

6. Insert the sound card driver disk in your disk drive.

7. Enter the drive address and driver name in the text box, and click OK.

8. Click OK.

Solution Two

To change the device's base address, consult your sound card's documentation. After changing the address, run the Add New Hardware Wizard by following these steps:

1. Click the Start button, choose Settings, and then click Control Panel.

2. Double-click the Add New Hardware icon.

3. Click Next, click Yes, and then click Next.

4. Click Yes when prompted to restart Windows.

Related KB article Q134559

Sound Blaster 16 Sound Card Causes Error Message

You upgrade Microsoft Windows 3.x to Windows 98 on a computer with a Creative Labs Sound Blaster 16 sound card installed, and you receive the following error messages when your computer starts:

Driver Unit Number = 0

Error CTSOUND1008: Invalid "/BLASTER=A:xxx" argument

Error: DIGN8002 The BLASTER environment settings are invalid

This problem occurs when Plug and Play configuration drivers for the Sound Blaster 16 sound card are being loaded from the AUTOEXEC.BAT and CONFIG.SYS files.

Solution

To solve this problem, follow these steps:

1. Click the Start button, click Run, enter *msconfig* in the Open box, and then click OK.

2. Click the Autoexec.bat window, and then type *rem* in front of the line that loads the Sound Blaster driver. For example, the line in your AUTOEXEC.BAT file might be similar to c:\vibra16\diagnose /s /w=c:\windows.

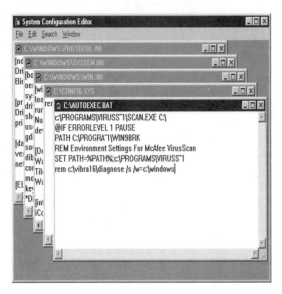

Figure 13-7. *The Autoexec.bat window in the System Configuration Editor.*

3. Click the Config.sys window, and then type *rem* in front of the line that loads the Sound Blaster driver. For example, the line in your CONFIG.SYS file might be similar to device=c:\vibra16\drv\vibra16.sys /unit=0 /blaster=a:220 i:10 d:3 h:7.

4. Choose Save from the File menu, close the program, and then restart your computer when you are prompted to do so.

Related KB article Q190171

Video

ActiveMovie 2.0 Does Not Display Video

You attempt to view a video file using ActiveMovie 2.0 and can hear audio and see the progress indicator move, indicating that the video is being played, but the video isn't displayed. This happens if you maximize the ActiveMovie window while the video file is being loaded.

Solution

Wait for the video file to load completely before you maximize the ActiveMovie window. If the ActiveMovie window is currently maximized, click the Restore button (the middle button in the upper right corner of the ActiveMovie window), and then maximize the window once the video file is completely loaded, and the video starts playing.

In ActiveMovie 1.0, the maximize button remains unavailable until the video file is completely loaded.

Related KB article Q186917

Digital Video Capture Device Doesn't Capture

You use a digital video capture device and can't use the capture feature.

This problem occurs when you use an Adaptec AHA-8940 1394 PCI host adapter and the Windows 98 driver for it.

Solution

Replace the Windows 98 driver with the Adaptec driver provided with the host adapter.

To remove the Windows 98 driver, follow these steps:

1. Click the Start button, choose Settings, and then click Control Panel.

2. Double-click the System icon, and then click the Device Manager tab.

3. Double-click the SCSI Controllers branch to expand it, and then click Adaptec AHA-8940 1394 PCI Host Adapter.

4. Click Remove, click OK, and then click Yes.

For information about how to install Adaptec drivers, consult the manufacturer or the host adapter's documentation.

Related KB article Q192172

Digital Video Playback from CD-ROM Jerky

You play digital video files from a CD-ROM and find frames are being dropped, resulting in jerky playback.

Solution

To smooth the playback, optimize the caching of the CD-ROM drive. First, however, you must determine if you are using a real-mode or a protected-mode driver to access the CD-ROM drive. To do so, follow these steps:

1. Click the Start button, choose Settings, and then click Control Panel.

2. Double-click the System icon.

3. Click the Device Manager tab.

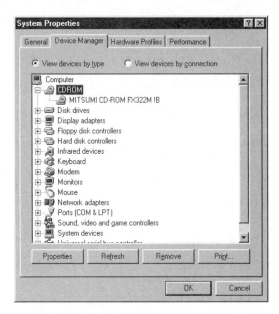

Figure 13-8. *The Device Manager tab in the System Properties dialog box.*

If a CD-ROM branch is listed, you are using protected-mode drivers. To optimize CD-ROM data caching using protected-mode drivers, follow these steps:

1. Click the Start button, choose Settings, and then click Control Panel.

2. Double-click the System icon.

3. Click the Performance tab, and then click File System.

4. Click the CD-ROM tab, and then select the appropriate speed for your CD-ROM drive in the Optimize Access Pattern For box.

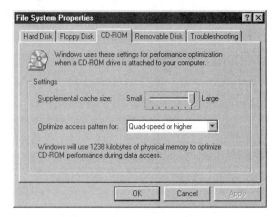

Figure 13-9. *The CD-ROM tab in the File System Properties dialog box.*

Note Selecting a speed that is faster than appropriate for your CD-ROM drive does not increase performance.

5. Be sure that the Supplemental Cache Size slider is set all the way to the right (the Large setting), and then click OK.

To optimize CD-ROM data caching using real-mode drivers, follow these steps:

1. Click the Start button, choose Settings, and then click Control Panel.

2. Double-click the System icon.

3. Click the Performance tab, and then click File System.

4. Click the CD-ROM tab, and then click the down arrow to open the Optimize Access Pattern For list.

5. Select No Read-Ahead, and then click OK.

If optimizing CD-ROM drive caching doesn't result in smoother video file playback, consider the following:

- Reduce the video hardware acceleration. For information about doing this, see KB article Q127139, "Troubleshooting Video Problems in Windows 95."

- Add RAM to your computer system.

- Upgrade to a faster CD-ROM drive.

- Upgrade to a faster video card.

Related KB article   Q149705

Mwave Sound Cards Cause Error Message When Playing .AVI Files

You play audio-video interleave (.AVI) files on an IBM Aptiva 2168-A92 or Acer computer with an outdated Mwave sound card driver and receive any of the following error messages:

> *A fatal exception 0E has occurred at 0028:<XXXXXXXX> in Vxd Vmwaudio*
>
> *(01)*
>
> *MMSYSTEM257 Invalid MCI device ID. Use the ID returned when opening the MCI device.*
>
> *MMSYSTEM296 The file cannot be played on the specified MCI device. The file may be corrupt, or not in the correct format.*

Solution

Contact IBM or Acer to inquire if an Mwave sound card driver update is available for your computer.

Related KB article   Q191195

QuickTime Version 1.1 or 2.0 Causes Errors Playing .MOV file

You install QuickTime version 1.1 or 2.0 for Windows, and you experience one of the following problems when you try to play an .MOV (video) file:

- A white line appears across the center of the screen.

- Two mouse pointers appear. The second pointer is stationary.

- Video scenes do not play correctly or do not appear at all.

- You play a video scene, and the display is corrupted when you move the mouse pointer over the video scene.

When you run the QuickTime for Windows (QTW) Setup program, QTW detects the video hardware and tries to program the hardware directly. If you are using a video adapter that uses the S3 chip set, the problems listed above occur.

Solution

Use a text editor such as Notepad to edit the QTW.INI file in the WINDOWS folder and add the following line to the [Video] section of the file:

Optimize=Driver

If the file has no [Video] section, add the section and the line listed above. The section should look like the following example:

[Video]

Optimize=Driver

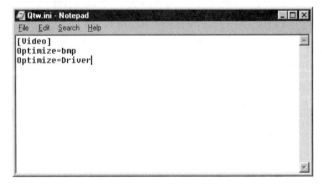

Figure 13-10.   *The QTW.INI file.*

Save the QTW.INI file, and then close it.

Related KB article Q126565

Video for Windows 1.1 Doesn't Work with Analog Video Capture Device

Programs that use the Microsoft Video for Windows 1.1 (VFW) interface cannot directly communicate with analog video capture devices that use the Windows Driver Model (WDM) video capture interfaces in Windows 98. Such analog capture devices can include PCI adapters with video decoder chips that use WDM drivers. This problem occurs because the VFW WDM Mapper files included with Windows 98 don't allow WDM-based analog capture devices to be used with the VFW 1.1 interface.

Solution

A supported fix that corrects this problem is now available from Microsoft but has not been fully regression tested and should be applied only to computers experiencing this specific problem. To resolve this problem immediately, contact Microsoft Technical Support to obtain the fix. If you are not severely impacted by this specific problem, Microsoft recommends that you wait for the next service pack that contains this fix.

For a complete list of Microsoft Technical Support phone numbers and information on support costs, please go to the following address on the World Wide Web:

http://support.microsoft.com/support/supportnet/default.asp

Related KB article Q192112

Video Media Causes Computer to Hang

You play video media, such as a DVD title, video clip (.AVI file), or movie clip (.MPEG file), and the computer stops responding to mouse and keyboard input, and the video media stops playing.

This problem occurs under the following conditions:

- Your video adapter uses hardware acceleration to play video media through the use of a video overlay. This is typically the case with DVD decoder hardware.

- Windows displays a system-modal dialog (message) box. When a system-modal dialog box is displayed, clicking any other window does not produce any response until the system-modal dialog box is closed.

The following actions cause a system-modal dialog box to display:

- You press Ctrl+Alt+Delete to open the Close Program dialog box.

- If the DVD or CD-ROM drive supports Media Event Status Notification (MESN), you press the Eject button on the DVD or CD-ROM drive while you are playing a DVD title or other files from the DVD or CD-ROM disc.

Under these conditions, video overlay produced by the video hardware is displayed on top of the system-modal dialog box. If the video frame covers the center portion of the screen, where a system-modal dialog box is typically displayed, it may completely cover the dialog box so that the dialog box cannot be seen.

Even though the system-modal dialog box is not visible on the screen in this case, it still accepts keyboard and mouse input if the correct keys are pressed, or if the mouse is clicked in the correct areas of the screen.

Solution One

You can cause the system-modal dialog box to appear on the screen by pressing Alt+Spacebar. Then you can read the message and click the appropriate button.

Solution Two

You can close the dialog box by pressing Alt+F4.

Solution Three

You can close the dialog box by pressing Esc, which is typically assigned to a Cancel button in the dialog box.

Solution Four

You can close the dialog box by pressing Enter, which activates the default button (typically the OK button).

Solution Five

You can close the dialog box by pressing the Spacebar, which activates the button that is currently selected (typically the OK button) in the dialog box.

Note You may be able to prevent this problem from occurring by adjusting the Hardware Acceleration settings for the graphics hardware.

Related KB article Q192809

Volume Control

Game Plays Sound Effects but Not Background Music

You upgrade to Windows 98 and notice that some games play sound effects but not background music.

Solution

To solve this problem, follow these steps:

1. Click the Start button, click Run, enter *sysedit* in the Open box, and then click OK.

2. Click the System.ini window, andscroll down to the Drivers section.

3. Type a semicolon (;) in front of the following items:

   - midi1=sxgb.drv

   - wave1=sxgb.drv

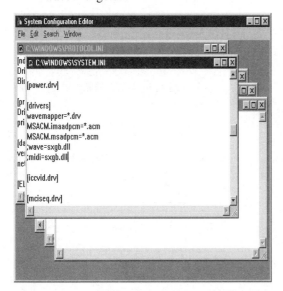

Figure 13-11.   *The System.ini window in the System Configuration Editor.*

4. Choose Save from the File menu and then close the program.

5. Restart the computer.

Related KB article Q190913

MIDI Mute Check Box Unavailable

You install DirectX 5.0 and find the Mute check box under MIDI (Musical Instrument Digital Interface) in the Volume Control tool is unavailable. This problem occurs if you are using a sound card with a Mixer chip found on some models of Creative Technology Ltd. sound cards.

Solution

In the Volume Control tool, move the Volume slider under MIDI all the way down.

The Mute check box under MIDI is available when you use older drivers for these sound cards, but the drivers actually implement a virtual MIDI playback mute by turning the MIDI volume down to zero. With these sound cards, if MIDI playback is muted and you attempt to record a MIDI file, no sound is recorded. However, it is possible to mute the playback volume of other devices (for example, CD Audio) without affecting the volume of the recording from those devices.

Related KB article Q173967

Volume Changes on ESS 1887 Sound Card Don't Stick

You change the playback volume level on an ESS 1887 sound card and restart your computer only to find the volume level back at its original setting. This problem occurs, because the ESS Record Waveout volume control saves its volume level information in the Registry, overwriting the standard Windows volume control information.

Solution

Use the Record Waveout volume control to adjust both playback and record volume settings.

Related KB article Q188179

Volume Control Not Available

You install Windows and find Volume Control isn't available. Tools such as Volume Control are installed based on the hardware detected during the installation of Windows. If the computer contains an ISA Plug and Play device that is not turned on by the BIOS, the device is not detected until after Windows is installed.

Solution One

Use the Custom Setup option when you install Windows. When you are prompted to select components, select Volume Control in the Multimedia section.

Solution Two

If Windows is already installed, follow these steps:

1. Click the Start button, choose Settings, click Control Panel, and double-click the Add/Remove Programs icon.

2. Click the Windows Setup tab, click Multimedia, and then click Details.

3. Select the Volume Control check box.

Figure 13-12.   *The Multimedia dialog box in the Add/Remove Programs tool.*

4. Click OK twice.

Related KB article Q163886

C H A P T E R   1 4

Starting Windows 98

Computer Stops Responding

Adaptec AHA-2940U2W Adapter and CD-RW Drive Cause Windows to Hang

You start Windows with an Adaptec AHA-2940U2W SCSI adapter with a SCSI CD-ROM Re-Writable (CD-RW) drive attached, and Windows stops responding (hangs). The reason is that the AIC78U2.MPD driver file included with the Adaptec AHA-2940U2W SCSI adapter is not completely compatible with Windows 98.

Solution

Download the 7800W9X.EXE file from the Adaptec web site. This self-extracting executable file contains updated drivers for the Adaptec AHA-2940U2W SCSI adapter.

Related KB article Q188810

ATI AGP Rage Pro Display Adapter Causes Computer to Hang

You try to start your computer, and your computer stops responding if an ATI AGP Rage Pro display adapter is installed.

Solution One

Disable your display adapter's hardware acceleration by following these steps:

1. Click the Start button, choose Settings, click Control Panel, and double-click the Display icon.

2. Click Advanced on the Settings tab, click the Performance tab, drag the slider to the None setting, click OK, and restart your computer if you are prompted.

Solution Two

Contact ATI to inquire about the availability of a fix or a Basic Input/Output System (BIOS) update.

Related KB article Q188163

External SCSI Device Connection Causes Computer to Hang

You attempt to start your Windows-based computer after connecting an external Small Computer System Interface (SCSI) device, and your computer stops responding (hangs) at the Windows logo screen. This behavior can occur if your computer contains a SCSI adapter with two internal ports and an external port and devices are connected to both internal ports.

Solution

Disconnect the external SCSI device and then restart your computer. For information about how to reconfigure your SCSI devices to avoid the external port, see the documentation included with your computer or SCSI adapter, or contact the computer's or adapter's manufacturer.

Related KB article Q193242

Logo Screen Spurs Computer Hang

You start Windows, and your computer stops responding (hangs) after the Windows logo screen is displayed. (Windows starts properly if you press and hold down the Ctrl key.) This problem can be caused by the following:

- An antivirus program warning screen might be hidden behind the Windows logo screen. This problem occurs if Windows is loading an antivirus program from the AUTOEXEC.BAT file to automatically check for a virus. The antivirus program detects that the COMMAND.COM file has changed as a result of the Windows installation and pauses the system to inform you and receive further instructions. To determine whether antivirus software is running, press the Esc key to close the Windows logo screen. This condition might occur with the following antivirus programs:

  - Microsoft Anti-Virus

  - Norton AntiVirus

  - Central Point Anti-Virus

- The display adapter installed in your computer is not properly handling the video mode switching that occurs when the Windows logo screen is displayed. This video mode switching does not occur when you choose Step-By-Step Confirmation from the StartUp menu because the Windows logo screen is not displayed. This problem is known to occur with the ATI Graphics Ultra Pro (Mach32) display adapter.

Solution One

If antivirus software is running, press the Esc key to close the Windows logo screen. If possible, choose the option that allows the program to update any affected files. This action prevents the pause from occurring when you start Windows.

Solution Two

Disable the logo screen. Add the line *Logo=0* to the [Options] section of the MSDOS.SYS file in the root folder of the physical boot drive.

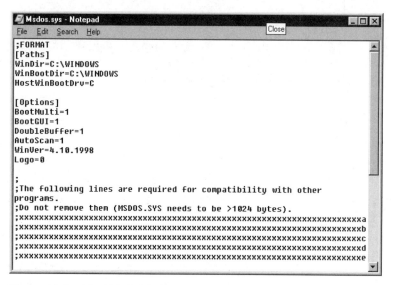

Figure 14-1. *The MSDOS.SYS file in Notepad.*

This method permanently prevents the logo screen from being displayed.

Solution Three

If disabling the logo screen solves the problem, you might be able to reconfigure the display adapter. Contact your display adapter's manufacturer for additional information.

Related KB article Q150516

Missing Device Reported or Windows Hangs at Logo Screen

You try to load Windows, and one of the following problems occurs: Either Windows stops responding (hangs) at the logo screen, or Windows reports the following error message:

Missing <device name> (where <device name> is a device such as HIMEM.SYS).

Make sure that the file is in your Windows folder and that its location is correctly specified in your CONFIG.SYS file.

These problems can occur if you have added the NOAUTO parameter to the dos= statement in the CONFIG.SYS file. For example:

```
DOS=HIGH,UMB,NOAUTO
```

This parameter can also cause your computer to hang at the first setup reboot because IFSHLP.SYS is not loaded.

Solution One

Remove the NOAUTO parameter from the dos= statement in the CONFIG.SYS file.

Figure 14-2. *The Config.sys tab of the System Configuration Utility.*

Solution Two

Add the required device= statements in the CONFIG.SYS file so that the necessary devices are loaded during startup.

Related KB article Q116253

POPDOS.EXE Causes Computer to Hang

You load the POPDOS.EXE Terminate-and-Stay-Resident (TSR) program in the AUTOEXEC.BAT file, and your computer stops responding when you start Windows.

POPDOS.EXE functions properly only if it is loaded at the top of conventional memory.

Solution One

Run POPDOS.EXE from an MS-DOS prompt in Windows, or run POPDOS.EXE in MS-DOS mode.

Solution Two

Prevent COMMAND.COM and DBLSPACE.BIN from loading at the top of conventional memory by following these steps:

1. Right-click the Start button, and choose Explore.

2. Choose Find from the Tools menu, and click Files Or Folders.

3. Enter *msdos.sys* in the text box, and click Find Now.

4. Right-click the MSDOS.SYS file icon, and choose Properties from the shortcut menu.

5. Clear the Read-Only and Hidden check boxes, and click OK.

6. Click the Start button, choose Programs, choose Accessories, and click WordPad.

7. Choose Open from the File menu, enter *msdos.sys* in the File Name text box, and click Open.

8. Add the line *LoadTop=0* to the [Options] section of the file.

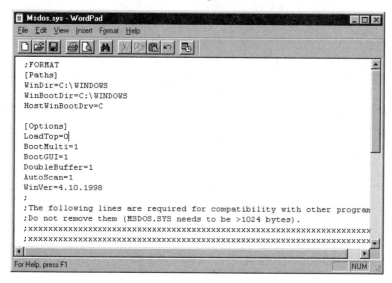

Figure 14-3.   *The MSDOS.SYS file in WordPad.*

9. Choose Save from the File menu, and close the program.

10. Return to Windows Explorer, and right-click the MSDOS.SYS file.

11. Choose Properties from the shortcut menu, select the Read-Only and Hidden check boxes again, and click OK.

12. Reboot your computer.

Related KB article Q134516

Toshiba Tecra 750 Computer Hangs

You start Windows 98, and your Toshiba Tecra 750 computer stops responding. This problem can occur if all the following conditions exist:

- Your computer contains an integrated drive electronics (IDE) CD-ROM drive.

- The IDE controller to which the CD-ROM drive is connected is using the driver included with Windows 98.

- You enable direct memory access (DMA) support for the CD-ROM drive.

This problem is caused by the IDE chip set used by Toshiba Tecra 750 computers.

Solution

To solve this problem, follow these steps:

1. Turn off your computer.

2. Remove the CD-ROM drive from your computer.

3. Restart your computer.

4. Install the Toshiba drivers for the IDE controller. If you do not have the drivers on a floppy disk, obtain them from Toshiba Technical Support or the Toshiba web site.

5. Shut down your computer.

6. Put the CD-ROM drive back in your computer.

7. Restart your computer.

For additional information or to inquire about the availability of an updated IDE chip set, contact Toshiba Technical Support.

Related KB article Q188195

Unrecoverable Page Fault Error Message and Computer Hangs

Your computer has a Hauppage Win/TV card installed, and your computer stops responding with an *Unrecoverable Page Fault* error message when you start Windows. This problem can occur if older S3 video adapter drivers are installed on your computer. Some older versions of the drivers for S3-based chip sets have compatibility problems with the drivers for the Win/TV hardware.

Solution

Install the Windows 98 S3 drivers or the most current drivers provided by your display adapter's manufacturer by following these steps:

1. Restart your computer. After your computer completes the Power On Self Test (POST), press and hold down the Ctrl key until you see the Windows 98 StartUp menu, and then choose Safe Mode.

2. Click the Start button, choose Settings, and click Control Panel.

3. Double-click the Display icon, click the Settings tab, and click OK.

4. Restart Windows normally.

5. Click the Start button, choose Settings, and click Control Panel.

6. Double-click the Display icon, click the Settings tab, and click Advanced.

7. Click the Adapter tab, and click Change.

8. Click Next, select the Display A List Of All The Drivers In A Specific Location So You Can Select The Driver You Want option, and click Next.

9. Click Show All Devices.

10. Select S3 in the Manufacturers box.

11. Select the appropriate model in the Models box, click OK, and click Next.

12. Click Next, click Next again, and click Finish.

13. Click Close, click Close again, and click Yes to restart your computer.

If these steps do not correct the problem, contact your display adapter's manufacturer for information about obtaining an updated Windows 98 driver.

Related KB article Q188160

XMS Cache Problem

You start Windows, and your computer stops responding and you receive the following error message:

XMS Cache Problem. Registry services may be inoperative this session.

This problem can occur if the Registry is too large to fit in memory.

Solution

Use the Windows Registry Checker (SCANREG.EXE) program to restore a copy of your previous Registry by following these steps:

Warning After you complete the following steps, you might have to reinstall some programs.

1. Restart your computer. After your computer completes the Power On Self Test (POST), press and hold down the Ctrl key until you see the Windows 98 StartUp menu, and then choose Safe Mode Command Prompt Only.

2. At the command prompt, type *scanreg /restore*, and then press Enter.

3. Click a Registry that has the word *Started* next to the date, and press Enter.

4. Press Enter to restart your computer.

Related KB article Q194731

Error Messages and General Startup Problems

Advanced Configuration and Power Interface Error Message

You try to start your Windows 98–based computer, and you receive an Advanced Configuration and Power Interface (ACPI) error message on a red screen.

This problem occurs when your computer has a hardware or Basic Input/Output System (BIOS) problem. ACPI error messages on a red screen are generated by a computer's BIOS.

Solution

Contact the manufacturer of your computer's BIOS to inquire about the availability of a fix for this problem.

Related KB article Q189432

Compaq Presario Starts Windows 98 with a Blank Dialog Box

You start Windows 98 on a Compaq Presario, and a dialog box containing no text appears. This problem can occur if the following lines are present in the [Drivers] section of the SYSTEM.INI file:

wave1=<path>\tamaudio.drv

mixer1=<path>\tamaudio.drv

Solution

Edit the SYSTEM.INI file, and disable the line that refers to the audio drivers by following these steps:

1. Click the Start button, choose Run, enter *system.ini* in the box, and click OK.

2. Press F3, enter *tamaudio* in the box, and press Enter.

3. Place a semicolon (*;*) at the beginning of each line that contains the phrase TAMAUDIO.DRV.

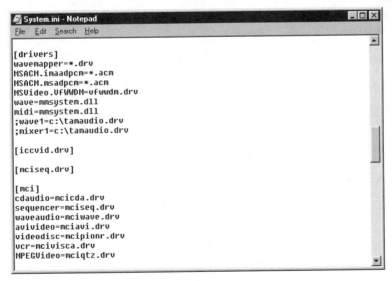

Figure 14-4. *The SYSTEM.INI file in Notepad.*

4. Choose Save from the File menu, and choose Exit from the File menu.

5. Restart your computer.

Related KB article Q191604

Display Blank or Unreadable

You start Windows and see nothing onscreen, or what you see is unreadable.

Solution

To solve this problem, follow these steps:

1. Restart your computer. After your computer completes the Power On Self Test (POST), press and hold down the Ctrl key until you see the Windows 98 StartUp menu, and then choose Safe Mode. Windows starts up in VGA mode.

2. Right-click the desktop, and choose Properties from the shortcut menu.

3. Click the Settings tab in the Display Properties dialog box.

4. Click OK. Windows notifies you that it will restart in VGA mode.

5. Click Yes, and restart your computer.

When your computer restarts, it will be running in VGA (640 x 480, 16-color) mode. You can now reset your display settings by right-clicking the desktop, choosing Properties, and clicking Settings. If the resolution you want to select is not available, choose another resolution (anything other than 640 x 480, 16-color), and let Windows restart. The full set of resolutions and color depths is available after you restart your computer.

Related KB article Q188481 or DISPLAY.TXT in your WINDOWS folder

Error Writing to Drive C Error Message

You start Windows 98 and receive the following error message on a blue screen:

Error writing to drive C:

This problem occurs when your computer's BIOS reports the interrupt request (IRQ) routing information incorrectly.

Solution

Disable IRQ steering by following these steps:

1. Restart your computer. After your computer completes the Power On Self Test (POST), press and hold down the Ctrl key until you see the Windows 98 StartUp menu, and then choose Safe Mode.

2. Click the Start button, choose Settings, and click Control Panel.

3. Double-click the System icon, click the Device Manager tab, and double-click the System Devices branch to expand it.

4. Click PCI Bus, and click Properties.

5. Click the IRQ Steering tab.

6. Clear the Use IRQ Steering check box.

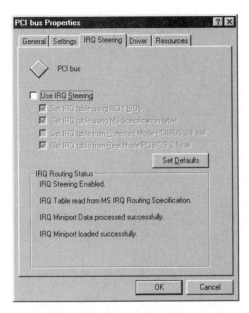

Figure 14-5.   *The PCI Bus Properties dialog box.*

7. Click OK, and click Yes to restart your computer when you are prompted.

Note Contact your computer's manufacturer to inquire about an update to address this problem.

Related KB article Q189000

Explorer Illegal Operation Error Message

You start Windows 98 and see the following error message:

> *Explorer:*
>
> *This program has performed an illegal operation and will be shut down.*
>
> *If the problem persists, contact the program vendor.*

If you click Details, you see the following information:

> *EXPLORER caused an invalid page fault in module EXPLORER.EXE at <address>.*

This problem can occur if the Windows 95 version of the EXPLORER.EXE file is located in the root folder of drive C.

Solution

Rename or delete the EXPLORER.EXE file in the root folder of drive C. For information about how to rename or delete a file, click the Start button, choose Help, click the Index tab, enter *files* in the box, and double-click either the Renaming or the Deleting topic.

Related KB article Q191609

Fatal Exception Error Message

You start Windows 98 and receive the following error message on a blue screen:

A Fatal Exception 0E has occurred at 0028:xxxxx in VXD IOS(04). The current application will be terminated.

This problem occurs when the SB16.VXD file is located in the WINDOWS\SYSTEM\IOSUBSYS folder.

Solution

Rename the SB16.VXD file in the WINDOWS\SYSTEM\IOSUBSYS folder by following these steps:

1. Restart your computer. After your computer completes the Power On Self Test (POST), press and hold down the Ctrl key until you see the Windows 98 StartUp menu, and then choose Safe Mode.

2. Click the Start button, choose Find, and click Files Or Folders.

3. Enter *sb16.vxd* in the Named box, and click Find Now.

4. On the list of found files, right-click the SB16.VXD file, which is located in the WINDOWS\SYSTEM\IOSUBSYS folder, and then choose Rename.

5. Type *sb16.old,* press Enter, and restart your computer.

Related KB article Q192925

Fatal Exception Error Message When Dr. Solomon's Anti-Virus Installed

You start Windows 98 and see the following error message:

Fatal Exception 0028 in VXD HELPWGRD

You see this error message if Dr. Solomon's Anti-Virus is installed on your computer, because Dr. Solomon's Anti-Virus is not compatible with Windows 98.

If Windows 98 Setup detects that Dr. Solomon's Anti-Virus is running, Setup unloads Dr. Solomon's Anti-Virus from memory and disables it so that it does not run when Windows 98 starts. If Setup is unable to detect that Dr. Solomon's Anti-Virus is running, the error message can occur when you attempt to create an emergency boot disk during Setup.

Solution One

Contact Dr. Solomon's to inquire about a possible update that fixes this problem.

Solution Two

Uninstall Dr. Solomon's Anti-Virus by following these steps:

Note If Windows 98 does not start up normally, try to start it in Safe mode. Restart your computer. After your computer completes the Power On Self Test (POST), press and hold down the Ctrl key until you see the Windows 98 StartUp menu, and then choose Safe Mode.

---

1. Click the Start button, choose Settings, click Control Panel, and double-click the Add/Remove Programs icon.

2. Click Dr. Solomon's Anti-Virus, click Add/Remove, and follow the onscreen instructions.

Solution Three

If you are unable to start Windows, rename the HELPWGRD.VXD file by following these steps:

1. Restart your computer. After your computer completes the Power On Self Test (POST), press and hold down the Ctrl key until you see the Windows 98 StartUp menu, and then choose Safe Mode Command Prompt Only.

2. Type the following commands at the command prompt, and press Enter after each line:

```
cd\
```

```
cd windows\system
```

```
ren helpwgrd.vxd helpwgrd.xxx
```

3. Restart Windows.

After you complete these steps, you see the following error message when you start Windows:

Cannot find a device file that may be needed to run Windows.

Helpwgrd.vxd

If you receive this error message, references to the HELPWGRD.VXD file might be in either the [386Enh] section of the SYSTEM.INI file or the Registry. To remove these references, follow these steps:

1. Click the Start button, and choose Run.

2. Enter *sysedit* in the Open box, and click OK.

3. Click the System.ini window.

4. Type in a semicolon (;) in front of the Device=Helpwgrd.vxd line if it exists.

5. Choose Save from the File menu, close the program, and restart your computer.

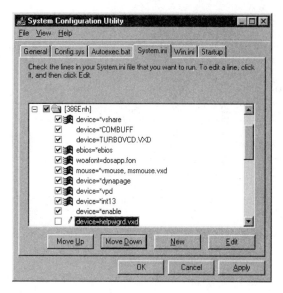

Figure 14-6. *The System.ini window of the System Configuration Editor.*

6. If you still receive the error message, use Registry Editor to remove the following Registry key:

```
HKEY_LOCAL_MACHINE\System\CurrentControlSet\Services\VXD\HELPWGRD
```

Warning Please read the Introduction for information about how to safely edit the Registry.

7. Click the Start button, choose Run, and enter *regedit* in the Run box. Click OK.

8. Navigate your way through the folders in the left pane until you locate the key just described.

9. Remove the Registry key.

10. Close Regedit.

11. Restart Windows.

Related KB article Q189610

GDI.EXE Error Message

You start Windows 98 and receive the following error message:

Error loading GDI.EXE. You must reinstall Windows.

After you receive this error message, your computer stops responding or restarts. This problem also occurs when you start Windows 98 in Safe mode. This problem can occur if you are using a VGA video adapter driver and one or more of the following files is missing or damaged:

```
Vgasys.fon
```

```
Vgaoem.fon
```

```
Vga850.fon
```

Solution

Rename the VGASYS.FON, VGAOEM.FON, and VGA850.FON files in the WINDOWS\FONTS folder, if they exist, and then extract new copies of these files from your original Windows 98 CD-ROM in to the WINDOWS\FONTS folder.

Related KB article Q188094

Illegal Operation Message When Windows Desktop Update Enabled

You start your computer and see the following error message if the Windows Desktop Update component is enabled:

This program has performed an illegal operation and will be shut down. If the problem persists, contact the program vendor.

You click Details and see one of the following messages:

Explorer caused an invalid page fault in module Explorer.exe at <address>.

Explorer caused an invalid page fault in module SHDOCVW.DLL at <address>.

This problem can happen whether you start Windows normally or in Safe mode.

Solution

The SHDOCVW.DLL file is missing, is damaged, or is the wrong version. The SHDOCVW.DLL file for Windows 98 is stamped 4.72.3110.3, 5/11/98, 2,128,000. To add or replace the file, follow these steps:

1. Restart your computer. After your computer completes the Power On Self Test (POST), press and hold down the Ctrl key until you see the Windows 98 StartUp menu, and then choose Command Prompt Only.

2. At the command prompt, type the following command, and then press Enter:

   ```
   ren <drive>:\<windows>\system\shdocvw.dll shdocvw.old
   ```

   where <drive> is the letter of the drive on which the WINDOWS folder is located and <windows> is the name of the folder in which Windows is installed. For example:

   ```
   ren c:\windows\system\shdocvw.dll shdocvw.old
   ```

Note This procedure assumes that you do not already have a SHDOCVW.OLD file on your hard disk. If this file already exists, use a filename extension that is not in use.

3. Extract the SHDOCVW.DLL file from your Windows CD to the WINDOWS\SYSTEM folder. For information, see KB article Q129605, "How to Extract Original Compressed Windows Files."

Note If you are unable to access your CD-ROM drive at a command prompt, load the real-mode CD-ROM driver and real-mode Microsoft CD-ROM Extensions driver (MSCDEX.EXE) in your CONFIG.SYS and AUTOEXEC.BAT files. For more information, see KB article Q135174, "Cannot Access CD-ROM Drive from MS-DOS Mode or Command Prompt."

4. Restart your computer.

Related KB article Q175930

Invalid System Disk Error Message

You boot your computer from startup or reboot in Setup, and you receive the following error message:

Invalid system disk Replace the disk, and then press any key

This problem is caused by one of the following conditions:

- The system is infected with the virus AntiCMOS.A.

- The system is running virus protection software.

- The system is using hard disk management software, such as Disk Manager, EZ-Drive, or Drive Pro.

- Setup was unable to copy the system files to the hard drive.

- Security software has disabled access to drive C.

Solution One

Use an antivirus program to detect and remove the virus, and then reinstall Windows. Boot-sector viruses infect computer systems by copying code to either the boot sector on a floppy disk or the partition table on a hard disk. During startup, the virus is loaded into memory. After the virus is in memory, the virus infects any noninfected disks accessed by the system.

Solution Two

Boot the system by using the Startup disk created during Windows Setup. Use the SYS command from the Startup disk to restore the system files to the hard disk.

Some computers use built-in antivirus software that must be disabled in the computer's CMOS settings. For information about changing CMOS settings, see your computer's documentation or contact the manufacturer.

Solution Three

If your system uses disk-management software, Windows might not in some cases detect disk management software and might overwrite the master boot record (MBR) information. See the documentation for the disk-management software you are using for information about restoring the MBR.

Also, check the SETUPLOG.TXT file for the following statement:

```
FSLog: BIOS Heads=:64:, BootPart Heads=:64:
```

The preceding number (64, in this example) might vary from computer to computer. If these two numbers are different, replace the system files on your hard disk by following these steps:

Warning If you are using Disk Manager or any other disk drive overlay program on a hard disk, make sure that the overlay driver is loaded before you use the SYS command on that hard disk. If the overlay driver is not loaded and you use the SYS command on the hard disk, the drive might not be recognized as being partitioned by the disk drive overlay program, and you can experience a data loss or inability to boot from the drive.

Note Although you can use the SYS command with OnTrack Disk Manager and later versions of MicroHouse EZ-Drive (or EZ-Max) after the overlay driver is loaded, earlier versions such as EZ-Drive 2.01s require operating system files to be copied to the overlay installation disk and installed by the overlay utility. In such cases, the overlay might be damaged if you use the SYS command on the hard disk.

---

1. Boot the system by using the Windows 95 or Windows 98 Startup disk.

2. At the MS-DOS command prompt, type the following lines:

```
c:

cd\windows\command

attrib c:\msdos.sys -s -h -r

copy c:\msdos.sys c:\msdos.xxx

a:

sys c:

attrib c:\msdos.sys -s -h -r

del c:\msdos.sys

copy c:\msdos.xxx c:\msdos.sys

attrib c:\msdos.sys +s +h +r
```

3. Remove the disk and reboot your computer.

Solution Four

If your system has security software enabled, this third-party software might lock access to one or more hard disks. If this software is installed, contact the manufacturer about how to remove it and safely restart Windows 98 Setup.

Related KB article Q128730

Mouse Driver Error Message

You start Windows, and the following error message is displayed in a full-screen MS-DOS window:

The mouse driver for MS-DOS cannot be loaded from an MS-DOS session within Windows. Exit Windows to load the mouse driver for MS-DOS.

After a few seconds, the window closes and Windows continues to load.

This error message occurs when MOUSE.COM or MOUSE.EXE is being loaded in the WINSTART.BAT file rather than in the AUTOEXEC.BAT file.

The WINSTART.BAT file is used to load terminate-and-stay-resident (TSR) programs that are required for Windows-based programs and are not needed in MS-DOS sessions. The WINSTART.BAT file should not be used to set environment variables.

Solution

Use a text editor, such as Notepad, to remove the line that loads the mouse driver from the WINSTART.BAT file in the WINDOWS folder, and then restart your computer.

Related KB article Q141442

Multiboot Warning Message

You start Windows and see the following error message before Windows starts normally:

Warning: Windows Multi-boot may not function correctly. Check for system files in your root directory with conflicting extensions.

This problem can occur if one or more of the following files exists in the root folder of the boot disk:

- AUTOEXEC.DOS
- AUTOEXEC.W40
- COMMAND.DOS
- COMMAND.W40
- CONFIG.DOS
- CONFIG.W40
- MSDOS.DOS
- MSDOS.W40

Solution

Rename the files with .W40 extensions to names with an extension other than .W40. Rename the files with .DOS extensions to names with an extension other than .DOS. When you boot Windows to the previous operating system, it renames the existing AUTOEXEC.BAT, CONFIG.SYS, COMMAND.COM, and MSDOS.SYS files to files with an extension of .W40. It then renames the previous versions of these files from the .DOS extension to the normal extension.

When you boot back into Windows, the AUTOEXEC.BAT, CONFIG.SYS, COMMAND.COM, and MSDOS.SYS files from the previous operating system are renamed with an extension of .DOS, and the .W40 files are renamed to their normal extensions.

These files do not prevent Windows from dual-booting.

Related KB article Q148921

Normal Mode Startup Fails

Windows doesn't boot or you receive an error message, such as a fatal exception or invalid VxD error message, during Windows startup.

Note If you have access to the Internet on another computer, you can use the Windows 98 Startup and Shutdown Troubleshooting Wizard, located at the following URL: *http://support.microsoft.com/support/tshoot/default.asp.*

Solution

If Windows 98 does not start normally, start it in Safe mode, and then step through the following startup process to see whether any devices do not load properly:

1. Restart your computer. After your computer completes the Power On Self Test (POST), press and hold down the Ctrl key until you see the Windows 98 StartUp menu, and then choose Safe Mode.

2. Click the Start button, choose Run, type *msconfig* in the Open text box, and click OK.

3. Click Selective Startup.

4. Try different boot options. To use a boot option, select or clear the appropriate check boxes. Follow the instructions after Table 14-1 to determine the cause of your problem.

Table 14-1. Troubleshooting Startup Options

Option	Boot A	Boot B	Boot C
Process Config.sys file	Yes	No	Yes
Process Autoexec.bat file	Yes	No	Yes
Process Winstart.bat (if available)	Yes	Yes	No
Process System.ini file	No	Yes	Yes
Process Win.ini file	No	Yes	Yes
Load Startup Group items	Yes	Yes	No

Note MSCONFIG cannot disable a file that has the read-only attribute, although it behaves as though it can. Check the properties for your files to make sure that none is set to read-only.

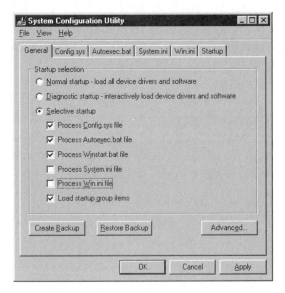

Figure 14-7. *The System Configuration Utility.*

If Windows 98 starts normally using the Boot A option, the SYSTEM.INI or WIN.INI file has a problem. To find which line in the SYSTEM.INI or WIN.INI file is causing the problem, go to step 5.

If Windows 98 starts normally using the Boot B option, Windows startup is failing on a terminate-and-stay-resident (TSR) program or driver loaded from the CONFIG.SYS or AUTOEXEC.BAT file. If Windows 98 starts normally using the Boot C option, Windows startup is failing on a program that is run during startup.

If Windows 98 does not start normally using any of the preceding boot options, Windows startup might be failing on a protected-mode driver, or you might have a Registry problem. Use System File Checker to check for damaged or replaced system files. To start System File Checker, click the Start button, choose Programs, click Accessories, click System Tools, click System Information, and choose System File Checker from the Tools menu.

5. Click the Start button, choose Run, enter *msconfig* in the Open text box, and click OK.

6. Click the WIN.INI tab, double-click the WINDOWS folder, clear the check boxes next to the load= and run= lines, and then click OK.

7. When you are prompted to restart your computer, click Yes.

If your computer starts properly, select the check boxes you cleared one by one, restarting after each one, until the problem reappears. Make a note of the line causing the problem. Select all of the check boxes, and then type a semicolon (;) in front of that line in the WIN.INI file using Notepad or the System Configuration Editor. Restart your computer.

Related KB article Q188867

Normal Mode Startup Fails Because of Loaded Driver or TSR

If Windows fails to start up normally but starts in Safe mode, the problem is a driver or TSR loaded from the CONFIG.SYS or AUTOEXEC.BAT file.

Solution

Determine whether your problem is caused by a driver or TSR in the AUTOEXEC.BAT file or the CONFIG.SYS file by following these steps:

1. Click the Start button, choose Run, type *msconfig* in the Open text box, and click OK.

2. Click Selective Startup, and clear the Process AUTOEXEC.BAT File check box.

3. Click OK, and restart your computer when you are prompted.

If the problem is solved, the problem driver or TSR is loaded from the AUTOEXEC.BAT file. If the problem is not solved, the problem driver or TSR is loaded from the CONFIG.SYS file. To determine which line in the AUTOEXEC.BAT or CONFIG.SYS file is loading the driver or TSR, follow these steps:

1. Click the Start button, choose Run, type *msconfig* in the Open text box, and click OK.

2. Click the AUTOEXEC.BAT or CONFIG.SYS tab, and then clear the check boxes for all non-essential drivers and programs.

Figure 14-8.   *The System Configuration Utility.*

3. Click OK, and restart your computer when you are prompted.

If the problem is solved, follow these steps:

1. Click the Start button, choose Run, type *msconfig* in the Open text box, and click OK.

2. On the AUTOEXEC.BAT or CONFIG.SYS tab, select the first check box in the list.

3. Click OK, and restart your computer when you are prompted.

If the problem is still solved, repeat steps 1–3, but select the next check box on the list. When the problem returns, the last check box you selected is loading the driver or TSR that is causing the problem. To fix your Windows startup problem, enable all of the lines, and then disable the line loading the problem TSR or driver using a text editor such as Notepad. If the line loads a program or driver you need, contact the manufacturer of the program or driver for further assistance.

If the problem is not solved, enable all lines, and then run Windows Registry Checker because the system Registry might have a problem. To start the Windows Registry Checker, click the Start button, choose Programs, click Accessories, click System Tools, click System Information, and choose Registry Checker from the Tools menu.

Related KB article Q188867

Normal Mode Startup Fails Because of Protected Mode Drivers

If Windows fails to start in Normal mode and the cause is not a program run at startup or a TSR or driver loaded from the AUTOEXEC.BAT or CONFIG.SYS, the problem is in a protected-mode driver.

Solution One

Determine whether this is the case by following these steps:

1. Click the Start button, choose Run, type *msconfig* in the Open text box, and click OK.

2. Click Advanced on the General tab.

3. Select a check box under Settings.

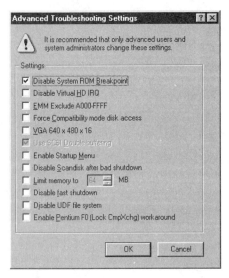

Figure 14-9. *The Advanced Troubleshooting Settings dialog box.*

4. Click OK, click OK again, and restart your computer.

If the problem is not solved, repeat steps 1–4, but select a different check box in step 3. When the problem is solved, the last check box you selected is causing the problem. For more information about advanced settings, see KB article Q181966, "System Configuration Utility Advanced Troubleshooting Settings." After resolving the problem with the checked item, clear the check box to allow your computer to boot normally.

If this process does not solve the problem, disable PCI bus IRQ steering in Windows. To do so, see KB article Q182628, "How to Disable PCI Bus IRQ Steering In Windows." If that does not solve your problem, see Solution Two.

Solution Two

Troubleshoot devices in Device Manager by following these steps:

1. Click the Start button, choose Settings, and click Control Panel.

2. Double-click the System icon.

3. Click the Device Manager tab, and then disable all devices under the following branches:

   - Display adapters
   - Floppy disk controllers
   - Hard disk controllers
   - Keyboard
   - Mouse
   - Network adapters
   - PCMCIA socket
   - Ports
   - SCSI controllers
   - Sound, video, and game controllers

To disable a device in Device Manager, follow these steps:

1. Double-click the branch containing the device you want, click the device, and click Properties.

2. Select the Disable In This Hardware Profile check box on the General tab, and click OK.

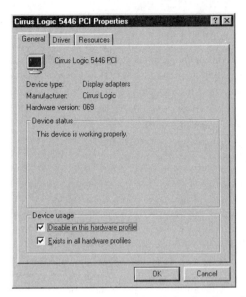

Figure 14-10. *The Properties dialog box for a device.*

3. Restart your computer.

If the problem is solved, enable the devices you disabled in step 3 in the following order, and then verify that no devices are conflicting:

- COM ports

- Floppy disk controllers

- Hard disk controllers

- Other devices

To enable a device and check for possible conflicts, follow these steps:

1. Double-click the branch containing the device you want, click the device, and click Properties.

2. Clear the Disable In This Hardware Profile check box on the General tab.

3. Click the Resources tab, and verify that no conflicts are listed under Conflicting Device List. Note that the Resources tab does not appear for each device.

4. Click OK, and restart your computer.

If the problem is not solved, run Automatic Skip Driver Agent to enable any device that was automatically disabled by the Automatic Skip Driver Agent. To start Automatic Skip Driver Agent, click the Start button, choose Programs, click Accessories, click System Tools, and click System Information. Then choose Automatic Skip Driver Agent from the Tools menu. For information about how to use Automatic Skip Driver Agent, see KB article Q186588.

If you still cannot get Windows to start properly, see Solution Three.

Solution Three

Check for a damaged static virtual device driver (VxD) by following these steps:

1. Restart your computer. After your computer completes the Power On Self Test (POST), press and hold down the Ctrl key until you see the Windows 98 StartUp menu, and then choose Step-By-Step Confirmation.

2. Press Y at each prompt up to and including the *Load all Windows drivers?* prompt, and then press N to respond to everything else, making sure that you write down a list of all the items trying to load after this point.

This process prevents VxDs from loading and VxDs in the WINDOWS\SYSTEM\VMM32 folder from overriding Windows internal VxDs (VxDs built into the VMM32.VXD file). If Windows boots properly, repeat the process, enabling one more driver until Windows no longer starts properly. Then enable all drivers except for the one causing the problem to check that there are no other damaged VxDs, and then use the System File Checker to extract that file from your Windows CD. For more information, see KB article Q129605, "How to Extract Original Compressed Windows Files."

For information about known hardware problems, see the HARDWARE.TXT file in the WINDOWS folder.

For additional troubleshooting assistance, see the BOOTLOG.TXT file in the root folder. The BOOTLOG.TXT file lists the loading status of all real-mode and protected-mode drivers. If Windows 98 does not start properly, the BOOTLOG.TXT file lists the last driver that loaded successfully and lists a *LoadFail* entry for each driver that failed to load before the problem occurred. Note, however, that some *LoadFail* entries in the BOOTLOG.TXT file are normal entries. For a listing of normal *LoadFail* entries in the BOOTLOG.TXT file, see KB article Q127970.

If you cannot solve the problem, contact Microsoft Technical Support.

Related KB article Q188867

Normal Mode Startup Fails Because of Startup Program

If Windows doesn't start in Normal mode, the problem is a result of a program that is run during startup.

Solution One

Determine which program is causing the problem by following these steps:

1. Click the Start button, choose Run, type *msconfig* in the Open text box, and click OK.

2. Click the Startup tab, and clear every check box to disable all startup items.

3. Click OK, and restart your computer when you are prompted.

If the problem is solved, follow these steps:

1. Click the Start button, choose Run, type *msconfig* in the Open text box, and click OK.

2. On the Startup tab, select the first check box in the list to enable that item.

3. Click OK, and restart your computer when you are prompted.

If the problem is still solved, repeat steps 1–3 and select the next check box on the list. When the problem returns, the last check box you selected is loading a program that is preventing Windows 98 from starting normally. Select all check boxes, then delete the program from the Startup folder on the Start menu. If the program is of importance, contact the program's manufacturer for additional assistance.

If you cannot solve the problem, see Solution Two.

Solution Two

A TSR loaded in the WINSTART.BAT file (if the WINSTART.BAT file exists) might also have a problem. Click the Selective Startup option, and clear the Process WINSTART.BAT File check box, if available on the General tab in System Configuration Utility. Click OK, and then restart your computer. If your system starts normally, your WINSTART.BAT file has a problem. To find the line loading the TSR causing the problem, click the Normal Startup opeion in the System Configuration Utility and then follow these steps:

1. Click the Start button, choose Programs, click Accessories, and click Notepad.

2. Choose Open from the File menu, enter *c:\windows\winstart.bat* in the File Name text box, and click OK.

3. Type *rem* in front of every line except the first to disable the lines, and then close Notepad. Click Yes when you're prompted to save your changes.

4. Restart your computer.

If your computer did not restart normally, the problem is in the first line. Type *rem* in front of the first line, and remove the *rem* commands from the rest of the lines to solve the problem.

If your computer restarted normally, remove the *rem* from the next line down and restart your computer. Continue this process until your computer no longer restarts normally. Then replace the last *rem* you removed and delete the remaining *rem* commands to enable your system to run normally. If the command you disabled is important, contact the program's manufacturer for additional assistance.

Related KB article Q188867

Not-Enough-Memory Error When Starting Windows or Windows Programs

You try to start Windows or a program in Windows and receive an error message indicating that it doesn't have enough memory.

Windows or programs in Windows cannot start if your computer does not have enough virtual or real memory. You can increase the virtual memory available to your computer by increasing the free space on the hard drive that contains your swap file.

Solution

Create more free space on your hard drive by deleting unimportant files (from the command prompt in MS-DOS). Follow these steps:

1. Restart your computer. After your computer completes the Power On Self Test (POST), press and hold down the Ctrl key until you see the Windows 98 StartUp menu, and then choose Command Prompt Only.

2. If your swap file is located on drive C:, continue with step 3. Otherwise, type the letter of the drive that contains your swap file (for example, *D:*), and press Enter.

3. At the C: prompt, type *dir* and press Enter. This step tells DOS to display a list of files in the current folder.

4. To delete a file, type *del file.ext*, where *file* is the name of the file you want to delete and *ext* is the file's extension. Be sure to place a space after *del* and a period between the file and its extension.

Note Delete only files that you have created or that you know are of no use. Do not delete any files in the WINDOWS folder.

---

5. To see another folder, type *CD dir* at the command prompt, where *dir* is the name of the folder you want to see.

6. Continue deleting unneeded files in other folders.

7. Reboot your computer.

Related KB article Q132571

Prerelease Version of Windows Expired Error Message

Your computer's date is set to 8/25/98 or later, you are running a beta version of Windows 98, and you see the following error message when you start Windows:

Error: this pre-release version of Windows has expired. Contact your vendor for a new version of Microsoft Windows 98. Press any key to continue.

When you press a key, the following message is displayed:

It's now safe to turn off your computer.

Solution

Change your computer's date by following these steps:

1. Write-protect the Windows 98 Emergency Startup Disk (ESD), and insert it in floppy drive A.

2. Start your computer, and then change your computer's date by using the computer's BIOS setup utility, or go to step 3.

Note For information about using your computer's BIOS setup utility, see your computer's documentation or manufacturer.

---

3. At the command prompt, type *date*, press Enter, type the correct date, and press Enter.

4. At the command prompt, type the line *sys c: a:*, and then press Enter.

5. Remove the ESD, and then restart your computer.

Related KB article Q180014

Protection Error Message

You start Windows and see either of the following error messages:

While initializing device <device name> Windows Protection Error

Windows Protection Error

A Windows Protection Error message indicates that an error occurred while loading a virtual device driver (VxD) before the desktop was loaded. In many cases, the error message indicates which VxD did not load, but in other cases, you might not be able to determine which VxD caused the problem.

Windows Protection Error messages are generated by any of the following conditions:

- A real-mode driver and a protected-mode driver are in conflict.

- The Registry is damaged.

- The WIN.COM or COMMAND.COM file is infected with a virus or is damaged.

- A driver is being loaded from the SYSTEM.INI file for which a protected-mode driver has already been initialized.

- A physical I/O or RAM address conflict exists.

- The CMOS settings for a built-in peripheral device (such as cache settings, CPU timing, hard disks, and so on) are incorrect.

- The Plug and Play feature of your computer's BIOS is not working correctly.

- The system cache or memory is malfunctioning.

- The motherboard is not working properly.

Solution

To solve this problem, follow these steps:

1. Restart your computer. After your computer completes the Power On Self Test (POST), press and hold down the Ctrl key until you see the Windows 98 StartUp menu, and then choose Safe Mode.

2. If the error does not occur in Safe mode, see KB article Q136337, "Troubleshooting Windows 95 Startup Problems."

3. If your computer is Plug and Play, reinstall Windows by using the setup /p I command.

Note For information about installing Windows, see KB article Q129260, "Windows 95 Setup: Description and Troubleshooting Steps."

4. Make sure that your computer's CMOS settings are correct.

Note For information about changing CMOS settings, see your computer's documentation or contact the manufacturer.

5. Install a clean copy of Windows in an empty folder. Choose the Custom installation option and do not let Setup detect the hardware in your computer. Install only a mouse, a VGA video adapter, and a keyboard.

If the error still occurs, it is most likely caused by faulty hardware.

The VxD that is generating the error message can be any VxD—either a default installed VxD or a third-party .386 driver being loaded from the SYSTEM.INI file. If you do not know which driver is causing the error message, create a BOOTLOG.TXT file and check to see which driver was last initialized. That driver is typically the one causing the problem.

Note You might also see a Windows protection error message when you restart Windows after installing a program or making a configuration change. For more information about this problem, see KB article Q157924, "Err Msg: 'IOS Failed to Initialize' on Boot."

Related KB article Q149962

Safe Mode Startup Fails

Windows doesn't boot in Normal mode or in Safe mode, and any of the following conditions is the cause:

- Your computer is infected with a virus.

- Your computer's CMOS settings are incorrect.

- A hardware conflict exists. These conflicts can include, but are not limited to, PCI BIOS settings, IRQ conflicts, redundant COM ports (for example, two COM1 ports or an internal modem set to the same COM port as an existing serial port), and defective RAM chips.

- A setting in the MSDOS.SYS file needs to be changed (for example, the Logo setting should be set to zero).

- You have a compressed drive that is unable to mount a compressed volume (CVF) file.

Solution One

To solve this problem, follow these steps:

1. Perform a virus check on your system.

2. Check your computer's CMOS settings. You might need to contact your computer's manufacturer to verify the settings.

3. Remove any recently installed hardware that might be causing a conflict.

4. Verify that no settings need to be changed in your MSDOS.SYS file. For more information about the MSDOS.SYS file, see KB article Q118579.

5. If you have a compressed drive, make sure that you can mount it. For more information about troubleshooting DriveSpace problems, see KB articles Q133175 and Q130018.

Solution Two

If you are still unable to start Windows 98 in Safe mode, run Windows Registry Checker (SCANREG.EXE) because the system Registry might have a problem. To start Windows Registry Checker, click the Start button, choose Programs, click Accessories, click System Tools, and click System Information. Choose Registry Checker from the Tools menu. For information about the Windows Registry Checker, see KB article Q183887.

Solution Three

If you are still unable to start Windows 98 in Safe mode after using Windows Registry Checker, install Windows 98 in a new, empty folder. This step should establish whether the problem is related to a remnant of the previous operating system (such as a configuration setting) or a hardware problem.

Related KB articles Q188867, Q118579, Q133175, Q130018, Q183887

ScanDisk Error Messages When Computer Not Shut Down Properly

You see one of the following error messages when Windows starts if your computer was not shut down properly or if an error occurs on a hard disk:

Windows was not properly shut down. One or more of your disk drives may have errors on it. Press any key to run ScanDisk on these drives.

One or more of your disk drives may have developed bad sectors. Press any key to run ScanDisk with surface analysis on these drives.

Solution

Press any key to allow ScanDisk to perform the necessary checks on all drives, and then choose to repair any errors that are found.

Note To shut down Windows, click the Start button, choose Shut Down, and click Shut Down. You should not turn off your computer while Windows is running unless the computer has stopped responding to mouse and keyboard input.

Related KB article Q152404

Starting Windows 98 Message Doesn't Appear

You start Windows, you do not see a *Starting Windows 98* message, and you cannot determine when to press the Ctrl key to display the Windows 98 StartUp menu. This problem happens because the prompt has been removed to allow for a faster startup of Windows 98.

Solution

Display the StartUp menu, by pressing and holding down the Ctrl key when your computer starts up.

Note If you press and hold down the Ctrl key when your computer starts, you might receive a keyboard error message. You can safely ignore this message.

If you want the Windows 98 StartUp menu to appear every time you start your computer, follow these steps:

1. Click the Start button, choose Run, enter *msconfig* in the Open box, and press Enter.

Figure 14-11. *The System Configuration Utility.*

2. Click Advanced on the General tab.

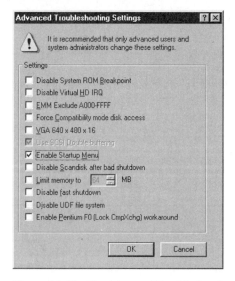

Figure 14-12. *The Advanced Troubleshooting Settings dialog box.*

3. Select the Enable StartUp Menu check box.

4. Click OK, click OK again, and click Yes.

Related KB article Q178548

StartUp Menu Missing Safe Mode with Network Support Command

You start your computer, and the Safe Mode With Network Support command is missing from the Windows 98 StartUp menu. This functionality is not supported in Windows 98.

Solution

Install the real-mode network drivers included with your network adapter. For information, see the documentation included with your network adapter.

Related KB article Q179128

System Registry Error Messages in Normal Mode

You start Windows 98 and see the following error message if you are not starting Windows in Safe mode:

Windows encountered an error accessing the system registry. Windows will restart and repair the system registry for you.

If you then click OK, you see the following error message:

Explorer caused an invalid page fault in module KERNEL32.DLL at 015f:bff711be. This program has performed an illegal operation and will be shut down.

If you then click Details, you see one of the following error messages:

Explorer caused an exception 6d007eh in module explorer.exe at 015f:<memory address>

Error loading Explorer.exe. You must reinstall Windows.

Visual C++ Runtime Library Error. Program C:\<%windir%>\Scanregw.exe, R6016, not enough space for thread data.

Solution

The disk that contains the Windows swap file does not have sufficient free disk space. First, determine which disk contains the swap file, and then increase the free disk space on that disk by following these steps:

1. Restart your computer. After your computer completes the Power On Self Test (POST), press and hold down the Ctrl key until you see the Windows 98 StartUp menu, and then choose Command Prompt Only.

2. At the command prompt, type *dir /s *.swp*, and press Enter. Note the swap-file name, disk letter, folder name, and date. It's usually a single file named WIN386.SWP and located in the root folder (C:\) or the WINDOWS folder (C:\WINDOWS).

3. If your computer has a single hard disk, drive C is the swap file disk; skip to step 9.

4. At the command prompt, type *<letter>:* (where <letter> is the next hard disk letter), and press Enter.

5. Type *dir /s *.swp*, and press Enter. Note the swap-file name, disk letter, folder name, and date.

6. If you have more hard disks to search, repeat steps 4 and 5. If you have no more hard disks to search, continue to step 7.

7. If you find one (or more) swap files on only one hard disk, this disk is the swap file disk; continue to step 8. If you find swap files on multiple hard disks, compare the date of each swap file. The hard disk that contains the swap file with the most recent date is the swap file disk.

8. At the command prompt, type *<letter>:* (where <letter> is the swap file disk letter), and press Enter. Delete each swap file on the swap file disk by following these steps:

9. At the command prompt, type *del <path>\<file name>* (where <path> is the swap file folder and <file name> is the swap file name), and press Enter. For example, type *del windows\win386.swp*.

10. If you have more swap files to delete, repeat step 9. If you have no more swap files to delete, continue to step 11.

11. Increase free disk space on the swap file disk by deleting nonessential files. To do so, type the following commands at the command prompt, pressing Enter after each command:

Warning If you are uncertain whether a file contains critical information, copy the file to a floppy disk before you delete it.

```
dir /w /p /s *.<extension>

del <path>\*.<extension>
```

where <extension> is the file extension of the files you want to delete, and <path> is the folder name containing the files you want to delete.) The following extensions might indicate nonessential files:

.BAK	.GIF	.OLD
.BMP	.HLP	.TMP
.CHK	.JPG	.TXT

12. Test to determine that your computer has sufficient free disk space to start normally. If you cannot start your computer normally, repeat step 11.

Related KB article Q193903

Terminate-and-Stay Resident Programs Not Supported Error Message

You start Windows on a computer that has McAfee BrightWorks version 2.00 installed, and you receive a message which says that Terminate and Stay Resident (TSR) programs are not supported in the Windows NetWare logon script processor.

Solution

This warning is irrelevant and does not cause any problems in running Windows or McAfee BrightWorks. The program the warning refers to is unloaded later in the script; therefore, this program does not affect McAfee BrightWorks.

Related KB article Q134479

TSR Causes Windows to Load Incompatible DOS/16M Module Error Message

You start Windows 98 and receive the following error message:

A TSR caused Windows to load an incompatible version of the DOS/16M interface module. Removing that TSR might make it possible to run Windows.

Solution One

If this message appears when you are running IBM Internet Connection 3.0, which is not compatible with Windows 98, remove or disable the device=dos16m.386 line in the [386Enh] section of the SYSTEM.INI file in the WINDOWS folder by placing a semicolon (;) at the beginning of the line. Then restart Windows 98.

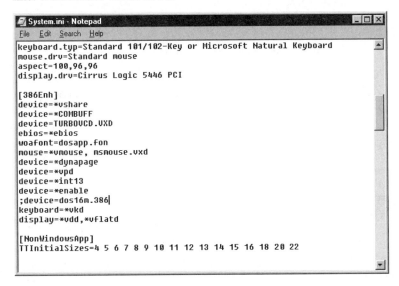

Figure 14-13. *The SYSTEM.INI file in Notepad.*

Solution Two

If TCP.SYS or DOSTCP.SYS is loading in the CONFIG.SYS file, remove or disable the TCP.SYS or DOSTCP.SYS line in the CONFIG.SYS file and then restart your computer.

Solution Three

If the AUTOEXEC.BAT file contains the line *call iicstart.bat*, remove or disable this line in the AUTOEXEC.BAT file and then restart your computer.

Solution Four

If the AUTOEXEC.BAT file contains the line *call startpcs*, remove or disable this line in the AUTOEXEC.BAT file and then restart your computer.

Related KB article Q136890

Unable to Install Java Packages Error Messages

You start your computer and see the following error message four times:

Unable to install java packages. The command line is invalid.

Cannot find file specified - Win32.cab

Cannot find file specified - xmldso4.cab

Cannot find file specified - dajava.cab

Cannot find file specified - osp.zip

This problem can occur for either of the following reasons:

- You used the SYSTEM.1ST file to test or correct problems with the Registry.

- Setup stopped responding, and you restarted your computer.

If you restarted your computer to finish Setup, the Virtual Machine (VM) for Java is functional, and the error message is not displayed after Setup is complete.

Solution One

Restore the original SYSTEM.DAT file.

Solution Two

If you permanently replaced your original SYSTEM.DAT file with the SYSTEM.1ST file, the VM for Java might no longer function. To install it from the Windows 98 CD-ROM, follow these steps:

1. Place the Windows 98 CD-ROM in your CD-ROM drive, click the Start button, choose Find, and click Files Or Folders.

2. Enter *java.inf* in the Named box, click your CD-ROM drive in the Look In box, and click Find Now.

3. Right-click the JAVA.INF file on the list of found files, and choose Install.

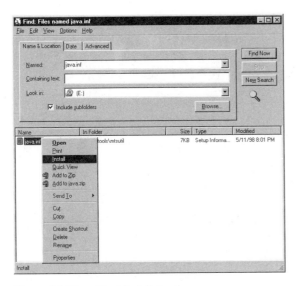

Figure 14-14. *The Find dialog box.*

4. Close Find.

If Windows 98 Setup stops responding (hangs) at RunOnce and you then restart your computer, RunOnce starts again, and the error messages might be displayed. However, VM for Java should already be installed, and after Setup finishes, the *Unable to install java packages* error message should no longer be displayed when you start your computer.

Eight entries in the RunOnceEx key install and register Java class files. The errors are generated because the installation files referenced are no longer available (they were deleted after the original installation).

Related KB articles Q180079 or Q188480 or MTSUTILS.TXT in the TOOLS\MTSULTILS folder on the Windows 98 CD-ROM

VFAT Device Initialization Failed Error Message

You start Windows, and it displays a blue screen and the following error message:

> *VFAT Device Initialization Failed. A device or resource required by VFAT is not present or is unavailable. VFAT cannot continue loading. System halted*

Solution One

This problem might occur because the IFSHLP.SYS file is missing from the WINDOWS folder. If so, extract a new WINDOWS folder.

Solution Two

This problem might occur because the CONFIG.SYS file points to the preceding version of the IFSHLP.SYS file. If so, follow these steps:

1. Restart your computer. After your computer completes the Power On Self Test (POST), press and hold down the Ctrl key until you see the Windows 98 StartUp menu, and then choose Safe Mode Command Prompt Only.

2. Use any text editor, such as EDIT.COM, to open the CONFIG.SYS file.

3. Remove the line that loads IFSHLP.SYS. (Windows automatically loads this driver when you start your computer.)

4. Save and close the CONFIG.SYS file.

5. Restart your computer.

Solution Three

This problem can occur because the IFSHLP.SYS statement was deleted from the CONFIG.SYS file after you reinstalled Windows.

When you're reinstalling Windows, Setup deletes the IFSHLP.SYS statement in the CONFIG.SYS file and does not replace it. Add the IFSHLP.SYS statement to the CONFIG.SYS file, by following these steps:

1. Restart your computer. After your computer completes the Power On Self Test (POST), press and hold down the Ctrl key until you see the Windows 98 StartUp menu, and then choose Safe Mode Command Prompt Only.

2. Use any text editor, such as EDIT.COM, to open the CONFIG.SYS file.

3. Add the following line to the CONFIG.SYS file:

```
device=<drive>:\<windows>\ifshlp.sys
```

where <drive> is the drive containing Windows and <windows> is the WINDOWS folder. For example, if Windows is installed in the WINDOWS folder on drive C, add the following line:

```
device=c:\windows\ifshlp.sys
```

4. Save and then close the CONFIG.SYS file.

5. Restart your computer.

Solution Four

This problem can occur if your computer has an incorrect [Paths] section in the MSDOS.SYS file. To solve this problem, follow these steps:

1. Restart your computer. After your computer completes the Power On Self Test (POST), press and hold down the Ctrl key until you see the Windows 98 StartUp menu, and then choose Safe Mode Command Prompt Only.

2. Type the following line at the command prompt:

```
attrib -s -h -r msdos.sys
```

3. Use any text editor, such as EDIT.COM, to open the MSDOS.SYS file.

4. Verify that the following lines in the MSDOS.SYS file are correct:

```
[Paths]

WinDir=<Windows>

WinBootDir=<Windows>

HostWinBootDrv=C
```

where <Windows> is the folder containing Windows. Note that if you are using disk-compression software (such as DriveSpace), you must change the drive letter in the HostWinBootDrv= line to the drive letter of the host drive.

5. Save and then close the MSDOS.SYS file.

6. Type the following line at the command prompt:

```
attrib +s +h +r msdos.sys
```

7. Restart your computer.

Solution Five

This problem can occur if the WINBOOT.INI file is present in the root folder of boot drive. If it is, follow these steps:

1. Restart your computer. After your computer completes the Power On Self Test (POST), press and hold down the Ctrl key until you see the Windows 98 StartUp menu, and then choose Safe Mode Command Prompt Only.

2. Delete the WINBOOT.INI file in the root folder of the boot drive, by typing *deltree winboot.ini* and then pressing Enter.

3. Restart your computer.

Related KB article Q139063

VMM32.VXD Error Message and Windows Starts at Command Prompt

You start your computer and see the following error message:

VMM32.VXD is required to run Windows. If this file is not in your PATH, you may need to reinstall Windows.

Your computer then starts at a command prompt.

Solution

The WINDOWS\SYSTEM folder is missing or renamed. Follow these steps:

1. At the command prompt, type *dir vmm32.vxd /s*, and then press Enter.

If the VMM32.VXD file is not found, you must install Windows again. If the VMM32.VXD file is found, note the folder in which the VMM32.VXD file is located, and then continue with step 2.

2. At the command prompt, type the following commands, pressing Enter after each command:

```
cd windows

ren <folder> system
```

where <folder> is the folder you noted in step 1.

3. Restart your computer.

Related KB article Q194679

Windows 95 Screen Appears During Windows 98 Startup

You start Windows 98, and the Windows 95 logo screen is displayed during the startup process.

This problem occurs when the Windows 95 version of the LOGO.SYS file is located in the root folder of drive C. Windows 98 no longer requires a LOGO.SYS file to display the default logo screen when you start Windows 98. If a valid LOGO.SYS file exists in the root of drive C, it is used.

Solution

Rename the LOGO.SYS file located in the root folder by following these steps:

1. Right-click the Start button, and choose Explore.

2. Choose Folder Options from the View menu.

3. Click the View tab, select the Show All Files option, and click OK.

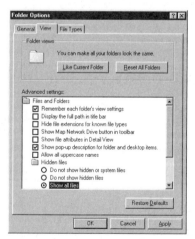

Figure 14-15. *The View tab of the Folder Options dialog box.*

4. Click the C: drive icon, and find the LOGO.SYS file in the drive's contents.

5. Right-click the file, and choose Rename from the drop-down list.

6. Enter a new name for the file in the text box, and click Enter.

Related KB article Q190645

Windows Boots Directly to Shutdown Screen

You start your computer and see the following message:

It's now safe to turn off your computer

This problem occurs when the VMM32.VXD or WININIT.EXE file is missing or damaged.

Solution

To solve this problem, follow these steps:

1. Restart your computer. After your computer completes the Power On Self Test (POST), press and hold down the Ctrl key until you see the Windows 98 StartUp menu, and then choose Command Prompt.

2. Enter the line *cd \windows\system* to change to the WINDOWS\SYSTEM folder.

3. Enter the line *ren vmm32.vxd vmm32.old*.

4. Reinstall Windows 98.

Related KB article Q141898

Missing File Error Messages

.386 or .VXD File Not Found

You start Windows, and an error message erroneously states that a .386 or .VXD file referenced in the SYSTEM.INI file cannot be found.

This error message occurs when the file in question is damaged. The message might be incorrect in stating that the file is referenced in the SYSTEM.INI file, because the file might be referenced in the Registry or be loaded by VMM32.VXD.

Solution

Locate and replace the file referenced in the error message by extracting it from your Windows 98 CD-ROM or disks.

Related KB article Q126574

COMMAND.COM Missing or Corrupt

You start your computer and see the following error message:

> *The following file is missing or corrupt: COMMAND.COM. Type the name of the Command Interpreter.*

This problem can occur if you install Windows 98 in a dual-boot environment with MS-DOS, install Windows 98 again, and then uninstall Windows 98. The Master Boot Record (MBR) might not be properly updated after you uninstall Windows 98. The MBR loads the JO.SYS file from the root folder of drive C. The JO.SYS file cannot load the MS-DOS versions of the MSDOS.SYS file and the COMMAND.COM file restored after you uninstall Windows 98. The JO.SYS file is used by Windows 98 in a dual-boot environment with MS-DOS.

Solution

Use the MS-DOS 6.x Upgrade Setup Disk 1 to restart your computer, and then use the SYS command on drive C by following these steps:

1. Place the MS-DOS 6.x Upgrade Setup Disk 1 in drive A, and then restart your computer.

2. Exit MS-DOS Setup by pressing the F3 key when MS-DOS Setup starts.

3. Type *sys c:* at the command prompt, and press Enter.

4. Restart your computer.

Related KB article Q187641

Command Prompt or File Missing Error Message Displayed

You start your computer, and it boots to a command prompt rather than to Windows. If you type *win* at the command prompt, Windows starts. If you try to start Windows normally or in Safe mode, you see an error message stating that files are missing. Both problems commonly indicate an incomplete installation of Windows.

Solution

Run Windows Setup again, and choose the Verify option when you are prompted. The Verify option causes Windows to check all files and replace any that are missing or damaged.

Windows might also boot to a command prompt if the MSDOS.SYS file contains the line BootGUI=0.

Note For more information, see KB article Q141721, "How to Boot to a Command Prompt by Default."

Related KB article Q149713

Device File Not Found

You start Windows and see this error message:

Cannot find a device file that may be needed to run Windows or a Windows application.

This error message occurs when the Windows Registry contains a reference to a device driver file and the file no longer exists on your system. Here are some possible reasons:

- A Windows virtual device driver (VxD) referenced in the Registry is missing or is damaged.

- One of the StaticVxD values in the Registry is blank or contains only spaces. If so, the error message does not name the missing device driver file.

Solution

Complete the following steps until you no longer see the error message:

1. If you have recently removed a program or component, reinstall the program or component, and then run the uninstall program if one is available. If it's not, contact the program's manufacturer to obtain uninstall instructions.

2. If the missing device driver has a .386 filename extension, disable in the SYSTEM.INI file the line referring to this device driver by placing a semicolon (;) at the beginning of the line. For example, if the line reads:

   ```
   device=Filename.386
   ```

   change it to the following:

   ```
   ;device=Filename.386
   ```

   and restart Windows.

3. If the missing device driver has a .VXD filename extension, it is a driver designed for use with Windows 98 and is referenced in the Windows Registry. In most cases, the associated program or component is also listed under the Add/Remove Programs icon in Control Panel. Following the instructions in step 1 should correct the problem.

4. If the error message still appears after following the instructions in step 1 or step 1 does not apply, use System File Checker to extract the missing file from the Windows 98 CD-ROM, by following the remaining steps.

5. Click the Start button, choose Programs, click Accessories, click System Tools, and click System Information.

6. Choose System File Checker from the Tools menu, click Extract One File From Installation Disk, and enter in the Specify The System File You Would Like To Restore box the name of the file you want to extract. Click the Start button.

7. In the Restore From box, enter the path to the WIN98 folder on your Windows 98 CD-ROM. Enter the destination folder in the Save File In box if necessary, and click OK.

8. Click OK, click OK again, and click Yes when you are prompted to restart your computer.

Note For more information about how to extract a file, see KB article Q129605.

9. If the specific device-driver file is not named in the error message, one of the StaticVxD values in the Registry is probably blank or contains spaces. The StaticVxD values are located in the following Registry keys:

`HKEY_LOCAL_MACHINE\System\CurrentControlSet\Services\VxD`

Warning Please read the Introduction for information about how to safely edit the Registry.

10. Click the Start button, choose Run, and enter *regedit* in the Run box. Click OK.

11. Navigate your way through the folders in the left pane until you locate the VXD folder. Use Registry Editor to locate and delete any StaticVxD value in the Registry that contains either invalid data or only spaces or is blank.

Figure 14-16.   *The Registry Editor.*

12. Close Regedit.

13. Restart Windows.

Related KB article Q132008

KRNL Files Not Found

You start Windows and see one of the following error messages:

Cannot find KRNL386.EXE

Cannot find KRNL286.EXE

Cannot find KRNL.EXE (version 3.0 only)

Cannot find or load required file KRNL386.EXE. The file was not found.

These messages indicate that Windows cannot find the kernel necessary to run 386 enhanced, standard, or real mode (version 3.0 only). The kernel provides system services such as memory and resource management. This problem can also occur if the WIN386.EXE file is in the WINDOWS folder. This file is run by WIN.COM, causing Windows to believe that the WINDOWS folder is the WINDOWS\SYSTEM folder.

Solution One

If Windows was not installed or uninstalled, follow these steps:

1. Boot with clean AUTOEXEC.BAT and CONFIG.SYS files.

2. Make sure that your WINDOWS folder is in your MS-DOS path.

3. Make sure that your path statement does not contain more than 128 characters.

4. Make sure that the correct kernel file indicated in the warning message exists in your WINDOWS\SYSTEM folder. If you are running a shared copy of Windows, make sure that the file is in the shared WINDOWS folder.

5. Add the WINDOWS\SYSTEM folder to your MS-DOS path.

6. Make sure that your MS-DOS version is compatible with your computer.

7. If you are using a shared installation of Windows on a network server, make sure that your personal WINDOWS folder and the shared WINDOWS folder are in your MS-DOS path and are listed in that order.

8. Ensure that you don't have any upper memory block (UMB) conflicts.

9. Rebuild the SYSTEM.INI file.

10. As a last resort, reinstall Windows.

Solution Two

If Windows was installed or uninstalled, follow these steps:

1. Remove the WIN386.EXE file from the WINDOWS folder. If no WIN386.EXE file is in the WINDOWS\SYSTEM folder, move the file from the WINDOWS folder to the WINDOWS\SYSTEM folder.

2. Restart your computer.

3. If this process doesn't solve the problem, follow the steps in Solution One.

Related KB article Q70467

PPWRPROF.DLL Not Found

You start Windows 98 and receive the following error messages:

RUNDLL Error loading POWRPROF.DLL. The system cannot find the file specified.

Error Starting Program A required .DLL file, POWRPROF.DLL was not found.

These error messages appear even when you disable LoadPowerProfile on the Startup tab in System Configuration Utility (MSCONFIG.EXE).

This problem occurs when the POWRPROF.DLL file in the WINDOWS\SYSTEM folder is missing or damaged.

Solution

Rename the POWRPROF.DLL file (if it exists) in the WINDOWS\SYSTEM folder, and then extract a new copy of the POWRPROF.DLL file from your original Windows 98 CD-ROM into the WINDOWS\SYSTEM folder by using System File Checker. To start System File Checker, click the Start button, choose Run, enter *sfc.exe* in the Open box, and click OK.

Related KB article Q188213

VMM32.VXD: Missing/Unable to Load Error

You start Windows and receive the following error message:

VMM32.VXD: Missing/Unable to Load. Press any key to continue.

Pressing any key causes the Shutdown screen to appear. This problem occurs when the UMAXIS11.386 file is being loaded in the SYSTEM.INI file. A UMAX scanner uses this file.

Solution One

Download the Patch for VMM32.VXD Error Message update from the UMAX web site, at *http://support.umax.com/scanners/index.htm*.

Solution Two

Until you can download the Patch for VMM32.VXD Error Message update, follow these steps:

1. Click the Start button, choose Run, enter *sysedit* in the box, and click OK.

2. Choose SYSTEM.INI from the Window menu.

3. Choose Find from the Search menu.

4. Enter *umaxis11.386* in the Find box, and press Enter.

5. Place a semicolon (;) at the beginning of the line that contains umaxis11.386.

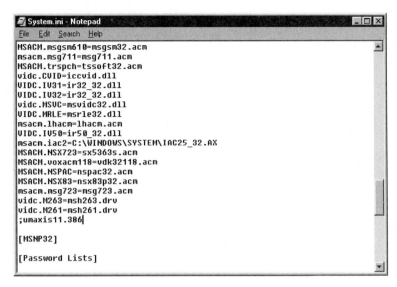

Figure 14-17. *The SYSTEM.INI file in Notepad.*

6. Choose Save from the File menu, and choose Exit from the File menu.

7. Restart your computer.

Related KB article Q191874

VVINESD.386 Not Found

You start your computer and see an error message on a black screen which says that the file VVINESD.386 cannot be found. This problem can occur if a previous installation of Banyan VINES was detected or if a Banyan VINES network client was incorrectly detected.

Solution

To solve this problem, follow these steps:

1. Use the System Configuration Editor (SYSEDIT.EXE) to disable the following line in the [386Enh] section of the SYSTEM.INI file (if it exists):

```
Device=c:\windows\vvinesd.386
```

2. Restart your computer. If you receive the error message again, continue to step 3.

3. Click the Start button, choose Settings, click Control Panel, and double-click the Network icon.

4. If any of the following network components is present, remove them:

- Banyan DOS/Windows 3.1 Client

- Banyan VINES ethernet protocol

- Banyan VINES token ring protocol

To do so, click a component, and click Remove. Repeat this sequence as needed until all the components have been removed.

5. Click OK, and click Yes. If you receive the error message again, continue to step 6.

Warning Please read the Introduction for information about how to safely edit the Registry.

6. Click the Start button, choose Run, enter *regedit* in the Run box, and click OK.

7. Navigate your way through the folders in the left pane.

8. Use Registry Editor to delete the vvinesd value under the following Registry key:

`HKEY_LOCAL_MACHINE\System\CurrentControlSet\Services\VXD\`

9. Close Regedit.

10. Restart Windows.

Related KB article Q194845

WIN386.EXE Not Found or Incompatible MS-DOS Version Startup Error Message

You start Windows and receive one of the following error messages if the root folder contains a WIN.COM file from an earlier version of Windows:

Cannot find Win386.exe needed to run in 386 enhanced mode; check to ensure the path is correct or reinstall Windows.

You have started your computer with a version of MS-DOS incompatible with this version of Windows. Insert a Startup diskette matching this version of Windows and then restart. The system has been halted. Press Ctrl+Alt+Delete to restart you computer.

Solution

Remove or rename the WIN.COM file in the root folder, and then restart your computer. If you have an earlier version of Windows installed on your computer and no WIN.COM file is in the folder for that version of Windows, move the WIN.COM file from the root folder to the folder containing the earlier version of Windows.

Related KB article Q153044

Programs or Devices Start Automatically

AUTOEXEC.BAT File Programs Not Started Automatically

After you install Windows, programs listed in the AUTOEXEC.BAT file are not started automatically when you start your computer. These programs generate the following error messages:

Bad command or file name

Path not found

The Setup program does not handle blank spaces in the PATH statement in the AUTOEXEC.BAT file correctly. Any PATH statement that contains spaces is considered incorrect, as shown in these examples:

Before running Setup

```
PATH=C:\Windows;C:\Program Files\Third Party Program
```

After running Setup

```
PATH=C:\Windows;C:\ProgramFiles\ThirdPartyProgram
```

Solution

Modify the AUTOEXEC.BAT file to add the missing spaces again by following these steps:

1. Click the Start button, choose Run, enter *sysedit* in the Open box, and click OK.

2. Choose AUTOEXEC.BAT from the Window menu.

3. Add the missing spaces to the PATH statement.

Note This problem can also affect other statements, such as SET statements. Make sure to correct any other lines with missing spaces.

---

4. Choose Exit from the File menu.

5. When you are prompted to save the modified AUTOEXEC.BAT file, click Yes.

6. Restart your computer.

Related KB article Q186927

Disabled Programs in WIN.INI File Still Run at Startup

You clear the Load= or Run= check box on the WIN.INI tab or the Load Startup Group Items check box on the General tab in the System Configuration Utility (MSCONFIG.EXE) dialog box, and programs still run when you start Windows 98.

Solution

The System Configuration Utility processes only the first load= and run= lines in the WIN.INI file. Eliminate multiple load= and run= lines by following these steps:

1. Click the Start button, choose Run, enter *win.ini* in the Open box, and click OK.

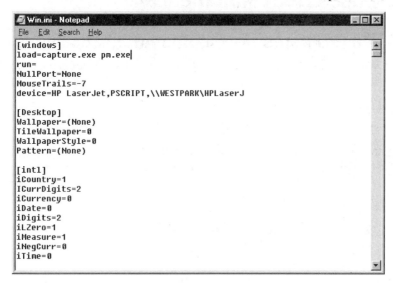

Figure 14-18. *The WIN.INI file in Notepad.*

2. For each additional load= and run= line in the [Windows] section, cut the text on the right side of the equal sign (=) and paste it on the end of the first load= or run= line. Be sure to separate each entry on the load= and run= lines with a space.

3. Delete each additional load= and run= line.

4. Close the WIN.INI file.

Related KB article Q194181

Disabled Program Shortcuts in Startup Folder Still Run

You use System Configuration Utility (MSCONFIG.EXE) to disable shortcuts in the STARTUP folder, and programs that have shortcuts in the STARTUP folder still run the next time you start Windows. This problem can happen if the DISABLED STARTUP ITEMS folder already exists and already contains a shortcut that is in the STARTUP folder.

Solution

Remove any shortcuts from the STARTUP folder that already exist in the DISABLED STARTUP ITEMS folder by following these steps:

1. Click the Start button, choose Settings, and click Taskbar & Start Menu.

2. Click the Start Menu Programs tab, and click Remove.

3. Double-click the STARTUP folder.

4. Click the shortcut you want to remove, and click Remove. Repeat this step for each shortcut in the STARTUP folder.

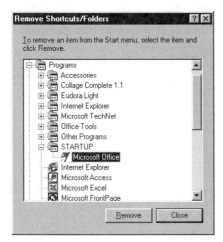

Figure 14-19. *The Remove Shortcuts/Folders dialog box.*

Note Only shortcuts that already exist in the DISABLED STARTUP ITEMS folder appear in the STARTUP folder.

5. Click Close, click OK, and restart your computer.

When you disable shortcuts in the STARTUP folder by clearing the Load Startup Group Items check box (on the General tab in the System Configuration Utility dialog box), the DISABLED STARTUP ITEMS folder is created, and shortcuts in the STARTUP folder are moved to it. If the DISABLED STARTUP ITEMS folder already exists and already contains a shortcut that is in the STARTUP folder, the shortcut is not moved to the DISABLED STARTUP ITEMS folder, and the program to which it points is run when you start Windows.

This problem can occur if shortcuts in the STARTUP folder are disabled and you reinstall a program that copies a new shortcut to the STARTUP folder. When you use System Configuration Utility to disable shortcuts in the STARTUP folder again, the shortcut is not moved to the DISABLED STARTUP ITEMS folder because it already exists.

When you select the Load Startup Group Items check box, the shortcuts are moved from the DISABLED STARTUP ITEMS folder back to the STARTUP folder, and the DISABLED STARTUP ITEMS folder is deleted.

Related KB article Q180129

Modem Tries to Connect to Internet Automatically

You start Windows, and your modem attempts to connect to your Internet service provider (ISP).

This problem can occur for any of the following reasons:

- You use a program that automatically checks for updated components or web pages.

- A program that dials your ISP is located in the STARTUP folder.

- Your computer is infected with a Trojan horse virus, such as SYSTEM32.EXE, that starts when you start your computer. Most antivirus programs do not detect and cannot remove Trojan horse viruses.

- Symantec WinFax is installed on your computer.

Solution One

Reconfigure the program that automatically checks for updated components or web pages so that it does not start automatically when Windows 98 starts. For information, see the original program documentation.

Solution Two

Remove the program that automatically checks for updated components or web pages from your STARTUP folder by following these steps:

1. Right-click the Start button, and choose Open.

2. Double-click the PROGRAMS folder.

3. Double-click the STARTUP folder.

4. Drag the program that automatically checks for updated components or web pages from the STARTUP folder to another folder. This step prevents the program from starting automatically when Windows starts.

Solution Three

Remove the SYSTEM32.EXE Trojan horse virus by following these steps:

Warning Please read the Introduction for information about how to safely edit the Registry.

1. Delete or rename the SYSTEM32.EXE file in the WINDOWS\SYSTEM folder.

2. Click the Start button, choose Run, enter *regedit* in the Run box, and click OK.

3. Navigate your way through the folders in the left pane.

4. Delete the SystemHandler value from the following Registry key:

   `HKEY_LOCAL_MACHINE\Software\Microsoft\Windows\CurrentVersion\Run`

5. Close Regedit.

6. Restart Windows.

Solution Four

Reconfigure Symantec WinFax by following these steps:

Warning Please read the Introduction for information about how to safely edit the Registry.

1. Close WinFax and the Controller.

2. Click the Start button, choose Run, enter *regedit* in the Run box, and click OK.

3. Choose Export Registry File from the Registry menu.

4. Click C:\ in the Save In box.

5. Enter *regold* in the File Name box, and click OK.

6. Change the following Registry keys to *N*:

   HKEY_LOCAL_MACHINE\Software\Microsoft\OLE\EnableDCOM

   HKEY_LOCAL_MACHINE\Software\Microsoft\OLE\EnableRemoteConnect

7. Close Regedit.

8. Restart Windows.

9. Reconfigure your modem in WinFax.

Solution Five

This problem can also occur if you are using a Lexmark printer. The Lexmark printer software might add LEXSTART.EXE to the Run key in the Registry to handle print commands you send to the printer. This problem can cause Dial-Up Networking to prompt you to dial your ISP.

Warning Please read the Introduction for information about how to safely edit the Registry.

1. Click the Start button, choose Run, enter *regedit* in the Run box, and click OK.

2. Navigate your way through the folders in the left pane until you locate the following Registry key.

   HKEY_LOCAL_MACHINE\SOFTWARE\Microsoft\Windows\CurrentVersion\Run

3. Remove the LEXSTART.EXE value from this Registry key.

4. Close Regedit.

5. Restart Windows.

Solution Six

If you are using Microsoft Personal Web Server 4.0, the Microsoft Distributed Transaction Coordinator (MSDTC) service might be loaded from the STARTUP folder. If you do not want to remove the MSDTC service from the STARTUP folder, configure Internet Explorer to connect to your ISP by using a local area network (LAN). Then, when you want to connect to the Internet, first connect to your ISP by using Dial-Up Networking, and then start Internet Explorer. To configure Internet Explorer to use a LAN, follow these steps:

1. Right-click the Internet Explorer icon on the desktop, and choose Properties.

2. Click the Connection tab, click Connect To The Internet Using A Local Area Network, and click OK.

3. If the MSDTC service is not being loaded from the STARTUP folder, open Regedit and remove the *Msdtc* value from the following Registry key:

   ```
   HKEY_LOCAL_MACHINE\Software\Microsoft\Windows\CurrentVersion\RunServices
   ```

Related KB article Q175312

MS-DOS-Based Program Starts When Restarting Computer

After you run a program in MS-DOS mode, you are not able to start Windows. Instead, every time you restart your computer, you see this message:

> *Windows 98 is now starting your MS-DOS-based program*

and then the MS-DOS-based program starts. This problem can occur if you run a program in MS-DOS mode and the program terminates abnormally.

Solution One

Restart your computer. After your computer completes the Power On Self Test (POST), press the Esc key to start Windows. If this does not solve the problem, try Solution Two.

Solution Two

Restart your computer. Let the MS-DOS-based program start, and then exit the program normally. If this does not work, trySolution Three.

Solution Three

Restore your original CONFIG.SYS and AUTOEXEC.BAT files by following these steps:

1. Restart your computer. After your computer completes the Power On Self Test (POST), press and hold down the Ctrl key until you see the Windows 98 StartUp menu, and then choose Safe Mode Command Prompt Only.

2. At the command prompt, type the following lines, pressing Enter after each line:

   ```
   ren config.sys config.app

   ren config.wos config.sys

   ren autoexec.bat autoexec.app

   ren autoexec.wos autoexec.bat
   ```

3. Restart Windows.

Related KB article Q187524

MS-DOS Program Starts Every Time Computer Restarts

An MS-DOS-based program you run in MS-DOS mode starts every time you restart your computer.

This problem occurs when the MS-DOS-based program terminates abnormally. For example, your computer restarts while the program is running.

Solution

Exit the MS-DOS-based program properly. Windows 98 should then start automatically. If it does not, follow these steps:

1. Restart your computer. After your computer completes the Power On Self Test (POST), press and hold down the Ctrl key until you see the Windows 98 StartUp menu, and then choose Safe Mode Command Prompt Only.

2. Type *win /wx* at the command prompt, and then press Enter.

Related KB article Q130448

MS-DOS Window Appears When Starting Windows 98

You upgrade to Windows 98, and an MS-DOS window opens every time you start Windows 98. When this problem occurs, the MS-DOS window contains the following error message:

Specified command search directory bad

This problem occurs when Cheyenne ARCSolo 1.0 is installed and attempts to run a program at startup.

Solution

Disable ARCSolo Recovery by following these steps:

1. Click the Start button, choose Run, enter *msconfig* in the Open box, and click OK.

2. Click the Startup tab.

3. Clear the ARCSolo Recovery check box.

4. Click OK.

5. Click Yes when you are prompted to restart your computer.

Related KB article Q188961

Program in Scheduled Tasks Folder Starts Unexpectedly at Startup

You start your computer, and a program starts unexpectedly if Scheduled Tasks has been configured to start a program when you start your computer.

Solution

Remove the program from the SCHEDULED TASKS folder by following these steps:

1. Click the Start button, choose Programs, click Accessories, click System Tools, and click Scheduled Tasks to open the SCHEDULED TASKS folder.

2. Double-click the program to open the program's dialog box.

3. Click the Task tab, and clear the Enabled (Scheduled Task Runs At Specified Time) check box.

Figure 14-20. *A scheduled task's properties dialog box.*

4. Click OK, and restart your computer.

Related KB article Q194529

Programs Don't Launch from STARTUP Folder

You start Windows, and either a folder other than the STARTUP folder launches programs or Programs in the STARTUP folder are not launched.

This problem occurs when the STARTUP folder has been renamed.

Solution

Rename the folder to STARTUP, and add or remove programs as necessary.

Related KB article Q141900

Text Sent to Printer or Printer Displays Error Code

You start Windows, and a small amount of text is sent to the local printer. The printer sometimes does not eject the page after the text is printed. The text varies but typically includes extended or unintelligible characters. The printer also displays an error code. On Hewlett-Packard LaserJet printers, *Error 22* is displayed. When you attempt to print a document, you receive a message that the printer is offline or out of paper.

This problem is also known to occur with the following printers:

- Canon BJC-5000
- Canon MultiPASS 5000

Solution

This problem occurs when the DRVWPPQT.VXD virtual device driver is loaded. To prevent this driver from being loaded, follow these steps:

Warning Do not implement this resolution if you have a tape backup device connected to a parallel (LPT) port on your computer.

1. Click the Start button, choose Find, and click Files Or Folders.

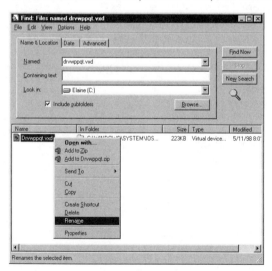

Figure 14-21. *The Find dialog box.*

2. If necessary, click the Name & Location tab.

3. Enter *drvwppqt.vxd* in the Named box, and click Find Now.

4. Rename all instances of the file by changing the filename extension. You must change the extension to prevent the driver from being loaded.

This file is installed by Seagate (formerly Arcada) Backup software and is typically in the WINDOWS\SYSTEM\IOSUBSYS folder as well as in the ARCADA\SYSTEM folder.

This driver is also installed by Windows 98 Backup. Backup is installed when you upgrade to Windows 98 if you have a previous version of Backup installed or if you choose to install Backup using the Custom installation option.

The driver detects tape devices connected to a parallel port. During the detection process, a string of text is sent through the parallel port to be interpreted by tape devices. Some printers interpret this string as printable text. The output might also be sent to the printer during modem or port detection.

Seagate (Arcada) Backup is manufactured by Seagate Software, a vendor independent of Microsoft; Microsoft makes no warranty, implied or otherwise, regarding this product's performance or reliability.

Related KB article Q157145

Welcome To Windows 98 Dialog Box Doesn't Disable

You cannot disable the Welcome To Windows 98 dialog box that appears when you start Windows, and another program that starts automatically when you start Windows displays a window that covers the Welcome To Windows 98 dialog box. This prevents you from being able to see the Show This Screen Each Time Windows 98 Starts check box.

Solution

To solve this problem, follow these steps:

1. Click the Start button, choose Programs, click Accessories, click System Tools, and click Welcome To Windows.

2. Clear the Show This Screen Each Time Windows 98 Starts check box, and close the Welcome To Windows 98 dialog box.

Figure 14-22.   *The Welcome To Windows 98 dialog box.*

Related KB article Q192399

Shutting Down and Restarting

BIOS Level Error on Main Board Message After Restart

You start your computer and receive a BIOS-level error message reporting an error on the main board.

This problem occurs on Peripheral Component Interconnect (PCI) computers with bus mastering PCI network cards and occurs only when the real-mode network has been started. The computer is unable to de-initialize the network adapter.

Solution

You can temporarily solve this problem by turning your computer off for 10 seconds and rebooting. To permanently solve this problem, contact the BIOS vendor to acquire an updated version.

Related KB article Q132852

Continuous Restarts on Startup

You start your computer, and Windows restarts continuously if WIN.COM is called from the AUTOEXEC.BAT file using the /W or /WX switch.

Solution

To prevent this problem, follow these steps:

1. Restart your computer. After your computer completes the Power On Self Test (POST), press and hold down the Ctrl key until you see the Windows 98 StartUp menu, and then choose Safe Mode Command Prompt Only.

Note For more information about Windows 98 startup, see KB article Q178548, "No 'Starting Windows 98' Message at Startup."

2. Type the following line, and then press Enter:

```
edit autoexec.bat
```

3. Locate and remove the line that reads:

```
win.com /W
```

or

```
win.com /WX
```

4. Save and then close the AUTOEXEC.BAT file.

5. Restart your computer.

The /W and /WX switches are typically used to restore the original CONFIG.SYS and AUTOEXEC.BAT files and to restart the computer after you restart your computer in MS-DOS mode. The /W switch on the WIN.COM line causes WIN.COM to rename the current CONFIG.SYS and AUTOEXEC.BAT files to CONFIG.APP and AUTOEXEC.APP, to restore the original CONFIG.SYS and AUTOEXEC.BAT files from the CONFIG.WOS and AUTOEXEC.WOS files, to delete the CONFIG.WOS and AUTOEXEC.WOS files, and then to display the following message:

Press any key to continue.

Pressing a key reboots your computer to Windows. If the /WX switch is used rather than the /W switch, WIN.COM performs the same steps but does not display the preceding message.

When the /W or /WX switches are used in the AUTOEXEC.BAT file after you restart your computer in MS-DOS mode, the original CONFIG.SYS and AUTOEXEC.BAT files are successfully restored from the CONFIG.WOS and AUTOEXEC.WOS files, and Windows starts normally after your computer is rebooted. However, if you use the /W or /WX switch in the AUTOEXEC.BAT file at any other time, the CONFIG.WOS and AUTOEXEC.WOS files do not exist, and the current CONFIG.SYS and AUTOEXEC.BAT files remain in the root folder of the boot drive. Because the /W or /WX switch remains in the AUTOEXEC.BAT file, Windows restarts continuously.

Note For additional information about the process that occurs when you restart your computer in MS-DOS mode, see KB article Q138996, "Description of Restarting Computer in MS-DOS Mode."

Related KB article Q148919

Ctrl+Alt+Delete in Shutdown Process Does Nothing

You press Ctrl+Alt+Delete when you see the *It's now safe to turn off your computer* message, and nothing happens. The reason is that Windows incorporates Fast Shutdown functionality, and keyboard interrupts are disabled during the shutdown process. As a result, pressing Ctrl+Alt+Delete does nothing.

Solution

To restart your computer, click Restart rather than Shut Down in the Shut Down Windows dialog box.

Related KB article Q186888

Disabling Floppy Disk Controller Causes Computer to Hang at Shutdown

You disable the Standard Floppy Disk Controller device in Device Manager, and your computer stops responding (hangs) when you shut it down. Your computer hangs while the shutdown screen is being displayed.

Solution

Turn your computer off manually after it hangs at the shutdown screen. Doing so should not cause any problems. The Standard Floppy Disk Controller device remains disabled when you restart your computer.

Related KB article Q193677

Fatal Exception Error on Shutdown

You try to shut down your Windows 98–based computer with a Compaq FX-series monitor, and you receive the following error message or one similar to it:

A Fatal Exception 0E has occurred at 0028:C001AEEB

This problem occurs because the version of Universal Serial Bus support software included with some FX-series monitors is not fully compatible with Windows 98.

Solution

Obtain and install the most current version of the Universal Serial Bus support software for FX-series monitors from Compaq. For information, contact Compaq or see the documentation included with your monitor or computer.

Related KB article Q189329

General Protection Fault Error Message or Hang During Shutdown

You try to shut down your computer, it stops responding, and you receive a general-protection (GP) fault error message in module CWBMIDI.VXD. This problem also occurs if you try to disable your Crystal Audio sound card in Device Manager.

This problem can occur if you are using a Crystal Audio sound card. Because the sound card is incorrectly detected during Windows 98 Setup, the correct device drivers might not be installed.

Solution

Obtain and install the most current version of the appropriate sound card drivers. For information, see the documentation included with your sound card or computer.

Related KB article Q188122

IBM Aptiva E84 or E56 Hangs After Cold Boot

You upgrade Windows 95 to Windows 98 on an IBM Aptiva E84 or E56 computer, and your computer stops responding when you turn it off and then back on (known as a *cold boot*).

Solution One

Restart your computer, press and hold down the Ctrl key until the Windows 98 StartUp menu appears, and then choose Safe Mode. After Windows 98 is loaded, click the Start button, choose Shut Down, click Restart, and click OK.

Solution Two

If your computer stops responding, restart it, and choose Normal from the Windows 98 StartUp menu.

Solution Three

Disable 32-bit disk access by following these steps:

1. Click the Start button, choose Programs, click Accessories, click System Tools, and click System Information.

2. Choose System Configuration Utility from the Tools menu.

3. Click Advanced on the General tab.

4. Select the Force Compatibility Mode Disk Access check box.

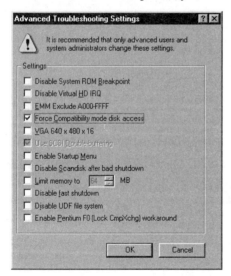

Figure 14-23.   *The Advanced Troubleshooting Settings dialog box.*

5. Click OK, click OK again, and click Yes when you are prompted to restart your computer.

Note Contact IBM Technical Support to inquire about the availability of a solution for this problem.

Related KB article Q190603

MS-DOS Mode Exit Causes Windows to Reboot

You restart Windows in MS-DOS mode using the current configuration (which does not require Windows to reboot before starting MS-DOS mode), and Windows reboots when you exit MS-DOS mode. This problem can occur if a real-mode device driver for MS-DOS mode is being loaded from the DOSSTART.BAT file. Your computer is restarted to remove the real-mode device driver from memory when you exit MS-DOS mode, and this behavior is by design.

Solution

If you want to prevent Windows from rebooting when you exit MS-DOS mode, disable the device driver in the DOSSTART.BAT file in the WINDOWS folder by placing the word *rem* at the beginning of the line.

Warning If you disable a device driver in the DOSSTART.BAT file, it is not available in MS-DOS mode. The device for which the device driver is loaded might not work in MS-DOS mode.

You can also load the real-mode driver in the AUTOEXEC.BAT file rather than the DOSSTART.BAT file. However, doing so causes the device driver to be loaded at all times.

Related KB article Q148795

MS-DOS Mode Restart Causes Computer to Hang or Restart Automatically

You restart your computer in MS-DOS mode and use NetBIOS (Network Basic Input/Output System) TCP/IP (Transport Control Protocol/Internet Protocol) Statistic (NBTSTAT) with any command-line switches, and either of the following occurs:

- Your computer restarts automatically.
- Your computer stops responding (hangs).

Solution

NBTSTAT is not designed to be used in MS-DOS mode. If your computer automatically restarts, EMM386.EXE is being loaded from the CONFIG.SYS file. If your computer hangs, EMM386.EXE is not being loaded from the CONFIG.SYS file.

Use NBTSTAT in an MS-DOS session within Windows. NBTSTAT is a command-line TCP/IP tool that is not designed to be used in MS-DOS mode, but in an MS-DOS session in the Windows environment.

Related KB article Q179239

MS-DOS Mode Restart Produces Lost File Error Message

You attempt to restart your computer in MS-DOS mode and see the following error message:

Cannot find the file 'C:\Windows\Exit to Dos.pif'. Make sure the file exists on your system and that the pathname and filenames are correct.

Solution

The Exit to DOS.PIF file in the WINDOWS folder is damaged. To delete it, follow these steps:

Note The Exit to DOS.PIF file is rebuilt every time you restart your computer in MS-DOS mode. If the Exit to DOS.PIF file is damaged, Windows is unable to rebuild it.

1. Click the Start button, choose Find, and click Files Or Folders.

2. Enter *exitto~1.pif* in the Named box, and click Find Now.

3. Right-click Exit To DOS.PIF on the list of found files, and then choose Delete.

Figure 14-24. *The Find dialog box.*

4. Close Find.

5. Click the Start button, choose Shut Down, click Restart In MS-DOS Mode, and click OK.

Related KB article Q193936

MSGSRV32 Error Message on Shutdown

You shut down or restart Windows 98 and receive one of the following error messages:

MSGSRV32.DLL caused a General Protection Fault in Module CM8330SB.DRV

MSGSRV32.EXE: An error has occurred in your program. To keep working anyway, click ignore and save your work in a new file. To quit this program, click Close. You will lose information you entered since your last save.

These error messages can occur if your computer uses a sound card based on the C-Media CMI8330 sound chip. This sound chip is used as the basis for several sound cards.

Solution

Contact your sound card's manufacturer to obtain an updated driver.

If you are unable to contact your sound card's manufacturer, you can try the C-Media Windows 98 sound card driver version 4.10.00.0152 or later, available at *http://www.cmedia.com.tw.*

If you are unable to obtain an updated driver for your sound card, disable your sound card by following these steps:

1. Restart your computer. After your computer completes the Power On Self Test (POST), press and hold down the Ctrl key until you see the Windows 98 StartUp menu, and then choose Safe Mode.

2. Click the Start button, choose Settings, click Control Panel, and double-click the System icon.

3. Click the Performance tab, and click File System.

4. Click the Troubleshooting tab, and select the Disable All 32-Bit Protected-Mode Disk Drivers check box.

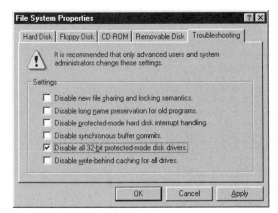

Figure 14-25.   *The Troubleshooting tab of the File System Properties dialog box.*

5. Click OK, and click OK again.

6. Restart your computer normally.

7. Click the Start button, choose Settings, and click Control Panel.

8. Double-click the System icon, and click the Device Manager tab.

9. Double-click the Sound, Video, And Game Controllers branch to expand it.

10. Click your sound card, and click Properties.

11. Select the Disable In This Hardware Profile check box.

12. Click OK, and click OK again.

Related KB article Q188803

NEC Versa 6000 or Fujitsu Laptop Doesn't Restart in MS-DOS Mode

You try to restart your Fujitsu or NEC Versa 6000 laptop computer in MS-DOS mode, and your computer shuts down but does not restart.

On NEC Versa 6000 computers, this problem occurs because of problems with the NEC mouse driver version 9.10.005 (released 8/7/96) from the Versa 6000 Hotload version 2.00.02.

On Fujitsu computers, this problem occurs because of problems with the original mouse driver (GPOINT.DRV).

Solution One

If you have an NEC Versa 6000 computer, obtain and install mouse driver version 9.10.008 or later. For information, contact NEC.

Solution Two

If you have a Fujitsu computer, obtain and install the most current version of the GPOINT.DRV file. For information, contact Fujitsu.

Related KB article Q188322

Power Button Doesn't Shut Down Computer Immediately

You press the power button to shut down your computer, and it does not shut down immediately if your computer has a sound card that uses Windows Driver Model (WDM) drivers and if you have configured the power button in your computer's CMOS settings to shut down your computer.

Solution

To shut down your computer, click the Start button, choose Shut Down, click the Shut Down option button, and click OK.

Related KB article Q194877

Restart-the-Computer Option Causes Windows to Hang

You restart your computer by using the Restart The Computer option in the Shut Down Windows dialog box, and Windows stops responding.

This problem occurs when your computer's BIOS expects IRQ 12 to be in use by a PS/2-style mouse port, but it is using instead a software-configurable hardware device (such as a Plug and Play adapter).

Solution

Either upgrade the BIOS in your computer or reserve an IRQ with Device Manager by following these steps:

1. Click the Start button, choose settings, and click Control Panel.

2. Double-click the System icon.

3. Click the Device Manager tab, and double-click Computer.

4. Click the Reserve Resources tab, click the Interrupt Request (IRQ) option, and click Add.

5. Click the IRQ you want to reserve.

6. Click OK, and close the program.

Related KB article Q135214

Shutdown Causes Computer with Cisco TCP/IP Suite 100 Stack to Hang

You are using Cisco TCP/IP Suite 100 as your Transmission Control Protocol/Internet Protocol (TCP/IP) stack, and, when you attempt to shut down Windows 98, your computer stops responding.

The Windows 98 shutdown process waits for a return from the NdisCloseAdapter variable call to the networking stack. Because the Cisco software does not recognize this call, your computer seems to not respond.

Solution One

Remove Cisco TCP/IP Suite 100, and then install Microsoft TCP/IP by following these steps:

1. Click the Start button, choose Settings, click Control Panel, and double-click the Network icon.

2. Click Cisco TCP/IP Suite 100 on the list of installed network components, and click Remove.

3. Click Add, click Protocol, and click Add.

4. Select Microsoft in the Manufacturers box, and select TCP/IP in the Network Protocols box.

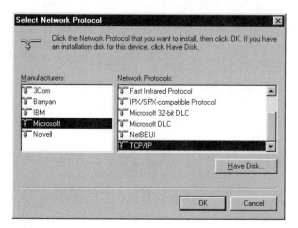

Figure 14-26. *The Select Network Protocol dialog box.*

5. Click OK, and restart your computer when you are prompted.

Solution Two

Cisco Systems suggests reverting to the version of the VNBT.386 file included with Windows 95 by following these steps:

1. Click the Start button, choose Find, and click Files Or Folders.

2. Enter *vnbt.386* in the Named box, and click Find Now.

3. Right-click the VNBT.386 file on the list of found files, choose Rename, and type a new name for the file, such as *vnbt.xxx*.

4. Close the Find window.

5. Extract into the WINDOWS\SYSTEM folder a new copy of the VNBT.386 file from your original Windows 95 disks or CD-ROM. You can find the VNBT.386 file in the following locations:

   - The WIN95_12.CAB cabinet file on the Windows 95 CD-ROM

   - The WIN95_18.CAB cabinet file on the Windows 95 OEM Service Release 2 (OSR2) CD-ROM

   - The WIN95_13.CAB cabinet file on disk 13 of the original Windows 95 DMF floppy disks

   - The WIN95_20.CAB cabinet file on disk 20 of the original Windows 95 non-DMF floppy disks

Note For information about using Extract, type *extract* at the command prompt.

Related KB article Q189880

Shutdown Causes Computer with Symantec Norton AntiVirus to Hang

You attempt to shut down Windows 98, and your computer stops responding. This problem can occur if you are using Symantec Norton AntiVirus with the Auto-Protect feature enabled.

Solution One

Disable the Norton AntiVirus Auto-Protect feature.

Solution Two

Obtain the latest LiveUpdate for Norton AntiVirus (SYMEVNT.EXE) from the Symantec web site. For more information about how to obtain LiveUpdate files, contact Symantec Technical Support.

Related KB article Q187324

Shutdown Command on Start Menu Causes Computer to Power Off

You use the Shut Down command on the Start menu to shut down Windows, and your computer automatically powers off after displaying the message *Please wait while your computer shuts down*.

Solution

This Advanced Power Management (APM) feature occurs only on computers with a Plug and Play BIOS that supports APM features. You have no way to change this feature. The hardware powers down in response to a software request.

Related KB article Q134841

Shut Down Windows Dialog Box Selects Last-Chosen Option

Clicking Start and then choosing Shut Down selects the option you chose the last time you shut down your computer.

Solution

Windows writes this information to the following Registry key every time your computer is shut down:

```
HKEY_CURRENT_USER\Software\Microsoft\Windows\CurrentVersion\Explorer\Shutdown
Setting
```

Create a shortcut to shut down your computer by following these steps:

1. Right-click the desktop, choose New from the shortcut menu, and click Shortcut.

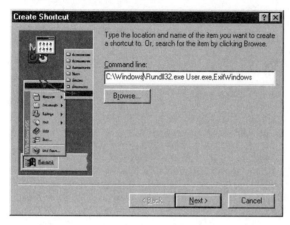

Figure 14-27. *The Create Shortcut dialog box.*

2. Enter the following line in the Command Line box, and click Next:

   `<Windows folder>\Rundll32.exe User.exe,ExitWindows`

   where <Windows folder> is the name of your WINDOWS folder.

3. Enter *Shut Down Windows* in the Select A Name For The Shortcut box, and click Finish.

Related KB article Q193624

Slow Shutdown or Logoff if Roaming Profiles Enabled

Shutting down or logging off takes an unusually long time if Roaming User Profiles are enabled and the TEMPORARY INTERNET FILES folder contains a large number of files.

Solution One

Empty your TEMPORARY INTERNET FILES folder every time you exit Internet Explorer by following these steps:

1. Click the Start button, choose Settings, and click Control Panel.

2. Double-click the Internet icon, and click the Advanced tab.

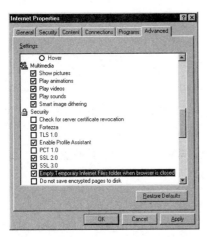

Figure 14-28. *The Advanced tab in the Internet Properties dialog box.*

3. Under Security, select the Empty Temporary Internet Files Folder When Browser Is Closed check box, and click OK.

Note This does not delete content in the COOKIES, HISTORY, or SUBSCRIPTION folders.

Solution Two

Maintain each user's temporary Internet files in the user's HOME folder. Although this solution still consumes server storage, it does not require that the files be copied to the server when users log off.

Solution Three

Maintain all users' temporary Internet files in a shared common folder. When you do so, all users' cookies are stored in the same location.

Solution Four

Maintain each user's temporary Internet files on the local drive in a location other than in the user's profile folder. This method is the most efficient. However, it does not allow a user's cookies to follow the user to other stations.

Internet Explorer 4.0 and 4.01 support Roaming User Profiles. This means that your personal Internet Explorer settings (Active Desktop, favorites, subscriptions, cache, and cookies) are stored on a Windows NT server and are copied to any Windows computer you log on to that is configured to use Roaming User Profiles. Your settings are copied back to the server when you shut down or log off your computer. If your TEMPORARY INTERNET FILES folder is large, shutting down or logging off your computer can take an unusually long time. Additionally, it can cause disk space problems on servers with many user profiles or with several user profiles that contain large TEMPORARY INTERNET FILES folders.

For additional information about Roaming User Profiles, see KB article Q142682, "How to Create and Copy Roaming User Profiles in NT 4.0," and visit the Microsoft web site, at *http:// www.microsoft.com/ntserver/nts/techdetails/default.asp*.

Related KB article Q179723

Windows Restart Displays Error Message or Causes Hang

You restart Windows while you are holding down the Shift key, and Windows stops responding or you receive an invalid page fault error message.

This problem can occur if either of the following conditions exists:

- Your computer contains a bus-mastering network adapter that does not respond properly to Windows shutdown procedures.

- Your computer contains a program, driver, or other hardware device that does not respond properly to Windows shutdown procedures.

Solution One

Do not hold down the Shift key while you are restarting your computer.

Solution Two

Disable fast shutdown by following these steps:

1. Click the Start button, choose Programs, click Accessories, click System Tools, and click System Information.

2. Choose System Configuration Utility from the Tools menu.

3. Click Advanced on the General tab.

4. Clear the Disable Fast Shutdown check box, click OK, and click OK again.

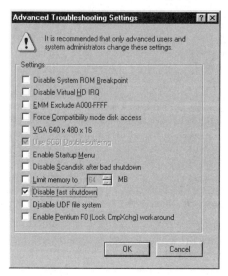

Figure 14-29. *The Advanced Troubleshooting Settings dialog box.*

5. Click Yes when you are prompted to restart your computer.

Solution Three

If you are using a bus-mastering network adapter, contact your adapter's manufacturer to inquire about the availability of updated drivers.

Related KB article Q186925

Startup and Boot Disk

Bad Command or Filename Error Message from Boot Disk

You start your computer with the boot disk included with Windows 98 (retail version), and you receive a *Bad command or filename* error message when you try to use any of the following commands:

- ATTRIB.EXE
- CHKDSK.EXE
- DEBUG.EXE
- EDIT.COM
- EXT.EXE
- FORMAT.COM
- HELP.BAT
- MSCDEX.EXE
- SCANDISK.EXE
- SYS.COM

This problem occurs because these files are not included as separate files on the boot disk nor are they extracted to a RAM drive for automatic use.

Solution

Start your computer by using a Windows 98 Startup disk, created by the Startup Disk option of the Add/Remove Program icon in Control Panel. The Startup disk automatically extracts these tools to a RAM drive when you start your computer.

Solution

Use a tool stored in the EBD.CAB file on the boot disk, and first extract the tool by using the appropriate method:

To extract the FORMAT.COM file to your boot disk, type the following command at the command prompt, and then press Enter:

```
extract ebd.cab format.com
```

This step extracts the FORMAT.COM file to your boot disk so that you can format your hard disk.

For all other commands, extract to the root folder of drive C the command you want to use, and then run the command by following these steps:

1. With the boot disk in drive A, restart your computer, type the following commands at the command prompt, and then press Enter after each one:

```
a:\

extract ebd.cab <toolname> /l c:\
```

where <toolname> is the name of the file or tool in the EBD.CAB file you want to use.

2. Use the tool you extracted in step 1. For information, type *<toolname> /?* and press Enter, where <toolname> is the name of the file or tool you extracted.

Related KB article Q191252

CD-ROM Access Limited

Your computer contains an integrated drive electronics (IDE) and small computer system interface (SCSI) CD-ROM drive, and you have access to only one CD-ROM drive when you start your computer by using the Windows 98 Startup disk.

This problem occurs because the IDE and SCSI CD-ROM drivers use Mscd001 as the driver ID.

Solution

Modify the CONFIG.SYS and AUTOEXEC.BAT files on the Windows 98 Startup disk so that each CD-ROM driver has a unique ID by following these steps:

1. Use a text editor, such as Notepad, to open the CONFIG.SYS file on the Windows 98 Startup disk.

2. Locate the line Device=btcdrom.sys /D:mscd001.

3. Change the line to *Device=btcdrom.sys /D:mscd002*.

4. Locate the line Device=aspicd.sys /D:mscd001.

5. Change the line to *Device=aspicd.sys /D:mscd003*.

6. Save and then close the CONFIG.SYS file.

7. Using the text editor, open the AUTOEXEC.BAT file on the Windows 98 Startup disk.

8. Locate the following line:

```
LH %ramd%:\mscdex.exe /D:mscd001 /L:%CDROM%
```

9. Change the line to:

```
LH %ramd%:\mscdex.exe /D:mscd001 /D:mscd002 /D:mscd003 /L:%CDROM%
```

10. Save the AUTOEXEC.BAT file, and then close the text editor.

Related KB article Q188391

Compression Driver Error Message

You start your computer by using a Windows 98 Startup disk, and you see the following error message:

The compression driver cannot be set up correctly.

Get a version from your vendor that is compatible with this version of Windows.

Or, after you start your computer by using a Windows 98 Startup disk, you are unable to gain access to a hard disk compressed with DriveSpace.

This problem occurs because Windows 98 Setup does not update the DriveSpace compression files (DRVSPACE.BIN and DBLSPACE.BIN) in the root folder of compressed drive C. When you create a Windows 98 Startup disk, the older compression files from compressed drive C are copied to the Startup disk.

The DRVSPACE.BIN and DBLSPACE.BIN files in the root folder of a compressed drive C are typically not used. When you start a computer with a compressed hard disk from the hard disk, the DRVSPACE.BIN or DBLSPACE.BIN file is loaded from the host drive (typically, drive H). Windows 98 Setup does correctly update the compression files in the root folder of the host drive.

The older compression files in the root folder of compressed drive C become a problem only when you create a Startup disk, because the system files are generally copied from the root folder of drive C rather than the root folder of the host drive for compressed drive C.

Solution

Copy the updated compression files to drive C, and then create a new Startup disk by following these steps:

1. Click the Start button, choose Programs, and click MS-DOS Prompt.

2. Type the following lines, pressing Enter after each line:

   ```
   attrib -s -h -r c:\d??space.bin

   ren c:\d??space.bin *.old

   copy <windows>\command\drvspace.bin c:\

   copy <windows>\command\drvspace.bin c:\dblspace.bin

   attrib +r +s +h c:\d??space.bin
   ```

   where <windows> is the folder containing Windows.

3. Click the Start button, choose Settings, and click Control Panel.

4. Double-click the Add/Remove Programs icon.

5. Click Create Disk on the Startup Disk tab.

Related KB article Q187218

Invalid System Disk Error Message

You boot from the Startup disk or reboot the first time in Setup, and you receive the following error message:

Invalid system disk Replace the disk, and then press any key

This problem is caused by one of the following conditions:

- The system is infected with the virus AntiCMOS.A.

- The system is running virus-protection software.

- The system is using hard disk management software such as Disk Manager, EZ-Drive, or Drive Pro.

- Setup was unable to copy the system files to the hard drive.

- Security software has disabled access to drive C.

Solution One

If the system is infected with the virus AntiCMOS.A, use an antivirus program to remove the virus, and reinstall Windows.

Solution Two

If the system is running antivirus software, follow these steps:

1. Boot the system by using the Startup disk created during Windows Setup.

2. Use the SYS command from the Startup disk to restore the system files to the hard disk.

Note Some computers use built-in antivirus software that must be disabled in your computer's CMOS settings. If you need to change CMOS settings, see your computer's documentation or contact the manufacturer.

Solution Three

If your system is running disk management software, follow these steps:

1. See the disk management software's documentation for the process required to restore the master boot record (MBR) information.

2. Follow the steps recommended to restore the MBR information.

3. Check the SETUPLOG.TXT file (as described in the following set of steps) for the following statement:

```
FSLog: BIOS Heads=:64, BootPart Heads=:64.
```

4. The preceding number (64, in this example) might vary from computer to computer. If these two numbers are different, replace the system files on your hard disk (as described next).

To check the SETUPLOG.TXT, follow these steps:

1. Click the Start button, choose Programs, and click Windows Explorer.

2. Click the C drive icon.

3. Choose Find from the Tools menu and Files Or Folders from the submenu.

4. Enter *setuplog.txt* in the Named Text box.

5. Click the SETUPLOG.TXT file icon, and read the file.

Follow these steps to reinstall Windows system files:

Warning If you're using Disk Manager or any other disk drive overlay program on a hard disk, make sure that the overlay driver is loaded before you use the SYS command on the hard disk.

1. Boot the system by using the Windows 95 or Windows 98 Startup disk.

2. At the MS-DOS command prompt, type the following lines, pressing Enter after each line:

```
c:

cd\windows\command

attrib c:\msdos.sys -s -h -r

copy c:\msdos.sys c:\msdos.xxx

a:

sys c:

attrib c:\msdos.sys -s -h -r

del c:\msdos.sys

copy c:\msdos.xxx c:\msdos.sys

attrib c:\msdos.sys +s +h +r
```

3. Remove the disk from the drive, and reboot your computer.

Related KB article Q128730

Not Enough Memory to Load RamDrive

You start your computer by using the Windows 98 Startup disk, you receive the message *Not Enough Memory to Load RamDrive,* and drive C contains the files that are normally loaded on the RAM drive. This problem can happen if your hard disk is partitioned with drive overlay software, such as OnTrack Disk Manager or EZBIOS EZ-Drive. When you start your computer by using the Windows 98 Startup disk, the drive overlay software is not loaded from your hard disk.

Solution

To solve this problem, follow these steps:

1. Restart your computer without the Windows 98 Startup disk in the floppy disk drive.

2. Follow the instructions onscreen to start your computer from the floppy disk. Although the method varies depending on the drive overlay software's manufacturer, most involve pressing either the Spacebar or the Ctrl key.

3. Insert the Windows 98 Startup disk in the drive when you are prompted.

Related KB article Q188886

Registry File Not Found Error Message

You attempt to start Windows 98 using the Startup disk, and you see the following error message:

Registry File was not found. Registry services may be inoperative for this session. XMS cache problem. Registry services may be inoperative this session.

You then see the following message on a blue screen:

VFAT Device Initialization Failed. A device or resource required by VFAT is not present or is unavailable. VFAT cannot continue loading. System Halted.

Solution

The Windows 98 Startup disk is designed for you to use to troubleshoot problems in starting Windows 98. You should not start Windows 98 from the Startup disk unless you are having problems starting Windows. Under normal conditions, start your computer from the hard disk.

You can, however, copy the MSDOS.SYS file from the hard disk to the Startup disk to start Windows 98 by using the Windows 98 Startup disk by following these steps:

1. Restart your computer by using the Windows 98 Startup disk.

2. Remove the system, hidden, and read-only attributes from the MSDOS.SYS file in the root folder of the Windows 98 Startup disk and the hard disk. To do so, type the following lines at the command prompt, pressing Enter after each line:

```
attrib -s -h -r a:\msdos.sys
```

```
attrib -s -h -r c:\msdos.sys
```

3. Rename the MSDOS.SYS file on the Windows 98 Startup disk by typing the following command and pressing Enter:

```
ren a:\msdos.sys msdos.xxx
```

4. Copy the MSDOS.SYS file from the hard disk to the Windows 98 Startup disk by typing the following command and then pressing Enter:

```
copy c:\msdos.sys a:\msdos.sys
```

5. Replace the system, hidden, and read-only attributes on the MSDOS.SYS file in the root folder of the Windows 98 Startup disk and the hard disk. To do so, type the following lines, pressing Enter after each line:

```
attrib +s +h +r a:\msdos.sys

attrib +s +h +r c:\msdos.sys
```

6. Restart your by computer by using the Windows 98 Startup disk.

The MSDOS.SYS file is a text file located in the root folder. The file contains a [Paths] section that lists the locations of other Windows 98 files, such as the Registry. When you create a Windows 98 Startup disk, the MSDOS.SYS file on the Startup disk contains only the line ;W98ebd.

Because the Startup disk contains only this line, you can use the Startup disk to start most computers and access a command prompt, but you cannot start Windows 98 because Windows cannot locate the IFSHLP.SYS file or the Registry. If you copy the MSDOS.SYS file from your hard disk to the Windows 98 Startup disk, you might not be able to use the Startup disk to start Windows 98 on another computer. This can be the case if Windows is installed in a different folder or on a different logical drive than the computer from which the MSDOS.SYS file is copied. However, you can still use the Startup disk to start another computer and access the command prompt by pressing and holding down the Ctrl key when your computer starts and then choosing Safe Mode Command Prompt Only from the StartUp menu.

Note For more information about the MSDOS.SYS file, see KB article Q118579, "Contents of the Windows MSDOS.SYS File."

Related KB article Q178947

CHAPTER 15

System Tools

Hot Topic

Control Panel

Accessibility Options ToggleKeys Turns Sound Down

You enable the Use ToggleKeys feature by using the Accessibility Options icon in Control Panel, and sounds are played very quietly or too quietly to be heard.

Solution

Do not enable the Use ToggleKeys feature.

Related KB article Q191458

Add New Hardware Tool Causes Windows to Stop Responding

You use the Add New Hardware tool in Control Panel, and your computer stops responding.

This problem occurs because of the incorrect interpretation of data stored in the computer's Basic Input/Output System (BIOS). On certain motherboards, Windows 98 cannot successfully complete the Plug and Play detection process.

Solution

You might be able to solve this problem by upgrading your computer's BIOS. For information about upgrading the BIOS, please contact the manufacturer of your motherboard.

Related KB article Q188308

Add New Hardware Tool Doesn't Work

You try to use the Add New Hardware tool, and your computer stops responding. Also, your computer hangs intermittently.

This problem occurs when you are using a 4 MB or 8 MB Hercules Thriller 3D video adapter with a Thriller 3D Basic Input/Output System (BIOS) version earlier than 1.04.141 (dated 3/26/98), and drivers earlier than version 0.85.3596 (dated 6/30/98).

Solution

Update the BIOS and drivers for your Hercules Thriller 3D card. For information about how to do so, look at the documentation included with your video adapter, or contact Hercules Technical Support.

Related KB article Q192299

Add New Hardware Tool Produces General Protection Fault Error Messages

You receive random general protection (GP) fault error message in MMSYSTEM.DLL or receive the following error message after you use the Add New Hardware tool in Control Panel:

Rundll32 — This program has caused an illegal operation and will be shut down.

This problem occurs when the Drivers=mmsystem.dll line is missing from the [boot] section of the SYSTEM.INI file.

Solution

To solve this problem, follow these steps:

1. Click the Start button, choose Run, enter *sysedit* in the text box, and then click OK.

2. Select the C:\WINDOWS\SYSTEM.INI window, and enter *Drivers=mmsystem.dll* in the [boot] section of the file.

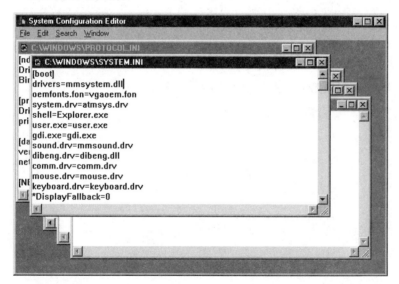

Figure 15-1. *The SYSTEM.INI file in System Configuration Editor.*

3. Choose Save from the File menu, close the program, and reboot the computer.

Related KB article Q138835

Add New Hardware Wizard Doesn't Detect Hardware

You attempt to run the Add New Hardware Wizard, and the progress indicator pauses at 15 percent and then skips to the end of the hardware-detection process without detecting any new hardware. This problem can occur if the SYSDETMG.DLL file is missing or damaged.

Solution

Extract to the WINDOWS\SYSTEM folder a new copy of the SYSDETMG.DLL from your original Windows 98 CD-ROM. For information about how to extract files, see KB article Q129605, "How to Extract Original Compressed Windows Files."

Related KB article Q192746

Add/Remove Programs Closes if Enter Key Pressed

You press Enter on the Startup Disk tab in the Add/Remove Programs dialog box to create a Windows 98 Startup disk, and the Add/Remove Programs Properties dialog box closes.

Solution

Rather than press Enter, press Alt+C or click Create Disk.

Figure 15-2.   *The Startup Disk tab in the Add/Remove Programs Properties dialog box.*

Related KB article   Q178634

Add/Remove Programs Icon Missing in Control Panel

You attempt to add or remove a component in Windows 95 or Windows 98, and you find that the Add/Remove Programs icon is missing in Control Panel or that the Windows Setup and Startup Disk tabs are missing when you use the Add/Remove Programs icon.

Solution

To repair or replace the APPWIZ.CPL or SETUPX.DLL file, follow these steps:

1. Click the Start button, choose Find, and then click Files Or Folders.

2. If the Add/Remove Programs icon is missing, enter *appwiz.cpl* in the Named box, and then click Find Now.

3. If the Windows Setup and Startup Disk tabs are missing, enter *setupx.dll* in the Named box, and then click Find Now.

4. On the list of found files, right-click APPWIZ.CPL or SETUPX.DLL, choose Rename from the shortcut menu, enter a new name for the file (such as *appwiz.xxx* or *setupx.xxx*), and then press the Enter key.

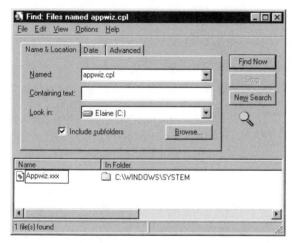

Figure 15-3. *The Find dialog box.*

5. Close the Find dialog box.

6. Extract the APPWIZ.CPL or SETUPX.DLL file from your Windows CD-ROM using System File Checker. For information about using System File Checker, see KB article Q129605, "How to Extract Original Compressed Windows Files."

7. Restart your computer.

Related KB article Q195064

Add/Remove Programs Missing Windows Setup and Startup Disk Tabs

If the SETUPX.DLL file is missing or damaged, the Windows Setup and Startup Disk tabs are missing from the Add/Remove Program Properties dialog box or the System icon in Control Panel does not work. The SETUPX.DLL file should be in the WINDOWS\SYSTEM folder.

Solution

To replace the SETUPX.DLL file, follow these steps:

1. Rename or remove the SETUPX.DLL file (if it exists) in the WINDOWS\SYSTEM folder.

2. Extract a new copy of the SETUPX.DLL file from your original Windows CD-ROM.

Note For information about using Extract, type *extract* at a command prompt, or see KB article Q129605, "How to Extract Original Compressed Windows Files."

3. Restart Windows.

Related KB article Q148793

Add/Remove Programs Prompts for Password

You attempt to add or remove a program or create a Windows 98 Startup disk using the Add/Remove Programs icon in Control Panel, and you are asked to enter a network share name, a drive letter, and a password. This problem occurs if you installed Windows 98 from a password-protected shared network drive.

Solution One

If you know the network share name, drive letter, and password of the shared network drive from which you installed Windows 98, enter this information in the appropriate boxes, and then click OK.

Note You must be logged on to the network to gain access to the shared network drive.

Solution Two

If you have the original Windows 98 CD-ROM or if the Windows 98 source files are located on your hard disk, use Registry Editor to change the value of SourcePath to the full path of the Windows 98 source files in the following Registry key:

```
HKEY_LOCAL_MACHINE\Software\Microsoft\Windows\CurrentVersion\Setup
```

For example, if you have the original Windows 98 CD-ROM, change the data value to <drive>:\win98, where <drive> is the letter of your CD-ROM drive.

Warning Please read the Introduction for information on how to safely edit the Registry.

To fix this problem, follow these steps:

1. Click the Start button, choose Run, enter *regedit* in the Run box, and then click OK.

2. Navigate your way through the folders in the left pane until you locate the preceding folder.

3. Change the value of SourcePath to the full path of your Windows 98 source files.

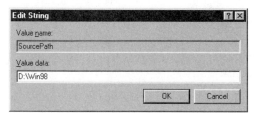

Figure 15-4. *The Edit String dialog box.*

4. Close Regedit.

5. Restart Windows.

Note This procedure changes the location of the Windows 98 source files for all operations that require Windows 98 files. For example, if you change the location of the Windows source files to your CD-ROM drive, you are always prompted for the Windows 98 CD-ROM for operations requiring Windows 98 files.

Related KB article Q186889

Add/Remove Programs Properties Dialog Box Missing Programs

You click the Windows Setup tab or the Install/Uninstall tab under the Add/Remove Programs icon in Control Panel, and you do not see any of the following programs:

- Microsoft Fax
- Microsoft Exchange
- Microsoft Windows Messaging
- Microsoft Mail

This problem can occur if the programs are not installed when you upgrade Windows 95 or Windows for Workgroups 3.1x to Windows 98.

Although they are not parts of the Windows 98 product, a version of Windows Messaging, Microsoft Fax, and a Microsoft Mail workgroup post office are included on the Windows 98 CD-ROM. These programs are made available so that you can reinstall files if the upgraded components become damaged. The use of these files on non-upgrade installations of Windows 98 has not been fully tested by Microsoft.

Windows Messaging is not intended to work with Exchange Server Client 5.0 and should not be installed on a computer on which it is installed.

Solution

If you have to install Windows Messaging, Microsoft Fax, or a Microsoft Mail workgroup post office, follow these steps:

1. Place your Windows 98 CD-ROM in the CD-ROM drive, and then open the folder TOOLS\OLDWIN95\MESSAGE\US.

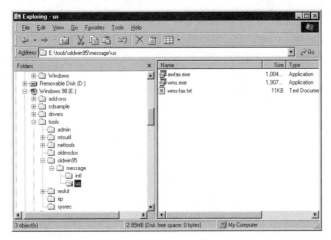

Figure 15-5. *Windows Explorer.*

2. Double-click the WMS.EXE file to install Windows Messaging and the Microsoft Mail workgroup post office utility.

3. Double-click the AWFAX.EXE file to install Microsoft Fax.

4. Restart Windows when you are prompted to do so.

Related KB article Q187549

Add/Remove Programs Unable to Create 5.25-Inch Startup Disk

You attempt to create a Windows 98 Startup disk using a 5.25-inch, 1.2 MB floppy disk, and you see the following prompt after files are copied to the floppy disk:

Please insert a blank floppy and label this disk 1

This problem occurs because creating a Windows 98 Startup disk using a 5.25-inch, 1.2 MB floppy disk is not supported. Although creating a Windows 98 Startup disk by using this type of floppy disk is not supported, it might be possible using two floppy disks.

Solution

Insert a second, formatted, 5.25-inch, 1.2 MB floppy disk in the floppy disk drive, and then click OK. Be sure to label this disk number two.

Related KB article Q191497

Add/Remove Programs Unable to Create Startup Disk

You are unable to create a Windows 98 Startup disk if any of the following conditions exists:

- Ten or more bad sectors are detected on the floppy disk.

- The first sector of the floppy disk is damaged.

- You are not using a high-density floppy disk.

- An antivirus program is running.

- A tape backup device is connected to the floppy controller.

- Your computer's CMOS settings are incorrect.

- You are having problems with the floppy disk drive. For more information about troubleshooting floppy disk problems, see KB article Q178133, "Troubleshooting Floppy Disk Drive Problems in Windows."

Solution One

If 10 or more bad sectors exist on the floppy disk or the first sector is damaged, you can try a different floppy disk. Alternatively, you can run ScanDisk for MS-DOS to try to repair the damaged sectors:

1. Restart your computer. After it completes the Power On Self Test (POST), press and hold down the Ctrl key until you see the Windows 98 StartUp menu, and then choose Command Prompt Only.

2. At the command prompt, type the *scandisk <drive>:* command, where <drive> is the letter of your floppy disk drive, and then press the Enter key.

3. When you are prompted to perform a surface scan, click Yes or press the Enter key.

4. Close ScanDisk after it is finished, and then restart your computer normally.

Solution Two

If you are not using a high-density floppy disk, replace your low-density floppy disk with a high-density floppy disk. Only a high-density floppy disk can be used to create a Windows 98 Startup disk.

Solution Three

Disable or uninstall any antivirus program installed on your computer. For information about how to do so, refer to the documentation included with the program.

Solution Four

Some older tape backup devices that attach to floppy controllers might prevent you from gaining access to the floppy disk drive. To work around this problem, disconnect the tape backup device from the floppy controller before you attempt to create a Windows 98 Startup disk, or disable the tape backup device's driver. For information about how to do either task, refer to the documentation included with your tape backup device.

Solution Five

Incorrect CMOS settings might also prevent you from creating a Windows 98 startup disk. To verify that the floppy disk drive settings are correct in your computer's CMOS, refer to the documentation included with your computer or floppy disk drive, or contact the manufacturer.

Related KB article Q191848

Control Panel Produces Couldn't Load CMF.DLL Error Message

You have the Xerox Color Manager program installed on a computer running Windows 3.1x and upgrade to Windows 95 or Windows 98, and you see the following error message when you open Control Panel:

Couldn't load Cmf.dll, check BinDir in Xcm.ini

If you then click OK, Control Panel opens normally.

Solution

To rename the Xerox Color Manager files, follow these steps:

1. Click the Start button, choose Find, and then click Files Or Folders.

2. In the Named box, enter *xcm*.cpl*, and then click Find Now.

3. Click the name of a file on the list. Click File, and then click the Rename option.

4. Change the extension of the filename from .CPL to *.OLD*, and press the Enter key.

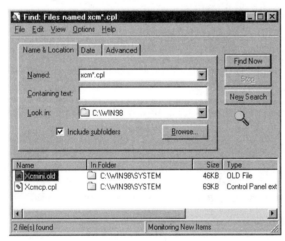

Figure 15-6. *The Find dialog box.*

5. Repeat steps 3 and 4 for each additional file on the list.

6. Close the Find box.

7. Restart your computer.

Related KB article Q191269

Desktop Shortcut Icon Launches Control Panel Slowly

You double-click a desktop shortcut linked to CONTROL.EXE to start Control Panel, and a 60- to 90-second delay occurs before Control Panel appears.

The CONTROL.EXE program was designed to be used with a shell component such as Program Manager or File Manager from an earlier version of Windows. When you are using Windows Explorer as the shell in Windows 98, starting CONTROL.EXE reloads much of the Windows 95 and Windows 98 shell components, resulting in a delay.

Solution One

To start Control Panel from the My Computer icon, follow these steps:

1. Double-click the My Computer icon on your desktop.

2. Double-click the Control Panel icon.

Solution Two

Start Control Panel from the Start menu: Click the Start button, choose Settings, and click Control Panel.

Solution Three

To create a shortcut to Control Panel from the Control Panel icon in My Computer, follow these steps:

1. Double-click the My Computer icon on your desktop.

2. Drag the Control Panel icon from the My Computer dialog box to the desktop.

3. When you're asked whether you want to create a shortcut, click Yes.

4. Double-click the Control Panel icon to start Control Panel.

Related KB article Q128702

Desktop Themes Icon Displays Invalid Page Fault Error Message

You attempt to change your desktop theme by using the Desktop Themes icon in Control Panel, and you see the following error message:

THEMES caused an invalid page fault in module <unknown>.

This problem can occur if the DefaultIcon Registry key is missing or damaged.

Solution One

Obtain the latest version of the THEMES.EXE file:

1. Click the Start button, and then click Windows Update.

2. After you're connected to the Windows Update web site, select the check boxes for the desktop themes you want to install.

3. Click Download, and then follow the instructions onscreen.

Solution Two

Re-create the DefaultIcon Registry key:

Warning Please read the Introduction for information on how to safely edit the Registry.

1. Click the Start button, choose Run, enter *regedit* in the Run box, and then click OK.

2. Navigate your way through the folders in the left pane until you locate the following key:

   ```
   HKEY_CURRENT_USER\Software\Classes\CLSID\{645FF040-5081-101B-9F08-00AA002F954E}\
   DefaultIcon
   ```

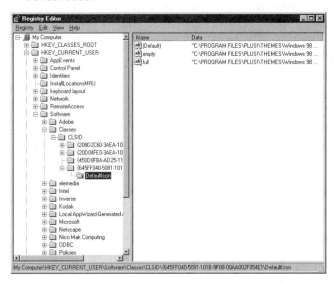

Figure 15-7. *The Registry Editor.*

3. Delete this key if it exists.

4. Close Regedit.

5. Restart Windows.

6. Click the Start button, choose Settings, click Control Panel, and then double-click Desktop Themes.

7. In the Theme box, click the desktop theme you want to use, and then click OK.

Related KB article Q190140

Error Message Occurs When Opening Control Panel After Upgrading from Windows 95

After you upgrade Windows 95 to Windows 98 and try to open Control Panel, you see the following error message:

An error occurred while Windows was working with the Control Panel

file <drive>:\<windows>\system\setnote.cpl

where <drive> is the drive on which Windows is installed, and <windows> is the folder in which Windows is installed. This problem can occur if IBM ViaVoice Gold version 4.3.0.1 is installed on your computer.

Solution One

Contact IBM Technical Support, and ask for an updated version of ViaVoice Gold.

Solution Two

To work around this problem, follow these steps:

1. Click the Start button, choose Find, and then click Files Or Folders.

2. In the Named box, enter *setnote.cpl*, and click Find Now.

3. If the file is displayed as SETNOTE on the list of found files, open My Computer, choose Folder Options from the View menu, and click the View tab. Under Files And Folders, clear the Hide File Extensions For Known File Types check box, and then click OK. The file is now displayed as SETNOTE.CPL.

4. On the list of found files, right-click the SETNOTE.CPL file, and then choose Rename.

5. Type a different name for the SETNOTE.CPL file (such as *setnote.xxx*), and then press the Enter key.

6. Close Find.

7. Using Registry Editor, delete the SETNOTE.CPL value in the following Registry key:

   ```
   HKEY_CURRENT_USER\Software\Microsoft\Windows\CurrentVersion\Explorer\
   DocFindSpecMRU
   ```

Warning Please read the Introduction for information on how to safely edit the Registry.

8. Click the Start button, choose Run, enter *regedit* in the Run box, and then click OK.

9. Navigate your way through the folders in the left pane until you locate the key just described, and then delete the SETNOTE.CPL value.

10. Close Registry Editor.

11. Restart Windows.

Microsoft has confirmed that this behavior is not caused by a problem in Windows 98, but might be caused by design changes in Windows 98. For more information about solving this problem, contact the program's manufacturer.

Related KB article Q190367

Fatal Exception Error Message Occurs When Opening or Closing Control Panel or Network Properties

If a scanner is installed in your computer, any or all of the following situations occur:

- When you attempt to open or close Control Panel or when you remove network components in the network properties and then restart Windows, you see the following error message:

   A fatal exception 0E has occurred at 0028:C029F7A1 in VXD IFSMGR(04) + 0000D4F1. The current application will be terminated.

   After receiving this error message, you can still use Control Panel, but the Volume icon no longer appears on the taskbar. This behavior also occurs in Safe mode.

- When you start Windows, you see the following error message:

   A fatal exception 0E has occurred at 028:C0282dB0 in VxD IFSMGR(03) + 0000 CF7C. The current application will be terminated.

- Windows Setup stops responding (hangs) while Control Panel is being configured.

Solution

These results can occur if the VHPSCAND.VXD file is located in the WINDOWS\SYSTEM folder rather than in the WINDOWS\SYSTEM\IOSUBSYS folder. To move the file, follow these steps:

1. Click the Start button, choose Programs, and then click Windows Explorer.

2. Choose Find from the Tools menu, choose Find, and then click Files Or Folders.

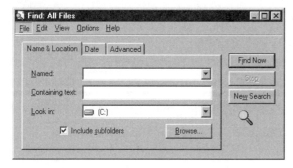

Figure 15-8.   *The Find dialog box.*

3. In the Named box, enter *vhpscand.vxd*, and then click Find Now.

4. If the VHPSCAND.VXD file is in the WINDOWS\SYSTEM folder, right-click the VHPSCAND.VXD file, and then click Cut.

5. Right-click the WINDOWS\SYSTEM\IOSUBSYS folder, and then click Paste.

6. Restart your computer.

Related KB article   Q175211

Fonts Shows Duplicate Fonts

After you upgrade Windows 3.x or Windows for Workgroups 3.x to Windows 98, the following bitmap fonts (.FON) are listed twice under the Fonts icon in Control Panel:

- MS Sans Serif

- MS Serif

- Small Fonts

- Courier

Other bitmap fonts are listed twice if you installed them separately. This problem occurs because the FONTREG.EXE file that is run during Windows 98 Setup incorrectly migrates Windows 3.x and Windows for Workgroups 3.x .FON files.

Solution

To delete duplicate bitmap fonts by using the Fonts icon, right-click the font you want to delete, and then choose Delete from the shortcut menu. Bitmap fonts listed twice in the Fonts icon are listed only once in programs.

Related KB article Q187658

Game Controllers Icon Behaves Unexpectedly

You double-click the Game Controllers icon in Control Panel and experience one of the following symptoms:

- The Game Controllers dialog box opens and then immediately closes.

- You receive the following error message:

    An error occurred while Windows was working with the Control Panel file ...\SYSTEM\JOY.CPL

This problem can occur if the DINPUT.DLL file is missing or damaged.

Solution

To solve this problem, follow these steps:

1. If it exists, rename the DINPUT.DLL file located in the WINDOWS\SYSTEM folder.

2. Extract to the WINDOWS\SYSTEM folder a new copy of the DINPUT.DLL file from your original Windows 98 CD-ROM. For more information about extracting files, see KB article Q129605, "How to Extract Original Compressed Windows Files."

Related KB article Q188106

General Protection Fault Occurs When Opening Control Panel

You open Control Panel and see the following error message:

EXPLORER caused a general protection fault in module qtw16.cpl at <address>

Your computer stops responding (hangs). This problem also occurs in Safe mode. The problem occurs if one or more Apple QuickTime for Windows files is missing or damaged.

Solution

Remove QuickTime for Windows:

1. Restart your computer. After your computer completes the Power On Self Test (POST), press and hold down the Ctrl key until you see the Windows 98 Startup menu, and then choose Safe Mode Command Prompt Only.

Note For more information about Windows 98 startup, see KB article Q178548, "No 'Starting Windows 98' Message at Startup."

2. At the command prompt, type the following lines, and press Enter after each one:

```
cd\windows\system

ren qt216.cpl qtw16.xxx
```

3. Restart your computer normally.

4. Click the Start button, choose Settings, click Control Panel, and then double-click the Add/Remove Programs icon.

5. Click the Install/Uninstall tab, click QuickTime For Windows, and then click Add/Remove.

To view QuickTime files, you must reinstall QuickTime for Windows. For information about how to do so, contact Apple Technical Support.

Related KB article Q193882

Icons Displayed Incorrectly in Control Panel

The icons in Control Panel appear in black or are the wrong icon. This problem can occur if the ShellIconCache file in the WINDOWS folder is damaged.

Solution

Reboot your computer. If this solution does not work, delete the SHELLICONCACHE folder from the Windows file. Because it's a hidden file, follow these steps to delete it:

1. Double-click the My Computer icon, and then choose Folder Options from the View menu.

2. Click the View tab, and select the Show All Files check box under the Hidden Files heading.

3. Click OK.

4. Click the Start button, choose Find, and click Files Or Folders.

5. Enter ShellIconCache in the Named text box, and click Find Now.

6. Right-click the SHELLICONCACHE folder, and choose Delete from the shortcut menu.

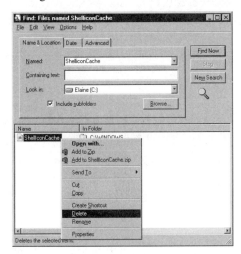

Figure 15-9. *The Find dialog box.*

7. Click Yes when you are asked whether you are sure that you want to send the folder to the Recycle Bin.

8. Right-click the Recycle Bin on the desktop, choose Empty Recycle Bin from the shortcut menu, and click Yes when it asks whether you are sure.

9. Reboot the computer.

Related KB article Q133733

Icons Missing in Control Panel

You open Control Panel from a shortcut or another program, and only the following five icons are available: Add New Hardware, System, Modems, ODBC, and Network.

This problem occurs when you are using an old version of the CONTROL.EXE file and should occur only with shortcuts that point specifically to CONTROL.EXE or 16-bit Windows-based programs that call CONTROL.EXE.

Solution One

Open Control Panel by clicking the Start button, choosing Settings, and clicking Control Panel. To create a shortcut to Control Panel, double-click My Computer, and then drag the Control Panel icon to the folder in which you want to create the shortcut.

Solution Two

Remove the shortcut that points to the CONTROL.EXE file. Verify that the CONTROL.EXE file in the WINDOWS folder is the current version. If it is not, remove or rename the file, and then extract the current file from the Windows disks or CD-ROM and place it in the WINDOWS folder. For more information about extracting files, see KB article Q129605, "How to Extract Original Compressed Windows Files."

Related KB article Q132885

Infrared Icon Reports Internal Error 45

You double-click the Infrared icon in Control Panel and receive the following error message:

Internal Error 45: Your infrared software has encountered an error, check infrared software settings under network properties.

This problem can occur if the Fast Infrared Protocol is missing or damaged.

Solution

Remove and then reinstall the Fast Infrared Protocol:

1. Click the Start button, choose Settings, and then click Control Panel.

2. Double-click the Network icon.

3. On the list of installed network components, click Fast Infrared Protocol, and then click Remove.

4. Restart your computer when you are prompted to do so.

5. Click the Start button, choose Settings, and then click Control Panel.

6. Double-click the Network icon.

7. On the Configuration tab, click Add.

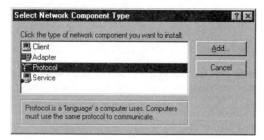

Figure 15-10. *The Select Network Component Type dialog box.*

8. Select Protocol, and then click Add.

9. In the Manufacturers box, select Microsoft, select Fast Infrared Protocol in the Network Protocols box, and then click OK.

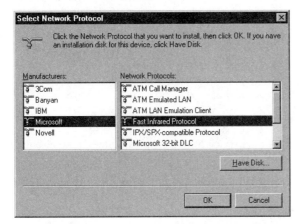

Figure 15-11. *The Select Network Protocol dialog box.*

10. Click OK, and then restart your computer when you are prompted to do so.

Related KB article Q191578

Microsoft Mail Post Office Missing from Control Panel

After you install Windows Messaging, Microsoft Exchange, or Microsoft Outlook, the Microsoft Mail Postoffice icon is missing in Control Panel if the WGPOADMN.DLL file and the WGPOCPL.CPL file are missing from the WINDOWS\SYSTEM folder.

Solution

To solve this problem, follow these steps:

1. Insert the Windows 98 CD-ROM in the CD-ROM drive, and then close the Windows 98 screen if it appears.

2. Click the Start button, and then choose Run.

3. In the Open box, enter the following command, and then press the Enter key:

```
<drive>:\tools\oldwin95\message\us\wms.exe
```

where <drive> is the drive letter assigned to your CD-ROM drive.

Related KB article Q182471

Mouse Properties Dialog Box Missing General Tab

You look at the Mouse Properties dialog box, and the General tab is missing. This behavior is by design. The purpose of the General tab in Windows 95 is to provide a location from which you can upgrade the mouse driver. However, the General tab can accommodate only one mouse. With the addition of Universal Serial Bus (USB) support in Windows 98, more than one pointing device is installed on the computer.

Solution

To upgrade the mouse driver in Windows 98, follow these steps:

1. Click the Start button, choose Settings, and then click Control Panel.

2. Double-click the System icon, click the Device Manager tab, and then double-click the Mouse branch to expand it.

3. Click the appropriate mouse, and then click Properties.

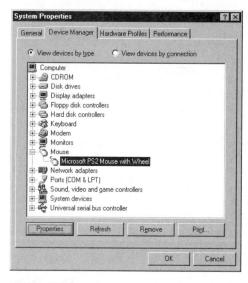

Figure 15-12. *The Device Manager tab in the System Properties dialog box.*

4. Click the Driver tab, and then click Update Driver.

5. Follow the instructions onscreen.

Related KB article Q186926

Network Icon Doesn't Open

You try to open the Network icon in Control Panel, and nothing happens, or you receive either of these two error messages:

Rundll caused an invalid page fault in netdi.dll

Rundll32 caused a general protection fault in krnl386.exe

This problem occurs when the NETDI.DLL file is missing or damaged.

Solution

Extract a new copy of the NETDI.DLL file from your original Windows disks or CD-ROM. For information about extracting files, see KB article Q129605, "How to Extract Original Compressed Windows Files."

Related KB article Q192323

System Properties Errantly Lists MMX CPU

You look at the System Properties dialog box in Windows 98 and notice that your non-MMX central-processing unit (CPU) is listed as an MMX CPU.

Solution

You can ignore the CPU information displayed in the System Properties dialog box. This issue does not affect the functionality of Windows 98 or the CPU and has been reported to occur with the following non-MMX CPUs:

- Intel Mobile Pentium Processor (Manufacturing Stepping is "mA4")

- S-Spec: Q0848, Q0849, Q0850, Q0851, Q0852, Q0853, SK119, SK120, SK121, SK122, SK123, SK124

Related KB article Q187613

System Properties Reports Memory Amount Incorrectly

You look at the Performance tab in System Properties, and notice that the amount of memory reported is different from the amount of memory installed in your computer.

Solution One

This problem might occur because HIMEM.SYS does not use the memory on your EISA computer. If you have an EISA computer, determine whether HIMEM.SYS is addressing all the available memory. For more information about this process, see KB article Q82712, "HIMEM.SYS /EISA Switch."

Solution Two

This problem might occur because a driver or program loading from the CONFIG.SYS or AUTOEXEC.BAT file claims a portion of random access memory (RAM).

To determine whether a real-mode device or program is claiming a portion of RAM, follow these steps to bypass the loading of the CONFIG.SYS and AUTOEXEC.BAT files:

1. Restart your computer. After your computer completes the Power On Self Test (POST), press and hold down the Ctrl key.

2. Choose Step-By-Step Confirmation from the StartUp menu.

3. Press Y at each prompt except for the following prompts, where you should press N:

```
Process your startup device drivers (CONFIG.SYS)?

Process your startup command file (AUTOEXEC.BAT)?
```

4. After Windows starts up, check the memory reported on the Performance tab in the System Properties dialog box.

5. The real-mode CD-ROM driver from Teac for its 4X CD-ROM drive loading in the AUTOEXEC.BAT file has the parameter xmssize= -1. This parameter can cause this behavior. To solve this problem, change the parameter to *xmssize=0*.

Solution Three

This problem might occur because a virtual device driver loading from the SYSTEM.INI file claims a portion of RAM.

To determine whether a virtual device driver being loaded from the SYSTEM.INI file causes this problem, replace the SYSTEM.INI file with a clean version. For more information about this topic, see KB article Q140441, "Creating a New SYSTEM.INI File Without Third-Party Drivers."

Solution Four

This problem might occur because a protected-mode driver causes the memory mismatch.

To determine whether this is the problem, follow these steps:

1. Click the Start button, choose Settings, click Control Panel, and then double-click the System icon.

2. Click the Device Manager tab.

3. Double-click a listed device, and then clear the Original Configuration (Current) check box. When you are prompted to restart the computer, click No.

4. Repeat step 3 for each listed device.

Note Do not repeat step 3 for devices listed on the System Devices branch. When you disable the hard disk controller, click Yes to restart the computer if the hard disk controller is a Peripheral Component Interconnect (PCI) device. PCI hard disk controllers cannot be loaded and unloaded dynamically.

5. Restart the computer.

6. After Windows starts up, check the amount of memory reported on the Performance tab in System Properties.

Solution Five

This problem might occur because the Registry is damaged. To determine whether the Registry is damaged, replace the current Registry with a backup copy. For more information about extracting files, see KB article Q131431, "How to Troubleshoot Registry Errors."

Solution Six

This problem might occur because a CMOS setting disables some of the RAM. Some computers have CMOS settings that can disable a portion of the computer's RAM or prevent Windows from recognizing the RAM.

One computer known to have this problem is the Cyrix 166. It has a CMOS setting labeled Hold To 15 MB RAM. If this setting is enabled, Windows reports only 15 MB of RAM on a computer that has more than 15 MB of RAM installed. To solve this problem on the Cyrix 166, disable the CMOS setting. This action causes Windows to recognize all the RAM in the computer.

Solution Seven

This problem might occur because the maxphyspage= setting in your SYSTEM.INI file is set to restrict Windows from using some of the installed memory. To solve this problem, remove or disable the maxphyspage= line in the SYSTEM.INI file, and then restart your computer. To disable the line, use a text editor, such as Notepad, to edit the SYSTEM.INI file and place a semicolon (;) at the beginning of the line.

Solution Eight

This problem might occur because RAMDRIVE.SYS is loading in the CONFIG.SYS file. Check your CONFIG.SYS file for a line containing RAMDRIVE.SYS. If you have this line, it means that you are using a RAM drive. To disable the RAM drive, remove or disable in the CONFIG.SYS file the line that contains *RAMDRIVE.SYS*. To disable the line, use a text editor, such as Notepad, to edit the CONFIG.SYS file and place a semicolon (;) at the beginning of the line.

Related KB article Q146912

Users Icon Missing from Control Panel

The Users icon is missing from Control Panel (even if you have enabled User Profiles) if you have used the TweakUI program to remove the Internet icon from Control Panel.

Solution

To use the TweakUI program to add the Internet icon to Control Panel, follow these steps:

1. Click the Start button, choose Settings, click Control Panel, and then double-click the TweakUI icon.

2. Click the Control Panel tab, select the INETCPL.CPL check box, and then click OK.

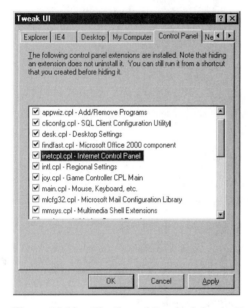

Figure 15-13.   *The Control Panel tab for the Tweak UI icon.*

3. Choose Refresh from the View menu, and then close TweakUI.

Related KB article Q193913

Device Manager

Circled Exclamation Point Next to Advanced Power Management Support Device

An exclamation point in a yellow circle is displayed next to the Advanced Power Management Support device in Device Manager, with the following status:

This device is not present, not working properly, or does not have all the drivers installed. See your hardware documentation (Code 10.)

This problem can occur if the Fast Shutdown option is enabled and you restart Windows while holding down the Shift key.

Solution One

Do not hold down the Shift key while restarting your computer.

Solution Two

To disable the Fast Shutdown option, follow these steps:

1. Click the Start button, choose Programs, click Accessories, click System Tools, and then click System Information.

2. Choose System Configuration Utility from the Tools menu.

3. Click the General tab, and then click Advanced.

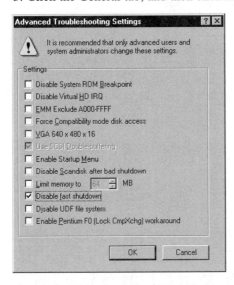

Figure 15-14.   *The Advanced Troubleshooting Settings dialog box.*

4. Select the Disable Fast Shutdown check box.

5. Click OK, and then click OK.

6. When you are prompted to restart your computer, click Yes.

On some computers, you can hold down the Shift key to restart Windows without restarting your computer. Although this strategy might work, the functionality is not supported in Windows 98. For information about other issues that can occur if you restart your computer while holding down the Shift key, see KB article Q186925, "Restarting Computer While Holding Down Shift Key Hangs Windows."

Related KB article Q193933

Circled Exclamation Point Next to PCMCIA Controller

After you install Windows 98, Device Manager displays a PCIC- (PC Card I/O Card) compatible PCMCIA controller with an exclamation point in a yellow circle. This problem can occur if you have a CardBus PCMCIA (Personal Computer Memory Card International Association) controller. These controllers are initialized to PCIC-compatible mode by the BIOS for backward compatibility. After Windows is installed, it disables PCIC compatibility mode in the BIOS and configures the controller to CardBus mode, but does not remove the PCIC-compatible controller from Device Manager.

CardBus controllers are designed to be compatible with older Intel PCIC controllers. To be compatible with older versions of Windows also, the controller is sometimes initialized in PCIC-compatible mode by BIOS vendors. In this case, Windows Setup detects a PCIC controller. Windows recognizes the CardBus controller and disables PCIC-compatibility mode and configures the controller to CardBus mode. Therefore, the PCIC-compatible controller in Device Manager displays the exclamation point in a yellow circle.

Solution

To remove the PCIC-compatible controller, follow these steps:

1. Click the Start button, choose Settings, click Control Panel, and then click the System icon.
2. Click the Device Manager tab in the System Properties dialog box.
3. Select the PCIC-compatible controller.
4. Click Remove, and then click Yes.
5. Click OK.

Microsoft is researching this problem and will post new information in the Knowledge Base as it becomes available.

Related KB article Q158906

Circled Exclamation Point Next to Plug and Play BIOS Device

After you upgrade from Windows 95 to Windows 98, an exclamation point in a yellow circle is displayed next to the Plug and Play BIOS device in Device Manager. If you look at the properties for the Plug and Play BIOS device, the following status is displayed:

This device is not working properly because the file (Bios.vxd) that loads the drivers for this device is bad (Code 8). To fix this problem, click Update Driver to update the driver for this device.

If you click Update Driver and attempt to search for a better driver, you see the following message:

The best driver is already installed.

This problem can occur if the Windows 95 version of the BIOS.VXD file is in the WINDOWS folder.

Solution

To delete the BIOS.VXD file, follow these steps:

1. Click the Start button, choose Find, and then click Files Or Folders.

2. In the Look In box, select the drive on which the WINDOWS folder is located.

3. In the Named box, enter *bios.vxd*, and then click Find Now.

4. On the list of found files, right-click the BIOS.VXD file in the WINDOWS folder, click Delete, and then click Yes.

5. Close Find.

6. Restart your computer.

Related KB article Q194175

Device Manager Reports an Error Code

To see the error codes the Device Manager reports, follow these steps:

1. Click the Start button, choose Settings, and then click Control Panel.

2. Double-click the System icon.

3. Click the Device Manager tab.

4. Double-click a device type (for example, double-click Modem) to see the devices in that category.

5. Double-click a device to see its properties. If an error code has been generated, the code appears in the Device Status box on the General tab.

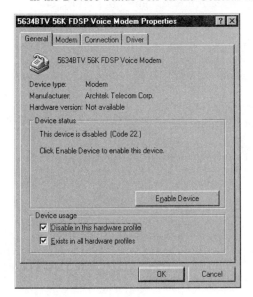

Figure 15-15. *The device status for a device.*

Solution One

Most of the error codes contain instructions for solving the problem. In several cases, the General tab also contains a Solution option for solving the problem.

For assistance in solving hardware conflicts, you can use Hardware Conflict Troubleshooter in the Windows 98 help system. To access the troubleshooter, click the Start button and choose Help. Then click the Contents tab, and click the Troubleshooters hyperlink. Click the Hardware Conflict hyperlink to start the troubleshooter.

Note For more information about troubleshooting hardware conflicts, see KB article Q133240, "Troubleshooting Device Conflicts with Device Manager."

Solution Two

For error codes 1–5, 7–10, 13, 17, 18–20, 22, 23, 26–28, and 31, you can also try removing the hardware device causing the error code and then running the Add New Hardware Wizard to reinstall the device. You can also try this method for Error Code 23 for hardware devices other than display adapters. To do so, follow these steps:

1. Select the device in Device Manager, and click Remove.

2. Double-click the Add New Hardware icon in Control Panel.

Note For error code 9, you might also have to ask the hardware manufacturer for the proper Registry settings for the device.

Solution Three

For error code 11, run the Automatic Skip Driver utility. To launch this utility, click the Start button, choose Run, enter *asd* in the Open text box, and then click OK.

You can use Automatic Skip Driver Agent to enable any device it has previously disabled, and Windows 98 then tries to use the device when you next restart your computer. If this device or operation does not start correctly, your computer stops responding. If you then restart your computer for a third time, Automatic Skip Driver Agent prevents the device or operation from running. When your computer starts up, click Details to identify the device or operation that does not start correctly and to display a suggested course of action.

Note Devices disabled by Automatic Skip Driver Agent to allow Windows to start up are recorded in the ASD.LOG file.

Solution Four

For error codes 4, 7, 8, 11, 17, 26, 27, 28, and 31, if the problem continues, contact the hardware manufacturer for an updated driver. For error code 26, you might be able to acquire the driver from the Microsoft Software Library.

Solution Five

For error codes 10 and 24, make sure that the device is firmly connected and that the adapter cards are properly seated.

Solution Six

For error code 19, if using the Check Registry option listed under the error message does not fix the problem, restart your computer in MS-DOS mode, and then type *scanreg /restore* at the command prompt.

After rebooting Windows, remove the device listing an error code, and then redetect it by using the Add New Hardware icon in Control Panel (see Solution Two).

Solution Seven

For error code 22, if the message says that the hardware was disabled by a Windows driver and the recommended solution doesn't work, try a clean boot, disabling as many drivers and programs as you can, to try to rule out any software interference. If you still have problems, contact your hardware manufacturer.

Solution Eight

For error code 30, remove the real-mode driver that is using the same IRQ as your device. To do so, click the Start button, choose Run, enter *msconfig* in the Open text box, and then click OK to open System Configuration. Click the Selective Startup option button, clear the Process CONFIG. SYS File and Process AUTOEXEC.BAT File check boxes, and restart your computer. If the problem goes away, you have a problem with a real-mode driver loaded from your AUTOEXEC.BAT or CONFIG.SYS files. Use the System Configuration Utility to determine which file is the problem, and then go through the problem file line by line in Notepad to eliminate the conflict.

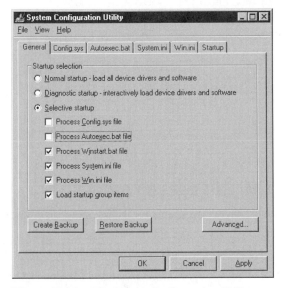

Figure 15-16. *The System Configuration Utility.*

Related KB article Q125174

Driver Names Identical for Windows 3.1 and Windows 98

After you install a Windows 3.1 device driver, the devices associated with the device driver appear on the Windows hardware lists in the Add New Hardware Wizard, Add Printer Wizard, and Install New Modem Wizard. It is difficult to distinguish between the Windows 3.1 driver and the Windows 98 driver on the hardware lists.

Solution

To remove all Windows 3.1 drivers from the hardware lists, rename all the OEM<n>.INF files in the WINDOWS\INF folder (where <n> is an incremental number starting at 0). Although this action does not affect the Windows 3.1 drivers you have installed, it does prevent you from reinstalling the drivers without the original OEMSETUP.INF files included with each driver. To rename the files, follow these steps:

1. Type the following commands at a command prompt, and press the Enter key after each line:

   ```
   cd \windows\inf

   ren oem?.inf oem?.xxx
   ```

2. If there are more than 10 OEM .INF files, you must also type the following command:

   ```
   ren oem??.inf oem??.xxx
   ```

Note Do not use the OEM*.INF wildcard designation in place of OEM?.INF and OEM??.INF. Doing so might cause the wrong files to be renamed.

---

3. If no OEM .INF files are in the WINDOWS\INF folder, you can force Windows to rebuild the entire driver information database by renaming the DRVDATA.BIN and DRVIDX.BIN files in the WINDOWS\INF folder. To do so, type the following commands at a command prompt, and press the Enter key after each line:

   ```
   cd \windows\inf

   ren drvdata.bin drvdata.xxx

   ren drvidx.bin drvidx.xxx
   ```

Related KB article Q137377

Duplicate Items Displayed for Dell XPi CD Latitude Laptop

After you upgrade a Dell XPi CD Latitude Laptop to Windows 98, you experience one or both of the following symptoms:

- Two PC Card (PCMCIA) devices are detected for every one inserted in your computer.

- An additional Texas Instruments Peripheral Component Interconnect (PCI) 1130 CardBus controller is displayed in Device Manager.

Solution

Obtain the A10 or later BIOS revision from the Dell Computer Corporation web site or from Dell Technical Support.

After you install the BIOS revision, device detection now functions properly, but two Texas Instruments PCI 1130 CardBus controllers are still displayed in Device Manager. This behavior is normal.

Related KB article Q191364

Mouse or Computer Hangs When Refresh Is Clicked

You click the Refresh option button in Device Manager, and the mouse stops responding (hangs) for a few seconds or the computer stops responding.

Solution

The computer (or mouse) is not hung. After pausing a few seconds, the system should work normally. SCSI controller drivers or SCSI device drivers might cause this behavior. To test it, disable the device or remove real-mode drivers for the device to see whether the behavior is minimized.

Related KB article Q158943

Resource Conflict Is Displayed in Device Manager

You look at a device in Device Manager, and an exclamation point in a yellow circle is displayed for the device. When you see the properties of the device, the status for the device reports Code 15, indicating a resource conflict, but the Resource tab for the device shows no conflicts.

This problem occurs when a resource conflict exists between the device and a device alias.

Solution

You can safely ignore the conflict. New devices you add to your computer can use Input/Output (I/O) addresses assigned to a device alias. For additional information about device aliases, see KB article Q180412, "Input/Output Addresses Are Used By Aliases in Device Manager."

You can also remove the resource conflict. For more information about how to troubleshoot device conflicts with Device Manager, see KB article Q133240, "Troubleshooting Device Conflicts with Device Manager."

Related KB article Q189877

Secondary Controller Drives Don't Function

After you restart your computer, the secondary controller on a CMD PCI-0640 PCI-to-IDE controller is no longer listed in Device Manager. When this situation occurs, devices on the secondary controller that use protected-mode drivers no longer function. This problem can be caused by incorrect settings in Device Manager for the CMD controller.

Solution

To configure the parent device correctly, follow these steps:

1. In Control Panel, double-click the System icon.

2. Click the Device Manager tab.

3. Double-click the Hard Disk Controllers branch to expand it.

4. Click the CMD PCI-0640 PCI-to-IDE controller, and then click Properties.

5. Click the Settings tab.

6. Select the proper configuration for the device.

Because of difficulties in detecting the chip sets on these controllers, extra settings have been added to ensure that they are properly configured at startup. You can choose from among the following settings:

- Default (Windows Auto Detect)
- Both IDE Channels Enabled
- Only Primary IDE Channel Enabled
- Only Secondary IDE Channel Enabled
- No IDE Channels Enabled

Related KB article Q159556

DriveSpace

Animated DriveSpace Pie Chart Isn't Displayed

You use DriveSpace to create a new compressed volume, and you can't see the animated DriveSpace pie chart.

This problem can occur if your computer is configured to use any of the following color schemes:

- High Contrast #1
- High Contrast #2
- High-Contrast Black

Solution

To select a different color scheme before starting DriveSpace, follow these steps:

1. Click the Start button, choose Settings, click Control Panel, and then double-click the Display icon.

2. Click the Appearance tab.

3. Select Windows Standard from the Schemes box, and click OK.

Figure 15-17. *The Appearance tab in Display Properties.*

Related KB article Q192572

CD-ROM or Network Drive Can't Be Examined

You try to use DriveSpace to create a new compressed volume, and you receive the following error message:

Error:

Windows cannot examine drive <n>. You should check the drive for errors using ScanDisk.

ID Number: DRVSPACE043

where <n> is the drive letter of a network share or a CD-ROM drive with a CD-ROM inserted. Note that this error message occurs twice for each mapped network drive or CD-ROM drive. This problem occurs because DriveSpace runs ScanDisk for Windows to check all drives (including mapped network drives and CD-ROM drives), but ScanDisk for Windows cannot check network or CD-ROM drives.

Solution

This problem does not affect the functionality of DriveSpace. To work around this problem, click OK twice for each mapped network drive or CD-ROM drive with a CD-ROM inserted. To prevent these error messages from occurring, remove all CD-ROMs from your CD-ROM drives and disconnect all network drives before running DriveSpace.

Related KB article Q186179

Disk Compression Tools Don't Uninstall

You use the Add/Remove Programs icon in Control Panel, and the Disk Compression Tools check box is missing from the System Tools dialog box if you already have disk compression installed.

Solution

To solve this problem (for example, if you want to reinstall disk compression tools), manually create an .INF file to restore the Disk Compression Tools check box:

1. Use any text editor, such as Notepad, to create a file with the following lines:

```
[version]

signature="$CHICAGO$""


[DefaultInstall]

AddReg=Enable.Drvspace


[Enable.Drvspace]

HKLM,%KEY_OPTIONAL%,"Dxxspace",,"dxxspace"

HKLM,%KEY_OPTIONAL%\dxxspace,INF,,"applets1.inf"

HKLM,%KEY_OPTIONAL%\dxxspace,Section,,"dxxspace""

HKLM,%KEY_OPTIONAL%\dxxspace,Installed,,"0"


[Strings]

KEY_OPTIONAL    =

"SOFTWARE\Microsoft\Windows\CurrentVersion\Setup\OptionalComponents"
```

2. Save the file, and then rename it to *dxxspace.inf.*

3. Right-click the file, and then choose Install from the shortcut menu.

4. Restart your computer.

Related KB article Q192351

Error Message Displayed When Attempting to Compress Drive with Long Folder Pathname

You experience one of the following four errors when you use DriveSpace:

- You upgrade a compressed drive from DriveSpace to DriveSpace 3 and receive the following error message:

  You cannot upgrade drive X because it contains errors. To upgrade this drive, first run ScanDisk on it, and then try again to upgrade it. ID Number: DRVSPACE 424

- You compress an existing uncompressed drive and receive the following error message:

  Drive X contains errors that must be corrected before the drive can be compressed. To correct them, run ScanDisk. ID Number: DRVSPACE 306

- You uncompress a compressed drive and receive the following error message:

  Drive X contains errors that must be corrected before the drive can be uncompressed. To correct them, run ScanDisk. ID Number: DRVSPACE 307

- You create a new empty compressed drive and receive the following error message:

  Drive C contains errors that must be corrected before the drive can be used to create a new compressed drive. To correct them, run ScanDisk. ID Number: DRVSPACE 308

This problem occurs when the drive contains a folder with a pathname that contains more than 66 characters.

Solution

To solve this problem, follow these steps:

1. Click the Start button, choose Programs, click Accessories, click System Tools, and then click ScanDisk.

2. Clear the Automatically Fix Errors check box, and then click the Start button.

   You will receive the error message:

   The <path> folder could not be opened in MS-DOS mode because its complete short name was longer than 66 characters

3. Make a note of the path that is longer than 66 characters, and then click Ignore. If you receive more than one of these messages, note each path.

4. When ScanDisk finishes, move each folder whose path contains more than 66 characters to another location with a shorter path.

5. Perform the DriveSpace operation you want.

6. When DriveSpace is finished, move to its original location each folder you moved in step 4.

Related KB article Q132883

FAT32 Drive Doesn't Compress

You try to compress a drive with DriveSpace or DriveSpace 3, and you receive the following error message:

Drive C cannot be compressed because it is a FAT32 drive.

ID Number: DRVSPACE738

Also, when you look at DriveSpace 3 properties, the size of a hard disk is listed as 2 gigabytes (GB) when the drive is larger than 2 GB. This problem might happen on FAT32 drives.

Solution

DriveSpace was designed to work with the FAT12 and FAT16 file systems and cannot be used with drives using the FAT32 file system. This feature is under review and will be considered for inclusion in a future release of Windows.

Related KB article Q150579

Real-Mode Memory Used By DriveSpace Not Reclaimed When Starting Windows

The real-mode (conventional or upper) memory that DriveSpace (DRVSPACE.BIN or DBLSPACE.BIN) uses is not reclaimed when you start Windows. This situation causes problems with MS-DOS-based programs that require more conventional memory than is available. DRVSPACE.BIN (or DBLSPACE.BIN) is normally unloaded from memory when the 32-bit DriveSpace driver (DRVSPACX.VXD) is initialized at Windows 98 startup.

This problem occurs for any of the following reasons:

- You boot to a command prompt and then start Windows by typing *win*. The real-mode memory that DRVSPACE.BIN (or DBLSPACE.BIN) uses cannot be reclaimed if you interrupt the normal Windows boot process.

- You load DRVSPACE.BIN (or DBLSPACE.BIN) in upper memory by using the following line:

```
devicehigh=<path>\drvspace.sys /move
```

  The real-mode memory that DRVSPACE.BIN (or DBLSPACE.BIN) uses cannot be reclaimed if it is loaded into an upper memory block (UMB).

- LoadTop=0 appears in the MSDOS.SYS file. A setting of 0 does not let Windows load DRVSPACE.BIN (or DBLSPACE.BIN) at the top of conventional memory (just below 640 KB). This setting prevents the unloading of DRVSPACE.BIN (or DBLSPACE.BIN) during Windows startup.

- The 32-bit DriveSpace driver (DRVSPACX.VXD) is not loaded. To determine whether it is loaded, run DriveSpace and then choose About DriveSpace from the Help menu. Table 15-1 lists by product the compression driver filenames, sizes, and versions as reported in DriveSpace. (*DBLSPACE.BIN* can be substituted for *DRVSPACE.BIN* in the table.)

Table 15-1.   Compression Driver Filenames, Versions, and Sizes in DriveSpace

Filename	Product	File size	About DriveSpace
DRVSPACE.BIN	Windows 95	71,287	Real-mode driver version 2
DRVSPACE.BIN	Microsoft Plus!	64,135	Real-mode driver version 3
DRVSPACX.VXD	Windows 95	54,207	32-bit driver version 2
DRVSPACX.VXD	Microsoft Plus!	61,719	32-bit driver version 3
DRVSPACE.BIN	Windows 98	68,871	Real-mode driver
DRVSPACX.VXD	Windows 98	57,642	32-bit driver

- DBLSPACE.BIN remains in memory if you are using a configuration consisting of DRVSPACE.INI and DBLSPACE.BIN. In this configuration, the DBLSPACE.BIN file is loaded as an installable device driver and is not transitioned to DRVSPACX.VXD. If you use both DBLSPACE.BIN and DRVSPACE.BIN with DRVSPACE.INI, DRVSPACE.BIN is given priority and this behavior does not occur.

Solution One

Start Windows normally. (Do not boot to a command prompt and start Windows by typing *win*.)

Solution Two

Change the command in the CONFIG.SYS file from

```
devicehigh=<path>\drvspace.sys  /move
```

to

```
device=<path>\drvspace.sys  /move
```

Note The syntax of this command is different if you use a third-party memory manager (such as Qualitas 386MAX or QuarterDeck QEMM).

Solution Three

Remove LoadTop=0 from the MSDOS.SYS file. For information about editing the MSDOS.SYS file, see KB article Q118579, "Contents of the Windows MSDOS.SYS File."

Solution Four

Rename the DRVSPACX.VXD file in the WINDOWS\SYSTEM\IOSUBSYS folder and then manually extract DRVSPACX.VXD from your original disks or CD-ROM. For information about extracting files, see KB article Q129605, "How to Extract Original Compressed Windows Files."

Note The DRVSPACE.BIN file for Windows 98 is located in the PRECOPY1.CAB file. The DRVSPACX.VXD file for Windows 98 is located in the WIN98_47.CAB file.

Related KB article Q134364

Uncompressing Drive Displays Error Message

You are uncompressing a drive compressed with DriveSpace, and you see the following error message:

Cannot Uncompress

The following files and subdirectories exist in both the root directory of drive <drive 1> and the root directory of drive <drive 2>:

<file 1>

<file 2>

<file 3>

Windows cannot uncompress drive <drive 1> because files or subdirectories with the same names exist on drive <drive 2>. Rename all conflicting files and subdirectories on drive <drive 1>, and then try again.

where <drive 1> is the drive letter of your compressed drive, and <drive 2> is the drive letter of your uncompressed drive.

This problem can occur if duplicate filenames are on both the compressed drive and the uncompressed drive. During the uncompression process, information from both the host drive and the compressed drive is restored to a single drive. To prevent data loss or damage, DriveSpace does not overwrite duplicate files.

Solution

Rename any duplicate files in the root folder of either drive, and then attempt to uncompress the compressed drive again.

Related KB article Q188087

FAT32 Converter

Command Prompt Drive Conversion Doesn't Work

You attempt to convert a drive to the File Allocation Table 32 (FAT32) file system from a command prompt, and you see the following error message:

You must run CVT32 to convert a drive to FAT32.

In Windows, click the Start button, point to Programs, point to Accessories, point to System Tools, and then click the FAT32 Converter Icon.

The conversion was canceled.

Solution

Add the /cvt32 parameter to the CVT.EXE command, and then run the conversion. For example, type *cvt <drive>: /cvt32* at the command prompt, where <drive> is the drive you want to convert, and then press the Enter key.

The /CVT32 parameter is designed to keep you from accidentally running the converter. Without this parameter, the utility does not run. The /WIN parameter can be used to run the converter in an MS-DOS window (also known as a virtual machine, or VM) in Windows 98, but it works only if no files are open on the specified volume. If the converter cannot prevent all possible file accesses by other system components and programs during the conversion, the conversion is canceled.

For additional information about using the FAT32 converter, see KB article Q180134, "How to Convert a Drive to FAT32 Using Drive Converter."

Related KB article Q184214

Computer Hangs on Startup After Conversion

After you install the FAT32 file system on a hard disk connected to an Adaptec 2940 or 3940 SCSI controller with a ROM BIOS version earlier than 1.23, the computer stops responding (hangs) when you start Windows. The SCSI ROM BIOS does not fully implement Interrupt 13 extensions, which causes IO.SYS to hang when booting.

Note This problem occurs only if the FAT32 file system is installed on the boot drive.

Solution

Upgrade the SCSI ROM BIOS to version 1.23 or later. Contact Adaptec for more information. Or repartition and format the drive without enabling large disk (FAT 32) support.

Related KB article Q156329

Drive Unavailable for Conversion

You attempt to convert a drive to the FAT32 file system, and the drive is either unavailable on the list of drives to convert or you see the following error message:

No drive can be converted to FAT32

This occurs because disks that are smaller than 512 MB (megabytes) cannot be converted to the FAT32 file system.

Solution

Choose a drive that is 512 MB or larger. Table 15-2 lists the cluster sizes of drives that are using the FAT32 file system:

Table 15-2.   Cluster Sizes by Drive Size

Drive size	Cluster size
Less than 512 MB	Not available
512 MB–8191 MB	4 KB
8192 MB–16,383 MB	8 KB
16,384 MB–32,767 MB	16 KB
32,768 MB and larger	32 KB

For information about the FAT32 file system, see KB article Q154997, "Description of FAT32 File System."

Related KB article Q179194

Iomega Zip Drive Error Message Occurs or Computer Hangs During Conversion

You attempt to convert your hard disk to the File Allocation Table 32 (FAT32) file system, you see the following message, and your computer stops responding (hangs):

Iomega Guest Driver Version 1.2 finding a drive letter for Iomega zip drive

If you restart your computer, you receive an error message that the FAT32 conversion process was not successful. This problem can occur if the Iomega Guest Driver program (GUEST.EXE) is automatically loading from the DOSSTART.BAT file in the WINDOWS folder.

Solution

To modify the DOSSTART.BAT file so that the Iomega Guest Driver program is not automatically loaded, follow these steps:

1. Restart your computer normally.

2. Click the Start button, choose Find, and then click Files Or Folders.

3. In the Named box, enter *dosstart.bat*, and then click Find Now.

4. On the list of found files, right-click DOSSTART.BAT, and then click Edit.

5. At the beginning of the GUEST.EXE line, enter *rem*, and press the Spacebar.

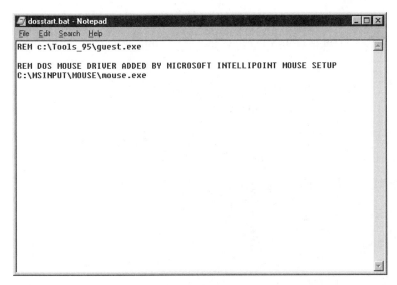

Figure 15-18. *The DOSSTART.BAT file.*

6. Choose Save from the File menu, and then choose Exit from the File menu.

7. Close the Find dialog box.

Related KB article Q194383

Memory Error Message Occurs or Computer Hangs During Conversion

You try to convert your hard disk to the FAT32 file system, and your computer stops responding before the conversion is complete, or you receive the following error message:

> *Not enough memory to convert the drive to FAT32. To free up memory, REM all statements in the Autoexec.bat and the Config.sys files.*

This problem can occur for either of the following reasons:

- Not enough free conventional memory is available.

- The folder structure is too large on the drive being converted to a FAT32 file system.

Solution

To increase the amount of free conventional memory, and then convert your hard disk to the FAT32 file system in real mode, follow these steps:

1. Click the Start button, choose Programs, click Accessories, click System Tools, and then click System Information.

2. Choose System Configuration Utility from the Tools menu.

3. On the AUTOEXEC.BAT tab, clear the check boxes of all nonessential drivers and programs.

4. On the CONFIG.SYS tab, clear the check boxes of all nonessential drivers and programs.

5. Click New, and then enter the following lines (note that you must click New before adding each line:

```
device=c:\<windows>\himem.sys
```

```
device=c:\<windows>\emm386.exe  /noems
```

```
dos=high,umb
```

where <windows> is the folder in which Windows 98 is installed.

Figure 15-19.   *The CONFIG.SYS file in the System Configuration Utility.*

Note If any of these lines already exists, select the line, and then click Edit to change it.

6. Using Find, check for the existence of the DBLSPACE.INI or DRVSPACE.INI file in the root folder of your physical boot drive (drive C or the host for drive C).

Note The DBLSPACE.INI and DRVSPACE.INI files are hidden files. To see hidden files, choose Folder Options from the View menu in Windows Explorer, click the View tab, select the Show All Files check box, and then click OK.

If either file exists, use a text editor, such as Notepad, to open the DBLSPACE.INI or DRVSPACE.INI file and search for the ActivateDrive= line. If the line exists, close the DBLSPACE.INI or DRVSPACE.INI file, and then add the following line to the CONFIG.SYS file:

devicehigh=c:\<windows>\command\drvspace.sys/move

If the line does not exist, close and then rename the DBLSPACE.INI or DRVSPACE.INI file to a different name, such as DBLSPACE.XXX or DRVSPACE.XXX.

7. Click OK, and then click Yes when you are prompted to restart your computer.

8. Click the Start button, choose Find, and then click Files And Folders.

9. Enter *exit to dos.pif*, and then click Find Now.

10. On the list of found files, right-click the EXIT TO DOS.PIF file, and then click Rename.

11. Type *old exit to dos*, and press the Enter key.

12. In the Named box, enter *dosstart.bat*, and click Find Now.

13. On the list of found files, right-click the DOSSTART.BAT file, and click Rename.

14. Type *old dosstart.bat*, and press the Enter key.

15. Run Drive Converter (FAT32), and try to convert your drive to the FAT32 file system again. If your drive is converted successfully, skip to step 24. If the problem persists, try increasing the amount of free conventional memory, and then convert your hard disk to the FAT32 file system in real mode. To do so, continue with step 16.

16. Click the Start button, choose Settings, and click Control Panel.

17. Double-click the Add/Remove Programs icon, and click the Install/Uninstall tab.

18. On the list of installed programs, click Delete Windows 98 Uninstall Information if it appears on the list, and then click Add/Remove.

19. Click Yes to delete the uninstall information, click OK, and then restart your computer.

20. Restart your computer. After your computer completes the Power On Self Test (POST), press and hold down the Ctrl key until you see the Windows 98 Startup menu, and then choose Command Prompt Only.

21. At the command prompt, type the following lines, pressing Enter after each one:

```
<drive>:

attrib suhdlog.dat -h -r

del suhdlog.dat
```

where <drive> is the drive letter of your physical boot drive (drive C or the host for drive C).

Note Steps 8–13 are required in order to remove the Windows 98 uninstall information. Drive Converter (FAT32) automatically removes Windows 98 uninstall information when it is started in Windows, but not when it is started in real mode (see step 14). Windows 98 cannot be uninstalled if your hard disk is converted to the FAT32 file system after you install Windows 98.

---

22. At the command prompt, type *CVT <drive>: /CVT32*, where <drive> is the letter of the drive you are converting to the FAT32 file system, and then press the Enter key.

23. Follow the instructions onscreen to convert your hard disk to the FAT32 file system.

Note If the conversion still is not completed successfully, the folder structure might be too large on the drive you are trying to convert. To work around this behavior, move some folders and files to another drive and repeat steps 14 and 15.

---

24. After your drive is converted to the FAT32 file system, Windows 98 starts up. Click the Start button, choose Programs, click Accessories, click System Tools, and then click System Information.

25. Choose System Configuration Utility from the Tools menu.

26. On the AUTOEXEC.BAT tab, select all the check boxes.

27. On the CONFIG.SYS tab, select all the check boxes.

28. Select the check boxes of the lines you typed in step 5 to clear them, and then click OK. Click No when you are prompted to restart your computer.

29. Click the Start button, choose Programs, click Accessories, click System Tools, and then click Disk Defragmenter.

30. Select the drive you converted to the FAT32 file system, and then click OK. Follow the instructions onscreen to defragment your drive, and then restart your computer.

Related KB article Q188561

Unable to Get a Lock Error Message Occurs

You try to convert a FAT16 partition on your Windows 98–based computer to the FAT32 file system, and you receive the following error message:

Drive converter was unable to get a lock on the drive.

This problem can occur if you are using EZ-BIOS/EZ-Drive version 9.03 or earlier to control your hard disk. These versions of the EZ-BIOS/EZ-Drive program do not support FAT32 partitions.

Solution

Contact the manufacturer of the your drive overlay program to inquire about a solution for this problem.

To determine whether your hard disk uses a drive overlay program, see KB article Q186057, "How to Tell If Drive Overlay Program Is Installed in Windows."

Related KB article Q191442

Maintenance Wizard and Disk Tools

Disk Cleanup Doesn't Display Files

You click Downloaded Program Files in Disk Cleanup and then click View Files, and nothing happens. This problem can occur if you are configuring the Disk Cleanup portion of Maintenance Wizard. If you configure Disk Cleanup using Maintenance Wizard and you click Temporary Internet Files or Recycle Bin and then click View Files, the files in the folders are displayed properly.

Solution

To view files in the WINDOWS\DOWNLOADED PROGRAM FILES folder by using Disk Cleanup, follow these steps:

1. Click the Start button, choose Programs, click Accessories, click System Tools, and then click Disk Cleanup.

2. In the Drives box, click the hard disk on which the DOWNLOADED PROGRAM FILES folder is located, and then click OK.

3. On the Disk Cleanup tab, click Downloaded Program Files, and then click View Files.

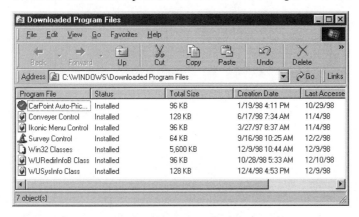

Figure 15-20.   *The DOWNLOADED PROGRAM FILES folder.*

Related KB article Q188099

Disk Defragmenter Displays Error Message

You try to defragment a FAT32 file system drive and receive the following error message:

> *Windows cannot defragment this drive. Make sure the disk is formatted and free of errors. Then try defragmenting the drive again. ID No: DEFRAG0026*

This problem occurs when a shortcut to an earlier version of Disk Defragmenter is on the desktop.

Solution

Right-click the shortcut to the earlier version of Disk Defragmenter on the desktop, and click Delete.

Related KB article Q155404

Disk Defragmenter Displays General Protection Fault Error Message

You try to run Disk Defragmenter from System Agent or Windows Task Scheduler, and you receive a general protection (GP) fault in module USER.EXE. This problem can occur if the task information for Disk Defragmenter has been damaged.

Solution

Delete the Disk Defragmenter task from System Agent or Task Scheduler, and then create a new task. For information about how to do so, click the Start button, choose Help, click the Index tab, type *task scheduler*, and then double-click the Adding Tasks topic.

Related KB article Q188182

Disk Defragmenter Repeatedly Fails to Complete

Disk Defragmenter for Windows 98 (DEFRAG.EXE) does not complete its task after repeated attempts. The reason is usually that an application is writing to the disk; Disk Defragmenter cannot share access to a drive with other tasks.

Solution

If DEFRAG doesn't work even when you run it immediately after booting, an application loading automatically at startup might be interfering with DEFRAG. To run DEFRAG before applications load at startup by adding a value for *DEFRAG.EXE /ALL* to the RunServicesOnce key in the Registry, follow these steps:

1. Select DEFRAG.INF found in the \TOOLS\MTSUTIL folder on the Windows 98 CD-ROM.

2. Right-click DEFRAG.INF, and then choose Install from the shortcut menu to add the value for DEFRAG.EXE /ALL to the Registry.

3. Restart your computer.

Related KB article Q188480 or MTSUTILS.TXT in the TOOLS\MTSULTILS folder on the Windows 98 CD-ROM

Disk Defragmenter Stops Responding

You try to run Disk Defragmenter on a compressed drive, and your computer stops responding. This problem can occur if you are running the PC-Cillin 95 version 3.x MONITOR.EXE program, an antivirus program that loads when you start up your computer.

Solution

Disable PC-Cillin 95 version 3.x before you start Disk Defragmenter. For information about how to disable MONITOR.EXE, consult the documentation included with PC-Cillin 95 version 3.x.

Related KB article Q186590

Hard Disk Low on Disk Space

Free disk space on your computer falls below a specific level (threshold), and you receive the following message or one similar to it:

Hard Disk is Low on Disk Space

You are running out of disk space on drive C.

To free space on this drive by deleting old or unnecessary files, click Disk Cleanup.

This problem can occur if the free disk space on your computer has dropped below the low disk space notification threshold associated with Disk Cleanup.

Solution

Either click Cancel to close the message, or click Disk Cleanup to start Disk Cleanup. Table 15-3 describes these thresholds in more detail.

Table 15-3.   Free Space Thresholds for the Disk Cleanup Utility

Disk size	Threshold percentage	Threshold space
<=512 MB	10.0	25.6 – 51.2 MB
<=1 GB	5.0	25.6 – 51.2 MB
<=2 GB	2.5	25.6 – 51.2 MB
<=4 GB	1.2	24.6 – 49.15 MB
<=8 GB	0.6	24.6 – 49.15 MB
<=16 GB	0.3	24.6 – 49.15 MB
<=32 GB	0.2	32.8 – 65.5 MB
>32 GB	0.1	32.8 – ???? MB

For example, if you have a 2 GB (gigabyte) hard disk, you receive the *Hard Disk Is Low on Disk Space* message when your free disk space is less than 51.2 MB (megabytes), or 2.5 percent of your total disk space.

Note These thresholds are not configurable.

Related KB article Q191824

Maintenance Wizard Tells You to Run FAT32 Converter

You start Windows, and Maintenance Wizard prompts you to run FAT32 Converter even though you previously chose not to convert to the FAT32 file system.

Solution One

To solve this problem, follow these steps:

1. Click the Start button, and choose Run.

2. Enter *c:\windows\tuneup.exe /r* in the Open box.

3. Click No when you are prompted to convert to FAT32.

Solution Two

Use Registry Editor to delete the following Registry key:

`HKEY_LOCAL_MACHINE\Software\Microsoft\Windows\CurrentVersion\Welcome\TuneUp`

To do so, follow these steps:

Warning Please read the Introduction for information on how to safely edit the Registry.

1. Click the Start button, choose Run, enter *regedit* in the Run box, and then click OK.

2. Navigate your way through the folders in the left pane until you locate the key just described.

3. Delete the key.

4. Close Regedit.

5. Restart Windows.

Related KB article Q194805

ScanDisk Closes When Monitor Shut Off

Your monitor turns off while ScanDisk is running, and ScanDisk closes when you press a key to turn your monitor back on.

This problem occurs when both the following conditions exist:

- You press Spacebar or Enter to turn your monitor back on.
- ScanDisk is the active program.

Solution

Press a key other than Spacebar or Enter to turn your monitor back on.

You can use the Power Management icon in Control Panel to specify the length of time you want your computer to be idle before your monitor turns off. If your monitor turns off while ScanDisk is running and is the active program, pressing Spacebar or Enter turns your monitor back on and closes ScanDisk because the Cancel option button is the active button.

Related KB article Q185500

ScanDisk Doesn't Use Previous Settings

When a scheduled ScanDisk session is started by Task Scheduler, the session does not use the settings you last selected in ScanDisk if you change settings within ScanDisk. These settings are not applied to a previously scheduled ScanDisk task in Task Scheduler.

Solution

Select the appropriate settings in the scheduled ScanDisk task in Task Scheduler:

1. Double-click the Task Scheduler icon on the taskbar.

2. Double-click the ScanDisk scheduled task.

3. Click Settings, and then click Advanced.

4. Select the settings you want, and then click OK.

5. Click OK twice.

The next time the scheduled ScanDisk task is started, the new settings are used.

Related KB article Q179369

ScanDisk Runs Slowly

You run Windows 98 Setup from within Windows, and the ScanDisk portion takes an unusually long time to check your hard disks. This problem can occur if you are loading DosIdle 2.00 in your AUTOEXEC.BAT file. DosIdle 2.00, a freeware program included with CpuIdle for Windows 95 and Windows 98, is designed to take advantage of the power-management features in your computer's BIOS.

Solution

To disable DosIdle before you install Windows 98, follow these steps:

1. Restart your computer. After your computer completes the Power On Self Test (POST), press and hold down the Ctrl key until you see the Windows 98 StartUp menu, and then choose Command Prompt Only.

2. At the command prompt, type *edit autoexec.bat*, and then press the Enter key.

3. Disable the line that loads the DOSIDLE.EXE file. To do so, type *rem* at the beginning of the line, and then press the Spacebar.

4. Press Alt+F, press S (to save), press Alt+F again, and then press X (to exit).

5. Restart your computer normally, and then run Windows 98 Setup.

Related KB article Q185659

Registry Tools and Issues

Backing Up Registry Error Message Occurs on Windows Startup

You start Windows and see the following error message:

Windows encountered an error while backing up the system Registry. Make sure you have enough space on the drive for three copies of the file c:\windows\user.dat. This error should not cause any loss of information, but if space is not made on the drive you may experience additional problems.

This error can occur for either of the following reasons:

- The hard disk containing Windows 98 does not have enough free space.

- A damaged driver is being loaded from the CONFIG.SYS or AUTOEXEC.BAT file.

Solution

Either free additional space on the hard disk containing Windows, or identify the driver causing the problem. To identify the driver, follow these steps:

1. Restart the computer.

2. Press and hold down the Ctrl key until you see the Windows 98 StartUp menu.

3. Choose Step-By-Step Confirmation.

4. Press Y at each prompt except for Process Your Startup Device Drivers (CONFIG.SYS) and Process Your Startup Command File (AUTOEXEC.BAT).

If the error message is no longer displayed, the problem is a driver being loaded from either the CONFIG.SYS or AUTOEXEC.BAT file. To determine whether the problem driver is being loaded from the CONFIG.SYS file, repeat steps 1 through 4, but press Y at the Process Your Startup Device Drivers (CONFIG.SYS) prompt. If the problem returns, a driver being loaded in the CONFIG.SYS file is damaged.

If the problem does not occur, repeat steps 1 through 4 again, but press Y at the Process Your Startup Command File (AUTOEXEC.BAT) prompt. After you identify the driver that is causing the problem, contact the driver's manufacturer for assistance, or reload the driver from the original disk.

When the CS.EXE driver (which loads in the CONFIG.SYS file) is damaged, is known to cause the preceding error message to be displayed. Other drivers might also cause this error message to be displayed.

Related KB article Q149632

Corrupted Registry Error Message Occurs During Windows 98 Setup

Windows 98 Setup stops responding during the file copy process, and you run Setup again and receive the following error message:

The Registry is corrupted and Windows must be installed to a new directory.

This error message can occur for any of the following reasons:

- Advanced Power Management (APM) shuts down your computer during the file copy process.

- A program (or programs) running during the file copy process conflicts with Windows 98 Setup.

- Your hard disk doesn't have enough free space to complete the installation.

- You are running the Symantec Norton Utilities Nprotect program (Protected Recycle Bin) during the file copy process.

Solution

To solve this problem, follow these steps:

1. Restart your computer. After your computer completes the Power On Self Test (POST), press and hold down the Ctrl key until you see the StartUp menu, and then choose Safe Mode Command Prompt Only.

2. Type the following lines at the command prompt, pressing Enter after each command:

```
cd \windows

attrib -r -s -h system.dat

attrib -r -s -h user.dat

ren system.dat system.bad

ren user.dat user.bad

copy \system.new system.dat

copy \user.new user.dat

cd\

deltree /y recycled
```

3. If APM shut down your computer, disable APM in your computer's BIOS before you start Windows 98 Setup. For information about how to do so, contact the manufacturer of your computer, or read the documentation included with your computer.

4. If programs were running during the file copy process, verify that only the necessary drivers or programs in the CONFIG.SYS or AUTOEXEC.BAT files are loaded before you start Windows 98 Setup. For information about how to do so, see KB article Q188867, "Troubleshooting Windows 98 Startup Problems and Error Messages."

5. If your hard disk doesn't have enough free space, verify that it has at least 195 MB (megabytes) of free space before you start Windows 98 Setup.

6. If the Norton Utilities Nprotect program is running, empty, and then disable the Norton Utilities Nprotect program before you start Windows 98 Setup. For information about how to do so, contact Symantec, or see the documentation included with Norton Utilities.

7. Restart your computer. After your computer completes the Power On Self Test (POST), press and hold down the Ctrl key until you see the StartUp menu, and then choose Safe Mode Command Prompt Only.

8. Run Windows 98 Setup again.

Related KB article Q189473

Damaged Registry Error Message Occurs on Windows Startup

Windows starts, and Registry Checker displays the following message:

Windows Registry is damaged. Windows will restart and try to fix the problem.

You click OK and receive the same message when Windows restarts.

This problem can occur if defective memory is in your computer. A defective memory chip can damage the Registry in memory. The Windows-based (or protected-mode) version of Registry Checker (SCANREGW.EXE) scans the Registry in memory for signs of damage. When this problem occurs, SCANREGW.EXE detects that the Registry is damaged in memory and marks it as such so that the real-mode Registry Checker SCANREG.EXE program is run the next time the computer starts. SCANREG.EXE alone might not detect any damage if the defective memory is not used in real mode and might allow Windows to start normally.

Solution One

Remove or replace memory chips in the computer to see whether the problem is solved.

Solution Two

Try limiting the amount of memory that Windows uses. If this action solves the problem, the problem is a defective memory chip. To limit the amount of memory Windows uses, follow these steps:

1. Restart your computer. After your computer completes the Power On Self Test (POST), press and hold down the Ctrl key until you see the Windows 98 Startup menu, and then choose Safe Mode.

2. Click the Start button, choose Programs, click Accessories, click System Tools, and then click System Information.

3. Choose System Configuration Utility from the Tools menu.

4. On the General tab, click Advanced.

5. Select the Limit Memory To check box, and set the value to 16 MB (megabytes).

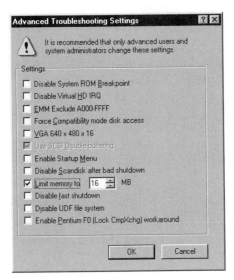

Figure 15-21. *The Advanced Troubleshooting Settings in the System Configuration Editor.*

Note Limiting memory to less than 16 megabytes might prevent Windows from loading. If you are unable to start Windows normally, start Windows in Safe mode, and then disable this option by pressing and holding the Shift key throughout the startup process.

6. Click OK, and then click OK again.

7. Restart Windows in the normal way.

Related KB article Q186909

Key Values Added Not Updated

You try to update a Registry key value by double-clicking a file with a .REG filename extension, and Windows adds the Registry key value in the file to the Registry as a new value, instead of updating the existing value. The Registry key value in the .REG file does not exactly match the value in the Registry. For example, if one of the values in the .REG file contains a trailing space but the corresponding value in the Registry does not, Windows considers them to be different values and adds the Registry key value from the file as a new value instead of updating the existing value.

Solution

Use Regedit to modify the Registry key values in the .REG file and the Registry so that they match exactly. If one of the values contains a trailing space, remove the trailing space from that value so that it matches the other value exactly.

Warning Please read the Introduction for information on how to safely edit the Registry.

Related KB article Q136783

MS-DOS Registry Checker Doesn't Display Time Stamp of Backups

You use the MS-DOS version of Registry Checker (SCANREG.EXE) to see the list of backup copies of your Registry, and some of the backups display a time stamp indicating the time they were created. This problem can occur if either of the following conditions exists:

- You use the Windows version of Registry Checker (SCANREGW.EXE) to create backup copies of your Registry. The Windows version of Registry Checker does not add a time stamp to backup copies of your Registry.

- You use the /comment=<text> command-line switch when you create backup copies of your Registry.

The lowest numbered RB0<nn>.CAB file might not be the earliest Registry backup. To locate the earliest backup, you must check the dates and times of the RB0<nn>.CAB files.

For additional information about how to use Registry Checker, click the Start button, choose Help, click the Index tab, type *registry*, and then double-click the Registry Checker topic.

Solution One

To create all Registry backups by using the MS-DOS version of Registry Checker without the comment=<text> command-line switch, type *scanreg /backup* at a command prompt, and then press the Enter key.

Solution Two

To see the time a Registry backup was created, follow these steps:

1. Click the Start button, choose Programs, and then click MS-DOS Prompt.

2. At the command prompt, look at the list of RB0<nn>.CAB files located in the <drive>:\<WINDOWS>\SYSBCKUP folder, where <nn> is a number between 00 and 99, <drive> is the drive letter on which the WINDOWS folder is located, and <windows> is the name of the folder in which Windows is installed. To do so, type the following commands at the command prompt, pressing Enter after each command:

```
cd \

cd <windows>\sysbckup

dir rb0*
```

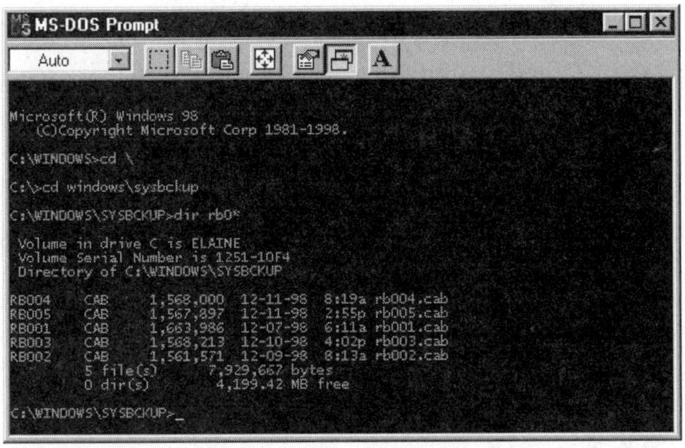

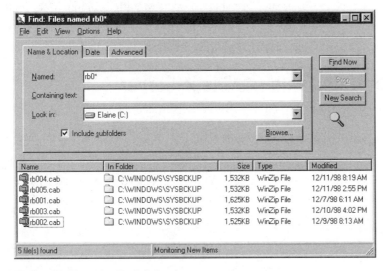

Figure 15-22. *The MS-DOS Prompt window.*

For each file listed, you see the filename and extension, size, and the time and date the file was created.

3. Close the command-prompt window.

Solution Three

To use the Find utility in Windows to locate and view the time a Registry backup was created, follow these steps:

1. Click the Start button, choose Find, and click Files Or Folders.

2. In the Named box, enter *rb0**, and click Find Now.

Figure 15-23. *The Find dialog box.*

If no files are displayed in the Find window, follow these steps:

1. In My Computer or Windows Explorer, choose Folder Options from the View menu.

2. Click the View tab.

3. Under Hidden Files, click Show All Files.

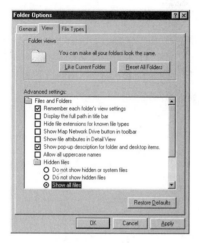

Figure 15-24.   *The Folder Options dialog box.*

4. Click OK.

5. Repeat steps 1 and 2.

The time the Registry backup was created is displayed in the Modified column in the Find window.

Related KB article Q184043

Policies Not Implemented with LANtastic Server

You have a system policy file stored on a LANtastic server, and the policies are not implemented on workstations that connect to the server. System policies are not supported on LANtastic 7.0 networks because network connectivity with the server is not established during the initial login.

When you start Windows, the portion of the startup process that processes the system policy file is run before the LANtastic network component. Windows cannot gain access to the system policy file because LANtastic connectivity has not yet been established.

Solution

Store the system policy file on a Microsoft Networking or Novell NetWare server.

Related KB article Q187220

Policy Editor Causes Error Message

You attempt to add a group to a policy file by using System Policy Editor (POLEDIT.EXE), and you experience one of the following problems:

- You attempt to save the policy file, and you receive the following error message:

  Unable to save <filename>: error 1010 occurred

- You attempt to open the policy file containing the group you added, and as many as three groups appear with similar names. The groups are distinguished only by random symbols appended to each group name.

This problem occurs when the group name contains more than 39 characters, and it occurs most often on Novell NetWare 4.x networks using NetWare Directory Services (NDS). When NDS is in use, NDS group names must be used rather than bindery-based group names.

Solution

Use 39 characters or fewer when you're naming groups.

Related KB article Q192938

Policy Editor Changes Applied to All Users and Computers, Not Just Default Ones

You use Policy Editor to change the default user or default computer settings and save the changes, and the changes are applied to all users and computers rather than to only the default user and computer.

Changes you make to the default user or computer affect every other user and computer in the policy file. The reason is that the changes are for every user, and Policy Editor makes these changes automatically.

When you log on, the default user or computer policies are first applied, and then the specific user or computer policies are applied, and they overwrite the defaults. It is not possible to avoid the default user or computer policies without overwriting them in the specific user or computer policies.

Solution

Microsoft recommends that you make all the modifications to the default user or computer and then make the modifications to individuals, groups, or computers. Note that any setting that is not enabled for individuals, groups, or computers is set by the default user or computer. If this is not what you want, you can remove the default user or computer from the policy file.

Related KB article Q185931

Policy Editor Produces Error Message When Saving Policy File

You are trying to save a policy file by using Policy Editor, and you see the following error message:

An error occurred writing the Registry. The file cannot be saved.

The folder has a long filename, or the file is not being saved with the .POL extension. A similar error can occur if you try to open a file from a folder with a long filename.

Solution

Enter the path and filename in the File Name box by using the MS-DOS (8.3) naming format. For example, type the following line:

C:\Mydocu~1\Config.pol

rather than this one:

C:\My Documents\Config.pol

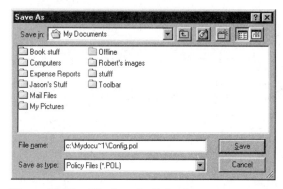

Figure 15-25. *The Save As dialog box.*

To determine the MS-DOS-format name for a folder, type *dir* at a command prompt to view the folder's name. Or right-click the folder in Windows Explorer, and then choose Properties from the shortcut menu. The MS-DOS name is listed on the General tab.

Related KB article Q164418

Registry Checker Displays Out-of-Memory Error Message

You run Registry Checker (SCANREG.EXE) with the /fix or /restore switch, and you receive an *out of memory* error message. You also receive this error message when SCANREG.EXE creates a backup copy of the Registry during Windows startup. This error message can occur if less than 340 KB (kilobytes) of free conventional memory is available. When you use SCANREG.EXE with the /fix or /restore switch, more than 340 KB of free conventional memory might be required, depending on the size of the Registry and the amount of damage.

Solution

Increase the amount of free conventional memory to more than 340 KB. You can use any of the following methods to increase the amount of free conventional memory:

- Restart your computer. After your computer completes the Power On Self Test (POST), press and hold down the Ctrl key until you see the Windows 98 StartUp menu, and then choose Command Prompt Only. Then run SCANREG.EXE with the /fix or /restore switch.

- Rename the AUTOEXEC.BAT and CONFIG.SYS files, restart your computer, press and hold down the Ctrl key until the Windows 98 StartUp menu appears, and then choose Command Prompt Only. Then run SCANREG.EXE with the /fix or /restore switch. After you run SCANREG.EXE, rename your AUTOEXEC.BAT and CONFIG.SYS files to their original names.

- Load all devices and terminate-and-stay resident (TSR) programs in upper memory, restart your computer, press and hold down the Ctrl key until the Windows 98 StartUp menu appears, and then choose Command Prompt Only. Then run SCANREG.EXE with the /fix or /restore switch. For information about loading devices and TSRs in upper memory, see KB article Q129605, "How to Increase Conventional Memory for MS-DOS Based Programs."

You might be able to run SCANREG.EXE with the /fix or /restore switch with as little as 320 KB of free conventional memory, depending on your configuration.

Related KB article Q187680

Registry Checker Doesn't Back Up Additional Files

You configure the Windows 98 Registry Checker to back up additional files, and the files are not backed up. This problem can occur when you do not capitalize the first letter of the Files= setting in the SCANREG.INI file.

Solution

Capitalize the first letter of the word *Files*. The remaining letters of the word *Files* must be lower-case letters. For example, to configure Registry Checker to back up the AUTOEXEC.BAT and CONFIG.SYS files, add the following line to the SCANREG.INI file:

```
Files=30,config.sys,autoexec.bat
```

Related KB article Q187321

Registry Checker Doesn't List Backup Copy of Registry

You use Registry Checker (SCANREG.EXE) to restore a backup copy of your Registry, and the backup from which you want to restore your Registry is not listed if Registry Checker is configured to maintain more than five Registry backups.

Solution One

Note Because you can restore Registry backups only from a command prompt, these solutions assume that you are already at a command prompt.

Configure Registry Checker so that only the last five Registry backups are stored in the WINDOWS\SYSBCKUP folder. Follow these steps:

1. At a command prompt, type the following lines, pressing Enter after each one:

   ```
   cd \
   ```

   ```
   cd \windows
   ```

   ```
   edit scanreg.ini
   ```

2. Locate the MaxBackupCopies= line.

3. Change the line to *MaxBackupCopies=5*.

4. Press Alt+F, press S (to save), press Alt+F, and then press X (to exit).

Solution Two

To restore a Registry backup later than the five listed in Registry Checker, rename earlier Registry backups until the backup from which you want to restore your Registry is one of the five listed. To do so, type the following commands at a command prompt, pressing Enter after each command, where <nn> is a number between 00 and 99:

```
cd\windows\sysbckup
```

```
ren rb0<nn>.cab rb0<nn>.xxx
```

Note The lowest-numbered Registry backup might not be the earliest. To determine the earliest Registry backup, check the date of the RB<nnn>.CAB file.

For example, the WINDOWS\SYSBCKUP folder contains seven Registry backups numbered RB000.CAB through RB006.CAB, where RB000.CAB is the earliest Registry backup and RB006.CAB is the latest. To cause Registry Checker to list the five latest backups, enter the following commands:

```
ren rb000.cab rb000.xxx
```

```
ren rb001.cab rb001.xxx
```

The *MaxBackupCopies=* line in the SCANREG.INI file determines the number of Registry backups maintained in the WINDOWS\SYSBCKUP folder. If the MaxBackupCopies= line is set to six or higher (five is the default), the correct number of Registry backups is maintained in the WINDOWS\SYSBCKUP folder, but Registry Checker can display only the five earliest backups.

Related KB article Q182841

Registry Checker Runs Slowly

You try to run Registry Checker with the /fix switch, and Registry Checker runs very slowly. Or, when you start your computer, you receive a message that says your Registry will be repaired, and this process runs very slowly. This problem can occur if you are using the QuarterDeck QEMM program as your memory manager program.

Solution

Start your computer with the Windows 98 Startup disk, and then run Registry Checker with the /fix switch.

Related KB article Q187636

System Information and Tools

Damaged System Files Error Message Occurs

You run Windows and receive an error message indicating that Windows has damaged system files.

Solution

To use System File Checker to extract a compressed file from the Windows 98 CD-ROM, follow these steps:

1. Click the Start button, choose Programs, click Accessories, click System Tools, and then click System Information.

2. Choose System File Checker from the Tools menu.

3. Click the Extract One File From Installation Disk option button, enter in the Specify The System File You Would Like To Restore box the name of the file you want to extract, and then click the Start button.

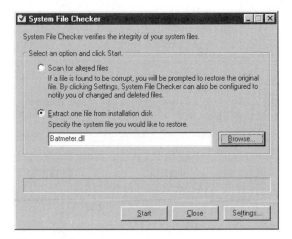

Figure 15-26. *The System File Checker.*

4. In the Restore From box, enter the path to the WIN98 folder on the Windows 98 CD-ROM, enter the destination folder in the Save File In box if necessary, and then click OK.

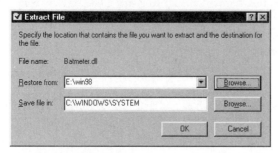

Figure 15-27.   *The Extract File dialog box.*

5. Click OK, click OK again, and then click Yes when you are prompted to restart your computer.

Related KB article Q129605

Dr. Watson Collects No Information

You use Dr. Watson to collect information about your computer when a program displays a fault error, and Dr. Watson does not collect any information if you are running a third-party program, such as Norton CrashGuard or CyberMedia First Aid 98, that is always active in memory.

Solution

Disable the third-party program before you use Dr. Watson. For information about how to do so, see the documentation included with the program.

Related KB article Q183809

Log File Not Saved by Clicking OK

You click OK when you fill out the optional information field to describe what you were doing at the time a log file was generated in order to send a report to a support technician, and the log file is not saved.

Solution

Choose Save or Save As from the File menu rather than clicking OK.

Related KB article Q184825

System Configuration Doesn't Disable Startup Files

You attempt to disable startup files by using System Configuration (MSCONFIG.EXE), and some or all of the files are still loaded when you start your computer. This problem can occur if any of the following files have the read-only attribute:

- AUTOEXEC.BAT
- CONFIG.SYS
- WIN.INI
- SYSTEM.INI
- WINSTART.BAT

Solution

To solve this problem, follow these steps:

1. Click the Start button, choose Programs, and then click MS-DOS Prompt.

2. At the command prompt, type the following commands, pressing Enter after each command:

   ```
   attrib c:\config.sys -r

   attrib c:\autoexec.bat -r

   attrib win.ini -r

   attrib system.ini -r

   attrib winstart.bat -r

   exit
   ```

3. Click the Start button, choose Programs, click Accessories, click System Tools, and then click System Information.

4. Choose System Configuration Utility from the Tools menu,.

5. Select the check boxes you previously cleared, click OK, and then click Yes when you are prompted to restart your computer.

6. Click the Start button, choose Programs, click Accessories, click System Tools, and then click System Information.

7. Choose System Configuration Utility from the Tools menu.

8. Clear the check boxes of the startup files you want to disable, click OK, and then click Yes when you are prompted to restart your computer.

Related KB article Q191547

System Configuration Options Don't Work on Compressed Drive

You run System Configuration on a computer with the entire hard drive compressed using DriveSpace, and the following items do not work:

- Diagnostic Startup—Interactively Load Device Drivers And Software

- Enable StartUp Menu

- Disable ScanDisk After Bad Shutdown

- Disable SCSI Double-Buffering

This problem occurs because DriveSpace swaps hard disk letters after the initialization of the compressed volume file (CVF). Because the System Configuration Utility is not aware of the drive letter swap, it edits the MSDOS.SYS file on the CVF rather than the MSDOS.SYS file on the host drive.

Solution

Edit the MSDOS.SYS file on the host drive (usually drive H) after DriveSpace is loaded. Note that DriveSpace hides the host drive by default. To make the host drive visible, follow these steps:

1. Click the Start button, choose Programs, click Accessories, click System Tools, and click DriveSpace.

2. Select the compressed drive for which the hidden drive is a host drive, and then choose Properties from the Drive menu.

3. Clear the Hide Host Drive check box.

4. Click OK.

After you've made the host drive visible, edit the appropriate line in the MSDOS.SYS file to enable or disable the feature you want. If the appropriate line does not exist, create it in the [Options] section of the MSDOS.SYS file. For more information about editing the MSDOS.SYS file, see KB article Q118579, "Contents of the Windows MSDOS.SYS File."

- To enable diagnostic startup, edit or add the line *orig_diag_BootMenu=1*. To disable the option, remove the line or change the value from 1 to 0 (zero).

- To enable the StartUp menu, edit or add the line *BootMenu=1*. To disable the option, change the value from 1 to 0 (zero).

- To disable automatic ScanDisk after an incorrect shutdown, edit or add the line *AutoScan=0*. To enable the option, change the value from 0 to 1.

- To enable SCSI double-buffering, edit or add the line *DoubleBuffer=1*. To disable SCSI double-buffering, change the value from 1 to 0 (zero).

Related KB article Q192723

System Configuration Reselects Startup File Check Box

You clear the check box next to a startup file (such as the CONFIG.SYS or AUTOEXEC.BAT file) on the General tab in System Configuration and then click Apply, and the check mark reappears in the check box.

This problem occurs when all the lines in a startup file are disabled or when all the lines in a startup file are deleted. There must be at least one line (or one line that is not disabled) in the startup file for System Configuration to process it.

Solution

Do not try to disable a startup file if all the statements in the file are disabled or have been deleted.

Related KB article Q185564

System File Checker Can't Find New Copy of Windows 98 File

You attempt to extract a new copy of a Windows 98 file by using System File Checker, and you see the following error message:

The file was not found. Verify that you have selected the correct 'Restore from' location and try again.

This message is displayed if one of the following happens:

- You specify the wrong path to the Windows 98 cabinet files.

- The file you are attempting to extract was created during Windows 98 Setup and is not in a Windows 98 cabinet file.

- You specify a path to a shared Windows 98 CD-ROM on a network.

Solution One

Specify the correct path:

1. Click the Start button, choose Programs, click Accessories, click System Tools, and click System Information.

2. Choose System File Checker from the Tools menu.

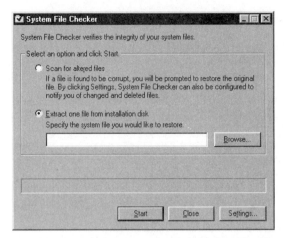

Figure 15-28. *The System File Checker dialog box.*

3. Click Extract One File From Installation Disk, enter the correct path to the cabinet files or click Browse to locate the files, and then click OK.

Note The Windows 98 cabinet files are in the WIN98 folder on the Windows 98 CD-ROM.

Solution Two

If you need a new copy of a file that was created during Windows 98 Setup, install Windows 98 again.

Solution Three

System File Checker does not support the extraction of files from a Windows 98 CD-ROM shared on a network. For System File Checker to work properly, the Windows 98 files should be shared from a hard disk.

Some files are created during Windows 98 Setup and cannot be extracted. System File Checker extracts files only from Windows 98 cabinet files. The following files are created during Windows 98 Setup and are not in the Windows 98 cabinet files:

CLASSES.ZIP	IE32DSW.OCX	M5DRVR32.EXE
COMPUTERINFO.OCX	IE32DSW.TXT	M5DRVR32.RST
CONTROL.INI	INDEX.DAT	M5IF32.DLL
CRYPT32.DLL	INTRO.DCR	MSBATCH.INF
DRVIDX.BIN	JAVAEE.DLL	MSMAIL.INI
EXCHANGE32.INI	JAVASNTX.DLL	MSTASK.DLL
ICWSCRPT.EXE	JSPROXY.DLL	MSOFFICE.INI

MSTASK.CNT	RIPAUX.DLL	TELEPHON.INI
MSTASK.EXE	RNAPH.DLL	VMM32.VXD
MSTASK.HLP	SELECTFILEDLG.OCX	VSREVOKE.DLL
MSTASK.INF	SETUP.INF	XOBGLU16.DLL
MSTINIT.EXE	SETUP.OLD	XOBGLU32.DLL
NDISLOG.TXT	SITE.INI	WAVEMIX.INI
POWERPNT.INI	SWADCMPR.X32	WININIT.INI
PROGMAN.INI	SWASTRM.X32	WINOA386.MOD
PROTOCOL.INI	SYSAGENT.EXE	WINTRUST.HLP
QTW.INI	TCLASSES.ZIP	

Related KB article Q180465

System File Checker Causes Errors

You use System File Checker (SFC.EXE) to restore a Windows 98 system file from a Windows 98 cabinet (.CAB) file (for example, the USER.EXE, GDI.EXE, or KRNL386.EXE file), and the wrong version of the file is extracted from the MINI.CAB cabinet file. This problem causes Windows to stop responding or you receive a *Windows Protection Error* message in Normal and Safe modes.

Note This problem occurs when System File Checker prompts you to restore a corrupt system file during a scan or when you extract and replace a system file by using System File Checker.

This problem occurs because the System File Checker baseline file (DEFAULT.SFC) contains incorrect information about the source cabinet file locations for some Windows 98 system files. As a result, System File Checker searches for the system file in the specified folder (if it is not in a cabinet file) and then in all cabinet files in the specified folder. System File Checker searches cabinet files by using their MS-DOS folder order and extracts the first instance found. The MINI.CAB cabinet file can appear in an MS-DOS folder listing before the correct Windows 98 cabinet file (for example, the correct cabinet file for the USER.EXE file is the WIN98_42.CAB cabinet file). If this situation occurs, System File Checker might first find the mini-Windows mode version of the system file in the MINI.CAB cabinet file.

Note The MINI.CAB cabinet file contains mini-Windows mode files used only by Windows 98 Setup and DriveSpace.

Solution

Restart your computer using the Windows 98 Startup disk, choose Start Computer With CD-ROM Support from the Windows 98 StartUp menu, and then re-extract the file at a command prompt by using EXTRACT.EXE. Note that EXTRACT.EXE does not search the MINI.CAB cabinet file by default. For more information about extracting files, see KB article Q129605, "How to Extract Original Compressed Windows Files."

Related KB article Q192832

System File Checker Defaults Not Restored

You click Settings in System File Checker and then click Restore Defaults on the Advanced tab, and the DEFAULT.SFC file is not restored. This problem occurs because you are not prompted to restart your computer. You must restart your computer for the DEFAULT.SFC file to be available.

Solution

Restart your computer after you run System File Checker.

Related KB article Q187543

System File Checker Detects Changes to Office Files

You look at the System File Checker log file (SFCLOG.TXT) and notice that some of the Office 7.0 for Windows 95 or Office 97 files are listed as updated. This occurs even if you have not made any changes to your Office files.

This problem occurs when the Tune-Up Application Start program (WALIGN.EXE) is run after Office is installed. This program modifies some of the properties of some Office files but does not update the System File Checker baseline information.

Solution

Update the System File Checker baseline information by clicking Update Verification Information when you are prompted.

Related KB article Q189292

System File Checker Detects Dr. Watson Deleted

You run System File Checker, and it detects that the DRWATSON.VXD file has been deleted. This problem can happen if Dr. Watson is running when System File Checker updates its verification information. Dr. Watson dynamically creates the DRWATSON.VXD file while it is running. The file is deleted when you close Dr. Watson.

Solution

Dr. Watson is not loaded by default. To start Dr. Watson automatically at startup, create a shortcut to the DRWATSON.EXE file in your Startup group.

Related KB article Q177982

System File Checker Displays Error Message When Extracting One File from Installation Disk

You attempt to extract a Windows 98 file using the Extract One File From Installation Disk option in System File Checker, and you see the following error message:

The file was not found.

Verify that you have selected the correct 'Restore from' location and try again.

This problem can occur if the file you are attempting to extract has a long filename, and its short filename alias is used on the Windows 98 CD-ROM or disks. System File Checker does not recognize long filenames when it searches for a file to extract.

Solution

To extract the file using its short filename and then rename the file to its long filename, follow these steps:

1. Table 15-2 lists files that use a short filename alias on the Windows 98 CD-ROM or disks. Note the long filename.

2. Click the Start button, choose Run, enter *sfc.exe* in the Open box, and then click OK.

3. Click Extract One File From Installation Disk, and then type the file's short filename.

4. Click the Start button.

5. Click Browse next to the Restore From box, click the folder in which the Windows 98 cabinet files are located, and then click OK.

6. Click Browse next to the Save File In box, click the folder in which you want to save the file, and then click OK.

7. Click OK, and then click OK again when you receive the following message:

    The file has been successfully extracted.

8. Click Close.

Windows 98 Setup uses setup information (.INF) files to install Windows 98 files. Table 15-4 lists both the files that use a short filename alias on the Windows 98 CD-ROM or disks and the .INF file used by Windows 98 Setup.

Table 15-4.   Long Filenames, Short Filenames, and INF Filenames Used by Setup

Long filename	Short filename	INF filename
3D Flower Box.scr	Ssflwbox.scr	Applets.inf
3D Flying Objects.scr	Ss3dfo.scr	Applets.inf
3D Maze.scr	Ssmaze.scr	Applets.inf
3D Pipes.scr	Sspipes.scr	Applets.inf
3D Text.scr	Sstext3d.scr	Applets.inf
Bach's Brandenburg Concerto No. 3	Bachsb~1.rmi	Mmopt.inf
Beethoven's 5th Symphony.rmi	Beetho~2.rmi	Mmopt.inf
Beethoven's Fur Elise.rmi	Fureli~1.rmi	Mmopt.inf
Black Thatch.bmp	Thatch2.bmp	Shell.inf
Blank Screen.scr	Scrnsave.scr	Applets.inf
BlueRivest.bmp	Rivets2.bmp	Shell.inf
Carved Stone.bmp	Egypt.bmp	Shell.inf
Confidential!.cpe	Confident.cpe	Awfax.inf
Curves and Colors.scr	Bezier.scr	Applets.inf
Dance of the Sugar-Plum Fairy.rmi	Danceo~2.rmi	Mmopt.inf
Debussy's Claire de Lune	Claire~1.rmi	Mmopt.inf
Flying Through Space.scr	Ssstars.scr	Applets.inf
Flying Windows.scr	Ssflywin.scr	Applets.inf
For Your Information.cpe	Fyi.cpe	Awfax.inf
Gold Weave.bmp	Gator.bmp	Applets.inf
Houndstooth.bmp	Hounds.bmp	Shell.inf
In the Hall of the Mountain King	Hallof_rmi	Mmopt.inf
Jungle Asterisk.wav	Jungleas.wav	Mmopt.inf
Jungle Close.wav	Junglecl.wav	Mmopt.inf
Jungle Critical Stop.wav	Junglecr.wav	Mmopt.inf
Jungle Default.wav	Junglede.wav	Mmopt.inf
Jungle Error.wav	Jungleer.wav	Mmopt.inf
Jungle Exclamation.wav	Jungleex.wav	Mmopt.inf
Jungle Maximize.wav	Junglema.wav	Mmopt.inf
Jungle Menu Command.wav	Jungleme.wav	Mmopt.inf
Jungle Menu Popup.wav	Jungle~2.wav	Mmopt.inf
Jungle Minimize.wav	Junglemi.wav	Mmopt.inf
Jungle Open.wav	Jungleop.wav	Mmopt.inf

Jungle Question.wav	Junglequ.wav	Mmopt.inf
Jungle Recycle.wav	Junglere.wav	Mmopt.inf
Jungle Restore Down.wav	Jungle~3.wav	Mmopt.inf
Jungle Restore Up.wav	Jungle~4.wav	Mmopt.inf
Jungle Windows Exit.wav	Jungle~1.wav	Mmopt.inf
Jungle Windows Start.wav	Junglewi.wav	Mmopt.inf
Metal Links.bmp	Mesh.bmp	Applets.inf
Mozart's Symphony No. 40	Mozart~2.Rmi	Mmopt.inf
Musica Asterisk.wav	Musicaas.wav	Mmopt.inf
Musica Close.wav	Musicacl.wav	Mmopt.inf
Musica Critical Stop.wav	Musicacr.wav	Mmopt.inf
Musica Default.wav	Musicade.wav	Mmopt.inf
Musica Error.wav	Musicaer.wav	Mmopt.inf
Musica Exclamation.wav	Musicaex.wav	Mmopt.inf
Musica Maximize.wav	Musicama.wav	Mmopt.inf
Musica Menu Command.wav	Musicame.wav	Mmopt.inf
Musica Menu Popup.wav	Musica~2.wav	Mmopt.inf
Musica Minimize.wav	Musicami.wav	Mmopt.inf
Musica Open.wav	Musicaop.wav	Mmopt.inf
Musica Question.wav	Musicaqu.wav	Mmopt.inf
Musica Recycle.wav	Musicare.wav	Mmopt.inf
Musica Restore Down.wav	Musica~3.wav	Mmopt.inf
Musica Restore Up.wav	Musica~4.wav	Mmopt.inf
Musica Windows Start.wav	Musica~1.wav	Mmopt.inf
Mystify Your Mind.scr	Ssmyst.scr	Applets.inf
Pinstripe.bmp	Pstripe.bmp	Shell.inf
Red Blocks.bmp	3dblocks.bmp	Applets.inf
Robotz Asterisk.wav	Robotzas.wav	Mmopt.inf
Robotz Close.wav	Robotzcl.wav	Mmopt.inf
Robotz Critical Stop.wav	Robotzcr.wav	Mmopt.inf
Robotz Default.wav	Robotzde.wav	Mmopt.inf
Robotz Error.wav	Robotzer.wav	Mmopt.inf
Robotz Exclamation.wav	Robotzex.wav	Mmopt.inf
Robotz Maximize.wav	Robotzma.wav	Mmopt.inf
Robotz Menu Command.wav	Robotzme.wav	Mmopt.inf

Robotz Menu Popup.wav	Robtoz~2.wav	Mmopt.inf
Robotz Minimize.wav	Robotzmi.wav	Mmopt.inf
Robotz Open.wav	Robotzop.wav	Mmopt.inf
Robotz Question.wav	Robotzqu.wav	Mmopt.inf
Robotz Recycle.wav	Robotzre.wav	Mmopt.inf
Robotz Restore Down.wav	Robotz~3.wav	Mmopt.inf
Robotz Restore Up.wav	Robotz~4.wav	Mmopt.inf
Robotz Windows Start.wav	Robotzwi.wav	Mmopt.inf
Robotz Windows Exit.wav	Robotz~1.wav	Mmopt.inf
Sandstone.bmp	Sand.bmp	Applets.inf
Scrolling Marquee.scr	Ssmarque.scr	Applets.inf
Stitches.bmp	Weave2.bmp	Shell.inf
The Microsoft Sound.wav	Ms_windowsstart.wav	Motown.inf
Tiles.bmp	Redtile.bmp	Shell.inf
Triangles.bmp	Pyramid2.bmp	Shell.inf
Urgent!.cpe	Urgent.Cpe	Awfax.inf
Utopia Asterisk.wav	Utopiaas.wav	Mmopt.inf
Utopia Close.wav	Utopiacl.wav	Mmopt.inf
Utopia Critical Stop.wav	Utopiacr.wav	Mmopt.inf
Utopia Default.wav	Utopiade.wav	Mmopt.inf
Utopia Error.wav	Utopiaer.wav	Mmopt.inf
Utopia Exclamation.wav	Utopiaex.wav	Mmopt.inf
Utopia Maximize.wav	Utopiama.wav	Mmopt.inf
Utopia Menu Command.wav	Utopiame.wav	Mmopt.inf
Utopia Menu Popup.wav	Utopia~2.wav	Mmopt.inf
Utopia Minimize.wav	Utopiami.wav	Mmopt.inf
Utopia Open.wav	Utopiaop.wav	Mmopt.inf
Utopia Question.wav	Utopiaqu.wav	Mmopt.inf
Utopia Recycle.wav	Utopiare.wav	Mmopt.inf
Utopia Restore Down.wav	Utopia~3.wav	Mmopt.inf
Utopia Restore Up.wav	Utopia~4.wav	Mmopt.inf
Utopia Windows Start.wav	Utopiawi.wav	Mmopt.inf
Utopia Windows Exit.wav	Utopia~1.wav	Mmopt.inf
Waves.bmp	Halftone.bmp	Shell.inf

Related KB article Q188183

System File Checker Displays Error Message When Extracting DESK.CPL from CD-ROM

You try to extract the DESK.CPL file from your Windows 98 CD-ROM by using System File Checker, and you receive the following error message:

The file was not found. Verify that you have selected the correct "Restore from" location and try again.

This problem occurs because the name of the DESK.CPL file on the Windows 98 CD-ROM is DESKW95.CPL.

Solution

Use System File Checker to extract the DESKW95.CPL file, and then rename the DESKW95.CPL file to *desk.cpl*.

Related KB article Q193312

System File Checker Displays Error Message When Improperly Closed

You start System File Checker, press Ctrl+Alt+Delete, click System File Checker, and then click End Task, and you see the following error message:

SFC caused an invalid page fault in module KERNEL32.DLL at 015f:bff7a115.

Solution

Close System File Checker normally rather than pressing Ctrl+Alt+Delete.

Related KB article Q186977

System File Checker Doesn't Prompt to Replace Old or Deleted Files

You run System File Checker using the default settings and are not prompted to replace older or deleted files if you have not enabled the following settings:

- Check for changed files
- Check for deleted files

If these settings are not enabled, System File Checker only appends the SFCLOG.TXT file and does not prompt you to make changes.

Solution

To enable these settings, follow these steps:

1. Click the Start button, choose Run, enter *sfc.exe* in the Open box, and then click OK.

2. Click Settings, and then select the Check For Changed Files and Check For Deleted Files check boxes.

Figure 15-29. *The System File Checker Settings dialog box.*

Note By default, System File Checker starts with those settings disabled. After you enable those settings, they remain the default settings.

3. Click OK, click Scan Files For Altered Files, and then click the Start button.

Related KB article Q182725

System File Checker Log File Entries Truncated

You look at the System File Checker log file (SFCLOG.TXT) and notice that some entries are truncated. For example, date entries are missing the last character representing the year. This problem can occur because the SFCLOG.TXT file has fixed limits for each column of information it displays. If the size of an entry exceeds the space allotted for that column of information, the entry might be truncated.

Table 15-5 shows the entry-size limitations in the SFCLOG.TXT file.

Table 15-5. Entry-Size Limitations in SFCLOG.TXT

Category	Characters
File	16
Change	11
Previous Version	11
Previous Date	9
New Version	11
New Date	9
CRC Match	6

Solution

Modify an entry to fit the allotted space. For example, you can modify your regional settings for short date format from MM/DD/YYYY to MM/DD/YY, and it prevents the entry from being truncated. To do so, follow these steps:

1. Click the Start button, choose Settings, click Control Panel, and double-click Regional Settings.

2. Click the Date tab, and then select mm/dd/yy in the Short Date Style box.

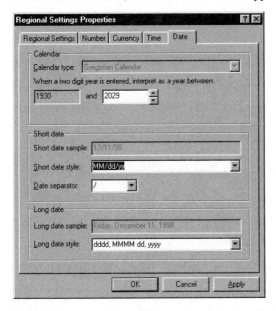

Figure 15-30. *The Regional Settings Properties dialog box.*

3. Click OK, and then close Control Panel.

Related KB article Q187367

System File Checker Shows Missing Folders

You click Add Folder on the Search Criteria tab in System File Checker (SFC.EXE), and the DOWN-LOADED PROGRAM FILES and OCCACHE folders are missing from the WINDOWS folder.

The DOWNLOADED PROGRAM FILES folder is included by default in System File Checker's search criteria, but this problem occurs if you remove it and then try to add it back to your search criteria. The OCCACHE folder, which does not exist unless you upgraded from Internet Explorer 3.x, is not included by default in System File Checker's search criteria, and this problem prevents you from being able to add it.

Solution

To remove the system attribute from the DOWNLOADED PROGRAM FILES (or OCCACHE) folder, add it to System File Checker's search criteria, and then add the system attribute back to the folder by following these steps:

1. Click the Start button, choose Programs, and then click MS-DOS Prompt.

2. At the command prompt, type the appropriate line, and then press the Enter key:

   ```
   attrib -s downlo~1
   ```

   or

   ```
   attrib -s occache
   ```

3. Click the Start button, choose Programs, click Accessories, click System Tools, and then click System Information.

4. Choose System File Checker from the Tools menu.

5. Click Settings.

6. Click the Search Criteria tab, and then click Add Folder.

7. Click Downloaded Program Files (or Occache), click OK, and then click OK again.

8. Click MS-DOS Prompt on the taskbar.

9. At the command prompt, type the appropriate lines, pressing Enter after each one:

   ```
   attrib +s downlo~1    exit
   ```

   or

   ```
   attrib +s occache    exit
   ```

Related KB article Q189413

System Information Can't Display Component Information

You run System Information and receive the following error message in the Software Environment and System Information sections:

Cannot Display Information

The Component which displays this information is not functioning properly or is not present on this machine.

This problem can occur if the MSISYS.OCX file is missing or damaged.

Solution

Extract into the WINDOWS\SYSTEM folder a new copy of the MSISYS.OCX file from your original Windows 98 CD-ROM by using System File Checker.

To start System File Checker, click the Start button, choose Run, enter *sfc.exe* in the Open box, and then click OK. For information about extracting files, see KB article Q129605, "How to Extract Original Compressed Windows Files."

Related KB article Q192867

System Information Displays Error Messages on Saving

You attempt to save your system information by using System Information, and you receive the following error messages:

Microsoft Visual C++ Runtime Library Runtime Error!

Program: FILES\COMMON FILES\MICROSOFT SHARED\MSINFO\MSINFO32.EXE Abnormal program termination

Msinfo32

This program has performed an illegal operation and will be shut down. If the problem persists, contact the program vendor.

You click Details and see the following information:

Msinfo32 caused an invalid page fault in module MFC40.DLL at <address>.

This problem occurs when the hard disk or partition to which you are attempting to save your system information doesn't have enough free space.

Solution

Choose a location with more free space, or increase the amount of free space on the hard disk or partition.

Related KB article Q192753

System Information Displays Incomplete Components Branch

If IntelliPoint 2.0 or later is installed on your computer and the POINT32.EXE program is running, you see incomplete information on the Components branch in System Information. This problem also occurs if you are running third-party mouse software.

Solution

Close the POINT32.EXE program and uninstall IntelliPoint by following these steps:

1. Press Ctrl+Alt+Delete, and then click Point32.

2. Click End Task.

3. Uninstall IntelliPoint using the Add/Remove Programs icon in Control Panel.

Windows 98 includes drivers that support wheel functionality for both IntelliPoint and Logitech wheel mice, and the mouse software is not required for wheel functionality (some features might require that the software be installed). For additional information, contact your mouse manufacturer.

Related KB article Q181509

System Information Reports Illegal Operation Error

You run the System Information tool and receive the following error message:

This program has performed an illegal operation and will be shut down. If the problem persists, contact the program vendor.

You click Details and receive the following error message:

MSINFO32 caused an invalid page fault in module KERNEL32.DLL at 015f:bff8XXXX

Solution

Extract a new copy of the MSINFO32.EXE file from your Windows 98 disks or CD-ROM. To use System File Checker to extract a new MSINFO32.EXE file from the Windows 98 CD-ROM, follow these steps:

1. Click the Start button, choose Run, enter *sfc.exe* in the Open box, and then click OK.

2. Select Extract One File From Installation Disk, enter *msinfo32.exe* in the Specify The System File You Would Like To Restore box, and then click the Start button.

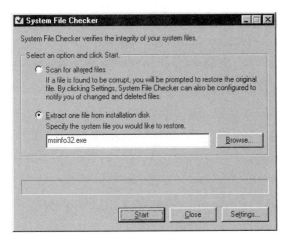

Figure 15-31. *The System File Checker dialog box.*

3. In the Restore From box, enter the path to the WIN98 folder on the Windows 98 CD-ROM.

4. If necessary, enter *<drive>:\Program Files\Common Files\Microsoft Shared\Msinfo* in the Save
File In box (where <drive> is the drive letter of the drive containing the Windows 98 PROGRAM
FILES folder), and then click OK.

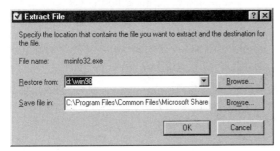

Figure 15-32. *The Extract File dialog box.*

5. Click OK, click OK, and then click Yes when you are prompted to restart your computer.

Note For more information about how to extract original compressed Windows files, see KB article
Q129605, "How to Extract Original Compressed Windows Files."

Related KB article Q191986

System Monitor Shows 100 Percent Kernel Processor Usage

You use System Monitor to monitor more than one occurrence of Kernel: Processor Usage, and the second and following occurrences of Kernel: Processor Usage show 100 percent processor usage.

Solution

Use only one occurrence of Kernel: Processor Usage in System Monitor, or use two separate occurrences of System Monitor.

Related KB article Q178563

Version Conflict Manager Deletes Original Windows 98 Files During Restoration

You use Version Conflict Manager to restore the newer versions of files that were overwritten by Windows 98 Setup, and the files are properly restored, but the original Windows 98 files are lost.

This problem can occur if you try to restore multiple files at one time.

When Windows 98 Setup detects that an existing version of a file is newer than the version being installed, the newer version is automatically replaced with the Windows 98 version and is moved to the WINDOWS\VCM folder. If you restore the newer version of the file by clicking it in Version Conflict Manager and then clicking Restore Selected Files, the newer version of the file is restored, and the Windows 98 version is moved to the WINDOWS\VCM folder with a .0?0 file extension. You can then restore the Windows 98 version of the file if you need to.

If you try to restore multiple files simultaneously, the newer versions of the files are properly restored, but the Windows 98 versions are not moved to the WINDOWS\VCM folder and are lost. This situation prevents you from being able to restore the Windows 98 version of the files.

Solution

Restore only one backup file at a time by using Version Conflict Manager. You might be able to recover the original Windows 98 files that were not backed up properly by using System File Checker. For information about how to use System File Checker, see KB article Q185836, "Description of the System File Checker Tool (SFC.EXE)."

For additional information about Version Conflict Manager, see KB article Q186157, "Description of the Version Conflict Manager Tool in Windows 98."

Related KB article Q184585

Windows Report Displays Error

You try to start Windows Report (WINREP.EXE) and you receive the following error message:

Error creating Eyedog.ocx control.

You run System Information (MSINFO32.EXE) and try to look at entries under the Hardware Resources branch or the Components branch, and you receive one of the following error messages:

Cannot Display Information

The component which displays this information is not functioning properly, or is not present on this machine.

Cannot Display Information

The component which displays this information is not functioning or is missing.

This problem occurs when the EYEDOG.OCX file, an ActiveX control, does not work correctly. It occurs when problems exist with the following files that this control uses:

- RICHED32.DLL

- RICHED.DLL

- RICHED20.DLL

Solution One

If WordPad is installed, follow these steps to uninstall WordPad and reinstall it:

1. Click the Start button, choose Settings, click Control Panel, and then double-click the Add/Remove Programs icon.

2. Click the Windows Setup tab, click Accessories (the word, not the check box), and then click Details.

3. Clear the WordPad check box, click OK, click OK again, and then follow the instructions onscreen to finish uninstalling WordPad.

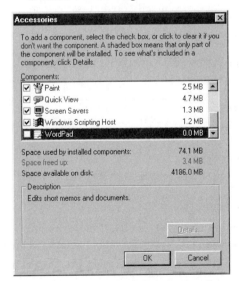

Figure 15-33. *The Accessories dialog box for the Add/Remove Programs icon.*

4. Click the Start button, choose Settings, click Control Panel, and then double-click the Add/Remove Programs icon.

5. Select the Windows Setup tab, click Accessories (the word, not the check box), and then click Details.

6. Select the WordPad check box, click OK, click OK again, and then follow the instructions onscreen to finish installing WordPad.

Solution Two

If WordPad isn't installed, follow these steps to install it:

1. Click the Start button, choose Settings, click Control Panel, and then double-click the Add/Remove Programs icon.

2. Select the Windows Setup tab, click Accessories (the word, not the check box), and then click Details.

3. Select the WordPad check box, click OK, click OK again, and then follow the instructions onscreen to finish installing WordPad.

Related KB article Q189589

Windows Report Doesn't Send Report

You create a report by using Windows Report and then click Next to send the report, and your report is not sent. Instead, you are prompted to save the report as a file on your computer.

This problem occurs because Windows Report sends a report only if the program is started by a support provider's web page. If you start this program yourself, a report is not sent.

Solution

Save your report as a file on your computer, and follow the instructions of your support provider to send the report, possibly by using e-mail.

Related KB article Q189316

Task Scheduler

Log File Doesn't Allow Deletion of Text

You try to delete text from the Task Scheduler log file SCHEDLOG.TXT by opening Task Scheduler, clicking Advanced, clicking View Log, selecting the text you want to delete and then pressing the Delete key, and you receive the following message:

The text in the C:\WINDOWS\SchedLog.Txt file has changed.

Do you want to save the changes?

If you click Yes and then click Save, you receive the following message:

C:WINDOWS\SchedLog.Txt already exists.

Do you want to replace it?

If you then click Yes, you receive the following error message:

Cannot create the C:\WINDOWS\SchedLog.Txt file.

Make sure that the path and filename are correct.

This problem can occur because the SCHEDLOG.TXT file cannot be modified while it is in use by Task Scheduler.

Solution

To disable Task Scheduler, edit the SCHEDLOG.TXT file, and then reenable Task Scheduler, by following these steps:

1. Click the Start button, choose Programs, click Accessories, click System Tools, and then click Scheduled Tasks.

2. Choose Stop Using Task Scheduler from the Advanced menu.

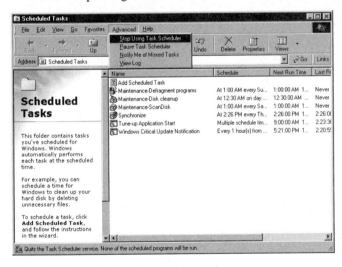

Figure 15-34. *The Scheduled Tasks window.*

3. Click Advanced, and then click View Log.

4. Edit the SCHEDLOG.TXT file by using Notepad, close the file, and then click Yes when you are prompted to save the file.

5. Click Advanced, and then click Start Using Task Scheduler.

6. Close the SCHEDULED TASKS folder.

Related KB article Q191427

Log File Inaccessible

You attempt to see the SCHEDLOG.TXT file by choosing View Log from the Advanced menu in Task Scheduler and the SCHEDLOG.TXT file does not open. You then see an error message similar to this one:

The document C:\Windows\SchedLog.txt is in use by another application and cannot be accessed.

This problem can occur if text (.TXT) files are associated with a program other than Notepad. When Task Scheduler is running, it constantly updates the SCHEDLOG.TXT file. Unlike Notepad, some text editors (such as WordPad) cannot open documents that are in use by another program.

Solution One

To temporarily disable Task Scheduler and then attempt to view the SCHEDLOG.TXT file again, follow these steps:

1. Open Task Scheduler.

2. Choose Stop Using Task Scheduler from the Advanced menu.

3. Look at the SCHEDLOG.TXT file.

4. When you are done, choose Start Using Task Scheduler from the Advanced menu.

Note You cannot work around this behavior by choosing Pause Task Scheduler from the Advanced menu.

Solution Two

To associate .TXT files with Notepad, follow these steps:

1. In My Computer or Windows Explorer, choose Folder Options from the View menu.

2. Click the File Types tab.

3. In the Registered File Types box, se;ect Text Document, and then click Edit.

4. Select Open from the Actions box, and then click Edit.

5. Enter the following path in the Application Used To Perform Action box:

    <drive>:\<windows>\notepad.exe

   where <drive> is the drive on which Windows is installed and <windows> is the folder in which Windows is installed.

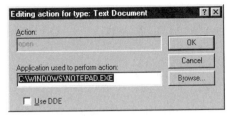

Figure 15-35.   *The Editing Action For Type: Text Document dialog box.*

6. Click OK, click Close, and then click Close again.

Related KB article Q187239

Program Doesn't Start

You use Task Scheduler to schedule a program, and the program does not start.

This problem occurs when your WINDOWS folder has the same name as the volume label of the hard disk on which the WINDOWS folder is located.

Solution

To change the volume label of the hard disk, follow these steps:

1. Double-click My Computer.

2. Right-click the hard disk that has the same name as your WINDOWS folder, and then click Properties.

3. In the Label box, enter a new name for your hard disk, and then click OK.

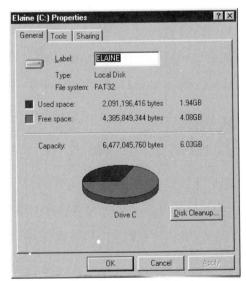

Figure 15-36.   *The Drive Properties dialog box.*

Related KB article Q190568

StarSight Loader Task Displays Could-Not-Start Status

You start Task Scheduler, and you see a task named StarSight Loader with a status of *Could not start* if you uninstall WebTV for Windows.

Solution

Right-click the StarSight Loader task, and then choose Delete from the shortcut menu. For information about StarSight Loader, contact StarSight.

Related KB article Q180059

Index

Stephen L. Nelson writes and consults about using computers for personal and business financial management. The author of over 50 books and more than 100 magazine articles, Nelson is the bestselling author on using computers for personal financial management. Nelson's books have sold more than 3 million copies in English and have been translated into eleven different languages.

Nelson, a certified public accountant, holds a bachelor of science degree in accounting from Central Washington University and a masters of business administration degree in finance from the University of Washington.

Nelson lives in the foothills east of Seattle, Washington, with his wife, Susan, and two children, Beth and Britt Marie.

Contributors

Mike Algozzine	Brian Lewis
James Drew	Jennifer Lindsey
David Gazjuk	Johnny Martinez
Chris Golden	Bill Miller
David Gordon	Thomas Montefusco
Jonathan Hoag	Robert Oppegaard
Joe Jeffcoat	Paul Peck
Becky Lawson	Eva Sanders

and PSS Desktop Systems Support Engineers

The manuscript for this book was prepared and submitted to Microsoft Press in electronic form. Text files were prepared using Microsoft Word 97. Pages were composed by Stephen L. Nelson, Inc., using Adobe PageMaker 6.5 for Windows, with text in Times and display type in Helvetica Narrow. Composed pages were delivered to the printer as electronic prepress files.

Cover Designer:	Patrick Lanfear
Interior Graphic Designer:	James D. Kramer
Technical Editors:	Kaarin Dolliver, Michael Furdyk, Jason Gerend, Michael Jang, Brian Milbrath
Developmental Editors:	Pat Coleman, Peter Dyson, Steve Nelson, Todd Young
Proofreaders:	Kevin Murray, Paula Thurman, Rebecca Whitney
Project Manager:	Jeff Adell
Principal Compositor:	Amy Calkins
Indexer:	Julie Kawabata

Keep fast answers
in your pocket!

MICROSOFT POCKET GUIDES are portable, reliable references to Microsoft Office 2000 applications, ideal for the frequent traveler or anyone seeking quick answers about each application's tools, terms, and techniques. To find everything you need to know to put Office 2000 to work today, trust MICROSOFT POCKET GUIDES—learning solutions, made by Microsoft.

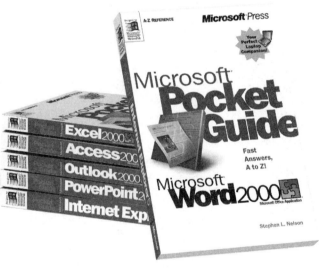

- MICROSOFT® POCKET GUIDE TO MICROSOFT EXCEL 2000
- MICROSOFT POCKET GUIDE TO MICROSOFT WORD 2000
- MICROSOFT POCKET GUIDE TO MICROSOFT ACCESS 2000
- MICROSOFT POCKET GUIDE TO MICROSOFT POWERPOINT® 2000
- MICROSOFT POCKET GUIDE TO MICROSOFT OUTLOOK™ 2000
- MICROSOFT POCKET GUIDE TO MICROSOFT INTERNET EXPLORER 5

mspress.microsoft.com

See clearly—
now!

Here's the remarkable, *visual* way to quickly find answers about the power-fully integrated features of the Microsoft® Office 2000 applications. Microsoft Press AT A GLANCE books let you focus on particular tasks and show you, with clear, numbered steps, the easiest way to get them done right now. Put Office 2000 to work today, with AT A GLANCE learning solutions, made by Microsoft.

- MICROSOFT OFFICE 2000 PROFESSIONAL AT A GLANCE
- MICROSOFT WORD 2000 AT A GLANCE
- MICROSOFT EXCEL 2000 AT A GLANCE
- MICROSOFT POWERPOINT® 2000 AT A GLANCE
- MICROSOFT ACCESS 2000 AT A GLANCE
- MICROSOFT FRONTPAGE® 2000 AT A GLANCE
- MICROSOFT PUBLISHER 2000 AT A GLANCE
- MICROSOFT OFFICE 2000 SMALL BUSINESS AT A GLANCE
- MICROSOFT PHOTODRAW® 2000 AT A GLANCE
- MICROSOFT INTERNET EXPLORER 5 AT A GLANCE
- MICROSOFT OUTLOOK® 2000 AT A GLANCE

mspress.microsoft.com

Optimize
Microsoft® Office 2000
with multimedia training!

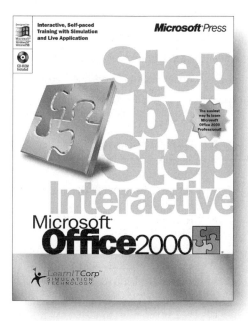

U.S.A.   **$29.99**
Canada $44.99
ISBN 0-7356-0506-8

MICROSOFT OFFICE 2000 STEP BY STEP INTERACTIVE is a multimedia learning system (in both audio and text versions) that shows you, through 20 to 30 hours of training, how to maximize the productivity potential of the Office 2000 programs: Microsoft Excel 2000, Word 2000, Access 2000, PowerPoint® 2000, Outlook® 2000, Publisher 2000, and Small Business Tools. If you already use Microsoft Office 97, this learning solution will help you make the transition to Office 2000 quickly and easily, and reach an even greater level of productivity.

mspress.microsoft.com

Stay in the *running* for maximum productivity.

These are *the* answer books for business users of Microsoft® Office 2000. They are packed with everything from quick, clear instructions for new users to comprehensive answers for power users— the authoritative reference to keep by your computer and use every day. THE RUNNING SERIES—learning solutions made by Microsoft.

- RUNNING MICROSOFT EXCEL 2000
- RUNNING MICROSOFT OFFICE 2000 PREMIUM
- RUNNING MICROSOFT OFFICE 2000 PROFESSIONAL
- RUNNING MICROSOFT OFFICE 2000 SMALL BUSINESS
- RUNNING MICROSOFT WORD 2000
- RUNNING MICROSOFT POWERPOINT® 2000
- RUNNING MICROSOFT ACCESS 2000
- RUNNING MICROSOFT INTERNET EXPLORER 5
- RUNNING MICROSOFT FRONTPAGE® 2000
- RUNNING MICROSOFT OUTLOOK® 2000

Microsoft®

mspress.microsoft.com

Register Today!

Return this
Microsoft® Help Desk For Microsoft Windows® 98
registration card today

Microsoft *Press*
mspress.microsoft.com

OWNER REGISTRATION CARD   0-7356-0632-3

Microsoft® Help Desk For Microsoft Windows® 98

_____   _____   _____
FIRST NAME   MIDDLE INITIAL   LAST NAME

_____
INSTITUTION OR COMPANY NAME

_____
ADDRESS

_____

_____   _____   _____
CITY   STATE   ZIP

                                                                    (   )
_____   _____
E-MAIL ADDRESS   PHONE NUMBER

U.S. and Canada addresses only. Fill in information above and mail postage-free.
Please mail only the bottom half of this page.

For information about Microsoft Press®
products, visit our Web site at
mspress.microsoft.com

Microsoft®*Press*